SOCIAL RESPONSIBILITY: CORPORATE GOVERNANCE ISSUES

RESEARCH IN INTERNATIONAL BUSINESS AND FINANCE

Series Editor: Thomas A. Fetherston

RESEARCH IN INTERNATIONAL BUSINESS AND FINANCE
VOLUME 17

SOCIAL RESPONSIBILITY: CORPORATE GOVERNANCE ISSUES

EDITED BY

JONATHAN A. BATTEN

Seoul National University, Korea

THOMAS A. FETHERSTON

University of Alabama, Birmingham, USA

2003

JAI
An imprint of Elsevier Science

Amsterdam – Boston – London – New York – Oxford – Paris
San Diego – San Francisco – Singapore – Sydney – Tokyo

ELSEVIER SCIENCE Ltd
The Boulevard, Langford Lane
Kidlington, Oxford OX5 1GB, UK

First edition 2003

Library of Congress Cataloging in Publication Data
A catalogue record from the British Library has been applied for.

ISBN: 0-7623-1025-1
ISSN: 0275-5319 (Series)

⊗ The paper used in this publication meets the requirements of ANSI/NISO Z39.48-1992 (Permanence of Paper).
Printed in The Netherlands.

CONTENTS

PART III: GOVERNANCE ACTION PROPOSALS

LIST OF CONTRIBUTORS

Tom Arnold	The E. Claiborne Robins School of Business, University of Richmond, USA
Jonathan A. Batten	College of Business Administration, Seoul National University, Korea
David Birch	Corporate Citizen Research Unit, Faculty of Arts, Deakin University, Australia
Hamparsum Bozdogan	Department of Statistics, University of Tennessee, USA
Bonnie Buchanan	University of Georgia, USA
David A. Carter	College of Business Administration, Oklahoma State University, USA
Sam Y. Chung	School of Business and Public Administration, Long Island University, New York, USA
Matthew F. Clarke	Centre for Strategic Economic Studies, Victoria University, Australia
M. Cary Collins	Department of Finance, University of Tennessee, USA
Yves Crama	School of Business Administration, University of Liège, Belgium
B. D. Craven	Department of Mathematics and Statistics, University of Melbourne, Australia
Eileen Davenport	Mira Szászy Research Centre for Maori and Pacific Island Development, University of Auckland, New Zealand
John Dobson	College of Business, California Polytechnic State University, USA

ix

x

Amitabh S. Dutta — Department of Financial and Information Systems, Columbus State University, USA

Kristina Eneroth — Department of Business Administration, Lund University, Sweden

Thomas A. Fetherston — University of Alabama, Birmingham, USA

Warren Hogan — School of Finance and Economics, University of Technology, Sydney, Australia

Marion Hutchinson — Faculty of Business and Law, School of Accounting and Finance, Deakin University, Australia

Phillip Hone — Department of Economics, Deakin University, Australia

Sardar M. N. Islam — Centre for Strategic Economic Studies, Victoria University, Australia

Jan Jonker — Nijmegen School of Management, University of Nijmegen, Netherlands

Jens Köke — University of Mannheim, Mannheim Research Institute for the Economics of Aging, Germany

Maryvonne Lassalle-de Salins — Department of Strategic Management, ESC-Toulouse, France

Luch Leruth — International Monetary Fund, Washington, DC, USA

Shu Ling Lin — Department of International Trade and Finance, Fu-Jen Catholic University, Taiwan

Will Low — Faculty of Arts, Auckland University of Technology, New Zealand

Tracy Murray Department of Economics,
University of Arkansas, USA

Lance Nail University of Alabama,
Birmingham, USA

Allan Purnell School of Accounting and Finance,
Deakin University, Australia

Jean Raar School of Accounting and Finance,
Deakin University, Australia

Luc Renneboog Department of Finance and Center for
Economic Research, Tilburg University,
The Netherlands

Thomas Schneeweis Department of Finance and Operations Management,
University of Massachusetts-Amherst,
USA

Peter W. Schroth Lally School of Management and Technology,
Rensselaer Polytechnic Institute, USA

Pasquale M. Sgro School of Ecomomics,
Deakin University,
Melbourne, Australia

Betty J. Simkins College of Business Administration,
Oklahoma State University, USA

W. Gary Simpson College of Business Administration,
Oklahoma State University, USA

Benny Simon Tabalujan Melbourne Business School,
The University of Melbourne,
Australia

Jean-Pierre Urbain Department of Quantitative Economics,
University Maastricht, Netherlands

James W. Wansley Department of Finance,
The University of Tennessee, USA

Soushan Wu College of Management,
Chang Gung University, Taiwan

PART I:
OVERVIEW

WHY GOVERNANCE AND SOCIAL RESPONSIBILITY MATTERS

Jonathan A. Batten and Thomas A. Fetherston

Exposition on and exploration of Corporate Governance is not new as is captured in Denis (2001). Surveys have been done on various germane topics such as the general subject of corporate governance by Shleifer and Vishny (1997); Murphy (1999) on executive compensation; Hermalin and Weisbach (2003) on boards of directors; Holderness (2001) on blockholders; and Karpoff (1998) and Romano (2000) on shareholder activism. Having laid the predicate of non-uniqueness of the general topic of "Corporate Governance" it is the goal of this work to contribute to the literature, which has evolved over the last twenty-five years. Even though there is a voluminous literature on "Corporate Governance" stemming from Jensen and Meckling (1976), it is still an unfinished work and still has room for further research and elucidation.

There has been extensive research interest in the realm of *Corporate Social Responsibility* with the outcome of this research providing tremendous progress and understanding. The goal of this volume is to provide further research insight on a topic, which still has not reached saturation in terms of analysis and understanding. The efforts in this volume will measurably add to the body of literature and understanding in the field. This volume is structured into three parts: a Global Overview section, a section with papers focusing the performance impact of Social Responsibility Procedures and a third section devoted to papers on implementation and measurement procedures. There are twenty-one papers in the volume with forty authors, many of whom are prominent in the field, contributing their effort to this volume.

Social Responsibility: Corporate Governance Issues
Research in International Business and Finance, Volume 17, 3–19
© 2003 Published by Elsevier Science Ltd.
ISSN: 0275-5319/PII: S0275531903170018

GLOBAL OVERVIEW

The *Sgro* paper explored process of globalization and its far-reaching social as well as economic effects. The term "globalization" is generally taken to mean an increase in international transactions in markets for goods, services and factors of production and a growth in institutions that straddle international borders. The author asserted that these developments have also meant that the corporate governance mechanisms have had to be reinforced to ensure fairness and transparency as well as social responsibility. Furthermore, he asserted that international infrastructure and institutions have to evolve to facilitate and ameliorate the effects of the growth in this world trade on the environment, sustainable development and bio-diversity. The author provided an overview of the current developments.

Globalization is predominantly an economic process but through its impact on culture, government and virtually all aspects of domestic policy making, it has a powerful social effect. It means an increase in international transactions in markets for goods, services and factors of production, plus the growth and expanded scope of many institutions that straddle international borders. It also includes foreign direct investment (FDI), multinational corporations (MNCs) and integration of the world capital flows.

There have been increased capital flows with the most pronounced being in portfolio investment. However, mobility of labour has not increased significantly over the same period. These global changes have been caused, inter alia, by changes in technology as well as changes in policy. Concerning capital mobility, it is clear that access to global capital helps countries develop but it is also true that capital can be withdrawn suddenly (as in the Asian Financial Crisis of 1997) resulting in widespread recession in those countries which affects the whole population.

The author pours light on many issues and provides food for further thought on some of the lessons that have been learned in the aftermath of the Asian Crisis of 1997.

IMPACT OF SOCIAL RESPONSIBILITY PROCEDURES

The *Carter, Simkins, and Simpson* analysis examined the relationship between board diversity and firm value for *Fortune 1000* firms excluding utilities and financial services firms. They defined board diversity as the presence of minorities (e.g. African-Americans, Asians, Hispanics, etc.) on the board of directors. Their research discussed three primary theories explaining the role of the board of directors. These three theories (agency Fama & Jensen, 1983), legalistic, and resource dependence (Zahra & Pearce II, 1989) have implications for how board diversity can enhance firm performance. The authors obtained data on board of director characteristics for (1997) from *Significant Data for Directors 1999: Board Policies and Governance Trends*, prepared by Directorship, a corporate governance-consulting firm. Additionally, they obtained accounting data used in this analysis from the COMPUSTAT database. They employed a data set of 494 firms with a complete set of all the data items out of 548 potential firms.

The major findings of their analysis on the relationship between board of director diversity and firm value are as follows. First, after controlling for size, industry, and other corporate governance measures, they found significant positive relationships between the fraction of minorities on the board and firm value. This result holds after controlling for potential endogeneity using two stage least squares regression analysis. Second, they found that the proportion of minorities on boards increases with firm size and board size but decreases as the number of insider's increases. Their results also suggest that firms making a commitment to increasing the number of minorities on boards also have more women on their boards. Overall, our results provide important evidence of the positive relation between firm value and diversity on the board of directors. This research is important because it highlights the need for firms to included diverse members on their board of directors.

The *Islam and Clarke* effort disputed the use of the many approaches existing within the literature to measure social welfare as the indicator of social, ethical and environmental performance using standard national accounts statistics. They argued that market preferences are a flawed approach. There is a need to develop an approach that is based on social choice perspectives, as there is a distinct difference in actions between citizens acting within the market and citizens judging and acting upon alternative social welfare states. The authors argued that there are several limitations of the extant literature within this area, including the reliance on aggregated preferences and lack of studies focusing on developing countries. A new approach, based on integrated systems analysis of the indicators for social, ethical and environmental performance, is developed by them and empirically applied to Thailand for a 25-year period (1975 to 1999). The approach developed by them in this chapter, the Total Systems Social, Ethical and Environmental Social Welfare (Total SSEE) index is characterized by a *systems approach*, *social choice theory* and *cost-benefit analysis*. A major limitation of the existing literature is that the underlying value judgments used in estimating welfare are not usually stated or clearly applied. This new approach overcomes this limitation, as all value judgments are made explicit within the specified social welfare function. This social welfare function, in turn, is derived from the principles of systems analysis, social choice theory and cost-benefit analysis. In this work, they integrated cost-benefit analysis and national income accounts measures of social welfare. They applied Social choice theory to welfare measurement in Thailand (Islam & Clarke,

2000, 2001) and extended it here. Social choice theory is a suitable starting point for measuring welfare within a systems analysis approach. However, as measuring welfare or quality of life is dependent on making social value judgments, a social welfare function is the most appropriate tool for undertaking this measurement. They identified certain adjustments, which can be made to GDP and justified these adjustments within a social welfare function.

The *Köke* study examined the impact of corporate governance and market discipline on productivity growth. He used a large panel of German manufacturing firms (841) over the years (1986–1996) and found that firms under concentrated ownership tend to show significantly higher productivity growth. The study analyzed the impact of five corporate governance mechanisms (ownership concentration, owner type, ownership complexity, financial pressure, and board size), product market competition, and their interactions on productivity growth. The study adds to the literature on four important respects: First, he considered a larger range of governance mechanisms and their relation to productivity growth than previous studies. Second, his study is the first to examine the impact of financial pressure (from creditors) on productivity growth for a continental European country. Due to the methodological similarity, our results are directly comparable to those of Nickell et al. (1997) obtained for the U.K. Third, he explicitly addressed potential endogeneity of the explanatory variables by using the GMM instrumental variables technique developed by Arellano and Bond (1991). This method is now standard in panel econometrics, however, it is not yet widely applied in studies on corporate governance with the exceptions of Nickell et al. (1997) and Januszewski et al. (2002). Finally, the data set used in this study is much larger than data sets used in previous work on corporate governance in Germany (Becht & Böhmer, 2000; Cable, 1985; Gross-Schuler & Weigand, 2001; Gorton & Schmid, 2000; Januszewski et al., 2002; Lehmann & Weigand, 2000).

The main findings were – Firms under concentrated ownership tend to show higher productivity growth, and this effect is larger when product market competition is intense. Hence, shareholder control and competition are complements. Financial pressure from creditors also has a positive impact on productivity growth, particularly for firms in financial distress. Under the impact of market discipline he found, productivity grows faster when competition in product markets is intense, but only when ownership concentration is high. He did not find evidence that the type of the owner, ownership complexity, or the size of the supervisory board is significantly related to productivity growth. Structures perform worse than other firms; and board size is not significantly related to productivity growth.

The *Crama, Leruth, Renneboog and Urbain* investigation described two broad systems of corporate governance existing in Continental Europe (the *insider* system) and in the U.K. (and the U.S., the *outsider* system). They emphasized a number of striking differences in concentration and nature of ownership between both systems. For example, in a typical Continental European country (majority) control is held by one shareholder or a small group of interlocked (corporate) shareholders, whereas Anglo-American companies are predominantly widely held. These discrepancies have important consequences in terms of agency costs and therefore, mechanisms have been developed in most countries to separate ownership (cash flow rights) and control (voting rights) both at the level of the firm and through corporate law. They demonstrated that traditional indices belonging to the Herfindahl family do not provide theoretically sound measures and have proposed to use another index (the Z-index, Banzhaf, 1965, 1966, 1968) based on the idea that shareholders are players in a voting game. They analyzed empirically the impact of the Z-index and Herfindahl indices on the financial performance of a stock and its risk. The data were a random sample of 250 companies quoted on the London Stock Exchange. All disclosed ownership stakes were retrieved from microfiche and hard copy annual reports. The risk measures were gotten from the Risk Measurement Service and betas have been calculated via a Vasicek Bayesian-updating procedure. Share price performance measures were drawn from the London Share Price Database. Accounting and firm specific characteristics data (including several non-risk security characteristics dividends, *P/E* ratio, etc.) are from Datastream.

Their results pointed to the fact that voting power, as measured by Z-indices, was tightly correlated to both share price performance and risk. The negative relation between the largest Z-index and corporate share price performance was explained by the fact that the voting power held by executive directors measures the degree of insider entrenchment, which has a negative impact on performance. Furthermore, the risk regressions showed that entrenched insider as well as large shareholders might seek higher levels of systematic risk. They also concluded that the classic Herfindahl indices inaccurately measure control that was reflected in the weaker relationship with performance.

The *Lin and Wu* study investigated the impact of Taiwanese corporate environmental performance on stock market valuation, based on an information usefulness perspective, accounting identity framework and shareholders' value pyramid theory. The analysis of their study was based on the perspective of information usefulness proposed by Lev and Ohlson (1982) and the accounting identity model developed by Modigliani and Miller (1958) and Landsman (1986). Their empirical results imply that corporate environmental performance positively affect its stock market valuation, which is supported by the green investor hypotheses. Besides, it suggested that investors perceive those firms who possess good environmental performance may get a better financial shape in the future. If the demand for better environmental performance firm's securities is greater, the market participants bid up share value, which is reflected in the premium of a firm's stock. Finally, the result confirms that corporate environmental capital investment seems to affect its stock market valuation through their environmental performance, and suggests that corporate with more environmental capital investment would enhance their stock market valuation. The empirical evidence is consistent with the shareholders' value pyramid theory proposed by Rappaport (1981). Based on these results, it concludes that mandated disclosure requirement is needed for truthful representation of environmental performance, and that strict enforcement of SEC's disclosure requirements in Taiwan would be desirable. The requirement of periodical quantitative information about environmental performance could be useful and beneficial to market participants. They propose further research be performed using time-series analysis to study the effect of within-firm's movement in environmental performance on shareholders' wealth.

The *Purnell, Raar and Hone* paper explored the activities of investment funds (the accounting and reporting by business activities concerned with conservation of wildlife are examined) that focus on socially responsible investment (SRI). These firms operate according to predetermined criteria for environmental, social and ethical issues. For investors in these funds, environmental stewardship issues are integrated with concern over financial resources and performance. In (1998) the Australian Accounting Standards Board and in (2001) the International Accounting Standards Board issued standards devoted to agriculture. Both standards deal with the reporting of managed biological assets and require application of essentially the same approaches despite the Australian standard requiring net market value while the International standard requires fair value.

The authors analyzed how one conservation firm Earth Sanctuaries Ltd. (ESL) applied AASB 1037 and then explored the implications for conservation firms operating in geographical locations outside Australia. Their examination found that it is appropriate to reconsider accounting guidelines provided by these standards in order to link the information relating to economic and environmental performance. They assert that transparency may be improved by a move closer to Elkington's (1997) triple bottom line reporting. They therefore contended that the issues arising from the use of AASB 1037 and IAS 41 need to be widely considered by all standard setters, particularly given the increasing attention to SRI. Further, they asserted that ESL and similar international conservation firms offer a unique opportunity for the accounting profession to link a triple bottom reporting approach with financial reports. They suggested it would be preferable for standard setters to identify any necessary change to aid transparency relating to corporate citizenship activities and financial performance, before practice introduces interpretations of IAS 41, which become "merely permitted" rather than being formally endorsed by the community and regulators. They also suggest that a reporting guideline for international conservation firms could be developed so that ambiguities are reduced and stakeholders do not have to shed light on accounting reports based on a practice that is merely "allowed".

In this chapter *Buchanan, Arnold and Nail* present a clinical examination of the corporate governance failures that led to the demise of HIH Insurance (Australia) and show that corporate governance failures are not endemic to the existing corporate governance system in the United States. Despite differences in corporate governance systems in the United States and Australia, the corporate governance failures that led to each country's largest bankruptcy are strikingly similar. WorldCom in the United States and HIH Insurance in Australia were both created by a rapid series of major acquisitions, failed after their last major acquisitions, and attempted to hide their declining performance with aggressive and/or fraudulent accounting practices.

The parallels between the histories and failures of HIH and WorldCom are striking, especially given that the companies were located in countries with differing corporate governance systems. The authors analyzed the corporate governance failures that aided the collapse of HIH and their similarities to the same failures at WorldCom. Specifically, they examined the similarities and differences between Australian corporate governance mechanisms and those in place in other developed markets and the role these mechanisms played in the failure of HIH. They then highlighted the elements of corporate governance which were ineffective in the case of HIH and show how these elements may be used to identify corporate governance weaknesses in other Australian firms and corporations in other developed countries. Previous research linked general corporate and insurance failures to unsupervised delegation of authority, rapid expansion, underpricing, reserve problems, false reporting, reckless management, rapid expansion, and incompetence. Following that direction, the authors found that these bankruptcies were less a result of economic Darwinism than preventable breaches of proper corporate governance.

The paper by *Islam* and *Craven* provides models and measurement computation methods for formulating sustainable growth and social welfare programs. Although the topics are not directly related to corporate governance they do provide insight on tangential topics. Sustainable growth relates to economic conditions of non-declining consumption or capital (whether man-made, natural, or environmental) over time.

The *Hutchinson* study investigated the relationship between a firm's risk and the effectiveness of the firm's corporate governance practices. The study focused on the efficiency of monitoring and incentive contracts, given certain characteristics of the firm. The study set out to determine whether risk firms with higher monitoring and levels of incentives are associated with higher firm performance. The data on the sampled firm's financial characteristics, management remuneration and share ownership were acquired from (1998/1999) company financial reports provided by Connect 4, an electronic database of the top 500 Australian company annual reports. Risk measures were obtained from the Australian Graduate School of Management (AGSM) risk measurement service of the University of New South Wales. The methods followed were consistent with prior research, executive directors are used as a proxy for executives (see Morck et al., 1988). Also the standard deviation of monthly returns and beta as a measure of firm risk (Aggarwal & Samwick, 1999; Carr, 1997) were used. The results suggested that executives might have greater risk bearing preferences when they are motivated and monitored. In other words, executives self-select firms that offer incentives and higher levels of total remuneration. In addition, the results demonstrated that a positive association between corporate controls and firm performance is associated with the level of firm risk.

The study tested the effectiveness of monitoring and incentive contracts for firms with risk, that is, the relationship of monitoring and incentive contracts to firm performance given the level of firm risk. The results of this study of 282 firms demonstrated how the relationship between firm risk and performance is associated with the monitoring and incentive contracts used by these firms. In particular, the results of this study showed that the negative association between risk and firm performance is weakened when firms have stronger monitoring and incentive mechanisms. The particular contribution of this study was to demonstrate that the role of corporate governance variables in firm performance should be evaluated in the context of the firm's risk. Furthermore, this study demonstrated that not all incentives available to firms are value increasing to all firms. Rather, greater firm performance is associated with the characteristics of the firm that endogenously determines the mix of monitoring and incentives selected by the firm.

The *Chung, Eneroth and Schneeweis* effort focused on the role of corporate reputation on a firm's current and future financial performance. In their study, the relationship between a firm's equity performance and reputation ratings published in the Economist (U.K.) and Fortune (U.S.) magazine were investigated for the period of (1990–1999). On a total return basis, monthly equity-returns of high-reputation firms were shown to outperform those of low-reputation firms both in the year prior and following the "reputation" reporting month. Other studies' results indicate that the size of a firm's market capitalization positively affects the firm's reputation (McGuire et al., 1990; Nanda et al., 1996; Shefrin & Statman, 1994, 1995). However, their study demonstrates that, unlike previous studies, it is primarily a firm's equity performance in the pre-survey and survey period that affects the published ranking of the firm's reputation and the published ranking has little impact on the firm's future risk-adjusted equity return.

The results of this study also indicate that a firm's equity performance in the survey period affects its reputation rating; that is, firms which perform poorly (well) in their equity performance in the survey period decline (rise) in their reputation rankings. This result is also indicative of "non-naive" respondents who use the equity market performance as a basis for reputation ratings. Thus, firm size is not a sole determinant of reputation ranking. The less than robust relationship between firms' risk-adjusted equity performance and their published rankings is also indicative of the lack of a market reaction to the information of reputation rankings. It is important to realize that information about individuals' view about a firm should be immediately reflected into the today's equity price. Only future unexpected changes in firms' corporate activities would affect future equity prices. Investors or corporate managers who use reputation rankings as a basis for future investment or as indicative of future risk-adjusted performance may only be capturing the expected returns underlying the fundamental risk and return patterns of the firm.

The *Low and Davenport* paper differentiates between social reporting and triple bottom line reporting. Using information and case studies from New Zealand, they contrasted the limited use of social reporting in the corporate sector with its more extensive use in the not-for-profit sector. They also outlined how social reporting and Triple Bottom Line Reporting (TBLR) are likely to move forward in parallel in New Zealand. The two competing approaches to social reporting acceptance are stand alone social reports based on the Social and Ethical Accounting, Auditing and Reporting standards (SEAAR) (ISEA, 2001) and Triple Bottom Line Reporting (Elkington, 1997). The triple bottom line refers to the organization's economic, environmental and social impacts, and therefore social reporting and triple bottom lining are clearly not mutually exclusive. However, the authors argued that social and ethical accounting, auditing and reporting as it is being practiced by a number of companies is not simply a complement to triple bottom line reporting, but tends to be qualitatively different, being process driven and requiring active, ongoing engagement with stakeholder groups.

The authors found that SEAAR and triple bottom line reporting have followed largely parallel lines of development in New Zealand. SEAAR has been adopted and developed primarily in the community/not-for-profit sector while TBLR has become the "standard" for the private sector so far. How and whether these two approaches to stakeholder engagement and accountability can come together, is therefore unclear, given the dearth of opportunity for cross-fertilization between the two sectors. The authors suggested the mediating factor might be the role government must play in indirectly encouraging social reporting by organizations of all types and directly financially supporting developments in both social auditing and TBLR.

However, the tentative conclusion of this study is that social auditing will continue to be favored by "values-driven" organizations (both private and not-for-profit) and TBLR will continue to be favored by mainstream companies.

IMPLEMENTATION OF CORPORATE GOVERNANCE MEASUREMENT

The *Schroth* work is the first in a series of papers in this volume dedicated to implementation of Corporate Governance measurement criteria. It describes the context of international anti-bribery and anti-deductibility efforts and the "business judgment rule" that protects directors from liability for mere negligence in most countries and the "new corporate law" or federalization of this area of the law in the United States, in part through the Foreign Corrupt Practices Act of (1977). It proceeds to the accounting and internal controls provisions of the two treaties and analysis of the national reports on this aspect of their implementation. The last section discussed the lessons to be drawn from this experience, noting in particular that it should provide valuable guidance to the drafters of corporate governance provisions in the planned United Nations convention against corruption and the possible Asian convention against corruption.

The author asserted the importance of transparency in the process. Transparency, in principle, management can be well informed without sharing its knowledge with others, but even to enforce this much, others must be able to determine whether management is well informed. One way – perhaps not the only way, but surely the simplest way – is to require that management be informed in a manner transparent to some suitable third party, such as shareholders and perhaps other stakeholders, independent auditors or a securities and exchange commission. On the other hand, transparency, in the limited sense of accurate accounts, is not enough, because accurate accounts may be silent on important matters. The real point must be to bring the information to the attention of management, so that management can behave responsibly, or, at least, be held accountable for its knowing failure to do so.

The focus of the *Birch* exegesis explores the aspirational rhetoric promulgating new directions for business to take with respect to corporate social responsibility and corporate citizenship. Senior CEOs of global companies have taken to this with considerable energy. However, at the end of the day, we are left facing the question whether the aspirations and visions are actually seriously embedded into the core business of the companies espousing the principles. The author focused his analysis on one major mining company, Rio Tinto (World's second largest mining company), and examines, through the *Rio Tinto Business with*

Communities programme (Rio Tinto, 2000, 2001, 2001b) the sort of enabling environment required to translate aspiration into everyday reality within a large global company.

A basic premise followed in this paper is that the fulfilling of responsibilities (to all those stakeholders who have contributed, and continue to contribute, to the survival and success of the company) effectively and the translation of leadership vision into core business reality is impossible without an enabling environment being put in place. Birch found Rio Tinto has clearly demonstrated at its most senior executive level a significant commitment to these developments. It has translated these commitments into policies, and publicly declared its commitment through its mandatory and non-mandatory reports each year. Furthermore, it has sought ways to engage with the communities in which it operates, and those which consider themselves to have either a direct or indirect interest in Rio Tinto's affairs, and has actively developed a comprehensive approach to stakeholder engagement, out of which has emerged the Business with Communities program which seeks to establish long-term partnerships with some of those key stakeholders. This partnership program has the potential to act as a significant enabling environment for the sharing and learning of new cultural vocabularies, through which the vision of the senior executives of the company can be translated into everyday core business. In effect, Rio Tinto provides a role model for other corporate citizens.

The *Murray and Lassalle-de Salins* paper explored the roles of a civil society in Trade Negotiations. They suggest that the apathy of the Uruguay Round where the early negotiations only drew the attention of those significantly and directly affected by the outcomes has changed. Hundreds of non-governmental organizations (NGOs) are now concerned about the issues of globalization and international trading relationships. Some groups criticize what they think is wrong with globalization while others are providing suggestions for improved outcomes. Both groups, however, perceive that the interests of the many are being excluded, i.e. that there is a democracy deficit.

The result has been protest. The protestors come from many occupations including trade unions fearing for jobs, farmers seeking a continuation of their subsidies, environmentalists concerned about ecological degradation and biodiversity, humanitarians calling for improved living conditions for the poor, supporters of animal rights and endangered species, and the list goes on. The views of the various NGOs are often contradictory, and some even internally inconsistent. The protestors mainly come from rich countries, but their interests are often global. Not all of civil society is civil, but neither is all of civil society wrong. Some NGOs are well intended, professionally managed, better funded than many of the governmental agencies dealing with particular international economic policy negotiations. Many NGOs have something of value to contribute. The authors suggested that to address the perceived problem, the WTO has taken steps to improve its relationships with civil society. However, the steps taken have been insufficient to conciliate its critics. International cooperation, by its very nature, requires that each Member country sacrifice a degree of national sovereignty. Such sacrifices must be offset by benefits coming from the resulting global governance. These trade-offs are seldom easy and are impossible to structure without imposing hardships on at least some groups in each society. As a follow-up to the points raised, the authors attempted to explore the methods used by Codex to include civil society in its deliberations leading to the elaboration of international food standards.

The *Dobson* effort delves into the discipline of behavioral finance and its adoption of an implicit prescriptive agenda. Behavioral finance does not merely describe financial market reality, it shapes it. Economic rationality is taken as the ideal toward to which individuals "should" strive. In this study, the author demonstrated that, as a behavioral ideal, economic rationality is unjustified both from a strictly economic perspective, and from a moral perspective. In short, there is nothing inherently "wrong" with economically irrational participants in the business environment. Indeed such participants will actually enhance the efficiency, and the ethicality, of business.

He argued that Behavioral finance does not merely describe financial market reality, it shapes it. Economic rationality is taken as the ideal toward which individuals "should" strive. In this paper Dobson asserted that, as a behavioral ideal, economic rationality is unjustified both from assuming away other motivations and thus elevating wealth-maximization to the status of a necessary law of nature, behavioral finance may be sanctioning behavior that society at large regards as, at best, morally questionable, and, at worst, strictly immoral. In the corporate milieu, by assuming unbridled self-interest, behavioral finance promotes unbridled self-interest. Furthermore, even if empirical evidence was to overwhelmingly support wealth maximization as the dominant motivation among contemporary economic agents (which, as we have just seen, it does not), behavioral finance's normative dimension would still obligate it to consider alternatives.

The *Tabalujan* paper focused on Indonesian corporate governance proposals from a legal-sociological perspective. The paper builds on two earlier papers. In the first paper (Tabalujan, 2001), he sketched the legal and business context of the Indonesian corporate governance framework during the 1990s, with specific reference to the banking sector. That paper demonstrated that, during the 1990s, despite some negative issues like cronyism and corruption, overall, significant improvements had been made in the "hardware" – the rules, institutions and technical framework – of Indonesian corporate governance. In the second paper (Tabalujan, 2002), he undertook three case studies relating to Indonesian banks, which showed that actual corporate governance behavior during the 1990s was far from the standard to be expected. He chose three banks (Bank Duta, Bank Summa & Bank Pikko) simply because banks were (and still are) among the most highly regulated companies in Indonesia and may thus be considered the bellwether of Indonesian corporate governance. In order to explain the significant divergence in the case studies between formal corporate governance principles on the one hand and actual corporate governance phenomena on the other, he postulated that the gap between stated principles and actual practice was due to the fact that Indonesian legal culture was not yet ready to embrace the changes brought about by reformist rules and institutions which sought to improve the Indonesian corporate governance system.

This paper elaborated further that, at least in Indonesia, culture matters to corporate governance. In particular, he focused on the recent work of Licht (1998, 2001). Licht et al. (2001) who utilizes insights from the field of cross-cultural psychology in order to create a framework of testable hypotheses, which can be used to examine the correlations between cultural value dimensions and corporate governance. Tabalujan is concerned that by not considering the impact of social and cultural factors, studies in the area may be inadvertently overstating the rate of progress in the growth of legal and corporate governance systems in these countries, while understating the actual problems faced by development initiatives and the time required to implement them – especially through ignorance of the cultural resistance which may stifle such initiatives.

The *Jonker* paper argued that at present, the "Corporate social responsibility" (CSR) movement is a "first generation" attempt to discuss and redefine the role and position of business organizations in contemporary society. He asserted that real encompassing CSR seems to require a different (world) view, one that takes into account the fundamental shift in societal power balances that has taken place in the past decades. Further, he suggested that it seems to imply a more "responsible" behavior of the business enterprise embedding a variety of nondescript social obligations. This perspective was based upon the generally accepted recognition that an enterprise operates within a societal network of stakeholders, who are influencing directly or indirectly the results of the enterprise.

He suggested that managing the sphere of influence of the firm has become a dynamic process as new transactions develop and change. Organizational Citizenship should lead to a mainstream business strategy to be conceived of as a responsible investment in social capital that generates a win-win for both the organization and for society. The meaning of the social responsibility of business is a *business strategy* – a way of determining direction and creating and maintaining relationships and structures that enhance performance. The bottom-line is that it will force businesses to rethink and redefine their societal and environmental responsibilities (whatever the specific meaning of consequences) without losing sight of their primary economic responsibilities. For many organizations, this will mean an alteration – if not fundamental shift – in their all too familiar business paradigm. The business case for CSR should interconnect the business aim and what needs to be done to ensure that the aim is achieved, through an adequate (corporate) strategy.

The *Batten and Hogan* contribution provides insight on the structures of corporate governance in banking and about the means by which bank boards and management secure the optimization of risk-reward structures. The authors assert that new developments reflecting legislative changes and proliferation of stakeholder interests emphasize the need for institutions to account for their social responsibilities beyond the maximization of shareholders' returns. New tasks for board and management are imposed by these requirements whether formal or otherwise. Yet there are complicated issues as to what these requirements mean and how they should be analyzed. While the analysis of obligations arising in the banking sphere reach well beyond the financial services sector, the concerns for establishing the basis for testing whether or not the new requirements or goals have been achieved are important. The paper sets out to establish what formal meanings may be attached to goals of social responsibility and their interpretations for testing outcomes. The authors' aim at providing a framework for discussion of what social responsibility means for banks and other deposit-taking institutions.

A debate on governance and social responsibility in banking is crucial given that they remain at the core of financial systems in both the developed and undeveloped world. A unique feature of bank operations is the settlement afforded by the payments system whereby banks may write cheques against themselves. In light of the essential culture of credit at the heart of banking operations then the structures of corporate governance should reflect the supervision and management of risks and credit especially so. The applicability of social responsibility concepts to banking activities was the key focus considered by the authors.

The *Dutta, Bozdogan, Collins and Wansley* effort introduced the use of Bozdogan's Informational Complexity (ICOMP) (Bozdogan, 1988, 1990a, b), criterion to help determine empirically for a sample of firms whether institutional ownership is endogenous or exogenous to the system of equations determining the relation between equity ownership and corporate policy. The new Informational Complexity ICOMP criterion for model selection is applicable to general multivariate linear and non-linear structural models. The authors provide a proof for ICOMP.

The authors conceptualized ICOMP's application to document the role of individual institutional investors as monitors of corporate management, they do not address the question whether such ownership, in general, is exogenously or endogenously determined. Researchers in the field of finance have put forward theoretical hypotheses whereby institutional owners (earlier referred to as "large shareholders", which could be either individuals or institutions) could function either endogenously or exogenously in determining the debt and dividend policies of firms. Thus, there is no clear-cut prior expectations on the role of institutional holdings in the joint determination of corporate ownership and corporate policy. In such a situation, ICOMP would be an ideal tool to help determine whether institutional ownership is endogenous (that is, a dependent variable) or exogenous (an explanatory variable only) to the system of equity ownership and corporate policy. In the field of economics, ICOMP has been used to measure food consumption in the Netherlands. They assert that the potential usage for this criterion is manifold. Any research situation in which two (or more) competing models need to be evaluated to determine which is better can use ICOMP to resolve the issue.

REFERENCES

Aggarwal, R. K., & Samwick, A. A. (1999). The other side of the trade-off: The impact of risk on executive compensation. *Journal of Political Economy, 107*(1), 65–106.

Arellano, M., & Bond, S. (1991). Some tests of specification for panel data: Monte Carlo evidence and an application to employment equations. *Review of Economic Studies, 58*, 277–297.

Banzhaf, J. F., III (1965). Weighted voting doesn't work: A mathematical analysis. *Rutgers Law Review, 19*, 317–343.

Banzhaf, J. F., III (1966). Multi-member electoral districts – Do they violate the "One-man – One vote's" principle? *Yale Law Journal, 75*, 1309–1338.

Banzhaf, J. F., III (1968). One man – 3,312 votes: A mathematical analysis of the electoral college. *Villanova Law Review, 13*, 304–332.

Becht, M., & Böhmer, E. (2000). Voting control in German corporations. Universite Libre de Bruxelles, Working paper.

Bozdogan, H. (1988). ICOMP: A new model selection criterion. In: H. H. Bock (Ed.), *Classification and Related Methods of Data Analysis* (pp. 599–608). Amsterdam: North-Holland.

Bozdogan, H. (1990a). On the information-based measure of covariance complexity and its application to the evaluation of multivariate linear models, Communications in Statistics. *Theory and Methods, 19*, 221–278.

Bozdogan, H. (1990b). Multisample cluster analysis of the common principal component model in K groups using an entropicstatistical complexity criterion. Invited paper presented at the International Symposium on Theory and Practice of Classification, Puschino, Soviet Union.

Cable, J. (1985). Capital market and industrial performance: The role of West German banks. *Economic Journal, 95*, 118–132.

Carr, L. L. (1997). Strategic determinants of executive compensation in small publicly-traded firms. *Journal of Small Business Management, 35*(3), 1–12.

Denis, D. K. (2001). Twenty-five years of corporate governance research . . . and counting. *Review of Financial Economics, 10*, 191–212.

Elkington, J. (1997). *Cannibals with forks: The triple bottom line of 21st century business.* London: Capstone Publishing.

Fama, E. F., & Jensen, M. C. (1983). Separation of ownership and control. *Journal of Law and Economics, 24,* 301–325.

Gorton, G., & Schmid, F. A. (2000). Universal banking and the performance of German firms. *Journal of Financial Economics, 58,* 29–80.

Gross-Schuler, A., & Weigand, J. (2001). Sunk costs, managerial incentives, and firm performance. *DIW Vierteljahresheft, 2,* 275–287.

Hermalin, B. E., & Weisbach, M. S. (Forthcoming, 2003). Boards of directors as an endogenously determined institution: A survey of the economic literature. *Economic Policy Review.*

Holderness, C. G. (2001). A survey of blockholders and corporate control. *Economic Policy Review.*

Institute for Social and Ethical Accountability (2001). Accountability quarterly (1st quarter). ISEA, London.

Islam, S., & Clarke, M. (2000). *Social Welfare and GDP: Can We Still Use GDP For Welfare Measurement?* Seminar paper presented at CSES, Victoria University (7 September).

Islam, S., & Clarke, M. (2001). Measuring the quality of life: A new approach empirically applied to Thailand. Paper presented at INDEX2001 Quality of Life Indicators Conference, Rome (2–5 October).

Karpoff, J. M. (1998). The impact of shareholder activism on target companies: A survey of empirical findings. Working paper, University of Washington.

Januszewski, S. I., Köke, J., & Winter, J. K. (2002). Product market competition, corporate governance, and firm performance: An empirical analysis for Germany. *Research in Economics* (forthcoming).

Jensen, M., & Meckling, W. (1976). Theory of the firm: Managerial behavior, agency costs and ownership structure. *Journal of Financial Economics, 3,* 305–360.

Landsman, W. (1986). An empirical investigation of pension and property rights. *Accounting Review* (October), 662–691.

Lehmann, E., & Weigand, J. (2000). Does the governed corporation perform better? Governance structures and corporate performance in Germany. *European Finance Review, 4,* 157–195.

Lev, B., & Ohlson, J. A. (1982). Market-based empirical research in accounting: A review, interpretation and extension. *Journal of Accounting Research* (Supplement), 249–322.

Licht, A. N. (1998). International diversity in securities regulation: Roadblocks on the way to convergence. *Cardozo Law Review, 20,* 227.

Licht, A. N. (2001). The mother of all path dependencies: Towards a cross-cultural theory of corporate governance systems. *Delaware Journal of Corporate Law, 26,* 147.

Licht, A. N. et al. (2001). Culture, law and finance: Cultural dimensions of corporate governance laws, social science research network working paper, June 2001, available from: http://papers.ssrn.com/sol3/papers.cfm?abstract_id=277613

McGuire, J., Schneeweis, T., & Branch, B. (1990). Perceptions of firm quality. *Journal of Management, 16,* 167–180.

Modegliani, F., & Miller, M. (1958). The cost of capital, corporation finance and the theory of investment. *American Economic Review* (June), 261–297.

Morck, R., Shleifer, A., & Vishney, R. W. (1988). Management ownership and market valuation: An empirical analysis. *Journal of Financial Economics, 20,* 293–315.

Murphy, K. (1999). Executive compensation. In: O. Ashenfelter & D. Card (Eds), *Handbook of Labor Economics* (Vol. 3). Amsterdam: North-Holland.

Nanda, S., Schneeweis, T., & Eneroth, K. (1996). Corporate performance and firm perception: The British experience. *European Financial Management, 2,* 197–221.

Nickell, S., Nicolitsas, D., & Dryden, N. (1997). What makes firms perform well? *European Economic Review, 41*, 783–796.

Rappaport A. (1981). Selecting strategies that create shareholders' value. *Harvard Business Review* (May–June), 139–149.

Tabalujan, B. S. (2001). Corporate governance of Indonesian banks: The legal and business contexts. *Australian Journal of Corporate Law, 13*, 67.

Tabalujan, B. S. (2002). Why Indonesian corporate governance failed – conjectures concerning legal culture. *Columbia Journal of Asian Law, 14*, forthcoming.

Tinto, R., & the Corporate Citizenship Research Unit (2000). *Corporate citizenship – A planned approach to business/community partnerships.* Melbourne: Deakin University and Rio Tinto Ltd.

Tinto, R. (2001). *Corporate citizenship in Australia. The Rio Tinto 'Business with Communities Program'.* Melbourne: Rio Tinto Ltd.

Tinto, R. (2001b). *Community relations. Global business, local neighbour.* London & Melbourne: Rio Tinto plc & Rio Tinto Ltd.

Romano, R. (2000). Less is more: Making shareholder activism a valued mechanism of corporate governance. Working paper, Yale Law School.

Shefrin, H., & Statman, M. (1994). Behavioral capital asset pricing theory. *Journal of Financial and Quantitative Analysis, 29*, 323–349.

Shefrin, H., & Statman, M. (1995). Making sense of beta, size, and book-to-market. *The Journal of Portfolio Management, 21*, 26–34.

Shleifer, A., & Vishny, R. W. (1997). A survey of corporate governance. *Journal of Finance, 52*, 737–783.

Zahra, S. A., & Pearce, J. A., II (1989). Board of directors and corporate financial performance: A review and integrative model. *Journal of Management, 15*, 291–334.

GLOBALISATION, THE ENVIRONMENT AND RECENT TRENDS IN INTERNATIONAL TRADE

Pasquale M. Sgro

ABSTRACT

The process of globalization has had far-reaching social as well as economic effects. The term "globalization" is generally taken to mean an increase in international transactions in markets for goods, services and factors of production and a growth in institutions that straddle international borders. This development has also meant that the corporate governance mechanisms have to be reinforced to ensure fairness and transparency as well as social responsibility. Finally, international infrastructure and institutions have to evolve to facilitate and ameliorate the effects of the growth in this world trade on the environment, sustainable development and bio-diversity. This paper provides an overview of the current developments in all these areas.

1. INTRODUCTION

International trade, as a share of gross domestic product (GDP), grew rapidly in the decade of the 1990s. In fact, it grew three times as fast as in the decade of the 1980s. As well, regional trade among developing economies has flourished before and after the Asian crisis of the late 1990s. An examination of trade statistics will show that between 1979 and 1988, world output grew at an average annual rate

Social Responsibility: Corporate Governance Issues
Research in International Business and Finance, Volume 17, 21–45
Copyright © 2003 by Elsevier Science Ltd.
All rights of reproduction in any form reserved
ISSN: 0275-5319/PII: S027553190317002X

of 3.4% while trade grew at 4.3%. Between 1989 and 1998, the growth in world output was an annual rate of 3.2% while trade expanded at 6.2%.

The increasing importance of trade has come about due to at least three reasons. First, the rapid improvements in transportation and communication technology make it easier and cheaper to reach new markets. Second, successive rounds of tariff and other trade barrier reductions have freed up trade in both developed and developing countries. Third, processing trade – trade involving goods where components cross borders more than once before reaching final buyers – has expanded rapidly.

Structurally, the composition of world trade has also changed with commodities displaced by manufacturing, which now accounts for about 70% of world exports, and growth in services which has become the leading sector for foreign investment and export growth. This growth in world trade has been caused by many factors such as trade liberalization, harmonized institutions and increasing competitiveness in many developing societies. A major influence is also the growth in the transnational network structure of much of the world's production. For example, the largest 100 transnational firms (excluding those in banking and finance) now account for about one-sixth of the world's productive assets.

There has also been an expansion of multinationals in the services sectors of banking, advertising, legal, freight and credit, which have created a world system of production and business services, so much so that their geographic spread is erasing their national identities.

Along with this growth in world trade, the development of international institutions has also expanded to improve the efficiency of world trade as well as providing a safety net to the developing countries and other countries facing economic crisis at various times. These international organizations arose at various times in response to certain needs and as a way of overcoming the transactions, implementation and enforcement costs which are substantial. It is a Coase-like theorem argument for the evolution of these organizations.

Globalization is predominantly an economic process but through its impact on culture, government and virtually all aspects of domestic policy making, it has a powerful social effect. The term "globalization" also generally means an increase in international transactions in markets for goods, services and factors of production, plus the growth and expanded scope of many institutions that straddle international borders. These institutions include firms, governments, international institutions and non-governmental organizations (NGO). It also includes foreign direct investment (FDI), multinational corporations (MNCs) and integration of the world capital flows.

There have been increased capital flows with the most pronounced being in portfolio investment. Mobility of labor has not increased significantly over the same period. These global changes have been caused, inter alia, by changes in technology as well as changes in policy. For example, improvements in both transportation and communication have aided globalization while with the presence of the Internet, these changes are accelerated. Policies on the other hand have moved in different directions over the last 100 years. International trade was restricted after World War I (1914–1918) and then opened up after World War II (1939–1945).

Since this growth in international trade and the integration of capital markets has occurred, who have been the main beneficiaries. Certainly as consumers, the individual on average income is better off since he/she has a greater variety of goods to choose from at affordable prices. However, we also know that the effect of trade is to redistribute income where the losers are likely to be the owners of a country's scarce factors. It may also mean that for less developed countries (LDCs), income inequality may be reduced.

Concerning capital mobility, it is clear that access to global capital helps countries develop but it is also true that capital can be withdrawn suddenly (as in the Asian Financial Crisis of 1997) resulting in widespread recession in those countries which affects the whole population. Some of the lessons that have been learnt in the aftermath of the Asian Crisis of 1997 are instructive. First, the focus of the authorities should be on institution building to provide appropriate prudential regulations and a strengthening of the supervisory arrangements. This includes reinforcing the corporate governance mechanism to ensure fairness and transparency as well as social responsibility. Second, bolster the regional financial markets that are linked to global markets. Third, use capital controls to influence capital inflow. This latter lesson applies particularly to those economies that have weak financial systems. Capital controls should be used until their financial systems become stronger.

In Sections 2–5, will discuss the development in the composition of trade as well as the international infrastructure and institutions that have evolved to facilitate and ameliorate the effects of this growth in world trade on the environment, sustainable development and bio-diversity. In Sections 6–8, will discuss aspects of globalization, regulation and corruption in international trade.

2. TRADE COMPOSITION

In the developed industrial countries, there has been a large expansion in trade in services. This has occurred partially in response to the shift of comparative advantage in the production of manufactured goods to Newly Industrialized Countries (NICs). Trade in services is predominantly concerned with financial

services, insurance, telecommunications, transportation, computer and professional services (e.g. architecture, engineering and law). Services now account
for about 60% of GNP in developed industrial countries while trade in services
accounts for 25% of world trade.

As a result of these developments, the reduction or elimination of barriers to services trade becomes a major priority in the Uruguay Round of GATT negotiations
(1986–1994). The General Agreement on Trade in Services (GATS) concluded as
an integral part of the Final Act of the Uruguay Round Table negotiations. GATS
provides, for the first time, a rules-based multilateral framework for liberalization
of trade in services including movement of persons both as service providers and
as consumers. The GATS agreement has a number of important principles to both
protect and ensure acceptance of agreed-to rules and regulations. These principles
are:

- *Transparency*. Full information about all rules and regulations governing
  economic transactions should be given to all potential competitors to enable
  them to fully assess their costs and benefits.
- *Due process*. Opportunity to comment and the right to pursue issues should be
  given to everyone affected by the proposed standards.
- *Proportionality*. The cost of standards should be proportional to the regulatory
  benefit expected from their implementation.
- *Minimizing distortions of trade*. The least trade-distorting method of achieving
  legitimate social objectives should be adopted.
- *National treatment*. Regulations should be applied to both domestic and foreign
  products equally.
- *Mutual recognition of testing results*. There should be mutual recognition of
  testing results with respect to the certification of technical standards and mutual
  recognition of applicable educational and professional experience with respect
  to the certification of professional experience by governments.

Despite the world growth in services trade, many developing countries remain
highly dependent on commodities for their trade, employment and income. There
is dependence on a few commodities rather than diversification and commodity
price instability has led to unstable commodity export earnings. However, since
agriculture still remains their main comparative advantage, commodity based
diversification offers the best chance for development. The competitiveness of
developing countries in the international commodity market could be enhanced
by the general reduction in protection and greater cooperation and help from the
developed countries would improve the supply reliability and quality. Agriculture
will still be the main source of foreign exchange earnings for developing
countries.

The growth in services trade has implications for migration management in both developed and developing countries. It is a source of job creation in labor surplus developing economies where by taking advantage of their low cost labor (including certain skill types) these countries can provide organized export of labor services. Since temporary movement of persons can be a partial substitute for longer-term migration, it can serve both the interests of developing and developed countries. This does imply a need for the harmonization of special visa and migration regimes to facilitate, monitor and manage trade-selected movements of service producers and consumers as distinct from longer-term migration for employment and permanent settlement.

The provision of most services demands close proximity in terms of both time and space, between the provider and the consumer. This implies for most services, delivery across countries cannot be completed without the movement of persons. There are, it should be pointed out, services that can be embodied in a material object and treated as goods such as a musical concert recorded on a video, computer software on a disk or banking services provided via a telecommunications system.

In general, we can distinguish between two categories of exports of labor services. In the first category, there are workers who reside, work and are paid abroad on specific assignments. In the second category, exporting firms combine management, technological know-how and personnel and provide their services as a package to the importing country. The globalization of the world economy along with outsourcing of services, transport and communications, have widened the potential export growth of this second category.

Trade-related labor mobility or access to markets by service providers is intimately related to the issue of licensing and certification requirements. Even if there are no immigration restrictions, the pressure of severe and non-transparent restrictions on the licensing of foreign professional and technical personnel can severely restrict exports. These restrictions can take many forms including requirements of nationality and residence, lack of recognition of degrees and denial of access to examinations for qualifications.

3. GLOBAL ECONOMIC ORGANIZATIONS

Three of the most important Global Economic Organizations are the World Trade Organization (WTO), the World Bank (WB) and the International Monetary Fund (IMF). Table 1 from Vines (1998) provides a summary of these organizations as well as their core role in the international community. There are similarities between the organizations but also important differences which will become apparent as we proceed.

PASQUALE M. SGRO

Table 1. Global Economic Regimes and Organizations: A Sketch Map.

Regime & Organization	Aspect of Regime and Activity of Organization	Type of Influence Wielded by Organization	Type of Sanctions That Support Influence	Organization Has Intellectual Leadership Capability?	Organization Has Policy Advice and Advocacy Capability?	Organization Has Access to Own Resources?
International Financial and Monetary System: IMF	Macroeconomic stability	Constraint on national policies	Conditionality; Informal only	Yes	Yes	Yes
	(1) Research and policy assistance					
	(2) Lending international exchange rate regime	International surveillance (very loose)				
	Solution to sovereign debt problems	Constraint on national policies	Conditionality			
	(1) Lending					
	(2) Debt restructuring?					
Development Policy: World Bank	Development assistance	Constraint on national policies		Yes	Yes	Yes
	(1) Research and policy assistance		Conditionality			
	(2) Lending "Other" development issues	?	?			
Global trading system: WTO	Solving collective action problems in trade	Global rules	Dispute settlement "Civil law" type. May become more difficult	Not yet	Not yet	No
	(1) Constraining domestic rent seeking					
	(2) "Strategic trade"	Regulatory structure				

Source: Vines (1998).

From World War II to almost the end of the 20th century, the international monetary system had functioned without a multilateral or international organization that dealt with trade issues between countries. Under the banner of the General Agreement on Tariffs and Trade (GATT), rules of the game were developed and "respected". Although GATT was an interim secretariat created through agreement amongst trading partners, it did not have the clout of the IMF or World Bank which were international organizations. In 1994, the Uruguay Round of trade negotiations ended under the GATT and agreement was reached to set up the World Trade Organization (WTO) which was born on 1st January 1995 and has the same legal and organizational standing as the IMF and World Bank. Although GATT was originally set up as an interim body to replace the failed International Trade Organization (ITO) that had been set up as a result of the Havana Charter of 1948 but subsequently was not supported by the USA, one of the few intact developed economies after World War II, ITO had been set up to ensure fairness in world trade, resolve disputes between members and institute coverage for the emerging markets in services, intellectual property rights and direct investment. Without support, ITO died and GATT became the major organization arbitrating on world trade until the WTO was formed fifty years later. Even though GATT did not have the legal status of an international economic organization, it nevertheless was able to achieve a great deal of liberalization of tariffs and trade as well as making the world economies more interdependent.

The WTO has its headquarters in Geneva, Switzerland, and is headed by a Director-General who heads the Secretariat and the General Council composed of representatives of each member state, which acts as required to review policy or settle disputes. The principles under which it operates are as follows. First, trade without discrimination, which binds members to grant to the products of other members treatment no less favorable than that accorded to the products of another country. Furthermore, once the goods have entered the market, they must be treated no less favorably than the equivalent domestically produced goods. It does however have provision for specific tariffs and other forms of protection under certain conditions. Second, predictable and growing access to markets which is intended to provide investors, employers, employees and consumers with a business environment that encourages trade, investment and job creation, choice and low prices in the market place. Related to this is the transparency of domestic laws, regulations and practices. Third, promoting fair competition and fair conditions of trade. Fourth, encouraging development and economic reform amongst all its members includes the developing and emerging economies that make up three-quarters of the WTO members. There are also provisions within WTO to favor developing and emerging economies in achieving these economic reforms. Its core role, therefore, is the writing of rules and enforcement of an explicit global regime whereby it provides a forum where rules can be written and a dispute settlement process where these rules can be enforced. For example, the Information Technology Agreement (ITA) concluded by members of the WTO in March 1997 should lead to a removal of tariffs on almost all types of information technology.

The main dispute-settling body of the WTO is the Disputes Resolution Body (DRB) where an aggrieved member may request the setting up of a Dispute Settlement Panel (DSP). The panel is set up with three members appointed from a panel of "well qualified" governmental and/or non-governmental individuals. Panels are required to complete their hearings and present their report within six months. In addition, panels are required to give "differential and more-favorable" treatment for the developing countries. The report is tabled and if none of the parties appeal, is adopted after sixty days. The appeals from the panels' cases are heard by a standing Appellate Body composed of "persons of recognized authority with demonstrated expertise in law, international trade and the subject matter of the covered agreements generally". An example of recent Dispute Panels are listed in Table 2.

Concerns about proliferating preferential arrangements such as NAFTA, APEC, EU and the like. Use of rules of origin and other protectionist measures within trading blocks has considerable potential for trade diversion and can therefore result in the establishment of more opportunities to multilateral trade liberalization. The development of these arrangements present a challenge for the WTO to ensure that these arrangements are compatible with an open multilateral system.

The IMF was a multilateral organization set up to administer the international monetary system as it was, to manage a specific system of rules about fixed exchange rates, which explicitly constrained the policies of member governments, in the global interest. Its current role has changed and today its two core activities (Table 1) are first, conducting research and offering advice on macroeconomic policies for industrial underdeveloped countries and second, to make loans to countries experiencing balance of payments problems. It is able to attach "conditionality" to its loans, ensuring that the well-researched advice will be heeded and repayments made since penalties for non-payment are quite heavy. The financial crisis of recent years, in Mexico in 1994, Asia 1997 and Russia and Brazil in 1998, have highlighted the instability of the liberalized market economy as well as the important role the IMF must play in such issues as coping with short-term capital flow and determining appropriate exchange rates for emerging economies. For example, free capital movements do not always bring about the optimum allocation of resources due to imperfect and asymmetrical information available to investors.

Table 2.   Recent Dispute Panels.

1	United States	Restrictions on imports of cotton and man-made fibre underwear. Complaint by Costa Rica (WT/DS24) involves U.S. restrictions on textile imports from Costa Rica.
2	United States	Measures affecting imports of woven wool shirts and blouses. Complaint by India (WT/DS33) concerns transitional safeguard measures imposed by the U.S.
3	European Communities	Regime for the importation, sale and distribution of Bananas. Complaints by Ecuador, Guatemala, Honduras, Mexico and the U.S. (WT/DS27) alleges violations of GATT Articles I, II, III, X, XI and CIII as well as other agreements.
4	European Communities	Measures affecting meat and meat products (hormones). Complaint by the U.S. (WT/DS26) alleges EU import restrictions violate GATT Articles III or XI and other agreements.
5	European Communities	Measure affecting meat and meat products (hormones). Complaint by Canada (WT/DS48) alleges EU import restrictions violate GATT Articles III or XI and other agreements (essentially the same as the U.S. claim WT/DS26).
6	Canada	Certain measures concerning periodicals. Complaint by the U.S. alleges Canadian prohibitions and/or restrictions on the importation of certain periodicals violate GATT Article XI.
7	Japan	Measures affecting consumer photographic film and paper. Complaint by the U.S. alleges Japan's laws, regulations and requirements affecting the distribution and sale of film violate GATT Articles III and X.

Source: http://www2/netdoor.com.au

The World Bank's original role was to channel capital to the war-torn global periphery in the face of a shortage on capital markets. Given the integration of global capital markets, this role is now superfluous. The present role of the World Bank is to bring together a lending, development research and assistance role through its International Bank of Reconstruction and Development (IBRD) and its concessional lending or aid role through its International Development Association (IDA). Essentially it sustains a global development policy role. It lends to governments for approved development projects and like the IMF, has conditionality via sanctions for countries not repaying loans.

Agreements on cooperation between the WTO, World Bank and IMF were reached in November 1996. These agreements provide for: (1) observer status to the WTO secretariat at IMF and World Bank meetings and vice versa; and (2) consultation between the staff of the three organizations concerning matters of mutual interest (essentially trade-policy related issues). Given the research resources of the World Bank and IMF, and the lack of such resources in the WTO, cooperation between the three organizations is essentially for a truly functioning global economic system.

4. THE ENVIRONMENT AND INTERNATIONAL TRADE AGREEMENTS

There have been widespread concerns about the natural resource use and environmental damage caused by the emphasis on trade and economic development. At the same time, trade policy discussions, including those in the WTO, have concentrated on the trade effects of environmental policies. The ongoing debate on trade and environmental policy distinguishes between domestic environmental problems where countries, it is argued, should be allowed to set their own standards. This does imply that low-income countries are free to choose lower air and water quality standards to develop a comparative advantage in pollution-intensive industries. The remedy in this case, however, is to correct the market failure and establish property rights rather than international trade policy, the argument being that environmental resources are not properly priced in the markets and since consumers do not bear the true cost of environmental resources, they tend to over-exploit. Where production and consumption decisions of one country impose environmental externalities on other countries (international environmental externalities), there is a stronger case for international trade policy intervention, although the more efficient solution would be to identify the source of the problem and take steps to internalize the environmental costs by getting the polluter to pay. Examples of this latter type of problem include global warming and biodiversity destruction which require multilateral cooperation such as a tax on carbon emissions. To protect endangered species, for example, there already exists the convention on International Trade in Endangered Species of Wild Flora and Fauna (CITES) which prohibits the trade in ivory, tiger skins and other products culled from endangered species. It requires that trade be subject to authorization by government-issued permits or certificates and was signed in 1975 by more than 125 countries. This restriction is based on certain types of trade and is to further sustainable development but may conflict with international trade law (the WTO).

There exist large differences across countries in environmental policies just as there are vast differences in other policies such as human rights, worker rights, education and health. In addition to the differences between countries in endowments of natural resources and environment, there are also differences in tastes and preferences for such endowments. As globalization increases, pressure to reduce trade barriers also increase. Part of this pressure reflects the concerns in countries with high environmental standards that higher production costs are making them less competitive compared with countries with lower standards. These differences are further highlighted as other traditional barriers to trade diminish. At the multilateral level, cooperative inter-governmental mechanisms for environmental policy have only recently been formed and will take time to become effective, while distorted world markets and a failure to apply economic instruments which support sustainable development is also a factor. The first-best remedy is to remove these market distortions which damage the environment and restrain development as well as devising mechanisms to internalize the environmental costs. An argument to justify applying trade restrictions is the case when environmental damage is directly and conclusively caused by trade. If the trade is in toxic waste, endangered species and other pollutant carrying products, the rules of GATT facilitates such actions. Article XX states that if the regulation is "necessary to protect human, animal or plant life or health" or "relating to the conservation of exhaustible natural resources" then it is permitted. However, to eliminate environmental damage efficiently it is still the case that the source of the problem be identified, internalize the environmental costs and get the polluter to pay. There have been a series of international agreements, with different groups of countries as signatories, tackling some of this more obvious environmental degradation that has occurred.

Due to the activities of the Canadian environmentalists in the early 1980s, and the U.S. and European environmentalists during the NAFTA debates in the early 1990s, the WTO set up the Committee on Trade and Environment (CTE) in Marrakesh in 1994. The mandate of this committee was to consider trade and environment's interrelationships and was directed to report to the first biennial meeting of the WTO which took place in Singapore in December 1996. The main issues discussed by the CTE were threefold. First, the relationship between trade and the various multilateral environmental agreements (MEAs) such as the Basel Convention and the Montreal protocol. The Basel convention on the Controls of Trans-boundary Movements of Hazardous Wastes and their Disposal, adopted in 1989, seeks to regulate the import and export of hazardous wastes to ensure that they are managed in an environmentally sound manner. The Montreal protocol on substances that deplete the ozone layer prohibits trade with parties that trade in ozone depleting substances and products harmful to the ozone layer. Second, the use of eco-labeling to convey information on harvesting processes with the product. Third, the relationship between market access and environmental measures. This last issue was of special interest to developing economies who were concerned that environmental laws would be used to limit their access to northern markets in the form of "green protectionism".

In addition to CITES and the Montreal and Basel Conventions, other International Environmental Agreements include the Convention on Biological Diversity

(CBD), the Framework Convention on Climate Change (FCCC) and the Kyoto Protocol and the North American Agreement on Environmental Cooperation (NAAEC).

The CBD was signed by over 150 governments at the Rio "Earth Summit" in 1992 and came into operation on the 29 December 1993. The aim of the agreement is to conserve the planet's biological diversity, ensure the sustainable use of its components, and promote the fair and equitable sharing of the benefits accruing from the use of genetic resources. The FCCC, which was also signed at the Rio Summit aims to limit or reduce emissions of greenhouse gases such as carbon dioxide. It came into operation in March 1994 and has been ratified by 176 countries. One of the aims of the Convention (Article 1) is to reduce the anthropogenic greenhouse gas emissions to 1990 levels by the year 2000. The third conference of the Parties to the Convention was held in December 1997 in Kyoto, Japan, where the countries adopted the Kyoto Protocol to the FCCC whereby developed countries committed legally binding targets to limit or reduce emissions of six major greenhouse gases, and an aggregate goal of a 5% reduction from 1990 levels by 2008–2012. There is still the unresolved issue of how to involve developing countries. This raises the issue of North-South equity and whether development will be hindered if countries are punished for emitting "excess" greenhouse gases. A possible source of conflict with international trade rules arises since the regulatory instruments that each country uses to meet the goals will be decided at the national level. There is also some debate on which trade measures will be used to enforce the convention.

The NAAEC was part of the NAFTA agreement which was signed by Canada, Mexico and the United States on 1 January 1994. The NAAEC was developed to support the environmental provision of the NAFTA by establishing a level playing field with a view to avoiding trade distortions and promoting environmental cooperation. The key objective of NAAEC is to promote sustainable development, encourage pollution prevention policies and practices and exercising compliance with environmental laws and regulations.

Most governments are disinclined to take environmental problems seriously. In fact, several of the MEAs have provisions that are against the WTO rules. To understand this conflict, it is useful to set out the three core GATT articles (which provided the foundation of the WTO regime). Article I: Most-Favored Nation Treatment (MFN) which prohibits members from disseminating between the product of others. Article II: National Treatment, prohibits dissemination between foreign and domestic producers. Article XI: Elimination of quantitative restrictions means that countries cannot restrict imports or exports by establishing quantitative limits, such as quotas or bans, to the flow of goods across its borders. For example, some MEAs seek to control or ban trade in endangered species, ozone depleting

Table 3.   Policy Effects of Trade and Bio-Diversity.

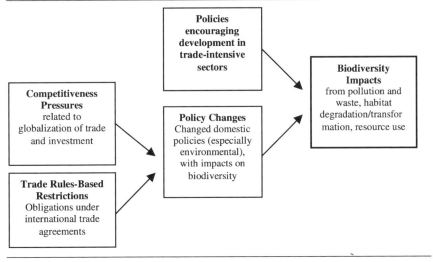

Source: Conway (1998).

substances and hazardous waste, however, such controls come into conflict with Article XI above which disallows quantitative restrictions. In order words, there is the primacy of trade policy objectives in the sense that the trade liberalization agreements establish a framework of rules and encourage trade patterns that effect public policy which in turn influence most of the objectives of MEAs. For example, the policy effects on biodiversity (in the CBD) are usefully summarized in Table 3. As part of the trade negotiations that occur periodically, the biodiversity impact of such negotiations should include an environmental impact assessment. This is especially important on new investments in particular sectors which are often linked to increases in habitat destruction, resource depletion and industrial pollution. The MEAs can play the role of mitigating some of the negative aspects of trade liberalization.

One of the major tasks for a sustainable global economy is to identify the areas of complementarity between specific MEAs and the WTO.

The UN Commission on Sustainable Development talks about "win-win-win" results (triple dividend) in terms of environmental trade and development gains. It argues that trade liberalization should be accompanied by environmental and resource management policies in order to achieve sustainable development. In order for developing countries to take full advantage of such policies, measures such as capacity building and improved access to finance and technology have been put in place by the international community. These policies should assist developing economies achieve agreed environmental targets.

5. LABOUR STANDARDS AND COMPETITIVE POLICY

Globalization has also led to a more liberal economic environment where issues such as labor standards, human rights, the environment, intellectual property rights, investment codes and competition policy are now considered legitimate topics in the trade debate.

The labor standards debate concerns the extent to which low wages and poor working conditions in developing countries constitutes an unfair advantage to them (relative to the developed countries) or merely reflect the inherent advantage of "surplus labor" economies. The environment debate concerns the different values placed on the environment by different countries and the extent of the benefits/costs that accrue to countries or regions most affected by such activities. Pricing these environmental costs to reflect the true economic costs to society is a technical issue. Just as important, however, is the institutional structure required to design, collect and implement the appropriate policies, such as a global carbon tax, while dispute resolution is seen as an important issue in this area. Arguments have also been put that the trade instrument is a potentially powerful sanction mechanism to enforce desirable changes in environmental policies. However, one has to be ever vigilant that this environmental concern is not used as a convenient devise to disguise protectionism. Intellectual property rights involve the practicalities of knowledge creation, control and ownership. For example, the appropriate valuation and treatment of indigenous knowledge is particularly relevant for developing economies.

The issues of competition policy and investment codes have been of more recent interest in the international community. The liberalization of capital markets along with competition policies that provide protection at the trade level, are ongoing debates in the WTO. For example, trade related investment policies and the need for new multilateral rules on investment (MRIs), particularly foreign direct investment, are seen as an issue for the new trade agendas. Presently there is no comprehensive international treaty or organization with a mandate over investment regulations, although there is a plethora of regional and bilateral agreements. The realization of the interrelationship between trade and investment had also led to the notion of market contestability (or market access). This concept emphasizes two essential ideas. First, a market is deemed internationally contestable when the conditions of competition allow unimpaired market access for foreign goods, services, ideas, investment and business people. Second, the investment mode of doing business is as important as trade because trade and investment are complementary ways of contesting markets. This debate is further complicated by the emergence of the new regionalism or what has come to be known as the "second regionalism".

The rules of the WTO are intended to strengthen cooperative behavior amongst countries. Given the interdependence in international trade between countries, such a set of rules should possess some desirable elements. These are set out in Table 4.

6. GLOBALIZATION AND REGIONALISM

Along with globalization, there has also been growth in the establishment and strengthening of regional corporations, or regionalism. Regionalism can be defined as a preferential reduction of trade barriers among countries that might, but need not be geographically contiguous. Discrimination not liberalization is the essential feature of regionalism. Some commentators distinguish between the "First Regionalism" in the 1960s and the "Second Regionalism" revived in the 1980s (Bhagwati, 1999). The first regionalism was heavily driven by the implementation of import-substitution policies at the regional level and was essentially protectionist in nature. The second regionalism is taking place in countries attempting to reinforce their outwardly orientated policies. The European Union (EU), the U.S.-Canada Free Trade Area to the North American Free Trade Agreement (NAFTA), the Asia-Pacific Economic Cooperation (APEC) and the Southern Cone Common Market (MERCOSUR) are just some examples of regional arrangements over these periods. The MERCOSUR was created by the Treaty of Ascuncion and signed by Argentina, Brazil, Paraguay and Uruguay in March 1991. These institutions and structures for cooperation can be almost seen as a reaction to globalization. That is, this new regionalism includes economic, political, social and cultural aspects and is much broader than the first regionalism immediately after World War II which was predominantly to do with free trade in goods. Furthermore, powerful regional arrangements and regional dispute settlement processes may pose a threat to orderly world trade in that there may be overlap and hence confusion as to which set of rules apply between WTO and regional obligations.

Traditionally regionalism was also seen as a harmonization of trade policies leading to deeper economic integration (the EU is a good example) with political integration seen as a possible future result. The current or modern regionalism has a number of dimensions (apart from the economic) including culture, security, and political. These dimensions all involve different degrees of change. For example, culture may take a long time while the transformation of the security regime may come sooner. Changes in the political regimes usually mean more

Table 4.   Elements of an Institutional Order for the World Economy.

	Type of Interdependence	Distortions, Disturbances	Rules
(1)	Exchange of goods and services	Protectionistic foreign trade policy (tariffs, import quotas, "voluntary" export restraints, strategic trade policy and industrial policy, anti-dumping, subsidies, product standards)	Trade rules, above all against new forms of protectionistic trade policy; country-of-origin principle for norms.
	- Goods	Calls for uniform social norms Market power of firms	No world-wide standardization possible. Competition rules. Free access to markets Competition authorities?
	- Services	Discrimination against foreign suppliers	National treatment
(2)	Factor migration	Not respecting property rights internationally reduces the incentive for technological progress	Property rights which protect new knowledge but permit gradual dissemination.
	- Technology		Governments compete using their infrastructure, tax system and regulations for mobile capita. Consequently, national self-interest impels countries to make themselves more attractive to outside capita. Aside from this, no international rules are necessary.
	- Capital	Risk of expropriation of foreign investments; tax competition for mobile capital	
	- Labor	Abrupt mass migrations	Free trade and free movements of capital as a substitute for labor migration. A right to emigrate (right to exit). Openness in immigration policy. Not achievable: a universal right of immigration.
(3)	Financial transactions	Volatility of exchange rates	Each country must keep the value of its money stable. Discretionary macroeconomic coordination is not possible unless each country submits itself to rules giving up sovereignty similar to the gold standard.
(4)	Diffusion of pollutants	Misuse of national environmental policy for strategic trade purposes; free rider behavior of individual countries in regard to global environmental problems.	International rules only for transfrontier and global environmental problems. National environmental problems are subject to national environmental policy. Separation between environmental policy and trade policy.

Source: Siebert (1998, p. 333).

democratization while economic policy changes move in the direction of opening up to trade.

Modern regionalism seemed to be as much concerned with political ambitions of establishing regional coherence and regional identity as with improving the movement of goods and services across national borders. A useful distinction can be made between three types of regions; core regions, peripheral regions and intermediate regions in between (Hattne, 1996).

The core regions are politically stable and dynamic. Europe is a good example, followed by North America and East Asia. The intermediate regions are closely linked to the core but are not yet as economically developed or as politically stable. These include Central Europe, Latin America and the Caribbean, China, South-East Asia and Oceania. The peripheral regions are politically turbulent and economically stagnant and their regional arrangements are ineffective and fragile. These include the post-Soviet area, the Balkans, the Middle East, South Asia and Africa.

At the political or foreign policy levels, regional trading blocs necessarily entail playing favourites and can lead to international factionalism. Furthermore, whatever their trade expansion perspectives, with respect to inter-regional trade, they do entail some measure of trade diversion thus distorting the efficient global allocation of resources. The rise of New Protectionism (especially quantitative restrictions) has been particularly pronounced in the USA and Europe in recent years with two of the main proponents of regional trading blocks (EU and NAFTA). However, one would expect that, over time, regional trading blocs will steadily move towards integration, through negotiation, with other trading blocs, while other blocs are already "open" to membership by subsequent parties. EU and OPEC are just two examples.

In general, the role of government in a modern world can be viewed as establishing infrastructure in the broadest sense – the educational, technological, financial, physical, environmental and social infrastructure of the economy. This infrastructure is necessary if markets are to operate in an economy and perform their role of increasing wealth and living standards. For developing and transition economies, governments face special problems on delivering these components of general infrastructure. Money markets are lacking and those that do exist may not function effectively, infrastructure problems are more severe and the capacity of governments to correct those markets failures is generally weaker.

Some on the other hand argue that governments also have a major role in "managing" globalization. That is, their role is to reduce risk and spread benefits through regulation, enforcement and redistribution of income and wealth. This expanded role is not easy as international markets become larger and stronger and multinational firms (with no allegiance to any particular country) expand.

7. REGULATORY REFORMS AND TRADE FACILITATION

To the extent that standards, technical regulations and certification systems differ across countries, they may act as a barrier to the free flow of trade. Hence, as a component of the move towards globalization and freer trade, regulatory reform has become an important issue. Additional reasons for this growing importance can be summarized as follows. First, the development of new products and services has made many regulations more ineffective in terms of the objective they were designed to achieve. That is, regulations that are product or service specific become more distortionary as they prevent the introduction of new goods or services. This is particularly the case in the provision of financial services. Second, new insights into the design of economically efficient regulations have been provided. It is now recognized that the various kinds of regulations providing different incentive structures make regulatory design much more important. Third, globalization of production and markets has made distinctions based on national origin difficult and increased the cost of regulation. Firms are able to locate closely linked production activities in different countries to take advantage of specific resources and characteristics in the different countries. Therefore large differences in national regulations will have a bearing on the production and can add to the costs. Regulatory reform can therefore lead to reductions in costs, larger economic growth and a higher standard of living. This will also apply to international trade as it promotes open national markets and global competition.

Conflict over reducing regulations and non-tariff barriers (NTBs) and encouraging competition can often arise between the priority of national sovereignty and total harmonization. The issue of domestic policy harmonization or convergence when it comes to trade regulations becomes much more involved since the effect on social welfare of harmonizing domestic policy is not as unambiguous as the usual welfare analysis of reducing tariffs and quotes. Competition also exists between agencies and governments as to whose set of regulatory policies should apply. As well, competition may apply between international voluntary standards bodies like the International Standards Organization (ISO) which is a non-government body and the International Labor Organization (ILO) on setting rules for maker protection and rights. In practice, much regulatory harmonization occurs as a result of private sector initiative whether at the firm or industry level.

Standards, testing and certification procedures can restrict international trade in many ways. Industry confronts additional costs in product modification that often has no value to consumers or public health, safety or environmental protection. The Uruguay Round produced the first binding set of rules governing technical barriers with a new Technical Barrier to Trade (TBT) agreement. In general, standards used in the production of goods vary by purpose, specificity, as well as development time. The majority of products traded on the world market are manufactured through voluntary consensus standards or through de facto industry standards. The voluntary standards are developed via discussion with manufacturers, consumers and other interested (including government) officials. Standards-developing bodies exist at the national and international level. For example, at the international level, the ISO and the International Electrotechnical Commission (IEC) develop voluntary consensus standards such as the ISO 9000 series on quality and the ISO 1400 series on the environment. These are not mandatory but can be used by governments to restrict or forbid imports. Standards, in some cases, are established to promote a public good.

Governments may also set mandatory standards at national, regional or local level. These standards are commonly referred to as technical regulations or regulatory standards. These relate to public health, safety or the environment and involve product testing and certification as an important part of the global trading system. Most international trade disputes involve demands by government for mandatory third-party certification. That is, the certification is to be carried out by organizations that are independent of any link to the manufacturer or purchaser. In fact, the provision of third-party testing services has become a highly profitable and growth industry in many countries.

A similar method to certification is product labelling where these labels, usually mandated by governments, specify the environmental impact of a product or the nutritional content of processed food (including genetically modified (GM) labels).

One of the main reasons why product standards have become more important is that global manufacturing requires standardized parts for production, leading to lower final costs to consumers as well as economies of scale when there are multiple markets. These standards also affect competition between global firms where firms, having accepted global standards, compete by differentiating their product or design and product features. They will also influence the pace of innovation as improvement in and new products are introduced.

The issues under discussion by the World Trade Organization (WTO) on trade facilitation, includes the following aspects: measures to reduce data and documentation requirements; measures to streamline and automate customs and other official interventions, and measures to build capacity in developing countries.

One of the concerns of firms involved in international trade is the lack of transparency and predictability of WTO members' rules and regulations governing import and export procedures. This lack of transparency causes delays as well as allowing discretionary (and sometimes corrupt) practices to flourish. Non-discrimination is the cornerstone of the General Agreement on Tariffs and Trade (GATT) and the WTO and should be a basic obligation in any trade foundation program to ensure fair and equal treatment to all traders. The concept of "least trade restrictions" should be applied to all import, export and customs procedures to ensure that those procedures are limited to the absolute minimum needed to carry out public policy objectives. Special and Differential Treatment (S&DT) provisions also exist in WTO to give developing countries extra time to comply with trade facilitation measures. A related issue is the interrelationship between product standards and free trade, and the recent bilateral, regional and multilateral trade talks involving developing economies and efforts to reduce technical and regulatory barriers. The removal of barriers to trade in standards, testing and certification could be viewed as a logical extension of global trade policy efforts in the latter half of the 20th century.

The U.S. and the European Union (EU) have taken a tentative first step towards reducing technical and regulatory barriers with the conclusion of the U.S.-EU Mutual Recognition Agreement (MRA) on product testing and certification. These MRAs address regulatory reform in product areas which are subject to relatively high government regulations. The MRA model focuses on third-party testing, inspection and certification in sectors regulated by governments through product approval systems.

Regulatory reform in international trade has also received a great deal of attention from the Organization for Economic Cooperation and Development (OECD) and WTO. Inappropriate regulations can result in substantial losses to both individual sectors of the economy and the economy as a whole. The type of sectoral features include higher costs, higher prices, misallocation of resources, a lack of product innovation and poor service quality. Analysis has been carried out that show that major productivity gain can be achieved in all sectors of our economy. Table 5 sets out some estimates of the gains from regulatory reform for a selection of OECD countries.

The 21 member economies in Asia-Pacific Economic Cooperation (APEC) have identified trade facilitation as one of its three priorities (the other two being trade and investment liberalization and economic and technical cooperation). For example, a significant part of the exports from APEC countries to the world markets involving electrical machinery and its appliances, industrial equipment and metal-working equipment, is subject to a duplication of testing and certification in every one of the member nations of APEC. The costs that accrue to any firm engaged in this export market are quite high.

An important factor in trade facilitation is the stability of the international financial institutions and the effective functioning of global capital markets. To ensure this effective functioning, transparency and accountability contribute to the improvements of the economic performance of both these markets and institutions.

Table 5.   Estimated Effects of Regulatory Reform: Summary (Percentage Change Relative to Baseline).

	United States	Japan	Germany	France	United Kindom	Netherlands	Spain	Sweden
Partial effects[a]								
Labour productivity	0.5	2.6	3.5	2.3	2.0	1.3	3.1	1.7
Capital productivity	0.5	4.3	1.3	3.3	1.4	2.9	3.1	1.3
Total factor productivity	0.5	3.0	2.8	2.7	1.8	1.8	3.1	1.5
Business sector employment	0.0	-1.0	-0.4	-0.4	-0.5	0.6	-0.7	-0.6
Wages	0.0	0.0	-0.1	0.0	0.0	-0.2	-0.1	0.0
GDP price level	-0.3	-2.1	-1.3	-1.4	-1.2	n.a.	n.a.	n.a.
Economy-wide effects[b]								
GDP	0.9	5.6	4.9	4.8	3.5	3.5	5.6	3.1
Unemployment	0.0	0.0	0.0	0.0	0.0	0.0	0.0	0.0
Employment	0.1	0.0	0.0	0.0	0.0	0.0	0.0	0.0
Real wages	0.8	3.4	4.1	3.9	2.5	2.8	4.2	2.1

Source: http://www.oecd.org//subject/regreform/economy.htm

[a] These effects are based on an aggregation of estimated sector-specific effects. They cover the business sector only.

[b] These effects include long-term and dynamic interactions in the economy as a whole and are based on simulations with a simplified macroeconomic model. The simulations for the Netherlands, Spain and Sweden are preliminary but the estimates nevertheless include some dynamic effects, and thus go beyond those reported in the individual Country Notes tables. For Spain, the estimates are based on 1990 cost structures, and subsequent reforms may have affected them to some degree.

Transparency refers to a process by which information about existing conditions, decisions and actions is made accessible, visible and understandable. It ensures that market participants have sufficient information to identify risk at the firm, national or international level. Accountability on the other hand refers to the need to justify and accept responsibility by decision-makers. It is a form of discipline on decision-makers intended to improve the quality of decisions taken.

It is useful to distinguish between transparency and accountability of three groups; the private sector, national authorities and international financial institutions. There is a significant degree of consensus in the international community on the objectives and elements of private sector disclosures. Through financial statements and other disclosures, firms should provide information that is material to investors' decisions. Such information should reflect the following elements:

- *Timeliness* – information of material importance should be disclosed on a periodic and timely basis, using a set of high quality, internationally acceptable accounting standards;
- *Completeness* – financial statements should cover all relevant transactions, both on and off the balance sheet;
- *Consistency* – accounting policies and methodologies should be applied consistently over time, and any changes should be identified and related effects disclosed;
- *Risk Management* – the strategies used to manage risks should be disclosed;
- *Audit and control processes* – firms should have effective systems of internal control, and financial statements should be reviewed annually by an independent auditor.

Poor disclosure practices in the private sector mainly stem from inadequate compliance with and enforcement of existing standards. At the national level, transparency and accountability require the provision of timely, comprehensive and accurate information about macroeconomic developments and policies. The IMF has established standards for this dissemination under its Special Data Dissemination Standards (SDDS) and the General Data Dissemination System (GDDS). For international financial institutions, following these internationally recognized disclosure standards is important. This would strengthen their credibility with both the national authorities and the public in general. Clearly there is also a need for confidentiality but this must be balanced against transparency. For example, the views of say the IMF on the sustainability of a member's current policies may be sensitive but policy advice and project assessments of multilateral development banks is less controversial.

8. CORRUPTION AND INTERNATIONAL TRADE

Corruption as an issue in international trade emerged in the 1990s. The problem of corruption has been around a long time and in fact dates back at least to the Romans. However, international institutions and governments of developed economies have only relatively recently decided to coordinate their efforts in trying to reduce or eliminate corruption. A manifestation of this interest by the IMF and OECD was the setting up of an independent non-profit organization in 1993 known as Transparency International (TI). This organization, through its agencies in more than 70 countries, works to strengthen civil society leadership and forge coalitions between government, business and academia in an effort to restrict corruption. It has participated in the development of the OECD Anti Corruption Convention which came into force in February 1999. This organization also produces an International Corruption Perception Index (ICPI) which seeks to rank countries according to their known record of behavior. There are various types of corruption from small time fraud and bribery to institutionalized and systemic corruption on a wide scale.

At a basic level, governments, as institutions, work to provide a framework in which conflict over property rights and obligations between various members of society can be resolved. That is, they provide laws and regulations to enable private individuals and groups to co-exist. This legal control over the implementation of law is akin to monopoly power over the public and private assets affected by the specific law. This monopoly power provides profits or rents to these officials.

This rent-seeking behavior is controlled by centuries of social, political, economic and legal developments so that, in most cases, we have a fairly strong legal, civil and moral code of behavior amongst public officials. Certainly it is acknowledged that this is the case in most western developed countries.

This however is not the case in all countries. It is not clear what causes corruption in some countries and not others although the World Bank and others are conducting large projects to try and determine this. Some features are however apparent. When corruption is prospering, there has emerged a convergence between the formal and informal rules that govern behavior in the public sector, even though every country has formal anti-corruption laws. What is clear, however, are the consequences of corruption.These include:

- Reduction in government revenue and increased expenditure, thus making sound fiscal management much more difficult;
- The watering down of legitimate regulation governing due diligence in industries covering finance, real estate, health and transport. Where corruption induces

excessive regulation to engineer monopoly rents, it further distorts market behavior;

- Individuals waste resources in pursuing monopoly rents, thus impeding genuine productive activity;
- There is a vast distortion of the distribution of wealth and income, and in particular results in inequitable taxation across disadvantaged groups;
- In distorting the equity of social administration and the legal system, corruption lessens the attraction of the free market for the exploited and can add to forces seeking the elimination of democracy;
- As managers seek to find their way around a plethora of empty rules and regulations imposed by officials in search of rents, distortion of entrepreneurial time results.

At a more decentralized level, corruption reduces investment and the rate of economic growth; expenditure on health and education as these service industries are less easily exploited; expenditure on current operating costs and maintenance of government production assets; the productivity of public investment; tax revenue and foreign direct investment, and public capital investment as it is easily exploited.

Given the awareness of corruption, international institutions are making efforts to try and control corruption. Both the World Bank and the IMF have adopted broad agendas in their administration of the up to US$100 billion and/reform programs they manage either directly or indirectly in their attempts to assist development/restructuring efforts in poorer countries. The evidence of such programs in action can be found most recently in the reform packages assembled for four of the five countries of East Asia hit in the recent crisis, Thailand, Indonesia, South Korea and the Philippines.

The OECD has instituted a program aimed at achieving worldwide uniformity in the illegal status of attempts by private sector organizations and individuals to participate in international trade and development activities through the use of or compliance in corruption. The approach seeks to make any cooperation by companies and other institutions in corrupt activities in foreign countries a major offence in their own domestic legal system. This would remove a major flaw in current laws in all countries bar the U.S. where, at present, such cooperation in foreign corruption is not illegal.

The development of the Internet in the early 1990s has provided a major new source of information gathering and dissemination that lends itself extremely well to the anti-corruption campaign. The efforts of Transparency International and other institutions to use this facility have achieved notable success. Further, TI's campaign to establish policy manuals for the creation of national integrity systems in all countries is now achieving worldwide acknowledgement as a pathway to the reassertion of rigorous standards in all countries.

REFERENCES

Conway, T. (1998). A framework for assessing the relationship between trade liberalization and bio-diversity conservation. Working Paper International Institute for Sustainable Development Canada: UNEP.

Hattne, B. (1996). Globalization, the new regionalism and East Asia. [http://www.une.edu/unupress/globalization.html]

Siebert, H. (1998). An institutional order for a globalizing world economy. In: K.-J. Koch & K. Jaeger (Eds), *Trade, Growth an Economic Policy in Open Economies* (pp. 331–349). Berlin: Springer Verley.

Vines, D. (1998). The WTO in relation to the fund and the bank: Competencies, agendas and linkages. Chapter 2 in: A. O. Krueger (Ed.), *The WTO as an International Organization*. Chicago: University of Chicago Press.

PART II:
CORPORATE GOVERNANCE AND
PERFORMANCE MEASURES

BOARD OF DIRECTOR DIVERSITY AND FIRM PERFORMANCE

David A. Carter, Betty J. Simkins and W. Gary Simpson

ABSTRACT

This study examines the relationship between board diversity and firm value for Fortune 1000 firms excluding utilities and financial services firms. Board diversity is defined as the presence of minorities (e.g. African-Americans, Asians, Hispanics, etc.) on the board of directors. This research discusses three primary theories explaining the role of the board of directors. These three theories (agency, legalistic, and resource dependence) have implications for how board diversity can enhance firm performance. The major findings of our analysis on the relationship between board of director diversity and firm value are as follows. First, after controlling for size, industry, and other corporate governance measures, we find significant positive relationships between the fraction of minorities on the board and firm value. This result holds after controlling for potential endogeneity using two stage least squares regression analysis. Second, we find that the proportion of minorities on boards increases with firm size and board size but decreases as the number of insiders increases. This research is important because it highlights the need for firms to include diverse members on their board of directors.

We have to look at the connection between diversity, the success of the board, and a successful company. We should look in a broader sense at good governance not just because it includes a broad spectrum of people, but because it means running a good company. That means the

Social Responsibility: Corporate Governance Issues
Research in International Business and Finance, Volume 17, 49–70
Copyright © 2003 by Elsevier Science Ltd.
All rights of reproduction in any form reserved
ISSN: 0275-5319/PII: S0275531903170031

numbers show up in the financials which, in turn, means that the issue is going to make a difference to shareholders.
Veronica A. Haggart
Corporate VP and Director of Government Relations at Motorola

1. INTRODUCTION

Is there a relationship between board of director diversity and firm performance? The above quotation implies that there should be a link. Furthermore, in the U.S., there is considerable pressure from professional groups and governmental agencies to increase board diversity. TIAA-CREF adopted a policy statement on corporate governance that states the board should be composed of "qualified individuals who reflect diversity of experience, gender, race and age" (TIAA-CREF, 1997). Diversity on the board is a key investment criterion for TIAA-CREF because they believe a diverse board will be less beholden to management. The National Association of Corporate Directors Blue Ribbon Commission recommends that gender, racial, age, and nationality diversity should be considered in the selection of directors (National Association of Corporate Directors, 1994). In addition, the State of Connecticut has formed several state commissions whose goal is to increase board diversity for firms operating in the state.

Pressures to increase diversity are not unfounded when one considers that 5.3% of directors at non-financial firms in the *Fortune 1000* firms are minorities, yet 31% of the total U.S. population consists of minorities (i.e. African Americans, Hispanics, Asians and Pacific Islanders, American Indians, Native Alaskans, and other racial minorities).[1] Furthermore, approximately one-half of *Fortune 1000* firms have no minorities on their board (Carter, Simkins & Simpson, 2003).

We build on three primary theoretical areas to argue that firm value can be positively affected by diverse boards of directors (e.g. containing members with a variety of backgrounds, experiences, etc.). Because minority directors are also likely to be outsiders of the firm, agency theory argues that they should be better monitors, helping to align the incentives of the firm's management with that of the shareholders. According to the legalistic theory, the purpose of boards is to protect the interests of the shareholders and direct the corporation. Individuals with a variety of backgrounds and viewpoints should be more adept in this function. Resource dependence theory views boards as the critical link between the firm and its environment, implying that directors are able to extract resources for company operations because of their professional connections and affiliations. Clearly, in a complex operating environment, a diverse board of directors should be more likely to accomplish this task.

Little empirical research has been conducted to date examining the linkage between firm performance and board diversity. We fill this gap in the literature by examining the relationship between board diversity and firm value using a sample of nonfinancial firms in the *Fortune 1000*.[2] Board diversity is defined as the percentage of minorities (i.e. African Americans, Asians, and Hispanics) on the board of directors and firm value is measured by Tobin's Q.[3] We control for possible endogeneity between firm value and diversity using two-stage least squares analysis. Overall, we find a positive significant relationship between board diversity and firm value. This results holds after controlling for size, industry, and other corporate governance measures. Our results are important because we present some of the first empirical evidence that indicates board diversity is associated with improved financial performance.

The remainder of the paper is organized as follows. Section 2 presents three theories of corporate governance and their implications for diversity and firm value. Section 3 examines prior empirical evidence on board composition, board diversity and firm value relevant to our study. Section 4 discusses the data and empirical methodology employed. The results of the empirical analysis are presented in Section 5 while Section 6 concludes the paper.

2. THEORY: CORPORATE GOVERNANCE AND BOARD DIVERSITY

In this section, we discuss three primary theories explaining the role of boards of directors. We then describe how these theories have implications for board diversity and firm value.[4]

2.1. Agency Theory

The best-known approach to understanding the link between board characteristics and firm performance is agency theory. Fama and Jensen (1983) point out that the board is the main mechanism to control and monitor managers, and hence reduce agency costs. They argue that the role of the board in an agency framework is to resolve agency problems between managers and shareholders by setting compensation and replacing managers that do not create value for the shareholders. One of the key elements of an agency view of the board is that outside board members will not collude with insiders to subvert shareholder interests because they have incentives to build reputations as expert monitors. Board independence is necessary to make decisions that are in the best interests of shareholders. The central question for our analysis is the impact board diversity would have on board independence. In other words, should we expect a more diverse board to be a better monitor of management and less probable to subvert the interest of shareholders?

Figure 1 illustrates how board diversity can enhance firm performance under the agency theory. [Note: For now, we only refer to the agency theory relationships of Fig. 1. Later we will discuss the Legalistic and Resource Dependence theories illustrated in the figure.] We extend the model of Zahra and Pearce (1989) to incorporate how diversity attributes such as board composition (i.e. the number of minority directors on the board), board characteristics (i.e. diverse director's experience, functional background, independence, etc.), board structure (i.e. board organization and committees in which diverse directors are involved), and board decision process (i.e. decision-making related activities) enhance the board roles of service, strategy and control. In turn, these board roles are theorized to result in improved strategic outcomes that enhance firm performance.

Agency theory provides a number of reasons why diversity might improve board effectiveness. First, diverse boards are potentially more independent because people with a different gender, ethnicity, or cultural background might ask questions that would not come from directors with more traditional backgrounds. In other words, a more diverse board might be a more activist board (i.e. be less beholden to management) because outside directors with non-traditional characteristics could be considered the ultimate outsider. Effective monitors of management must be independent and not part of the "good old boy" network. Increasing diversity is a step in the direction of more independence.[5] However, we should point out that a different perspective might not necessarily result in more effective monitoring because diverse board members may be marginalized.

A second way diversity can impact the board is in its structure. Diverse members appointed to the four most influential and powerful board committees (e.g. audit, nominating, compensation, or executive committees) can improve monitoring (Braiotta & Sommers, 1987; Securities and Exchange Commission, 1980). This allows diverse members to have a substantial impact in board roles. Kesner (1988) finds that members of the four key committees are more likely to be outsiders and that the composition of these committees differs significantly from that of the overall board. She argues that this is necessary for effective monitoring. If, for example, a diverse member is only asked to serve on an unimportant committee, then tokenism may be occurring because the diverse member monitors minor issues with little impact on firm performance. This implies that when minorities are asked to serve on key committees, the firm is serious about board diversity issues.

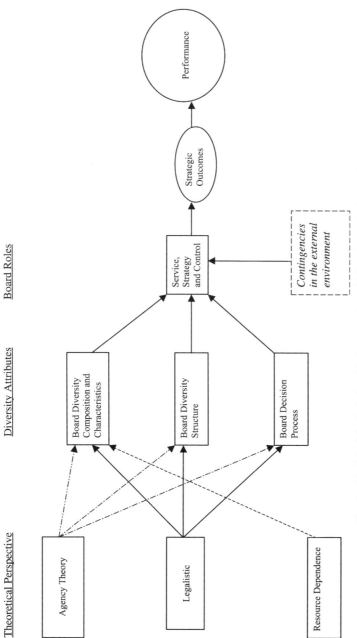

Fig. 1. Model of the Relationship between Board Diversity and Firm Performance.

Third, the board decision process might be enhanced by including diverse members. A recent Conference Board study found that diversity on boards enhances the strategic planning process (Brancato & Patterson, 1999). As Sheila Wellington, President of Catalyst, points out: "A group of people with the same background, the same experience is going to come up with a predictable group of solutions to problems – not a good idea in the world we live in. Different points of views yield a wider approach to decision making". (Shultz, 2000). Enhancing the strategic decision making ability of the board will improve board monitoring in this area. While heterogeneity on the board may initially produce more conflict in the decision making process, the variety of perspectives that emerges cause decision makers to evaluate more alternatives and more carefully explore the consequences of these alternatives (Robinson & Dechant, 1997). Existing literature does not fully define the monitoring value of this strategic decision-making, but advocates believe that it becomes evident when critical decisions are being made. Examples of such critical choices are acquiring a new firm, divesting a division, or negotiating a takeover bid (Baysinger & Butler, 1985; Kosnik, 1987).

In summary, while agency theory helps us understand how board diversity can improve monitoring and thus enhance firm performance, it does not provide us with specific characteristics and composition required. This is consistent with Hermalin and Weisbach's (2000) comments regarding more general board characteristics: "Although such principal-agent modeling provides many insights, it is not particularly useful for explaining board-specific phenomena: For example, why the ratio of insiders to outsiders matters or changes: or why management seems to have such influence in the selection of directors?"

2.2. Legalistic Theory

As the name implies, this theory emphasizes that boards contribute to the performance of the firm by fulfilling their legally mandated responsibilities. The two broad roles of the board implied under this theory are: (1) representing and protecting the interests of shareholders; and (2) directing the corporation without interfering in day-to-day operations. Under this theory, the implementation of these roles includes selecting and monitoring the CEO, assuring that the firm acts in the best interests of shareholders, providing guidance and advice to top management, and monitoring management and company performance. This theory adopts a broad view of company performance and emphasizes not only financial, but also social and systemic outcomes.

Empirical research on this theory has found that boards do not always fulfill their legally mandated responsibilities, do not effectively ask management about company goals and objectives, fail to evaluate CEO performance thoroughly, and are not successful in adequately reviewing managerial decisions before approving them.[6] These shortcomings have brought about efforts to reform boards in a number of ways, one of which is to broaden the representation of different stakeholders on the board. This includes increasing the number of outside directors and increasing diversity on the board.

As illustrated in Fig. 1 for the Legalistic theory, we theorize that board diversity may help overcome some of the above shortcomings. This theory, like the agency theory, has implications for diversity attributes of the board (i.e. composition and characteristics, structure, and decision process) that indirectly impact firm performance. For instance, research shows that diversity can increase innovation and problem solving. This in turn should help improve board performance. As Theodore Jadick, Managing Partner, Heidrick & Struggles states (see Brancato & Patterson, 1999): "We've never been more active than now in rebuilding corporate boards.... But if you ask what are the hottest items, I'd say number one, it's global operating types; two, diversity".

2.3. Resource Dependence Theory

The resource dependence theory views boards as crucial boundary spanners that provide important information to management (Zahra & Pearce II, 1989). As shown in Fig. 1, this theory has implications for diversity attributes concerning board composition and characteristics. This theory implies that directors are able to extract resources for successful company operations because of their professional connections and affiliations. In essence, the directors are viewed as the link between the firm and the environment, and this link should improve the firm's efficiency and performance.

To illustrate this theory, consider Ford Motor Company. Ford states that diversity in firm leadership positions (including the board) helps cultivate and retain a diverse workforce. Furthermore, Ford finds that diversity helps the firm in key global markets because the firm better understands the needs and issues within local cultures and communities. Joginder Singh, Director of Business Strategy at Ford states: "In our industry, all the main players have similar strategies, products and services. The difference going forward that provides a competitive advantage is in the area of intellectual capital, the way our people tackle challenges with new and creative thinking. If we are able to bring together a diverse set of minds and apply them to automotive challenges, we'll have an amazing kaleidoscope of ideas to choose from" (Sulaiman-Eason, 2001). In addition, Sun Oil's CEO, Robert Campbell states: "Often what a woman or minority person can bring to the board is some perspective a company has not had before – adding some modern-day reality to the deliberation process. Those perspectives are of great value, and often missing from an all-white, male gathering. They can also be inspiration to the company's diverse workforce" (Campbell, 1996).

This theory and its implications for board diversity allude to a multidimensional definition of company performance that includes financial, systemic, and social components. Directors provide vital links to other companies and hence, increase coordination among organizations. This results in reduced transaction costs and improved access to critical information and resources. Included in this theory is the importance of interlocking board relationships.[7] It should be noted that in our empirical analysis, we focus strictly on financial measures of company performance.

2.4. Contingencies in the External Environment

One additional way we argue that diversity can enhance the role of the board is in the handling of contingencies in the external environment. As illustrated with the dashed-line box in Fig. 1, contingencies are expected to impact the board roles of service, strategy and control, which in turn impact strategic outcomes and ultimately firm performance. For example, when the environment is volatile and hostile, creating favorable links with external stakeholders becomes an important part of the service role. Developing strategies to handle contingencies in a hostile environment is an important part of the strategy and control roles. Diversity should improve the effectiveness of these links.

The following two examples further illustrate our points. First, clothing maker Abercrombie & Fitch was forced to pull a new line of Asian-themed t-shirts from their stores nationwide after Asian-Americans protested that the shirts carried a racist message (Kong, 2002). The t-shirts carried caricatures of Asians in conical hats along with questionable slogans. The firm has been the target of other consumer complaints; we believe that if the firm increased their board diversity, such problems would not occur and their firm would improve their relationship with consumers.

The second example illustrates demographic changes that occur in the external environment. Improving board diversity increases the board's knowledge and sensitivity of the changing marketplace. For instance, Betsy Saunders was a relatively new board member for a supermarket company when the directors discussed the failure of "apron droppers" advertising (i.e. specials so enticing that women drop their aprons and rush to the store to buy the specials). The board debate was whether to change the day of those sales or the placement of the ads. Only Saunders thought to question the premise of the sales themselves.

3. PRIOR EMPIRICAL RESEARCH

A number of studies have been published in recent years examining board composition and characteristics, including the number of directors on the board, the percentage of outside directors on the board, the ownership position of inside directors, board size, board committee structure, and the number of meetings held annually.[8] The facet of board composition most often studied is board independence (i.e. the number of outside directors relative to inside directors on the board) (Hermalin & Weisbach, 2000). This aspect of board composition is relevant to our research because a more diverse board is likely to be a more independent or activist board.

Baysinger and Butler (1985) test the relationship between the percentage of independent directors and a relative measure of return on equity. They find that boards with more outsiders outperformed other firms and conclude that boards with both insiders and outsiders produce the best financial value. Hermalin and Weisbach (1991) compare the percentage of outsiders on boards to a relative measure of Tobin's Q. They conclude that there is no relationship between the percentage of outsiders on the board and firm value. Yermack (1996), Bhagat and Black (1999), and Agrawal and Knoeber (1996) find a negative correlation between Tobin's Q and the proportion of independent directors on the board. Rosenstein and Wyatt (1990) use event study methodology and find a very slight increase in stock prices when a company appointed an additional outside director. MacAvoy and Millstein (1999) argue that the mixed results have followed from concentrating on periods when boards were largely irrelevant and using unreliable proxies for board independence. Using other independence measures, MacAvoy and Millstein find a positive relationship between board independence and financial value. Given the mixed results for research in this area, Hermalin and Weisbach (2000) argue that "Overall, there is little to suggest that board composition has any cross-sectional relation with firm value".

A few studies have examined the relationship between cultural or racial diversity of employees and firm performance. Keys, Turner and Friday (2002) examine firms identified as diversity promoters and find that these firms exhibit significantly greater return on equity and buy-and-hold returns when compared to a control sample. Furthermore, they find that the wealth impact is positively related to the proportion of diversity among top-level managers. Wright, Ferris, Hiller and Kroll (1995) calculate significant positive excess returns when firms were recognized with U.S. Department of Labor awards for affirmative action programs and significant negative excess returns when firms announced discrimination settlements in lawsuits. Richard (2000) identifies a positive relationship between a firm's ROE and employee diversity for firms following a growth strategy.

Interestingly, only a few academic studies published to date investigate the relationship between board diversity and firm performance. This is most likely due to the fact that diversity data for board members is very difficult to obtain. Shrader, Blackburn and Iles (1997) investigate the relationship between the percentage of female board members and two accounting measures of financial value (e.g. ROA and ROE) for a sample of approximately 200 *Fortune 500* firms. A major weakness in their analysis is that they control indirectly for firm size, but include no other control variables in a simple OLS regression equation. The authors find a significant negative relationship between the percentage of women on the board and firm value in some tests. Zahra and Stanton (1988) use canonical analysis to test the relationship between the percentage of ethnic minority directors and several accounting measures of financial value (e.g. ROE and EPS). However, they find no statistically significant relationship. Carter, Simkins and Simpson (2003) uncover a positive relationship between board diversity (measured by women and minorities on the board) and firm value when examining financial and nonfinancial firms in the *Fortune 1000*. Their results support the view that diversity and shareholder value creation are positively associated. Farrell and Hersch (2002) analyze the determinants of a firm adding a woman to its board. They find an inverse relation between the likelihood of a woman being added to a board and the percentage of women on the board in the previous year. Their results imply that gender affects the choice of directors being added to the board.

Overall, the few studies examining board diversity and firm value have found mixed results. Our goal is to improve on prior research in examining the relation between board diversity, measured by the percentage of minorities on the board, and firm value. The following section discusses our data sources and the methods used to investigate this relationship.

4. DATA AND EMPIRICAL METHODOLOGY

4.1. Data Sources and Description

In this investigation of board of director diversity and firm value, we draw our sample from publicly traded *Fortune 1000* firms, excluding utilities and financial services firms. We obtain data on board of director characteristics for 1997 from *Significant Data for Directors 1999: Board Policies and Governance Trends*, prepared by Directorship, a corporate governance-consulting firm. Additionally, we obtain accounting data used in this analysis from the COMPUSTAT database. There are 548 firms with a complete set of board of director data, however, due to

Table 1. Descriptive Statistics for Sample Firms.

Variable	Number of Firms	Mean	Standard Deviation
Total assets ($ millions)	548	7,042	22,177
Duality of CEO and board chair	548	0.757	0.429
Number of annual board meetings	548	7.219	2.695
Age of directors	548	59.913	3.874
Number of directors	548	10.542	2.642
Number of inside directors	548	2.772	1.557
Percentage of insiders on board	548	0.267	0.137
Number of women directors	548	1.053	0.817
Percentage of women on board	548	0.096	0.072
Number of minority directors	548	0.599	0.725
Percentage of minorities on board	548	0.053	0.065

Note: This table presents descriptive statistics for sample firms. The sample is drawn from the *Fortune 1000* firms, excluding utilities and financial services firms. Data related to board of director characteristics are taken from *Significant Data for Directors 1999: Board Policies and Governance Trends*, compiled by Directorship.

missing accounting data, the sample is reduced to 494 firms with a complete set of all the data items.

Descriptive statistics for our sample firms are provided in Table 1. The sample firms in our sample tend to be large, with an average size of $13.3 billion in total assets. There tends to be a concentration of control, in the sense that the chair of the board is also the CEO in over 75% of the firms. The mean board size is 10.5 directors, of whom, on average, 2.8 are insiders, 1.1 are women, and 0.6 are minorities. The mean age of the board is almost 60 years and they meet a little over seven times per year.

We present a breakdown of the number of minorities on boards in Table 2. In our sample, 290 firms (52.9%) do not have any minorities on their boards of directors. There are 196 firms (35.8%) with a single minority director. Fifty-four firms (9.9%) have two minority directors, while eight firms (1.5%) have three board members that are minorities. There are no firms with four or more minority directors. Overall, 47.1% of the firms (258 firms) have one or more minority directors.

4.2. Testing the Relationship Between Firm Performance and Board of Director Diversity

To investigate the relationship between firm value and minority representation on boards of directors, we develop an empirical model that not only includes a measure of whether there are minority board members but also includes corporate

Table 2.   Breakdown of Minorities on Boards of Directors.

Number of Minority Directors	Number of Firms with Minority Directors	Percentage of Firms with Minority Directors
0	290	52.9%
1	196	35.8%
2	54	9.9%
3	8	1.5%
4+	0	0.0%
Total firms with minority directors	258	47.1%

Note: This table presents a breakdown of the number of minorities on boards of directors for sample firms. The sample is drawn from the *Fortune 1000* firms, excluding utilities and financial services firms. There are a total of 548 firms in the sample. Data related to board of director characteristics are taken from *Significant Data for Directors 1999: Board Policies and Governance Trends*, compiled by Directorship.

governance related variables that other researchers have found to be linked to firm performance. For instance, in an investigation of board activity, Vafeas (1999) finds a negative relationship between firm value and the number of board meetings. Yermack's (1996) results suggest an inverse relationship between firm value, as measured by Tobin's Q, and the size of the board of directors. Morck, Shleifer and Vishny (1988) and McConnell and Servaes (1990) find a significant, nonlinear, relationship between firm value and ownership by insiders. The importance of the monitoring role by outside directors is shown by Brickley, Coles and Terry (1994) and Borokhovich, Parrino and Trapani (1996). Finally, Perry (1999) finds evidence that stock-based compensation plans for directors provide incentives to monitor management. Therefore, based on prior research, we include the following control variables: board size (natural logarithm of the number of directors), the logarithm of the number of meetings annually, CEO/chair duality, a dummy variable indicating whether directors receive stock compensation, insider ownership, and the percentage of insiders on the board. Additionally, we include a measure of firm size (e.g. natural logarithm of total assets), return on assets (ROA), and one-digit SIC dummies in our model.

To analyze the effect of minority board members on firm performance, we estimate the following relationship:

Firm Value $= f$(Firm Size, Board Size, Number of Board Meetings, CEO/Chair

Duality, Management Stock Compensation, Insider Ownership,

Inside Directors, Return on Assets, Minority Directors),   (1)

where we use the approximation of Tobin's Q (see Chung & Pruitt, 1994) to measure firm value. We use both an indicator variable equal to 1 if a firm has at least one minority director, and zero otherwise, and the percentage of minorities on the board as our measures of board of director diversity. Estimation of Eq. (1) allows us to test the following null hypothesis:

Hypothesis. The presence of minority directors does not affect firm value.

Rejection of the null hypothesis implies that having a diverse board of directors affects firm value. If the null hypothesis is rejected, the estimated relationship could be either positive, suggesting firm value is enhanced by the presence of minorities on boards of directors or negative, implying that the presence of minorities on boards reduces firm value. Failure to reject the null hypothesis suggests that board of director diversity does not significantly influence value. It should be pointed out that either significant negative or non-significant estimates do not mean that minorities make poor directors. Rather, these results may imply that firms are using minority directors as "window dressing", or that the culture of the firm is not conducive to their success as directors.

4.3. Corporate Governance Characteristics and Board Diversity

In addition to investigating the relationship between firm value and board diversity, we also explore the determinants of board of director diversity estimating the following functional relationship:

$$\text{Board Diversity} = f(\text{Firm Size, Board Size, Age of Board, CEO/Chair Duality,}$$
$$\text{Inside Directors, Firm Value, Women Directors}). \qquad (2)$$

We also control for different industry characteristics by including one-digit SIC dummy variables in our model. CEO/chair duality, age, and the percentage of insiders on the board capture various aspects of board independence. Boards with little independence, as characterized by chairs that are also the CEO, older directors, and more insiders, will likely be more resistant to minority directors, who are more likely to be outsiders. Thus, we expect each of these variables to be negatively related to the percentage of minorities on the board. We also expect that firms having a higher percentage of women on their boards have made a commitment to increasing board diversity. Therefore, we include the percentage of women as an explanatory variable in our model investigating the presence of minorities on the board.

We estimate Eq. (2) using three different methods: OLS, logit, and Tobit. The estimates of the relationship between corporate governance characteristics and the percentage of minorities on boards of directors are reported in Table 3. The dependent variable in the OLS estimations is the percentage of minorities on the

Table 3. Determinants of the Percentage of Minorities on Boards of Directors for Sample Firms.

	OLS	Logit	Tobit
Constant	0.0389	−0.5692	−0.0151
	(0.1651)	(6.6189)	(0.3511)
Size (natural logarithm	0.0129***	0.4427***	0.0236***
of total assets)	(0.0026)	(0.1072)	(0.0051)
Board size (natural	0.0030	2.0277***	0.0503**
logarithm of number			
of directors on board)	(0.0115)	(0.4843)	(0.0240)
Duality of chair and	0.0079	0.3200	0.0186
CEO			
	(0.0062)	(0.2489)	(0.0128)
Natural logarithm of the	−0.0259	−2.0806	−0.0772
average age of			
directors			
	(0.0413)	(1.6658)	(0.0880)
Percentage of insiders	−0.0677***	−2.9442***	−0.1623***
on board			
	(0.0200)	(0.8506)	(0.0433)
Percentage of women	0.1754***	7.1645***	0.3741***
on board			
	(0.0386)	(1.6146)	(0.0794)
Natural logarithm of	0.0021	0.0467	0.0027
Tobin's Q			
	(0.0034)	(0.1344)	(0.0067)
One-digit SIC dummies	Yes	Yes	Yes
N	534	534	534
R^2	0.196		
F-Statistic (χ^2 for Logit)	9.74***	107.74***	

Note: This table provides estimates of the determinants of minority directorships. The dependent variable in the OLS and tobit estimations is the percentage of minorities on the board of directors. The dependent variable in the logit model is coded as a 1 if there are one or more minority on the board of directors, and zero otherwise. The standard errors are reported in parentheses, beneath the parameter estimates. The sample is drawn from the *Fortune 1000* firms, excluding utilities and financial services firms. Data related to board of director characteristics are taken from *Significant Data for Directors 1999: Board Policies and Governance Trends*, compiled by Directorship.
Significance at the 10, 5, and 1% levels is indicated by *, **, and ***, respectively.

board. The same dependent variable is used in the Tobit estimation, except that it is treated as being censored at zero. The dependent variable in the logit model is coded as a 1 if there are one or more minorities on the board of directors, and zero if not.

Size, as measured by the natural logarithm of total assets, is positive and significant in all three estimations indicating that larger firms are more likely to have minorities on their boards of directors. The estimates for the percentage of insiders on the board are negative and highly significant in all three models. This result suggests that boards made-up of significant numbers of insiders are likely to have smaller numbers of minority directors. This may be because minorities are more likely to be outsiders and thus opposed by insiders in their effort to gain membership on the board. We also find significant positive relationships between the percentage of minorities on boards and board size (logarithm of the number of directors) and the presence of women on the board. The latter result suggests that firms making a commitment to include more minorities on their boards are also more likely to include female directors. In the next section, we present our results examining the relationship between board of director diversity and firm value.

5. RESULTS

In this section, we present the empirical results for our investigation of the relationship between board of director diversity and firm value. We present *t*-tests for differences in means for firms with and without minorities on their boards. The comparisons of means are presented in Table 4. Table 5 presents the results for OLS estimation of Eq. (1). Finally, we present 2SLS estimates of the relationship between firm value and board of director diversity in Table 6.

5.1. Comparisons of Firms with and without Diverse Boards

In Table 4, we present *t*-tests of differences in means for firms with and without minorities on their boards. On examination of Table 4, it is readily apparent that significant differences exist for several variables. Firms with minority directors are larger ($11.3 billion in total assets versus $3.3 billion), have larger boards (11.5 directors vs. 9.7 directors), have more annual meetings (7.5 vs. 7.0), and have a greater proportion of female directors (12.0% vs. 7.5%). Firms with minority directors also perform better, as measured by Tobin's Q (1.83 vs. 1.40). Finally, firms with minorities on their boards have fewer inside directors than those that do not have minority directors (0.237 vs. 0.293).

Table 4. Comparison of Means for Firms With and Without Minority Directors.

Variable	Firms with no Minority Directors (N = 290)	Firms with at Least one Minority Director (N = 258)	Difference	t Statistic
Total assets	3,250.3	11,303.0	−8,052.7	4.07***
($ millions)	(4,359.6)	(31,479.0)		
Average age of	58.72	59.13	−0.41	1.26
directors	(4.44)	(3.12)		
Board size	9.67	11.52	−1.85	8.76***
(number of	(2.51)	(2.44)		
directors on				
board)				
Number of annual	6.97	7.50	−0.53	2.35**
board meetings	(2.76)	(2.59)		
Percentage of	0.293	0.237	0.056	4.98***
insiders on	(0.147)	(0.119)		
board				
Percentage of	0.075	0.120	−0.045	7.75***
women on	(0.072)	(0.065)		
board				
Duality of CEO	0.717	0.802	−0.085	2.34**
and board chair	(0.451)	(0.399)		
Tobin's Q	1.396	1.827	−0.431	2.75***
	(1.530)	(2.025)		

Note: This table presents tests of differences in means for several variables, between firms with and without representation of minorities on their boards of directors. The sample is drawn from the *Fortune 1000* firms with utilities and financial services firms excluded. Data related to board of director characteristics are taken from *Significant Data for Directors 1999: Board Policies and Governance Trends*, compiled by Directorship.
Statistical significance at the 10, 5, and 1% levels is indicated by *, **, and ***, respectively.

Because differences in firm value and corporate governance may be related to both size and industry, we use multivariate statistical techniques (e.g. regression) to control for these factors. These results are discussed in the following section.

5.2. Regression Results: Board of Director Diversity and Firm Value

Table 5 reports the results of the OLS regression of Eq. (1). The dependent variable in all four models is the natural logarithm of Tobin's Q. In models (1) and (2), we use an indicator variable, coded as 1 if there are one or more minority directors, and 0 otherwise, to measure minority representation on the board. In models (3)

Table 5. OLS Estimates of the Relationship Between Firm Value and the
Presence of Minorities on Boards of Directors.

Variable	Board Diversity Measure = Minority Director Indicator Variable		Board Diversity Measure = Percentage of Minorities on Board	
	(1)	(2)	(3)	(4)
Constant	−1.1160***	−0.9869**	−1.1989***	−1.0699***
	(0.3843)	(0.4149)	(0.3771)	(0.4072)
Size (log of total assets)	0.0938***	0.0811**	0.0903***	0.0784**
	(0.0325)	(0.0323)	(0.0327)	(0.0325)
Board size (log of	0.0935	0.0578	0.1398	0.1009
number of directors)	(0.1454)	(0.1450)	(0.1421)	(0.1422)
Log of number of	−0.0143	−0.0204	−0.0110	−0.0173
annual board meetings	(0.0962)	(0.0958)	(0.0961)	(0.0957)
Duality of CEO and	−0.1806**	−0.2028***	−0.1821**	−0.2035***
board chair	(0.0749)	(0.0744)	(0.0749)	(0.0744)
Stock compensation	0.1361*	0.1313*	0.1376*	0.1328*
	(0.0815)	(0.0806)	(0.0814)	(0.0805)
Insider ownership	−0.0518	−0.0876	−0.0627	−0.1016
percentage	(0.5418)	(0.7706)	(0.5413)	(0.5377)
Insider ownership	0.3199	0.4887	0.3287	0.5011
percentage squared	(0.7755)	(0.7706)	(0.7750)	(0.7701)
Percentage of insiders	−0.0134	−0.0829	−0.0024	−0.0760
on board	(0.2542)	(0.2550)	(0.2544)	(0.2551)
Minority director	0.1331*	0.1220*		
indicator	(0.0700)	(0.0708)		
Percentage of			1.0659**	0.9562*
minorities on board			(0.5170)	(0.5205)
Return on assets (ROA)	0.0551***	0.0542***	0.0552***	0.0543***
	(0.0044)	(0.0043)	(0.0044)	(0.0043)
One-digit SIC indicator variables	No	Yes	No	Yes
N	494	494	494	494
Adjusted R^2	0.286	0.307	0.287	0.308
F-Statistic	20.76***	14.64***	20.85***	14.68***

Note: This table presents OLS results for the relationship between firm value and the presence of minorities on the board of directors. The sample is drawn from the *Fortune 1000* firms, excluding utilities and financial services firms. Data related to board of director characteristics are taken from *Significant Data for Directors 1999: Board Policies and Governance Trends*, compiled by Directorship. The dependent variable is the natural logarithm of Tobin's *Q*, calculated using the method suggested by Chung and Pruitt (1994). Standard errors are reported in parentheses, beneath the parameter estimates.
Significance at the 10, 5, and 1% levels is indicated by *, **, and ***, respectively.

and (4), we measure board of director diversity using the percentage of minorities on the board. We include one-digit SIC dummy variables in models (2) and (4) to control for differences in industries.

The OLS results suggest several variables may be related to firm value. First, in all four models, the estimated coefficient for size is positive and significant. Interestingly, we find significant negative coefficient estimates for CEO/board chair duality. This result provides evidence that a CEO who is also board chair may not be an effective monitor. Consistent with prior research, we find a positive relationship between firm value and management stock compensation. Importantly for this research, we find significant positive relationships between both measures of board diversity and firm value. This results suggests a positive association between firm performance and the presence of a diverse board of directors.

Hermalin and Weisbach (2000) argue that endogeneity may be an important econometric issue when investigating board composition and value. This is due to the fact that while board diversity might affect firm value, firm value might also affect board diversity. If this is the case, estimation of Eq. (1) using OLS can produce biased coefficient estimates. To control for this possibility, we estimate the following system of equations using 2SLS:

$$\text{Firm Value} = f(\text{Firm Size, Board Size, Number of Board Meetings,}$$
$$\text{CEO/Chair Duality, Management Stock Compensation,}$$
$$\text{Insider Ownership, Inside Directors, Return on Assets,}$$
$$\text{Minority Directors)}, \tag{3a}$$

$$\text{Board Diversity} = f(\text{Firm Size, Board Size, Age of Board, CEO/Chair Duality,}$$
$$\text{Inside Directors, Firm Value, Women Directors)}. \tag{3b}$$

The 2SLS results are reported in Table 6. As with the OLS results, the dependent variable in all models is the natural logarithm of Tobin's Q. In models (1) and (2), we use the indicator variable as before to measure minority representation on the board. The percentage of minorities on the board is used in models (3) and (4) to measure board of director diversity. To control for differences in industries, we include one-digit SIC dummy variables in models (2) and (4).

Overall, the results of the 2SLS estimations are similar to the OLS results, although there is no longer a significant relationship between firm size and performance. As before, we find a significant negative relationship between firm value and CEO/chair duality, suggesting that firm value declines when CEOs are also board chairs. We also find significant positive estimates for stock compensation and return on assets. Importantly, we find significant positive estimates for both

Table 6. 2SLS Estimates of the Relationship Between Firm Performance and the Presence of Minorities on Boards of Directors.

Variable	Board Diversity Measure = Minority Director Indicator Variable		Board Diversity Measure = Percentage of Minorities on Board	
	(1)	(2)	(3)	(4)
Constant	−0.5443	0.0535	−0.9292**	−0.6764
	(0.4805)	(0.6460)	(0.4195)	(0.4898)
Size (log of total assets)	0.0498	0.0090	0.0302	0.0007
	(0.0395)	(0.0478)	(0.0436)	(0.0509)
Board size (log of	−0.1210	−0.2795	0.1004	0.0694
number of directors)	(0.1815)	(0.2184)	(0.1527)	(0.1597)
Log of number of	−0.0291	−0.0574	−0.0141	−0.0304
annual board				
meetings	(0.1014)	(0.1105)	(0.1026)	(0.1072)
Duality of CEO and	−0.1944**	−0.2356***	−0.2026***	−0.2359***
board chair	(0.0791)	(0.0861)	(0.0804)	(0.0845)
Stock compensation	0.1479*	0.1383	0.1562*	0.1478*
	(0.0859)	(0.0920)	(0.0873)	(0.0903)
Insider ownership	0.0961	0.2611	0.0535	0.1128
percentage	(0.5740)	(0.6319)	(0.5799)	(0.6093)
Insider ownership	0.2749	0.2711	0.3092	0.3892
percentage squared	(0.8163)	(0.8844)	(0.8273)	(0.8628)
Percentage of insiders	0.2237	0.3715	0.2915	0.3525
on board	(0.2882)	(0.3486)	(0.3001)	(0.3462)
Minority director	0.6368***	0.9738***		
indicator	(0.2399)	(0.3686)		
Percentage of			5.3029***	6.6500**
minorities on board			(1.9275)	(0.5205)
Return on assets (ROA)	0.0530***	0.0544***	0.0527***	0.0545***
	(0.0047)	(0.0050)	(0.0048)	(0.0049)
One-digit SIC indicator	No	Yes	No	Yes
variables				
N	494	494	494	494
Adjusted R^2	0.269	0.255	0.264	0.262
F-Statistic	19.12***	11.53***	18.68***	11.96***

Note: This table presents 2SLS results for the relationship between firm value and the presence of minorities on the board of directors. The sample is drawn from the *Fortune 1000* firms, excluding utilities and financial services firms. Data related to board of director characteristics are taken from *Significant Data for Directors 1999: Board Policies and Governance Trends*, compiled by Directorship. The dependent variable is the natural logarithm of Tobin's Q, calculated using the method suggested by Chung and Pruitt (1994). For brevity, we omit the second regression in the system.
Standard errors are reported in parentheses, beneath the parameter estimates. Significance at the 10, 5, and 1% levels is indicated by *, **, and ***, respectively.

the minority director indicator variable and the percentage of minorities on the board. These results provide important evidence of the relationship between firm value and the presence of minorities on boards of directors.

6. CONCLUSION

Our research examines the relationship between board of director diversity and firm value for *Fortune 1000* firms, excluding utilities and financial services firms. We define board diversity as the presence of minority directors (e.g. African-Americans, Asians, and Hispanics). Our most important finding is that after controlling for size, industry, and other corporate governance measures, we find statistically significant positive relationships between the presence of minorities on the board and firm value. We also find that the fraction of minorities directors increases with firm size and board size but decreases as the number of insiders increases. Our results also suggest that firms making a commitment to increasing the number of minorities on boards also have more women on their boards. Overall, our results provide important evidence of the positive relation between firm value and diversity on the board of directors.

NOTES

1. U.S. population data was obtained from the 2000 U.S. Census. Statistics on board of director diversity are based on the results of our research study using 1997 data.
2. It is important to note what this paper does not do. We do not evaluate the issue of equity and board diversity. Our goal is to explore the economic implications of board diversity and leave the sociological and political implications to others.
3. Tobin's Q is the ratio of the firm's market value to the replacement cost of its assets and is a measure of the value added by the firm's activities.
4. For a detailed review of these theories and empirical evidence, refer to Zahra and Pearce (1989).
5. See the National Association of Corporate Directors (NACD). Report of the NACD Blue Ribbon Commission on Director Professionalism, 1996, 15–19.
6. See Jensen (1993), Zahra and Pearce (1989), among others, for additional discussion of these issues.
7. The interlock approach focuses on a company's interface with its competitors. An interlock occurs when an individual sits as a member of the board of directors of two companies.
8. Refer to Hermalin and Weisbach (2000), Bhagat and Black (1999) and Shultz (2000) for a review of the evidence on corporate boards.

REFERENCES

Agrawal, A., & Knoeber, C. R. (1996). Firm value and mechanisms to control agency problems between managers and shareholders. *Journal of Financial and Quantitative Analysis, 31*, 377–397.

Baysinger, B. D., & Butler, H. N. (1985). Corporate governance and the board of directors: Value effects of changes in board composition. *Journal of Law, Economics and Organization, 1*, 101–124.

Bhagat, S., & Black, B. (1999). The uncertain relationship between board composition and firm value. *Business Lawyer, 54*, 921–963.

Borokhovich, K., Parrino, R., & Trapani, T. (1996). Outside directors and CEO selection. *Journal of Financial and Quantitative Analysis, 31*, 337–355.

Braiotta, L., Jr., & Sommers, A. A. (1987). *The essential guide to effective corporate board committees.* Englewood Cliffs, NJ: Prentice-Hall.

Brancato, C. K., & Patterson, D. J. (1999). Board diversity in U.S. corporations: Best practices for broadening the profile of corporate boards. The Conference Board, Research Report 1230-99-RR.

Brickley, J., Coles, J., & Terry, R. (1994). Outside directors and the adoption of poison pills. *Journal of Financial Economics, 34*, 371–390.

Campbell, R. H. (1996). Letters to the editor: CEO vs. Nun: It's a draw. *Wall Street Journal* (August 12), Section A.

Carter, D. A., Simkins, B. J., & Simpson, W. G. (2003). Corporate governance, board diversity, and firm value. *Financial Review, 38*, 33–53.

Chung, K. H., & Pruitt, S. W. (1994). A simple approximation of Tobin's *Q. Financial Management, 23*, 70–74.

Fama, E. F., & Jensen, M. C. (1983). Separation of ownership and control. *Journal of Law and Economics, 24*, 301–325.

Farrell, K. A., & Hersch, P. L. (2002). Additions to corporate boards: Does gender matter? University of Nebraska-Lincoln, Working Paper.

Hermalin, B. E., & Weisbach, M. W. (1991). The effects of board composition and direct incentives on firm value. *Financial Management, 20*, 101–112.

Hermalin, B. E., & Weisbach, M. S. (2000). Boards of directors as an endogenously determined institution: A survey of the economic literature. University of California at Berkeley, Working Paper.

Jensen, M. C. (1993). The modern industrial revolution, exit, and the failure of internal control systems. *Journal of Finance, 48*, 831–880.

Keys, P. Y., Turner, P. A., & Friday, S. S. (2002). Shareholder benefits of diversity. University of Delaware, Working Paper.

Kong, D. (2002). Abercrombie & Fitch pulls T-shirts, but Asian-Americans still protest. *Associated Press Newswires* (April 18).

Kosnik, R. D. (1987). Greenmail: A study of board performance in corporate governance. *Administrative Science Quarterly, 32*, 163–185.

MacAvoy, P. W., & Millstein, I. M. (1999). The active board of directors and Its effect on the value of the large publicly traded corporation. *Journal of Applied Corporate Finance, 11*, 8–20.

McConnell, J., & Servaes, H. (1990). Additional evidence on equity ownership and corporate value. *Journal of Financial Economics, 27*, 595–612.

Morck, R., Shleifer, A., & Vishny, R. W. (1988). Management ownership and market valuation: An empricial analysis. *Journal of Financial Economics, 20*, 293–315.

National Association of Corporate Directors (1994). *Report of the NACD Blue Ribbon Commission on value evaluation of Chief Executive Officers, Board, and Directors.* Washington, DC.

National Association of Corporate Directors (1996). *Report of the NACD Blue Ribbon Commission on director professionalism.* Washington, DC.

Perry, T. (1999). Incentive compensation for outside directors and CEO turnover. Arizona State University, Working Paper.

Richard, O. C. (2000). Racial diversity, business strategy, and firm value: A resource-based view. *Academy of Management Journal, 43,* 164–177.

Robinson, G., & Dechant, K. (1997). Building a business case for diversity. *Academy of Management Executive, 11,* 21–30.

Rosenstein, S., & Wyatt, J. G. (1990). Outside directors, board independence and shareholder wealth. *Journal of Financial Economics, 26,* 175–191.

Securities and Exchange Commission (1980). Staff Report on Corporate Accountability. Washington, DC: U.S. Government Printing Office.

Shrader, C. B., Blackburn, V. B., & Iles, P. (1997). Women in management and firm financial value: An exploratory study. *Journal of Managerial Issues, 9,* 355–372.

Shultz, S. F. (2000). *The board book.* New York: AMACOM.

Sulaiman-Eason, M. (2001). Driving new initiatives home at Ford Motor Company. *Profiles in Diversity Journal, 3,* 10–11.

TIAA-CREF Policy Statement on Corporate Governance (1997). New York.

Vafeas, N. (1999). Board meeting frequency and firm value. *Journal of Financial Economics, 53,* 113–142.

Wright, P., Ferris, S. P., Hiller, J. S., & Kroll, M. (1995). Competitiveness through management of diversity: Effects on stock price valuation. *Academy of Management Journal, 38,* 272–287.

Yermack, D. (1996). Higher market valuation of companies with a small board of directors. *Journal of Financial Economics, 40,* 185–211.

Zahra, S. A., & Pearce, J. A., II (1989). Board of directors and corporate financial performance: A review and integrative model. *Journal of Management, 15,* 291–334.

Zahra, S. A., & Stanton, W. W. (1988). The implications of board of directors' composition for corporate strategy and value. *International Journal of Management, 5,* 229–236.

INDICATORS FOR SOCIAL, ETHICAL AND ENVIRONMENTAL PERFORMANCE: USING SYSTEMS ANALYSIS-BASED SOCIAL CHOICE THEORY FOR SOCIAL WELFARE MEASUREMENT

Sardar M. N. Islam and Matthew F. Clarke

ABSTRACT

Though many approaches exist to measure social welfare as the indicator of social, ethical and environmental performance within the literature, the most common approach is to use standard national accounts. There is a need to develop an approach that is based on social choice perspectives as there is a distinct difference in actions between citizens acting within the market and citizens judging and acting upon alternative social welfare states. Such an approach, based on integrated systems analysis of the indicators for social, ethical and environmental performance will be developed in this chapter and empirically applied to Thailand for a 25-year period, 1975 to 1999. This new approach is based on certain cost-benefit adjustments to GDP for the indicators of social, ethical and environmental performance. There are stark differences between GDP and social choice adjusted GDP rates for this period, not only in the overall change in the levels of social welfare but in the

Social Responsibility: Corporate Governance Issues
Research in International Business and Finance, Volume 17, 71–87
© 2003 Published by Elsevier Science Ltd.
ISSN: 0275-5319/PII: S0275531903170043

manner that these levels rise and fall during the period under review. This chapter concludes that GDP can be used as an indicator of social welfare if the GDP estimates are undertaken within a cost-benefit analysis framework based on social choice perspectives and systems analysis.

1. INTRODUCTION

Though many approaches exist within the literature to measure social welfare as the indicator of social, ethical and environmental performance, the most common approach is to use standard national accounts. This chapter disputes the use of this set of statistics and argues that market preferences are a flawed approach. There is a need to develop an approach that is based on social choice perspectives as there is a distinct difference in actions between citizens acting within the market and citizens judging and acting upon alternative social welfare states.

Qualitative estimation of the state of welfare in an economy is a well-developed discipline in economics. There are various methods for estimating aggregate welfare measures (Daly & Cobb, 1990; Hicks, 1940; Morris, 1979; Nordhaus & Tobin, 1973; Pigou, 1962; UNDP, 1990). Measurement of welfare is conditional on the methodology and value judgements adopted in evaluating and estimating economic and social activities (Sen, 1979, 1985).

There are several limitations in the existing literature within this area, including the reliance on aggregated preferences and lack of studies focusing on developing countries. A new approach, based on integrated systems analysis of the indicators for social, ethical and environmental performance, is developed in this chapter and empirically applied to Thailand for a 25-year period (1975–1999). The approach developed in this chapter, the Total Systems Social, Ethical and Environmental Social Welfare (Total SSEE) index is characterised by a *systems approach, social choice theory* and *cost-benefit analysis.* A major limitation of the existing literature is that the underlying value judgements used in estimating welfare are not usually stated or clearly applied. This new approach overcomes this limitation, as all value judgements are made explicit within the specified social welfare function. This social welfare function, in turn, is derived from the principles of systems analysis, social choice theory and cost-benefit analysis.

This new approach is based on certain cost-benefit adjustments to the most common standard national account, Gross Domestic Product (GDP) for the indicators for social, ethical and environmental performance. This approach is justified because of its normative values and its plausible results. There are stark differences between GDP and social choice adjusted GDP rates for this period, not only in the overall change in the levels of social welfare but in the manner that these levels rise and fall during the period under review. This chapter concludes that GDP can be used as an indicator of social welfare if the GDP estimates are undertaken within a cost-benefit analysis framework based on social choice perspectives and systems analysis. Such a social choice adjusted GDP figure is a more accurate measure of social welfare than unadjusted GDP; the increase in social welfare in Thailand over this 25-year period is not as much as is evidenced by economic growth/GDP increase over this period. This chapter therefore represents a significant contribution to welfare economics and indicators literature – through the operationalisation of social choice theory and welfare economics for improved measurement and understanding of social welfare dynamics of a nation.

Within this first part, Section 1 has introduced the chapter. Section 2 reviews the use of standard national accounts as the conventional measure of social welfare and notes the limitations of this approach. Section 3 discusses the importance of Systems Analysis within this new approach before Section 4 introduces Social Choice Theory. Section 5 reviews methodology and quantification of the separate social, ethical and environmental adjustments to GDP. The results and analysis of these adjustments are discussed in Section 6, and Section 7 concludes this chapter.

2. GDP AS A MEASURE OF SOCIAL WELFARE AND ITS LIMITATIONS

The most widely used aggregate standard national accounts is GDP. From its inception, GDP has been used as a measure of social welfare (McLean, 1987). High GDP is considered a measurement of high social welfare. Similarly, a high level of growth in GDP, economic growth, is considered a measure of the increase in social welfare.

Social welfare has been defined in many ways (Sen, 1985). A widely accepted definition is that social welfare is a function of consumption (Slesnick, 2001). Within this framework there are legitimate reasons for GDP and other aggregate standard national account statistics, such as national income, to be used as a measure of social welfare (Hicks, 1940; Pigou, 1962). These aggregate statistics measure what is produced within the economy and therefore are a measure of economic activity. If social welfare is delineated into two parts, economic and non-economic, there is an "unverified probability" that economic welfare is a barometer of the "index of total welfare" (Pigou, 1962, p. 12). Thus, if the economic welfare of the country is clearly associated with the size of the national dividend, so too is total social welfare.

When economists explicitly or implicitly accept the identification of economic welfare with the supply of goods and services, they effectively ignore the differences between economic and non-economic welfare and the fact that activities affecting economic welfare favourably may conceivably affect non-economic welfare unfavourably (Abramovitz, 1961). Therefore, whilst economic growth might increase economic welfare, it may reduce non-economic welfare. The cumulative effect on social welfare may be positive, negative or neutral (Islam et al., 2001), but this approach assumes it to be positive.

GDP is based on the calculation of prices and quantities:

$$\text{GDP} = q \cdot p \qquad (1)$$

where: q is a vector of outputs $(n \times 1)$, $[q^1, q^2, \ldots, q^n]$; p is a vector of prices $(1 \times n)$, $[p^1, p^2, \ldots, p^n]$.

By observing how individuals allocate a certain sum of money over a specified period of time, data can be collected on people's preferences for particular consumption bundles (Hufschmidt et al., 1983).

At an aggregate level, GDP is the summation of all individuals' revealed preferences. Just as revealed preferences can indicate whether the welfare of an individual has increased or decreased, thus, so too can GDP indicate this for the entire economy. GDP as (1) is a consumption bundle for a given period. Changes in (1) are implicitly assumed to indicate changes in social welfare.

GDP as a measure of social welfare faces the limitations inherent in its own construction, the inherent faults of price indexes (Islam & Clarke, 2002), and also from a feminist perspective in that it totally ignores such activities as breastfeeding and informal sectors that are usually undertaken by women and children (Waring, 1987). Finally, GDP is limited as it aggregates individual preferences assuming that such an aggregation represents an optimal social outcome. Despite Adam Smith's *invisible hand*, individuals operating selfishly do not guarantee optimal social outcomes. To find an optimal level of social welfare it is not always possible to simply aggregate individual preferences. It cannot however be assumed that individual preferences revealed within the market place can be aggregated to reflect socially optimal outcomes in terms of social welfare. Firstly, individual preferences may be made without full knowledge. Preferences between A and B may be expressed without knowing that C is an option or that B has hidden consequences. However, even assuming full (albeit imperfect) knowledge, individual preferences may not result in optimal welfare outcomes in the first instance (Ehrlich et al., 1999). Individual preferences are not necessarily welfare (or utility) enhancing choices (Broome, 1999; see also Sen, 1977; Stoleru, 1975). In terms of the environment, unless individual and social incentives are aligned with one another, then optimal environmental outcomes will not be assured (Ehrlich et al., 1999). This is primarily because the environment is a public good (Sen, 1999; Smith, 1988).

It is possible for individuals to make decisions both as individuals within the market place and make decisions as citizens in a society (Sen, 1995). As citizens, individuals can prioritise certain value judgements such as equity and freedom. When social choice decisions are made over individual market decisions, socially optimal outcomes are more likely. Therefore social choices can be made by the individual within a new framework which considers alternatives from a social perspective that includes other considerations other then their own well-being (Sen, 1995).

3. THE SYSTEMS ANALYSIS APPROACH AND COST-BENEFIT ANALYSIS

Society is a complex and dynamic state resulting from a number of interconnected and evolving, dynamic systems or domains (Bossel, 1999; Colfer & Byron, 2001; Dopfer, 1979; Slesnick, 2001). In addition to the economy, these systems may include social, ethical and environmental systems, which can be represented by an integrated social environmental and ethical system; the SEE system. The concentration on only one of these systems to assess, measure and plan social welfare improvements is inadequate.

Systems analysis incorporates the non-linear outcomes of the interaction within a systems based economy (Omerod, 1994). A systems analysis approach is adopted within this study to allow the social welfare impacts of changes in the social, ethical and environmental performance to be fully considered. It is assumed that numerical estimates of these sub-systems are possible (see Clarke, 2002).

Aggregated standard national accounts are a measure of the aggregation of the different parts of the economic sub-system. Therefore, changes in unadjusted GDP reflect only changes in that particular sub-system. As society is systems based however, the changes in the economy (as indicated by increasing or decreasing GDP or national income) have an impact on the social, ethical and environmental sub-systems as well. These changed sub-systems then continue to impact on the economic and the dynamic inter-relationships. These inter-relationships are not direct and casual, and it cannot be assumed that a positive movement in the economic sub-system results in a positive movement within the other sub-systems.

This new understanding of society as a system impacts on those attempting to plan paths of increased development or welfare. Under this criteria, a focus on increasing the aggregate value will only add to society's welfare if it does not come at the expense of other sub-systems such as the environment. "GDP is now mainly a measure of how fast resources are squandered and converted into money flows, irrespective of their effect on society" (Bossel, 1999, p. 12). Therefore, increases in unadjusted GDP are likely to impact negatively on at least one of the other sub-systems, social, ethical or environmental. Likewise, activities within one sub-system (such as the environment) impact on other areas within that same domain (Arbhabhirma et al., 1988).

Further, a concentration on the importance of unadjusted GDP or economic growth as a measure of society's welfare is also fraught with danger as unadjusted GDP is simply the aggregation of one sub-system of many that in total make up society. The inter-relatedness of these sub-systems means that achieving increased economic growth may be obtained at the direct expense of one or more other sub-systems which will feedback not only to future economic consequences but will also have immediate welfaristic consequences.

The systems approach can be operationalised through the adjusting of aggregated standard national accounts so that the impacts of the separate costs and benefits of economic growth for all sub-systems are incorporated if we assume the measurability of the various sub-systems (Clarke & Islam, forthcoming; Islam & Clarke, 2001, 2002).

Cost-benefit analysis is a useful framework to rank social states (or projects) when the forces of private profitability are unable to rank according to social orderings (Boadway & Bruce, 1984). It has several components or elements. The first component is to consider all the direct economic and non-economic inputs and outputs. Social states (or projects) considered within a cost-benefit analysis framework have economic inputs and outputs that would be considered in a financial analysis, but they also have non-economic inputs and outputs that also need to be fully captured. These may include time saved, risk taking or health improvements.

The second component then is to consider all the indirect costs and benefits. These indirect effects are primarily externalities that are not captured elsewhere in the economy. They include such things as pollution, which affects third parties, and the production-consumption relationship.

Having identified all the direct and indirect, economic and non-economic costs and benefits, the third component of cost-benefit analysis is to then assign monetary values to these effects. The monetary value of the direct, economic costs and benefits are found within the market. However, a variety of techniques have been developed (i.e. hedonic pricing, border prices, willingness to pay, etc.) to calculate the prices of indirect, non-economic costs and benefits. These are known as *shadow prices*. By assigning monetary values to these non-economic goods, they can be considered with the economic costs and benefits to determine the final ranking.

The final component of cost-benefit analysis is to sum all these impacts for each period but to also convert all these current values into a present value. This is achieved through the use of time preferences and social discount rates (Boadway & Bruce, 1984).

Cost-benefit analysis will be incorporated in this paper to consider the desirability of economic growth. This will account for both economic and non-economic, direct and indirect effects and concerns of economic growth on social welfare through identifying and incorporating these effects, then assigning monetary values through the use of market prices and shadow prices, and using social time preferences for intertemporal welfare comparisons. This will make the cost-benefit analysis of economic growth an appropriate tool to rank different social states.

4. SOCIAL CHOICE THEORY

Social choice theory has a long history (see Sen, 1999 for a survey). The difficulties in making a judgement on the state of social welfare have long been recognised (Borda, 1780, reprinted 1953; de Condorcet, 1785). Bergson (1938) first suggested that social choices could be discussed within a social welfare function. Arrow (1951) formulated the difficulties and inconsistencies of doing so within his "impossibility theorem". Arrow showed through using axiomatic set theory that it was not possible to make a non-dictatorial social choice that satisfied a set of axioms of reasonableness. An alternative theorem was developed by Sen (1966, 1970, 1973 and subsequently added to by others, see Hammond, 1976) that argued that Arrow's set of axioms of reasonableness were not reasonable and it was possible to make non-dictatorial social choice decisions. Arrow's analysis is based on some restrictive assumptions, which are not necessary in operational social choice making in real life environments. The impossibility theorem therefore shows the mathematical impossibility of aggregating non-aggregatable entities (ordinal preferences), not a social choice impossibility since no social institutional mechanism is adopted in the aggregation process. Social choices are made through institutions, not abstract mathematical aggregations. These institutions may include parliamentary democracy, majority voting in other forms, or the free market (Islam, 2001).

Social choices can be estimated using expert opinion (or analyst), government formulated public policy, or specific interviews of individuals on social welfare outcomes. The methodology for each technique is well established (Islam, 2001). Using one, or a combination of the above, it is possible to determine the social choice perspectives on various social welfare issues. As the State maintains the functions of allocation, regulation and distribution (Musgrave, 1959), the State has a role to enforce these social choice preferences and "incarnate the moral and political will of the people" (Stoleru, 1975, p. 1). This is done in two stages: (1) *quantification* of individual preferences; and (2) the *weighting* of these individual preferences by weights determined by some form of consensus (i.e. majority voting for particular social structures, etc.). Perhaps more importantly, with regards to certain concepts, such as sustainability, individual preferences will not achieve these outcomes and the State (or analyst) must interpret and then act upon these social preferences (Pezzey, 2001, 2002). That this emphasis be placed on achieving an optimal social outcome should not be considered unusual. "Samuelson's (1956) consensus model of the household assumes that all members pool their resources and work in concert to maximise a common utility function" (Slesnick, 2001, p. 32). Social choice extends this consensus from the household to the society.

Social choice theory therefore is concerned with the study of issues surrounding social welfare on the basis of individual preferences but also considering the requirement for an optimal social outcome. Social choice theory is concerned with defining and measuring social welfare consistent with individual preferences for improving social welfare conditions but in which society's preferences are paramount.

5. THE NEW APPROACH: TOTAL SSEE SOCIAL WELFARE INDEX

GDP is an aggregation of individual preferences made within the market place. However, as has been discussed, these market preferences are not always socially optimal. Further, as social welfare is affected by social, ethical and environmental sub-systems, in addition to the economic sub-system, standard national accounts fail to adequately measure social welfare. Therefore, an adjusted measure of GDP based on social choice theory and systems analysis within a cost-benefit analysis framework, can operationalise this analysis of society. Adjustments can be made to GDP so that social choice and all sub-systems are included in the final aggregation.

In the existing literature, national income accounts and cost-benefit analysis measures are separated. It is often argued that cost-benefit analysis provides a more accurate measure of social welfare effects of policies, projects or economic states compared to national income accounts (see for example Pearce & Nash, 1981). In the present chapter it will be shown that the limitations of national income accounts can be overcome, to a significant extent, by integrating cost-benefit analysis and national income accounts measures of social welfare.

Social choice theory has been applied to welfare measurement in Thailand (Islam & Clarke, 2000, 2002). The following democratic social welfare function is developed and empirically applied for a 25-year period between 1975 and 1999.

$$\text{SW Total SSEE}_t = \frac{\text{GDP}_t + \text{So}_t + E_t + \text{En}_t}{(1+r)^t} \tag{2}$$

where: SW Total SSEE = Social Welfare of the Total System of Social, Ethical and Environmental sub-systems; GDP = Gross Domestic Product; W = welfare; t = time; r = discount rate; En = net benefit of the environmental sub-system; So = net benefit of the social sub-system; E = net benefit of the ethical sub-system.

This social welfare function is an expression of the costs and benefits of economic growth. Normally GDP is a criterion of a social welfare function, but in this social welfare function, the costs and benefits of GDP are used. This index is therefore not the sum of individual welfare but rather a function of the costs and benefits of economic growth. This makes it possible to specify a social welfare function that includes components of a social, economic and environmental (SEE) system.

This index is a socially preferable measure of social welfare as it has incorporated social choices on the social, ethical and environmental sub-systems. This measure is not based on traditional welfare criteria as Pareto optimality, but rather highlights issues of equity, distribution, fairness and compensation. The use of a cost-benefit analysis framework is necessary to use these alternative criteria.

These components include the social, ethical and environmental sub-systems. GDP is an aggregation of monetary exchanges within the economic sub-system and does not clearly capture the impact these exchanges have on the other sub-systems. As social welfare is a function of the entire SEE system, the social welfare definition takes into account changes within each sub-system. The following adjustments have been selected based on the work of previous studies that have adjusted GDP in order to more accurately measure social welfare (Daly & Cobb, 1990; Islam & Clarke, 2002; Nordhaus & Tobin, 1973; Sametz, 1968). These adjustments should be considered when applying social choice theory to a country such as Thailand (other adjustments might be necessary for different countries) to measure changes in social welfare occurring within a SEE system.

Social Sub-system

- Income distribution (based on Atkinson's equally distributed equivalent level of income).
- Public expenditure on education (75% of government expenditure on education).
- Public expenditure on health (50% of government expenditure on health).
- Private expenditure on health (50% of private expenditure on health).

- Urbanisation (based on estimates that 18% of urban income is spent on obtaining fresh water and overcoming medical problems caused by air pollution).
- Commuting (estimated at US$219 annually per car registered in Bangkok).
- Government streets and highways (based on 50% of government expenditure on roads).
- Consumer durables (based on 10% of private expenditure on consumer durables).
- Debt (based on 50% of the interest paid on public debt).

Environmental Sub-system

- Air pollution (based on previous studies estimating costs of air pollution).
- Water pollution (based on previous studies estimating costs of water pollution).
- Noise pollution (based on 1% of GDP).
- Loss of forests (based on cost of 886 baht per hectare of forest lost to deforestation).
- Non-renewable resources (based on previous studies estimating costs of the depletion of non-renewable resources).
- Long-term environmental damages (based on previous studies estimating costs of long-term environmental damage).

Ethical Sub-system

- Commercial sex work (based on 3% of GNP).
- Corruption (based on estimations of government corruption as percentage of government budget).

See Clarke (2002) for a full explanation of the methodologies used to numerically estimate these adjustments.

Obviously as all of these sub-systems inter-relate, some adjustments may cross-over various components. However, for simplicity, it is of interest to categorise the adjustments within only one of the sub-systems.

A Case Study: Measurement of Social Welfare in Thailand

Thailand has achieved remarkable growth over the last three decades. These sustained increases in GDP have played a major role in reducing absolute poverty levels, measured in terms of income levels from nearly one third of the population in (1975) to less than 10% in 1999 (Warr, 2001). But at the same time, income inequality increased (Clarke, 2001).

Within this general environment of high economic growth, Thailand is an interesting country to apply a GDP adjusted social welfare function for determining changes in quality of life within a SEE system.

The results of this application of social choice theory to quality of life measurement using a SEE system are significantly different to simple standard of living measures. Through the application of social choice theory to welfare via a social welfare function, the new measure of welfare can no longer be considered a version of GDP. It is now a measure of a SEE system and not just a reflection of national accounts. Therefore many of the limitations of GDP as a measure for development or welfare are overcome. These limitations include time preference concerns, aggregation concerns and the exclusions of non-welfare concerns (Islam, 2001; Sen, 1985). The new measure of welfare is no longer an aggregation of preferences because it explicitly takes into account value judgements through the use of a cost-benefit analysis framework.

6. RESULTS OF THE TOTAL SEE SOCIAL WELFARE INDEX

When a Total SSEE index is used to measure social welfare, a different result is achieved than that found using unadjusted GDP per capita to measure standard of living. Table 1 compares the Total SSEE per capita and GDP per capita calculations for the period 1975 to 1999 in constant (1988) prices.

This Total SSEE shows an end total increase of just over double during this period. It is interesting to compare this with the unadjusted GDP figure that increased by more than three times over the same period.

An adjusted GDP democratic social welfare function provides a more realistic description of welfare. Not only does Total SSEE increase at a slower rate, but is also decreases at times when GDP is actually increasing. The Total SSEE rose and fell throughout the 1980s, effectively being unchanged in 1986 from the 1979 figure. In comparison, GDP rose over 40% during this same period.

Both GDP and the Total SSEE rose steadily during the next decade though at significantly different rates. Within this period, the divergence between the two indices becomes quite apparent. This is shown in Fig. 1.

Both indices peak in 1996. This is just prior to the financial crisis of 1997. After 1996 both indices begin to fall. Whilst GDP per capita has shown the propensity to increase in 1999, Total SSEE has not increased but fallen by another 10%. It is too early to confirm whether this is a trend or a fluctuation. However, by

Table 1.   Comparison of Total SSEE Index per Capita and GDP per Capita in
Thailand, 1975–1999 (1988 Prices in 000,000 Baht Except per Capita Figures).

Year	Social	Ethical	Environment	Total SSEE Index	Total SSEE Index per Capita	GDP per Capita
1975	331842	−24116	−86055	221671	5229	14662
1976	363119	−26362	−85708	251049	5809	15754
1977	388797	−29030	−142814	216953	4900	16942
1978	427773	−31815	−152304	243654	5388	18237
1979	440068	−33381	−77447	329240	7140	18819
1980	461013	−35231	−82224	343558	7316	19458
1981	477326	−37075	−87778	352473	7362	20206
1982	497694	−37682	−94795	365217	7477	20883
1983	510856	−40005	−95357	375494	7583	21729
1984	515187	−42178	−103939	369070	7296	22504
1985	523127	−43951	−111730	367446	7094	22996
1986	528024	−46248	−96285	385491	7278	23722
1987	583552	−50789	−102979	429784	7978	25561
1988	657776	−57594	−111997	488185	8882	28380
1989	718965	−64090	−119705	535170	9576	31316
1990	765265	−71273	−144164	549828	9765	34565
1991	810049	−77202	−157070	575777	10108	37073
1992	857132	−82948	−164696	609488	10547	39506
1993	954830	−90271	−174799	689760	11824	42765
1994	1064806	−98332	−185197	781277	13221	45174
1995	1180788	−106962	−195065	878761	14779	48511
1996	1240733	−113180	−210948	916605	15247	51489
1997	1201253	−114104	−217620	869529	14298	49691
1998	1058342	−98926	−220998	738418	12013	45348
1999	1003719	−101929	−209435	692355	11228	45789

Source: Clarke (2002).

drawing on the results of other studies (Daly & Cobb, 1990; Jackson et al., 1997), predictions may be made that this new divergence could be expected.

What is obvious, is that quality of life as defined by the Total SSEE index can rise and fall independently of movements of GDP. Therefore, social welfare does not have a direct and positive relationship with GDP. For policy makers, the implications of this are serious. Policies aimed at increasing economic growth can no longer be justified in terms of seeking to increase welfare. Policies that result in economic growth may actually reduce welfare. In light of this, policy makers will need to re-evaluate their underlying assumptions and motivations.

There are a number of ways to analyse the results of such an application. Issues of equity can be studied. For example, the major reason why GDP as a welfare measurement is different to the Total SSEE index is that income has been adjusted

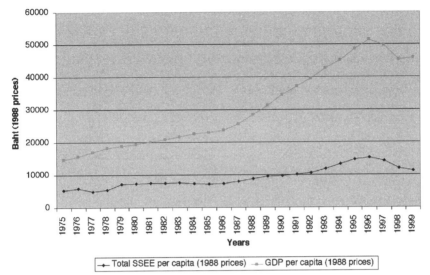

Fig. 1. Comparison of Total SSEE Index and GDP per Capita in Thailand (1975–1999) (1988 Prices in Baht).

for inequality in its distribution. As a result, if society's welfare in Thailand were to be increased, consideration should be given to the distribution of income. By reducing this inequality, the welfare of Thailand would increase dramatically.

Few other studies of welfare exist for Thailand (see Islam & Clarke, 2002; Kakwani, 1999 for exceptions) however a number of studies focusing on individual aspects of welfare such as poverty levels and the environment have been undertaken (Riggs, 1995). Popular approaches to measuring standard of living based on GDP indicate that welfare has increased dramatically over the past three decades. However, the use of GDP as a measure of welfare does not take into account the effects of changes to the social, ethical or environmental sub-system impacts during that time.

The results from the Total SSEE are intuitively correct. Social welfare during the 1980s has increased, but not evenly, with dips and falls perhaps related to increased inequality of income distribution. The benefits of economic growth have been positive but the costs of this growth have also been accounted for. Certainly, the Total SSEE has not increased as dramatically as the GDP measure of welfare would suggest. It is suggested that the Total SSEE measure of social welfare is a suitable welfare indicator within a SEE system.

This chapter has adopted a social choice approach to measuring social welfare. Implicit in this approach are certain value judgements. By expressing the definition of welfare as a social welfare function, these value judgements become explicit in estimating and evaluating welfare changes. The omission of such considerations in conventional measures, such as GDP, is thus rectified resulting in this measure of welfare being more plausible than GDP and so more useful to policy makers.

As Sen (1999) has stated repeatedly, social choice theory is concerned with the normative assessment of economic states and outcomes. The present chapter has applied the social choice theory to the GDP based welfare measurement of economic development in Thailand. This approach has been innovative and appropriate since it has produced plausible estimates of welfare in the Thai economy and has provided useful information and insights into the processes and changes of development dynamics in Thailand and the normative implications of these. The adoption of the systems approach has also been useful since this adoption has assisted in identifying, quantifying and measuring the various components that influence welfare both systematically and rigorously.

This new approach provides an intuitive correct measure of changes of social welfare within Thailand over a 25-year period. Social welfare has risen but not as much as suggested when social welfare is a function of GDP on which most studies of Thai social welfare rely (see Kakwani, 1997). Social planners can improve their governance and social responsibility of improving social welfare by adopting such a framework that casts a wider net over influencing factors such as the social, ethical and environmental ones.

7. CONCLUSION

This chapter has incorporated social choice theory, systems analysis and cost-benefit analysis to develop and empirically apply an indicator for social, ethical and environmental performance for Thailand for a 25-year period (1975–1999). It has argued that the process of increasing social welfare is dependent on a complicated set of interrelationships between a number of systems, of which the economy is but one. It has further argued that social choice theory is still a legitimate method of operationalising this new approach through the adjustment of GDP to take account of these systems. The value judgements on the determinants of welfare are explicitly defined in this chapter and set out in a social welfare function by adopting social choice theory.

Social choice theory is a suitable starting point for measuring welfare within a systems analysis approach. However, as measuring welfare or quality of life is dependent on making social value judgements, a social welfare function is the most appropriate tool for undertaking this measurement. This chapter has identified certain adjustments which can be made to GDP and justified these adjustments within a social welfare function so that changes to development or welfare can be measured within a SEE system.

The results of this study are *intuitively* correct. Whilst social welfare has increased in Thailand, this increase has been *moderate* and *steady*. Adjusting GDP and defining it as a social welfare function to analyse the SEE system not only highlights the limitation of the current use of GDP within mainstream social sciences, but it also offers insights into the constitution of an ideal society. A society must harmonise its various sub-systems. Social planners will be able to identify how best to balance the needs of the various sub-systems in order to move in a positive direction. An adjusted GDP social welfare function is a positive step towards understanding an ideal society. Though this approach was applied to Thailand, it is *generally applicable to measure social welfare under any circumstances*. Therefore, the present study makes a significant contribution to operationalise social choice theory and to enhance the practical significance of welfare economics, especially for measuring, analysing and understanding social welfare dynamics of a nation.

REFERENCES

Abramovitz, M. (1961). The welfare interpretation of secular trends in national income and product. In: M. Abramovitz et al. (Eds), *The Allocation of Economic Resources*. Stanford: Stanford University Press.

Arbhabhirma, A., Phantumvarit, D., Elkington, J., & Ingkasuwan, P. (1988). *Thailand: natural resources profile*. Singapore: Oxford University Press.

Arrow, K. (1951). *Social choice and individual value*. New York: John Wiley & Sons.

Bergson, A. (1938). A reformulation of certain aspects of welfare economics. *Quarterly Journal of Economics* (February).

Boadway, R., & Bruce, N. (1984). *Welfare economics*. Oxford: Basil Blackwell.

Borda, J. (1780 – reprinted in 1953). Memoire sur les elections au scrutin', histoire de l'academic royale des sciences. (Translated by A. de Grazia). *Mathematical Derivation of an Election System, 44*, 42–51.

Bossel, H. (1999). *Indicators for sustainable development: Theory, method, applications*. International institute for sustainable development. Winnipeg.

Broome, J. (1999). *Ethics out of economics*. Cambridge: Cambridge University Press.

Clarke, M. (2001). Does economic growth reduce poverty? A case study of Thailand. Poster prepared for UNU/WIDER development conference, *Growth and poverty*. Helsinki (25–26 May).

Clarke, M. (2002). *Is economic growth desirable? Measuring social welfare for Thailand*. Ph.D. thesis. Melbourne: Victoria University.

Clarke, M., & Islam, S. (forthcoming). Measuring social welfare: Application of social choice theory. Accepted for publication in *Journal of Socio-economics*.

Colfer, C., & Byron, Y. (2001). *People managing forests: The link between human well-being and sustainability*. Baltimore: John Hopkins University Press.

de Condorcet, M. (1785). *Essai sur l' application de l'analyse a la probabilitie des decisions rendues a la plualite des voix*. Paris: Imprimerie Royal.

Daly, H., & Cobb, J. (1990). *For the common good*. Boston: Beacon Press.

Dopfer, K. (1979). *The new political economy of development: Integrated theory and Asian experiment*. Melbourne: Macmillian Press Ltd.

Ehrlich, P., Wolf, G., Daily, G., Hughes, J., Daily, S., Dalton, N., & Goulder, L. (1999). Knowledge and the environment. *Ecological Economics, 30,* 267–284.

Hammond, P. (1976). Equity, arrow's conditions and rawls' difference principles. *Econometrica, 44,* 793–804.

Hicks, J. (1940). The valuation of social income. *Economica, 7,* 104–124.

Hufschmidt, M., James, D., Meister, A., Bower, B., & Dixon, J. (1983). *Environment, natural systems, and development*. Baltimore: Johns Hopkins University Press.

Islam, S. (2001). *Optimal growth economics*. Amsterdam: North Holland Publishing Co.

Islam, S., & Clarke, M. (2000). Social welfare and GDP: Can we still use GDP for welfare measurement? Seminar paper presented at CSES, Victoria University (7 September).

Islam, S., & Clarke, M. (2001). Measuring the quality of life: A new approach empirically applied to Thailand. Paper presented at *INDEX2001 quality of life indicators conference*, Rome (2–5 October).

Islam, S., & Clarke, M. (2002). The relationship between economic development and social welfare. *Social Indicators Research, 57,* 201–228.

Jackson, T., Laing, F., MacGillivray, A., Marks, N., Ralls, J., & Stymne, S. (1997). *An index of sustainable economic welfare for the United Kingdom 1950–1996*. Centre for environmental strategy, University of Surrey, Guildford.

Kakwani, N. (1997). Welfare based approaches to measuring real economic growth with application to Thailand. Discussion paper 14, school of economics, The University of New South Wales, Sydney.

Kakwani, N. (1999). Poverty and inequality during the economic crisis in Thailand. *Indicators of well-being and policy analysis*, Vol. 3, No. 1 (January), NESDB, Bangkok.

McLean, I. (1987). Economic wellbeing. In: R. Madock & I. McLean (Eds), *The Australian Economy in the Long Run*. New York: Cambridge University Press.

Morris, M. (1979). *Measuring the condition of the world's poor: The physical quality of life Index*. New York: Pergamon.

Musgrave, T. (1959). *The theory of public finance*. New York: McGraw-Hill.

Nordhaus, W., & Tobin, J. (1973). Is growth obsolete? In: M. Moss (Ed.), *The Measurement of Economic and Social Planning, Economic Growth*. New York: National Bureau of Economic Research.

Omerod, P. (1994). *The death of economics*. London: Faber and Faber.

Pearce, D., & Nash, C. (1981). *The social appraisal of projects*. London: Macmillan.

Pezzey, J. (2001). *Sustainability policy and environmental policy*. Mimeo, centre for resource and environmental studies, Australian National University, Canberra.

Pezzey, J. (2002). *Concern for sustainable development in a sexual world*. Mimeo, centre for resource and environment studies, Australian National University, Canberra.

Pigou, A. (1962). *The economics of welfare* (4th ed.). London: Macmillian.

Riggs, J. (Ed.) (1995). *Counting the costs*. Singapore: Institute of southeast Asian studies.

Sametz, A. (1968). Production of goods and services: The measurements of economic growth. In: E. Sheldon & W. Moore (Eds), *Indicators of social change*. New York: Russell Sage Foundation.

Sen, A. (1966). A possibility theorem on majority decisions. *Econometrica, 34.*

Sen, A. (1970). *Collective choice and social welfare*. Amsterdam: North-Holland.

Sen, A. (1973). *On economic inequality*. London: Oxford University Press.

Sen, A. (1977). Rational fools: A critique of the behavioural foundations of economic theory. *Philosophy and Public Affairs, 6,* 317–344.

Sen, A. (1979). Personal utilities and public judgements: Or what's wrong with welfare economics. *Economic Journal, 89.*

Sen, A. (1985). *Commodities and capabilities.* Amsterdam: North-Holland.

Sen, A. (1995). Environmental evaluation and social choice: Contingent valuation and the market analogy. *The Japanese Economic Review, 46,* 23–37.

Sen, A. (1999). The possibility of social choice. *The American Economic Review* (June), 349–378.

Slesnick, D. (2001). *Consumption and social welfare.* Cambridge: Cambridge University Press.

Smith, V. (1988). The influence of resources and environmental problems on applied welfare economics. In: V. Smith (Ed.), *Environmental Resources and Applied Welfare Economics.* Resources for the future, Washington, DC.

Stoleru, L. (1975). *Economic equilibrium and growth.* Amsterdam: North-Holland.

UNDP (1990). *The human development report*, UNDP. New York.

Waring, M. (1987). *Counting for nothing.* Wellington: Bridget William Books.

Warr, P. (2001). Poverty reduction and sectoral growth: Evidence from southeast Asia. Paper presented for the WIDER development donference, Growth and development, Helsinki (25–26 May).

CORPORATE GOVERNANCE, MARKET DISCIPLINE, AND PRODUCTIVITY GROWTH

Jens Köke

ABSTRACT

Using a large panel of German manufacturing firms over the years 1986–1996, this study examines the impact of corporate governance and market discipline on productivity growth. We find that firms under concentrated ownership tend to show significantly higher productivity growth. Financial pressure from creditors influences productivity growth positively, particularly for firms in financial distress. Regarding market discipline, productivity grows faster when competition in product markets is intense, but only when ownership concentration is high. We do not find evidence that the type of the owner, ownership complexity, or the size of the supervisory board is significantly related to productivity growth.

1. INTRODUCTION

In a recent survey, Bartelsman and Doms (2000) identify four factors that are likely to influence productivity growth at the micro level: (1) government regulation altering the incentives for innovating, market entry, and gaining market share; (2) managerial ability and firm ownership determining the firm's choices on technology and inputs; (3) technology and human capital affecting efficiency in

Social Responsibility: Corporate Governance Issues
Research in International Business and Finance, Volume 17, 89–122
© 2003 Published by Elsevier Science Ltd.
ISSN: 0275-5319/PII: S0275531903170055

production; and (4) (international) competition on product markets making firms learn faster about new technologies. This study examines empirically the role of corporate governance and product market competition (and their interaction), which are two important determinants of managerial behavior. Corporate governance is understood and measured as the system of firm's ownership structure, capital structure, and board structure.[1]

Empirical work on corporate governance, competition, and their relation to productivity is accumulating. Studies examining the role of competition include Green and Mayes (1991) and Nickell (1996) for the U.K., Klette (1999) for Norway, Bottasso and Sembenelli (2001) for Italy, and Caves (1992), Porter (1992), and Börsch-Supan (1999) for a range of industrialized countries. Studies investigating the role of ownership structure encompass Nickell et al. (1997) for the U.K., and Gross-Schuler and Weigand (2001) and Januszewski et al. (2002) for Germany; Nickell and Nicolitsas (1999) examine the role of capital structure. Another strand of literature investigates different corporate governance mechanisms, such as the structure of the board (e.g. Yermack, 1996); however, empirical studies on board structure typically examine the impact on firm value or some accounting measure, but not the impact on productivity. A study that examines the impact of corporate governance (shareholder control and financial pressure), product market competition, and their interactions on productivity growth in U.K. firms is Nickell et al. (1997). Januszewski et al. (2002) conduct a similar analysis for German firms; however, they neglect the role of creditors. In contrast to the U.K., lending relationships in Germany are often characterized as long-term and comparatively stable, ensuring lending even to ailing firms (Mayer, 1988). Recently, this German "housebank" system has been criticized as too inflexible in times of rapid economic change; hence, new evidence on creditors' governance role is desirable.[2]

Using a panel of 841 German manufacturing firms over the years 1986–1996, this study analyzes the impact of five corporate governance mechanisms (ownership concentration, owner type, ownership complexity, financial pressure, and board size), product market competition, and their interactions on productivity growth. The present study adds to the literature on four important respects: First, we consider a larger range of governance mechanisms and their relation to productivity growth than previous studies. Second, to our knowledge this study is the first to examine the impact of financial pressure (from creditors) on productivity growth for a continental European country. Due to the methodological similarity, our results are directly comparable to those of Nickell et al. (1997) obtained for the U.K. Third, we explicitly address potential endogeneity of our explanatory variables by using the GMM instrumental variables technique developed by Arellano and Bond (1991). This method is now standard in panel econometrics, however, it is not yet widely applied in studies on corporate governance with the exceptions of Nickell et al. (1997) and Januszewski et al. (2002). Finally, the data set used in this study is much larger than data sets used in previous work on corporate governance in Germany (Becht & Böhmer, 2000; Cable, 1985; Gorton & Schmid, 2000; Gross-Schuler & Weigand, 2001; Januszewski et al., 2002; Lehmann & Weigand, 2000).

Our main findings are: Firms under concentrated ownership tend to show higher productivity growth, and this effect is larger when product market competition is intense. Hence, shareholder control and competition are complements. Financial pressure from creditors also has a positive impact on productivity growth, particularly for firms in financial distress. But we cannot confirm that financial pressure and competition stand in a substitutive relationship, as documented by Nickell et al. (1997) for the U.K. Similar to Franks and Mayer (2000) and Januszewski et al. (2002), we cannot confirm that firms controlled via cross ownership or pyramid structures perform worse than other firms; and board size is not significantly related to productivity growth.

The paper is structured as follows: Section 2 briefly reviews the literature on corporate governance and market discipline, and how these monitoring mechanisms are related to productivity growth. The aim is to formulate a set of testable hypotheses. Section 3 describes the data sources used and how corporate governance and market discipline are measured in this study. Section 4 gives some preliminary evidence on the relation of corporate governance and market discipline to productivity growth. Section 5 presents an empirical model of productivity growth and details on the GMM estimation procedure. Section 6 contains the estimation results and Section 7 concludes.

2. HYPOTHESES

The classical problem of corporate governance is the separation of ownership and control. The literature on corporate governance discusses a variety of mechanisms that are supposed to alleviate this agency conflict. A common feature of all mechanisms is that they aim to align the interests of managers and owners of a firm (Shleifer & Vishny, 1997). In the following, we discuss mechanisms covered extensively in the literature and deduct hypotheses that are to be tested in the empirical analysis.[3] We distinguish between the firm's ownership structure, capital structure, board structure, and product market competition.

We expect that productivity growth is affected as follows:

Hypothesis 1. Concentrated ownership increases productivity growth.

Hypothesis 2. The impact of ownership concentration is stronger when a firm is owned by a non-financial firm as a large blockholder, but weaker when a firm is owned by a large private or public blockholder.

Hypothesis 3. Complex ownership decreases productivity growth.

Hypothesis 4. A large fraction of bank debt increases productivity growth.

Hypothesis 5. The impact of bank debt is stronger when performance is poor.

Hypothesis 6. Small board size increases productivity growth.

Hypothesis 7. Intense product market competition increases productivity growth.

The first hypothesis (H1) follows Shleifer and Vishny (1986) who argue that a large block provides the owner with an incentive to collect information and to monitor management. A large blockholder also has enough voting control to put pressure on management. In contrast, in firms with a dispersed shareholder structure free-riding behavior should make monitoring too costly (Grossman & Hart, 1980). The evidence on monitoring by blockholders indicates that large shareholders indeed play an active role in corporate governance. For Japan, Kaplan and Minton (1994) find that poorly performing management is more likely to be replaced by a large blockholder. For Germany, Franks and Mayer (2000) find little association of ownership concentration with managerial dis-ciplining. Lehmann and Weigand (2000) find a negative relation of ownership concentration and accounting-based profitability. In contrast, Januszewski et al. (2002) show that ownership concentration is positively related to productivity growth.

The second hypothesis (H2) is concerned with the type of the controlling block-holder. Pound (1988) notes that institutional investors such as banks should be effective monitors because they have frequent business contacts to their clients; on the other hand, these investors might become entrenched and support incumbent management. Therefore, investment or pension funds could be better monitors than banks or insurers. Similarly, non-financial firms as blockholders can be effective monitors when their investment is strategic; when operating in the same industry, information asymmetries are lower. In contrast, private blockholders typically have only limited access to monitoring competency within their family. For the U.S., the evidence on the role of institutional investors is mixed (Black, 1998). For Belgium, Renneboog (2000) finds that industrial companies resort to disciplinary actions when performance is poor. For Germany, focusing on earnings-based performance measures Edwards and Nibler (2000) cannot find evidence that the role of banks is different from that of other large corporate shareholders; in contrast, Gorton and Schmid (2000) and Lehmann and Weigand (2000) find a positive impact. Focusing on productivity, Gross-Schuler and Weigand (2001) cannot find a consistent impact of any particular type of owner. In contrast, Januszewski et al. (2002) find that financial institutions as blockholders are harmful for productivity growth.

The third hypothesis (H3) addresses the role of ownership complexity for corporate monitoring. Franks and Mayer (1995) note that cross holdings can exclude small investors from the control over management. Bebchuk et al. (2000) adds that pyramids and cross ownership function as anti-takeover devices, and therefore shelter management from capital market pressure. Ownership structures are particularly complex in continental Europe and Japan (La Porta et al., 1999). For Germany, Franks and Mayer (2000) cannot find evidence that managerial disciplining is smaller in firms controlled by pyramids, and Januszewski et al. (2002) cannot find evidence that productivity growth is lower for firms controlled by cross-held blockholders.

The fourth hypothesis (H4) focuses on the firm's capital structure and its effect on performance. Jensen (1986) argues that debt financing reduces free cashflow and therefore has a disciplinary effect on management. Management can use high leverage to signal credibly that they maximize profits. Likewise, any disciplinary impact creditors have on management should be the greatest when a large fraction of debt is bank debt. Previous evidence indicates that high gearing has a positive impact on performance (see Cable, 1985; Gross-Schuler & Weigand, 2001, for Germany; Nickell & Nicolitsas, 1999, for the U.K.; Renneboog, 2000, for Belgium).

The fifth hypothesis (H5) recognizes that creditors are concerned about avoiding failure of the provided loans, but much less concerned about monitoring their client firms to ensure that they maximize profits (Stiglitz, 1985). Therefore, we expect banks to interfere in particular when performance is poor and when they are in a strong creditor position, i.e. when a large proportion of debt is bank debt. Similar arguments are put forward by Mayer (1988). He shows that institutionalized lending relationships, as exemplified by the German housebank system (see Edwards & Fischer, 1994, for a detailed discussion), reduce information asymmetries, and as a consequence allow for (new) long-term lending even in times of financial difficulties.

The sixth hypothesis (H6) follows Jensen (1993) who argues that smaller boards control more effectively and therefore have a positive impact on performance. For the U.S., Yermack (1996) confirms that board size is negatively correlated with firm value. In Germany with its two-tier board structure, a supervisory board is required by law for public corporations, and in some cases also for private corporations. The number of supervisory board members is also regulated by law, with a minimum of three and a maximum of 21 members, depending on firm size and industry; for details, see Hopt (1997). Since firm's discretion is low regarding the size of the board, any empirical relation is likely to be weak.

Finally, the seventh hypothesis (H7) recognizes that even in the presence of weak internal monitoring, fierce product market competition may act to align managers' goals with the aim of efficient production; Allen and Gale (2000) provide a review. For example, Hart (1983) shows that an increase in product market competition reduces managerial slack. Other theoretical studies show that competition has no or a positive impact on agency costs. The empirical evidence is less ambiguous. Green and Mayes (1991), Caves (1992), Nickell et al. (1997), Bottasso and Sembenelli (2001), and Januszewski et al. (2002) document that increased product market competition is associated with higher productivity or higher productivity growth. In a recent study with Norwegian establishment-level data, Klette (1999) provides evidence for the positive relationship between price-cost margins, as a measure for product market competition, scale economies, and productivity.

3. DATA AND MEASUREMENT ISSUES

The sample used in the empirical analysis is based on firm-level data covering the years 1986–1996. The unbalanced panel comprises 841 German corporations operating in the manufacturing sector, with a total of 5,329 firm years. In contrast to most previous empirical studies on corporate governance in Germany we do not restrict our analysis to listed corporations, but also include non-listed corporations. This is significant because it alleviates the selection bias caused by restricting the analysis to listed firms (Börsch-Supan & Köke, 2002). For a detailed description of sample selection, see the Appendix.

The sample is fairly representative for the universe of large German corporations. Taking the number of all incorporated German firms in the year 1992 as a reference, coverage is high for listed firms (48.9%), all of which are public corporations. The sample includes all firms listed on any German stock exchange that mainly operate in the manufacturing sector. For non-listed firms, coverage is small for public corporations (8.9%) and weak for private corporations (0.02%). However, choosing corporations with total sales exceeding 100 million DM as the benchmark, the sample includes 66.1% of all large public corporations, and more than 3% of all large private corporations. For a more detailed analysis of sample representativeness, see Tables A2 and A3.

Below we explain the economic principles that guide the construction of the variables used in this study; for precise definitions, see Appendix.

3.1. Measuring Corporate Governance

To measure corporate governance, this study uses data on ownership structure, capital structure, and board structure. In the following, we explain how these measures are constructed to test the hypotheses formulated in Section 2. We also provide some descriptive statistics.

The main variable used to measure ownership is an indicator whether a firm has an ultimately controlling owner or not (CONTROL). This measure takes into account complex ownership structures which are frequently encountered in large German firms. Therefore, it is not only based on measures of direct ownership, which can be misleading particularly for conglomerates (Becht & Böhmer, 2000; Köke, 2001). Similarly, it clearly identifies one single owner. This allows us to classify firms according to the type of their ultimate owner. For a detailed description of the concept of control, which is applied to identify the ultimate owner of each sample firm, see Appendix.

To illustrate our main measure of ownership, Table 1 describes how average ownership concentration evolves over time. Besides CONTROL, Table 1 also

Table 1.   Ownership Concentration.

	Mean			Median	
	CONTROL	BLOCK	HERF	BLOCK	HERF
1986	80.2%	59.2%	46.3%	53.9%	36.1%
1987	84.3%	65.2%	53.4%	68.0%	50.0%
1988	86.0%	68.4%	57.6%	75.7%	57.8%
1989	87.3%	70.9%	60.3%	77.3%	60.3%
1990	88.9%	71.5%	60.9%	77.3%	60.4%
1991	89.6%	72.8%	62.3%	79.6%	63.4%
1992	90.6%	74.9%	65.1%	83.9%	70.4%
1993	91.7%	78.8%	70.2%	95.0%	90.3%
1994	91.0%	81.0%	74.1%	99.0%	98.0%
1995	90.5%	81.4%	75.1%	100.0%	100.0%
1996	90.2%	81.2%	74.9%	99.9%	99.8%
Average	89.2%	75.7%	66.9%	90.0%	81.0%
Correlation with CONTROL	1.000	0.641	0.511	0.641	0.511

Note: Concentration of ownership in a given year for the period 1986–1996. Measures of ownership concentration include the average size of the largest share block (BLOCK), the average Herfindahl index of owner concentration (HERF), and the fraction of firms for which an ultimate owner can be identified applying the concept of control (CONTROL). The size of the largest block and the sum of the three largest blocks are calculated at the direct level of ownership. The sample comprises 841 firms.

presents two alternative measures of ownership concentration commonly used in the literature: the size of the largest block (BLOCK) and the Herfindahl index (HERF) calculated for all large share blocks. Note that BLOCK as well as HERF refer to the direct level of ownership. We find that ownership is highly concentrated. Examining ownership at the ultimate level, we identify a controlling owner for, on average, 89.2% of sample firms during the years 1986–1996. At the direct level of ownership, the largest block is also very large with 75.7% at the mean and 90.0% at the median. Similarly high concentration is found when using the Herfindahl index. Both BLOCK and HERF are highly correlated with CONTROL. Hence, collinearity problems would be likely when using all three measures simultaneously in the empirical analysis. The degree of ownership complexity in large German firms makes CONTROL a more appealing measure of ownership concentration, hence CONTROL is our preferred measure of ownership concentration in this study.

In addition, we measure ownership complexity (CROSS, PYRAMID) and we identify the type of the ultimate owner for each sample firm (TYPE). The largest fraction of firms is ultimately controlled by a non-financial firm (41.7%) or a private owner (36.7%). Only 4.4% of sample firms are ultimately controlled by a bank, and 2.3% are controlled by other financial institutions. Note that actual voting power of banks might be greater in practice when banks make use of proxy voting. However, recent evidence suggests that proxy voting is extremely unlikely to significantly enhance bank voting power (Edwards & Nibler, 2000). Government agencies control 4.1% of the firms in our sample, and 10.8% of firms have dispersed ownership. Regarding ownership complexity, 7.5% of sample firms are controlled by a firm that belongs to the well-known web of German industrial and financial conglomerates (Wenger & Kaserer, 1998), and 50.2% of sample firms are controlled through a pyramid with at least one intermediate firm between the ultimate owner and the sample firm.

Regarding capital structure, the main measure used in this study is the ratio of bank debt to total debt (BANK). On average, 27.4% of the total debt burden consists of bank debt. As additional measures we use the ratio of total debt to total assets (DEBT), the ratio of total debt to book value of total equity (LEVERAGE), and the ratio of operating earnings to interest payments (COVERAGE). Our measure of board structure is an indicator whether the number of directors on the supervisory board is equal to the legally specified minimum or whether it is greater (SMALL). As discussed in detail in the Appendix, this minimum number depends on industry and firm size, but also on other firm characteristics, which are not observable to the researcher. Since not all sample firms have a supervisory board, we use an indicator whether such a board exists (BOARD). In our sample, 74.3% of firms have a supervisory board, and in 76.4% of firms the supervisory board consists of the legally specified minimum number of directors.

3.2. Measuring Market Discipline

To measure market discipline, this study uses data on product market competition. The main variable used to measure competition is the firm's rents from production (RENT), which can be interpreted as an ex post measure of market power. The motivation for using this measure is that firms operating in less competitive markets should be able to sell their products well above marginal cost, and therefore earn higher rents after covering their expenses (on capital, labor, and materials). The abstract definition of production rents, R_t, is as follows:

$$R_t = \frac{S_t - r_t^K p_t^K K_t}{Q_t} \tag{1}$$

The denominator, Q_t, is real output (value added), $p_t^Y Y_t - p_t^M M_t$.[4] The numerator is a measure of the firm's real operating surplus, S_t, less real cost of capital, $r_t^K p_t^K K_t$. In this notation, Y_t is nominal output, L_t, K_t, and M_t are nominal labor, capital, and materials inputs, while p_t^Y, p_p^L, p_p^K, and p_t^M are the corresponding prices. Finally, r_t^K is the user cost of capital, define as $r_t^K = \delta + r_t$, where δ is the depreciation rate and r_t is the risk-free market interest rate.

In the literature (e.g. Nickell, 1996), raw operating surplus, S_t, is measured by "earnings before interest, taxes, and depreciation" (also known as EBITDA). This quantity contains a number of balance-sheet items that can potentially distort the economic content of this variable, resulting in values of EBITDA that are downward-biased measures of raw operating surplus. This problem is particularly severe in Germany, where firms are entitled to retain a large fraction of earnings to build up reserves. In our sample, this effect is large enough to make the mean of the rents variable negative in the pooled sample, with the implication that, loosely speaking, a large number of firms make losses most of the time. Similar to Lehmann and Weigand (2000), we therefore do not use balance-sheet EBITDA as a measure of raw operating surplus. Instead, we use an economic definition of raw operating surplus: sales less costs for materials and labor, hence $S_t = p_t^Y Y_t - p_t^M M_t - p_t^L L_t$. In economic terms, this definition is equivalent to the definition of EBITDA. With this in mind, the abstract definition of firm rents in (1) can be re-written in terms of observable quantities as follows:

$$R_t = \frac{(p_t^Y Y_t - p_t^M M_t - p_t^L L_t) - r_t^K p_t^K K_t}{p_t^Y Y_t - p_t^M M_t} \tag{2}$$

In addition to firm-specific rents, we use the market share of the six largest suppliers (CR6) and the respective Herfindahl index (HHI), both measured at the four-digit industry level, as proxy variables for competition. As a proxy for competition from abroad we use the ratio of imports to total market size (i.e. the sum of domestic production and imports), measured at the two-digit industry level (IMPORT).

98   JENS KÖKE

There are two important caveats with respect to all measures of competition used in this paper. First, we acknowledge that these variables do not reflect some important facets of competition, namely potential entry and firm conduct. Second, as we do not have firm-specific data on market shares, we can only assign companies to their primary four-digit industry group, but we cannot adjust Herfindahl indices and concentration ratios using firms' market shares.

To illustrate our measures of competition, Table 2 describes the intensity of competition using all of these measures, separately for the 22 two-digit manufacturing

Table 2. Firm- and Industry-Specific Measures of Competition.

	Firm Level		Industry Level		Observ.	
	RENT	CR6	HHI	IMPORT	Total	Percent
Food (15)	45.8%	33.1%	4.2%	18.7%	676	12.7%
Tobacco (16)	48.6%	97.8%	20.3%	10.2%	55	1.0%
Textiles (17)	16.7%	45.2%	6.2%	46.4%	228	4.3%
Clothing (18)	55.2%	20.6%	1.4%	61.2%	84	1.6%
Leather (19)	46.7%	33.3%	3.2%	63.2%	24	0.5%
Wood (20)	36.0%	19.6%	1.6%	24.0%	30	0.6%
Paper (21)	30.1%	47.8%	6.7%	27.7%	168	3.2%
Publishing, printing (22)	30.9%	23.6%	1.9%	5.5%	57	1.1%
Coal, oil processing (23)	41.1%	81.8%	14.9%	38.4%	63	1.2%
Chemicals (24)	39.1%	60.1%	10.6%	26.1%	564	10.6%
Rubber/plastic products (25)	28.4%	34.2%	3.8%	19.6%	318	6.0%
Rock, stone, glass (26)	30.1%	51.9%	8.5%	17.6%	326	6.1%
Metals (27)	10.9%	56.7%	10.9%	26.2%	308	5.8%
Metal products (28)	27.6%	25.7%	2.7%	14.8%	280	5.3%
Machinery (29)	20.2%	37.9%	5.0%	16.7%	941	17.7%
Equation for data processing (30)	27.3%	80.7%	23.5%	60.2%	191	3.6%
Equation for power generation (31)	21.6%	42.6%	6.5%	31.1%	230	4.3%
Equation for broadcasting and TV (32)	23.0%	60.5%	12.6%	48.4%	188	3.5%
Medical and optical instruments (33)	20.2%	41.2%	6.7%	33.6%	124	2.3%
Cars, car parts (34)	26.8%	67.5%	12.7%	20.8%	246	4.6%
Other vehicles (35)	2.6%	67.7%	19.2%	59.7%	163	3.1%
Furniture, jewelry, toys (36)	38.5%	32.4%	3.4%	25.7%	65	1.2%
Average	28.4%	46.6%	7.9%	26.1%	5,329	100.0%
Correlation with RENT	1.000	−0.034	−0.028	−0.067	–	–

Note: Firm- and industry-specific measures of competition, separately by two-digit industry. Measures of competition include the ratio of total operating surplus less costs of capital to value added (RENT), the market share of the six largest suppliers (CR6), the Herfindahl index of producer concentration (HHI), and the ratio of imports to total market size (IMPORT). The sample comprises 841 firms.

industries contained in the sample. We find that German manufacturing firms earned rents of about 28% during the years 1986–1996. On average, the six largest suppliers cover about 47% of the domestic market, and imports make up for about one fourth of the total market. Table 2 also indicates some remarkable differences between industries. Imports represent a large fraction of the total market in clothing, leather, equipment for data processing, and other vehicles (e.g. ships). The market share of the six largest suppliers is low in clothing, wood, publishing and printing, and metal products; in turn, concentration is extremely high in tobacco. Correspondingly, industries with low RENT are textiles, metals, and other vehicles. As we could expect, RENT is negatively correlated with industry concentration and import penetration. However, this correlation is weak. This implies that the empirical analysis should include firm-level as well as industry-level measures of competition.

4. PRELIMINARY EVIDENCE

We begin our empirical analysis with some suggestive evidence based on a simple measure of productivity growth. In a first step, we estimate a standard two-factor Cobb-Douglas production function with value added as the dependent variable, labor and capital as independent variables (i.e. we indirectly account for materials as third input factor), and we interpret the residuals from this static regression as a measure of relative firm productivity (i.e. relative to the regression mean).[5] The concept of relative productivity has a long tradition in applied productivity analysis; see Doms et al. (1995) for an application. In a second step, we calculate the first difference of the predicted residuals to obtain a measure of productivity growth.

To get a first impression of the effects of corporate governance and market discipline on productivity growth, we split the sample into two groups: firms with positive and negative productivity growth. In Table 3 , we report means of some key measures of corporate governance and market discipline for both splits. One reason for considering growth instead of levels of productivity is that some of our variables for corporate governance and market discipline should be highly endogenous to the level of productivity. Since productivity growth is less persistent than productivity levels, the endogeneity problem may be less severe if lagged values of corporate governance and market discipline are used; see also the discussion in Nickell (1996). In the econometric analysis reported below, we use productivity growth as dependent variable and address the potential endogeneity by using an instrumental variables approach. Here we simply use all variables that are supposed to explain productivity growth with a one year lag. Taking into

Table 3.   Bivariate Analysis of Corporate Governance, Market Discipline, and
Productivity Growth.

Forward-looking Horizon Performance	0 years		2 years		4 years	
	Negative	Positive	Negative	Positive	Negative	Positive
Owner concentr. (BLOCK)	73.7%**	75.4%	69.3%***	72.6%	65.4%***	71.7%
Ultimate owner (CONTROL)	88.9%	89.0%	87.6%	88.0%	84.3%*	87.5%
Owner (TYPE = private)	39.4%*	37.0%	43.2%	40.4%	43.4%	40.3%
Owner (TYPE = financial firm)	6.6%	6.6%	7.0%	5.8%	7.0%	5.5%
Owner (TYPE = non-fin. firm)	39.8%	40.9%	35.2%**	39.6%	31.6%***	39.9%
Owner (TYPE = government)	3.0%**	4.5%	2.2%	2.2%	2.3%	1.8%
Cross ownership (CROSS)	7.8%	7.1%	7.0%	7.2%	6.7%	6.7%
Pyramid (PYRAMID)	45.6%***	50.4%	40.0%	42.5%	36.0%**	40.6%
Bank debt (BANK)	28.7%	27.8%	29.8%*	31.5%	31.1%	29.5%
Debt ratio (DEBT)	40.8%*	41.8%	39.6%	40.7%	39.2%	39.4%
Ind.-adj. return on assets (ROA)	4.7%***	−0.5%	4.7%***	−0.3%	4.4%***	0.6%
Financial distress (LOSS)	1.2%	1.4%	0.4%**	1.1%	0.3%	0.9%
Small board (SMALL)	75.2%	77.1%	76.8%	75.3%	75.7%	74.8%
Industry concentration (CR6)	47.6%**	46.2%	50.1%*	48.5%	50.1%	48.5%
Industry concentration (HHI)	8.3%***	7.6%	8.9%**	8.3%	8.7%	8.3%
Rent (RENT)	32.0%***	26.2%	32.0%***	26.9%	30.4%***	27.6%
Number of obs.	1,493	1,481	1,087	905	622	504

Note: Bivariate analysis of corporate governance and market discipline and their relation to productivity
growth. Productivity growth is approximated by the first difference in the residuals from pooled
OLS estimation of a two-factor Cobb-Douglas production function including time and two-digit
industry dummies. Productivity growth is measured at three forward-looking time horizons: zero
years (residual in year t), two years (average of residuals in years t through $t + 2$), and four years
(average of residuals in years t through $t + 4$). All other variables are observed in year $t − 1$.
The test statistics are heteroskedastic t-tests of equal means.
*, **, *** indicates significance at the 0.10, 0.05, and 0.01 levels, respectively. For definitions, see
Appendix.

account that corporate governance and market discipline might affect productivity
growth in the long run rather than in the short run, we report results for three
different forward-looking time horizons: zero years, two years, and four years.
For example, for a time horizon of two years we calculate productivity growth as
the average of productivity growth in year t, year $t + 1$, and year $t + 2$.

We find strong support for hypothesis H1 that firms under concentrated
ownership show significantly higher productivity growth (Table 3). For our
measure of ownership concentration at the direct level, BLOCK, this result holds
irrespective whether we consider short- or long-run productivity growth. However,
for our measure of ownership concentration at the ultimate level, CONTROL, this
holds only for long-run productivity growth, a five-year average. Regarding the

type of ultimate owner, we find that a significantly larger fraction of firms under control of a private owner belongs to the group of firms with lower productivity growth. This suggests that productivity in privately-controlled firms tends to grow more slowly. Vice versa, productivity grows faster in firms under control of a non-financial firm; this supports hypothesis H2. In addition, productivity growth is higher in firms controlled through a pyramid. We find no indication that cross ownership has an adverse impact on productivity growth.

Regarding our measures of capital structure, there is weak evidence that firms are more productive when a large fraction of total debt is bank debt and when the total burden of debt is high. This implies that financial pressure from creditors appears to play some role in disciplining management. This notion is supported by the results on two measures of performance: firms tend to show significantly higher productivity growth when industry-adjusted return on assets is low or when operating income (EBITDA) is negative. Hence, the preliminary evidence supports hypotheses H4 and H5. Regarding board size, we do not find evidence that productivity grows faster in firms with small boards.

Moreover, Table 3 indicates that firms facing intense competition show higher productivity growth. Both of our industry-level measures of competition, the market share of the six largest suppliers (CR6) and the Herfindahl index of producer concentration (HHI), are significantly lower for firms with high productivity growth. The same holds for our measure of firm-level competition (RENT). Since all three measures are inverse measures of competition, these results strongly support hypothesis H7. Note that this result holds irrespective of whether we consider short-run or long-run productivity.[6]

In summary, the preliminary evidence suggests that in German manufacturing some elements of corporate governance, such as ownership concentration and bank debt, as well as market discipline reflected by product market competition, are positively related to productivity growth. However, this descriptive analysis is purely bivariate and ignores all potential endogeneity problems. In the remainder of this paper, we address these problems in a dynamic model of productivity growth estimated with instrumental variable techniques.

5. AN EMPIRICAL MODEL OF PRODUCTIVITY GROWTH

In this section, we derive an empirical model of productivity growth from the firm's production function, modelling explicitly the sources of total factor productivity. Specifically, we model the level of total factor productivity as a function of the firm's cumulated experience with corporate governance and market discipline.

We therefore assume that productivity is shaped by the compound effect of past conditions under which the firm operated, such as intense product market competition or tight shareholder control. For vivid evidence on the compound effect of competition on productivity differentials between industrialized nations, see Porter (1992).

The starting point of our model, which is very similar to the one used by Nickell et al. (1997), is a Cobb-Douglas production function with two factor inputs,

$$Y_{it} = L_{it}^{\beta_L} K_{it}^{\beta_L} A_{it}, \tag{3}$$

where Y_{it} is value added, L_{it} is labor, K_{it} is capital, and A_{it} is a measure of total factor productivity for firm i in year t. Since we use value added as the output measure, which is defined as total sales less materials costs, we implicitly allow for materials as a third input.

As we are interested in the determinants of total factor productivity growth, we transform the production function (3) into a regression equation in several steps. First, we take logs and include lagged output besides the inputs of capital and labor, using a weight λ. This expansion takes into account potential persistence in output. We also include a fixed firm effect, α_i, to allow for unobserved firm heterogeneity. Since output can have a stochastic component, we add an error term, ϵ_{it}, which is assumed to be serially uncorrelated over time. This yields our basic log-linear empirical production function, with small letters denoting logs:

$$y_{it} = \lambda y_{it-1} + (1 - \lambda)\beta_L l_{it} + (1 - \lambda)\beta_K k_{it} + (1 - \lambda)a_{it} + \alpha_i + \epsilon_{it}. \tag{4}$$

Second, taking first differences eliminates the fixed firm effect α_i. We obtain the differenced growth version of the Cobb-Douglas production function in Eq. (3):

$$\Delta y_{it} = \lambda \, \Delta y_{it-1} + (1 - \lambda)\beta_L \, \Delta l_{it} + (1 - \lambda)\beta_K \, \Delta k_{it} + \Delta\alpha_{it} + \Delta \epsilon_{it}. \tag{5}$$

Finally, we specify the sources of productivity growth by using the level of corporate governance and product market competition in year $t - 1$. Employing these variables in levels to explain productivity growth is appropriate here because we assume that the level of total factor productivity is influenced by the compound effect of all past states of corporate governance and competition. In particular, we specify productivity growth with our variables of interest, which follow from the hypotheses derived in Section 2. These variables include measures of ownership structure (CONTROL, CROSS, TYPE), capital structure (BANK), financial distress (LOSS), board structure (SMALL), and product market competition (RENT). Note that all of these variables enter with a one-year lag. To take into account cyclical effects on productivity growth, we add a contemporaneous industry-specific proxy variable that measures capacity utilization (CYCLE), and time effects μ to filter out productivity shocks. To control for growth effects related to firm size but unrelated to corporate governance and market discipline, we include lagged total assets (ASSET). Thus, productivity growth is modeled as

$$\Delta a_{it} = (\mu_t - \mu_{t-1}) + \gamma_1 \text{CYCLE}_{it} + \gamma_2 \text{ASSET}_{it-1} + \beta_1 \text{CONTROL}_{it-1}$$
$$+ \beta_2 \text{CROSS}_{it-1} + \beta_3 \text{TYPE}_{it-1} + \beta_4 \text{BANK}_{it-1} + \beta_5 \text{LOSS}_{it-1}$$
$$+ \beta_6 \text{SMALL}_{it-1} + \beta_7 \text{RENT}_{it-1}. \tag{6}$$

The empirical model of productivity growth is given by Eq. (5) together with Eq. (6). The structure of this model corresponds to the differenced panel model with lagged endogenous variables considered by Arellano and Bond (1991). They propose a generalized method of moments (GMM) estimator that allows to exploit lags of the lagged dependent variable as well as lags of the explanatory variables as instruments. In our application, using this approach addresses the potential endogeneity problems with respect to the corporate governance and market discipline variables that enter the right-hand side of Eq. (5).[7]

Arellano and Bond (1991) show that endogenous variables lagged two or more periods are valid instruments, provided there is no serial correlation in the time-varying component of the error terms in Eq. (4); we test this condition for all specifications. The instruments we use are y_{it-j} for $j = 2$, and second lags of CONTROL, DEBT, CR6 and ASSET.[8] We test for instrument validity using a Sargan test of over-identifying restrictions.[9] We report those tests together with the estimation results and standard errors that are robust with respect to general heteroskedasticity in the next section.

While the Arellano-Bond approach can in principle deal with potential endo-geneity problems in our application, there is a caveat. Blundell and Bond (1998) show that in autoregressive models with persistent series, the first-difference esti-mator can be subject to finite sample bias as a result of weak instruments. They argue that this bias could be greatly reduced by estimating a model with equations in both levels and first differences. We do not apply such a GMM system estimation procedure here because, as discussed above, we assume that the level of corporate governance and market discipline influences productivity growth. This suggests to use a first-difference estimator. This approach also has the advantage that we do not have to compare levels of productivity across firms and industries, but only changes in productivity. The disadvantage of potential finite sample bias remains, although our sample is much larger compared with those used for previous studies.

6. ESTIMATION RESULTS

In the following, we examine the effects of corporate governance and market discipline on productivity growth. Section 6.1 presents estimation results for our empirical model of productivity growth. All regressions are estimated using the

GMM method developed by Arellano and Bond (1991). First, we look at the impact of corporate governance (Table 4), then we investigate additional effects of market discipline and their interactions with corporate governance (Table 5). Section 6.2 examines the sensitivity of our main findings.

6.1. Effects of Corporate Governance and Market Discipline

Starting with the analysis of firms' corporate governance, we hardly find any significant effect on productivity growth. Model (1) in Table 4 shows that ownership structure, measured either by ownership concentration, type of owner, or ownership complexity, is not significantly related to productivity growth. Hence, we do not find support for Hypotheses H1, H2, nor H3.[10] Note that this result contradicts the descriptive evidence from Section 4, where firms' ownership structure appears to be related to productivity growth. Note also that we obtain this result as long as not taking into account product market competition. As shown below, interacting corporate governance and competition changes this result.

Examining capital structure in Model (2), we find that the fraction of bank debt is positively related to productivity growth. This suggests that firms in which banks are potentially more influential are subject to tighter discipline, resulting in higher productivity growth. Hence, banks as creditors appear to perform an important monitoring function; this supports Hypothesis H4.

Taking into account that banks' influence should be particularly strong when the borrower's performance is poor, Model (3) additionally includes an indicator of financial distress (LOSS) and interacts bank debt and this measure of poor performance. We find that bank debt alone does not show any significant impact on productivity growth any longer. But the interaction of poor performance and bank debt is significantly positive. This suggests that a large fraction of bank debt has a disciplinary effect, but only when performance is poor. This result supports Hypothesis H5.

Turning to the third main element of governance, the board structure, we cannot confirm that board size is significantly related to productivity growth (H6). Controlling for the fact that not all sample firms have a supervisory board (BOARD), our indicator for small board size (SMALL) is positive but insignificant. As mentioned in Section 2, this result could be expected because in Germany the size of supervisory boards is tightly regulated by law, prescribing minimum and maximum numbers of directors. Hence, firm's discretion is low regarding the size of the board. Therefore, in the subsequent analysis we do not consider board size any longer.

Table 5 additionally considers the impact of product market competition and its interaction with corporate governance. We do not include variables measuring

Table 4.   Effects of Corporate Governance on Productivity Growth.

Independent Variables	Dependent Variable: Output Growth (Δy_{it})			
	Model (1)	Model (2)	Model (3)	Model (4)
Lagged output growth (Δy_{t-1})	0.027	0.028	0.002	0.001
	(0.159)	(0.159)	(0.133)	(0.132)
Labor growth (Δl_t)	0.803***	0.806***	0.801***	0.795***
	(0.165)	(0.165)	(0.159)	(0.161)
Capital growth (Δk_t)	−0.100	−0.114	−0.156	−0.132
	(0.228)	(0.223)	(0.202)	(0.213)
Business cycle (CYCLE$_t$)	0.012	0.012	0.010	0.010
	(0.019)	(0.019)	(0.019)	(0.019)
Owner concentration (CONTROL$_{t-1}$)	−0.014	−0.002	0.014	0.017
	(0.036)	(0.035)	(0.035)	(0.036)
Owner (TYPE$_{t-1}$ = private)	0.024	0.014	0.017	0.016
	(0.042)	(0.040)	(0.039)	(0.039)
Owner (TYPE$_{t-1}$ = financial)	−0.114	−0.111	−0.113	−0.107
	(0.090)	(0.091)	(0.088)	(0.087)
Owner (TYPE$_{t-1}$ = government)	0.141	0.141	0.110	0.107
	(0.199)	(0.199)	(0.198)	(0.200)
Cross ownership (CROSS$_{t-1}$)	−0.060	−0.059	−0.052	−0.052
	(0.065)	(0.065)	(0.064)	(0.064)
Bank debt (BANK$_{t-1}$)		0.105**	0.007	−0.003
		(0.053)	(0.049)	(0.047)
Financial distress (LOSS$_{t-1}$)			−0.898	−0.877
			(0.954)	(0.959)
BANK$_{t-1}$ × LOSS$_{t-1}$			8.237**	8.199**
			(3.855)	(3.865)
Board (BOARD$_{t-1}$)				0.001
				(0.048)
Small board (SMALL$_{t-1}$)				0.026
				(0.031)
Total assets (ASSET$_{t-1}$)	0.010	0.011	0.010	0.008
	(0.013)	(0.013)	(0.011)	(0.012)
Listed (LISTED$_t$)	0.029	0.018	0.030	0.022
	(0.027)	(0.028)	(0.025)	(0.026)
Intercept	−1.315	−1.263	−1.192	−1.185
	(1.798)	(1.597)	(1.761)	(1.753)
Number of obs.	3,647	3,647	3,647	3,647
Instrument validity (Sargan test)	$p = 0.497$	$p = 0.456$	$p = 0.315$	$p = 0.286$
First-order correlation of residuals	$p = 0.027$	$p = 0.027$	$p = 0.015$	$p = 0.015$
Second-order correlation of residuals	$p = 0.418$	$p = 0.414$	$p = 0.430$	$p = 0.429$
Constant returns to scale (Wald test)	$p = 0.301$	$p = 0.279$	$p = 0.223$	$p = 0.261$

Note: GMM regression results relating measures of corporate governance to productivity growth. Estimates are obtained using the Arellano and Bond (1991) method. All regressions include time and two-digit industry dummies. Instruments are y_{it-j} for $j = 2$ and the second lags of CONTROL, DEBT, CR6, and ASSET. Asymptotic standard errors (reported in parentheses) are robust to general cross-section and time-series heteroskedasticity.

*, **, *** indicates significance at the 0.10, 0.05, and 0.01 levels, respectively. For definitions, see Appendix.

Table 5.   Effects of Corporate Governance and Market Discipline on
Productivity Growth.

Independent Variables	Dependent Variable: Output Growth (Δy_{it})					
	Model (5)		Model (6)		Model (7)	
	Interaction	RENT$_{t-1}$	Interaction	RENT$_{t-1}$	Interaction	RENT$_{t-1}$
Lagged output growth (Δy_{t-1})	−0.019		−0.025		−0.025	
	(0.133)		(0.130)		(0.122)	
Labor growth (Δl_t)	0.825***		0.833***		0.833***	
	(0.167)		(0.166)		(0.161)	
Capital growth (Δk_t)	0.438		0.467		0.446*	
	(0.329)		(0.328)		(0.248)	
Business cycle (CYCLE$_t$)	0.011		0.012		0.012	
	(0.019)		(0.019)		(0.019)	
Owner concentration (CONTROL$_{t-1}$)	0.231**	−0.684**	0.255**	−0.757**	0.367***	−1.072***
	(0.114)	(0.319)	(0.109)	(0.300)	(0.118)	(0.335)
Bank debt (BANK$_{t-1}$)	0.189***		0.484*	−1.019	0.082*	
	(0.072)		(0.277)	(0.783)	(0.047)	
Financial distress (LOSS$_{t-1}$)					−1.924	
					(1.001)	
BANK$_{t-1}$ × LOSS$_{t-1}$					8.776**	
					(3.726)	
Total assets (ASSET$_{t-1}$)	0.020		0.022		0.019*	
	(0.015)		(0.015)		(0.011)	
Listed (LISTED$_t$)	0.054**		0.060**		0.063**	
	(0.026)		(0.027)		(0.028)	
Intercept	−1.270		−1.467		−1.522	
	(1.587)		(1.579)		(1.784)	
Number of obs.	3,647		3,647		3,647	
Instrument validity (Sargan test)	$p = 0.206$		$p = 0.153$		$p = 0.377$	
First-order correlation of residuals	$p = 0.029$		$p = 0.028$		$p = 0.021$	
Second-order correlation of residuals	$p = 0.524$		$p = 0.486$		$p = 0.513$	
Constant returns to scale (Wald test)	$p = 0.464$		$p = 0.392$		$p = 0.356$	

Note: GMM regression results relating measures of corporate governance and market discipline to productivity growth. Estimates are
obtained using the Arellano and Bond (1991) method. All regressions include time and two-digit industry dummies. Instruments are
y_{t-j} for $j = 2$ and the second lags of CONTROL, DEBT, CR6, and ASSET. Asymptotic standard errors (reported in parentheses)
are robust to general cross-section and time-series heteroskedasticity.
*, **, *** indicates significance at the 0.10, 0.05, and 0.01 levels, respectively. For definitions, see Appendix.

ownership complexity and the type of the ultimate owner any longer because we could not find evidence that they affect productivity growth (Table 4).[11] Note that the magnitude of the input coefficient on labor is hardly affected, and the input coefficient on capital remains insignificant. As in Table 4, the latter result is likely due to measurement error in capital stock, a common problem in productivity analysis. Note also that the coefficient on bank debt remains significantly positive.

The main result from Table 5 is that intense product market competition has a positive impact on productivity growth, but only in the presence of a strong ultimate shareholder. Model (5) shows that firms for which rents – our inverse firm-level measure of competition – are low experience higher productivity growth; however, this direct effect of rents is insignificant. But when we interact rents with our measure of tight owner control (CONTROL), as suggested by Nickell et al. (1997), we find that the interaction term is significantly negative. At the same time, the sign of ownership concentration is significantly positive. Taken together, tight control by an ultimate owner has a positive impact on productivity growth, and that this effect is enhanced when competition on product markets is fierce. Hence, when taking into account competition we find strong support for Hypothesis H1. The evidence also supports Hypothesis H7, but only for firms under tight control.

Note that our industry-level measure of competition is not significantly associated with productivity growth. The business cycle proxy is also insignificant. These insignificant coefficients might be due to the fact that time and industry dummies absorb most of the variation in these industry-level variables. Also, we cannot assign industry-level competition variables to firms perfectly because we only have industry codes for the firms' primary products, as noted above.

In Model (6) we additionally interact rents with financial pressure (BANK), as also suggested by Nickell et al. (1997). We find that the positive impact of bank debt on productivity growth remains, but the interaction term is insignificant. This suggests that bank influence is not enhanced by fierce product market competition. Instead, in Model (7) we interact bank debt with our indicator of financial distress, as suggested by Model (3) of Table 4. As in Model (3), we find a significantly positive interaction term. This indicates that banks are in a position to influence productivity growth particularly when firm performance is poor; again this strongly supports Hypothesis H5. Note that the positive impact of shareholder control and its negative interaction with competition remains.

All versions of our GMM model are generally supported by the standard battery of specification tests. The Sargan tests do not reject the hypothesis of instrument validity. Also, the tests for second-order serial correlation of the residuals do not reject the null of zero correlation. Wald tests cannot reject the hypothesis of constant returns to scale. Finally, in all specifications we report, the slope coefficients and the sets of time and industry dummy variables are jointly significant according to our Wald tests (not reported). Finally, note that firm size, which is included in all models as a control, does not have a significant impact on productivity growth. The dummy for listed firms is significantly positive in some of the specifications.

6.2. Sensitivity of Results

To check the sensitivity of our main findings, we conduct a range of robustness tests. One concern is the selection of variables measuring corporate governance and market discipline. Table 6 examines whether two alternative measures of ownership concentration, the largest block (BLOCK) and the Herfindahl index

Table 6. Robustness Tests: Different Measures of Ownership Structure.

Independent Variables	Dependent Variable: Output Growth (Δy_{it})					
	Model (5)		Model (5a)		Model (5b)	
	Interaction	RENT$_{t-1}$	Interaction	RENT$_{t-1}$	Interaction	RENT$_{t-1}$
Lagged output growth (Δy_{t-1})	−0.019		−0.023		−0.021	
	(0.133)		(0.129)		(0.131)	
Labor growth (Δl_t)	0.825***		0.833***		0.835***	
	(0.167)		(0.166)		(0.166)	
Capital growth (Δk_t)	0.438		0.506		0.518*	
	(0.329)		(0.344)		(0.346)	
Business cycle (CYCLE$_t$)	0.011		0.012		0.012	
	(0.019)		(0.019)		(0.019)	
Industrial concentration (CR6$_{t-1}$)	0.083		0.087		0.090	
	(0.093)		(0.095)		(0.096)	
Rent (RENT$_{t-1}$)	−0.127		−0.664		−0.479	
	(0.258)		(0.597)		(0.445)	
Owner concentration (CONTROL$_{t-1}$)	0.231**	−0.684**	0.505**	−1.518**	0.419**	−1.258**
	(0.114)	(0.319)	(0.250)	(0.719)	(0.178)	(0.507)
Largest block (BLOCK$_{t-1}$)			−0.520	1.576		
			(0.456)	(1.332)		
Herfindahl index (HERF$_{t-1}$)					−0.382	1.142
					(0.330)	(0.943)
Bank debt (BANK$_{t-1}$)	0.189***		0.154***		0.149**	
	(0.072)		(0.058)		(0.059)	
Total assets (ASSET$_{t-1}$)	0.020		0.019		0.020	
	(0.015)		(0.014)		(0.014)	
Listed (LISTED$_t$)	0.054**		0.063**		0.063**	
	(0.026)		(0.030)		(0.031)	
Intercept	−1.270		−1.089		−1.198	
	(1.587)		(1.600)		(1.620)	
Number of obs.	3,647		3,647		3,647	
Instrument validity (Sargan test)	$p = 0.206$		$p = 0.273$		$p = 0.262$	
First-order correlation of residuals	$p = 0.029$		$p = 0.030$		$p = 0.030$	
Second-order correlation of residuals	$p = 0.524$		$p = 0.493$		$p = 0.485$	
Constant returns to scale (Wald test)	$p = 0.464$		$p = 0.352$		$p = 0.335$	

Note: GMM regression results relating measures of corporate governance and market discipline to productivity growth. Estimates are obtained using the Arellano and Bond (1991) method. All regressions include time and two-digit industry dummies. Instruments are y_{it-j} for $j = 2$ and the second lags of CONTROL, DEBT, CR6, and ASSET. Asymptotic standard errors (reported in parentheses) are robust to general cross-section and time-series heteroskedasticity.
*, **, *** indicates significance at the 0.10, 0.05, and 0.01 levels, respectively. For definitions, see Appendix.

(HERF), have an additional impact on productivity growth besides our preferred measure (CONTROL). In contrast to CONTROL, which measures concentration at the ultimate level of ownership, these alternative measures refer to the direct level of ownership. Taking Model (5) from Table 5 as the reference, we cannot find evidence that BLOCK or HERF have any additional impact on productivity growth. The other coefficients do not change qualitatively.

Next, we test the sensitivity of our finding that in Germany the impact of financial pressure is not enhanced or reduced when competition is intense, in particular because Nickell et al. (1997) find that they are substitutes. Table 7 examines whether two alternative measures of financial pressure, the debt ratio (DEBT)

Table 7. Robustness Tests: Different Measures of Capital Structure Interacted with Competition.

Independent Variables	Dependent Variable: Output Growth (Δy_{it})					
	Model (6)		Model (6a)		Model (6b)	
	Interaction	RENT$_{t-1}$	Interaction	RENT$_{t-1}$	Interaction	RENT$_{t-1}$
Lagged output growth (Δy_{t-1})	−0.025		−0.029		0.009	
	(0.130)		(0.126)		(0.150)	
Labor growth (Δl_t)	0.833***		0.793***		0.838***	
	(0.166)		(0.153)		(0.168)	
Capital growth (Δk_t)	0.467		0.541*		0.543	
	(0.328)		(0.307)		(0.336)	
Business cycle (CYCLE$_t$)	0.012		0.014		0.012	
	(0.019)		(0.019)		(0.019)	
Industrial concentration (CR6$_{t-1}$)	0.104		0.135		0.111	
	(0.097)		(0.104)		(0.100)	
Rent (RENT$_{t-1}$)	0.168		0.731		−0.006	
	(0.246)		(0.540)		(0.352)	
Owner concentration (CONTROL$_{t-1}$)	0.255**	−0.757**	0.233**	−0.636**	0.290**	−0.837**
	(0.109)	(0.300)	(0.102)	(0.284)	(0.121)	(0.331)
Bank debt (BANK$_{t-1}$)	0.484*	−1.019	0.486*	−0.682	0.464*	−0.773
	(0.072)	(0.783)	(0.289)	(0.798)	(0.279)	(0.803)
Debt ratio (DEBT$_{t-1}$)			0.177	−1.605		
			(0.486)	(1.415)		
Interest coverage (COVERAGE$_{t-1}$)					0.000	0.000
					(0.001)	(0.002)
Total assets (ASSET$_{t-1}$)	0.022		0.016		0.022	
	(0.015)		(0.013)		(0.016)	
Listed (LISTED$_t$)	0.060**		0.053**		0.076**	
	(0.027)		(0.028)		(0.034)	
Intercept	−1.467		−1.601		−1.623	
	(1.579)		(1.623)		(1.762)	
Number of obs.	3,647		3,647		3,647	
Instrument validity (Sargan test)	$p = 0.153$		$p = 0.161$		$p = 0.285$	
First-order correlation of residuals	$p = 0.028$		$p = 0.030$		$p = 0.032$	
Second-order correlation of residuals	$p = 0.486$		$p = 0.512$		$p = 0.193$	
Constant returns to scale (Wald test)	$p = 0.392$		$p = 0.284$		$p = 0.324$	

Note: GMM regression results relating measures of corporate governance and market discipline to productivity growth. Estimates are obtained using the Arellano and Bond (1991) method. All regressions include time and two-digit industry dummies. Instruments are y_{t-j} for $j = 2$ and the second lags of CONTROL, DEBT, CR6, and ASSET. Asymptotic standard errors (reported in parentheses) are robust to general cross-section and time-series heteroskedasticity.

*, **, *** indicates significance at the 0.10, 0.05, and 0.01 levels, respectively. For definitions, see Appendix.

and interest coverage (COVERAGE), have an additional impact on productivity growth besides our preferred measure (BANK). Taking Model (6) from Table 5 as the reference, we find that both alternative measures are not significantly related to productivity growth, and all other results remain qualitatively unaffected.

In Table 8, we use two alternative measures of firm-level competition to address potential endogeneity issues. RENTA is the average of the firm's rents over the past two years. This time aggregation should smooth short-run firm-specific shocks that affect output directly and hence affect rents. RENTI is the year-specific average of our firm-specific rents measure across the respective three-digit industry. This

Table 8.   Robustness Tests: Different Measures of Firm-Level Competition.

Independent Variables	Dependent Variable: Output Growth (Δy_{it})					
	Model (7)		Model (7a)		Model (7b)	
	Interaction	CONTROL$_{t-1}$	Interaction	CONTROL$_{t-1}$	Interaction	CONTROL$_{t-1}$
Lagged output growth (Δy_{t-1})	−0.025		−0.048		−0.004	
	(0.122)		(0.124)		(0.131)	
Labor growth (Δl_t)	0.833***		0.828***		0.816***	
	(0.161)		(0.159)		(0.160)	
Capital growth (Δk_t)	0.446*		0.296		−0.009	
	(0.248)		(0.216)		(0.195)	
Business cycle (CYCLE$_t$)	0.012		0.011		0.009	
	(0.019)		(0.091)		(0.019)	
Industry concentration (CR6$_{t-1}$)	0.125		0.110		0.096	
	(0.094)		(0.091)		(0.088)	
Rent (RENT$_{t-1}$)	0.130	−1.072***				
	(0.223)	(0.335)				
Rent, time average (RENTA$_{t-1}$)			0.289	−1.011***		
			(0.255)	(0.337)		
Rent, ind. average (RENTI$_{t-1}$)					−0.184	−0.608**
					(0.297)	(0.295)
Owner concentration (CONTROL$_{t-1}$)	0.367***		0.341***		0.203*	
	(0.118)		(0.116)		(0.105)	
Bank debt (BANK$_{t-1}$)	0.082*		0.070		0.053	
	(0.047)		(0.048)		(0.048)	
Financial distress (LOSS$_{t-1}$)	−1.924*		−1.760*		−1.041	
	(1.001)		(0.958)		(0.963)	
BANK$_{t-1}$ × LOSS$_{t-1}$	8.776**		8.831**		8.373**	
	(3.726)		(3.751)		(3.844)	
Total assets (ASSET$_{t-1}$)	0.019*		0.017		0.010	
	(0.011)		(0.011)		(0.010)	
Listed (LISTED$_t$)	0.063**		0.054**		0.043	
	(0.028)		(0.026)		(0.027)	
Intercept	−1.522		−1.442		−1.033	
	(1.784)		(1.750)		(1.696)	
Number of obs.	3,647		3,647		3,647	
Instrument validity (Sargan test)	$p = 0.377$		$p = 0.265$		$p = 0.576$	
First-order correlation of residuals	$p = 0.021$		$p = 0.018$		$p = 0.015$	
Second-order correlation of residuals	$p = 0.513$		$p = 0.432$		$p = 0.435$	
Constant returns to scale (Wald test)	$p = 0.356$		$p = 0.579$		$p = 0.312$	

Note: GMM regression results relating measures of corporate governance and market discipline to productivity growth. Estimates are obtained using the Arellano and Bond (1991) method. All regressions include time and two-digit industry dummies. Instruments are y_{it-j} for $j = 2$ and the second lags of CONTROL, DEBT, CR6, and ASSET. Asymptotic standard errors (reported in parentheses) are robust to general cross-section and time-series heteroskedasticity.
*, **, *** indicates significance at the 0.10, 0.05, and 0.01 levels, respectively. For definitions, see Appendix.

cross-sectional aggregation also wipes out firm-specific shocks, and therefore avoids potential endogeneity problems associated with the rents variable. Taking Model (7) from Table 5 as the reference, we find that the interaction of rents and ownership concentration remains significantly negative. In addition, the positive impact of shareholder control as well as the positive interaction of bank debt and financial distress remain. However, using the industry-adjusted measure of rents in Model (7b), the direct impact of bank debt turns insignificant. Overall, this robustness check gives us some confidence that our general approach – controlling for endogeneity problems using an instrumental variables GMM method – is appropriate.

To check whether our finding regarding financial pressure is robust against the definition of creditor influence, we examine two alternative measures, the debt

Table 9. Robustness Tests: Different Measures of Capital Structure Interacted with Financial Distress.

Independent Variables	Dependent Variable: Output Growth (Δy_{it})					
	Model (7)		Model (7a)		Model (7b)	
	Interaction	CONTROL$_{t-1}$	Interaction	CONTROL$_{t-1}$	Interaction	CONTROL$_{t-1}$
Lagged output growth (Δy_{t-1})	−0.025		−0.017		−0.016	
	(0.122)		(0.123)		(0.118)	
Labor growth (Δl_t)	0.833***		0.852***		0.845***	
	(0.161)		(0.149)		(0.147)	
Capital growth (Δk_t)	0.446*		0.512		0.502**	
	(0.248)		(0.244)		(0.234)	
Business cycle (CYCLE$_t$)	0.012		0.012		0.012	
	(0.019)		(0.019)		(0.018)	
Industry concentration (CR6$_{t-1}$)	0.125		0.130		0.138	
	(0.094)		(0.095)		(0.092)	
Rent (RENT$_{t-1}$)	0.130		0.068		0.097	
	(0.223)		(0.231)		(0.237)	
Owner concentration (CONTROL$_{t-1}$)	0.367***		0.370***		0.372***	
	(0.118)		(0.122)		(0.122)	
RENT$_{t-1}$ × CONTROL$_{t-1}$	−1.072***		−1.049***		−1.074***	
	(0.335)		(0.346)		(0.350)	
Financial distress (LOSS$_{t-1}$)	−1.924*		−1.119		−1.732	
	(1.001)		(1.969)		(0.117)	
Bank debt (BANK$_{t-1}$)	0.082*	8.776**	0.161**	9.488**	0.117	9.365**
	(0.047)	(3.726)	(0.081)	(4.172)	(0.084)	(3.929)
Debt ratio (DEBT$_{t-1}$)			−0.215	−1.780		
			(0.144)	(4.283)		
Leverage (LEVERAGE$_{t-1}$)					−0.021	−0.108
					(0.041)	(0.447)
Total assets (ASSET$_{t-1}$)	0.019*		0.020*		0.020*	
	(0.011)		(0.010)		(0.011)	
Listed (LISTED$_t$)	0.063**		0.062**		0.061**	
	(0.028)		(0.028)		(0.027)	
Intercept	−1.522		−1.479		−1.489	
	(1.784)		(1.772)		(1.794)	
Number of obs.	3,647		3,647		3,647	
Instrument validity (Sargan test)	$p = 0.377$		$p = 0.254$		$p = 0.269$	
First-order correlation of residuals	$p = 0.021$		$p = 0.024$		$p = 0.022$	
Second-order correlation of residuals	$p = 0.513$		$p = 0.497$		$p = 0.500$	
Constant returns to scale (Wald test)	$p = 0.356$		$p = 0.216$		$p = 0.230$	

Note: GMM regression results relating measures of corporate governance and market discipline to productivity growth. Estimates are obtained using the Arellano and Bond (1991) method. All regressions include time and two-digit industry dummies. Instruments are y_{it-j} for $j = 2$ and the second lags of CONTROL, DEBT, CR6, and ASSET. Asymptotic standard errors (reported in parentheses) are robust to general cross-section and time-series heteroskedasticity.
*, **, *** indicates significance at the 0.10, 0.05, and 0.01 levels, respectively. For definitions, see Appendix.

ratio (DEBT) and leverage (LEVERAGE). Table 9 shows the results. Again using Model (7) from Table 5 as the reference, we find that these alternative measures do not have any additional explanatory power for productivity growth, and our main findings are unchanged. Only when using leverage as alternative measure, the direct impact of bank debt becomes insignificant.

Since the measure of industry-level competition (CR6) is insignificant across all specifications, we consider two alternative measures described in Section 3.2.

Using the Herfindahl index of producer concentration (HHI) instead, its coefficient is also insignificant and the other coefficients remain similar. Using the import ratio as a measure of foreign competition in addition to CR6 or HHI, its coefficient remains insignificant as well, and the other coefficients hardly change. This lack of explanatory power in industry-level measures of competition is likely due to measurement problems, which are hard to overcome with currently available data, as mentioned above.

All of our results are robust against alternative definitions of the capital stock. We experimented with capital stock measures constructed using the method applied by Nickell (1996) and Nickell et al. (1997). They also apply a perpetual inventory method, but they do not assume a constant rate of depreciation. We experimented with annual depreciation rates of 4 and 12%, but our estimation results turned out to be robust.

Finally, we experimented with alternative sets of instrumental variables. Our main results regarding the impact of corporate governance and market discipline are robust against variations of the lag length chosen for the instruments. They are also robust against using additional instruments, particularly the second lags of all time-varying measures of ownership structure and competition. In summary, we are confident that our main findings as presented in Section 6.1 are generally not sensitive against alternative specifications of explanatory variables or alternative sets of instruments.

7. CONCLUSIONS

This study analyzes the impact of five corporate governance mechanisms (owner concentration, owner type, owner complexity, financial pressure, and board size) and market discipline (product market competition) on productivity growth. We use a panel of 841 German manufacturing firms over the years 1986–1996.

We find that firms under concentrated ownership tend to show higher productivity growth, and this effect is larger for firms earning lower rents. Since we use rent as an inverse measure of the intensity of product market competition, this means that firms in more competitive markets show higher productivity growth, but only when owner control is tight. Our finding regarding the beneficial effect of competition is in line with evidence from the U.K. (Nickell et al., 1997), Italy (Bottasso & Sembenelli, 2001), Germany (Gross-Schuler & Weigand, 2001; Januszewski et al., 2002), and other major Western economies (Caves, 1992; Porter, 1992). Our finding that tight owner control has a disciplinary effect is consistent with evidence from Japan (Kaplan & Minton, 1994), the U.K. (Nickell et al., 1997), and Germany (Januszewski et al., 2002). However, we find that owner control and intense product market competition are complements; this stands in sharp contrast to Nickell et al. who find that they are substitutes.

Furthermore, also financial pressure from creditors has a positive impact on productivity growth. We find weak evidence that productivity grows faster for firms showing a large fraction of bank debt, and strong evidence that productivity grows faster when bank debt is high and at the same time firm performance is poor. Hence, creditors seem to be in a position to influence management decisions, which in turn affect productivity growth. And the creditors' position appears to be particularly strong for firms in financial distress. This disciplinary effect of financial pressure is consistent with evidence from Germany on the early 1970s (Cable, 1985), and with recent evidence from the U.S. (Zingales, 1998), the U.K. (Nickell & Nicolitsas, 1999), and Belgium (Renneboog, 2000).

We cannot confirm that the type of the ultimate owner has a particular impact on productivity growth. Likewise, we do not find evidence that complex ownership structures (e.g. cross ownership or pyramid structures) or large board size have an adverse impact on performance. One reason for the insignificant relation of board size and performance could be that the size of German supervisory boards is tightly regulated by law. Hence, board size is likely to be determined by other factors such as firm size and industry, not necessarily by considerations regarding optimal governance structure. We also cannot find evidence that financial pressure from creditors acts as a substitute for competition. This finding contrasts with Nickell et al. (1997) who document a substitutive relationship. In summary, our results suggest that corporate governance (ownership and capital structure of a firm) as well as market discipline (product market competition) are important governance devices. The combination of these mechanisms forms the basis for higher productivity growth.

Our findings have two policy implications. First, the beneficial impact of increased product market competition on productivity growth implies that competition policy should aim at fostering competition. In the European context this means that remaining obstacles to an integrated Internal Market should be removed. This is even more relevant as intense competition appears to reinforce the beneficial impact of tight owner control, which is prevalent in continental Europe (La Porta et al., 1999). Second, we find a beneficial impact of creditors on productivity growth. While we do not explicitly test for the impact of "housebank" relations, our results suggest that lending relationships in Germany cannot simply be dismissed as too inflexible and outdated, as often argued. However, we also find that creditors' influence depends on a strong creditor position, measured as a large fraction of bank debt. This implies that reduced bank lending, for example as a consequence from increased securitization of loans, could negatively affect the banks' incentives or ability to monitor. One way to address a potential decline in monitoring by creditors could be to strengthen other parties involved in corporate governance. In the U.S. and the U.K. we observe an increasingly active participation of small shareholders such as pension funds, which appear to be able to influence particular corporate decisions (Carleton et al., 1998; Smith, 1996). For Germany, institutional investment continues to rise as well, not at least due the current transition in the pension system. The bottom line for public policy is to ensure a fair treatment of minority shareholders.

Finally, our findings have implications for future empirical research. First, we find a positive impact of ownership concentration on productivity growth, but only when we consider ownership at the ultimate level, not at the direct level. This suggests that ultimate ownership matters, not direct ownership. Hence, studies relying on measures of direct ownership, which are typically more easily to obtain, might come to misleading results. Second, we find that ownership concentration does not affect productivity growth when not taking into account product market competition. Only when using competition measures as well, we find a significant impact. This is a good example of a missing variables problem (Börsch-Supan & Köke, 2002). Hence, studies investigating only one or a few of all mechanisms that potentially affect productivity growth might come to misleading results as well. Third, this study does not investigate whether the threat of a takeover has a disciplinary effect on managerial behavior. This is an important question because takeovers can be disciplinary (Jensen, 1988), and due to the repeal of the corporate capital gains tax the number of acquisitions and divestitures in Germany is expected to increase considerably.

NOTES

1. For theoretical analyses on the role of ownership structure, see Shleifer and Vishny (1986), on the role of capital structure, see Jensen (1986), and on the role of competition, see Hart (1983). We discuss these theoretical arguments in Section 2.

2. Gross-Schuler and Weigand (2001) examine the impact of financial pressure on the level of productivity for German corporations. However, they neglect the role of the board and they do not consider interactions between different governance mechanisms.

3. In the literature, particularly in studies on financial economics, the goal is typically not to explain productivity but some other measure of firm performance. But since high productivity can help lower the costs of a firm, high productivity should also be in the shareholders' interest. However, due to varying performance measures used in the empirical studies discussed below, the results of these studies are sometimes not directly comparable.

4. We have also used real sales, $p_t^Y Y_t$, in the denominator to check for robustness. All results reported below remain qualitatively unchanged.

5. To estimate this production function using OLS, we also include time and two-digit industry dummies; see Table 3.

6. This result also holds when RENT is measured relative to total sales instead of value added, when RENT is measured as the average over two consecutive years, or when RENT is measured as average rent within each three-digit industry.

7. An alternative estimation approach for dynamic panel data models is the standard instrumental variables (IV) estimator proposed by Anderson and Hsiao (1981). However, since we have modeled the influence of corporate governance and market discipline on productivity growth using the parameterization in Eq. (6), the Anderson-Hsiao IV estimator is not readily applicable in our setting.

8. We also experimented with additional instruments, using all time-varying measures of ownership structure or competition. However, our main results did not change qualitatively; see Section 6.2.

9. Following Arellano and Bond (1991), we use the two-step version of the GMM estimator for obtaining the Sargan test statistic, while coefficient estimates are based on the one-step version. Arellano and Bond report that the one-step Sargan test is sensitive to heteroskedasticity, tending to over-reject the null.

10. When we use PYRAMID instead as a measure of ownership complexity, we still do not find a significant relation.

11. To check for robustness, we re-estimated all regressions in Table 5, including these additional ownership characteristics. We still could not find any consistent relation between these measures and productivity growth. At the same time, none of our main findings in Table 5 is qualitatively altered.

12. In 1985 several changes were introduced in German corporate law (§289 HGB), most of them triggered by the European Community's Fourth Company Law Directive on the harmonization of national requirements pertaining to financial statements.

13. See Köke (2000) for a more detailed analysis of selection, entry, and attrition biases in a panel of firms that is very similar to the one used here.

14. A 50% majority is sufficient to dismiss management after their regular period of office. But a majority of 75% is required to dismiss management during its period of office (§103 (1) AktG).

ACKNOWLEDGMENTS

Financial support from the German Science Foundation (DFG) is gratefully acknowledged (grant no. BO 934, 7-2). Matthias Braun and Gregor Führich provided excellent research assistance. Helpful comments from Axel Börsch-Supan, Friedrich Heinemann, Tereza Tykvová, and Joachim Winter are appreciated.

REFERENCES

Allen, F., & Gale, D. (2000). Corporate governance and competition. In: X. Vives (Ed.), *Corporate Governance: Theoretical and Empirical Perspectives*. Cambridge: MIT Press.
Anderson, T. W., & Hsiao, C. (1981). Estimation of dynamic models with error components. *Journal of the American Statistical Association, 76*(375), 598–606.

Arellano, M., & Bond, S. (1991). Some tests of specification for panel data: Monte Carlo evidence and an application to employment equations. *Review of Economic Studies, 58*, 277–297.

Bartelsman, E. J., & Doms, M. (2000). Understanding productivity: Lessons from longitudinal micro data. *Journal of Economic Literature, 38*, 569–594.

Bebchuk, L. A., Kraakman, R., & Triantis, G. (2000). Stock pyramids, cross ownership, and dual class equity. In: R. K. Morck (Ed.), *Concentrated Corporate Ownership* (pp. 295–315). Chicago.

Becht, M., & Böhmer, E. (2000). Voting control in German corporations. Universite Libre de Bruxelles, Working Paper.

Black, B. S. (1998). Shareholder activism and corporate governance in the United States. In: P. Newman (Ed.), *The New Palgrave Dictionary of Economics and Law*. London: Macmillan Reference.

Blundell, R., & Bond, S. (1998). Initial conditions and moment restrictions in dynamic panel data models. *Journal of Econometrics, 87*, 115–143.

Bond, S., Harhoff, D., & van Reenen, J. (1999). Investment, R&D, and financial constraints in Britain and Germany. Institute for Fiscal Studies, London, Working Paper.

Börsch-Supan, A. (1999). *Capital productivity and the nature of competition*. Brookings Papers on Economic Activity (Microeconomics), 205–244.

Börsch-Supan, A., & Köke, J. (2002). An applied econometricians' view of empirical corporate governance studies. *German Economic Review, 3*(3), 295–326.

Bottasso, A., & Sembenelli, A. (2001). Market power, productivity and the EU single market program: Evidence from a panel of Italian firms. *European Economic Review, 45*, 167–186.

Cable, J. (1985). Capital market and industrial performance: The role of West German banks. *Economic Journal, 95*, 118–132.

Carleton, W. T., Nelson, J. M., & Weisbach, M. S. (1998). The influence of institutions on corporate governance through private negotiations: Evidence from TIAA-CREF. *Journal of Finance, 53*(4), 1335–1362.

Caves, R. E. (1992). *Industrial efficiency in six nations*. Cambridge: MIT Press.

Doms, M., Dunne, T., & Roberts, M. J. (1995). The role of technology use in the survival and growth of manufacturing plants. *International Journal of Industrial Organization, 13*(4), 523–542.

Edwards, J., & Fischer, K. (1994). *Banks, finance, and investment in Germany*. Cambridge: Cambridge University Press.

Edwards, J., & Nibler, M. (2000). Corporate governance: Banks versus ownership concentration in Germany. *Economic Policy, 15*(2), 237–267.

Franks, J., & Mayer, C. (1995). Ownership and control. In: H. Siebert (Ed.), *Trends in Business Organization* (pp. 171–200). Tübingen: Mohr.

Franks, J., & Mayer, C. (2000). Ownership and control of German corporations. London Business School and University of Oxford, Working Paper.

Gorton, G., & Schmid, F. A. (2000). Universal banking and the performance of German firms. *Journal of Financial Economics, 58*, 29–80.

Green, A., & Mayes, D. (1991). Technical inefficiency in manufacturing industries. *Economic Journal, 101*, 523–538.

Grossman, S. J., & Hart, O. D. (1980). Takeover bids, the free-rider problem, and the theory of the corporation. *Bell Journal of Economics, 11*, 42–64.

Gross-Schuler, A., & Weigand, J. (2001). Sunk costs, managerial incentives, and firm performance. *DIW Vierteljahresheft, 2*, 275–287.

Hart, O. D. (1983). The market mechanism as an incentive scheme. *Bell Journal of Economics, 14*(3), 366–382.

Hopt, K. J. (1997). The German two-tier board (Aufsichtsrat): A German view on corporate governance. In: K. J. Hopt & E. Wymeersch (Eds), *Comparative Corporate Governance: Essays and Materials* (pp. 3–20). Berlin: Walter de Gruyter.

Januszewski, S. I., Köke, J., & Winter, J. K. (2002). Product market competition, corporate governance, and firm performance: An empirical analysis for Germany. *Research in Economics* (forthcoming).

Jensen, M. C. (1986). Agency costs of free cash flow, corporate finance and takeovers. *American Economic Review, 76*, 323–329.

Jensen, M. C. (1988). Takeovers: Their causes and consequences. *Journal of Economic Perspectives, 2*, 21–48.

Jensen, M. C. (1993). The modern industrial revolution, exit, and the failure of internal control systems. *Journal of Finance, 48*(3), 831–880.

Kaplan, S. N., & Minton, B. (1994). Appointments of outsiders to Japanese boards: Determinants and implications for managers. *Journal of Financial Economics, 36*(2), 225–258.

Klette, T. J. (1999). Market power, scale economies and productivity: Estimates from a panel of establishment data. *Journal of Industrial Economics, 47*(4), 451–476.

Köke, J. (2000). *Control transfers in corporate Germany: Their frequency, causes, and consequences.* Centre for European Economic Research, Mannheim, ZEW Discussion Paper, No. 2000–67.

Köke, J. (2001). New evidence on ownership structures in Germany. *Kredit und Kapital, 34*(2), 257–292.

La Porta, R., Lopez-de-Silanes, F., & Shleifer, A. (1999). Corporate ownership around the world. *Journal of Finance, 54*(2), 471–517.

Lehmann, E., & Weigand, J. (2000). Does the governed corporation perform better? Governance structures and corporate performance in Germany. *European Finance Review, 4*(2), 157–195.

Mayer, C. (1988). New issues in corporate finance. *European Economic Review, 32*, 1167–1189.

Monopolkommission (1996). *Wettbewerbspolitik in Zeiten des Umbruchs: Hauptgut-achten 1994/1995.* Baden-Baden, Nomos.

Nickell, S. (1996). Competition and corporate performance. *Journal of Political Economy, 104*(4), 724–746.

Nickell, S., & Nicolitsas, D. (1999). How does financial pressure affect firms? *European Economic Review, 43*, 1435–1456.

Nickell, S., Nicolitsas, D., & Dryden, N. (1997). What makes firms perform well? *European Economic Review, 41*, 783–796.

Porter, M. E. (1992). *The competitive advantage of nations.* London: MacMillan.

Pound, J. (1988). Proxy contests and the efficiency of shareholder oversight. *Journal of Financial Economics, 20*, 237–265.

Renneboog, L. (2000). Ownership, managerial control, and the governance of companies listed on the Brussels stock exchange. *Journal of Banking and Finance, 24*(12), 1959–1995.

Shleifer, A., & Vishny, R. W. (1986). Large shareholders and corporate control. *Journal of Political Economy, 94*(3), 461–488.

Shleifer, A., & Vishny, R. W. (1997). A survey of corporate governance. *Journal of Finance, 52*(2), 737–783.

Smith, M. P. (1996). Shareholder activism by institutional investors: Evidence from CalPERS. *Journal of Finance, 51*(1), 227–252.

Stiglitz, J. (1985). Credit markets and the control of capital. *Journal of Money, Credit, and Banking, 17*(2), 133–152.

Wenger, E., & Kaserer, C. (1998). The German system of corporate governance: A model which
    should not be imitated. In: S. W. Black & M. Moersch (Eds), *Competition and Convergence in
    Financial Markets* (pp. 41–78). Amsterdam: Elsevier.
Yermack, D. (1996). Higher market valuation of a company with a small board of directors. *Journal
    of Financial Economics, 40,* 185–211.
Zingales, L. (1998). Survival of the fittest or the fattest? Exit and financing in the Trucking industry.
    Journal of Finance, 53(3), 905–938.

APPENDIX

Sample Selection

The data set used in this analysis rests on three pillars. The first main pillar –
balance sheet data used to estimate productivity growth – comes from Hoppenstedt's Balance Sheet Database (henceforth, BSD). An important feature of this
data source is that it contains information on listed and non-listed corporations,
both public (Aktiengesellschaft, AG) and private (Gesellschaft mit beschränkter
Haftung, GmbH). We take 1986 as the starting year because a change in
disclosure rules makes data from annual reports before and after the year 1986
incompatible.[12] The last year of the sample is 1996. For the period 1986–1996,
BSD contains 5,604 firms (31,294 firm years) for which consolidated balance
sheet data are available. We eliminate all firms that do not operate primarily
in the manufacturing sector because productivity in industries such as financial
(bank or insurance) or non-financial services (wholesale or retail trade) is hard to
compare with productivity in manufacturing. We also eliminate firms operating in
the utility, traffic, and telecommunications industries, which were predominantly
government-owned during the period of observation. Selection by industry leaves
us with data on 1,835 firms.

The second main pillar – data on ownership structure and board size – is
constructed from annual reports published by former Bayerische Hypotheken-
und Wechsel-Bank (in short, Hypobank). These reports contain information on
direct ownership of common stock for all listed and large non-listed German
corporations. Hypobank reports the size and the name of a direct owner when
the size of the ownership block exceeds 5%. However, the Hypobank data on
direct ownership rights cannot readily be used because ownership complexity
of German firms requires to examine ultimate firm ownership, as pointed out
by Böhmer (2000), Köke (2000), and Lehmann and Weigand (2000). Therefore,
this study reconstructs voting rights information in a bottom-up approach from
information on direct ownership rights (see Section 3.1).

After matching ownership data, we are left with a sample of 1,090 firms. Because of missing values for important balance sheet items, another 122 firms must be eliminated. This selection procedure generates a sample of 968 firms (5,563 firm years) with at least one year of balance sheet and ownership data during the years 1986–1996. Since the dynamic panel estimator, which we apply in the empirical analysis, requires at least three consecutive years of data, we further eliminate 127 firms for which we have less than three years of consecutive data. The final sample contains 841 firms (5,329 firm years).

The third main pillar – measures of product market competition – rests on several sources of data. Information on supplier concentration at the four-digit industry level is obtained from biennial reports of the Federal Anti-Trust Commission (Monopolkommission, 1996). Information on the value of imports and domestic production at the two-digit industry level is obtained from the Federal Statistical Office (Statistisches Bundesamt, Außenhandelsstatistik and Produktionsstatistik, Fachserie 4, Reihe 3.1). Based on these industry-level data we construct measures of competition, domestic and from abroad. In addition, we construct a firm-specific measure of competition based on balance sheet data (see Section 3.2).

Sample attrition is a concern since it might result in selection biases. To test for a potential selection bias, we analyze information on firms' survival status. For firms leaving the sample before 1996, information is obtained from BSD and telephone interviews. We find that 91 out of 146 firms that exit the sample before 1996 still existed in 1996 without a change in ultimate ownership – they simply changed their name or stopped reporting due to reasons determined within the firm. In 29 cases, operation was shut down due to liquidation or bankruptcy. In 24 cases, a firm had been taken over by another entity. And in two cases operation was shut down voluntarily. Hence, the majority of firm exits from the sample is not related to firm failure or acquisition.[13]

Concept of Control

The identification of the ultimate owner for each firm is based upon German corporate law and involves two steps. First, we identify the ultimate owner for each direct shareholder using the following three rules. Rule 1 (strong ownership rule): A chain of control is pursued to the next level if the shareholder being analyzed is owned to 50% or more by a shareholder on the next level, while all other shareholders on the next level own less than 50%. Rule 2 (weak ownership rule): If rule 1 does not apply, a chain of control is pursued to the next level if the shareholder being analyzed is owned to 25% or more by a shareholder on the next level, while all other shareholders on the next level own less than 25%. Rule 3 (stop rule): If neither rule 1 nor rule 2 applies, a chain of control is not pursued further. These rules guarantee that no more than one ultimate owner is identified for each direct shareholder. Note that if a shareholder has split his ownership stake in a particular company into several smaller stakes, for example into two blocks of 50% held by two subsidiary firms, we combine these smaller stakes into one single block. We set the first cutoff point at 50% because German law allows an investor owning 50% of all shares to appoint management.[14] The second cutoff point is set at 25% because an investor owning 25% of the shares has the right to veto decisions. In a second step in determining the ultimate owner for each sample firm, we apply the three rules to all direct share-holders. This allows us to identify one single shareholder that is in ultimate control. When no single shareholder fulfills the criteria, this firm is seen to have no ultimate owner.

Definition of Variables

In the following, we describe how the variables used in the empirical analysis are constructed. All variables used in this study are appropriately de ated and measured in prices of 1991. Sources of price and cost indexes and other aggregate variables are given below, together with details on how we constructed each variable used in the empirical analysis.

Value Added
The firm's value added, Y_t, is defined as output (total sales) less total materials costs. Real values are obtained using a two-digit industry-specific producer price index published by the Federal Statistical Office (Statistisches Bundesamt, Fachserie 17, Reihe 2, 1998) for output, and a combined input price index for materials. The latter does not vary by industry.

Capital Stock
The firm's capital stock, K_t, is defined as replacement costs of tangible assets including machines, buildings, and land, deflated using a combined input price index for capital goods and land, weighted by their empirical distribution (Statistisches Bundesamt, Fachserie 17, Reihe 2, and Fachserie 17, Reihe 4, 1998). Replacement costs of capital are calculated using the method of Bond et al. (1999). They adjust the historical cost values for in ation and then apply a perpetual inventory method with a constant annual depreciation rate of $\delta = 0.08$. Specifically,

$$p_t^K K_t = (1 - \delta) p_{t-1}^K K_{t-1} \frac{p_t^K}{p_{t-1}^K} + p_t^K I_t, \qquad (A.1)$$

where K_t is the capital stock, p_t^K is the price index for capital goods, It is real investment and d the depreciation rate. The starting value is the net book value of tangible assets, adjusted for inflation in previous years.

Labor
The firm's labor input, L_t, is defined as the total number of employees.

Business Cycle Proxy
To control for business cycle effects, we use a survey-based index of capacity utilization at the two-digit industry level as a proxy variable (CYCLE). This index is part of the ifo Geschäftsklima and was obtained from the ifo Institut für Wirtschaftsforschung, Munich.

Corporate Governance: Ownership Concentration
The construction of our preferred measure for ownership concentration (CONTROL), as well as two alternative measures (BLOCK and HERF) are discussed in Section 3.1 and below.

Corporate Governance: Type of Owner
We classify firms into five ownership categories (TYPE): private (including partnerships and foundations), financial firms (including banks and insurers), non-financial firms, government authorities. If a firm has no ultimate owner according to the concept of control (see below), the ownership category is "dispersed."

Corporate Governance: Ownership Complexity
Ownership complexity is measured with an indicator variable for cross ownership (CROSS) and pyramids (PYRAMID). CROSS takes the value of one if a firm's ultimate owner is part of the web of industrial and financial German firms identified by Wenger and Kaserer (1998) and if the ultimate owner indirectly owns a share block in itself, zero otherwise. PYRAMID takes the value of one when a firm is controlled via a pyramid, with at least one intermediate firm between the ultimate owner and the sample firm, zero otherwise.

Corporate Governance: Financial Pressure
Financial pressure is measured using three alternative measures of creditor influence on management and a measure of financial distress. BANK is the ratio of bank debt to total debt, DEBT is the ratio of total debt to total assets, LEVERAGE is the ratio of total debt to the book value of total equity, and COVERAGE is the ratio of operating earnings before interest, taxes, and depreciation (also known as EBITDA) to interest payments. Financial distress (LOSS) is an indicator variable that takes the value of one when a firm reports negative EBITDA, zero otherwise.

Corporate Governance: Board Size

Board size is measured with an indicator variable for small boards (SMALL) that takes the value of one if the firm's supervisory board has the minimum number of directors required by law, zero if the number of directors is larger than minimum. To control for the fact that not all sample firms have a supervisory board, we also include BOARD, an indicator variable that takes the value of one for firms having a board, zero otherwise. Determining the minimum number of directors is a complex process as different laws are to be applied, depending on firm size and industry (Stock Corporation Law, Iron and Steel Codetermination Law (1951), Amendment to Codetermination Law (1967), Law on Codetermination (1976)). In addition, a firm belonging to a group company (Konzern) can be subject to codetermination laws and therefore must comply with different requirements regarding board size, even when firm size is smaller than the thresholds specified in codetermination laws. However, a group company cannot be identified from our data; groups can only be identified by consulting individual corporate charters. Hence, SMALL might contain some classification error for subsidiaries of conglomerates.

Market Discipline: Industry-Level Competition

We use three measures to proxy for industry-level competition. As a measure of foreign competition, we use import penetration (IMPORT), defined as the ratio of the total value of imports to total market size. The latter is the sum of imports and domestic production, measured at the two-digit industry-level. Regarding industry concentration, we use the market share of the largest six producers, CR6, and the Herfindahl index of producer concentration, HHI, both of which are measured for four-digit output classes. This information is obtained from biennial reports of the German Federal Antitrust Commission, as reported in Monopolkommission (1996). Note that we cannot assign both competition measures perfectly to each firm for two reasons. First, for the construction of this measure, the Antitrust Commission uses information on firms' sales in individual market segments. Hence, there are several competition measures for each firm depending on sales structure. Unfortunately, our main source of data, the Hoppenstedt database, assigns firms only to one industry, the primary product market. Hence, our competition measure may contain some classification error for large firms. Second, the classification of industries used by the Antitrust Commission differs from the industry classification used in the Hoppenstedt database (European NACE code). Therefore, we had to assign some firms on an individual basis.

Market Discipline: Firm-Level Competition

The construction of our measure for firm-specific rents (RENT) is discussed in Section 3.2.

CORPORATE CONTROL CONCENTRATION MEASUREMENT AND FIRM PERFORMANCE

Yves Crama, Luc Leruth, Luc Renneboog
and Jean-Pierre Urbain

ABSTRACT

Traditionally share price returns and their variance have been explained by factors linked to the operations of the company such as systematic risk, corporate size and P/E ratios or by factors related to the influence of the macro-economic environment. In these models, the institutional environment in terms of concentration and nature of voting rights, bank debt dependence and corporate and legal mechanisms to change control have rarely been included. In this paper we have a dual objective. We first highlight the large discrepancies among corporate governance environments. We conclude that there is a need for a theoretically well-grounded measure of corporate control applicable to all systems and we define such a measure. Secondly, the impact of ownership structure on the share price performance and corporate risk is empirically analysed for companies listed on the London Stock Exchange. Within Europe, the U.K. corporate landscape is particularly interesting because of its widely-held nature and the liquidity of the market for controlling rights. Our results point to the fact that voting power, as measured by Z-indices, is tightly correlated to both share price performance and risk. The negative relation between the largest Z-index and corporate share price

Social Responsibility: Corporate Governance Issues
Research in International Business and Finance, Volume 17, 123–149
ISSN: 0275-5319/PII: S0275531903170067

performance is explained by the fact that the voting power held by executive directors measures the degree of insider entrenchment which has a negative impact on performance. This negative relation is compensated when outside shareholders (e.g. industrial companies, individuals or families) own substantial voting power and may actively monitor the firm. This is because with a counterbalancing pole of control, the largest shareholder is forced to compromise and maximize firm's profits rather than his or her own utility function. The risk regressions show that entrenched insider as well as large shareholders may seek higher levels of systematic risk. It may be that these shareholders prefer risky high growth strategies which are providing higher levels of private benefits for these types of shareholders at the expense of small shareholders. We also conclude that the classic Herfindahl indices inaccurately measure control, which is reflected in the weaker relationship with performance.

1. INTRODUCTION

Traditionally, share price returns and their variance have been explained by factors linked to the operations of the company such as systematic risk, corporate size and P/E ratios (as in Fama & French, 1992, among many examples) or by factors related to the influence of the macro-economic environment (e.g. Chen, Roll & Ross, 1986). In these models, the institutional environment in terms of concentration and nature of voting rights, bank debt dependence and corporate and legal mechanisms to change control have rarely been included. In fact, empirical research on the dynamics of ownership and its impact on corporate performance in European economies has only become possible in recent years. Indeed, while detailed data on ownership for listed corporations in Anglo-American markets have been available for some decades, the European Commission's Transparency Directive of 1988 (88/627/EEC) has only gradually been integrated into the national legislation of continental European countries.[1] Even so, each country retained the right to modulate the Commission's directive according to its own specific requirements with the result that ownership disclosure regulation of voting rights differs substantially across countries in terms of notification thresholds and frequency.[2] In this paper we have a dual objective. Firstly, we focus on highlighting the large discrepancies among corporate governance environments. As environments differ widely, we conclude that there is a need for a theoretically well-grounded measure of corporate control applicable to all systems and we define such a measure. Secondly, the impact of ownership structures on the share price performance and corporate risk is empirically analysed for companies listed on the London Stock Exchange. Within Europe, the U.K. corporate landscape is particularly interesting because of its widely-held nature and the liquidity of the market for controlling rights. Our results point to the fact that voting power, as measured by Z-indices, is tightly correlated to both share price performance and risk. The negative relation between the largest Z-index and corporate share price performance is explained by the fact that the voting power held by executive directors measures the degree of insider entrenchment which has a negative impact on performance. This negative relation is compensated when outside shareholders (e.g. industrial companies, individuals or families) own substantial voting power and may actively monitor the firm. This is because with a counterbalancing pole of control, the largest shareholder is forced to compromise and maximize firm's profits rather than his or her own utility function. The risk regressions show that entrenched insider as well as large shareholders may seek higher levels of systematic risk. It may be that these shareholders prefer risky high growth strategies which are providing higher levels of private benefits for these types of shareholders at the expense of small shareholders. We also conclude that the classic Herfindahl indices inaccurately measure control, which is reflected in the weaker relationship with performance.

The paper is organised as follows. Section 2 discusses the main differences in ownership structures in Europe. The section draws upon the research results of the European Corporate Governance Network.[3] In Section 3, we show that voting rights are but one element – albeit an important factor – in the corporate governance framework and we highlight the role of corporate law, minority protection, courts and banks. Section 4 focuses on a key issue in any economic analysis of corporate governance, i.e. the definition of *effective measures of control in complex ownership structures*, possibly characterised by multiple, intertwined layers of shareholding. We briefly discuss the weaknesses of classical approaches to this issue (via raw voting rights or Herfindahl indices) and we propose an alternative measure of control based on the Banzhaf index which we call the *Z-index*. We illustrate why the *Z-index* more adequately captures each shareholder's negotiating or voting power. On the basis of a sample of U.K. companies, Section 5 provides an econometric illustration of the importance of control dispersion on some key economic variables (beta and returns). We also briefly illustrate how the *Z-index* can be applied in the case of Continental European economies. Conclusions are presented in Section 6.

2. OWNERSHIP CONCENTRATION AND VOTING BLOCKS

2.1. Insider Versus Outsider Corporate Governance Systems

In spite of the relative paucity of data on voting structures, some striking features emerge from a simple cross-country comparison. For example, Table 1 highlights the major difference in ownership concentration between continental Europe and

Table 1. Concentration of Voting Rights by Country.

	Studies (2001) Eur. Corp. Governance Network	Sample co's All Quoted	Disclosure Threshold	Total Ownership Concentr.		Largest Shareholding		Shareholder Classes with Largest Percent of Voting Rights	
				Mean	Median	Mean	Median	Most	2nd Most
Austria	Gugler, Kalss, Stomper and Zechner	50 listed (all)	5%	65.5	60.0	54.1	52.0	Domestic co's	Fx co's/bks
Belgium	Becht, Chapelle and Renneboog	150 listed (all)	5%	63.4	66.5	55.8	55.5	(Fin)Holding co's	Ind&com Co's
France	Bloch and Kremp	40 listed (CAC)[a]	5%	52.0	30.0	29.4	20.0	(Fin)Holding co's	Ind&com Co's
Germany	Becht and Boehmer	374 listed (all)[b]	5%	<65%	<65%	n.a.	52.1	Companies	Fin. Inst.
Italy	Bianchi, Bianco and Enriques	216 listed (all)	2%	68.4	62.3	51.9	54.5	Companies	Individuals
Netherlands	De Jong, Kabir, Mara and Roell	137 listed (all)	5%	62.5	69.8	42.8	43.5	Administr. office	Fin. Inst.
Spain	Crespi and Garcia-Cestona	193 listed (all)	5%	65.1	63.2	40.1	34.2	Domestic co's	Fx co's
U.K.	Goergen and Renneboog	250 listed[c]	3%	40.8	39.0	15.2	10.9	Institutions	Directors
U.S.	Becht	1309 (NYSE)	5%	ca 30%	n.a.	<5%	<5%	Institutions	Individuals

This table presents total ownership concentration of all large shareholders and of the largest shareholder. The ownership classes which hold (cumulatively) the largest percentage of equity in the average listed company are also exhibited. Ownership data capture both direct and indirect (ultimate) shareholdings: all voting rights controlled directly and indirectly possibly via a cascade of intermediate holdings are added. In other words, alliances based on share stakes are taken into account. The companies in these studies are listed and exclude financial institutions.

All studies (a.o.) forthcoming in Barca and Becht (2001): The Control of Corporate Europe. Oxford Univ. Press.

[a] For all 680 French listed firms, the largest owner controls an average of 56% of voting rights. Companies which are part of an index have to assure sufficient. Liquidity; hence, the high free float and smaller blockholdings. For comparison: the median largest voting block of a DAX30 company amounts to 11.0%.

[b] All listed from the official market.

[c] Random sample of all non-financial firms listed on the LSE.

the Anglo-American countries. In the former, all large (disclosing) shareholders combined own more than 60% of the equity capital,[4] in the latter these control only about 40% of the voting rights. The differences in voting rights held by the largest shareholder are even more remarkable: the largest owner in the median U.K. listed company holds a stake of less than 15% and this stake is less than 5% in the U.S. In contrast the largest shareholder (or group of large shareholders) controls 40–54% of the voting rights on the continent. About 85% of the listed non-financial companies in Continental Europe have a large shareholder which holds at least a blocking minority (25%) and in about half the companies, one shareholder owns an absolute majority.

The high concentration of ownership in Continental European equity markets is only one manifestation of what is known as an *insider system* with the following characteristics: (i) the corporate sector has controlling interests in itself because companies are often shareholders of other ones; (ii) the number of listed companies is small compared to the size of the economy; (iii) and the capital market is illiquid because controlling blocks are held by a few dominant shareholders. Worse still, in spite of all the efforts made to simplify corporate structures, there remains a large number of holdings or interlocked companies, which de facto deter any attempt by outsiders to control any of them (Renneboog, 2000). Thus, while given an opportunity to participate in equity returns, outside investors have little hope to trade and acquire control. In contrast, the Anglo-American system is labelled as an *outsider system*. In that system, the number of listed companies is large; the process of acquiring control (not only participate in equity return) is effectively market-oriented (i.e. there is a liquid capital market with frequently traded ownership and control rights); and there are few corporate holdings or interlocked patterns of ownership. Finally, there are few major, controlling shareholdings and these are rarely associated with the corporate sector itself (La Porta et al., 1999; Wymeersch, 1994).

2.2. Cash Flow Versus Voting Rights

Although equity markets in Continental Europe indeed display some similarity, they also markedly differ with regard to a number of criteria. We concentrate on two of them. Firstly, as shown in Table 1, the nature of the main shareholders varies from country to country. Obviously, each category of shareholder has different incentives or abilities to exert control. For example, there is little evidence that institutional investors undertake any disciplinary actions against poorly performing management (Stapledon, 1996). In contrast, corporate shareholders might value dominant shareholding positions, not only for the financial return of their investment, but also for other potential benefits of control, especially when a customer or supplier relation exists with the target company (Barclay & Holderness, 1989).

Secondly, the complexity of ownership structures also varies across countries. Germany, for example, is characterised by complex shareholdings around and within industrial groups (Becht & Boehmer, 2001) while the French system is characterised by ownership cascades of financial groups and cross-company shareholdings (Bloch & Kremp, 2001). In Italy, long pyramids controlled by state or family-owned corporations are typical (Bianchi et al., 2001). More than a third of listed and non-listed Belgian companies are controlled by financial holdings companies (Becht et al., 2001) while in most Dutch listed companies, the separation of ownership and control is almost absolute, as blocks of voting rights are not held by shareholders but by an Administration Office (De Jong et al., 2001). Finally, although state controlled ownership has decreased substantially in Spain since 1995, state holding companies still own a golden-share in strategic sectors (Crespi & Garcia, 2001).

These differences have important implications in terms of the one-share-one-vote principle. *Ownership pyramids*, for instance, allow power concentration with limited investment, since controlling a target company can be achieved via a number of subsidiaries and a chain of 51% of their voting rights. With one intermediate holding, the ultimate shareholder retains absolute control while only receiving 25% ($= 0.51 \times 0.51$) of the cash flow.[5] Whereas legal restrictions have impeded the occurrence of ownership cascades in the U.K. (Goergen & Renneboog, 2003), they are common practice in Belgium, France or Italy. Another way of amassing voting power is through *voting pacts* and *proxy votes*. For example, voting pacts are not uncommon in Germany (Chirinko & Elston, 1996) and German banks commonly use proxy votes of the shares deposited in their custody (called the "Depotstimmrecht", see for example Wenger & Kaserer, 1997).[6]

Still, a number of mechanisms exist to erode voting power, such as the imposition of *voting caps*. An extreme case is the Netherlands where under the "structural governance regime", non-voting certificates are distributed to ordinary shareholders while the voting power is given to a foundation controlled by company insiders (De Jong et al., 2001). In Germany, Belgium or Spain, a decision by the board of directors can limit any percentage of voting power to, e.g. 5%.[7] Whereas *dual class shares* are frequently used to separate ownership and control in Sweden (Agnblad et al., 2001), this has been actively discouraged in the U.K. by the LSE (Brennan & Franks, 1997). Finally, since the take-over wave in the 1980s, several *poison pills* like shelf registration of equity,[8] issuing bonds cum warrants or convertible bonds, are frequently used to dilute the voting power of "hostile" shareholders.

Table 2. Ownership and Voting Power: Structure and Consequences.

Panel A: Dispersed Ownership and Dispersed Voting Power
   where: U.S., U.K.
   advantages: a. portfolio diversification and liquidity, b. take over possibility
   disadvantages: insufficient monitoring: free riding problem
   agency conflicts: management vs. shareholders

Panel B: Dispersed Ownership and Concentrated Voting Power
   where: countries where a stake holder can collect proxy votes and shareholder coalitions are
      allowed.
   advantages: a. monitoring of management, b. portfolio diversification and liquidity;
   disadvantages: a. violation of one-share-one-vote, b. reduced take over possibility
   agency conflicts: controlling block holders vs. small shareholders

Panel C: Concentrated Ownership and Dispersed Voting Power
   where: any company with voting right restrictions
   advantages: protection of minority rights
   disadvantages: a. violation of one-share-one-vote, b. low monitoring incentives, c. low
      portfolio diversification possibilities and low liquidity, d. higher cost of capital, e. reduced
      take over possibilities
   agency conflicts: management vs. shareholders

Panel D: Concentrated Ownership and Concentrated Voting Power
   where: Continental Europe, Japan, in any company after take over.
   advantages: high monitoring incentives
   disadvantages: a. low portfolio diversification possibilities and low liquidity, b. reduced take
      over possibilities
   agency conflicts: controlling block holders vs. small shareholders.

2.3. Corporate Governance and Agency Costs

Both the insider and outsider corporate governance systems present weaknesses and advantages which can be analysed in terms of the principal-agent theory (see Table 2). The Anglo-American system, characterised by high dispersion of voting and cash flow rights and called the "Weak owners, strong managers" – case by Roe (1994), may induce free riding[9] on control. As a single small shareholder only benefits from performance improvements in direct proportion to the cash flow rights, he or she may not find it profitable to monitor management while a large shareholder will necessarily feel differently. This situation may result in agency conflicts between management and shareholders.[10] Still, the large free float allows investors to take advantage of portfolio diversification possibilities and introduces the discipline of the (hostile) take-over market.[11]

   Concentration of ownership and voting rights, on the other hand, stimulates corporate governance actions against under-performing management, but may lead to expropriation of the rights of minority shareholders as discussed in panel D of Table 2. Furthermore, share liquidity is reduced due to the low free float and hostile take-overs are virtually ruled out.

Panels B and C of Table 2 present the other combinations of concentrations of ownership and voting rights which can be attained by some of the instruments described above to amass or dilute voting power. For example, when shareholder coalitions or proxy votes are allowed, the supervisory power of a block of shareholders vis-à-vis management increases, but the agency conflicts shift from shareholder-management towards large versus minority shareholders.

3. CORPORATE GOVERNANCE: SYMBIOSIS OF FINANCIAL MARKETS AND CORPORATE LAW

The discussion above points to the difficulty in explaining corporate governance systems on the basis of conventional theories. In this section, we shall emphasise this critical point before moving on to a discussion of the methodology we use to measure control. Indeed, neither transaction costs theory,[12] nor principal agent theory,[13] nor the theory of implicit contracting[14] nor the theory of vertical integration[15] can fully explain why two governance systems (Continental European and Anglo-American) have emerged or, in a more refined way, why Continental European countries differ in terms of structure and concentration of ownership (cash flow rights) and voting rights. In the previous section, we have shown that the weaknesses of both systems have been partially dealt with through mechanisms separating cash flow and voting rights. In addition however, governments, regulators and stock exchanges have often found it necessary to develop a legal environment able to limit the inconveniences (e.g. agency costs) induced by the corporate governance system.

In fact, historic evolution of regulation has shaped ownership structures, capital markets and corporate governance systems (for a path-dependence theory; see Bebchuk & Roe, 1999). Not surprisingly, there are two broad legal traditions; the common law system, found in Anglo-American countries and the Commonwealth, and the civil law tradition of Continental Europe and its sphere of influence (former colonies). These two legal systems are different in terms of shareholder protection, adherence to the one-share-one-vote principle and creditor protection. According to La Porta et al. (1997, 1998, 2000), the common law system appears to provide stronger shareholder and creditor protection.[16] But legal origin can also explain differences in corporate governance systems and the degree of capital market development. In common law countries, the ratio of external capital to GDP is higher, as are the ratio of corporate debt to GDP and the number of listed domestic firms and initial public offerings as a proportion of the corporate population. Whether or not the institutional environment has a momentous impact on economic activity has been explored by a number of authors. In particular, Carlin and Mayer (2001) investigate the relation between economic growth, R&D investment and fixed income formation, on the one hand, and the presence of bank-firm relations, development of security markets, degree of ownership concentration and the legal system on the other. For a sample of companies in 20 countries, there is little influence of banking activity and ownership concentration on economic growth, but they find that legal protection of investors and development of securities markets matter.

A seemingly logical implication of the discussion above is that it would be extremely difficult to develop a set of corporate governance regulations applicable to all EU countries without undertaking the difficult task of concomitantly dismantling the existing country-specific mechanisms that currently provide shareholder protection. Indeed, several attempts made in that direction had to be withdrawn. For example, the mandatory take-over bid requirement for all listed companies included in the first draft of the 13th Company Law Directive was dropped. The consequence would have been a weakening of direct monitoring resulting from reduced voting block sizes (Becht, 1999). The 5th Company Law Directive (now abandoned) aimed at imposing the one-share-one-vote rule on all European companies. As dual class shares would also have been ruled out, there was a danger that shareholders would have reacted by relying increasingly on pyramids and voting pacts in order to retain control, thereby reducing market liquidity.

4. EFFECTIVE MEASURES OF CONTROL

4.1. The Weakness of Herfindahl Indices

The previous discussion underlines the difficulty of apprehending the whole intricacy and diversity of the issues surrounding corporate governance. In this context, a most fundamental question appears to be that of *measuring* the extent to which a given company is controlled by each of its (ultimate) shareholders and to measure the dispersion of control among shareholders. A number of indices have been proposed to answer this question. Most of these indices belong to the Herfindahl family, i.e. they focus on the (square of the) proportion of shares owned by the largest direct shareholder(s) in the company. We claim, however, that such indices do not provide a theoretically sound measure of dispersion.

Let us first tackle the case of the Anglo-American or "outsider" system. Consider a target company whose capital is first diluted from five shares to seven shares, then

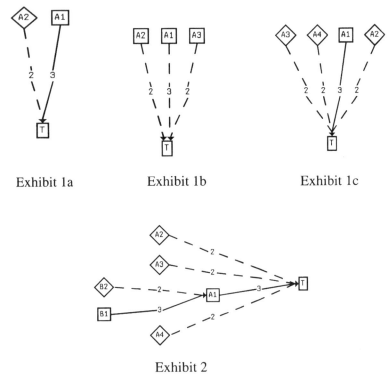

Exhibit 1a   Exhibit 1b   Exhibit 1c

Exhibit 2

Fig. 1. Ownership Concentration Indices in Insider and Outsider Systems.

from seven to nine shares, as illustrated in Exhibits 1a to 1c (in Fig. 1). It is easy
to verify that company A1 has full control over the target in Exhibit 1a, no more
control than any other shareholder in Exhibit 1b[17] (meaning that dilution leads
to less concentration of control in this case), but more than any other shareholder
in Exhibit 1c[18] (meaning that dilution leads to higher control concentration in
this case). Yet, each successive dilution yields Herfindahl indices which wrongly
diagnose less concentration, mostly due to the fact that the proportion of shares
owned by company A1 steadily decreases in the process.[19] In addition, since
Herfindahl indices concentrate on the largest shareholders and totally disregard the
float, they fail to integrate a very important element of the potential disciplinary
effect of coalitions of small shareholders in the outsider system.

Let us next consider the case of the Continental European (or insider) system.
By definition, Herfindahl indices can only tackle one layer of shareowners. While
this may be a good approximation of reality in outsider systems, a simple look at

Exhibit 2 (Fig. 1) reveals that it is clearly insufficient in more complex, multi-layered (pyramid) ownership structures. Indeed, should one compute the Herfindahl index on the basis of the largest direct shareholder or take into account the presence of B1 and B2? If we do the latter, A2 (or A3 or A4 indifferently) becomes the largest shareholder since B1 would only have the equivalent of $9/5$ ($= 3 \times 3/5 < 2$) direct shares. In practice, however, B1 has more control over T than any other shareholder and a Herfindahl index would fail to diagnose it. Similarly, corporate law fails to capture the whole complexity of the issue. Banking commissions and other regulatory bodies usually rely on rather simple concepts of corporate control, whereby owners are classified into a small number of distinct categories. For instance, a shareholder is said to detain majority control if he controls (directly or indirectly) more than 51% of the shares; he has at least a blocking minority if he controls between 25 and 50% of the shares (and could be considered to have more control if he has the ability to remove administrators); otherwise, he is viewed as having no control at all. There are many situations, however, where such rules prove unsatisfactory. A striking example occurs when a single individual (call him for instance Bill Gates) owns 20% of the shares of a company (call it Microsoft), while the remaining 80% of the shares are totally dispersed among an "ocean" of small investors. In such a case, the main share-holder typically rules the company, while legal regulations would consider him as possessing no significant control. Alternatively, it may happen that a corporate shareholder with more than 50% shares in a subsidiary is himself owned by a dispersed group of shareholders, in which case, it is highly debatable whether the subsidiary is controlled or not.

Thus, it appears difficult to build indices of corporate control that succeed in providing effective and consistent estimates of ownership dispersion, especially when studying a variety of corporate governance systems. Promising attempts, however, have been made to handle this question within a formal game theoretic framework. The idea is here to model shareholders as *players* in a *voting game*, and to use classical *power indices* (such as Shapley indices, see e.g. Crespi & Renneboog, 2001; Owen, 1982) to measure the extent of their control over a target company. Intuitively, such power indices reflect the relative ability of each player (or shareholder) to impose his will to the target company through coalitions with other players. This approach has been applied to the study of corporate control by a few authors (see Cubbin & Leech, 1983; Gambarelli, 1991; Zwiebel, 1995). Yet, their investigations are mostly theoretical and/or restricted to the analysis of a single layer of shareowners.

We propose here to use the Banzhaf index, which measures the ability of a voter to swing the decision in his or her own favour. More precisely, the Banzhaf index of a player can be defined as the probability that the outcome of the voting process changes when the player changes her mind unilaterally, under the assumption that all vectors of votes are equally likely (see Banzhaf, 1965, 1966, 1968). Although there are technical differences between the Banzhaf Index and the Shapley value, both indices essentially capture the same phenomenon and often yield nearly equivalent measures of power. However, we found the Banzhaf Index easier to compute algorithmically, especially in the case of complex structures. The reader interested in a detailed discussion of the differences between the Banzhaf Index and the Shapley value is referred to Dubey and Shapley (1979) and Felsenthal and Machover (1998). Thus, we have computed an index (the Z-index) largely based on Banzhaf's methodology. For the computation of the Z-index, we have assumed that the float was constituted of a large number of small voters. This is not always done as it is often assumed that only large shareholders matter, in which case the float is neglected by normalizing the total number of shares to the sum of the shares held by the largest identified shareholders.

4.2. How to Compute the Z-Index: An Illustration

We illustrate the computation of the Z-index in the simple cases displayed in Fig. 1. Let us first consider Exhibit 1a, and assume that there is one issue concerning T on which shareholders have to vote "yes" or "no". Assuming that votes are not correlated, there are four (2^2) possible voting strings as shown in Table 3 . Among these, there are two where (A1) changes her mind while (A2) does not and the result of the vote changes in both occasions. On the other hand, although (A2) changes her mind twice as well, the final vote does not change in either occasion, reflecting the absolute incapacity of (A2) to affect the outcome. The Z-index is computed as the ratio between the number of swings in the final outcome induced by each player over the total number of swings in the final outcome induced by all players. It is equal to 100% (2/2) for (A1) and 0% (0/2) for (A2), reflecting that (A1) has full control over T, which can be readily spotted in this very simple case. Let us move to Exhibit 1b where there are eight (2^3) possible voting strings among which four correspond to situation where (A1) changes her mind while the others do not. Thus, (A1) can induce two swings in the final outcome when changing her mind four times. The same holds for both other players, so that a change in the final outcome caused by one single change of mind can only occur in six instances. Thus, the Z-index for each player is the same and equal to 2/6 or 1/3. Consider now Exhibit 1c. This time there are 16 (2^4) possible voting strings. A similar computation, detailed in Table 3 shows that the Z-index has now increased for (A1) from 1/3 to 1/2 while the Z-index of all three other players has gone down to 1/6. Thus, in contrast to the traditional indices as the Herfindahl, the Z-index provides results

Table 3. Computation of Z-indices – An Illustration.

String #	Possible Voting Choices				Outcome (T)
	(A1)	(A2)	(A3)	(A4)	
Panel A					
1	Y	Y			Y
2	Y	N			Y
3	N	Y			N
4	N	N			N
Results	Number of possible strings =				4
	Number of swings for (A1) =				2
	Number of swings for (A2) =				0
	Total number of swings =				2
	Z-index (A1) =		(= 2/2)		1
	Z-index (A2) =		(= 0/2)		0
Panel B					
1	Y	Y	Y		Y
2	Y	Y	N		Y
3	Y	N	Y		Y
4	Y	N	N		N
5	N	Y	Y		Y
6	N	Y	N		N
7	N	N	Y		N
8	N	N	N		N
Results	Number of possible strings =				8
	Number of swings for (A1) =				2
	Number of swings for (A2) =				2
	Number of swings for (A3) =				2
	Total number of swings =				6
	Z-index (A1) =		(= 2/6)		0.333
	Z-index (A2) =		(= 2/6)		0.333
	Z-index (A2) =		(= 2/6)		0.333
Panel C					
1	Y	Y	Y	Y	Y
2	Y	Y	Y	N	Y
3	Y	Y	N	Y	Y
4	Y	Y	N	N	Y
5	Y	N	Y	Y	Y
6	Y	N	Y	N	Y
7	Y	N	N	Y	Y
8	Y	N	N	N	N
9	N	Y	Y	Y	Y
10	N	Y	Y	N	N

Table 3. *(Continued)*

String #	Possible Voting Choices				Outcome (T)
	(A1)	(A2)	(A3)	(A4)	
11	N	Y	N	Y	N
12	N	Y	N	N	N
13	N	N	Y	Y	N
14	N	N	Y	N	N
15	N	N	N	Y	N
16	N	N	N	N	N
Results	Number of possible strings =				16
	Number of swings for (A1) =				6
	Number of swings for (A2), (A3), (A4) =				2
	Total number of swings =				12
	Z-index (A1) =		(= 6/12)		0.5
	Z-index (A2), (A3), (A4) =		(= 2/12)		0.166

which are fully consistent with the intuition discussed in the previous subsection. In particular, the control held by (A1) goes down then up as the capital is diluted.

In order to make the case that the Z-index can be used in the more complex structures of the insider systems, we consider Exhibit 2 of Fig. 1 where there are only five players because the vote of (A1) is fully determined by the vote of (B1) and (B2). A similar mechanism based on the analysis of 32 possible voting strings shows that the Z-index is 1/2 for (B1), 1/6 for (A2), (A3), and (A4) and 0 for (B2).

Using a sample of French companies, we have computed the Z-index for the main (possibly indirect) shareholder and compared it with the percentage of shares held by the largest direct shareholder. We display here two exhibits (see Fig. 2). In the first exhibit, we show the relationship between the Z-index for the main shareholder and the percentage of shares held when the latter is below 50% (about 35 companies). It is readily apparent that the relation between both indicators is highly nonlinear. In the second exhibit, we display the Z-index of the main indirect shareholder for a sample of about 70 companies in which the largest direct shareholder owns more than 50%. Note that this does not imply a Z-index of 1 because the majority direct shareholder may feature a dispersed ownership structure itself.[20] Actually, the graph in Fig. 2 suggests that this must often be the case. Thus, it clearly appears that the Z-index provides a strikingly different picture of shareholding structures from that based on the Herfindahl concept. The above discussion also shows that the Z-index (or any index of a similar nature) would provide a sound measure for all systems of corporate governance.

In the next section, we use the Z-index to analyse the impact of corporate ownership dispersion on the financial performance of U.K. firms.

**Shareholder < 50%: control (Z index)
by ultimate main shareholder vs
shares held by largest <u>direct</u>
shareholder**

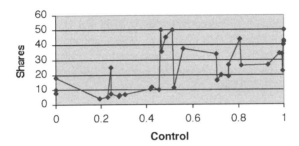

Note: In the graph below, firms are ranked according to the amount of control held by
their largest ultimate shareholder (control is on the vertical axis while firms are
numbered on the horizontal axis).

**Shareholder > 50%: control (Z index)
detained by ultimate main shareholder**

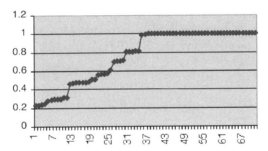

Fig. 2. Control Versus Ownership for a Sample of French Companies.

5. EMPIRICAL RESULTS

We have already discussed the main features of the corporate governance system
that prevails in the U.K. We are now going to describe some of the relationships
that emerge between the financial characteristics of firms, on the one hand, and

either Herfindahl or Z-indices on the other, as they emerge from an empirical study of a panel of listed British firms.[21]

5.1. Data Sources

A random sample of 250 companies quoted on the London Stock Exchange was selected and (yearly) data relative to these companies were collected in the pre-Cadbury period (1988–1993). All disclosed ownership stakes were retrieved from microfiche and hard-copy annual reports: these include all beneficial and non-beneficial shareholders with stakes of 3% or more, as well as all directors' shareholdings. Whenever a nominee was mentioned as major shareholder, the individual, corporation or institution behind the nominee shareholding was identified by contacting the companies' finance managers. The risk measures are from the Risk Measurement Service and betas have been calculated via a Vasicek Bayesian-updating procedure. Share price performance measures are from the London Share Price Database. Accounting and firm specific characteristics data (including several non-risk security characteristics dividends, P/E ratio, etc.) are from Datastream.

Table 4 shows the ownership distribution of the random sample of U.K. firms. Panel A shows that in most firms (187 out of 250) institutional shareholder own large stakes. The second most important category consists of executive directors. The largest share stake across categories is around 13%. Panel B shows that, although institutions are omnipresent, their stakes are smaller (usually below 10%), whereas a higher proportion of the share stakes above 10% is controlled by executive directors. It should be mentioned that blockholders owning large stakes often deliberately remain below the 30% threshold which triggers a mandatory bid on all other shares.

5.2. Tests and Results

In order to illustrate the importance of ownership dynamics in the economy, we report here on two specific issues. First, we investigate the possible link between the performance of a stock and the ownership structure of the firm at the previous period. Performance is measured by annual return, i.e. by the ratio called *Return_t* in Table 4: (capital gain plus dividend) to (value of the stock at the previous period). Four types of control indices are used to capture the ownership structure of each firm:

* $Z1$ denotes the *Z-index* of the largest shareholder;
* $Z2$ denotes the *Z-index* of the second largest shareholder;

Table 4. Ownership Distribution by Category of Owner.

Panel A: Ownership concentration and voting power of large shareholders by shareholder category.
1992

	Average Based on Total Number of co's with a Shareholding for This Category of Owner				Average Based on Total Number of Sample Companies			
	Numb. of co's with Large Owners	% Equity	Shapley	Herfindahl	All Sample Companies	% Equity	Shapley	Herfindahl
1. Banks								
Largest	62	5.7%	0.16		204	1.7%	0.05	
Sum		6.2%	0.18	0.04		1.9%	0.05	0.01
2. Investment and pension funds								
Largest	139	6.0%	0.20		204	4.1%	0.14	
Sum		8.9%	0.27	0.08		6.1%	0.18	0.06
3. Insurance co's								
Largest	173	8.4%	0.26		204	7.2%	0.22	
Sum		17.1%	0.46	0.11		14.5%	0.39	0.09
Total institutions								
Largest	187	8.4%	0.32		204	7.2%	0.29	
Sum		24.4%	0.68	0.18		22.4%	0.62	0.16
4. Industrial cos								
Largest	86	12.8%	0.34		204	5.4%	0.14	
Sum		14.3%	0.36	0.13		6.0%	0.15	0.06
5. Families and individuals								
Largest	31	10.7%	0.19		204	1.6%	0.03	
Sum		16.4%	0.27	0.07		2.5%	0.04	0.01
6. Government								
Largest	6	5.7%	0.03		204	0.2%	0.00	
Sum		5.7%	0.03	0.04		0.2%	0.00	0.00
7. Executive directors								
Largest	103	8.1%	0.16		204	4.1%	0.08	
Sum		11.6%	0.21	0.07		5.9%	0.11	0.04

Table 4. (Continued)

1992	Average Based on Total Number of co's with a Shareholding for This Category of Owner				Average Based on Total Number of Sample Companies			
	Numb. of co's with Large Owners	% Equity	Shapley	Herfindahl	All Sample Companies	% Equity	Shapley	Herfindahl
8. Non-executive directors								
Largest	58	10.3%	0.21		204	2.9%	0.06	
Sum		14.5%	0.26	0.08		4.1%	0.07	0.02
Total directors								
Largest	118	10.3%	0.21		204	4.1%	0.12	
Sum		17.3%	0.31	0.10		10.0%	0.18	0.06

Panel B: Ownership distribution by category of owner

250 firms	[3%, 10%]			[10%, 25%]			[25%, 50%]			[50%, 75%]			[75%, 100%]		
	Mean (Tot.)	Mean (Cat.)	No. of Invest.	Mean (Tot.)	Mean (Cat.)	No. of Invest.	Mean (Tot.)	Mean (Cat.)	No. of Invest.	Mean (Tot.)	Mean (Cat.)	No. of Invest.	Mean (Tot.)	Mean (Cat.)	No. of Invest.
Banks	0.29	1.11	60	0.02	1.00	4	0.00	1.00	1	0.00	0.00	0	0.00	0.00	0
Investment funds	1.06	1.63	219	0.04	1.00	9	0.00	0.00	0	0.00	0.00	0	0.00	0.00	0
Insurance co's	2.01	2.57	414	0.22	1.21	46	0.02	1.00	4	0.00	0.00	0	0.00	0.00	0
Total Institutions	3.35	3.76	691	0.29	1.26	59	0.02	1.00	5	0.00	0.00	0	0.00	0.00	0
Industrial co's	0.31	1.14	64	0.11	1.05	22	0.04	1.00	9	0.01	1.00	2	0.00	1.00	1
Families/indiv.	0.22	1.84	46	0.03	1.40	7	0.02	1.00	4	0.00	0.00	0	0.00	0.00	0
Executive dir.	0.24	1.40	49	0.14	1.38	29	0.04	1.14	8	0.00	1.00	1	0.00	0.00	0
Non-exec. dir.	0.26	1.71	53	0.08	1.23	16	0.02	1.00	5	0.00	1.00	1	0.00	0.00	0
Total directors	0.50	1.85	102	0.22	1.55	45	0.06	1.30	13	0.01	1.00	2	0.00	0.00	0
All shareholders	4.42	4.69	910	0.65	1.51	133	0.15	1.11	31	0.02	1.00	4	0.00	1.00	1

Note: Panel A shows the sum of the large ownership stakes by category of owner and the largest shareholding. Panel B shows the average number of large shareholders by shareholder category and by size of equity stake. Mean (tot.) and Mean (cat.) stand for the average stake by class of shareholder whereby the denominator is, respectively, the total number of companies and the total number of companies with a shareholder of this category. No. of invest. stands for the number of investors in this category. Source: Annual reports.

- *Herf1* denotes the square of the percentage of shares detained by the largest shareholder;
- *Herf5* denotes the sum of squared percentages of shares detained by the five largest shareholders.

The other variables appearing in the regression (Table 4) are included to control for firm specific characteristics. Firstly, we control for corporate size measured by the level of employment ($Empl_{t-1}$) and market capitalisation ($Mcap_{t-1}$) as in Demsetz and Lehn (1985). This way, we incorporate the small firm effect on returns and on risk. The small firm effect has been documented by many studies: small firms are expected to generate higher returns than predicted by the capital asset pricing models as such models understate small firms' riskiness. As the correlation between the employment and market size is low, the results do not suffer from multicollinearity. Secondly, we include future growth in relation to current profitability as measured by the price-earning ratio (PE ratio$_{t-1}$). A third control variable represents the systematic risk of the stock as measured by its Beta ($Beta_{t-1}$) and we control for industry effects by including a dummy for the sector of activity ($Sector_t$). Note that a Z-index is defined for each firm's shareholder while Herfindahl indices correspond to a distribution of ownership for the firm. Thus, while *Herf1* and *Z1* may correspond to the same unique financial link when the largest direct shareholder also happens to be the largest ultimate shareholder, there is no such similarity between the Z-indices and Herfindahl indices of higher order. In a second model, we investigate the possible link between the systematic risk of a stock, as measured by its Beta, and the above indices of ownership structure. Thus, we have obtained three econometric equations (with either *H1* and *H2*; or *Z1* and *Z2*; or *Z1* only, respectively) explaining returns and three explaining the Beta. Given the presence of missing observations for some years and/or firms in the sample, the models (fixed effects models with time/year specific dummies) were estimated from an unbalanced panel by feasible GLS using estimated cross-section residual variances. Heteroskedasticity robust *t*-test statistics (in absolute value) are reported in parentheses. The higher the *t*-test statistics, the more significant the variable is. The main results are summarised in Table 5.

The relation between ownership concentration, as measured by voting power indices, and performance is expected to be positive, provided that large shareholders assume a monitoring task to ensure that management focuses its efforts on the maximisation of corporate value (Roe, 1994). If, however, large shareholders use their voting dominance to safeguard private benefits of control and to extract rents from the company, large shareholder concentration may be have a detrimental effect on the share price return. Empirical research has not shown convincing evidence of large shareholder monitoring. For example, neither Franks et al.

Table 5. Impact of Ownership Dynamics on the Risk and Financial Performance of a Stock.

	Dependent Variables					
	$Return_t$	$Return_t$	$Return_t$	$Beta_t$	$Beta_t$	$Beta_t$
Explanatory variables						
$Z1_{t-1}$	−3.3510***	–	−7.0417***	0.1222***	–	0.1184***
	(2.51)		(4.55)	(22.414)		(19.341)
$Z2_{t-1}$	24.3068***	–	–	0.1019***	–	–
	(11.31)			(18.783)		
$Herf1_{t-1}$	–	0.0088	–	–	−0.00003	–
		(1.688)			(1.509)	
$Herf5_{t-1}$	–	−0.1131**	–	–	0.00005***	–
		(2.299)			(3.215)	
Control variables						
$Empl_{t-1}$	0.0007***	0.0006***	0.0007***	0.000004***	0.000004***	0.000004***
	(24.010)	(21.378)	(34.77)	(13.108)	(15.281)	(17.3118)
$Mcap_{t-1}$	−0.0226***	−0.0214***	−0.0218***	−0.00005***	−0.00005***	−0.00005***
	(46.392)	(45.108)	(12.71)	(65.050)	(32.671)	(60.459)
$PE\ ratio_{t-1}$	0.3415***	0.1806***	0.2813***	−0.0010***	−0.0009***	−0.0008***
	(15.081)	(7.550)	(12.71)	(21.215)	(12.458)	(18.074)
$Beta_{t-1}$	39.0118***	34.388***	37.8001***	–	–	–
	(17.096)	(8.803)	(15.96)			
$Sector_t$	0.8963***	0.9661***	0.8734***	−0.0003	−0.0009	0.0002
	(4.9894)	(2.258)	(4.890)	(0.456)	(1.144)	(0.236)
No. of observations	767	767	767	782	782	782
Adjusted R^2	0.16	0.16	0.16	0.78	0.76	0.78

Notes: $Z1$ denotes the Z-index of the largest shareholder; $Z2$ denotes the Z-index of the second largest shareholder; $Herf1$ denotes the square of the percentage of shares detained by the largest shareholder; $Herf5$ denotes the sum of squared percentages of shares detained by the five largest shareholders. Given the presence of missing observations for some years and/or firms in the sample, the models (fixed effects models with time/year specific dummies, not reported in this table) were estimated from an unbalanced panel by feasible GLS using estimated cross-section residual variances. Heteroskedasticity robust t-test statistics (in absolute value) are reported in parentheses. The higher the t-test statistics, the more significant is the variable.

(2001) nor Faccio and Lasfer (1999) find evidence that large shareholders are involved in corporate governance actions like managerial disciplining, but confirm that executive ownership entrenches management. For Continental Europe where blockholders are more prominent, there is evidence that the presence of substantial shareholders has a detrimental impact on corporate returns. For example, Banerjee et al. (1997) and Renneboog (2000) show that respectively large French and Belgian holding companies do not monitor their investments and are not well monitored, which may account the discount compared to their market break-up value. Thus, if large shareholders pursue private benefits of control and if the codes of conduct and corporate law do not sufficiently curb the extraction of corporate rents by large shareholders, this may be reflected in lower corporate returns. Similarly, the presence of dominant large shareholder combined with inefficiencies initiated by private benefits (like the choice of a non-optimal investment policy) may increase systematic risk.

Table 5 shows that the Z-indices are highly significant in both models tested. The Z voting power index of the largest shareholder is negatively correlated with return. This implies that a company with strong concentration of voting power in the hands of one single shareholder generates a lower return than a widely-held firm. An analysis of the type of shareholders with the highest voting power reveals that it is the large pivotal shareholdings (and hence high Z-indices) held by executive directors who are directly responsible to the negative sign. This suggests that executive directors owning large ownership stakes succeed in building entrenched positions such that the corporate focus on not on value maximisation. Several papers found strong evidence that directors can extract private benefits of control at the detriment of shareholders (Dyck & Zingales, 2001; Johnson et al., 2000) or manage to insulate themselves from any corporate monitoring even in the wake of poor performance (Crespi & Renneboog, 2001; Franks et al., 2001; Zwiebel, 1995). In contrast, when managers have less discretion as a result of smaller relative voting stakes, the negative relation between control and return is reversed indicating that large monitoring shareholders have a beneficial impact on corporate performance. The presence of a large second shareholder may reduce potential rent extraction by directors and hence have a positive impact on the share price return. In other words, when there exists a counterbalancing pole of control (both *Z1* and *Z2* are high), utility functions are usually different and the best compromise is then to maximize profits. This balancing effect clearly appears as the coefficient of *Z2* is significantly positive while that of *Z1* is significantly negative.

By contrast, the coefficients of *Herf1* is not significant and *Herf5* is only statistically significant at a lower levels. The Herfindahl index measuring the dispersion of control of the largest five shareholders shows that more diffuse ownership has a negative impact on the returns. We find strong statistical significance for our control variables[22]: high risk and strong growth opportunities are reflected in positive returns in the next period. Large firms, measured by numbers of employees generated higher returns, which is in line with the reverse size effect of the early 1990s.

The beta-regressions of Table 5 report that high shareholder voting power (measured by the Z-indices of the largest and second largest shareholder) are positively correlated to systematic risk. This finding suggests that the presence of large dominant shareholders – both directors and outsiders, like corporations and institutions – chose to take on higher levels of risk than widely-held firms. Both directors and other classes or large shareholders may opt to undertake additional risk because for these shareholders not only the financial return on their investment is important but also other benefits of control which may come at the detriment of (small) shareholders. Let us consider two examples of expropriation of shareholder rights. La Porta et al. (2000) give some examples of "tunnelling";

they show that large corporate shareholders can influence sales or investments such that, e.g. setting low transfer pricing or spinning off of assets below market value siphons off corporate value to companies of which the large shareholders own 100% of the voting rights. Directors may also tempted to investment in high-risk investment projects which aim at corporate growth rather than corporate value. The reason is that remuneration schemes in the U.K. have been shown to be more size-sensitive than performance-sensitive (see e.g. Muphy, 1999).

6. CONCLUSION

This paper has described two broad systems of corporate governance existing in Continental Europe (the *insider* system) and in the U.K. (and the U.S., the *outsider* system). We have emphasised a number of striking differences in concentration and nature of ownership between both systems. For example, in a typical Continental European country, (majority) control is held by one shareholder or a small group of interlocked (corporate) shareholders, whereas Anglo-American companies are predominantly widely held. These discrepancies have important consequences in terms of agency costs and therefore, mechanisms have been developed in most countries to separate ownership (cash flow rights) and control (voting rights) both at the level of the firm and through corporate law. The complexity of apprehending the numerous and intricate issues related to corporate governance has led us to focus on the need to adequately measure the extent to which a company is controlled by its shareholders. We have shown that traditional indices belonging to the Herfindahl family do not provide theoretically sound measures and have proposed to use another index (the Z-index) based on the idea that shareholders are players in a voting game.

In order to illustrate the importance of ownership dynamics on the economy, we analysed empirically the impact of the Z-index and Herfindahl indices on the financial performance of a stock and its risk. Given the widely held nature of companies listed on the London Stock Exchange, the importance of the role played by potential shareholder coalitions, and the availability of data, the equations have been estimated for the U.K. Our results point to the fact that voting power, as measured by Z-indices, is tightly correlated to both share price performance and risk. The negative relation between the largest Z-index and corporate share price performance is explained by the fact that the voting power held by executive directors measures the degree of insider entrenchment which has a negative impact on performance. This negative relation is compensated when outside shareholders (e.g. industrial companies, individuals or families) own substantial voting power and may actively monitor the firm. This is because with a counterbalancing pole of control, the largest shareholder is forced to compromise and maximize firm's profits rather than his or her own utility function. The risk regressions show that entrenched insider as well as large shareholders my seek higher levels of systematic risk. It may be that these shareholders prefer risky high growth strategies which are providing higher levels of private benefits for these types of shareholders at the expense of small shareholders. We also conclude that the classic Herfindahl indices inaccurately measure control, which is reflected in the weaker relationship with performance.

NOTES

1. The following countries adopted the disclosure regulations: Belgium in 1989; Spain in 1989, France in 1989, Italy in 1974 with adaptation in 1992, Netherlands in 1992, Germany in 1995.

2. For instance, shareholdings exceeding 2% of the equity capital (voting rights) are to be disclosed in Italy whereas, in most other European countries the notification threshold is at 5%. Furthermore, disclosure frequency in, e.g. Belgium and the U.K. differs: in the former changes in ownership need to be reported as soon as the new threshold transgresses any subsequent threshold of 5% (5%, 10%, 15% etc.) of equity whereas in the U.K., a change of 1% in a large shareholding (of more than 3%) triggers disclosure.

3. The European Corporate Governance Network consists of researchers from, among others: Banque Nationale de Paris, Banca d'Italia, University of Oxford, Princeton University, Tilburg University, Free University of Brussels (ECARE), Catholic University of Leuven, University of Vienna, Autonomous University of Barcelona, University of Groningen, Humboldt University Berlin, University of Manchester, Stockholm School of Economics, University of Milan. The ECGN is financed by the European Union and Fondazione E. Mattei (Milan). The Network consists of about 25 researchers at 18 universities and National Banks in 9 European countries.

4. In France, total ownership concentration in CAC40 or DAX30 companies is lower because relatively high free float is required.

5. This example illustrates the major difference between voting rights and cash flow rights. Through control leverage, it is possible to detain control over a large number of entities while only investing little money (and being entitled to a small portion of the cash flows).

6. Wenger and Kaserer (1997) mention that in a 1992 survey of the 24 largest German companies, banks controlled over 80% of the votes.

7. Usually, the board of directors can only install voting caps after prior consent of the annual general meeting. This authority can be delegated for a limited amount of time. In addition, the installation of voting caps can only happen under specific conditions e.g. when the company is threatened by a hostile take over. In the only three hostile take-over attempts since WWII, voting caps were used in each case (Franks & Mayer, 2001).

8. With prior consent of the shareholders at an annual meeting, the board of directors can issue new equity, place it with "friendly" shareholders and thus dilute the share stakes of other shareholders.

9. For a theoretical discussion of the free riding problem of dispersed shareholdings. See for example, Shleifer and Vishny (1986), Hart (1995b).

10. Low monitoring resulting from voting rights dispersion might be compensated by increased bank monitoring. In spite of the close connections between banks and industry in Germany, which include ownership states, positions on the supervisory board and proxy votes, several studies show that German banks have provided less finance to industry than in UK banks (Edwards & Fisher, 1994; Edwards & Ogilvie, 1996). Furthermore, Edwards and Nibler (2000) do not find a positive effect of bank ownership of equity on the profitability of German firms.

11. The hostile take-over market in the U.S. has been considered as a disciplinary device to correct managerial failure. Empirical research supports this view for the U.S. (Martin & McConnell, 1991). In contrast, the targets of hostile take-overs in the 1980s were not poorly performing, but mostly average or good performers (e.g. Franks & Mayer, 1996).

12. Pioneered by Coase in the 30s and further developed by e.g. Williamson (1983).

13. See for example: Jensen and Meckling (1976), Milgrom and Roberts (1992).

14. The theory of implicit contracting is well described in by Grossman and Hart (1982, 1986) Hart and Holmstrom (1987), Hart and Moore (1990), Hart (1995a).

15. See, e.g. Alchian and Demsetz (1972).

16. In countries with the common law system, La Porta et al. (1997, 1998) build an index which captures shareholder protection and increases when: shareholders are not required to deposit their shares prior to annual meetings; shareholders can mail proxy votes; cumulative voting is allowed; minority protection legislation is strong; and small shareholders can call extra-ordinary meetings. Regarding creditor protection, this index increases when the rule of absolute priority is followed in case of financial distress. However, Franks et al. (2001) conjecture that even within the Anglo-American countries there are substantial differences in corporate control regulation. Essentially, this would be because the relative cost of control is higher in the U.K. than in the U.S. because of stronger minority protection legislation than in the U.S., where the reliance on courts is higher.

17. Because any two shareholders jointly detain a majority of shares.

18. Because when the main shareholder colludes with any other shareholder, they jointly detain a majority, whereas all three small shareholders should collude in order to counter A1, a clearly more difficult task.

19. Although this example may appear overly simplified, we have been able to identify a number of real-world cases where control over companies behaves as described here.

20. Leaving aside the issue of the possible existence of a blocking minority.

21. Note that one should be careful before drawing definitive conclusions given the potential pitfalls that apply to this type of standard cross-sectional studies of stock returns (see inter alia, Kan & Zhang, 1999; Kim, 1995).

22. Note that the regressions are not suffering from multicollinearity as the correlations between Z-indices and Herfindahl indices, as well as among the control variables is low and not statistically significant.

REFERENCES

Agnblad, J., Berglof, E., Hogfeldt, P., & Svancar, H. (2001). The Swedish model at a crossroads – Family and bank control through dual class shares meets international capital. In: F. Barca &

M. Becht (Eds), *The Control of Corporate Europe* (pp. 228–258). Oxford: Oxford University Press.

Alchian, A., & Demsetz, H. (1972). Production, information costs and economic organization. *American Economic Review, 62*, 777–795.

Banerjee, S., Leleux, B., & Vermaelen, T. (1997). Large shareholdings and corporate control: An analysis of stake purchases by French holding companies. *European Financial Management, 3*, 23–43.

Banzhaf, J. F., III (1965). Weighted voting doesn't work: A mathematical analysis. *Rutgers Law Review, 19*, 317–343.

Banzhaf, J. F., III (1966). Multi-member electoral districts – Do they violate the "One man – One vote's" principle? *Yale Law Journal, 75*, 1309–1338.

Banzhaf, J. F., III (1968). One man – 3,312 votes: A mathematical analysis of the electoral college. *Villanova Law Review, 13*, 304–332.

Barclay, M., & Holderness, C. (1989). Private benefits from control of public corporations. *Journal of Financial Economics, 25*, 371–395.

Bebchuk, L., & Roe, M. (1999). A theory of path dependence in corporate governance and ownership. *Stanford Law Review, 52*, 127–170.

Becht, M. (1999). European corporate governance: Trading off liquidity against control. *European Economic Review, 43*, 1071–1083.

Becht, M., & Boehmer, E. (2001). Ownership and control in Germany. In: F. Barca & M. Becht (Eds), *The Control of Corporate Europe* (pp. 128–153). Oxford: Oxford University Press.

Becht, M., Chapelle, A., & Renneboog, L. (2001). Shareholding cascades: The separation of ownership and control in Belgium. In: F. Barca & M. Becht (Eds), *The Control of Corporate Europe* (pp. 71–105). Oxford: Oxford University Press.

Bianchi, M., Bianco, M., & Enriques, L. (2001). Ownership, pyramidal groups and separation between ownership and control in Italy. In: F. Barca & M. Becht (Eds), *The Control of Corporate Europe* (pp. 154–187). Oxford: Oxford University Press.

Bloch, L., & Kremp, E. (2001). Ownership and voting power. In: F. Barca & M. Becht (Eds), *The Control of Corporate Europe* (pp. 106–127). Oxford: Oxford University Press.

Brennan, M., & Franks, J. (1997).Underpricing, ownership and control in initial public offerings of equity securities in the U.K. *Journal of Financial Economics, 45*, 391–413.

Carlin, W., & Mayer, C. (2001). Finance, investment and growth. Working paper, University of Oxford.

Chen, N., Roll, R., & Ross, S. (1986). Economic forces and the stock market. *Journal of Business, 59*, 386–403.

Chirinko, R. S., & Elston, J. (1996). Banking relationships in Germany: Empirical results and policy implications. In: *Federal Reserve Bank of Chicago, Rethinking Bank Regulation: What Should Regulators Do?* (pp. 239–255). Chicago: Federal Reserve Bank of Chicago.

Crespi, R., & Garcia, M. (2001). Ownership and control: A Spanish survey. In: F. Barca & M. Becht (Eds), *The Control of Corporate Europe* (pp. 207–227). Oxford: Oxford University Press.

Crespi, R., & Renneboog, L. (2001). United we stand: Coalition formation and shareholder monitoring in the U.K. Discussion paper centre, Tilburg University.

Cubbin, J., & Leech, D. (1983). The effect of shareholding dispersion on the degree of control in British companies: Theory and measurement. *The Economic Journal, 93*, 351–369.

De Jong, A., Kabir, R., Mara, T., & Roell, A. (2001). Ownership and control in the Netherlands. In: F. Barca & M. Becht (Eds), *The Control of Corporate Europe* (pp. 188–206). Oxford: Oxford University Press.

Demsetz, H., & Lehn, K. (1985). The structure of corporate ownership: Causes and consequences. *Journal of Political Economy, 93*, 1155–1177.

Dubey, P., & Shapley, L. S. (1979). Mathematical properties of the Banzhaf power index. *Mathematics of Operations Research, 4*, 2–28.

Dyck, A., & Zingales, L. (2001). Private benefits of control, and international comparison. Working paper, University of Chicago.

Edwards, J., & Fisher, K. (1994). *Banks, finance and investment in Germany*. Cambridge: Cambridge University Press.

Edwards, J., & Nibler, M. (2000). Corporate governance in Germany: The role of banks and ownership concentration. *Economic Policy, 31*, 237–260.

Edwards, J., & Ogilvie, S. (1996). Universal banks and German industrialization: A reappraisal. *Economic History Review, 49*, 427–464.

Faccio, M., & Lasfer, M. A. (1999). Managerial ownership, board structure and firm value: The U.K. evidence. Working paper, City University.

Fama, E., & French, K. (1992). The cross-section of expected stock returns. *Journal of Finance, 47*(2), 427–466.

Felsenthal, D., & Machover, M. (1998). *The measurement of voting power*. London: Edward Elgar Publishing Inc.

Franks, J., & Mayer, C. (1996). Hostile takeover and the correction of managerial failure. *Journal of Financial Economics, 40*, 163–181.

Franks, J., & Mayer, C. (2001). Ownership and control of German corporations. *Review of Financial Studies, 14*, 943–977.

Franks, J., Mayer, C., & Renneboog, L. (2001). Who disciplines management in poorly performing companies? *Journal of Financial Intermediation, 10*, 209–248.

Gambarelli, G. (1991). Political and financial applications of the power indices. In: G. Ricci (Ed.), *Decision Processes in Economics* (pp. 84–106). Berlin and Heidelberg: Springer-Verlag.

Goergen, M., & Renneboog, L. (2001). Strong managers and passive institutional investors in the U.K. In: F. Barca & M. Becht (Eds), *The Control of Corporate Europe* (pp. 259–284). Oxford: Oxford University Press.

Goergen, M., & Renneboog, L. (2003). Why are the levels of control (so) different in German and U.K. companies? Evidence from initial public offerings. *Journal of Law, Economics and Organization, 19*(1), 141–175.

Grossman, S., & Hart, O. (1982). Corporate financial structure and managerial incentives. In: J. McCall (Ed.), *The Economics of Information and Uncertainty*. Chicago: University of Chicago Press.

Grossman, S. J., & Hart, O. (1986). The cost and benefits of ownership: A theory of vertical and lateral integration. *Journal of Political Economy, 94*, 691–719.

Gugler, K., Kalss, S., Stomper, A., & Zechner, J. (2001). The separation of ownership and control: An Austrian perspective. In: F. Barca & M. Becht (Eds), *The Control of Corporate Europe*. Oxford: Oxford University Press.

Hart, O. (1995a). Corporate governance: Some theory and implications. *Economic Journal, 105*, 678–689.

Hart, O. (1995b). *Firms, contracts, and financial structure. Clarendon lectures in economics*. Oxford and New York: Clarendon Press.

Hart, O., & Holmstrom, B. (1987). The theory of contracts. In: T. Bewley (Ed.), *Advances in Economic Theory* (pp. 71–155). New York and Melbourne: Cambridge University Press.

Hart, O., & Moore, J. (1990). Property rights and the nature of the firm. *Journal of Political Economy, 98*, 1119–1158.

Jensen, M., & Meckling, W. (1976). Theory of the firm: Managerial behavior, agency costs, and ownership structure. *Journal of Financial Economics, 3*, 305–360.

Johnson, S., La Porta, R., Lopez-de-Silanes, F., & Shleifer, A. (2000). Tunnelling, NBER working paper 7523.

Kan, R., & Zhang, C. (1999). Two-pass tests of asset pricing models with useless factors. *Journal of Finance, 54*, 203–236.

Kim, D. (1995). The errors in variables problem in the cross-section of expected stock returns. *Journal of Finance, 50*, 1605–1634.

La Porta, R., Lopez-de-Silanes, F., Shleifer, A., & Vishny, R. (1997). Legal determinants of external finance. *Journal of Finance, 52*, 1131–1150.

La Porta, R., Lopez-de-Silanes, F., Shleifer, A., & Vishny, R. (1998). Law and finance. *Journal of Political Economy, 106*, 1113–1155.

La Porta, R., Lopez-de-Silanes, F., Shleifer, A., & Vishny, R. (1999). Ownership around the world. *Journal of Finance, 54*, 471–517.

La Porta, R., Lopez-de-Silanes, F., Shleifer, A., & Vishny, R. (2000). Investor protection and corporate governance. *Journal of Financial Economics, 58*, 3–27.

Martin, J., & McConnell, J. (1991). Corporate performance, corporate takeovers and management turnover. *Journal of Finance, 46*, 671–687.

Milgrom, P., & Roberts, J. (1992). Economics, organization and management. *Journal of Finance, 47*(3), 1121–1140.

Muphy, K. (1999). Executive compensation. In: O. Ashenfelter & D. Card (Eds), *Handbook of Labor Economic*. Amsterdam: North-Holland.

Owen, G. (1982). *Game theory*. New York: Academic Press.

Renneboog, L. (2000). Ownership, managerial control and the disciplining of poorly performing companies listed on the Brussels Stock Exchange. *Journal of Banking and Finance, 24*, 1959–1995.

Roe, M. (1994). *Strong managers, weak owners*. The political roots of American corporate finance. New York: Princeton University Press.

Shleifer, A., & Vishny, R. (1986). Large shareholders and corporate control. *Journal of Political Economy, 94*, 461–488.

Stapledon, G. (1996). *Institutional shareholders and corporate governance*. Oxford: Clarendon Press.

Wenger, E., & Kaserer, C. (1997). The German system of corporate governance – a model which should not be imitated. American institute for contemporary German studies, the Johns Hopkins University, WP 14, Washington, DC.

Williamson, O. E. (1983). Organizational form, residual claimants, and corporate control. *Journal of Law and Economics, 26*, 351–380.

Wymeersch, E. (1994). Elements of comparative corporate governance in Western Europe. In: M. Isaksson & R. Skog (Eds), *Aspects of Corporate Governance*. Stockholm: Juristforlaget.

Zwiebel, J. (1995). Block investment and partial benefits of corporate control. *Review of Economic Studies, 62*, 161–185.

THE EFFECTS OF CORPORATE ENVIRONMENTAL PERFORMANCE AND ENVIRONMENTAL CAPITAL INVESTMENT ON STOCK MARKET VALUATION IN TAIWAN

Shu Ling Lin and Soushan Wu

ABSTRACT

This paper investigates the effects of corporate environmental performance and its environmental capital investment on stock market valuation in Taiwan's manufacturing industry during 1991–2000.

The present empirical results suggest those better environmental performance views as the potential environmental asset of corporations. Furthermore, more corporate investment on environmental capital would be lending some credence to the existence of a demand by some green investors. The results support the existence of a premium in the stock valuation of corporations that disclose better environmental performance and higher environmental capital investment. This implies that the disclosure of audited environmental information of a non-financial nature in a corporate annual report could be beneficial to market participants. The current results suggest that corporate with good environmental performance will enhance their stock market valuation.

Social Responsibility: Corporate Governance Issues
Research in International Business and Finance, Volume 17, 151–171
Copyright © 2003 by Elsevier Science Ltd.
All rights of reproduction in any form reserved
ISSN: 0275-5319/PII: S0275531903170079

1. INTRODUCTION

There has been an increasing social awareness among investors with respect to corporate pollution during the past two decades. Concern about the environment has led many individuals or institutional investors to restrict their investments to firms that are perceived to have ethical or sustainable development in their social behavior (Jaggi & Freedman, 1982).

In such a context, Cormier et al. (1993) suggest that there is two mutually reinforcing trends that can influence a firm's stock valuation. First, corporations with a worse environmental performance will generate less free cash flows in the future, since they will be forced to invest in additional anti-pollution equipments. Furthermore, corporations with bad environmental performance will likely face increasingly costly sanctions and penalties imposed by government upon their polluters. That is, corporations with a bad environmental performance thus face a potential liability that should decrease the free cash flows in the future and their stock valuation, and vice versa. Secondly, it is assumed that green investors have influence in the stock market and that they bid up share value of firms with good environmental performance. The green investors' behavior will be reflected in the premium at which a firm's stock is selling, since the demand for their securities is greater.

Compared to the traditional yardsticks used by investors for assessing the value of a company,[1] the World Business Council for Sustainable Development (WBCSD, 1996) proposes an environmental yardstick by using environmental drivers.[2] The WBCSD argues that the new index can evaluate corporate performance effectively. In the same way, the financial community can reduce its risks by integrating environmental considerations into its investment decisions. Owing to that, a financial valuation model can be extended to include environmental drivers. Rappaport (1981) suggests that one might start with an analytical model, shareholders' value pyramid, which is built on three value contributors: sales growth, cost management and capital deployment. Four value drivers, including strategy, operational fitness, stakeholder satisfaction and product, support these in turn. The contention of Rappaport's (1981) study is that, in the well-managed company, environmental performance will be woven into each of the four value drivers. The financial value is represented by the free cash flow. In other words, the total of all future free cash flows defines corporate shareholders' value.

However, the environmental movement in Taiwan is still in its youth and most companies do not yet adopt long-term plans to reduce pollution. On the empirical ground, the effects of corporate environmental performance or environmental capital investment on its stock performance in Taiwan are not clear. The purpose of this study is to investigate the effects of corporation's environmental performance on the stock market valuation, and the relationship between corporate environmental capital investment and stock market valuation in Taiwan during 1991–2000. Good environmental performance behavior is inferred from a new environmental performance index, higher Eco-productivity index (EPI) or lesser traditional yardsticks, in this study. The EPI is computed by the indexed turnover in product values per year over the actual pollutant emission per year. The analysis of this study is based on the perspective of information usefulness proposed by Lev and Ohlson (1982) and the accounting identity model developed by Modegliani and Miller (1958) and Landsman (1986).

Section 2 reviews the literatures and develops hypotheses for this study. Section 3 presents the empirical model and describes the sample. Section 4 presents the empirical results. Finally, the results' implications are concluded in Section 5.

2. LITERATURE REVIEW AND HYPOTHESES DEVELOPMENT

2.1. Literature Review

Several legislative actions have been aimed at abating industrial pollution since 1969 in American, and the U.S. Securities and Exchange Commission (SEC) has been engaged in developing pollution disclosure requirements to ensure adequate disclosure of pollution information. The political, regulatory, social, and economic pressures are expected to encourage management to become more socially responsible and pay greater attention to environmental consequences of corporate activities. Jaggi and Freedman (1992) point out that pollution abatement activities may involve substantial amounts of capital expenditures, which would have an impact on the economic performance of firm. Consequently, there may be a stock market reaction that would influence management decisions relating to pollution abatement activities.

Questionnaire and field studies show that many investors do have green concerns, as shown by their interest in environmental performance information or by their investment objectives. From Longstreth and Rosenbloom's (1973) survey of 115 institutional investors, 57% of respondents base their investment decisions both on economic and environmental information consideration. In the studies of Buzby and Falk (1978) and Rockness and Williams (1988), mutual fund managers are surveyed and a need for social information, especially the environmental performance information, is found. The results from these surveys strongly suggest that there exist a sizeable clientele of investors that actively look, and are thus willing to pay a premium, for green investment. Jaggi and Freedman (1982) call this argument as "the green investor hypotheses".

Empirical confirmation that firms respond to green investors' concerns can be summarized as follows. Chow (1983) and Foster (1986) find that if the investors evaluate information that is positive and beneficial to firms' reputation, corporations would disclose such information in their annual report or press releases. This argument is referred to as *the user utility concept*, proposed by Arnold (1990). Arnold (1990) indicates that social disclosures are influenced by stakeholders' demand for information. If management perceived that stakeholders are demanding disclosure of certain type of social information, it would provide such information to meet the perceived needs. Consequently, the investors' demand for information should alter corporate reporting behavior. On the contrary, Bowman and Haire (1975), Ingram and Frazier (1980), and Zéghal and Ahmed (1990) evaluate the level of social information disclosed in corporate annual reports. Their results indicate that the level of social information disclosure is relatively low among public help corporations and suggest that there is not much demand for social information by investors. However, Cormier et al. (1993) find that environmental performance is a business risk and information about it is required to value a firm. This argument is based on *the political economy concept*, suggested by Guthrie and Parker (1990), who consider social disclosures to be a social, political and economic tool for management. Disclosure of environmental information would be influenced by the management's desire to advance the corporate political or ideological goals, and to mitigate the effects of public pressures for mandated disclosure requirements.

About the effect of environment performance information on the stock market, Belkaoui (1976) evaluates if the disclosure of pollution control expenses is associated with a relative improvement in stock market performance. The results indicate that the disclosure of environmental information, which is computed as pollution control expenses as a percentage of sales, has a positive effect on the security prices. Ingram (1978) studies stock market reactions to social information events using a sample of 287 *Fortune 500* firms. The result shows that the information content of corporate social information events is conditional upon industry- and firm-specific characteristics. Besides, Spicer (1978), Shane and Spicer (1983) evaluate the impact of environmental pollution-based performance on security returns. Spicer (1978) concludes that firms having better pollution control performance tend to have greater profitability, a larger size and higher price/earnings ratio than firms with poorer environmental performance. Shane and Spicer (1983) explore those firms whose bad environmental performance experienced a drop in their stock price during the two-day period before the disclosure. They also observe that firms with positive environmental performance significantly outperformed their competitive counterparts. Furthermore, Anderson and Frankle (1980), Freedman and Jaggi (1982, 1986) study the effect of social data reporting on security returns focusing on the broader social disclosure. Anderson and Frankle (1980) find that the stock price of a sample of *Fortune 500* firms reacted positively to the disclosure of social information in the annual report from 1971 to 1972. On the contrary, Freedman and Jaggi (1982, 1986) indicate that since there is no significant stock market reaction, the social information has no incremental information content.

Maloney and McCormick (1982) derive a positive theory of environmental quality regulation and suggest that negative and strict environmental regulations can actually enhance a producer's wealth, by indirectly limiting competition through raised product price and the profits of its producers. The study shows that after controlling for contemporaneous events (e.g. change in price), firms experienced a significant increase in stock market value for the period around the decision. Hughes et al. (1986) further modifies Maloney and McCormick's argument by considering the differential effects of the new regulation among firms and adopts a longer perspective. They do not find a strong evidence of value enhancement. Cormier et al. (1993) shows that Maloney and McCormick's results are highly sensitive to event window considered or differential firm characteristics. Freedman and Stagliano (1991) find that the stock prices of textile-cotton firms are negatively affected by the stricter standard of U.S. Supreme Court decisions. The negative market reaction suggests that the additional investments required by additional regulation be expected to generate negative cash flows. This result is consistent with Hughes et al. (1986), but contradicts Maloney and McCormick (1982).

The relationship between environmental information and economic performance has provided conflicting results. Bragdon and Marlin (1972) report that there is positive correlation between pollution control and a company stock's performance, which is measured by EPS growth, average return on equity and average return on investment. Spicer (1978) includes some market variables in the analysis, and shows that the most profitable large companies tend to have the best pollution control records, and that these companies, in general, are judged by investors to be less risky in terms of both total and systematic risk. However, Christiansen and Haveman (1981) analyze the contribution of environmental regulations to slow-down in productivity growth by reviewing studies that estimate pollution control costs and their impact on productivity growth. They conclude that environmental regulations could have major adverse output and productivity impacts on certain sectors or industries. They point out that these impacts are localized and do not have a significant impact on macroeconomic performance, and indicate that the pollution performance in certain industries has a negative impact on company stock performance. Furthermore, Belkaoui (1976), Ingram (1978), Anderson and Frankle (1980), Jaggi and Freedman (1982), and Shane and Spicer (1983) examine investors' reaction to pollution disclosures. The results of these studies indicate that disclosure of social information, especially environmental pollution information, triggers investor reaction as reflected in stock price movements.

Overall, the above empirical researches seem to suggest that disclosure of environmental performance information is valuable, since there are indications that green investors consider it in their decision making. The disclosure of social information or the release of other relevant financial information can thus cause any observed market reaction. Moreover, corporations can observe stock market fluctuations around information releasing dates. However, the evaluation of market reactions to social disclosure events relying on the event study methodology is not entirely consistent with the hypothesis. Since only short-term effects are considered, it does not necessarily imply the existence of a long-term premium or discount. Based upon this, Cormier et al. (1993) attempt to use cross-sectional valuation approach to investigate the relationship between the pollution index and a firm's stock valuation. The results show that market participants as providing information about its environmental liabilities interpret a firm's pollution performance. Moreover, their results weakly support the existence of a premium in the stock valuation of firms, and suggest that the disclosure of audited social information of non-financial information in a firm's annual report could be beneficial to market participants.

2.2. Hypotheses Development

This study relies on a cross-sectional pooling valuation approach, which attempts to directly estimate the market premium assigned to corporations with good environmental performance. The sample includes Publicity Corporation in Taiwan's manufacturing industry in the period of 1991–2000. The environmental information is transformed into EPI and actual/standard pollutant emission that is directly comparable across sample firms for relative performance purposes. In addition, this paper proposes a multiple regression valuation approach, by attempting to define corporate stock market value in terms of financial and environmental variables. This allows a direct assessment of environmental information's usefulness for corporate stock market valuation purposes. The following alternative hypothesis is developed.

The first hypothesis takes directly into consideration the current environmental potential assets that may result from positive environmental performance, and vice versa.

Hypotheses 1. There exists a relationship between a corporation's environmental performance and its stock valuation, which is inferred from the current potential assets by market participants. That is, there exists a positive relationship between EPI and stock valuation of the sample corporations. Conversely, There exists a negative relationship between traditional yardsticks (actual pollutant emission/Standard pollutant emission) and stock valuation of the sample corporations.

Within the framework of the green investor hypotheses, the study proposes the following hypothesis:

Hypotheses 2. There exists a relationship between the common shares of corporations with a positive environmental performance (higher EPI or lesser traditional yardsticks) sell at a premium compared with counterparts, and vice versa.

Finally, to explore the relationship between corporate stock market valuation and its environmental capital investment, the following hypothesis is proposed.

Hypotheses 3. There exists a positive relationship between corporation's corporate stock market valuation and its environmental capital investment.

Acceptance of the above alternative hypotheses would support the argument that there exists a relationship between environmental performance, environmental capital investment and corporate stock market valuation. The sign of coefficient will indicate whether the relationship is positive or negative.

The next section discusses the empirical model and sample selection.

3. EMPIRICAL MODEL

3.1. Measure of Environmental Performance

Environmental pollution information about the sample corporation is collected by the annual report of *Taiwan Economic Journal (TEJ)* over the 1991–2000 period. For each corporation, sample measures of various sources of industrial pollution record are disclosed by the report of Business Council of Sustainable Development (BCSD) in Taiwan. For example, suspended solids, average concentration of sulphurous anhydride, biochemical oxygen demand (BOD), chemical oxygen demand (COD), etc. Consumption of energy and resources for each product is also disclosed. Combining these environmental pollution records would assume additive or multiple properties that are not evident.

To obtain a single measure of a firm's environmental pollution record, the WBCSD (1996) proposes an Eco-productivity index (EPI). It relates the scale of its production as an indexed turnover to the consumption of each of its major environmental indicators: water, energy and raw material consumption. The EPI is an indicator of the company's success in producing more per unit of input. A rise in the EPI demonstrates that it has succeeded in using a particular resource more efficiently. The results in resource savings yield both environmental and financial benefits. According to the definition of WBCSD (1996), the EPI indexed turnover equals to "*the product or service value per environmental influence* over *the resource consumption*".

In order to conduct empirical analysis and inter-firm comparison, this study proposes the following model for EPI and traditional index as follows, separately.

$$\text{EPI} = \left(\frac{\text{Product Value per Year}}{\text{Pollutant Emission per Year}} \right) \times 100 \tag{1}$$

$$\text{Traditional yardsticks} = \left(\frac{\text{Actual pollutant emission per Year}}{\begin{array}{c}\text{Standard pollutant emission}\\\text{announced by EPA per Year}\end{array}} \right) \times 100 \tag{2}$$

3.2. Measure of Stock Market Valuation

The study's cross-sectional polling design relies upon the accounting identity equation, which is derived and rearranged by Modegliani and Miller (1958, 1966), and Landsman (1986). For any given firm:

$$\text{Market Value (MV) of Equities} = \text{MV (Assets)} - \text{MV (Liabilities)} \tag{3}$$

Since the market value of total assets and of its components are not directly observable, Landsman (1986) suggests that the market value of net monetary working capital, inventories and fixed assets can be a priori assumed to be close to their respective book value. Concerning intangible assets, it is likely that the book value figure is not representative of current market conditions and does not reflect the firm's growth potential. Zarowin (1990) indicates that the price-earnings ratio captures the firm's growth potential and therefore reflects the value of its intangible assets. Consequently, the price-earnings ratio is used as a proxy for the market value of intangible assets in this study. Cormier et al. (1993) propose that all debts and preferred stock instruments are monetary items, because of their thin trading, whose market value are not available and also highly unreliable, hence the market value eventually converges to their book value. Besides, this study does not try to explain the relationship between market value of debt and interest rates, so the fluctuation in market interest rates to affect the book value of long-term debt is not concerned in this study. Based on these facts, book value is used in this study to proxy for the market value of all debts and preferred stock securities.

By transforming Eq. (3) from a theoretical model into an empirical model and incorporating a firm's relative environmental performance index, that is the EPI as a potential asset into the accounting identity, the following regression model is shown as following:[3]

$$MV(Equities)_{i,t} = \alpha_0 + \alpha_1 BV(NWC)_{i,t} + \alpha_2 BV(FA)_{i,t} + \alpha_3 (P/E)_{i,t}$$
$$+ \alpha_4 (EP)_{i,t} + \alpha_5 BV(LT-Debts)_{i,t} + \varepsilon_{i,t} \qquad (4)$$

where $NWC_{i,t}$: the *net monetary working capital* of the ith firm at time t; $FA_{i,t}$: the *fixed assets* of the ith firm at time t; $(P/E)_{i,t}$: the *price/earnings ratio* of the ith firm at time t; $EP_{i,t}$: the *eco-productivity index (EPI) and traditional yardsticks* (*actual pollutant emission/standard pollutant emission*) of the ith firm at time t; $Debts_{i,t}$: the *long-term debts* of the ith firm at time t; $\varepsilon_{i,t}$: the residual error term of the ith firm at time t; t: 1, 2, and 3 represent the years of 1991–2000.

Based on the above analysis, the predicted signs of regression coefficients in Eq. (4) of net monetary working capital, fixed assets, the *P/E* ratio, and EPI are "+", while the debts is "−".

However, Eq. (4) does not explicitly indicate the magnitude (in NT\$) of the potential asset faced by firms because of their environmental pollution behavior. In other words, Eq. (4) does not directly indicate if a firm is selling at a premium or discount because of its good or bad environmental performance, as would predict the green investor hypotheses by Hypothesis 2. Consequently, Beaver et al. (1989) suggest that deflating all the financial variables in Eq. (5) by the book value of stockholders' equity would provide such evidence and would also control the econometric problems caused by within-sample differences in firm size. The dependent variable then becomes the premium (discount) paid over book value by investors for a firm's common stock and allows for direct testing of Hypothesis 2. The new multiple regression equation with equity deflator shows as follows:

This equation evaluates the usefulness of environmental performance information, which implies that market's assessment of the positive environmental performance as a potential asset.

In order to investigate the relationship between environmental capital investment and corporate stock market valuation, this study proposes the following empirical model:

$$\frac{\text{MV(Equities)}_{i,t}}{\text{BV(Equities)}_{i,t}} = \beta_0 + \beta_1 \left(\frac{\text{BV(NWC)}_{i,t}}{\text{BV(Equities)}_{i,t}} \right) + \beta_2 \left(\frac{\text{BV(FA)}_{i,t}}{\text{BV(Equities)}_{i,t}} \right)$$

$$+ \beta_3 (P/E)_{i,t} + \beta_4 (\text{EP})_{i,t} + \beta_5 \left(\frac{\text{BV(LT-Debts)}_{i,t}}{\text{BV(Equities)}_{i,t}} \right) + \theta_{i,t}$$

(5)

$$\text{MV(Equities)}_{i,t} = \gamma_0 + \gamma_1 \text{Time} + \gamma_2 \text{BV(ECI)}_{i,t} + \gamma_3 (\text{Size})_{i,t}$$

$$+ \gamma_4 (\text{Beta})_{i,t} + \zeta_{i,t}$$

(6)

where $\text{ECI}_{i,t}$: the *environmental capital investment* of the ith firm at time t; $\text{Size}_{i,t}$: the corporate size, which is calculated by *log (Total Assets) and used as a controlled variable*; $\text{Beta}_{i,t}$: the risk evaluation of the ith firm at time t and used as a controlled variable.

Finally, in order to further explore the effects of different environmental performance, this study considers penalty fees as controlled variable for the sample corporations.

$$\text{MV(Equities)}_{i,t} = \gamma_0 + \gamma_1 \text{Time} + \gamma_2 \text{BV(ECI)}_{i,t} + \gamma_3 (\text{Penalty})_{i,t}$$

$$+ \gamma_4 (\text{Size}) + \gamma_5 (\text{Beta})_{i,t} + \omega_{i,t}$$

(7)

where $\text{Penalty}_{i,t}$: the *penalty fees* of the ith firm at time t, used as a controlled variable.

3.3. Sample and Data Collection

Since the EPI and traditional yardsticks are used as proxy for the corporate environmental performance record, only firms whose environmental discharges and emission information are disclosed in the BCSD reports in Taiwan are included in the sample. The sample includes 30 publicity corporations during 1991–2000 in Taiwan's manufacturing industry. All data are extracted from the sample firms' year-end financial statements, except for the market value of equity and beta, which are the number of common shares outstanding at year-end times the common stock price at year-end from *Taiwan Economic Journal (TEJ)*. Besides, the EPI of this study is measured by the *product value* of the sample firms over its *COD (BOD) dispersion in water or NO_x (SO_x) emission in air*.

3.4. Statistical Method

In addition to an ordinary least-squares regression, a robust estimation by Yule-Walker estimates for error term autocorrelations is used to control the potential problems caused by outliers. Furthermore, the weighted least square (WLS) regression for heteroscedasticity variance of the error term is also performed to test Hypotheses 1–3, respectively. The following reports the current empirical results.

4. EMPIRICAL RESULTS

4.1. Market Valuation Regression (With No Deflator) – Hypothesis 1

The descriptive statistics of the entire group of samples indicate that the standard deviation of *MV* (*Equities*) and *Fixed Assets* are large. This shows that the change of sample corporation stock market value and its size between 1991 and 2000 periods is tremendous. Besides, the results of descriptive statistics show that all variables have the correct sign. This indicates that the control variable in the model is appropriate (Table 1).

Table 1. Descriptive Statistics of Full Samples for Stock Market Valuation Model.

Variable	N	Mean	Std Dev	Sum	Minimum	Maximum
With No Equity Deflator (1991–2000)						
MV (Equities)	39	73946186	1.1527E8	2.8839E9	4342396	6.782E8
Year	39	6.6923	2.2729	261.0	1.0000	10.0000
BV (WC)	39	4391260	7594443	1.7126E8	−5541200	24302000
BV (FA)	39	19653845	19694884	7.665E8	4059380	89566000
P/E Ratio	39	16.9264	22.6469	660.1	−80.3600	64.8400
EPI	39	67004.6	205162	2613178	4.5500	945795
BV (LT-DEBT)	39	9657278	9730769	3.7663E8	268453	43676593
WPI	33	6502168	9325857	2.1457E8	1179.0	35000000
With Equity Deflator (1991–2000)						
MV (E)	39	1.774949	1.015013	69.223000	0.445000	5.626000
Year	39	6.692308	2.272882	261.000000	1.000000	10.000000
BV (WC)	39	0.096641	0.261575	3.769000	−0.619000	0.735000
BV (FA)	39	0.659462	0.349692	25.719000	0.111000	1.471000
P/E Ratio	39	16.926410	22.646910	660.130000	−80.360000	4.840000
BV (D)	39	0.328256	0.242891	12.802000	0.013000	1.095000

Table 2. The Effects of EPI on Stock Market Valuation & Market to Book
Premium – Weighted Least Square (1991–2000).

Independent Variable	No Equity Deflator	With Equity Deflator
Intercept	-51210067	1.8950
	$(0.0069)^{***}$	$(0.0002)^{***}$
Time	5189711	-0.0036
	$(0.0313)^{**}$	(0.9375)
BV (Net working capital)	2.3196	-0.6595
	$(0.0806)^{*}$	(0.2569)
BV (Fixed assets)	4.2393	-1.0012
	$(0.0001)^{***}$	$(0.0464)^{**}$
Price/Earnings ratio	2132697	0.0275
	$(0.0022)^{***}$	$(0.0115)^{**}$
Eco-productivity index (EPI)[a]	177.9018	0.000002321
	$(0.0009)^{***}$	$(0.0001)^{***}$
BV (Long-term debts)	-6.0612	-0.2734
	$(0.0005)^{***}$	(0.7552)
Number of observations	39	39
Adjusted R-square	82.69%	91.32%
F statistics	27.615	59.644
p-value	$(0.0001)^{***}$	$(0.0001)^{***}$
Durbin-Watson value (H_0: $\rho_a = 0$)	2.0728	1.9253

Dependent variable: Stock market valuation of equities in NT$000 (No equity deflator) & Market-to-Book Premium (Market Value/Book Value) in NT$000 (With equity deflator), separately.
Parenthesis shows the *p*-value. Since the terms of *book value of preferred stock* and *ages of fixed assets* are not significant in the first regression, these variables have been dropped from the analysis.
[a] The EPI is calculated by productive value per year/actual pollutant emission per year for the sample corporation in its publicly annual reports.
* Significant at 10% level.
** Significant at 5% level.
*** Significant at 1% level.

Tables 2 and 3 show the results of the weighted least square regression from Eq. (4) for EPI and traditional yardsticks, separately. An analysis of the correlation matrix and collinearity diagnostics show that the maximum value of variance inflation factors (VIF) is below 10, the minimum value of tolerance is above 0.1, the minimum value of Eigenvalue is above 0.01, and the maximum value of Condition Index is below 30. These results do not suggest the presence of any multicollinearity problems. Besides, Durbin-Watson tests also do not indicate any obvious autocorrelation problems either. The results are quite robust with an adjusted *R*-square of 82.69 and 99.12% for the results of EPI and traditional yardsticks, separately. Besides, the Fisher-Snedecor statistics of 27.615 and

Table 3. The Effects of Traditional Yardsticks (Actual Pollutant Emission/Standard Pollutant Emission) on Stock Market Valuation & Market to Book Premium – Weighted Least Square (1991–2000).

Independent Variable	No Equity Deflator	With Equity Deflator
Intercept	29849877	1.8283
	$(0.0703)^*$	$(0.0001)^{***}$
Time	−9207321	0.0477
	$(0.0001)^{***}$	(0.2488)
BV (Net working capital)	−0.1373	−0.1482
	(0.8898)	$(0.0275)^{**}$
BV (Fixed assets)	8.4790	−1.6849
	$(0.0002)^{***}$	$(0.0009)^{***}$
Price/Earnings ratio	−173043	0.0163
	(0.3615)	(0.1132)
Actual emission/Standard emission[a]	−321.2223	5.0762E-8
	$(0.0326)^{**}$	$(0.0007)^{***}$
BV (Long-term debts)	0.0683	0.2696
	(0.9503)	(0.7307)
Number of observations	33	33
Adjusted R-square	99.12%	91.71%
F statistics	533.699	53.179
p-value	$(0.0001)^{***}$	$(0.0001)^{***}$
Durbin-Watson value (H_0: $\rho_a = 0$)	1.949	1.9339

Dependent variable: Stock market valuation of equities in NT$000 (No equity deflator) & Market-to-Book Premium (Market Value/Book Value) in NT$000 (With equity deflator), separately.
Parenthesis shows the *p*-value. Since the terms of *book value of preferred stock* and *ages of fixed assets* are not significant in the first regression, these variables have been dropped from the analysis.
[a] Data of standard emission announced by the Environmental Protection Agency (EPA) in Taiwan.
* Significant at 10% level.
** Significant at 5% level.
*** Significant at 1% level.

533.699 those are significant at the 1% level. All coefficients have the predicted signs. The control variables, the *year* is positive significantly in Table 2, but negative and statistically significant in Table 3.

The coefficients for *net working capital* and *fixed assets* are significantly positive at the 10 and 1% level with value that are significantly different from 1.0. The value of these coefficients indicate that assets' book value do not closely approximate their market value. It shows that accounting-based book value seemingly cannot be inferred to be impounded in a firm's market valuation, which obviously is not consistent with the results obtained in the study of Harris and Ohlson (1990). The coefficient for *long-term debts* is significantly negative and closes to −6.

The slight discount can be explained by market interest rates being higher than nominal interest rates for many companies in the period 1991–2000. The coefficient for *long-term debts* is negative at −6.0612 in Table 2. This would suggest that the lower the financial leverage of a firm, the greater the valuation granted to its common shares. This result is consistent with the argument of Myers (1977), who argues that firms with more assets on the balance sheet have greater ratios of financial leverage than firms having most growing opportunities not yet reflected on the balance sheet.

The coefficient for the *price/earnings ratio* is positive significantly in Table 2, but negative insignificantly in Table 3. This can be inferred to the sample that includes mostly traditional resource-based corporations, many of which are in their mature stage of life cycle that means the growth is very limited. The *EPI* coefficient is positive and statistically significant at 1% level at 177.9018 in Table 2. This indicates that the greater level of *EPI* environmental performance produced by a firm, the higher its stock market valuation. On the side of traditional yardsticks, the *actual/standard pollutant emission* coefficient is negative and statistically significant at 5% level at −321.2223 in Table 3. This indicates that the greater level of *actual/standard pollutant emission* environmental performance produced by a firm, the lesser of its stock market valuation.

Thus, from the market valuation regression, the results indicate that market participants who provide information about its potential environmental assets enhance the corporate environmental performance. Moreover, the result does seem to be robust while considering that other regression coefficients have reasonable value that is consistent with economic reality.

Overall, the empirical evidence is thus supportive of Hypothesis 1.

4.2. Premium to Book Value Regression (With Equity Deflator) – Hypothesis 2

The results of a weighted least square regression with all financial variables being deflated by the book value of stockholders equity is shown in Tables 2 and 3.

Diagnostic tests do not suggest the presence of obvious multicollinearity and auto-correlation problems. The results are quit robust with an adjusted R-square of 91.32 and 91.71% for *EPI* and *traditional yardsticks*, separately. The Fisher-Snedecor statistics of 59.644 and 53.179 are significant at the 1% level. All coefficients have the predicted signs expect for *net working capital* and *fixed asset*. Since *the age of fixed assets* and *BV (Preferred Stock)* are not significant in the above market valuation regression, these controlled variables are dropped.

The coefficients for *net working capital* and *fixed assets* are significantly negative at the 5 and 1% level in Table 3, respectively. The two coefficients are significantly

Table 4. Descriptive Statistics of Full Samples (The Relationship between Corporate Environmental Capital Investment and Stock Market Value (1991–2000)).

Variable	N	Mean	Std Dev	Sum	Minimum	Maximum
MV (Equities)	300	17008493567	34962976555	5.1025481E12	0	209965100000
Year	300	5.500000	2.877080	1650.000000	1.000	10.000000
Penalty	300	417570	1069750	125270907	0	9900000
ECI	300	152270033	1254574339	45681009760	0	20673373000
Size	300	6.969126	0.524294	2090.737905	5.828	8.320109
Beta	300	0.812989	0.546826	243.896800	−2.514	2.848900

different from 1.0. It is expected that the *net working capital* and *fixed assets* should negatively contribute to any stock premium. A large share of these assets must imply potential depreciation of the firm's stock. It may explain a significant share of its market-to-book premium. The coefficient for *year* is not significantly different from zero and thus does not contribute to any stock premium.

The coefficient for the *P/E ratio* is positive and statistically significant in Table 2. It shows that a unit increase in *P/E ratio* leading to a 0.0275 increase in the market premium. The result is consistent with the evidence obtained from the market valuation regression. Finally, The coefficient of *EPI* is positive and statistically significant at the 1% level. This indicates that the green market participants do bid up the stock prices of firms with good environmental performance.

Overall, the empirical evidence is supportive of Hypothesis 2 about the influence of green investors. This implies that environmental performance seems to affect a firm's market valuation and its market-to-book premium, which implicitly confirms that environmental performance, has a multi-dimensional impact on firms' stock prices through the green market participants (Table 4).

4.3. Relationship between Stock Market Valuation and Environmental Capital Investment – Hypothesis 3

Table 5 shows the results of weighted least square estimations for full sample corporations, as indicated in Eqs (5) and (6).

After correction by Yule-Walker estimation and weighted least square estimation, diagnostic tests do not suggest the presence of obvious multicollinearity, autocorrelation or heteroscedasticity. These results are quite robust with an adjusted *R*-square close to 61.16% and a Fisher-Snedecor statistics that are all significant at the 1% level. All coefficients have the predicted signs. Since the control variable,

Table 5. The Relationship between Corporate Stock Market Valuation and Environmental Capital Investment *For Full Sample* – Weighted Least Square Estimation (1991–2000).

Independent Variable	No Controlled Variable	With Controlled Variable[a]
Intercept	−2.6886	−2.4940
	(0.0001)***	(0.0001)***
Time	−44823109	−476070504
	(0.3555)	(0.3063)
Environmental capital investment	6.2842	6.1439
	(0.0001)***	(0.0001)***
Penalty fees		6433.7406
		(0.0001)***
Corporate size	41310279169	38158960272
	(0.0001)***	(0.0001)***
Beta	−633858071	−657173844
	(0.7973)	(0.7973)
Number of observations	300	300
Adjusted *R*-square	61.16%	64.29%
F statistics	95.498	91.016
P-value	(0.0001)***	(0.0001)***
Durbin-Watson value (H_0: $\rho_a = 0$)	2.0056	2.0140

Dependent variable: Stock market valuation of equities in NT$000.
Parenthesis shows the *p*-value.
[a] This study uses penalty fees, size, and beta as controlled variables.
*** Significant at 1% level.

the *penalty fees and size*, are significant in Eqs (5) and (6) at 1% level, it implies that *environmental capital investment* (*ECI*) has a positive impact on corporate stock market valuation through these controlled factors. The coefficient of *ECI* of the current year is shown as 6.2842 and statistically significant at the 1% level. This indicates that the information content of more investment on environmental capital would be a positive impact on corporate stock market valuation. This implies that market participants expected the firm that poses higher environmental capital investment; its environmental performance would be better than its counterpart. Then, the stock price would be bidded up.

Furthermore, the full sample corporations are subdivided into two groups, that is, the water pollutant emission and the air pollutant emission in Tables 6 and 7 . The empirical results are the same as Table 5. The coefficient of *ECI* of the current year is shown as 40.3272 for industry in water emission and 3.2695 for industry in air emission, separately. They are both statistically significant at the 1% level.

Table 6. The Relationship between Corporate Stock Market Valuation and Environmental Capital Investment *For Industry Subdivided in Water Emission*[a] – Weighted Least Square Estimation (1991–2000).

Independent Variable	No Controlled Variable	With Controlled Variable[b]
Intercept	−1.7118	−1.7095
	$(0.0001)^{***}$	$(0.0001)^{***}$
Time	−60450267	−63648533
	(0.8704)	(0.8638)
Environmental capital investment	40.7233	40.3272
	$(0.0001)^{***}$	$(0.0001)^{***}$
Penalty fees		521.4699
		(0.6175)
Corporate size	26173586072	26122812677
	$(0.0001)^{***}$	$(0.0001)^{***}$
Beta	1958271647	1894754037
	(0.3201)	(0.3378)
Number of observations	250	250
Adjusted *R*-square	67.60%	67.50%
F statistics	105.331	87.549
p-value	$(0.0001)^{***}$	$(0.0001)^{***}$
Durbin-Watson value ($H_0: \rho_a = 0$)	1.9946	1.9943

Dependent variable: Stock market valuation of equities in NT$000.
Parenthesis shows the *p*-value.
[a] The subdivision criteria of emission in water and air industry are based on the ETDC (Eastern Technology Development Center) in Taiwan, 2001. The emission in water includes the Food, Textile, Electronic, Chemical, Glass, Car, Rubber, Plastic, and Electrical industry.
[b] This study uses penalty fees, size, and beta as controlled variables.
*** Significant at 1% level.

This indicates that the information content of more investment on environmental capital would be a positive impact on corporate stock market valuation.

Thus, the empirical evidence is supportive of Hypothesis 3.

The current results confirm that environmental capital investment seems to affect corporate stock market valuation through their environmental performance, which is consistent with the argument of the shareholders' value pyramid theory, suggested by Rappaport (1981). That is, the more investment on environmental capital, the better the environmental performance that represents the financial value of a proactive investment strategy. Therefore, more future free cash flows lead to higher corporate stock market valuation. This implies that the disclosure of audited corporate environmental performance in corporate annual report could be beneficial to investors and market participants.

Table 7.   The Relationship between Corporate Stock Market Valuation and
Environmental Capital Investment *For Industry Subdivided in Air
Emission*[a] – Weighted Least Square Estimation (1991–2000).

Independent Variable	No Controlled Variable	With Controlled Variable[b]
Intercept	$-4.4172E+11$	-2.7490
	$(0.0001)^{***}$	$(0.0001)^{***}$
Time	-3315388643	-2881586909
	$(0.0673)^{*}$	$(0.0539)^{*}$
Environmental capital investment	2.0141	3.2695
	(0.2835)	$(0.0402)^{**}$
Penalty fees		18761
		$(0.0001)^{***}$
Corporate size	68803817002	43143603311
	$(0.0001)^{***}$	$(0.0001)^{***}$
Beta	-1474621663	5451797097
	(0.8553)	(0.4243)
Number of observations	50	50
Adjusted R-square	73.38%	82.05%
F statistics	28.561	39.088
p-value	$(0.0001)^{***}$	$(0.0001)^{***}$
Durbin-Watson value (H_0: $\rho_a = 0$)	2.3241	2.1766

Dependent variable: Stock market valuation of equities in NT$000.
Parenthesis shows the p-value.
[a] The subdivision criteria of emission in water and air industry are based on the ETDC (Eastern Technology Development Center) in Taiwan, 2001. The emission in air includes the Metal, and Electronic Machinery industry.
[b] This study uses penalty fees, size, and beta as controlled variables.
* Significant at 10% level.
** Significant at 5% level.
*** Significant at 1% level.

5. CONCLUSION

This study investigates the impact of corporate environmental performance disclosed on its stock market valuation, based on an information usefulness perspective, accounting identity framework and shareholders' value pyramid theory. The empirical results imply that corporate environmental performance positively affect its stock market valuation, which is supported by the green investor hypotheses. In addition, it suggests that investors perceive those firms who possess good environmental performance may get a better financial share in the future. If the demand for better environmental performance firm's securities is greater, the market participants bid up share value, which is reflected in the premium of a firm's stock. Finally, the result confirms that corporate environmental capital investment seems to affect its stock market valuation through their environmental performance, and suggests that corporate with more environmental capital investment would enhance their stock market valuation. The empirical evidence is consistent with the shareholders' value pyramid theory proposed by Rappaport (1981).

Based on these results, it concludes that mandated disclosure requirement is needed for truthful representation of environmental performance, and that strict enforcement of SEC's disclosure requirements in Taiwan would be desirable. The requirement of periodical quantitative information about environmental performance could be useful and beneficial to market participants.

In the future, it would be interesting to perform a time-series analysis to study the effect of within-firm's movement in environmental performance on shareholders' wealth.

NOTES

1. The traditional yardsticks used by investors for assessing the environmental performance of a company is the actual pollutant emission/standard pollutant emission announced by the Environmental Protection Agency (EPA) in Taiwan.

2. The environmental driver proposed by WBCSD (1996) includes the environmental performance into the strategy and vision of corporate operational fitness and manufacturing process. Those value drivers then contribute cost deduction and promote sales growth. Finally, the share price of a firm would be enhanced. (Rappaport, 1981), "Selecting strategies that create shareholders' value", *Harvard Business Review* (May–June), 139–149.

3. Since the term of BV (Inventory) is highly correlation with other explanatory variables, BV (Inventory) has been dropped in Eq. (4). Besides, the terms of BV (Preferred Stock) and Ages of Fixed Assets are not significant in initial regression analysis, so these two variables have been dropped too.

ACKNOWLEDGMENTS

The author acknowledges the help of data summarized from the students of Fu-Jen Catholic University; they are Yi-Chia Su, Ya Tzu Lin, Wei Jen Pi, Chung Yuan Yueh, Hsin Yi Ai, and Ya Huei Wang.

REFERENCES

Anderson, J. G., & Frankle, A. W. (1980). Voluntary social reporting: An iso-beta portfolio analysis. *Accounting Review* (July), 467–479.

Arnold, P. (1990). The state and political theory in corporate disclosure research: A response to Guthrie and Parker. *Advances in Public Interest Accounting, 3*, 177–182.

BCSD (1999). *Road map to sustainability: Environmental milestones of BCSD member companies.* Taiwan.

Beaver, W., Eger, C., Ryan, S., & Wolfson, M. (1989). Financial reporting, supplemental disclosures, and bank share prices. *Journal of Accounting Research* (Autumn), 157–178.

Belkaoui, A. (1976). The impact of the disclosures of the environmental effects of organizational behavior on the market. *Financial Management* (Winter), 26–31.

Bowman, E. H., & Haire, M. (1975). A strategic posture toward corporate social responsibility. *California Management Review* (Winter), 49–58.

Bragdon, H. H., & Marlin, J. (1972). Is pollution profitable? *Risk Management* (April), 9–18.

Buzby, S., & Falk, H. (1978). A survey of the interest in social responsibility information by mutual funds. *Accounting, Organization and Society* (March), 191–201.

Chow, C. W. (1983). The impacts of accounting regulations on bondholder and shareholders' wealth, the case of the securities act. *Accounting Review* (July), 485–520.

Christiansen, G., & Haveman, R. (1981). The contribution of environmental regulations to the slowdown in productivity growth. *Journal of Environmental Economics and Management, 8*, 381–390.

Cormier, C., Magnan, M., & Morard, B. (1993). The impact of corporate pollution on market valuation: Some empirical evidence. *Ecological Economics, 8*, 135–155.

Foster, G. (1986). *Financial statement analysis.* Englewood Cliffs, NJ: Prentice-Hall International.

Freedman, M., & Jaggi, B. (1982). Pollution disclosures, pollution performance and economic performance. *Omega, 10*, 167–176.

Freedman, M., & Jaggi, B. (1986). An analysis of the impact of corporate pollution disclosures included in annual financial statements on investors. *Advances in Public Interest Accounting, 1*, 193–212.

Freedman, M., & Stagliano, A. J. (1991). Differences in social-cost disclosures: A market test of investor reactions. *Accounting, Auditing and Accountability Journal, 4*(1), 68–82.

Guthrie, J., & Parker, L. D. (1990). Corporate social disclosure practice: A comparative international analysis. *Advances in Public Interest Accounting, 3*, 343–352.

Harris, T., & Ohlson, J. A. (1990). Accounting disclosures and the market's valuation of oil and gas properties: Evaluation of market efficiency and functional fixation. *Accounting Review* (October), 764–780.

Hughes, J. S., Mogat, W. A., & Ricks, W. E. (1986). The economic consequences of the OSHA cotton dust standards: An analysis of stock price behavior. *Journal of Law and Economics* (April), 29–59.

Ingram, R. W. (1978). An investigation of the information content of certain social responsibility disclosures. *Journal of Accounting Research* (Fall), 270–285.

Ingram, R., & Frazier, K. (1980). Environmental performance and corporate disclosure. *Journal of Accounting Research* (Autumn), 614–622.

Jaggi, B., & Freedman, M. (1982). An analysis of the information content of pollution disclosures. *Financial Review* (September), 142–152.

Jaggi, B., & Freedman, M. (1992). An examination of the impact of pollution performance on economic and market performance: Pulp and paper firms. *Journal of Business Finance & Accounting, 19*(September), 697–713.

Landsman, W. (1986). An empirical investigation of pension and property rights. *Accounting Review* (October), 662–691.

Lev, B., & Ohlson, J. A. (1982). Market-based empirical research in accounting: A review, interpretation and extension. *Journal of Accounting Research* (Supplement), 249–322.

Longstreth, B., & Rosenbloom, D. (1973). *Corporate social responsibility and the institutional investor.* Praeger.

Maloney, M. T., & McCormick, R. E. (1982). A positive theory of environmental quality regulation. *Journal of Law and Economics* (April), 99–123.

Modegliani, F., & Miller, M. (1958). The cost of capital, corporation finance and the theory of investment. *American Economic Review* (June), 261–297.

Modegliani, F., & Miller, M. (1966). Some estimates of the cost of capital to the electric utility industry, 1954–1957. *American Economic Review* (June), 333–391.

Myers, S. C. (1977). Determinants of corporate borrowing. *Journal of Financial Economics* (November), 147–175.

Rappaport, A. (1981). Selecting strategies that create shareholders' value. *Harvard Business Review* (May–June), 139–149.

Rockness, J. W., & Williams, P. F. (1988). A descriptive study of social responsibility mutual funds. *Accounting, Organizations and Society, 13,* 397–411.

Shane, P., & Spicer, B. (1983). Market response to environmental information produced outside the firm. *Accounting Review* (July), 521–538.

Spicer, B. (1978). Investors, corporate social performance and information disclosure: An empirical study. *Accounting Review* (January), 94–111.

WBCSD (1996). *Environmental performance and shareholder value.* Switzerland.

Zarowin, P. (1990) What determines earnings-price ratios: Revisited. *Journal of Accounting, Auditing and Finance* (Summer), 439–454.

Zéghal, D., & Ahmed, S. A. (1990). Comparison of social responsibility information disclosure media used by Canadian firms. *Accounting, Auditing and Accountability, 3,* 38–53.

VALUATION AND REPORTING OF NATIVE FAUNA IN MONETARY TERMS: COMPATIBILITY BETWEEN A MARKET-BASED SYSTEM AND NATURAL RESOURCES?

Allan Purnell, Jean Raar and Phillip Hone

ABSTRACT

A change in community values and priorities has introduced ethical, environmental and social issues into the way in which business conducts its activities. There are an increasing number of managed investment funds focusing on socially responsible investment (SRI) by concentrating on firms that operate according to predetermined criteria for environmental, social and ethical issues. For investors in these funds environmental stewardship issues are integrated with concern over financial resources and performance. In this paper the accounting and reporting by business activities concerned with conservation of wildlife are examined.

The world of accounting has functioned for many years with relatively few accounting standards devoted to specialised industry needs. In 1998 the Australian Accounting Standards Board and in 2001 the International Accounting Standards Board issued standards devoted to agriculture. Both standards deal with the reporting of managed biological assets and require

Social Responsibility: Corporate Governance Issues
Research in International Business and Finance, Volume 17, 173–198
ISSN: 0275-5319/PII: S0275531903170080

application of essentially the same approaches despite the Australian standard requiring net market value while the International standard requires fair value.

In this paper we analyse how one conservation firm Earth Sanctuaries Ltd. (ESL) has applied AASB 1037 and then we explore the implications for conservation firms operating in geographical locations outside Australia. It is suggested that AASB 1037 and indeed IAS 41 may not provide value appropriate information for investor decisions relating to accounting profits for such firms. Our examination shows that it is appropriate to reconsider accounting guidelines provided by these standards in order to link the information relating to economic and environmental performance. Transparency may be improved by a move closer to Elkington's (1997) triple bottom line reporting. We therefore contend that the issues arising from the use of AASB 1037 and IAS 41 need to be widely considered by all standard setters, particularly given the increasing attention to SRI.

1. INTRODUCTION

Socially Responsible Investing (SRI) can be defined as the integration of an individual's investment objectives with his/her commitment to social concerns such as social justice, economic development, peace or a health environment (U.K. Social Investment Forum).[1] Screening practices for SRI adopt positive or negative categories to include or exclude publicly traded securities from the investment portfolios of individual managed funds. Conservation and agriculture fit into the category of positive screening when selecting the shares of firms that are viewed as making a positive societal contribution (Allen Consulting Group, 2000). Based on its conservation platform, Earth Sanctuaries Ltd. (ESL), a public listed firm would fall into the positive screening category.

> The truth is, environmental problems do not automatically create opportunities to make money. At the same time, the opposite stance – that it never pays for a company to invest in improving its environmental performance – is also incorrect (Reinhardt, 1999, p. 150).

The community views heritage and conservation activities as a "public good" that are usually managed by government bodies (Barton, 2000). Australian wildlife is controlled by legislation insomuch as they cannot be commercially sold. As a commercial conservation and eco-tourist operation, with values based on corporate citizenship and indeed the maintenance of native fauna in the public interest, ESL are required to report their financial performance to external parties according to Australian accounting standards.

The Australian community has come to the realisation that declining species of wildlife are a public good. "The population of northern hairy-nosed wombats has been declining and was around 100 animals in 2000" (Woodford, 2001, p. 141), all found at a single location in Queensland. This animal is Australia's most rare mammal. The Western Plains Zoo in central New South Wales had been trying to establish the breed in captivity. In October 2000, a conservation team met at Western Plains Zoo and decided the only hope for the northern hairy-nosed wombat was to consider locking them away from the outside world with a predator-proof fence" (Woodford, 2001, p. 132). Almost two years later, construction of the fence commenced in September 2002 and is to be completed in November 2002 at a cost of $0.4 m.

In January 1985 John Wamsley opened Warrawong Sanctuary near Adelaide. A man of vision, Wamsley established a further eight sanctuaries and provided the management of another sanctuary. His vision led to the world's only listed company, Earth Sanctuaries Ltd. with a core business activity of conservation. The approach was simple. Fence off the land with feral-animal-proof fencing, kill off all the feral animals within the fenced area and then re-establish populations of endangered animals.

Wombats and feral-animal-proof fencing seem quite remote from accounting for cattle, hazelnut groves and forests. The latter undertakings are activities we are most likely to associate with accounting for agriculture, along with crops, dairy, poultry and pigs. Indeed cattle, hazelnut groves and forests activities are the basis of the illustrations in Australian accounting standard AASB 1037: Self-Generating and Regenerating Assets AASB 1037. But AASB 1037 also seems able to be applied to native fauna once perimeter fencing controls them.

The Australian accounting standard was available to the standard setters who developed International Accounting Standard 41: Agriculture IAS 41. And now IAS 41 is being evaluated by an increasing range of national accounting bodies with a view to introducing a standard on agriculture. Native fauna are also found in some of these countries; could IAS 41 be applicable to them?

The primary objective of our paper is establish the value relevance, in terms of use, of AASB 1037, and the potential use by international conservation firms of IAS 41 for:

(a) decision usefulness in terms of concerned stakeholders' prediction of earnings quality and future cash flows, and
(b) sustainable wildlife population, and the development of organisational capabilities to support sustainable outcomes.

The issues and questions are:

- Is AASB 1037 the appropriate financial reporting standard to provide interested parties with a fair and reasonable picture of the financial position of conservation firms like ESL?
- Do regulations restricting the sale of wildlife in the market prevent wildlife from being commercial assets? (Barton, 2000; SAC4, 1992).
- Does the use of AASB 1037 provide managers with an incentive structure that is consistent with the conservation objectives of the company?
- Should the profession define key accounting concepts for corporate citizenship activities relating to conservation?

In the next section of this paper we provide a brief introduction to agricultural activity and the role of accounting standards in that activity. The third section contains a summary of AASB 1037 and IAS 41. These summaries highlight the aspects of the standards that are critical to any analysis. In the fourth section we review and discuss how AASB 1037 has been interpreted and applied by ESL. Section 5 evaluates how meaningful the profit and the asset values derived from application of AASB 1037 are for shareholders and outside parties who are interested in wildlife breeding operations. In Section 6 we highlight the plurality of paradigms that exist for conservation firms operating as commercial public companies, and the citizenship performance issues relating to the use of IAS 41 in a similar manner to AASB 1037. Finally in Section 7, we conclude with a summary and suggest some principles that could be used in re-designing a valuation standard for a commercial organisation engaged in wildlife conservation.

A complete comparison between IAS 41 and AASB 1037 is outside the scope of this paper, as is the full evaluation of a diverse range of possible implementations of those standards. Our research method is primarily through a single case study.

2. AGRICULTURAL ACTIVITY

2.1. Standards Devoted to Agriculture

The world of accounting has functioned for many years with relatively few accounting standards devoted to specialised industry needs. Agriculture is a large employer in many countries and a major sector of the economy. Its impact on: (a) the economy, has fallen in recent decades; and on (b) employment, has fallen further. Nevertheless agriculture is still a major sector albeit of mainly small operations, such as the family farm.

History professor at Yale John McNeill has written an environmental history of the twentieth century, showing how humans have altered their world. The modern expansion of agriculture is one of the driving forces behind changes in the earth's vista.

> The general transformation of farming after 1940, of which mechanisation and the Green Revolution were parts, both shaped the twentieth century and reflected its dominant tends. It was energy- and knowledge-intensive. It replaced simpler systems with more complex ones, involving distant inputs and multiple social and economic linkages. It reduced family and regional autonomy, enmeshing farmers in a world of banks, seed banks, plant genetics, fertilizer manufacturers, extension agents and water bureaucrats. It transplanted what worked in the West and Japan to other societies. It sought to harness nature tightly, to make it perform to the utmost, to make it maximally subservient to humankind, or at least some subset thereof. And it sharply increased its output, making us dependent upon its perpetuation. As of 1996, to feed ourselves without these changes, we would have needed to find additional prime farmland equal in area to North America (McNeill, 2001, p. 227).

Accounting and financial reporting represent ways an organisation communicates with society and its shareholders, thereby legitimating its actions. Agricultural production presents varying and often unique accounting issues because of the diverse range of activities undertaken. In addition, accountants are in the unique position to be able to translate environmental impacts into information that can be measured in dollar terms. Although accountants presently find they need to make some information available in qualitative terms because not all information can be quantified in monetary terms.

While some official pronouncements have existed in a small number of countries, principally Canada, the United States and New Zealand, the development of standards has not followed. Malaysian accounting standard (MAS 5): Accounting for Aquaculture became effective on 1st January 1992. However, the world's first acknowledged standard, the Australian standard AASB 1037: Self-Generating and Regenerating Assets was issued in 1998 and became effective in 2001.

Why might standards not be forthcoming? In the United Kingdom, for example, the greater part of agricultural business is to do with seasonal crops and horticulture. Thus, maturity to a point of sale frequently follows an annual cycle, and established accounting practice based on the historical cost concept is acceptable to the banks and the revenue authorities. Standards were not needed.

2.2. Conservation – Attitudes and Opportunities

The Australian community has demonstrated concern about environmental quality over many years. At the start of the last century Australian society was concerned with natural resource development for commercial purposes by the farming, mining and timber industries and the preservation of visually attractive and unique settings through the establishment of parks. Today, Australian society seems far more concerned with reducing risks to biodiversity and the protection of a wider range of natural ecosystems than was the case 20 or 30 years ago. Moreover, there appears to be evidence that the demand for environmental quality is growing overtime.[2] Society's preferences for the environment have changed as its understanding of the role and threats to native flora and fauna have changed and the threats to our well being from wars and economic disruption have tended to decline. These trends are not restricted to Australia and are evident in all developed economies (for example, Baldock & Lowe, 1996; MAFF, 2000).

In response to the community's increasing demand for environmental quality the Federal and State governments have re-evaluated the efficacy of their responses to natural resource management issues. For example, there have been numerous government inquiries on environmental issues over the last 20 years and some elections have been dominated by environmental concerns. (Reports include Industry Commission, 1997; SEAC, 1996.) One of the outcomes of this policy process has been that consensus seems to be forming around the notion that Australia's traditional model of reliance on the national park system is unlikely to be sufficient to meet either the threats that confront biodiversity or the demands of the electorate. The use of market instruments rather than direct government supply and or quantitative regulations has been widely promoted in policy circles as a feasible, low cost approach to delivering the high level of environmental outcomes that are being demanded by society (ABARE, 1998; Brown & Adger, 1994; Bureau of Transport Economics, 1998; Industry Commission, 1997).

The use of market-based policy instruments is consistent with the belief that environmental problems exist because of problems with the structure of the property rights systems. Resources that lack efficient property rights systems tend to be over-exploited and degraded. The establishment of property rights allows individual decisions on environmental values to be harnessed through the market system.

Examples of this policy direction include the establishment of new markets for a wide range of resources including irrigation water in Australia, native game species in Zimbabwe and the USA, air pollution in the USA and the current debate concerning the trade in Carbon Credits and Greenhouse Gas emission permits. The actions of private individuals, and "not for profit" groups such as Nature Conservancy in the USA and Trusts for Nature in Australia, in acquiring land and water rights for environmental purposes are other examples (see Moran et al., 1991 for a discussion of some of the approaches).

Historian John McNeill (2001, pp. 314–323) lists dominant features of twentieth century economic history as: industrialisation, Fordism, and economic integration (globalism). Interestingly he does not mention the rising impact of recreation/tourism/leisure. Changing community values now make recreation/tourism/leisure a major sector of the economy and present many potential commercial opportunities.

Concern over fauna conservation and embryonic eco-tourism initiatives in Australia have spawned a particularly interesting commercial operation involving native fauna conservation. This and other similar ventures will bring on the need to set out principles for the valuation of biological assets. Wildlife in peril needs to be "valued" in order to provide impetus for their survival. It is not clear that values provided from within a traditional accounting framework will foster conservation and meet needs of investors providing the capital to enable these activities.

Investors in Australia have a publicly listed company with the stated objective of maximising shareholder returns by "... conserving Australia's unique biodiversity in a commercial environment..." (ESL, 2000a). ESL was registered as a public company in 1993 and listed on the Australian Stock Exchange in 2000. ESL is attempting to make profits for its shareholders by establishing private sanctuaries where native animals are protected, bred, displayed and ultimately traded. There is an argument that sanctuaries and the native animals they contain are important commercial assets for ESL and this needs additional coverage in public financial statements released by the company. There is a further argument that successful conservation attempts by ESL represent performance that should be reported as part of the profit and loss of each reporting period.

The appropriateness of Accounting Standard (AASB 1037) – Self-Generating and Regenerating Assets to account for fauna will be considered in the following sections. As ESL has already applied this standard their situation was studied and the accounting treatment for fauna under conservation was examined, together with the role of reported information in the relationship between business risks and good corporate governance.

3. ACCOUNTING STANDARDS FOR LIVING ASSETS

3.1. History and Scope of AASB 1037

AASB 1037 was first applied to the reporting of all self-generating and regenerating assets (SGARAs) for the financial years on or after 30th June 2000. The intended scope of the standard was to remedy a gap in the reporting of a special class of inventory. AASB 1019, the Accounting Standard applicable to inventory reporting, specifically excludes "... inventories that are self-generating and regenerating assets, although it is applicable to non-living produce derived from self-generating and regenerating assets..." such as felled logs (Parker, 2001, p. 694).

Issued prior to an international standard, AASB 1037, defines SGARAs as non-human living self-generating and regenerating assets. These include assets with short production cycles such as wheat as well as longer-term production cycles assets like apple trees. The standard also covers the living assets of stud breeders and aqua culturists. SGARAs are those held primarily for profit, either by sale in their own right or to generate produce that is available for sale. Attention is directed within the standard to the case of national parks or gardens and the problem accountants face in attempting to measure reliably, the SGARAs separately from the land value on which they are attached. In this context the standard permits the exclusion of SGARAs that are held primarily for purposes of "ecology" and "environment" rather than income generation.

The standard setters suggested a further level of classification of SGARAs to indicate to the external user, management's investment intention in assets of this type, e.g. held for sale, or breeding purposes. Sub-classification is also considered appropriate for SGARAs that are either leased or over which the individual reporting entity has other controlling rights. Asset recognition occurs when it is probable (i.e. can be expected on the basis of available evidence or logic, a 50% or greater chance) that a future economic benefit will eventuate from the SGARAs.

During the development of the Standard, views were expressed that:

(a) the Standard should not apply to SGARAs with short-term production cycles;
(b) the Standard should not apply to long-term bearer-SGARAs such as grape vines, which are equivalent to plant and equipment;
(c) non-SGARAs to which SGARAs are inextricably linked (for example, the land upon which trees grow in a forest and the infrastructure within the forest) should be treated as a whole and not separated;
(d) the determination of net market value of SGARAs is subjective in the absence of active and liquid markets; and
(e) changes in the net market value of SGARAs should be recognised directly in equity, consistent with the general treatment of revaluation increments and decrements for property, plant and equipment.

The standard was hailed as beneficial to companies involved with: (a) livestock, forestry and vineyards, which rely on the natural environment as their source of business, through an increase in the ability to attract equity capital as a source of funding; and (b) endangered species, by which a valuation would provide a greater appreciation of their worth to society and thus aid their protection (Cummings, 2000, p. 30).

3.2. Measurement of SGARAs

AASB 1037 requires that measurement of SGARAs be at net market value at the end of the accounting period, and displayed as a separate asset classification in the position statement. Basically AASB 1037 applies to SGARAs that are for sale, either in their own right, or used to generate produce that will ultimately be sold. The approach adopted by the standard setters is that any increments (or decrements) in the net market value of SGARA's be recognized as revenue (or expenses) in the performance statement. In the case of a "bearer-SGARA", the production of a separate SGARA (which may also be a "bearer-SGARA" itself) "...typically results in a reduction in the net market value of the SGARA..." (Parker, 2001, p. 1193). At the same time, an increment in the net market value of the new SGARA will be recorded as revenue (less costs of extraction). Arguably, a physical capital maintenance concept underpins AASB 1037. Changes in volume and value are recognized in the performance statement.

The net market value of SGARAs is the amount a firm, as a going concern, would expect to receive from their disposal in an active and liquid market after costs of realization are deducted. Where no active or liquid market exists, the options provided in the standard for "best indicator" measures of net market value are:

- net market value of related assets. In the case of an orchard this would apply to the net market value of apple trees ascertained by allocating the total net market value between SGARAs and non-SGARAs;
- net present value of cash flows to be generated by the SGARAs discounted by a rate reflective of the risk associated with them. Cash inflows represent those flows anticipated from either the asset or their produce, with the outflows excluding re-establishment costs, e.g. replanting trees in a native forest following harvest;
- net market value of same or similar assets; and
- cost – when market prices are not reliably determinable.

3.3. Required Disclosure

AASB 1037 requires firms to disclose SGARAs over which the firm has rights of control. It includes any SGARAs over which these rights of control may be restricted by either regulatory or external requirements.

If "best indicator" measurements are used, the reporting entity is required to provide information on the method adopted, and any significant assumptions made in the determination. The firm is also required to disclose if the valuation is based on an independent valuation or a director's valuation. In order to identify the particular economic attributes of specific classes of SGARAs relative to the firm, the performance statement should include separate details on the net increment (decrement) attributable to each.

3.4. History and Scope of IAS 41

The International Acccounting Standard IAS 41, prepared to practical guidance to accountants on reporting agricultural operations will become operative for the financial period ending on or after 1st January 2003. However, a national standard based on the principles contained in IAS 41 is already operative in Singapore. Other countries have outstanding exposure drafts on agriculture.

The Australian Accounting Standards Board said they decided to issue a standard ahead of the International Accounting Standards Committee (IASC) (now International Accounting Standards Board, IASB) due to the uncertain timing of the IASC project and a perceived urgent need for guidance for Australian entities that control SGARAs. Australian implementation experience should benefit the IASC as it moves to finalise its Agriculture project. The IASC are themselves seeking feedback on IAS 41 and any difficulties it raises for users.

The scope of IAS 41 is restricted to animals (and plants) capable of biological transformation. It focuses on a managed transformation and thereby restricts itself to agricultural concerns rather than dealing with all living assets. The specialised principles for agricultural inventory, contained in the standard, apply only until the biological transformation process is complete. In the case of animals this means that they are slaughtered. Obviously this concept cannot apply to native fauna that are subject to conservation. When dealing with fauna, what could the biological transformation process be interpreted to cover? Would that mean the birth of additional wombats, and if so when can we judge the birthing process to be complete? Does this mean that "newborn" wombats are not covered by the principles of the standard but the breeding stock is covered by the principles? If a breeding stock of wombats is acceptable, is an ever-increasing breeding stock acceptable?

3.5. Measurement and Disclosure Required by (IAS 41)

AASB 1037 requires the use of net market value (NMV). It is fairly uncompromising but the standard is pragmatic enough to realise that NMV may have to be established from a variety of approaches.

IAS 41 requires the use of fair value (FV) measured at the point of "harvest". The primary indicator of fair value should be net market value. From FV it is necessary to deduct transaction costs. The effect is the same as for AASB 1037, even if the wording differs. In select specified circumstances IAS 41 does allow the use of depreciated cost (paragraph 30). This approximation for FV has no equivalent in the Australian standard. Under AASB 1037, all assets recognised must be measured at NMV (paragraph 5.2).

The change in fair value of biological assets is a more relevant indicator of the performance of an enterprise engaged in agricultural activities than is profit or loss measured on the traditional historical-cost basis, which recognises no profit until a sale takes place. But what is the agriculturalist's concept of agricultural profit – is it the net amount of cash generated, or a benefit accruing from the process of biological transformation? Many observers question whether agriculture is an appropriate type of business for introducing earlier recognition of profit, i.e. before it is realised through the sale of the product.

The IASC Steering Committee on Agriculture prepared a Draft Statement of Principles (DSOP). This DSOP identified a tension over how the change in the carrying amount of a group of biological assets should be allocated. It suggested they should be allocated between: (i) the physical change in biological assets – reported in the income statement; and (ii) the change in fair values – reported in the statement of non-owner movements in equity. This has some similarity to the recommendations in the Australian Discussion Paper No 23: Accounting for Self-Generating and Regenerating Assets.

Many observers and industry representatives believe it is necessary to appropriately distinguish between increases in the value of assets and operating profit. While a comprehensive income approach is welcomed there is nevertheless a desire to distinguish results of operations from changes in equity as a result of movements in values. Arguably the required reconciliations of IAS 41, results in greater disclosure of the increases in value of assets as distinct from operating profit although these are not included in the face of the reports.

3.6. Comparing AASB 1037 and IAS 41

As indicated in our introduction, we make no attempt to comprehensively compare AASB 1037 against IAS 41. Our interest is restricted to matters that relate to the values and increases in those values, for living assets. Indeed the living assets in which we are interested are native fauna. This paper does not put emphasis on flora or crops.

4. EARTH SANCTUARIES LTD. AND AASB 1037

4.1. ESL Background

John Wamsley and his wife Proo Geddes opened Warrawong Sanctuary near Adelaide, South Australia on January 1st 1985. The sanctuary had been developed since 1979 when Wamsley had acquired the land in a rundown condition. ESL was registered as a private company in 1988 and absorbed the existing environmental activities of Wamsley who became the company's managing director. ESL converted to a publicly listed company in 2000. (Details of the company can be found in the ESL published prospectus, ESL, 2000a.)

The primary objective of ESL is to maximise returns to shareholders through activities aimed at conserving Australia's biodiversity. At the time of floating the company, ESL reported that their main income earning activities would involve running sanctuaries and related tourist facilities, environmental consultancies together with breeding and trading in native fauna. Until the end of 2001, ESL operated/managed four sanctuaries in as tourist ventures in South Australia and New South Wales (NSW). Three further "commercial" sanctuaries were planned for Little River, the Blue Mountains and the Gold Coast – areas near major cities with heavy tourist flows. In total, ESL was operating or developing a total of ten sanctuaries prior to a major reorganisation early in 2002.

The company has an issued capital of $29 million. While ESL has nearly 7000 shareholders in total, the directors' holdings represent 40% of the company's capital. The market value of shares in ESL, after listing, proved to be volatile. They gained little support from institutional investors. The share price reached a top price of $2.50 on the opening day of its trading, however in mid-January 2002 the share price reached a low of 16.5 cents, before recovering to trade around twenty cent figures.

In the accounting periods 1995–1998, prior to AASB 1037, ESL produced supplementary Economic Accounts, a selection of which are displayed in Table 1. Also included in Table 1 is information from 1999 to 2001 following the introduction of their application of AASB 1037. The supplementary accounts enabled ESL to present financial measurements for the natural assets under their control. Figures presented were categorised into natural assets of wildlife, habitat and vegetation. The Economic Valuation Reserve created within the set of supplementary Economic Accounts at 30th June 1998, amounted to 691% of total Shareholder's Funds in the "conventional" accounts. Table 1 also includes information from the period when AASB 1037 was applied.

The Economic Accounts represent an interesting attempt by ESL to inform investors of the value of the entity that could not otherwise be depicted in

Table 1. ESL Selected Items: 1995–2001.

	Imputed Accounts Constructed				AASB 1037 Applied		
	1995 ($000)	1996 ($000)	1997 ($000)	1998 ($000)	1999 ($000)	2000 ($000)	2001 ($000)
Vegetation	14,875	15,370	16,194	16,562			
Wildlife	12,156	17,515	19,523	31,084			
Habitat	4,806	17,515	19,523	31,084			
Intangibles etc.	928	689	1,941	2,617			
Property and plant and other	6,750	7,026	8,609	12,009			
Total non-current asset value in *economic* accounts	39,515	58,115	65,790	93,356			
Australian fauna					3,845	5,905	5,412
Other assets	6,314	7,272	8,885	12,135	15,883	26,763	17,549
Total non-current asset value in *financial* accounts	6,314	7,272	8,885	12,135	19,728	32,668	22,961
Equity issued and paid up (including premiums)	4,740	6,154	8,914	10,588	15,568	29,334	30,018
Operating profit before tax	84	61	106	147	1,238	2,055	(13,648)
Increase in Australian fauna					1,049	2,060	(493)
Percentage increase in Australian fauna					37.5%	53.6%	(8.3%)
Increase in economic valuation reserve	29,521	16,270	7,641	25,251			
Percentage increase in economic valuation reserve	N/A	55.1%	16.7%	47.3%			

Source: Adapted from Hone et al. (2001) which was based on data extracted from ESL annual reports and a table by Burritt and Cummings (1999, p. 8), also compiled using data from ESL annual reports.

Table 2.   ESL: Sources of Revenue 1999–2001.

	1999		2000		2001 As Published		2001 Assuming no Reclassification	
	$000	%	$000	%	$000	%	$000	%
Source								
Ecotourism	1,132	48.9	1,286	34.8	1,280	87.5	1,280	41.0
Interest	14	0.6	116	3.1	118	8.1	118	3.7
Donations	253	10.9	120	3.3	19	1.3	19	0.6
Other	72	3.1	115	3.1	45	3.1	45	1.4
Increment in NMV of Australian fauna	845	36.5	2,060	55.7	[a]		1,670	53.3
REVENUE	2,316	100.0	3,697	100.0	1,462	100.0	3,122	100.0

Source: This table is based on data extracted from ESL annual reports.
[a] In 2001 a decrement of $493,000 was recorded as a result of adoption of categories used by Environment Australia. This decrement equates to 33.7% of the recorded revenue for the period.

conventional accounts. With the advent of AASB 1037, ESL was able to present figures for the natural assets under their control as part of the "normal" accounting process. The difference in figures from the two approaches is interesting. In either case a reader of the financial reports had to refer to the notes to the accounts to get a complete picture revealing value of the natural assets.

ESL, one of the first firms to use AASB 1037, applied the standard from 1st July 1998. The standard did become operative for all companies until 30th June 2001. The principal sources of ESL's revenue since adoption of AASB 1037 are shown in Table 2. Increases in the value, in accordance with AASB 1037, of native fauna held by the sanctuaries are clearly a significant component. In 2000, increases of a single species, the Southern Hairy-Nosed Wombat accounted for nearly $1 million of the reported a pre-tax operating profit of almost $2.06 million (ESL, 2000b).

4.2. Recording Wildlife as SGARAs

ESL has treated wildlife within their sanctuaries as SGARAs under the meaning of AASB 1037. As there is no tradeable market for these fauna, ESL valued the animals using as a "best indicator" for net market value, the estimate of the recovery of sanctuary costs in re-establishing species populations and associated translocation expenses (ESL, 2000b). They classified animals on the basis of their "risk status" and derived three valuation categories:

• "threatened" species valued for 1998/1999/2000 at $1,250 per animal;
• "rare" species valued for 1998/1999/2000 at $2,500 per animal; and
• "endangered" species valued for 1998/1999/2000 at $5,000 per animal.

In the year ended 30th June 2001 ESL increased SGARA values by 10% and adjusted categories for reassessment of risk status, in accordance with the terminology used by National Parks and Wildlife of Australia. The new "risk status" and valuation categories were:

- "rare" species valued for 2001 at $1,375 per animal;
- "vulnerable" species valued for 2001 at $2,650 per animal; and
- "endangered" species valued for 2001 at $5,500 per animal.

This reassessment was a contributor to a dramatic reversal in profit performance for 2001 when a loss of $13.65 million was reported. A write-down of sanctuary assets by $10.5 million occurred. In addition, ESL considered their trading activities were "disappointing" during this period.

A key issue of ESL's operations is the establishment of species numbers, and in accordance with AASB 1037, an increase in revenue is obtained as a result of increasing numbers. The revenue is not realised and under current wildlife provisions, is in actual fact unable to be realised. In terms of realized funds, or cash flow, ESL have a number of cash flow generating activities alongside their conservation objectives namely: guided walks and tours, outdoor education, food and beverage sales, accommodation, gift shop sales, native nursery sales, conferences, weddings, filming and photography, consulting services, contract services, contract management, and donations.

4.3. Relevance and Reliability

The fundamental concept underpinning financial statement reporting is the objective of decision-usefulness. The merits of reporting practices open to ESL are discussed in this regard. We continue by identifying issues where the qualitative characteristics of relevance and reliability may be further supported. These are:

- The classification of wildlife as an asset;
- Measurement approach used to value fauna included in the position statement; and
- Inclusion of unrealized gains in the performance statement.

4.4. Wildlife – Are They Commercial Assets?

Statement of Accounting Concepts 4 (SAC4) defines an asset as "future economic benefits controlled by the entity as a result of past transactions or other past events" (paragraph 14). In contrast, Pearce (1993) suggests the valuation of assets necessary to preserve biodiversity for future generations is based on the human perception of their intrinsic value. To a reporting entity such as ESL, the wildlife do qualify as providing future service potential, as without these animals the business operations would not be conducted. However, commercial conservations organisations such as ESL occupy a unique and challenging position. They are accountable for the stewardship of the natural assets – native fauna. At the same time, they are responsible for the financial performance outcomes from these operations. The outcomes of the former have a longer-term perspective, while those of the latter are usually of shorter term.

SAC4 dictates that an item reported in financial statements as an asset must be obtained as a result of a past transaction or other past events, which includes an appropriation – a non-reciprocal transfer. ESL gained its fauna stocks from wild capture, or obtained them from breeding programs run by other bodies. They fenced a habitat area, removed all other threats, thus ensuring their survival and encouraging procreation in a protected environment. Exchangeability is not an essential characteristic in the determination of an asset. ESL holds a licence for purposes of increasing the population of native species of fauna, but is restricted from selling the animals or using them for slaughter. However, for purposes of the defining of an asset according to the SAC4 asset definition, ESL may be considered to have control over these wildlife.

AASB 1037 applies to SGARAs other than SGARAs that are held for the primary purpose of aesthetics, heritage, ecology, the environment, or recreation (paragraph 2.1). AASB 1037 applies to SGARAs that are held primarily for profit, for example, SGARAs held primarily for sale in their own right or held to generate produce for sale (paragraph 2.1.1). Commercial operations similar to that of ESL presently profit from eco-tourism and not sale of animals.

The principles in this standard may be appropriate for SGARAs that are not held primarily for profit (for example, SGARAs that are a component of a national park, public botanical garden or public recreational park). However, measurement techniques available to the entity may not be sufficiently developed to reliably measure the net market value of SGARAs separately. For example, techniques may not be adequately developed to reliably measure the net market value of SGARAs in national parks separately from the non-biological assets (such as land) to which they are attached (paragraph 2.1.1). It is possible to question whether fauna that cannot be sold by ESL might add to the value of the land it owns.

ESL has reported fauna under their conservation management as SGARAs on their position statement. The appropriate classification within the statement is the next point for discussion.

4.5. Wildlife – Are They an Inventory Item?

AASB 1037 was developed to remedy a gap in reporting inventory as the relevant accounting standard, AASB 1019, excluded self-generating and regenerating assets. AASB 1037 is applicable to SGARAs with short production cycles, e.g. wheat and other crops, and is also applicable to SGARAS with lengthy production cycles such as grape vines. SGARAs are not interchangeable in the marketplace, are held for future economic benefit in the longer term, and the standard aligns financial performance with a biological change – not exchange.

ESL and similar operations are concerned with stewardship of (the inventory of) native fauna – i.e. of natural assets. For accountability of financial performance, inventory is held to generate revenue in an ensuing accounting period. Inventory can be raw materials, work in process, by-products or a finished product held for sale, exchange, rent, or other related economic benefits. If under regulatory requirements ESL and other similar commercial operations are unable to sell, rent or re-licence the threatened, rare or endangered wildlife, then any characterization in the financial reports as an item of item of inventory, can be questioned. There are no estimations of sales, harvesting or other cash-related revenue that can be directly identified with the biological increases. Hence, classification in the Statement of Financial Position should be entirely as a non-current asset.

Assets that are to be reported must be measured. Two studies have reported that then-existing SGARA measurement practices would have to change in order to ensure compliance with AASB 1037 (Dowling & Godfrey, 2001; Herbohn et al., 1998). Both studies questioned whether substantially increased consistency would be achieved in the way SGARAs are measured in "traditional" agricultural situations. The studies examined the practices relating to forestry (timber), grapevines, livestock and crops. Our next point for discussion is the likelihood of meaningful measurement where fauna is identified as an asset to be recorded.

5. ACHIEVING MEANINGFUL QUANTIFICATION

5.1. Identification and Measurement of Asset

Placing a monetary value on natural assets can signal that they are marketable and exchangeable in the market place. This is not the case for native fauna controlled by ESL. In an effort to overcome this, ESL attached intrinsic values to the fauna by categorising them into "rare", "threatened" and "endangered" characteristics.

ESL identifies the commodity providing greater future economic benefit as the individual animal, and attach a monetary measure to each animal. As net market value was not relevant in this case, a surrogate dollar amount was determined according to: (a) species; and (b) its intrinsic characterization (rare, threatened, or endangered). The total dollar amount for each species and intrinsic group was based on the number of animals and multiplied by the relevant dollar amount applicable to each.

Given that the conservation of native wildlife is now a commercial operation and the annual report is prepared under the concept of financial maintenance, the distinction between the individual animal and its species group, or sanctuary, may be somewhat hazy. The individual animal may not be the asset generating the greater future economic benefit to ESL. The asset "sanctuary" may be the preferable option. This appears to be the item generating the greater future economic benefits, the marketable commodity, and the security suitable for external lending requirements should the need arise to fund further sanctuaries.

AASB 1037 requires SGARAs to be measured at net market value or some other reliable best indicator. For ESL, the primary mission underpinning their business activities is breeding for conservation purposes of rare, endangered or threatened species. There is no active and liquid market for this native fauna and in this circumstance AASB 1037 suggests that net present value as the best measurement indicator. Net present value requires the subjective evaluation of management intentions including the choice of risk and related discount rates, and is more applicable to economic values and propensity of the firm's cash flows.

ESL have measured net market value as "recovery of sanctuary costs in re-establishing species populations and associated translocation expenses" including of capture the native fauna in the wild. Breeding associated costs are more consistent and provide the basis for an intra-firm comparable trend while an increasingly sophisticated investor group may find this measurement more readily understandable. If these animals continue to be classified as an asset, it is suggested that breeding costs may be the more appropriate monetary measurement to provide a more reliable and indeed relevant to decision makers.

5.2. Revenue Generation and Capital Maintenance

Under AASB 1037, whichever method is chosen for net market value, the net increments (decrements) are adjusted in the profit and loss account as revenues (expenses). ESL's potential to generate revenue is controlled by its ability attract tourists and clients to the subordinate activities of the firm. ESL is accountable for the financial capital contributed by the shareholders and also the stewardship (i.e. physical maintenance) of the natural capital. The biological changes affect the physical operating capacity of the firm.

In terms of wealth accumulation, the income measurement is a symbol of the successful financial performance of a firm (Lee, 1989). Although ESL stakeholders, and indeed their investors, may be primarily concerned with their conservation activities, the financial performance provides insights into the longer-term and ongoing prospects of the firm.

To ensure continued viability ESL will need to reinvest in order to maintain and extend operations and thereby eventually increase wealth. ESL measure the revenue attached to native fauna on the unrealised changes in wildlife stock volumes and prices. Using an increase in wildlife stock volumes is consistent with the conservation objectives underpinning ESL goals and objectives – physical capital maintenance, albeit of natural capital. However, non-realisable revenues will not directly assist in reinvestment opportunities. In fact, pressure from share-holders may encourage higher dividend rates diverting cash funds from activities that may add to financial sustainability and potential growth. Furthermore, included with the unrealised gains though changes in stock volumes are the realizable gains from the cash flow generating activities. Combining realisable and non-realisable revenues may not enhance relevance for user decision-making objectives, and introduces an additivity problem. The inclusion of non-realisable (and somewhat subjective) gains (losses) in profit and loss calculations, and the associated ratio analyses, may indirectly influence the decisions of uninformed stakeholders. In order to aid transparency in this regard, it may be preferable for ESL to distinguish the realizable revenue associated with tourist activities, from the holding gain profit associated with wildlife increases. In so doing, stakeholders would be provided more relevant information for their individual decision-making needs. Reaching conservation goals through an increase in wildlife stock numbers may impose a requirement for larger sanctuaries to accommodate and nurture the animals. These can only be provided by additional monetary commitments. Access to cash is e obtained by: (a) an increase in shareholder equity; (b) loans through lending institutions; or (c) cash resulting from operations. Increased equity is obtained subject to the risk preferences of individual shareholders; loans will increase ESL's debt to equity ratio and require cash inflows to service the debt. Increasing the transparency of reports in this regard can only assist informed decisions.

6. INCENTIVE IMPACTS

While there are a number of criteria upon which the performance of managers can be assessed, the maximisation of longer-term shareholder value is an important performance criterion for the management for most, if not all, public companies. The value of a share in a public company reflects the market's assessment of the net present value of the total returns that flow from the ownership of the share. In this context, total returns refers to both the monetary and non-monetary returns that are expected to flow from a share of ownership of the company. The monetary returns are reflected in the dividend stream plus capital gains. The non-monetary returns influence share prices through two processes.

First, they have a direct impact on the shareholders personal assessment of the value of the share through the sense of personal satisfaction that flows from being associated with organisations and efforts that they believe to be worthy. These "warm inner glows" motivate numerous actions in society including donations to charities and the willingness of consumers to pay premiums for environmentally sound goods or services. The development of ethical investment funds is evidence of the finance community's assessment of the size of this market segment. Over a period of time, with growing affluence and increasing concern with environmental issues, the number of potential investors that are willing and able to pay for these sentiments is likely to grow.

Second, potential investors who have no personal interest or commitment to environmental issues can be expected to factor the sentimental values of the rest of the community into their assessments of the likely future capital gains from holding stocks in companies that are likely to viewed as environmentally sound. That is, in assessing the value of shares in companies like ESL, investors will be sensitive to other people's "warm inner glows" just as they would to the future dividend stream.

Therefore, community concern about the environment is likely to be a key driver in determining the longer-term value of ESL. The level of commercial returns the company makes from tourism and consulting will be sensitive to the level of community interest in Australian environmental issues. Moreover, share prices will reflect these commercial returns plus the company's environmental conservation factor.

In seeking to maintain and build shareholder value, management needs to capitalise on, and promote, the environmental image of the company. Clearly this will involve visibly achieving environmental objectives that the community supports. Unfortunately, the achievement of profit, as measured by ESL, may be inconsistent with the achievement of environmental objectives held by current and future investors and consumers.

The longer-term profitability of ESL will be influenced by the company's ability to trade in, and in particular export, native wildlife. This is currently tightly controlled with the ownership of native wildlife being specifically prohibited by Australian law. While the relaxation of these trade restrictions could transform ESL's profit position, the trade in native wildlife is an extremely controversial issue in environmental circles. To the extent to which this trade is opposed by potential future investors, the opening up of this trade would tend to reduce the intrinsic value of shares in ESL. The net impact of the development of a true trade in wildlife on the value of ESL would depend on the extent to which the increase in profits that come from the change is offset by this reduction in value due to the confrontation with environmental sensitivities.

At a more fundamental level it can also be argued that there is a very real prospect that the incentive structures implied within ESL's asset valuation approach are incongruous to the environmental objectives of many of their potential investors. Under the current valuation structure, ESL makes profits by breeding wildlife. The more at risk the wildlife is, the greater the gain to be had through the expansion in numbers. If ESL is successful in its breeding programs they (and other members of this potential industry) will confront the issue of determining the most profitable numbers of rare animals to hold and breed.

An expansion in numbers that moves the species from "endangered" to "rare" would reduce the potential value of that new progeny from $5,500 per head to $2,650 per head. Importantly, this reduction in value would apply to all existing stock as well as newly-bred stock. The net result of a successful breeding program for any endangered species could be a halving in the capital value of the breeding stock. If the program is really successful and the species classification is reduced to "threatened" the value of each unit of stock would fall to $1,375.

It is quite conceivable that the potential investors in this industry would like to see all animals move from "endangered" to "rare" to "threatened" and ultimately off the ESL valuation list entirely. The achievement of profits, as defined by ESL, may become inconsistent with this objective. In the extreme, the pursuit of profits could motivate the management of ESL to advocate policies and actions that increase, rather than reduce, the risk species confront. In this case, the net result could be that successful profit maximisation would reduce shareholder value rather than increase it. Paradoxically, increasing profits may not result in greater financial security for investors.

Divergences between the imputed values used by ESL and the actual values that consumers and/or investors place on particular species is also possible. These divergences are more likely to occur when a cost-based valuation approach is used than when a market exchange approach is adopted. Market exchange valuations directly link values to consumer preferences. This linkage is likely to be lost in cost-based approaches. For example, the legless lizard may be an endangered species and therefore of high value to ESL but of little interest to tourists or many investors. Conversely, charismatic species such as Koalas may be "threatened" and therefore of a lesser value to ESL but of critical importance to tourists and many investors.

To the extent to which the cost valuations do not accurately reflect consumer or investor valuations, the pursuit of profits encourages management to depart from a mix of species that would maximise the value of the program to tourists and investors. That is, a breeding program that accentuates reported profits would not be consistent with maximising profits from tourism or optimising the sustainable conservation values of investors.

It is also worth considering if tourism profits would expand or fall if ESL is successful in reducing the risks to endangered wildlife. That is, how does the tourism income from demonstrating successful wildlife breeding compare with the tourism income from viewing rare or endangered species? The answer is not obvious and is beyond the scope of this paper.

7. IAS 41 AND COMMERCIAL CONSERVATION

ESL has said that it has a standing order for a pair of platypuses for a price yet to be negotiated from an aquarium in Japan who have invested around $500,000 in their business, but cannot fulfill the order, due to the prohibition in the trade of native species (Cummings, 2000, p. 31). In South Africa, certain native species bred in captivity can be traded, such as the Black Rhino, for as much as US$35,000, and a Cheetah for as much as US$28,000. The UN Convention on International Trade in Endangered Species (CITIES) only prohibits trade in endangered species "removed from the wild", not those "bred in a controlled environment".

It is interesting to speculate what price Australian animals might command if government restrictions prohibiting trade in endangered species were removed and captive-bred animals were sold. But it is also interesting to speculate whether black rhinos would be profitably recorded by South African game reserves if Statement of GAAP AC 137, Agriculture, which is based on IAS 41, and is effective from 1 January 2003. Clearly a sale reinforces the quality of any profit recognised.

What might happen if rhino are unable to be sold because of a change in regulation within South Africa? Would an IAS 41-based-standard allow recognition of profit from growth in numbers and growth in value? This, of course, is untested speculation but there would seem no clear prohibition by IAS 41, despite its closer alignment with tradition agricultural activity. It is thought that a racehorse owned by a racing syndicate lies outside the provisions of IAS 41 but is clearly covered, as a living asset, by AASB 1037.

It does seem that ESL could well continue their present reporting approaches if they came under the jurisdiction of IAS 41. It may be, however, more difficult to claim that the accounting standard requires application of values to their fauna. ESL and similar operations might need to draw strong analogies between their operation and the definition of agricultural activity provided in IAS 41. Such an analogy might work against their environmental credentials. Their level of disclosure might be increased slightly because of requirements in the International standard. The question of what value to assign to living assets would remain a vexing question. To all intents and purposes, NPV is the same as fair value less costs incurred for the sale transaction.

Assigning a value to endangered animals assists the cause of conservation through recognising that the animals have a "value". For ESL, part of the attraction of SGARAs is the positive publicity that they can engender. If ESL were to prepare reports using IAS 41 they might still gain some acceptance because they are promoting the cause that animals need to be valued, and recognised for that value. The soundness of the method used to achieve and report those values may well go unquestioned. Ideally, of course, animals should just be valued for the diversity they add to our environment.

8. CONCLUSION

The listing of ESL on the Australian Stock Exchange in May 2000 represented an interesting development in the range of SRI investment options available to Australians by offering an opportunity to supply funds for conservation activities that deal directly with risks to biodiversity. Undertaking a dynamic change in commercial operations to capture environmental values, ESL provides SRI investors with the prospect of earning financial returns and also intrinsic personal satisfaction from their supply of funds.

In this paper we have evaluated the measurement of ESL's performance. It is concluded that the application of AASB 1037 to place a monetary valuation on wildlife with a consequential inclusion in the financial Statement of Performance as unrealised profits, may not aid insights to management's financial performance or indeed their stewardship of these fauna. The use of AASB 1037 requires the recording of non-realised operating profits using a capital maintenance concept of physical operating capacity based on an increase in the volume of wildlife stock.

The native animals bred and contained on ESL land are controlled but not legally owned by the firm, but are central to the earning of future income. Much of the cash income that ESL will earn through tourism and education programs is dependent on the extent and mix of the wildlife on their sanctuaries. An increase in wildlife stock numbers is associated with the targets integral to their corporate citizenship objectives. However, the inclusion of: (a) wildlife as quasi inventory items; and (b) unrealised profits may not enhance the relevance and reliability of the financial information communicated to external parties.

It is suggested that, in this difficult area, an appropriate reporting approach would involve establishing separate accounts for: (a) management decision making; and (b) regulatory reporting purposes. The accumulating and reporting of information, relevant to internal decision making needs, should value the increase in native animals at the NPV of the deemed contribution to the future income earning potential of the sanctuaries.

The process of maximising shareholder and corporate citizenship is likely to be further enhanced if "traditional" financial results are supplemented by separate and detailed physical accounts – a move toward Elkington's 1997 triple bottom line reporting approach. These physical accounts can record the extent to which conservation firms, have made progress in pursuing the environmental objectives that are valued by current and potential future SRI investors. The information required here would include non-monetary information on changes in individual species, together with estimated changes for the following period. Adopting this approach is considered to aid reliability and comparability, insomuch as concerned stakeholders are offered greater insights into assessing the financial performance of management and the fulfilment of their stewardship role in preserving the "public assets" i.e. native fauna for the benefit of future generations.

Applying AASB 1037 and attaching monetary values to individual wildlife, assumes that the asset providing future economic benefits to the firm is indeed the wildlife. However as ESL and other similar conservation firms are legally restricted from offering wildlife for sale, we suggest the "future economic benefit to the entity" is the sanctuary – the combination of land and wildlife. On the 14th January 2002 Earth Sanctuaries announced to the Australian Stock Exchange its intention to completely restructure the business and seek a buyer for some, or indeed all of its assets. This statement was further supported in the 2001 reports. Since the release of these reports ESL have sold, or made arrangements to sell seven sanctuary properties in order to reduce debt (Milne, 2002), somewhat substantiating the point of view that the sanctuary is the asset providing the "future economic benefit".

The issues have greater import now as the uptake of IAS 41 principles by national standard setters may bring the question of accounting for the conservation of fauna to a wider audience. Singapore introduced a standard on agriculture late in 2001 and South Africa has a standard to become operative in 2003. New Zealand has an outstanding exposure drafts on agriculture. Former Eastern Block countries are moving to adopt International accounting standards and agriculture is often thought to be the key to their transformation to a capitalist economy.

Our paper has focused on the appropriateness of AASB 1037 for the assets and income of a firm pursuing commercial conservation activities. While our case study was isolated to commercial conservation there are interesting aspects that future research efforts could explore such as plantation forests, which also fall under the control of AASB 1037 and IAS 41. There is much to examine and much to learn form this interesting case study in the use of "cutting edge" accounting requirements.

ESL and similar international conservation firms offer a unique opportunity for the accounting profession to link a triple bottom reporting approach with financial reports. It would be preferable for standard setters to identify any necessary change to aid transparency relating to corporate citizenship activities and financial performance, before practice introduces interpretations of IAS 41, are which become "merely permitted" rather than being formally endorsed by the community and regulators. A reporting guideline for international conservation firms could be developed so that ambiguities are reduced and stakeholders do not have to shed light on accounting reports based on a practice that is merely "allowed".

NOTES

1. Cited in "The Allen Consulting Group", 2000, page 1.
2. The establishment of the Natural Heritage Trust and the widespread support it has received are evidence of these changes in values and perceptions.

ACKNOWLEDGMENTS

The authors wish to thank participants at the European Accounting Association (EAA) Copenhagen, April 2002 and the 11th International Congress on Social and Environmental Accounting Research, Melbourne, April 2002, and colleagues, particularly Brad Potter at Deakin University for comments on earlier versions of this paper. Comments on an earlier paper *The Valuation of Native Wildlife and AASB 1037: The Case of Earth Sanctuaries Limited* by participants at the conference on Governance and corporate Social Responsibility in the New Millennium, Deakin University 26–27th November have also assisted.

REFERENCES

AASB (1997). *Exposure draft ED83: Self-generating and regenerating assets*. Melbourne: Australian Accounting Standards Board.

ABARE (1998). Emissions trading in Australia: Developing a framework. ABARE Research Report 98.1. Canberra: AGPS.

Baldock, D., & Lowe, P. (1996). The development of European agri-environmental policy. In: M. Whitby (Ed.), *The European Environment and CAP Reform. Policies and Prospects for Conservation*. Wallingford: CAB International.

Barton, A. D. (2000). Accounting for public heritage facilities, assets or liabilities of the government. *Accounting, Auditing and Accountability Journal*, *13*(2), 219–235.

Brown, K., & Adger, W. N. (1994). Economic and political feasibility of international carbon offsets. *Forest Ecology and Management*, *68*, 217–229.

Bureau of Transport Economics (1998). Trading greenhouse emissions: Some Australian perspectives. Occasional Paper 115, Canberra.

Burritt, R. L., & Cummings, L. S. (1999). Environmental accounting, economic values and financial reporting, the case of Earth Sanctuaries Ltd. Paper presented at the AAANZ conference. Cairns, Australia.

Cummings, L. (2000). Accounting for crops. *Australian CPA*, *70*(8), 30–31.

Dowling, C., & Godfrey, J. (2001). AASB 1037 Sows the seeds of change: A survey of SGARA measurement methods. *Australian Accounting Review*, *11*(1), 45–51.

Earth Sanctuaries Ltd. (2000a). *Prospectus*.

Earth Sanctuaries Ltd. (2000b). *Annual Report*.

Herbohn, K. F., Peterson, R., & Herbohn, J. L. (1998). Accounting for forestry assets: Current practice and future directions. *Australian Accounting Review*, *8*(1), 54–66.

Hone, P., Purnell, A., & Raar, J. (2001). The valuation of native wildlife and AASB 1037: The case of Earth Sanctuaries Ltd. Paper presented at corporate governance and citizenship conference. Deakin University (November).

Industry Commission (1997). A full repairing lease, inquiry into ecologically sustainable land management. Draft Report, Canberra: AGPS.

Lee, T. (1989). *Income and value measurement: Theory and practice*. London, England: Van Nostrand Reinhold (International).

MAFF (2000). *Towards sustainable agriculture*. London, England: Ministry of Agriculture, Fisheries and Food.

McNeill, J. R. (2001). *Something new under the sun*. London: Penguin Books.

Milne, C. (2002). There's still life in earth sanctuaries. *Australian Financial Review* (July 5).

Moran, A., Chisholm, A., & Porter, M. (Eds) (1991). *Markets, resources and the environment*. North Sydney: Allen and Unwin.

Parker, C. (Tech. Ed.) (2001). *Accounting Handbook* (Vol. 1). Melbourne: Pearson Education.

Pearce, D. (1993). *Economic values and the natural world*. London, England: Earthscan.

Reinhardt, F. L. (1999). Bringing the environment down to earth. *Harvard Business Review* (July–August), 149–157.

SEAC (State of the Environment Advisory Council) (1996). *Australia: State of the environment 1996*. Melbourne: CSIRO Publishing.

The Allen Consulting Group (2000). *Socially responsible investment in Australia*. ISBN: 059-783-3709.

Woodford, J. (2001). *The secret life of wombats*. Melbourne: Text Publishing.

BEWARE THE IDES OF MARCH:
THE COLLAPSE OF HIH INSURANCE

Bonnie Buchanan, Tom Arnold and Lance Nail

ABSTRACT

Despite differences in corporate governance systems in the United States and Australia, the corporate governance failures that led to each country's largest bankruptcy are strikingly similar. WorldCom in the United States and HIH Insurance in Australia were both created by a rapid series of major acquisitions, failed after their last major acquisitions, and attempted to hide their declining performance with aggressive and/or fraudulent accounting practices. In this paper we present a clinical examination of the corporate governance failures that led to the demise of HIH Insurance and show that corporate governance failures are not endemic to the existing corporate governance system in the United States.

1. INTRODUCTION

The collapse of HIH Insurance in March 2001 is the biggest financial collapse in Australia's corporate history. As of March 15, 2001, liquidators estimated that the deficiency for the HIH Group is between $3.6 billion and $5.3 billion.[1] Six months before its collapse, HIH Insurance was Australia's second biggest insurer. As a publicly traded stock, HIH Insurance had only a ten-year history – growing rapidly through a series of acquisitions. The failure of HIH is largely attributable to its last major acquisition, FAI Insurance, and its aggressive accounting practices. Despite

Social Responsibility: Corporate Governance Issues
Research in International Business and Finance, Volume 17, 199–221
ISSN: 0275-5319/PII: S0275531903170092

the decline of HIH, its CEO received a multimillion dollar severance package when he resigned in the year before its bankruptcy. The fallout since the HIH collapse has been immense because it has triggered a rise in global reinsurance premiums. Domestically, the HIH collapse has impacted housing construction where builders who had previously been covered by HIH had to seek replacement coverage. The collapse also deprived approximately half of Australia's doctors of malpractice insurance and thousands of small businesses lost liability coverage.

WorldCom is the largest bankruptcy in U.S. history. Prior to its collapse in 2002, WorldCom was a leading telecommunications giant and the second largest provider of long distance services in the U.S. WorldCom's bankruptcy was due in large part to one of its last major acquisitions, MCI Communications, and fraudulent accounting practices. WorldCom was created from a merger between two communications companies in 1993 and grew exponentially through dozens of acquisitions over its nine-year history. The CEO of WorldCom also received a multimillion dollar severance package upon his resignation in the months before the bankruptcy that led to thousands of layoffs and cast further doubts on the strength of the domestic and international telecommunications industry.

The parallels between the histories and failures of HIH and WorldCom are striking, especially given that the companies were located in countries with differing corporate governance systems. In this paper we analyze the corporate governance failures that aided the collapse of HIH and their similarities to the same failures at WorldCom. Specifically, we examine the similarities and differences between Australian corporate governance mechanisms and those in place in other developed markets and the role these mechanisms played in the failure of HIH. We then highlight the elements of corporate governance which were ineffective in the case of HIH and show how these elements may be used to identify corporate governance weaknesses in other Australian firms and corporations in other developed countries.

The remainder of our study is organized as follows: Section 2 presents a comparison of corporate governance systems in place in major developed markets, Section 3 details the industry and firm-specific factors relevant to the demise of HIH, Section 4 highlights the corporate governance failures that led to the collapse of HIH, and Section 5 concludes.

2. OVERVIEW OF DEVELOPED COUNTRIES' CORPORATE GOVERNANCE SYSTEMS

As LaPorta et al. (2000) show, corporate governance systems are the strongest (or most effective) in those countries offering the highest levels of legal protection to stockholders. Among these countries with the highest levels of legal protection, the

United States (U.S.), the United Kingdom (U.K.), Germany, and Japan have been compared and contrasted for their differences in corporate governance systems. Of interest in comparative studies is why these developed countries have such variance in their corporate governance systems and the advantages and disadvantages to each system.

While different in some aspects, corporate governance systems in the U.S. and U.K. (and Canada as well) are more similar than different and researchers often classify them as the same when compared to systems in place in Germany and Japan (see Kaplan, 1994a, b).[2] The defining characteristics of this "Anglo-American" corporate governance system is its external mechanisms and open market orientation. These two characteristics are intertwined to form an active external market for corporate control and managerial labor. As Manne (1965) points out, poor corporate governance will lead to a depressed stock price and a takeover opportunity whereby managers of the acquired firm are replaced. Fama (1980) furthers this concept of external market discipline with his theory of "ex post settling up". Under this theory, managers who have been terminated because of their firms' poor performance face a harsh labor market and generally do not achieve the same level of status or compensation as before the termination. These external market mechanisms are designed to encourage managers to act in shareholders' best interests. Corporate governance changes may occur rapidly in the Anglo-American model, causing Kaplan (1994a) to term this model a "short term" corporate governance system.

Other characteristics common in the U.S./U.K. model include a single board of directors with a mix of management (inside) and non-management (outside) members. The chief executive officer (CEO) almost always serves on the board – often as chairman.[3] In the U.K., and increasingly in the U.S., the boards' audit and compensation committees are comprised of outside directors. CEOs are generally shareholders in their firms, but the levels of holdings vary greatly.

In contrast, the German and Japanese corporate governance systems are better described as long-term relationship models. External control mechanisms are minimal, but shareholdings are more concentrated – often held by financial institutions with a major presence on firms' boards. In Germany the board structure is bifurcated into a supervisory and management board. This is somewhat similar to the Anglo board/management structure but with notable exceptions. First, the two boards are mutually exclusive. Thus, the supervisory board, which oversees the management board, is a board of strictly outside directors. Second, the supervisory board appoints and charges the management board. This differs from the Anglo model where the CEO generally has some, or even total, control over the selection of the board of directors. Third, CEOs in Germany tend to have less absolute power over their corporations than in the U.S./U.K. model.[4]

The CEO and/or chairman of the board also has less power in Japanese corporate governance systems where decision by consensus is the norm. Board structure and function is different from both the Anglo and German models. Dominated by inside directors, the boards of Japanese companies are largely made up of current and former employees who tend to have negligible ownership stakes in the firm. As in the German system, shareholdings are concentrated and institutional ownership is higher than in the U.S./U.K. However, institutional shareholders tend to be less proactive in the Japanese system.[5]

Australia is a developed country with a corporate governance system combining elements of both the external and internal control mechanisms described above. The general structure of the Australian corporate governance system is a hybrid of the Anglo-American, German, and Japanese models. As pointed out by Suchard et al. (2001), Australian corporate governance mixes the Anglo board structure with the internal "relationship" corporate governance mechanisms seen in Germany and Japan. Australian firms have a single board of directors comprised of inside and outside members. Following the 1991 Bosch Report, directors are classified into three categories: executives, independent non-executives, and non-independent non-executives. The dichotomy of classification of non-executives relies on a comprehensive list of current and past relationships between the director and firm. Directors are deemed independent only if they have no current or prior relationship with the firm as an employee, professional advisor, or having no other contractual relationship to the company.

However, Australian firms tend to have less diffuse shareholdings than in the U.S. and U.K. Australian markets also differ in that hostile takeovers are rare and not viewed as a source of external discipline as in the U.S./U.K. model. Rather, the few blockholders with the large concentrations of shares are expected to serve as monitors of the firm much as in the case in Germany and Japan. This mixture of a board structure designed to be monitored by open and external governance mechanisms with closed and internal monitoring mechanisms has led some to question the effectiveness of the Australian corporate governance system.[6] The HIH collapse highlights some of the shortcomings of the Australian corporate governance system.

3. RELEVANT INDUSTRY AND FIRM INFORMATION

3.1. The Australian Insurance Industry

The Australian insurance industry represents 2% of the international market in general insurance and is ranked the 11th largest market in the world. For the year ending 2000 there were 161 Australian Prudential Regulation Authority (APRA) licensed private sector insurers and reinsurers writing insurance inside Australia. Panel A of Table 1 indicates how these private sector insurers are classified.

Table 1.

Type of Insurer	Number of Insurers	
Panel A: Classification of Licensed Private Sector Insurers and Reinsurers inside Australia, Year: 2000.		
Direct Underwriters	104	
Mortgage Insurers	17	
Captive Insurers	6	
Reinsurers	30	
s.37 exempt Insurers	4	
Total	161	
	Dec 1999	Dec 2000
Panel B: Summary Statistics for the Australian Insurance Industry 1999–2000 (in Millions $Aust).		
Premium Revenue	$18,379,291	$19,035,745
Less: outwards reinsurance expense	3,935,729	4,757,772
Net premium revenue	14,443,562	14,277,973
Claims Expense	20,583,455	17,725,196
Less: reinsurance and other recoveries revenue	7,144,384	5,715,936
Net Claims Expense	13,439,071	12,009,260
Underwriting expenses	3,933,455	3,763,382
Underwriting result	−2,928,964	−1,494,669
Plus investment revenue rising from: Interest	1,384,330	1,491,894
Dividends	285,193	449,321
Rent	76,155	52,130
Plus other revenue	123,977	132,431
Plus changes in net market value on investments	482,738	1,570,750
Less general and administration expenses	811,678	669,643
Profit/loss from general insurance	−1,388,249	1,532,214
Plus: profit/loss from business other than general insurance	30,039	87,439
Operating profit/loss before extraordinary items and income tax	−1,358,210	1,619,653
Less: income tax expense attributable to operating profit	−121,453	100,409
Operating profit/loss after income tax	−1,236,757	1,519,244
Plus: profit/loss on extraordinary items net of tax	−21,535	−34,064
Operating profit/loss after extraordinary items and income tax	−1,258,292	1,485,180

Source: Australian Prudential Regulation Authority. Data are in Australian dollars.

Table 1 also provides details regarding the insurance industry as a whole. 1999 was not a particularly good year for the insurance industry due to a series of natural disasters. However, 2000 proved to be a much better year. Despite the improving economic environment, insurer New Cap Re failed while others struggled significantly (e.g. Reinsurance Australia Corporation and GIO Insurance). In the following year, HIH Insurance, Australia's second largest insurer, went into provisional liquidation.

The U.S. telecommunications industry, while not so affected by events of nature, witnessed a severe decline beginning in the late 1990s. Sources of financing so readily available in earlier years to WorldCom, industry leader AT&T, and even upstarts such as Global Crossing for financing their acquisition programs and/or capital investments dried up as the capital markets realized that the long distance business was in decline, prior acquisitions had not lived up to promised potential, and the quality of certain telecom assets (especially fiber optics) were coming under increasing scrutiny. Global Crossing preceded WorldCom to bankruptcy by a matter of months in 2002.

3.2. The History of HIH Insurance

HIH Insurance began in 1968 when Ray Williams and Michael Payne established MW Payne Underwriting Agency Pty. Ltd in Australia. After being acquired by a British insurer in 1971, the firm that became HIH was spun-off as a publicly-traded firm on the Australian Stock Exchange in 1992. Through a decade of multiple acquisitions, mergers, and name changes, HIH diversified into many insurance sectors with operations in multiple countries. Table 2 provides a detailed history.

By 2001, the HIH group consisted of 217 subsidiaries with operations in a number of countries. Within the HIH group the three largest licensed insurance companies were HIH Casualty and General Insurance Limited, FAI General Insurance Company Limited and CIC Insurance Limited. HIH Insurance Limited was the listed holding company. Prior to its collapse, HIH Insurance's principal activities in Australia and internationally were general insurance underwriting, the operation of insurance underwriting agencies, investment funds management, financial services and property. The company also managed workers' compensation schemes in New South Wales, Victoria and South Australia.

Evidence of HIH's aggressive approach to accounting surfaced as early as 1992 in a due diligence report by Ernst and Young performed for CIC Holdings while in merger talks with CE Heath International (an earlier version of HIH). Heath was found to have understated liabilities by $18 million and under-reserved by $41 million (much of this sum constitutes a "prudential margin", a very common

Table 2. Chronology of Key Events at HIH Insurance.

1968	Ray Williams and Michael Payne establish M. W. Payne Underwriting Agency Pty Ltd.
1971	M. W. Payne Underwriting Agency acquired by CE Heath Plc. of the U.K.
1980	Ray Williams appointed to board of CE Heath Plc.
1987	CE Heath Plc. establishes workers compensation underwriting operation in California, USA.
1989	Business of CE Heath Plc. transferred to CE Heath International Holdings Ltd. (CE Heath), with 90% shareholding retained by CE Heath Plc.
1992	CE Heath lists on the Australian Stock Exchange. This results in 45% of the issued capital owned by the public, 44% by CE Heath plc and 11% by CE Heath directors and staff.
1993	CE Heath commences operations in the U.K.
1993	CE Heath sells its workers compensation underwriting operation in California, USA.
1995	CE Heath acquires CIC Insurance Group ("CIC"). CIC Holdings becomes Winterthur Holdings Australia Ltd., a wholly owned subsidiary of Winterthur Swiss Insurance Company ("Winterthur Swiss").
1996	CE Heath changes its name to HIH Winterthur International Holdings Limited ("HIH Winterthur"). HIH acquires Utilities Insurance.
1997	HIH Winterthur repurchases the workers compensation subsidiary in California, Heath Cal, subsequently named HIH America Compensation and Liability Insurance Company ("HIH America").
1997	HIH Winterthur acquires Colonial Ltd. General Insurance operations in Australia and New Zealand. HIH becomes Australia's largest writer of bank assurance.
January 1998	HIH Winterthur acquires Solart in Argentina.
February 1998	HIH Winterthur establishes representative office in Beijing, China. HIH Winterthur acquires minority interest (24.46% stake) in Nam Seng Insurance Plc. of Thailand.
April 1998	HIH Winterthur acquires the Cotesworth Group Ltd. in London, U.K., a managing agency of four Lloyds syndicates.
June 1998	HIH America acquires Great States Insurance Co. of Arizona, USA.
July 1998	Winterthur Swiss announces it is selling its 51% shareholding in HIH Winterthur to the public. HIH shares trade around $2.85.
August 1998	Sale of shareholding complete.
September 1998	HIH Winterthur announces proposed takeover of FAI Insurance Ltd. Adler family unloads 14.3% stake. HIH announces it had purchased the Adler family stake. Shares trade around $2.50.
September 1998	HIH blacklists stockbroking analysts who disputed the assessment of the company.
October 1998	HIH Winterthur becomes HIH Insurance Ltd.
January 1999	S&P downgrades HIH's corporate credit rating from A to A⁻ FAI takeover complete.
February 3, 1999	HIH's converting notes make a strong debut on ASX.
March 3, 1999	HIH enters formal negotiations for the sale of its 45% stake in FAI Life. HIH posts a 39% fall in 1998 net profit.
March 4, 1999	HIH announces it has suffered a 39% profit plunge.

Table 2.   (*Continued*)

March 26, 1999	HIH's earnings potential receives an upward rating by stockbroking analysts.
April 1999	As result of Sydney hailstorm, expected total loss of $27 million. The group also estimates its net loss due to reinsurance to be no more than $10 million.
April 21, 1999	HIH steps up sale of non-core asset, Oceanic Coal. Shares fall to $1.99.
June 30, 1999	New financial year-end used. Changed from Dec. 31 to June 30.
August 26, 1999	HIH posts $58.8 million loss in the six months to June.
September 15, 1999	HIH continues to pay dividends despite heavy losses. However, dividends had been slashed in half.
February 1, 2000	HIH ceases to be a substantial shareholder in OAMPS.
February 3, 2000	A$^-$ rating confirmed by Standard & Poor's.
March 2000	HIH returns to profitability for the first half of 1999/2000.
March 2, 2000	HIH announces plans to develop the St. Moritz Hotel in NY with Millenium Partners.
March 3, 2000	HIH sells about half of it to St. Moritz investment.
March 28, 2000	HIH takes a 10% stake in Safe Trade, an internet insurer.
March 29, 2000	HIH decreases its interest in Armourglass (from 10.55% to 8.91%).
March 31, 2000	HIH decreases holding in Acclaim Uranium NL (12.10% to 10.8%).
April 5, 2000	HIH decreases its interest in Armourglass (8.91% to 7.64%).
May 8, 2000	HIH decreases its interest in Acclaim Uranium (10.8% to 9.60%).
June 15, 2000	Share price falls to new low of $0.96.
June 20, 2000	Announcement that Rodney Adler, an executive non-director had topped up his holding in the company to 1.86%.
July 1, 2000	Goods and Services Tax (GST) introduced in Australia.
September 2000	Joint venture with Allianz announced. HIH sells part of its domestic personal lines to Allianz for $500 million.
September 12, 2000	George Sturesteps and Michael Payne resign as directors of HIH.
October 12, 2000	Dominic Fodera resigns as director of HIH. Also in October, the U.S. business is placed in run-off. Ray Williams, CEO, announces his retirement.
November 2000	S&P downgrade HIH credit rating to BBB$^+$. Some Asian operations are also sold. HIH also enters managing general agency agreement with Gerling Group.
December 15, 2000	HIH annual general meeting. Ray Williams steps down as director of HIH and Randolph Wein is appointed the new CEO. Shareholders call for resignation of Rodney Adler from HIH board.
February 22, 2001	ASX trading halt to HIH shares. Speculation that HIH will lose up to $500 million.
February 26, 2001	HIH resumes trading. Rodney Adler resigns. ASIC raids HIH offices.
February 27, 2001	Trading halted at HIH's request. ASIC hands HIH documents to ASX. S&P lowers HIH Credit rating.
March 1, 2001	HIH shares suspended until interim profit released.
March 6, 2001	QBE forms joint venture with HIH in corporate insurance, takes 60% stake.
March 9, 2001	Allianz buys remainder of retail insurance venture for $125 million.
March 14, 2001	NRMA buys HIH workers' compensation business for $130 million.
March 15, 2001	HIH puts itself into provisional liquidation and estimates $800 million half year loss.
May 16, 2001	ASIC launches its biggest ever investigation, seizing HIH documents.
May 21, 2001	Federal Government announces a Royal Commission into what is at the time Australia's biggest corporate collapse.

Source: Australian Financial Review and HIH Royal Commission Website.

prudent insurance company practice of reserving approximately 20% more capital beyond what is necessary to cover expected liabilities).[7]

Ray Williams, CEO of Heath, disagreed with the need for a prudential margin. A second report by an independent expert was drafted and recommended that the merger still take place. The independent expert was Alan Davies of the public accounting firm Arthur Andersen. Davies later became HIH's lead auditor in 1996 when the former auditor, Dominic Fodera, became HIH's finance director.[8]

Similarly, WorldCom had been accused by former employees of accounting improprieties for overbooking revenue and not writing off bad accounts receivable in a lawsuit that was dismissed a couple of years prior to the bankruptcy. The controller and CFO were later indicted for accounting fraud for understating expenses by more than U.S.$3 billion. Arthur Andersen also served as the auditor of WorldCom.

Despite the aggressive accounting and the potential agency issues with auditors, the beginning of the end of HIH focuses on a particular acquisition in 1998. HIH initiated a formal takeover of domestic insurer FAI Insurance Ltd. in September 1998, completing the takeover in January 1999. According to its annual report, HIH's strategy was to secure a major market share position in the Australian general insurance industry and to diversify its distribution channels. A major stakeholder in FAI, the Adler family, sold their 45 million shares, or 14.2% stake, in FAI to HIH for $34 million. HIH Insurance announced it had purchased the Adler family stake and would make a bid for the remaining shares of the company. The terms of the offer were one HIH share and $2.25 cash for every six FAI shares. At the time, this would value FAI at approximately $300 million. At the time of the proposed acquisition, HIH announced that it intended to retain FAI's personal lines insurance business as a discrete unit within HIH and would retain the FAI brand name in its retail operations. The reinsurance program would also be consolidated, both companies' corporate insurance portfolios would be merged, and the IT systems would be integrated. After the FAI takeover, the HIH group accounted for more than 10% of the general insurance business in Australia. Rodney Adler, CEO of FAI, was then named a director at HIH.

In early 1999, HIH announced that it had suffered a 39% profit plunge in the year through December. Declining premium rates, record low interest rates and the second worst year on record for natural disasters were given as reasons for the profit plunge. Such disasters included storm and flood damage along Australia's East Coast, Hurricanes' George and Mitch, Canadian ice storms, and a large scale power outage in New Zealand. As a result of these disasters, claims expenses increased sharply and the core underwriting resulted in a loss of $73.4 million for 1998 with catastrophe losses totaling $36 million. CEO Ray Williams claimed that 90% of the 2.5% increase in the group's combined ratio (a measure of claims and expenses to net earned premium) was attributable to the catastrophe claims. The group's combined ratio grew from 102.7% to 105.2%. FAI Insurance recorded an unaudited loss of $50–$60 million for the six months to December and suffered a $22 million loss on investments for the first quarter. Despite this, by the end of March 1999, HIH's earnings potential had received an upward rating by stock analysts.

However, the credit quality of HIH had already been downgraded from A to A⁻ by Standard and Poors in January 1999 due to concerns over the acquisition of FAI. HIH attempted to allay the fears of the rating agencies by issuing subordinated debt with quasi-equity characteristics because it hoped to neutralize rating agencies' concerns about its indebtedness, while also addressing shareholders' concerns of dilution by a straight equity issue.

Yet, losses continued to mount during the year and the stock price continued to drop. By June, shares had slipped below the $2 mark. Then in August, HIH posted a $58.8 million loss for the first six months of 1999. Two losses stood out at this time – a $50.1 million loss on the sale of FAI's former asset, Oceanic Coal, and a $50 million abnormal loss related to the introduction of the Goods and Services Tax (GST) that would take place in Australia on July 1, 2000. Despite these losses, HIH still intended to pay dividends and, according to media reports, was aiming at a 70% to 80% payout ratio. Analysts had determined that HIH would have to generate at least $80 million in retained earnings in order to make this dividend payment. During this period, HIH changed its financial year-end from December 31 to June 30, justifying the decision because of the need to standardize internal reporting periods following the takeover of FAI Insurance so that investors could make more meaningful comparisons with competitors.

At the start of 2000, HIH benefited by offloading part of its stake in the telephone company One.Tel for about $35 million (One.Tel would also later collapse in 2001). In January, the company also sold part of its business in Argentina and ceased to be a substantial shareholder in a number of companies. Also in January, HIH decided to sue former clients in order to recover an alleged overpayment of funds.

Reported profits for the last two quarters of 1999 exceeded expectations by about $10 million. HIH pointed to an improved underwriting result, $25 million in cost savings from the integration of FAI Insurance, and disposal of that acquisition's last major non-core asset as reasons for the improvement. However, reinsurance, which represented 5% of HIH's business, contributed a $16.6 million loss as a result of exposure to the European windstorms in December. Standard and Poors confirmed HIH's credit rating of A⁻ in February.

As the year progressed, so did the negative news events for HIH. At the end of May, HIH denied claims that it had withheld from its shareholders relevant information about two takeover offers and a potentially expensive indemnity case.

By the middle of June 2000, HIH shares were trading at half the price they had been twelve months earlier. HIH management attributed the drop in share price as an irrational response to negative publicity aimed at HIH Insurance in the media. At the end of June, analysts expressed concerns regarding HIH's ability to pay its claims. In July HIH suffered more profit downgrades by analysts based on concerns of lower investment income and an expectation that predicted premium rate increases would not occur.

Several news events continued the decline of HIH's stock price. On September 11, HIH shares were suspended from trading as the company delayed its profit announcement. Three days later, two news events caused a further 20% slide in stock price. First, reported financial results for the first two quarters of 2000 were far worse than expected by analysts. Second, HIH announced a deal to sell its personal lines business to German insurer Allianz. The terms were that 51% would be owned by Allianz and 49% by HIH. HIH would receive $200 million at the time of the deal and proportional earnings for up to five years. After the five years Allianz would have an option to buy HIH's interest, while HIH could sell its 49% interest at any time during the following five years for $125 million.

The negative market reaction stemmed from investors' belief that HIH was selling its best assets – its personal lines business. Although this action would return HIH to its original focus of corporate insurance, analysts were concerned about the long-term viability of the company and grew suspicious of its accounting practices. HIH shares slumped another 30% the day after these announcements.

In order to support the stock during this downfall, CEO Williams bought 1.05 million shares and another board member bought 227,000 shares. At about the same time, director and former FAI CEO Rodney Adler began selling shares.

The stock's decline was not reversed by Williams' stock purchases or his strategic decisions and so he tendered his resignation on October 12. The company concurrently announced other restructuring moves, including that Australian executives would no longer sit on the board of HIH, reducing the size of its board from 11 to 7. The reason cited was that such a change was aimed at increasing the independence of the board. The capital markets greeted this news favorably and Adler continued selling shares soon thereafter.

Some media outlets began speculating that HIH's crisis was linked to the FAI takeover from two years prior. Apparently, no formal review of FAI's books occurred before HIH launched its $300 million takeover. Instead, the decision to buy FAI was based on a review of publicly available information such as annual reports and company results without a due diligence effort. After the takeover of FAI, HIH shut down several of FAI's insurance books. However, in the two-year period subsequent to the takeover, claims from those books had swollen to approximately $400 million, indicating that FAI was effectively insolvent when HIH bought it.

In November Standard and Poors dropped the credit rating of HIH from A⁻ to BBB⁺ – attributing the downgrade to a lower quality balance sheet that had emerged as a result of the deterioration in the FAI book of business and poor underwriting performance in HIH's U.K. and U.S. operations. In response to the downgrade, HIH constructed a revival plan that included abandoning its loss-making U.S. workers' compensation business and placing its Asian operation (estimated to be worth $80–$90 million) up for sale. Once the restructuring was completed, HIH consisted of: the Australian corporate insurance line, a minority stake in the Allianz joint venture and business in New Zealand and London.

A new CEO, Randolph Wein (former head of Asian Operations), was announced on December 15, 2000. At the shareholders meeting, investors jeered the former CEO when it was announced he would receive an estimated $5 million payout. In February 2001, the new CEO announced a flatter management structure for HIH Insurance. Rodney Adler, who had sold the last of his shareholdings in late December 2000, resigned at the end of February, 2001. The Australian Securities and Investment Commission (ASIC) announced an investigation of his share trading shortly afterwards.

WorldCom Chairman and CEO Bernard Ebbers also negotiated a multimillion dollar severance package when he was forced to resign in the months preceding the bankruptcy. WorldCom also later announced that the board had previously approved a multimillion dollar loan from the firm to Ebbers. While not illegal at the time, approval of loans of this magnitude to a company executive called into question the fiduciary responsibility of the board.

Shares in HIH were suspended on February 22, 2001 and again on February 27, 2001. Standard and Poors lowered HIH's credit rating from BBB⁺ to BBB⁻ and retained a credit watch on the company. The Australian Securities and Investment Commission (ASIC) also launched an investigation into HIH's market disclosure. Amongst speculation that HIH's half-year loss to December would be between $100 and $500 million, the Australian Stock Exchange (ASX) commenced delisting talks with HIH at the start of March 2001.

On March 7, HIH announced that it had sold a majority part of its corporate insurance operation to insurer QBE, who would effectively pay $36 million for the right to 60% of HIH's $600 million in premiums. What QBE would not take on was HIH's liabilities. Allianz bought the remainder of HIH's retail venture for $125 million and NRMA bought HIH's worker's compensation business for $130 million. On March 12, 2001 the Australian Prudential Regulation Authority (APRA) announced that it had already provided notice to HIH as to why it should be investigated. Amongst estimates of a half-year loss of $800 million, HIH put itself into provisional liquidation on March 15, 2001 and representatives from KPMG

Fig. 1. This Plot shows Share Price Data for HIH Insurance, the Australian Insurance Sector, and the Australian All Ordinaries Index (ASX) for the Period January 1, 1992–March 15, 2001. The Data is Weekly Indexed with an Initial Index Set Equal to 100. *Source:* DATASTREAM.

were appointed liquidators to the company and 17 of its controlled entities. A temporary form of administration, provisional liquidation gives a company time for the provisional liquidators to review a corporation's operations and assess its financial position.

Figure 1 displays the share price for the period 1992–2001. Data for the Australian Insurance sector index and the Australian All Ordinaries Index are also contained in Fig. 1.

4. CORPORATE GOVERNANCE ISSUES

Previous research links general corporate and insurance failures to unsupervised delegation of authority, rapid expansion, underpricing, reserve problems, false reporting, reckless management, rapid expansion, and incompetence. In this section we examine the legal and organizational framework, including the principles and processes, by which HIH was governed. In addition, we also focus on the accountability and relationships of key participants in the direction and control of the company – the board of directors and management. First of all, we will describe the legal and regulatory framework in which an Australian insurance firm, like HIH, operates.

4.1. The Regulatory Environment of the Australian Insurance Industry

The Australian insurance industry is regulated by Federal, State and Territory legislation. The Federal regulatory structure is made up of three key authorities: the Treasury, the Australian Prudential Regulation Authority (APRA) and the Australian Securities and Investment Commission (ASIC). The Treasury sets regulatory policy including drafting legislation. Prudential regulation of the industry is undertaken by APRA and market conduct is regulated by ASIC.

APRA first became aware of HIH's aggressive accounting in 2000 when a former HIH finance executive, Jeff Simpson, provided a report that essentially stated that HIH was already financially insolvent. Simpson noted that the APRA appeared understaffed and under-skilled (Main, 2002b). Inquiries after the HIH collapse noted that Arthur Andersen approved HIH's financial statements knowing that large losses were not being reported (Sykes, 2002a). The situation is similar to that in the U.S. where several corporate failures of firms audited by Arthur Andersen could not be pre-empted by the Securities and Exchange Commission (SEC) because of their claimed understaffing.

ASIC's responsibility in regard to HIH deals primarily with the public disclosure of financial reports, corporate executive conduct, and the conduct of market participants. Although ASIC has not to date aggressively pursued the potentially fraudulent financial reporting of HIH and FAI, Rodney Adler has faced prosecution and investigation in regards to corporate misconduct and insider trading.

Before it can launch a formal investigation into a business, APRA must give an insurer 14 days notice. APRA allegedly gave HIH notice on March 1, 2001 that it was preparing an investigation – a decision triggered by HIH's failure to file its December report. On March 14, HIH went to the Supreme Court and placed itself into provisional liquidation without prior notice to APRA. On the next day the APRA investigation began.

4.2. Board Structure and Compensation

A cornerstone of corporate governance is an understanding of the powers, accountability and relationships of those who participate in the direction and control of a company. The participants include the board of directors and management. As of September 2001, Australian Stock Exchange (ASX) Listing Rule 4.10.3 requires that a listed company's annual report contain a statement of the main corporate governance practices it has in place.

In addition to executive directors, an Australian board of directors may include non-executive directors. The main role of the executive directors is to carry out day-to-day management of the company's business. Consequently, executive directors are usually full-time employees of a company and are usually its senior management. Executive directors also have directorial duties of the company and may also have additional duties as part of their employment contract. On the other hand, non-executive directors are not employed by the company and are engaged on a part-time basis. Rather than focused or specialized in any particular area of a company's operations, the non-executive director is intended to have a broad and independent view of the company's operations.

Farrar (2002) examined the corporate governance practices of the top 100 listed Australian companies. He found that all the companies surveyed stated whether directors were executive or non-executive. Farrar also found that the average board size was 9.6 members, comprising 2.2 executive directors and 7.4 non-executive directors. The 2000 Korn/Ferry Report states that Australian boards were made up of an average of five non-executive and two executive directors. This board structure is similar to that found in Anglo-American firms.[9]

"Corporate Practices and Guidelines" claims that independence is more likely to be assured if the director is not a substantial shareholder of the company, is not retained as a professional adviser by the company, is not a significant supplier to or customer of the company, has not been employed by the company within the last few years, and has no significant contractual relationship with the company otherwise than as a director. Of concern in the case of HIH Insurance was that it was led by its founders and non-executive board member, Rodney Adler, who was the son of the founder of FAI Insurance, the company that has been referenced as a determining factor in the collapse of the HIH Group.

Stapledon and Lawrence (1996) investigate the issue of independent directors in an Australian context. The disadvantages of independent directors include: some independent directors are still too closely allied to management, their position is weakened where the chairperson is not an independent director, they lack detailed knowledge of the company's business, they have limited time to spend on the directorship and they are sufficiently linked with shareholders.

Lawrence and Stapledon (1999) later explain that using independent directors is one element of a broader tapestry of monitoring devices and rules which should serve to reduce agency costs in a corporation. Lawrence and Stapledon however find that independent Australian directors do not appear to have added value in the period 1985–1995.

According to the Korn/Ferry Report, the average remuneration for non-executive directors in Australian listed companies was $A52,760 as of 2000. As can be seen in Table 3, the direct compensation of the directors of HIH was well above this average. Additionally, several directors held substantial equity stakes in the firm. Of course, linking director remuneration to share price presents a number of inherent dangers. For one, it can lead to a disproportionate focus on short-term performance and pre-occupation with supporting the share price.

Amongst other HIH board failings was the attendance of some directors at board meetings. Throughout 1998 and the first six months of 1999, Michael Payne, the retired co-founder and CEO of HIH and chairman of the reinsurance committee, attended only four of 24 board meetings.

4.3. Accounting Issues

The Australian Accounting Standards Board (AASB) sets the accounting standards for Australian companies. According to AASB standards, companies must provide in their annual report a profit and loss statement, a balance sheet and a statement of cash flows. Under AASB standards, the financial statements must indicate a "true and fair view" of the financial position and performance of the company. An Australian company also has various semiannual reporting obligations. The law after July 1, 1998 also requires that a company's annual financial report (or its concise version) must be audited and lodged with the Australian Securities and Investment Commission within three months of the end of the financial year.

The case of HIH also refocused attention on the controversial issue of the independence of the auditors from their clients. The board of HIH had three former partners of Arthur Andersen, HIH's auditor. In October 2000, the auditor signed off on HIH's financial statements, indicating the company had assets of $8.32 billion against liabilities of $7.38 billion, giving it net assets of approximately $940 million. Andersen received $1.7 million for its work as auditor to the HIH group for the 12 months ended June 30, 2000.

In retrospect, certain items on HIH Insurance Group's balance sheet requires further scrutiny. Shareholders' funds in the 2000 annual report were estimated to be $939 million, but *the supporting were of suspect value*. In the 2000 annual report HIH's assets included intangibles of approximately $500 million, the bulk of which represented goodwill for FAI. On the liabilities side, there was approximately $500 million in borrowings. The substantial amount of debt carried by HIH is troubling. An insurance company's investment portfolio holds the premiums the company

Table 3. HIH Board Composition, Executive Compensation and Executive Shareholdings.

	Key Announcements	Compensation ($Aust)	Ordinary Shares	Options	Convertible Notes
1998/1999 Annual Report					
Non-Executive Directors					
G. A. Cohen (Chairman)		324,600	55,806		4,260
C. P. Abbott		204,386	59,647		
R. S. Adler	Appointed April 16, 1999	4,311,945	5,500,000		
J. H. Gardner	Appointed December 2, 1998	31,377	46,894		
A. W. Gorrie		200,862			
N. R. Head		142,140			
E. W. Heri	Resigned effective October 15, 1998				
M. W. Payne	Retired as Executive June 30, 1998, appointed Non-Executive July 9, 1998	271,936	133,611	376,000	8,467
W. E. Schurpf					
R. H. Stitt	Resigned effective April 15, 1998	128,180	40,810		1,129
Executive Directors					
R. Williams (CEO) and Deputy Chairman		1,460,350	10,336,383	500,000	19,200
T. Cassidy		916,777	6,941,213	400,000	10,000
D. Fodera		799,870	348,871	520,000	5,024
G. Sturesteps		986,294	6,242,061	320,000	9,700
H. R. Wein		517,687			
1999/2000 Annual Report					
Non-Executive Directors					
G. A. Cohen (Chairman)		216,090	61,566		4,260
C. P. Abbott		86,400	209,832		
R. S. Adler		53,000	5,753,670		
J. H. Gardner		57,000	112,713		

Table 3. (*Continued*)

	Key Announcements	Compensation ($Aust)	Ordinary Shares	Options	Convertible Notes
A. W. Gorrie	Resigned November 19, 1999	32,307			
N. R. Head	Resigned November 19, 1999	6,796			
M. W. Payne	Resigned effective September 12, 2000	133,317			
R. H. Stitt		63,514	140,260		1,129
Executive Directors					
R. Williams (CEO)	Resigned effective December 15, 2000	1,147,692	12,222,715	500,000	19,200
T. Cassidy	Resigned effective October 12, 2000	671,900			
D. Fodera	Resigned effective October 12, 2000	677,128			
	Appointed Chief Operating Officer				
G. Sturesteps	Resigned effective September 12, 2000	707,286			
H. R. Wein (new CEO)	Appointed new CEO December 15, 2000	648,328	4,233		

Note: For the 1998/1999 annual report there were 12 directors on the board, three less than the maximum number provided for under the company's constitution. For the 1999/2000 annual report, the Board of HIH had seven directors (5 Non-Executives and 2 Executives), eight less than the maximum number provided for under the company constitution.
On October 13, 2000 it was announced by HIH Chairman Geoffrey Cohen that Australian executives would no longer serve on the board. This meant that Terry Cassidy and Dominic Fodera would step down. Around this time Dominic Fodera was appointed Chief Operating Officer.

Source: Australian Financial Review and HIH Annual Reports. Data are in Australian dollars.

collects from its policy holders and generates investment income as an internal source of capital. Thus, there is little reason for an insurance company to seek external debt except for one-time purposes such as a takeover. Compared with the previous year, HIH's debt had risen by $170 million in 1999–2000 (a nearly 50% increase). According to its cash flow statements, HIH's premium income dropped 15%, or $486 million.

The HIH offer for FAI Insurance was at a 43% premium to FAI's market capitalization. Of the $300 million HIH paid for FAI, $157 million was for net assets and $143 million came in the form of goodwill. By June 30, 2000, HIH's goodwill had increased to $555.9 million and analysts estimated that $405.3 million of that total was related to FAI assets. Thus, within 18 months of FAI takeover, the net assets acquired from FAI were valued at a loss of over $100 million. This prompted the managers of HIH to consider legal action to determine if the financial position of FAI had been intentionally overstated at the time of the acquisition. Interestingly, FAI had also used Andersen as its auditor.

FAI was not the sole contributing factor to HIH's growing problems. On the reinsurance side, according to press reports, by June 2000, HIH had run out of reinsurance cover and presumably did not have a sufficient prudential margin nor sufficient assets to cover its claims. HIH's expansion into the competitive Lloyd's market (with losses of approximately $150 million) and U.S. workers' compensation sector are other possible reasons. One accounting issue that received some scrutiny from analysts was the decision by HIH to treat its increase in reserving as a goodwill item. While an acceptable accounting treatment, such a practice would be reflected in a company's profit and loss statement under more conservative accounting practices.

The main concern with insurance companies' published accounts is with their reserving, or the amount that the insurer shows as its liability for outstanding claims. Three of the most important factors include the actuary's estimate of the dollar value of future claims (based on claims experience and probability), the inflation rate by which that estimate may be increased, and the interest rate at which the estimate should be discounted. Clearly, this calculation is open to some educated guesswork and subjectivity. Once the insurance company has calculated its outstanding claims in the manner described it will normally add a prudential margin of 10–25%. HIH did not add this prudential margin to their reserve balance. This practice made HIH look stronger than its industry peers allowing a stronger credit rating until the string of catastrophic events depleted its shallow reserves.

Another subjective accounting practice potentially abused by the managers of HIH is how the actuarial assumptions of outstanding claims are determined. A small change in interest rates or assumptions about claims frequency can make

Table 4. Financial Highlights at HIH Insurance Group (1996–2000).

	12 months to June 1996	12 months to June 1997	12 months to June 1998	12 months to June 1999	12 months to June 2000
Premium (revenue earned-gross(excl. VWA)	1135.8	1343.0	1841.3	2318.4	2962
Premium revenue earned – net	888.5	1067.0	1300.5	1662.2	1995.4
Claims incurred and expenses	905.4	1094.5	1344.8	1808.4	2098.9
Combined ratio	101.9%	102.6%	103.4%	108.8%	105.2%
Underwriting Profit/Loss	(16.9)	(27.5)	(44.3)	(146.3)	(103.5)
Goodwill amortization	(4.7)	(5.2)	(7.3)	(17.2)	(35.3)
Interest expense	(1.8)	(4.8)	(4.7)	(17.9)	(31.5)
Investment return on shareholders' funds	26.1	95.8	31.4	71.1	60.4
Operating Profit after income tax, abnormal and extraordinary items	59.2	78.3	37.5	(39.8)	18.4
Dividend/share (cents)	13.0	15.0	16.0	12.0	6.0
Earnings/share (cents)	20.5	25.6	9.9	(0.4)	(0.6)
Net tangible asset backing per share –diluted[a]	1.23	1.38	1.66	1.02	0.67
Return on Equity	15.4%	16.3%	6.5%	−5.0%	2.0%
	31.12.97	30.6.99	30.6.00		
Other Financial Items					
Inflation Rate (%)	5.0	5.0	3.8		
Discount Rate (%)	6.2	6.1	6.4		
Outstanding Claims Details					
Expected Future claim payments (undiscounted)	$2,377.3	$4,4598.7	$4,922.9		
Liability for Outstanding Claims (Aust$m)	$1,956.6	$4,051.5	$4,430.9		

Note: According to the HIH annual report, the weighted average expected term to settlement from the balance date of the outstanding claims is estimated to be 2.6–2.7 years. The inflation and discount rates displayed were used in measuring the consolidated outstanding claims liability for the succeeding and subsequent years.
Source: HIH annual report.
[a] Adjusted for full effect of Convertible and Converting Note Issues, where applicable.

large differences to the present value of outstanding claims, in turn changing the net assets of the insurance company quite dramatically. The rate of interest is important particularly when it is compounded over long periods. For example, the lower the inflation rate and the higher the discount rate used, the lower the dollar value will be of the outstanding claims. In the case of HIH Insurance, the inflation rate estimate for 2000 was 3.8%, down from the 1999 estimate of 5% (see Table 4). The discount rate HIH used in 2000 was 6.4% versus 6.1% for 1999. This 1.5% increase in the gap could have reduced claims reserves by as much as $100 million. Revising the two adjustments to the inflation rate and discount rate alone would have wiped out $360 million of HIH's shareholders' funds. Thus, these minor movements in rates could have artificially inflated the capital base by more than one third.

Again, the parallel situation existed at WorldCom. The aforementioned aggressive turned fraudulent accounting practices at WorldCom allowed them to maintain their investment grade debt rating and issue a U.S.$11.8 billion bond issue in May 2002, just months before the bankruptcy. An internal auditor found the accounting fraud after the resignation of Ebbers and reported it to the board who eventually investigated the fraud. Arthur Andersen never uncovered the fraud, but did receive U.S.$4.4 million in audit fees and another U.S.$12.4 million in consulting fees from WorldCom in the year before the bankruptcy. In both cases, debt was increased as a source of capital on the basis of inflated accounting numbers and lofty bond ratings.

5. CONCLUSION

The bankruptcies of HIH and WorldCom demonstrate that certain corporate governance failures are common across different corporate governance systems. Both were the largest bankruptcies in their respective countries and the factors that led to both failures were relatively the same – a rapid acquisition program, one large problematic acquisition, aggressive and/or fraudulent accounting, increased leverage obtained on the basis of inflated accounting numbers, and a lack of independence with respect to the board of directors and auditors.

In the wake of these bankruptcies, the regulatory agencies in both countries are taking a more proactive role in overseeing corporate governance. The Australian government established a rescue package to compensate resident individuals and small businesses. In addition, the Australian government announced a Royal Commission to report on the HIH failure. At the time of this writing, the HIH Royal Commission was still in progress. However, in the meantime civil proceedings had been brought against three directors (Rodney Adler, Ray Williams, and Dominic Fodera). All were found to have breached their duties as directors under the Corporations Act. Adler and Williams were jointly held liable to pay compensation of more than $7 million and were banned from being involved in company management for terms of 20 years and 10 years respectively.

In the United States, criminal charges have been brought against WorldCom controller David Myers and CFO Scott Sullivan. At the time of this writing, Myers had pleaded guilty to accounting fraud. This bankruptcy, along with other high profile corporate governance failures that led to bankruptcies at Enron, Global Crossing, and Adelphia, sparked a movement towards tighter monitoring of the corporate governance mechanisms in place in the U.S. Namely, the Sarbanes-Oxley bill requires the independence of auditors by disallowing auditing firms from offering consulting services to their clients. Also, the New York Stock

Exchange and Securities and Exchange Commission have enacted more stringent corporate governance practices.

This case illustrates how corporate failures are inextricably linked to corporate governance failures, regardless of the corporate governance system in place. We show that the major factors to the bankruptcies of HIH and WorldCom were corporate governance failures – too rapid of an acquisition program, poor integration of a takeover target, accounting malfeasance, and a lack of board and auditor independence. While market conditions did play a role in the demise of these companies, many of their competitors remain. Thus, these bankruptcies were less a result of economic Darwinism than preventable breaches of proper corporate governance. As these abuses span different corporate governance systems, they are not the result of the system at hand and may be addressed internationally. As the same corporate governance abuses occur repetitively, the confidence of all investors is undermined and international economic interests are at stake, not just individual companies and their shareholders.

NOTES

1. All values and prices throughout this article are expressed in Australian dollars unless stated otherwise.
2. The U.S. and U.K. are becoming closer given the similar recommendations of the Cadbury and Hampel Committees in the U.K. and the revised 2002 listing requirements in the U.S.
3. Although the dual CEO/chairman role is becoming less frequent in both countries.
4. For further comparisons, see John and Senbet (1998).
5. For further comparisons, see Kang and Shivdasni (1995).
6. See Shawn Donnan, "Flaws and failures behind some fine facades". *Financial Times*, June 8, 2001.
7. See Sykes (2002b).
8. See Main (2002a) for more detail on these relationships.
9. See Yermack (1996).

REFERENCES

Australian Financial Review (various editions).
Bosch, H. (Ed.) (1991). *Corporate practices and conduct Information Australia*. Melbourne: F.T. Pitman.
Donnan, S. (2001). Flaws and failures behind some fine facades. *Financial Times* (June 8).
Fama, E. F. (1980). Agency problems and the theory of the firm. *Journal of Political Economy, 88*, 228–307.
Farrar, J. (2002). *Corporate governance in Australia and New Zealand*. Oxford University Press.

HIH Insurance Annual Reports (1999–2000).

http://www.treasury.gov.au

http://www.asic.gov.au

http://www.apra.gov.au

John, K., & Senbet, L. M. (1998). Corporate governance and board effectiveness. *Journal of Banking and Finance, 22*, 371–403.

Kang, J. K., & Shivdasni, A. (1995). Firm performance, corporate governance and top executive turnover in Japan. *Journal of Financial Economics, 38*, 29–58.

Kaplan (1994a). Top executive rewards and firm performance: A comparison of Japan and the United States. *Journal of Political Economy, 102*, 510–546.

Kaplan (1994b). Top executives, turnover and firm performance in Germany. *Journal of Law, Economics and Organization, 10*, 142–159.

Korn/Ferry (2000). *International boards of directors in Australia and New Zealand 2000.* Korn/Ferry International.

LaPorta, R., Lopez-de-Silanes, F., Shleifer, A., & Vishny, R. (2000). Investor protection and corporate governance. *Journal of Financial Economics, 58*(1–2), 3–27.

Lawrence, J., & Stapledon, G. (1999). Do independent directors add value? Research Report, CCLSR, University of Melbourne.

Main, A. (2002a). HIH cut corners from the start: Inquiry. *Australian Financial Review* (June 18), 1 of News Section.

Main, A. (2002b). APRA told of HIH insolvency. *Australian Financial Review* (July 12), 1 of News Section.

Manne, H. G. (1965). Mergers and the market for corporate control. *Journal of Political Economy, 73*, 110–120.

Stapledon, G., & Lawrence, J. (1996). Corporate governance in the top 100. Research Report. CCLSR, University of Melbourne, Melbourne.

Suchard, J., Singh, M., & Barr, R. (2001). The market effect of CEO turnover in Australian firms. *Pacific-Basin Finance Journal, 9*, 1–27.

Sykes, T. (2002a). How the HIH audit report came to be signed. *Australian Financial Review* (April 2), 11 of Companies and Markets Section.

Sykes, T. (2002b). Resurrected report raises doubts about HIH's solvency. *Australian Financial Review* (June 22), 12 of Companies and Markets Section.

Yermack, D. (1996). Higher market valuation of companies with a small board of directors. *Journal of Financial Economics, 40*, 185–212.

MODELS AND MEASUREMENT OF SUSTAINABLE GROWTH AND SOCIAL WELFARE

Sardar M. N. Islam and B. D. Craven

ABSTRACT

This paper develops mathematical models and computational methods for formulating sustainable growth and social welfare programs, and discusses approaches to computing the models. Computer experiments on modifications of the Kendrick–Taylor growth model, using the optimal control packages SCOM (Craven & Islam, 2001) and RIOTS_95 (Schwartz, 1996), analyse the effects of changing the discount factor, time scale, and growth factor. These packages enable an economist to experiment, using his own computer, on the results of changing parameters and model details.

1. INTRODUCTION

The terms *sustainability of growth*, and *social welfare* that ensure intergenerational equity, are controversial. In recent literature, Hamiltonian-based measures of social welfare have been used to define the concept of sustainable growth. In the mainstream economic interpretation, where social welfare is measured in terms of pure economic variables such as income or consumption, *sustainable growth* relates to economic conditions of non-declining consumption or capital (whether man-made, natural, or environmental) over time. *Sustainable growth* has been formalised in different ways. In the optimal growth literature, sustainable

Social Responsibility: Corporate Governance Issues
Research in International Business and Finance, Volume 17, 223–251
© 2003 Published by Elsevier Science Ltd.
ISSN: 0275-5319/PII: S0275531903170109

consumption is characterized by the *golden age*, representing the maximum consumption possible without reducing the potential for the same level of consumption in the future. Given the numerical orientation of this study, the objective function here has cardinality, measurability and intergenerational utility and welfare comparability implications. Several other definitions of sustainability have been given (Faucheux, Pearce & Proops, 1996). Conceptual and theoretical studies of sustainability are well advanced. In spite of several operational numerical studies of this issue (e.g. Islam, 2001), there is still a strong need for operational methods for sustainability modelling. This paper presents several operational models and methods for sustainable growth and welfare, in order to explore a range of optimal control models in welfare economics.

2. WELFARE MEASURES AND MODELS FOR SUSTAINABILITY

Various theoretical articles (Faucheux, Pearce & Proops, 1996; Smulders, 1994) have incorporated sustainability in optimal growth models. In terms of optimal control theory, sustainable consumption or welfare for an autonomous infinite-horizon problem has been described by a Hamiltonian function (see Heal, 1973, 1998; Leonard & Long, 1994).

Consider an infinite-horizon model, formulated as optimal control:

$$V(a, b) := \text{Max} \int_a^\infty e^{-\rho t} f(x(t), u(t)) \, dt$$

subject to:

$$x(a) = b, \dot{x}(t) = m(x(t), u(t)).$$

Here $x(t)$ is the state function (e.g. capital), $u(t)$ is the control function (e.g. consumption), and $u(t)$ is unconstrained. Denote by $\lambda(t)$ the costate function, and by $\Lambda(t) = \lambda(t) e^{\rho t}$ the current-value costate function. The current-value Hamiltonian is:

$$h(x(t), u(t), \Lambda(t)) = f(x(t), u(t)) + \Lambda(t) m(x(t), u(t)).$$

Denote the optimal functions by $x^*(t)$, $u^*(t)$, $\Lambda*(t)$. Under some restrictions (see Section 3.3), including the requirement (usually fulfilled) that $\lambda(t) = O(e^{-\beta t})$ as $t \to \infty$ for some $\beta > 0$, and no constraints on the control $u(t)$, it may be shown that:

$$h(x^*(t), u^*(t), \Lambda^*(t)) = -\rho V(t, x^*(t)) = -\rho e^{-\rho \tau} V(0, x^*(t)) \to 0 \quad \text{as} \quad t \to \infty.$$
$$(1)$$

The proofs in Weitzman (1976), Leonard and Long (1994) and Heal (1998) are incomplete, and do not state some necessary restrictions. Although the two functions $h(x^*(t), u^*(t), \Lambda^*(t))$ and:

$$\delta^{-1} \int_t^\infty f(x^*(\tau)), u^*(\tau) e^{-\delta(\tau - t)} \, d\tau$$

satisfy the same first-order differential equation, their equality only follows if they satisfy a common boundary condition, namely both $\to 0$ as $t \to \infty$, which follows from Eq. (1).

Weitzman (1976) and subsequent authors have interpreted $V(t, x^*(t))$ as the stock of *total wealth*, and also $h(x^*(t), u^*(t), \Lambda^*(t))$ as the *interest on total wealth*, which may be taken as a measure of sustainable income, utility or social welfare.

There are many criticisms of this approach to measurement of sustainable welfare and sustainability (Arronsson, Jacobson & Lofgren, 1997; Brekke, 1997; Heal, 1998; Land Economics, 1997). The Hamiltonian approach assumes very restrictive and unrealistic conditions, including: (i) constant discount rate, technology, and terms of trade; (ii) time autonomous dynamic systems in continuous time; (iii) no constraints on the control or state functions; (iv) positive social time preferences; and (v) convex optimal control models (so that necessary optimality conditions are also sufficient). The assumption of a single capital good may not be necessary. Some aspects of this approach need more attention, including transversality conditions, and conditions when the Hamiltonian approaches zero for large times. Overtime and intercounting comparisons are not possible; the consumption path has a single peak, and this is not sustained; and the *dictatorship of the present* is embedded in the model. If non-autonomous dynamics are considered, thus assuming $\dot{x}(t) = m(x(t), u(t), t)$ where $m(\cdot)$ depends explicitly on t, then $x(t)$ and $u(t)$ will *not* generally tend to limits $x(\infty)$ and $u(\infty)$ as t tends to infinity; this is the case with the Kendrick–Taylor model considered in Section 5. For an autonomous model, the limits (if they exist) must satisfy $0 = m(x(\infty), u(\infty))$.

Work on computational models and methods for sustainable growth is generally less advanced, although some simple approaches have been tried (see Cesar, 1994; Land Economics, 1997; Smulders, 1994). The object of the present paper is to develop some mathematical and computational models and methods for sustainable growth, within the framework of welfare economics (Arrow et al., forthcoming). They include the elements of an optimal growth program (Islam, 2001) such as an objective function, time horizon, time preference and terminal constraints.

There are several ways to embed *sustainability* into the mathematical formulation of a computable optimal growth model. These include the following:

(a) Including environmental factors and consequences in the model, e.g. by dynamic equations, or suitable constraints, for resource supply and exhaustion, pollution generation, etc. (see Cesar, 1994; Heal, 1998). See Section 5.1.
(b) Appropriate specification of the objective function, to express the principles or criteria for sustainable growth (see Section 3.1).
(c) Modelling intergenerational equity, reflected in social time preference, by suitably modified discount factors (see Section 3.2).
(d) Considering a long-term planning horizon, or an infinite horizon in an optimal growth model, so as give suitable weight to the long-term future, as well as to the short-term, e.g. by Rawls (1972) or Chichilnisky (1977) (see Sections 3.2 and 3.3).

The paper is structured as follows. In Sections 3 and 4, some mathematical models and methods are provided, for including sustainability in an optimal growth model. The Kendrick–Taylor model is modified in Section 5 to incorporate sustainability criteria. The results of computational experiments are presented in Section 6. Conclusions and computational recommendations are given in Section 7.

3. MODELLING SUSTAINABILITY

3.1. Description by Objective Function with Parameters

Sustainability should be studied within a social choice framework. The present discussion assumes the possibility of a social choice by a social welfare function (objective function). This function may contain utilitarian and non-welfaristic elements of social choice. It must incorporate, in some suitable form, the concerns for sustainability. If a description using a single objective is sought, that of Chichilnisky (1996) is as plausible as any available. It includes a parameter α, which must be chosen to set the balance between short-term and long-term. This objective function may be written:

$$\alpha \int_0^\infty U(c(t), k(t), t)e^{-\rho t} \, dt + (1 - \alpha)\lim_{t \to \infty} U(c(t), k(t), t),$$

perhaps with some replacement for the discount factor (see Section 4.2). This model assumes that limits exist (so excluding any oscillatory models), and it is not computable as it stands, because of the infinite time range. As remarked in Section 2, the assumed limits as $t \to \infty$ will normally require that the function *m* in the dynamic equation, and also the utility U, do not depend explicitly on t. Moreover, some bounds on the variables should be adjoined, (compare Rawls), and some lower bound on consumption (thus introducing a further parameter). Note that capital $k(t)$ and consumption rate $c(t)$ are vector functions — though scalar functions may be considered first to simplify the discussion. Note that environmental factors may enter as components of capital; for example, if $p(t)$ is some measure of environmental degradation, then $-p(t)$ could be a component of $k(t)$.

However, a model with a single objective may not represent important aspects of the system being modelled. An alternative approach adjoins constraints, containing parameters. For example, consider a growth model with consumption $u(t)$ and capital stock $k(t)$, and with some floor specified for the consumption. This may relate to a minimum consumption as a function of time, or among various consumers. Some simple examples are as follows.

(a) $\text{Max}_{u,x} \Phi(x(T))$ subject to $(\forall t)u(t) \geq b_1,$

$$x(0) = x_0, \dot{x}(t) = m(x(t), u(t), t)(t \in [0, T]).$$

Here the parameter b describes the minimum consumption level allowed.

(b) $\text{Max}_{u,x,b} b$ subject to $(\forall t)u(t) \geq b_1,$

$$x(0) = x_0, \dot{x}(t) = m(x(t), u(t), t)(t \in [0, T], \Phi(x(T))) \geq \Phi_0.$$

Minimum consumption is maximized, subject to a minimum level for the final capital. A simple special case, with $x(t) \in R$ and $u(t) \in R$, is:

$$\text{Max}_{u,x,b} b \quad \text{subject to } (\forall t)u(t) \geq b_1,$$

$$x(0) = x_0, \dot{x}(t) = \alpha x(t) - u(t) \quad t \in [0, T], x(T) \geq x_T,$$

at which the optimum (supposing the constraints to be feasible) is evidently at $u(\cdot) = b_1$.

(c) Denoting Pareto maximum by $P_{\max}$, consider:

$$P_{\max} x, u, b\{b, \Phi(x, T)\} \quad \text{subject to } (\forall t)u(t) \geq b, b \geq b_0,$$

$$x(0) = x_0, \dot{x}(t) = m(x(t), u(t), t)(t \in [0, T] \cdot \Phi(x(T))) \geq \Phi_0.$$

(d) A variant of (a) considers a bound on average consumption:

$$T^{-1} \int_0^T c(t) \, dt \geq b_2$$

(with $b_2 > b_1$ in (a)). This constraint may be included as a penalty cost, by introducing a new state variable $y(t) := \int_0^t T^{-1} c(s) \, ds$, and then the constraint

$y(T) \geq b_2$ enters as a penalty cost of the form $\mu[-y(T) + b_3]_+$ added to the total cost to be minimized. (Here $[\cdot]_+$ replaces negative vector components by zeros, and $b_3 \approx b_2$.)

Note that examples (a) and (b) will give single elements of the set of Pareto maxima. Several values of the parameter b might be considered, in order to discuss a tradeoff between consumption and capital. A similar remark applies to the parameter α in the Chichilnisky model.

Some other Pareto maxima may be obtained by maximizing a weighted combination $\omega_1^T b + \omega_2 \Phi(T)$. While this is often proposed, some criterion for choosing the weights would be required. It may be more meaningful to consider a parameter such as b instead.

3.2. Modified Discounting for Long-term Modelling

A model must maintain a suitable balance between short-term and long-term utility. Consider an optimal control model with a state $x(\cdot)$ (e.g. a capital function) and a control $u(\cdot)$ (e.g. a consumption function), and a time horizon T, of the form:

$$\int_0^T e^{-\delta t} f(x(t), u(t)) \, dt + \Phi(x(T)).$$

A variant considers $\int_0^\infty$ and $\lim_{t \to \infty} \Phi(x(T))$. The traditional discount factor $e^{-\delta t}$ gives negligible value to the far future, so this is not a sustainable model. If the discount factor is omitted, then the model may not be comparable with models for alternative investment of resources, since it does not allow for possible growth when profits are reinvested.

The $e^{-\delta t}$ discount factor assumes that money can be invested so as to grow at a compound-interest rate $e^{\delta t}$. But such real growth can only happen over a fairly short time horizon, during which suitable investments may be available, perhaps with some limit on the amount invested. The continued exponential growth shown in some datasets for longer time periods merely describes monetary inflation. A continued exponential growth in real terms will soon meet resource constraints (e.g. Forrester), or social constraints (e.g. a financial collapse). When a particular activity, or enterprise, is modelled, there is always assumed some *background* of other activities (in the sector, industry, etc.), that are not being described in detail, but rather in some aggregated way. Without a *background* to invest money in, discounting has no meaning.

A more realistic discount factor would not assume indefinite real growth; instead, some saturation effect would appear. A better description is required for *background growth*, meaning the growth available in the larger system, of which the model being studied forms a part. If $g(t)$ describes the background growth, then a possible description is given by: $\dot{g}(t) = \delta g(t)/(1 + \rho t)^2$. This growth starts as exponential, but later approaches saturation. For this growth rate, $g(t) = g(0)\exp(\delta t/(1 + \rho t))$. Thus $g(t)/g(0) \to e^{\delta/\rho}$ as $t \to \infty$; qualitatively, saturation starts to matter at about time $1/\rho$. The discount factor is then $\sigma(t) = 1/g(t)$. Of course, there are other functions than this one with the desired qualitative properties. But, lacking numerical data on saturation, it is appropriate to choose a simple function.

Another possible description for *background* growth assumes a maximum level for capital, and a logistic function for its growth rate, thus: $\dot{g}(t) = \delta g(t)[1 - \beta g(t)]$, $g(0) = g_0$. This integrates to:

$$g(t) = \frac{ae^{\delta t}}{1 + \beta a e^{\delta t}} \quad \text{where } g_0 = \frac{a}{1 + \beta a}, a = \frac{g_0}{1 - \beta g_0}.$$

Thus, as $t \to \infty$, $g(t) \to 1/\beta$, the assumed maximum level. This model may be more plausible than the previous one where the saturation is a given function of time t. The discount factor is then $\sigma(t) := 1/g(t) = e^{-\delta t} + \beta a$. Thus it tends to a positive constant value for large times.

Heal (1998, p. 98) considers a class of discount factors $\Delta(t)$ satisfying $\Delta'(t)/\Delta(t) \to 0$ as $t \to \infty$, for which the term $\lim_{t \to \infty} \Phi(x(T))$ does not affect the optimum. The classical exponential discount factor does not satisfy this condition; the modified discount factor $1/g(t)$ given above satisfies it. Then Heal's criterion is satisfied for both the functions $\sigma(\cdot)$ proposed here, since:

$$\frac{\dot{\sigma}(t)}{\sigma(t)} = \frac{-\delta}{1 + \rho t} + \frac{\delta \rho}{(1 + \rho t)^2} \quad \text{or} \quad \frac{-\delta}{1 + \beta a e^{\delta t}},$$

and each of these $\to 0$ as $t \to \infty$.

The Strotz phenomenon (see Chakravarty, 1969, p. 41) shows that only with an exponential discount factor can a certain balance be achieved between an optimum path starting at time 0 and an optimum path starting at a later time. Unfortunately this is incompatible with giving proper weight to the more distant future.

3.3. Infinite Horizon Model

Optimal control models of the form:

$$\text{Min}_{u(\cdot),x(\cdot)} F(x, u) := \int_0^\infty e^{-\rho t} f(x(t), u(t), t) \, dt$$

subject to:

$$x(0) = x_0, \dot{x}(t) = m(x(t), u(t), t), a(t) \leq u(t) \leq b(t)(t \geq 0),$$

have often been considered in recent economic literature (sometimes as Max $F(x, u) \Leftrightarrow$ Min$-F(x, u))$, often without explicit bounds on the control $u(t)$, and often with $e^{-\rho t}$ as the only explicit dependence on t. However, for the infinite horizon, it may not be obvious whether a minimum, or maximum, is reached; and the Pontryagin theory of optimal control is commonly presented only for a finite time horizon, since some assumptions about uniform approximation over the whole time domain are involved. For an infinite horizon, some further restrictions are required for validity. The present discussion assumes limiting behaviour as $t \rightarrow \infty$, which ensures that the infinite-horizon problem is closely approximated by a problem with finite horizon T. Consequently, any weight attached to the distant future must be expressed by a separate term in the objective, as e.g. in the Chichilnisky model.

Assume that a mininum is reached, at $(x^*(t), u^*(t))$. The discount factor $e^{-\rho t}$ is needed, so that $F(x, u)$ is finite. Following the approach in Craven (1995), the differential equation with initial condition is expressed in abstract form as $Dx = M(x, u)$; the Hamiltonian is:

$$h(x(t), u(t), t, \lambda(t)) := e^{-\rho t} f(x(t), u(t), t) + \lambda(t) m(x(t), u(t), t),$$

and the integral of the Hamiltonian equals $H(x, u, \theta) := F(x, u) + \theta M(x, u)$, where θ is a Lagrange multiplier vector, and $\lambda(t)$ is a function representing θ.

Assume that $x^*(t)$, $u^*(t)$, and $\lambda^*(t)$ (from the adjoint equation below) tend to limits as $t \rightarrow \infty$, with $\lambda^*(t) = O(e^{-\beta t})$ as $t \rightarrow \infty$; $f(., ., .)$ and $m(., ., .)$ are twice differentiable functions, such that the second derivatives $f_{xx}(x(t), u(t), t)$, $m_{xx}(x(t), u(t), t)$, $f_{xu}(x(t), u(t), t)$, $m_{xu}(x(t), u(t), t)$ are bounded int, whenever $(x(t), u(t))$ are near to $(x^*(t), u^*(t))$.

Note that an oscillatory optimum control is thus excluded; and the exponential decay terms mean that the infinite horizon is closely approximated by problem over $(0, T)$, for some suitable finite T.

The steps in the proof, based on (Craven, 1995) are as follows; only the significant changes for an infinite horizon need be detailed.

(a) Obtain first-order necessary conditions;
(b) From (a), deduce the adjoint differential equation:

$$-\dot{\lambda}(t) = \left(\frac{\partial}{\partial x}\right) h(x(t), u(t), t, \lambda(t)), \quad \lambda(t) \rightarrow 0 \quad \text{as} \quad t \rightarrow \infty.$$

Here $\lambda(t)$ is assumed to represent θ, subject to verification that the differential equation obtained is solvable; the calculation using integration by parts is valid, under the assumptions on limits as $t \to \infty$.

(c) A linear approximation:

$$H(x, u, \theta) - H(x^*, u, \theta) = H_x(x^*, u^*, \theta^*)(x - x^*) + o(||u - u^*||)$$

holds, given the bounded second derivatives, noting that a term $e^{-\rho t}$ is present in F_x, and $e^{-\beta t}$ in θM_x; here $||u - u^*|| = \int_0^\infty |u(t) - u^*(t)| \, dt$. The *quasimin* property follows:

$$H(x, u^*, \theta) - H(x^*, u^*, \theta) \geq o(||u - u^*||).$$

(d) Assume that control constraints, if present, are a constraint on $u(t)$ for each time separately. If $h(x^*(t), \ldots, t, \lambda^*(t))$ is *not* minimized at $u^*(t)$ (possibly except for a set E of t for which $\int_E dt = 0$), then a standard proof (not depending on the domain of t) shows that the quasimin is contradicted.

Suppose now that an endpoint term $\lim_{T \to \infty} v(x(T))$ is added to the objective function. This has the effect of adding $v(x(t))\delta(t - T)$ to f, then letting $T \to \infty$. In consequence, the boundary condition for the adjoint equation becomes:

$$\lambda(t) - v'(x(t)) = O(e^{-\beta t}) \quad \text{as} \quad t \to \infty.$$

If $x(t)$ tends to a limit as $t \to \infty$ (which implicitly assumes that f and m do not explicitly contain t), and $v(\cdot)$ is continuous, then the limit of $v(x(T))$ exists. This remark applies to the Chichilnisky criterion in Section 4.2.

4. APPROACHES THAT MIGHT BE COMPUTER

4.1. Computing for a Large Time Horizon

As discussed in Section 3.1, it is appropriate to discuss optimization models with parameters — required to take account of the several conflicting objectives that exist — and the question of what happens to the optima when these parameters are varied provides a further stage of exploration. However, the model must be somewhat recast, in order that a computer package can handle it, whether RIOTS_95 (Schwartz, 1996) or any other. Assuming that the limits as $t \to \infty$ exist, a *nonlinear time* transformation $t = \psi(\tau)$ may be applied, so as to compress the time scale for large times t (when little is changing). A computation requires a discretization of the time interval into finitely many subinervals, and such a transformation considerably reduces the number of subintervals required (see Craven, 1995).

4.2. The Chichilnisky Criterion with a Long Time Horizon

If a discount factor $e^{-\rho t}$ is retained, then the Chichilnisky model may be approximated, for some large T, by:

$$\text{Max } \alpha \int_0^T e^{-\rho t} U(c(t), k(t))\, dt + \alpha U(c(T), k(T))\rho^{-1} e^{-\rho T} + (1-\alpha)V(k(T))$$

subject to:

$$k(0) = k_0; \dot{k}(t) = m(c(t), k(t)), c_U \geq c(t) \leq c_L (0 \leq t \leq T); k(T) \geq k_T.$$

The second term is an estimate of the contribution for times beyond T; a similar estimate is the *salvage value* cited in (Chakravarty, 1969). The following assumptions are made:

- the utility $U(., .)$ and the dynamics function $m(., .)$ have no explicit dependence on time t;
- T is assumed large enough that $c(T)$ and $k(T)$ approximate their limits as $\rightarrow \infty$;
- the term in $e^{-\rho t}$ estimates the integral from T to ∞;
- the lower bound c_L *on* consumption is assumed constant (achievable by scaling $c(t)$);
- the upper bound c_U is included to bound the region where an algorithm must search;
- the utility V applicable at time T may, but need not, be the same as U.

Note that the utility V depends on the final capital $k(T)$, but not on the final consumption $u(T)$, since $u(T)$ is not of significance, but rather the whole curve of consumption versus time.

The constraint $k(\infty) \geq k_T$ may be replaced by a penalty term:

$$\tfrac{1}{2}\mu[k(\infty) - k_T + \mu^{-1}\epsilon]_+^2,$$

where μ is a positive parameter, and $[\cdot]_+$ replaces negative components by zero; $\epsilon \geq 0$ will be adjusted, so as to fulfil the constraint exactly. According to the theory of *augmented Lagrangians* (see the discussion in Craven, 1978), ϵ relates to a Lagrange multiplier. If $c(t)$ does not meet its bounds, then the inactive constraints on $c(\cdot)$ can be omitted. According to the Pontryagin theory, with some regularity assumptions because of the infinite domain (notably that the limits exist), an optimum satisfies the differential equation for $\dot{k}(t)$, the adjoint differential equation:

$$-\dot{\lambda}(t) = -e^{-\rho t} U_k(c(t), k(t)) + \lambda(t)m_k(c(t), k(t), t),$$

$$\lambda(\infty) = \mu[k(\infty) - k_T + \mu^{-1}\epsilon]_+ - (1 - A)V_k(k(\infty);$$

and (from the Pontryagin principle):

$$-\alpha e^{-\rho t}U_c(c(t), k(t)) + \lambda(t)m_k(c(t), k(t), t)(0 \le t < T).$$

The adjoint differential equation is required for computing the gradient of the objective.

When T is large, and the only explicit time dependence is the discount factor, it may be useful to transform the time scale nonlinearly by:

$$t = \psi(\tau) := -\rho^{-1}\log(1 - \beta\tau), \quad \text{where } \beta = 1 - e^{-\rho T};$$

this maps $\tau \in [0, 1]$ to $t \in [0, T]$; $dt/d\tau = (\beta/\rho)(1 - \beta\tau)^{-1} = (\beta/\rho)e^{\rho t}$. Denoting $u(\tau) := c(\psi(\tau))$ and $x(t) := k(\psi(\tau))$, the problem is transformed to:

$$\text{Max } J(u) := \alpha \int_0^1 U(u(\tau), x(\tau))\,d\tau + \alpha U(u(1), x(1))\rho^{-1}e^{-\rho T}$$

$$+ (1 - \alpha)V(u(1), x(1)) = \alpha \int_0^1 [U(u(\tau), x(\tau))$$

$$+ \delta(\tau - 1)W(u(\tau), x(\tau)]\,d\tau$$

where $W(u(\tau), x(\tau) := U(u(\tau), x(\tau)\rho^{-1}e^{-\rho T} + \alpha^{-1}(1 - \alpha)V(x(\tau))$ subject to:

$$x(0) = k_0; \quad \dot{x}(\tau) = \left(\frac{\beta}{\rho}\right)\frac{m(u(\tau), x(\tau), \psi(\tau))}{1 - \beta\tau}(0 \le t \le T),$$

$$c_U \ge u(t) \ge c_L(0 \le \tau \le 1); \quad x(1) \ge k_T.$$

Here $\dot{x}(\tau)$ means $(d/d\tau)x(\tau)$.

The adjoint differential equation is then:

$$-\dot{\lambda}(t) = -\alpha U_x(u(\tau), x(\tau)) + \left(\frac{\beta}{\rho}\right)\frac{m_x(u(\tau), x(\tau), \psi(\tau))}{1 - \beta\tau};$$

$$\lambda(1) = -\left(\frac{\alpha}{\rho}\right)e^{-\rho T}U_x(u(1), x(1)) - (1 - \alpha)V_x(u(1), x(1))$$

$$+ \mu[k(T) - k_T + \mu^{-1}\epsilon]_+$$

The gradient of the the objective is then computed (when $z(1) = 0$) from:

$$J'(u)z = -\alpha \int_0^T \left[U_u(x(\tau), u(\tau)) + \left(\frac{\beta}{\rho}\right)\lambda(\tau)\frac{m_u(u(\tau), x(\tau))}{1 - \beta\tau}\right]z(\tau)\,d\tau$$

4.3. Chichilnisky Model Compared with Penalty Term Model

In the approximated Chichilnisky model considered in Section 4.2, the second term with $e^{-\rho T}$ estimates $\int_T^\infty e^{-\rho t} U(c(t), k(t)) \, dt$, in the case when $c(T)$ and $k(T)$ are close to limiting values. (For the Kendrick–Taylor model discussed below in Section 5, there are no limiting values.) The comparison for a discount rate $\rho = 0.03$ and horizon $T = 20$ years):

$$\int_0^T e^{-\rho t} \, dt = \rho^{-1}(1 - e^{-\rho T}) \approx 0.55 \quad \text{with} \quad e^{-\rho T} \approx 15.04$$

shows that the term is unimportant, if U and V are of comparable size.

Neglecting it, the objective reduces to:

$$\alpha \left\{ \int_0^T e^{-\rho t} U(c(t), k(t)) \, dt + \alpha^{-1}(1 - \alpha) V(k(T)) \right\}.$$

If $k(\cdot)$ has only one component, then a reasonable choice for $V(k(T))$ would be:

$$-\xi[k(T) - k^{\#}]^2 \quad \text{or} \quad -\xi[k(T) - k^*]_+^2,$$

where μ is a suitable positive parameter. (Of course, another form than quadratic could be chosen; the quadratic is convenient to compute.) The two versions describe attainment of a target, or perhaps exceeding it. Then the objective becomes:

$$\alpha \left\{ \int_0^T e^{-\rho t} U(c(t), k(t)) \, dt + \tfrac{1}{2}\mu[k(T) - k^{\#}]^2 \right\},$$

with $\mu = 2\xi\alpha^{-1})1 - \alpha)$, and perhaps $[\cdot]$ replaced by $[\cdot]_+$.

This may be compared with adding to the integral a penalty term, to represent an endpoint constraint $k(T) = k_T$ (or $k(T) \geq k_T$). The penalty term has the same form, with k^* differing a little from k_T, the difference depending on μ and on a Lagrange multiplier in the optimization. In fact, the SCOM package handles an endpoint constraint in exactly this way.

It follows that the modified Chichilnisky model may be studied as a parametric problem, with μ and k^* as parameters.

4.4. Pareto Optimum and Intergenerational Equity

Intergenerational equity (and sustainability) can be interpreted in terms of Pareto optimality.

Consider now two objective functions, say:

$$F^1(x, u) := \int_0^T e^{-\rho t} f(x(t), u(t)) \, dt \quad \text{and} \quad F^2(x, u) := \Phi(x(T))$$

to describe, in some sense, utilities for the present generation and a future generation, where $x(t)$ denotes rate of consumption, and $k(t)$ denotes capital (both may be vectors). Assume that these functions are constrained by a dynamic equation for $(d/dt)x(t)$, and bounds on $u(t)$. Suppose that (x^*, u^*) is a *Pareto maximum* point of this model. Then (assuming some regularity of the constraint system), Karush-Kuhn-Tucker necessary conditions, or equivalent Pontgryagin conditions, hold for (x^*, u^*) exactly when these conditions hold for a single objective function $\tau_1 F^1(\cdot) + \tau_2 F^2(\cdot)$, for some nonnegative multipliers τ_1, τ_2, not both zero. Different points in the (large) set of Pareto optima correspond to different choices of the multipliers. For the two-objective problem, the costate becomes a matrix function $\Lambda(t)$, and the Pontryagin maximum principle considers a Pareto maximum of a vector Hamiltonian:

$$F^1(x, u), F^2(x, u)) + \Lambda(t)(\text{RHS of dynamic equation})$$

with respect to $u(t)$ (see Craven, 1999).

This may be compared with the parametric version of Chichilnisky's criterion:

$$\alpha F^1(x, u) + (1 - \alpha) F^2(x, u) = \alpha[F^1(x, u) + \beta F^2(x, u)], \quad \beta = \alpha^{-1}(1 - \alpha).$$

Each choice of α, or β, gives a different Pareto maximum point.

4.5. Computing with a Modified Discount Factor

If the discount factor is modified to $e^{-\rho t} + \kappa$, then integration over an infinite time domain will give infinite values. Instead, the following model may be considered:

$$\text{Max } \alpha \int_0^T [e^{-\rho t} + \kappa] U(c(t), k(t)) \, dt + (1 - \alpha) V(k(T))$$

subject to $k(0) = k_0$; $\dot{k}(t) = m(c(t), k(t), t), c_U \geq c(t) \geq c_L (0 \leq t \leq T); k(T) \geq k_T$.

Here, $\kappa > 0$, and some finite time horizon T must replace ∞. With the same time transformation as above (for computation), the transformed problem becomes:

$$\text{Max } \alpha \int_0^1 (1 + \kappa(1 - \beta\tau)^{-1})U(u(\tau), x(\tau)) \, d\tau + (1 - \alpha)V(u(1), x(1))$$

$$= \alpha \int_0^1 (1 + \kappa(1 - \beta\tau)^{-1})U(u(\tau), x(\tau)) + \delta(\tau - 1)\alpha^{-1}(1 - \alpha)V(x(\tau)) \, d\tau$$

subject to $x(0) = k_0;\ \dot{x}(\tau) = (\beta/\rho)m(u(\tau), x(\tau), \psi(\tau))/(1 - \beta\tau)(0 \leq \tau \leq 1)$.

5. COMPUTATION OF THE KENDRICK–TAYLOR MODEL

5.1. The Kendrick–Taylor Model

The Kendrick–Taylor model for economic growth (Kendrick & Taylor, 1971) has the form:

$$\text{Max}_{c(\cdot),k(\cdot)} \int_0^T a e^{-\rho t} c(t)^\theta \, dt$$

subject to:

$$k(0) = k_0, \quad \dot{k}(t) = \zeta e^{\delta t} k(t)^\beta - \sigma k(t) - c(t), \quad k(T) = k_T.$$

Here $c(t)$ denotes consumption, and $k(t)$ denotes capital (including man-made, natural, environmental, and human). Some computational results for this model are given in Craven and Islam (2001) and Islam and Craven (2001).

Since the model includes a growth factor $e^{\delta t}$, it may be appropriate (see Chakravarty, 1969) to choose the terminal value k_T to increase exponentially with T. If $k(t) = k_0 e^{\omega t}$ and $c(t) = c_0 e^{\omega t}$, then the dynamic equation is satisfied only when $\omega = \delta/(1 - \beta)$ and $k_0 \omega = k_0^\beta - \sigma k_0 - c_0$. Then the objective function remains finite as $T \to \infty$ when $\rho > \theta\omega$, thus when $\rho > \theta\delta/(1 - \beta)$. (An analogous criterion is given by Chakravarty (1969, p. 99) for a different model, only partly described.) Since the growth of $c(t)$ is dominated by the discount factor, the optimal objective tends to a limit as $T \to \infty$. So here an infinite-horizon model may be approximated by a finite-horizon model; but it does not describe sustainable growth over an infinite horizon, since the exogenous growth factor $e^{\delta t}$ can only be sustained for a limited time.

5.2. *Extending the Kendrick–Taylor Model to Include a Long Time Horizon*

This model is now modified to use the modified discount factor from Section 3.2. This gives the formulation:

$$\text{Max}_{c(\cdot),k(\cdot)} \int_0^T a[e^{-\rho t} + \kappa]c(t)^\theta \, dt$$

subject to:

$$k(0) = k_0, \quad \dot{k}(t) = \zeta e^{\delta t} k(t)^\beta - \sigma k(t) - c(t), \quad k(T) = k_T.$$

This formulation differs from the model in Kendrick–Taylor only by the inclusion of the positive parameter κ. In order to compare with previous results, the following numerical values are considered:

$$a = 10, \quad T = 10, \quad \rho = 0.03, \quad \theta = 0.1, \quad f = 10, \quad k_0 = 15.0, \quad \zeta = 0.842,$$

$$\beta = 0.6, \quad \sigma = 0.05, \quad k_T = 24.7.$$

However, larger values of the horizon T become relevant. The parameter κ depends on the relative weighting to be given to the longer-term in relation to the short-term. Since $e^{-\rho t}$ is small when $t \geq 2/\rho$, the ratio of the two could be taken as:

$$\frac{\int_{2/\rho}^T \kappa \, dt}{\int_0^{2/\rho} e^{-\rho \tau} \, dt} \approx \kappa \rho T.$$

A possible value for this parameter would be 0.5. Otherwise:

$$\int_0^T \kappa \, dt = \int_0^T e^{-\rho t} \, dt$$

when $\kappa \approx 0.86$.

In a more general model, $c(t)$ and $k(t)$ would take vector values; however, single components for $c(t)$ and $k(t)$ will be considered here.

With the modified discount factor $e^{-\rho t} + \kappa$, integration over an infinite time domain will give infinite values. So the horizon T must here be finite (though it may be large). An alternative to the terminal constraint $k(T) = k_T$ is a terminal objective term, giving an objective function:

$$\int_0^T a[e^{-\rho t} + \kappa]c(t)^\theta \, dt + \varphi(c(T)).$$

With the same time transformation as in Section 4.2, and writing $\tilde{c}(\tau) = c(t)$ and $\tilde{k}(\tau) = k(t)$, the objective function and dynamic equation become:

$$\left(\frac{\beta}{\tau}\right) \int_0^1 a\left[1 + \frac{\kappa}{1 - \beta\tau}\right] \tilde{c}(\tau)^\theta \, d\tau + \varphi(\tilde{c}(1))$$

$$\tilde{k}(0) = k_0, \dot{\tilde{k}}(\tau) = \frac{(\beta/\rho)[\zeta e^{\delta t}\tilde{k}(\tau)^\beta - \sigma\tilde{k}(t) - \tilde{c}(t)]}{1 - \beta\tau}.$$

5.3. Chichilnisky Variant of Kendrick–Taylor

The Chichilnisky formulation does not directly apply to the Kendrick–Taylor model, because $\lim_{t \to \infty} x(t)$ is not available. However, the modified version of Section 4.2, with $e^{-\rho t}$ discount and some large horizon T, may be considered for the Kendrick–Taylor model. If the endpoint constraint is replaced by a penalty cost $V(x(T)) := [x(T) - k_T]^2$, then the nonlinear time transformation leads to:

$$U(u(\tau), x(\rho)) = u(\tau)^\theta; \quad W(u(\tau), x(\tau)) = u(\tau)^\theta \rho^{-1} e^{-\rho T}$$

$$+ \alpha^{-1}(1 - \alpha)[x(t) - k_T]^2; \quad x(0) = k_0, \dot{x}(\tau)$$

$$= \frac{(\beta/\rho)[\zeta(1 - \beta\tau)^{-\delta/\rho}x(\tau)^\beta - \sigma x(\tau) - u(\tau)]}{1 - \beta\tau}.$$

However, because of the growth term $e^{\delta t}$ in the dynamic equation, there is no infinite-horizon version of the Kendrick–Taylor model, and the time transformation was not obviously useful here. Computations omitting this growth term may be of interest – see Section 6(c).

5.4. Transformation of the Kendrick–Taylor Model

In view of some numerical instability encountered when computing the Kendrick–Taylor model for time horizons $T > 10$, the following transformation (see Islam & Craven, 1995) of the model to an equivalent, more computable, form may be used. Set $q(t) = e^{\sigma t}k(t)$ and $\theta = \sigma + \delta - \beta\sigma$; then:

$$\dot{q}(t) = e^{\sigma t}(\zeta e^{\delta t}k(t)^\beta - \sigma k(t) - u(t) + \sigma k(t));$$

$$\dot{x}(t) = \gamma\zeta e^{\theta t}(x(t))^{(\beta+\gamma-1)/\gamma} - \gamma u(t),$$

where:

$$u(t) = e^{\sigma t}q(t)^{\gamma-1}c(t) = e^{\sigma t}(x(t))^{(\gamma-1)/\gamma}c(t).$$

Choosing $\gamma = 1 - \beta$, the problem in the new functions $x(t)$ and $u(t)$ becomes:

$$\text{Min} \int_0^T a e^{-\nu t} u(t)^\epsilon x(t)^\mu \, dt$$

subject to:

$$\dot{x}(t) = \gamma \zeta e^{\theta t} - \gamma u(t), \quad x(0) = k_0^\gamma, \quad x(T) = k_T^\gamma,$$

where $\nu = \rho + \epsilon \sigma$ and $\mu = \epsilon(1 - \gamma)/\gamma$. The dynamic equation now does not involve fractional powers. Note that this transformation does *not* preserve any bounds on $c(t)$.

Using the data from Section 5.2, with $k(0) = 15.0$,

$$\gamma = 0.4, \quad \nu = 0.035, \quad \mu = 0.15, \quad x(0) = 2.9542, \quad \theta = 0.04$$

If $T = 10, k(0) = 15.0, k(T) = 24.7$, then $x(T) = 4.4049$. If $T = 20$ then $k(T)$ may be considered as $15.0 + 2(24.7 - 15 - 0) = 34.4$, then $x(T) = 6.1424$.

6. COMPUTER PACKAGES AND RESULTS OF COMPUTATION OF MODELS

6.1. Packages Used

Optimal solutions for these sustainable growth models may be computed, using appropriate computer packages for optimal control. The packages used were SCOM (Islam & Craven, 2001), and also RIOTS_95 (Schwartz et al., 1997), to validate the SCOM results by comparison with another package. In the SCOM package, the control function is approximated by a step-function, constant on each of N subintervals of the time period, with e.g. $N = 20$; this is known (Craven, 1995) to be an adequate approximation. Function values and gradients are computed, by solving differential equations; then the MATLAB *constr* package for mathematical programming is used to compute the optimum. For the models considered here, the gradients given by the theory were not useful (see discussion in Section 8), and finite-difference approximations were provided by *constr*. Another suitable package for optimal control is OCIM (see Craven, de Haas & Wettenhall, 1998).

For analysing the results of all model computations, we have followed the common practice in economic growth economics, where the arbitrary effects of terminal constraints are avoided by ignoring the results of the last time periods, thus from when the variables start to tend towards the terminal constraints (see for example Land Economics Journal, 1997).

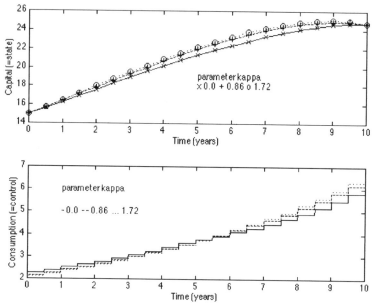

Fig. 1. Changing the Discount Parameter.

The following computations were done with modifications of the Kendrick–Taylor model.

6.2. Results: Comparison of the Basic Model Solution with Results for Modified Discount Factor

Results computed with the SCOM package were obtained for the discount factor $e^{-\rho t} + \kappa$ for capital (upper graph of Fig. 1) and consumption (lower graph), for a ten year time horizon, for the three cases:

(a) $\kappa = 0.00$ Objective = 98.1;
(b) $\kappa = 0.86$ Objective = 196.0;
(c) $\kappa = 1.72$ Objective = 243.9.

Within each graph, (a) is the lowest curve, and (c) is the highest. Note that the objective values are not comparable, since the different discount factors measure utility on different scales.

In order to assess the accuracy of these computations, Fig. 2 compares the computed consumptions computed by the SCOM and the RIOTS_95 packages.

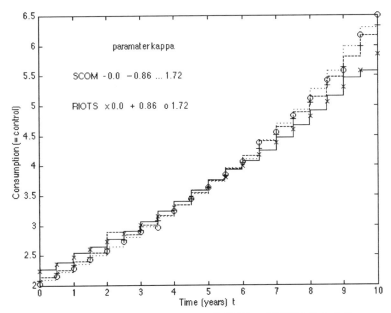

Fig. 2. Effect of Discount Parameter – ROITS and SCOM Calculations.

The following values were obtained for objective functions:

κ	0.0	0.1	0.8639	1.7278
RIOTS_95 calculation	98.08	109.46	196.41	294.74
SCOM calculation	98.08		195.96	293.85

The results for the two packages are in substantial agreement. As remarked in Craven and Islam (2002), the optimal curve of capital is insensitive to small rapid fluctuations in the consumption (the control function), so a step-function approximation to the control is sufficient.

Increasing the parameter kappa in the modified discount factor, so as to give more weight to later times, decreases the consumption for earlier times and increases it for later times, and also increases the rate of capital growth.

6.3. Results: Effect of Increasing the Horizon T (cf. Section 5.2)

Figures 3 and 4, computed by SCOM using the transformation of the Kendrick–Taylor model from Section 5.4, show capital and consumption for a

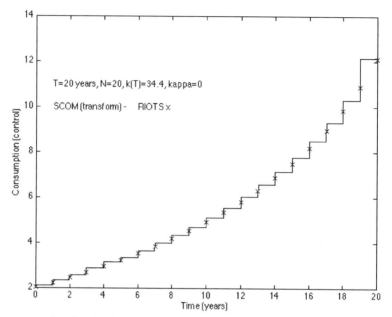

Fig. 3. Consumption, 20 Years, Compare RIOTS and SCPM.

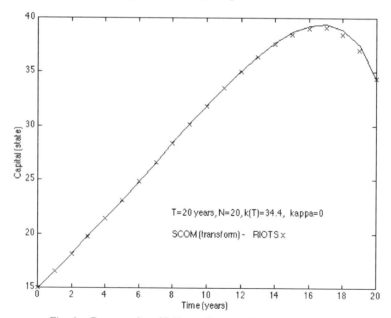

Fig. 4. Consumption, 20 Years, Compare RIOTS and SCOM.

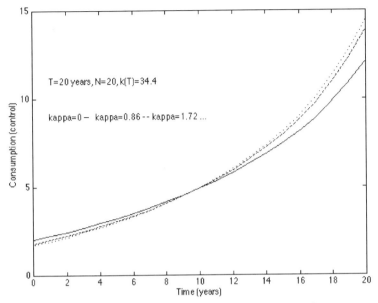

Fig. 5. Consumption, 20 Years, Vary Kappa, RIOTS.

horizon of T increases from 10 to 20 years, and with the final capital value $k(T)$ increased from $k(10) = 24.7$ to $k(20) = 34.4$ (obtained from $k(0) + 2(24.7 - k(0))$). For comparison, results from RIOTS_95 are also plotted.

Consider the numerical values:

$$a = 10, \quad \rho = 0.03, \quad \epsilon = 0.1, \quad \zeta = 0.842, \quad \delta = 0.02, \quad \sigma = 0.05,$$

$$k_0 = 15.0, \quad T = 20, \quad k_T = 34.4.$$

Then:

$$\gamma = 0.4, \quad \nu = 0.035, \quad \mu = 0.15, \quad x(0) = 2.9542, \quad x(T) = 4.1174, \quad \theta = 0.04.$$

Figures 5 and 6 (computed with RIOTS_95) show the result of increasing the parameter kappa in the modified discount factor. As with a ten year horizon, the consumption is decreased for earlier times and increased for later times. The capital growth is increased, then brought down to the target of $k(20) = 34.4$.

6.4. Results: Effect of Omitting the Growth Term in the Dynamic Equation

The result of making $\delta = 0$ in the growth term $e^{\delta t}$ is shown in Figs 7 and 8. As a check on accuracy, Figs 9 and 10 show the result of increasing the number N of

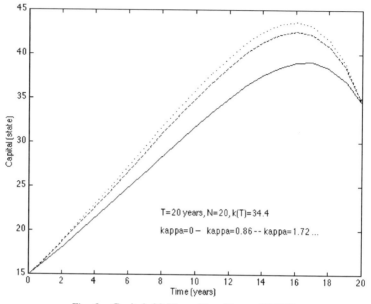

Fig. 6. Capital, 20 Years, Vary Kappa, RIOTS.

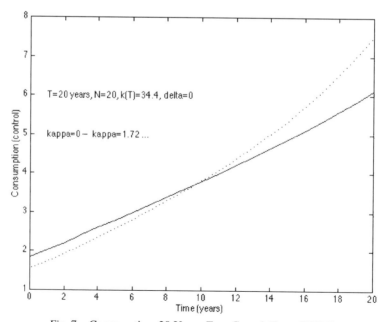

Fig. 7. Consumption, 20 Years, Zero Growth Term, RIOTS.

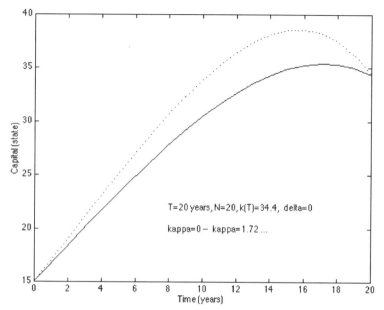

Fig. 8. Capital, 20 Years, Zero Growth Term, RIOTS.

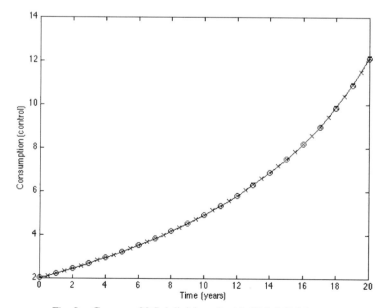

Fig. 9. Compare 20 Subdivisions 0 with 40 Subdivisions *x*.

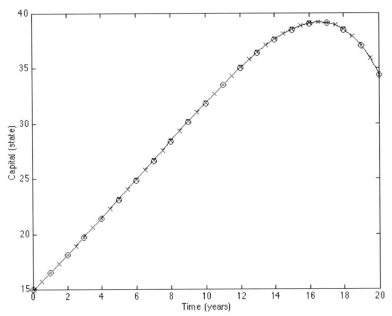

Fig. 10.   Compare 20 Subdivisions 0 with 40 Subdivisions x.

subdivisions from 20 to 40 (for the case $\kappa = 0$, $T = 20$, $k(T) = 34.4$, growth term present). The calculations agree closely.

6.5. Results: Parametric Approach (see Section 4.2)

Figures 11 and 12 show the effect of changing the parameter $k(T)$, the specified capital at the final time $T = 20$ of the calculation. The discount parameter κ was kept as 0. The final capital $k(T)$ could be brought up to 55, with some loss in consumption.

The effect of changing the exponent β in the dynamic equation was studied in Islam and Craven (2001).

6.6. Results: The Modified Chichilnisky Approach

The modified Chichilnisky approach of Sections 4.2 and 4.3, with a large but finite horizon T, may be applied to the Kendrick–Taylor model. As discussed in Section 4.3, the second term of the objective may be neglected. So this modified

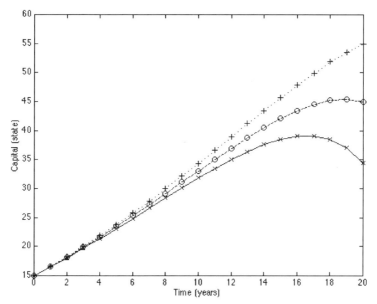

Fig. 11. Capital – Changing Endpoint $k(T)$.

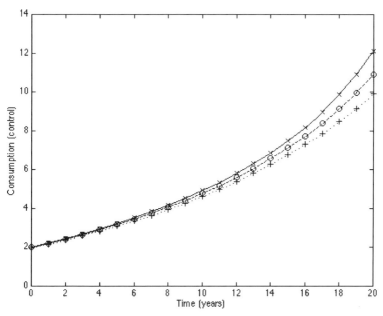

Fig. 12. Consumption – Changing Endpoint $k(T)$.

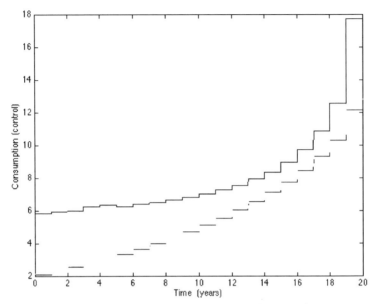

Fig. 13. Effect of Endterm Weighting on Consumption.

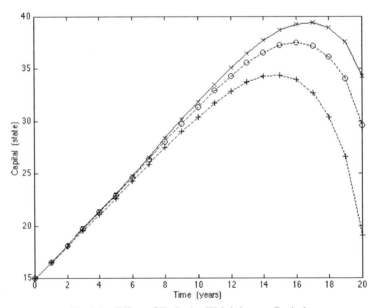

Fig. 14. Effect of Endpoint Weighting on Capital.

Chichilnisky problem may be studied as a parametric problem, with μ and k^* as parameters. Figures 13 and 14 show consumption and capital, computed by SCOM for the Kendrick–Taylor model with horizon $T = 20$ years (and the discount parameter $\kappa = 0$), with the endpoint term included, and the target $k(T) = 34.4$. The three cases are:

$\mu = 10$ (lower graph); $\quad \mu = 0.1$ (middle graph); $\quad \mu = 0.02$ (upper graph).

The case $\mu = 10$ was used previously in SCOM to reach the target $k(20) = 34.4$ accurately.

Clearly, decreased weight for the endpoint term reduces capital, and increases consumption.

7. EXISTENCE, UNIQUENESS AND GLOBAL OPTIMALITY

In an optimal control model for an economic growth problem, there is usually no way to prove existence in advance. The following procedure deals with this question.

Assuming (for the moment) that an optimum exists, one may first construct Pontryagin necessary conditions, then find a solution to these necessary conditions. This solution is not always an optimum; however it is an optimum if the problem satisfies convex, or *invex*, conditions (see Craven, 1995). The Kendrick–Taylor model is certainly not convex, but does satisfy *invex* conditions (see Islam & Craven, 2001). Therefore the solution obtained to the Pontryagin conditions is indeed an optimum.

8. CONCLUSIONS

Several models of sustainability in optimal growth models are described, with computational methods. Two optimal control packages were used, Schwartz's RIOTS_95 and Craven's SCOM, to test and validate the results. The model results have a turnpike property, as shown in Islam and Craven (2001). The computed results show time paths of economic variables which show relatively higher values of consumption or welfare during the later part of the planning horizon. The results for the two computing packages were in good agreement.

Computations with versions of the Kendrick–Taylor growth model presented some difficulties because of implicit constraints in the model (see Craven & Islam, 2001). An optimization calculation must compare various consumption functions, and some produce negative values for capital, so an optimum is not reached.

This difficulty arose for a 20 year horizon, and was avoided with the RIOTS_95 package by computing using finite differences for gradients, and with SCOM by a mathematical transformation of the model to an equivalent and more stable form.

From a comparison of the original form of the Kendrick–Taylor model with other, more sustainable, forms, there are some implications as to sustainable growth. Effects of changing the discount factor to give more weight to the distant future, of omitting the exogenous growth factor in the dynamic equation, and of varying the target for endpoint capital, are presented in the graphs. While the Chichilnisky model is not directly computable because it involves an infinite time horizon, a modified version with a large finite horizon can be computed. This version is equivalent to attaching a penalty cost when a capital target is not reached. The solutions so obtained are Pareto maxima of a two-objective problem, considering both a short-term objective and a long-term objective.

The computational experiments in this paper, using several different models for optimal growth, show that sustainability of growth and social welfare can conveniently be modelled empirically for policy analysis, and which specify growth paths which are sustainable and ensure intergenerational equity, altruism and fairness.

REFERENCES

Aronsson, T., Johansson, P., & Lofgren, K. (1997). *Welfare measurement, sustainability and green national accounting: A growth theoretical approach, new horizons in environmental economic series*. Cheltenham: Edward Elgar.

Arrow, K., et al. (forthcoming). *Handbook of social choice and welfare*. Amsterdam: North-Holland.

Brekke, K. A. (1997). *Economic growth and the environment: On the measurement of income and welfare*. Cheltenham: Edward Elgar.

Cesar, S. (1994). *Control and game models of the greenhouse effect*. Heidelberg: Springer-Verlag.

Chakravarty, S. (1969). *Capital and development planning*. Cambridge, MA: MIT Press.

Chichilnisky, G. (1977). Economic development and efficiency criteria in the satisfaction of basic needs. *Applied Mathematical Modeling, 1*.

Chichilnisky, G. (1996). An axiomatic approach to sustainable development. *Social Choice and Welfare, 13*(2), 219–248.

Craven, B. D. (1978). *Mathematical programming and control theory*. London: Chapman & Hall.

Craven, B. D. (1995). *Control and optimization*. London: Chapman & Hall.

Craven, B. D. (1999). Multicriteria optimal control. *Asia-Pacific Journal of Operational Research, 16*, 53–62.

Craven, B. D., de Haas, K., & Wettenhall, J. M. (1998). Computing optimal control. *Dynamics of Continuous, Discrete and Impulsive Systems, 4*, 615.

Craven, B. D., & Islam, S. N. (2001). Computing optimal control on MATLAB: The SCOM package and economic growth models. In: A. Rubinov & B. Glover (Eds), *Optimization and Related Topics* (pp. 61–70). Dordrecht: Kluwer.

Faucheux, S., Pearce, D., & Proops, J. (1996). *Models of sustainable development*. Hants, UK: Edward Elgar.

Heal, G. M. (1973). *The theory of economic planning*. Amsterdam: North-Holland.

Heal, G. (1998). *Valuing the future: Economic theory and sustainability*. New York: Columbia University Press.

Islam, S. N. (2001). *Optimal growth economics: An investigation of the contemporary issues, and sustainability implications*. Amsterdam: North-Holland, Series – Contributions to Economic Analysis.

Islam, S. N., & Craven, B. D. (2001). Computation of non-linear continuous optimal growth models: Experiments with optimal control algorithms and computer programs. *Economic Modelling: The International Journal of Theoretical and Applied Papers on Economic Modelling, 18,* 551–568.

Kendrick, D. A., & Taylor, L. (1971). Numerical methods and nonlinear optimizing models for economic planning. In: H. B. Chenery (Ed.), *Studies in Development Planning*. Cambridge, MA: Harvard University Press.

Land Economics (1997). Special issue on Sustainability.

Leonard, D., & Long, V. V. (1994). *Optimal control theory and static optimization in economics*. Cambridge, UK: Cambridge University Press.

Rawls, J. (1972). *A theory of justice*. Oxford: Clarendon.

Schwartz, A. (1996). Theory and inmplementation of numerical methods based on Runge-Kutta integration for solving optimal control problems, Dissertation. Berkeley: University of California.

Schwartz, A., Polak, E., & Chen, Y. (1997). Recursive integration optimal trajectory solver 95: A MATLAB toolbox for solving optimal control problems (Version 1.0 for Windows). http://www.turnpike.net/~RIOTS.

Smulders, J. A. (1994). Growth, market structure, and the environment, Ph.D. thesis, Tilburg University, Tilburg.

Weitzman, M. C. (1976). On the welfare significance of national product of a dynamic economy. *Quarterly Journal of Economics, 20,* 156–162.

MONITORING AND INCENTIVES OF EXECUTIVES IN RISKY FIRMS: A TEST OF THE ASSOCIATION WITH FIRM PERFORMANCE

Marion Hutchinson

ABSTRACT

This study investigates the relationship between a firm's risk and the effectiveness of the firm's corporate governance practices. Previous research investigating the relationship between corporate controls and firm performance has been mixed and often weak. Therefore, this study sets out to determine the efficiency of monitoring and incentive contracts given certain characteristics of the firm. That is, the study sets out to determine whether risk firms with higher monitoring and levels of incentives are associated with higher firm performance.

The results of this study of 282 firms demonstrate how the relationship between firm risk and performance is associated with the monitoring and incentive contracts used by these firms. In particular, the results of this study showed that the negative association between risk and firm performance is weakened when firms have stronger monitoring and incentive mechanisms. The particular contribution of this study is to show that the role of corporate governance variables in firm performance should be evaluated in the context of the firm's risk.

Social Responsibility: Corporate Governance Issues
Research in International Business and Finance, Volume 17, 253–272
© 2003 Published by Elsevier Science Ltd.
ISSN: 0275-5319/PII: S0275531903170110

1. INTRODUCTION

Agency theory suggests that, given certain characteristics of the firm and the organisational environment, firms adopt particular corporate control systems to eliminate agency costs (Bathala & Rao, 1995). However, previous research investigating the relationship between corporate controls and firm performance has been mixed and often weak (Bloom & Milkovich, 1998; Coles et al., 2001; Core et al., 1999; Dalton et al., 1998; Hermalin & Weisbach, 1991; Jensen & Murphy, 1990; Kosnik & Bettenhausen, 1992). A potential explanation for these conflicting and/or weak results may be the failure to consider the effect of the characteristics of the organisational environment on the link between the firm's control system and performance.

It is suggested in this paper that there is a basic negative association between an exogenous variable, firm risk, and firm performance (see Bloom & Milkovich, 1998). Subsequently, the study examines whether certain corporate governance variables could affect this relationship. No attempt is made to infer any causality between corporate governance variables and firm performance. Based on theory, the paper demonstrates that the negative association between risk and firm performance is weaker for firms with more non-executive directors, higher management share ownership and higher management remuneration/compensation. Because governance controls are a firm-level response to a complex environment, they may not impact on financial performance, which may be a function of the dynamics of the industry (Gomez-Mejia & Wiseman, 1997). Control mechanisms are simultaneously and endogenously determined so that economies in agency costs are attained. Therefore, links to performance are not necessarily directional as other factors may determine the level of control mechanism. Therefore, the objective of this research is to determine the efficiency of monitoring and incentive contracts given the level of risk of the firm.

In this study, it is suggested that different monitoring and incentive contracts are optimal for different firms, for the simple reason that each firm faces its own management problems, and hence finds its own solution. "Each firm has different governance needs depending on its economic and regulatory environment, as well as exogenously determined market forces that may also discipline management" (Vafeas & Theodorou, 1998, p. 384).

The results of this study using multiple regression analysis show that monitoring and incentives weaken the negative relationship between the firm's risk and performance. In particular, the results of this study showed the importance of a non-executive director dominated board, higher levels of management share ownership and remuneration on the efficiency of the risky firm. This result suggests that firm performance increases when executives are monitored and compensated for increased levels of risk.

This paper contributes to the literature in several ways. This study adds to prior research by looking at the firm's monitoring and incentive contracts as a collection of controls available to firms, accordingly this study overcomes some of the limitations of prior research. In addition, this research adds to corporate governance-firm performance literature by demonstrating that the corporate governance and performance relationship is associated with an organizational environment variable, that is, firm risk. It is posited in this study that there is a negative association between the level of firm risk and firm performance and that, it is this basic relationship that is modified, as a result of different corporate governance variables. An implication of the results is that risky firms should consider more internal control mechanisms to enhance firm performance.

2. BACKGROUND AND HYPOTHESES DEVELOPMENT

2.1. Firm Risk and Corporate Governance

Firm risk affects the forecasting and planning activities of decision makers, and is therefore related to both the principal and the agent's monitoring and compensation contracting preferences. Firm risk refers to the underlying volatility in the firm's earnings stream and has been identified as a source of agency conflict (Bathala & Rao, 1995). In an effort to reduce these agency conflicts, firms use supervisory and incentive alignment mechanisms that alter the risk and effort orientation of agents to align them with the interests of principals (Tosi & Gomez-Mejia, 1989). These controls are designed to motivate a risk and effort-averse agent to exert unobservable effort in an environment characterized by uncertainty (Banker et al., 1996; Brickley et al., 1997). The control question encompasses how this risk is shared between the principal and the agent.

Typically, firm risk refers to variability in organizational returns and increased chance of corporate ruin (Bloom & Milkovich, 1998). Indeed, prior research has found a significantly negative relationship between firm risk and performance (e.g. Bloom & Milkovich, 1998; Core et al., 1999). The measure of firm risk adopted in this study refers to the underlying volatility in the firm's earnings stream. This interpretation of firm risk is adopted because managers are exposed to both systematic and unsystematic risk. Managers typically have limited opportunity to diversify, partly due to the fact that they receive shares in their own company. Therefore the risk that they are exposed to is the total risk[1] rather than the systematic risk intrinsic in a diversified portfolio (Carr, 1997). Shareholders can select a diversified portfolio that eliminates the unsystematic risk.[2] This implies that the agent, whose compensation mix includes firm-specific stock, has to bear the total risk. Therefore executives are interested in the variance in their own firm's stock and earnings; hence variance is the appropriate measure when testing the principal-agent model (Aggarwal & Samwick, 1999).

Prior research testing the relationship between firm risk and corporate controls has been mixed. For instance, some researchers found a decreased incidence of incentives such as share ownership and stock options were associated with firm risk (Aggarwal & Samwick, 1999; Beatty & Zajac, 1994; Bloom & Milkovich, 1998). In contrast, others found a positive relationship between risk and the use of incentives and stock options (Sanders & Carpenter, 1998; Stroh et al., 1996). In addition, Bathala and Rao (1995) found that board composition was affected so that the number of external members reduced with the level of risk.

2.2. Corporate Governance and Firm Performance

The efficiency of employment contracts is dependent on several factors. In particular, Beatty and Zajac (1994, p. 313) suggest the following:

(1) The ability of firms to use executive compensation contracts to address managerial incentive problems is hampered by risk-bearing concerns that stem from the risk aversion of top executives.
(2) This problem is particularly severe for riskier firms.
(3) Firms seek to address this problem by structuring their boards of directors to ensure sufficient monitoring of managerial behavior, given the magnitude of the agency problem.

Previous research investigating the relationship between corporate controls and firm performance has been mixed and often weak (Agrawal & Knoeber, 1996; Baliga et al., 1996; Bloom & Milkovich, 1998; Coles et al., 2001; Core et al., 1999; Dalton et al., 1998; Evans & Weir, 1995; Hermalin & Weisbach, 1991; Jensen & Murphy, 1990; Kren & Kerr, 1997; Kosnik & Bettenhausen, 1992). This paper sets out to demonstrate how prior research may have benefited by evaluating the association between corporate governance and firm performance from the perspective of the firm's level of risk.

It is posited in this study that there is a negative association between the level of firm risk and firm performance. It is this basic relationship that is modified when firms adopt different corporate governance controls. Consequently, this study sets out to determine whether board monitoring and incentives employed by firms with volatile earnings is associated with financial performance. The research question is whether board monitoring and the extent to which incentive contracts contain shares and higher remuneration reduces owner-manager conflict.

2.3. Firm Risk, Board Composition and Firm Performance

Prior research has failed to arrive at a consensus regarding the relationship between board monitoring and firm performance (see Dalton et al., 1998, for a summary). For example, Evans and Weir (1995) only found support for the relationship between frequency of meetings and profitability. Coles et al. (2001) results demonstrate a negative relationship between the proportion of outside directors and firm performance. Baliga et al. (1996) discovered no evidence of a relationship between duality and firm performance while Coles et al. (2001) report a positive relationship between duality and firm performance. Agrawal and Knoeber (1996) found control mechanisms were interdependent and that outside board membership was negatively related to firm performance. In contrast, Kren and Kerr (1997) did not find that a higher proportion of outsiders maintain a closer link between corporate performance and executives' pay. Therefore, it is likely that board composition is unlikely to have a direct impact on firm performance. Rather, it is feasible that the relationship between board composition and firm performance is associated with the level of firm risk. It has been suggested in the literature that firms with high risk are subject to greater agency conflicts and therefore need more external board membership monitoring (Bathala & Rao, 1995). However, Bathala and Rao (1995) found a negative relationship between the proportion of outsiders and volatility.[3]

With a higher percentage of executive directors on the board and the volatility of the firm's income stream it becomes difficult to assess the outcome of management's decisions. This gives rise to higher agency costs associated with the potential for opportunistic behaviour. Therefore, it is likely that high-risk firms will have lower performance as a result of the inability to monitor managers' behavior.

In order to safeguard their investment in the firm, shareholders and debtholders of high-risk firms will demand a higher proportion of non-executive directors to monitor managers' actions to ensure their actions are value increasing. Managers will be unable to fund future projects unless they can make a credible commitment to shareholders and/or creditors that agency costs will be controlled. One way of achieving this is to have non-executive directors appointed to the board. Therefore, it is expected that firm performance will increase as a function of risk and non-executive director board-dominance. In other words a positive relationship among higher firm risk, proportion of non-executive directors and firm performance is expected. In addition, previous research has struggled to find a significant relationship between board composition and firm performance (see a summary in Dalton et al., 1998). This could be due to the failure of previous studies to consider whether the relationship between board composition and firm performance is associated with the characteristics of the firm. The previous arguments lead to the following proposition:

H1. The negative relationship between the level of firm risk and firm performance is weakened by a higher proportion of non-executive directors on the board.

2.4. Firm Risk, Incentives and Firm Performance

Agency theorists argue that incentive contracts may be designed in response to agency problems (Fama & Jensen, 1983; Jensen & Meckling, 1976). Incentives, both compensation and equity, are governance controls which provide targets, such as financial results, for managers to achieve. This type of control approximates a market contracting arrangement, entailing little monitoring or security holder direction. The principal's objective is to construct an incentive contract that aligns the agent's interests with those of the principal. However, even an efficient system of incentive alignment will still result in some interest divergence, that is, the residual loss. Therefore, the incentive compensation, the cost of monitoring and the residual loss represent the agency costs. Two forms of incentives are considered in this study, remuneration and share ownership.

2.4.1. Remuneration
Researchers have argued that CEO's will pursue their own interests rather than shareholders when their reward does not coincide with that of shareholders (e.g. Jensen & Murphy, 1990). Subsequently, prior research has tested the sensitivity of CEO pay to changes in performance. This argument suggests that an effective governance mechanism that aligns the goals of management with shareholders will be one where a change in shareholder wealth will lead to a significant change in CEO compensation. However, prior research has failed to find consistent and significant relationships between executives' remuneration and firm performance (e.g. Crawford, Ezzell & Miles, 1995; Jensen & Murphy, 1990; Murphy, 1993).

In addition, the results of prior studies testing the relationship between risk and compensation contracts have been mixed. Beatty and Zajac (1994) found that riskier firms have a lower proportion of incentive compensation to total compensation. Munter and Kren (1995) found that uncertainty was negatively related to outcome-based compensation schemes. Stroh et al. (1996) found that during high levels of risk, organisations use variable pay rather than higher fixed cash compensation. Aggarwal and Samwick (1999) found that executives in volatile firms have less performance-based compensation. Bloom and Milkovich

(1998) found that three of four measures of risk[4] were negatively related to the use of incentive pay. Core et al. (1999) suggests that firm risk, in terms of information and operating environment, is an important determinant of the level of CEO compensation.

Prior research (e.g. Aggarwal & Samwick, 1999; Core et al., 1999) suggests that executives of volatile firms will receive higher remuneration to encourage them to accept higher uncertainties, of their environment and subsequently of their compensation. Subsequently, managerial risk aversion would imply that managers of firms with volatile earnings would receive higher compensation as recompense for accepting uncertainty. Therefore, the higher level of compensation will weaken the negative relationship between firm risk and performance. That is, the higher levels of remuneration will act as an incentive to accept the risk of the firm. This leads to the following hypothesis:

H2. The negative relationship between firm risk and performance will be weaker for firms with higher levels of executive total remuneration.

2.4.2. Management Share-Ownership

Share ownership can be an important source of incentives and power for executives as well as outside shareholders. It typically bestows voting rights, which can give internal and external shareholders a voice in the governance of a corporation. Distribution of stock among these stakeholders can, therefore, have a significant impact on corporate actions that are dependent on shareholder voting. It therefore follows that share ownership aligns the interests of executives with shareholders, as executives are less likely to engage in actions that are not in the interests of shareholders.

Two views are expressed regarding the impact of managerial share ownership on shareholder welfare. Some authors (e.g. Beatty & Zajac, 1994; Stulz, 1988) have argued that managerial share ownership should be viewed with caution because substantial managerial share ownership can have undesirable risk-bearing properties. That is, as executives have already invested their non-diversifiable human capital in the firm, increased share ownership transfers additional risk to executives. This approach suggests that this additional risk can lead to risk avoiding behavior on the part of executives, which is not in the interest of shareholders. This argument suggests that executives would have low share ownership in firms with high risk.

In contrast, theoretical and empirical works based on a positivist approach to agency theory have advocated stock ownership as a means to align the interest of top executives with that of shareholders (Jensen & Meckling, 1976; Singh & Harianto, 1989). That is, if executives own stock in a company they are less likely to take actions that are not in the interests of shareholders. However, the research investigating the relationship between firm performance and share ownership has been mixed (see, e.g. Hermalin & Weisbach, 1991; Morck et al., 1988; Zhou, 2001).

Several factors suggest that the relationship between the firm's risk and executive share ownership may be associated with firm performance. Management share-ownership will ensure managers undertake risk-bearing strategies that will increase firm performance. As firms with volatile earnings have the potential to yield large earnings and the realization of the earnings may be delayed, deferred management earnings via share ownership will act as an effective incentive and alignment mechanism. Therefore, it is likely that managerial share ownership has the potential to motivate management to undertake risky projects so that performance will be greater for these firms. In addition it is expected that, low risk firms have stable earnings and as a consequence, there will be less need to motivate executives to seek out risky but profitable investments. This leads to the following hypothesis:

H3. The negative relationship between firm risk and firm performance will be weaker at higher levels of executive share ownership.

3. RESEARCH DESIGN

Data. Archival data on the sampled firm's financial characteristics, management remuneration and share ownership was acquired from 1998/1999 company financial reports provided by Connect 4, an electronic database of the top 500 Australian company annual reports.[5] Risk measures were obtained from the Australian graduate school of management risk measurement service of the University of New South Wales.

3.1. Independent Variables

The traditional measure of the monitoring by board members is the proportion of external directors to internals directors. Prior research has identified external board members as non-executive directors (Conyon & Peck, 1998; Weir, 1997). Board composition is measured as the ratio of non-executive directors to executive directors on the board of directors. NED = non-executive directors divided by total number of directors. The higher the ratio, the greater the proportion of non-executive directors on the board. Following the Australian stock exchange listing rule 3C, non-executive and executive directors are identified and disclosed in either the corporate governance statement or the director's report in the company's annual report.

Executives' remuneration is measured as total reported remuneration divided by the number of executives, which equals the average total remuneration of executives.[6] This measure therefore controls in part for size as a contributing factor to the total remuneration paid to executives. Total remuneration does not include share or share option valuations. It is argued that management share-ownership will ensure managers will undertake risk-bearing strategies that will increase share value. Management share ownership is measured as the total number of ordinary shares held by executive directors divided by the total number of issued ordinary shares and labeled SHARE%. Consistent with prior research, executive directors are used as a proxy for executives[7] (see Morck et al., 1988).

Prior research has used the standard deviation of monthly returns and beta as a measure of firm risk (Aggarwal & Samwick, 1999; Carr, 1997). Therefore, the relevant proxies for firm risk are total variance measures (Core et al., 1999). The primary measure of risk used in this study is the total risk of the firm. This is measured as the standard deviation of the rate of return on equity for the company and labeled RISK. It is expressed as a rate of return per month, and is computed from the (continuously compounded) equity rates of return for the company's equity.[8] Such rates of return are distributed approximately normally. This measure encompasses both systematic and unsystematic risk (Carr, 1997). To test the validity of the results BETA was also used. Beta is the slope coefficient from a simple linear regression of the company equity rate of return on that of the market index, where both are measured as deviations from the risk free rate.

3.2. Dependent Variable

Performance measures include, among other things, return on equity, return on assets, earnings per share, Tobin's Q and profit margin. Previous studies (e.g. Gomez-Mejia et al., 1997) have suggested using factor analysis to integrate various measures of firm performance. However, it may be suggested (Carr, 1997) that one measure should be used independently as many of the measures are highly correlated because they are derived from the same financial data. Executive compensation literature suggests that managers' prefer accounting-based performance measures (see Gomez-Mejia & Balkin, 1992, pp. 204–205) because they are easier to control than external or market-based measures, which are subject to exogenous economic factors (Elitzur & Yaari, 1995). The value of stock arises from three sources, changes to expected cash flows, predictable return variation due to changes in discount rates, and changes to discount rates. In contrast, a firm's current operating performance and changes to its expected future cash-generating ability determine accounting earnings (Sloan, 1993, p. 64). Sloan's (1993) study demonstrated that earnings reflect firm-specific changes in value and are less sensitive to market-wide movements in equity values. Given this distinction between accounting and market-based outcome measures, it seems reasonable to argue that firm performance should be measured using accounting-based measures as they are more likely to reflect the outcome of managers' actions.

In this study, firm performance is measured using return on equity (ROE) for 1999, to demonstrate the relationship between the corporate governance controls adopted in 1998 and the subsequent firm performance in 1999. ROE is measured as income after tax and before abnormal items is divided by total equity minus outside equity interests. Although managerial discretion may affect accounting returns through smoothing and accounting manipulations in the short run, in the long run accounting and market measures of returns should reflect the same economic factors for the firm (Carr, 1997).

3.3. Control Variables

A firm that has high leverage is likely to be viewed as a firm that may have liquidity problems and therefore potentially more risky. DEBT is measured as current and non-current borrowings divided by total equity. This ratio indicates how firms choose to finance operations. The lower the ratio, the greater the protection for lenders, who rank before shareholders. Because book values are used to write debt contracts this measure more accurately proxies for debt holder and shareholder conflicts than market-based measures (Skinner, 1993).

Firm size is included as a control variable in the analysis because it has been found to be associated with various firm characteristics. Firm size is measured as the book value of total assets. A natural logarithmic transformation is performed to normalize data and the transformed variable is labeled LNASSET.

It is likely that specific industries adopt particular corporate governance practices. Therefore it would be expected that there would be an association with industry type and board composition and directors' shareholdings. To account for this relationship industry type is included as a control variable. The INDUSTRY variable is categorized according to the 24 Australian stock exchange (ASX) codes for each of the listed companies in the sample.

The current financial performance of the firm is likely to be associated with future performance. Following preliminary testing, to improve the robustness of the model, ROE for 1998 was included in the regression model. Including this variable creates a lagged variable, which captures, at least in part, the dynamic adjustment of ROE.

4. RESULTS AND DISCUSSION

4.1. Data Screening

The criteria used to develop the sample for testing the hypotheses is presented in Table 1. Following the elimination of firms that did not have values on all criteria, the sample size was reduced to 282. Panel B shows the frequency of industries in the sample, which is representative of the total sample. Of the 282 firms the highest contributing industry type is miscellaneous industrials (12.8%) closely followed by gold (12.1%).

Descriptive statistics and correlations are provided in Table 2. The mean score for the standard deviation of monthly returns (firm risk) is 10.48, suggesting the volatility of the firm's income. The average proportion of non-executive directors (NED) is 69%, as disclosed in the 1998 annual reports. Executive directors own 7% of the sampled firms' total issued shares with a maximum of 89% and a minimum of 0%. Executives receive an average of $216,920 per annum in total remuneration with a maximum of $1,127,579.[9] The firms' average size ($1,194,233,000), Debt (56%) and ROE (1% for 1999 and 7% for 1998) is also shown in the table.

The Pearson's correlation coefficients for the variables of interest are given in the Table 2 below. The correlation matrix reveals a negative correlation between RISK and firm performance (ROE 99) providing support for the proposition of a negative association between risk and firm performance. Performance taken together with the negative association with size suggests that risky firms are small and struggling firms. Risk is also negatively associated with board monitoring (NEDS) and executives' total remuneration. ROE 99 is positively correlated with assets (size).

4.2. Multivariate Tests

Regression analysis is used to test and evaluate the contribution and significance of the hypotheses. The regression tests whether the level of corporate controls moderates the negative association between firm performance and firm risk.

The results of testing the hypotheses are reported in Table 3. The model explains 29% of the variation in the sampled firms' ROE. The results reported in Table 3

Table 1. Screening Criteria and Firm Observations.

	Firm observations
Panel A: Screens applied to data for	
1. Financial statement data reported in Connect 4	437
Observations eliminated because:	
2. Missing values for ROE 1999	42
	395
3. Missing values for RISK	36
	359
4. Missing values for executive directors share ownership	24
	335
5. Missing values for executive's total remuneration	31
	304
6. Missing values for DEBT	22
TOTAL	282

Firm observations	Frequency	%
Panel B: Industry type per ASX code		
Alcohol & tobacco	10	3.5
Chemicals	14	5.0
Developers & contractors	16	5.7
Diversified industrials	12	4.3
Diversified resources	5	1.8
Energy	23	8.2
Engineering	8	2.8
Food and household	8	2.8
Gold	34	12.1
Health care & biotechnology	13	4.6
Infrastructure & utilities	5	1.8
Investment & financial services	17	6.0
Media	18	6.4
Miscellaneous industrials	36	12.8
Other metals	15	5.3
Paper & packing	5	1.8
Property trusts	3	1.1
Retail	13	4.6
Telecommunications	5	1.8
Tourism & leisure	12	4.3
Transport	4	1.4
TOTAL	282	100%

Table 2. Pearsons' Correlation and Descriptive Statistics ($N = 282$).

	ROE 98 1	ROE 99 2	DEBT 3	LNASSET 4	NED 5	SHARE% 6	TR 7	RISK 8
1	1.00	0.341**	0.031	0.112	−0.024	−0.049	−0.076	−0.010
2	0.341**	1.00	0.019	0.166**	0.107	0.038	0.040	−0.197**
3	0.031	0.019	1.00	0.287**	0.088	0.089	0.135*	−0.089
4	0.112	0.166**	0.287**	1.00	0.265**	−0.196**	0.445**	−0.510**
5	−0.024	0.107	0.088	0.265**	1.00	−0.320**	0.103	−0.262**
6	−0.049	0.038	0.089	−0.196**	−0.320**	1.00	−0.064	0.099
7	−0.076	0.040	0.135*	0.445**	0.103	−0.064	1.00	−0.195**
8	−0.010	−0.197**	−0.089	−0.510**	−0.262**	0.099	−0.195**	1.00
				9				
Mean	0.075	0.014	0.561	1,194,233	0.693	0.072	216,921	10.480
Median	0.098	0.090	0.444	201,274	0.750	0.002	186,322	8.850
Std. Dev.	0.575	0.883	0.679	4,293,288	0.204	0.140	145,389	5.279
Min.	−3.142	−13.724	0.00	2,726	0.00	0.00	0.00	3.30
Max.	7.939	3.356	8.08	54,484,000	1.00	0.89	1,127,579	32.90
Percentiles								
25	0.037	0.035	0.171	72,672	0.600	0.0001	150,163	6.80
50	0.098	0.090	0.444	201,274	0.750	0.002	186,322	8.850
75	0.149	0.149	0.722	692,678	0.833	0.069	242,594	12.83

1 ROE 98 = ROE for 1998
2 ROE 99 = Earnings after tax before abnormals/total equity for 1999
3 DEBT = Current and non current borrowings/total equity
4 LNASSET = Log of assets to normalize
5 NED = Ratio of non-executive directors to total directors
6 SHARE% = Executive directors share holdings to total shares
7 TR = Executives total remuneration/number of executives earning >$100,000
8 RISK = The standard deviation of the rate of return on equity for the company
9 TOTAL ASSETS = Total assets $'000 (unlogged)

*Correlation is significant at the 0.05 level (1-tailed).
**Correlation is significant at the 0.01 level (1-tailed).

reveal that the performance of the firm is negatively and significantly related to firm risk thus providing support for examining the stated hypotheses. The results of testing the stated hypotheses suggest that the negative association between firm risk and firm performance is weakened at higher levels of monitoring and incentives. More specifically, a higher proportion of non-executive directors on the board successfully monitor managers' behavior. Higher levels of firm performance confirm this conclusion, therefore H1 is supported. The results also show that the negative relationship between risk and performance is weakened at higher levels of executive remuneration. The result was significant, thus supporting H2. This result

Table 3. Regression Model for Interactive Effects of RISK on ROE ($N = 282$).

	Predicted Sign	Coefficients (B)	t	Sig.	VIF
(Constant)		0.501	0.700	0.485	
ROE 98	+	0.696	7.215	0.000	1.390
DEBT	−	−0.0010	−1.341	0.181	1.240
LNASSET	+	0.0532	1.332	0.184	2.128
NED	?	−0.863	−1.511	0.132	6.099
SHARE%	?	−2.363	−2.289	0.023	9.423
TR	?	−0.0000	−1.675	0.095	5.989
RISK	−	−0.141	−4.702	0.000	11.316
RISK × NED	+	0.122	2.928	0.004	10.553
RISK × SHARE%	+	0.270	3.117	0.002	9.916
RISK × TR	+	0.0000	1.888	0.060	7.458
Alcohol & tobacco		0.0515	0.126	0.900	2.604
Chemicals		−0.0721	−0.186	0.852	3.197
Developers & contractors		0.0246	0.065	0.948	3.497
Diversified industrials		−0.0718	−0.180	0.857	2.925
Diversified resources		−0.131	−0.271	0.787	1.858
Energy		0.0478	0.130	0.897	4.611
Engineering		−0.0574	−0.134	0.894	2.305
Food and household		−0.129	−0.299	0.765	2.307
Gold		0.195	0.537	0.592	6.317
Health care and biotechnology		0.0767	0.194	0.847	3.121
Infrastructure and utilities		0.0015	0.003	0.998	1.828
Investment and financial services		−0.0082	−0.022	0.983	3.658
Media		−0.109	−0.293	0.770	3.778
Miscellaneous industrials		−0.0023	−0.006	0.995	6.266
Other metals		−0.933	−2.390	0.018	3.472
Paper and packing		−0.0165	−0.034	0.973	1.815
Property trusts		−0.0443	−0.079	0.937	1.505
Retail		−0.0108	−0.028	0.978	3.042
Telecommunications		0.117	0.244	0.807	1.824
Tourism and leisure		0.0122	0.031	0.976	2.916
Transport		−0.0779	−0.152	0.879	1.662
R^2	0.289				
Adjusted R^2	0.201				
F	3.285			0.000	

RISK×NED = Interactive term = risk×ratio of non-executive directors to total directors.
RISK×SHARE% = Interactive term = risk×percentage of executive directors share holdings to total shares.
RISK×TR = Interactive term = risk×executives' total remuneration.

suggests that executives are compensated for accepting higher levels of uncertainty of their environment, which in turn provides incentives for executives to adopt value-increasing strategies. The results reported in Table 3 also demonstrate a significant and positive interaction of RISK and executive directors' shareholdings on firm performance. The result shows that firm performance increases at higher levels of firm risk and executive directors' shareholdings, thus supporting H3. The positive relationship between risk and share ownership on ROE shows that using share ownership as an incentive to align agent and principal goals may reduce agency costs and risk avoiding behavior. This result suggests that decision-makers in high-risk firms adopt value-increasing strategies when they have some ownership in the firm.

4.3. Sensitivity Analysis

To test the validity of the results of testing the hypotheses, additional tests were carried out. The regression was run using BETA as the measure of market risk. However, the interactions when testing these hypotheses were not significant.[10] As a further sensitively test, the sampled firms were categorized as high-risk firms (75 percentile) and low-risk firms (25 percentile) and separate regressions were run with the corporate governance variables as the independent variables. The industry variable was dropped from the analysis because too many variables make the relative precision of individual coefficients worse and the resulting loss of degrees of freedom reduce the power of the tests performed on the coefficients. The results reported in Table 4 show a positive relationship between the corporate governance

Table 4. Regression Model: Dependent Variable: ROE 0.99.

	Low Risk ($N = 69$)			High Risk ($N = 70$)		
	Coefficients (B)	t	Sig.	Coefficients (B)	t	Sig.
(Constant)	−0.0095	−0.116	0.908	−3.876	−2.112	0.039
ROE 98	0.682	8.647	0.000	0.519	2.812	0.007
Debt	0.0001	0.486	0.629	−0.0023	−1.105	0.273
LNASSET	0.0061	0.999	0.322	0.212	1.228	0.224
NED	−0.0388	−0.747	0.458	1.522	1.649	0.104
SHARE%	−0.0073	−0.061	0.952	2.278	1.550	0.126
TR	−0.0000	−0.581	0.563	0.0000	0.685	0.496
R^2	0.679			0.189		
Adjusted R^2	0.648			0.112		
F	21.908		0.000	2.443		0.035

measures of board composition, share ownership and remuneration and firm performance for the high-risk firms. In contrast, the relationship between the corporate controls and firm performance is negative for low-risk firms. Although this result is not significant, the results support the interpretation of the results provided in Table 3. That is, that the negative association between risk and firm performance is weaker for firms with more non-executive directors, higher management share ownership and higher management remuneration/compensation. Very simply, the weaker negative association is expected because each of the corporate governance variables identified and examined are more effective for firms with high risk than firms with low risk, ceteris paribus. A reason for this is that firms with more earnings variability or risk (less earnings variability or low risk) are more difficult (less difficult) to monitor and corporate governance mechanisms play a more important (less important) role.

5. CONCLUSIONS

The results of testing the hypotheses suggest that assuming an agent is risk-averse does not capture the full range of attitudes and behaviors agents' exhibit under risk. The results suggest that executives may have greater risk bearing preferences when they are motivated and monitored. In other words, executives self-select firms that offer incentives and higher levels of total remuneration. In addition, the results demonstrate that a positive association between corporate controls and firm performance is associated with the level of firm risk.

This study tested the effectiveness of monitoring and incentive contracts for firms with risk, that is, the relationship of monitoring and incentive contracts to firm performance given the level of firm risk. The hypotheses are premised on the notion of basic negative association between risk and performance based on prior research. The hypotheses predict that the negative association is weaker for firms with:

(1) a higher proportion of non-executive directors on the board,
(2) higher management shareholdings, and
(3) higher management remuneration.

The results based on a sample of 282 large Australian companies support all these hypotheses.

5.1. Limitations and Future Research

Limitations of this study include sample bias and cross-sectional analysis. The sample was not randomly chosen as the data was collected from the top 500 (in terms of market capitalization) Australian publicly listed companies. A wider sample of firms, both small and large, might add additional information for testing the relationships posited in this study.

Cross-sectional analysis of the data does not determine causality of association. Ideally the data collection should cover at least two to five years. The hypotheses presented in this research also imply that firms will change their incentive contracts over time as the relative level of firms' risk varies. If the risk changes for a given firm over time, theory predicts changes associated with the firm's incentives. To test the preference of firms for a particular incentive contract would require time-series analysis.

This research tested the notion that risk is a major variable that is associated with an individual's motivation and acceptance of incentive contracts and is therefore related to firm performance. Risk can be measured in many ways. The measure used in this study is designed to indicate the total risk of the firm. However, a multidimensional measure of risk may indicate a stronger association with incentive contracts and firm performance. This research has shown that risk is associated with firms' strategic performance relationships. Researchers may gain a better understanding of the conditions under which agency predictions hold and test the efficiency of contracts by examining different sources of risk and how they are related to corporate governance decisions. A fertile area of research is to examine the dimensions of risk and their relationship to organisational strategies and outcomes.

Despite the limitation of this research due to the experimental design, the findings provide insight into the choice of board monitoring and incentive contracts adopted by firms and the efficacy of the controls in terms of firm performance. The particular contribution of this study is to show that not all incentives available to firms are value increasing to all firms. Rather greater firm performance is associated with the characteristics of the firm that endogenously determine the mix of monitoring and incentives selected by the firm.

NOTES

1. Total risk consists of systematic risk, which is a measure of how the asset (share) covaries with the economy, and unsystematic risk, which is independent of the economy.
2. CAPM theory suggests that shareholders can diversify away all risk except the risk of the economy as a whole, which is undiversifiable (Copeland & Weston, 1988).
3. Volatility was measured as the coefficient of variation of earnings before interest and tax.
4. Both systematic and unsystematic income stream volatility and systematic stock market return volatility.

5. The top 500 companies in terms of market capitalization.

6. Annual reports include the total remuneration paid to executives earning greater than $100,000.

7. Firms only report executive directors' share ownership in the financial reports as part of the corporate governance disclosure requirements of the Australian stock exchange.

8. It is measured over the four-year period ending in the last month of 1998. All measurable monthly returns in the four-year interval are included. Individual monthly returns measure total shareholder returns for the company, including the effects of various capitalization changes such as bonus issues, renounceable and non-renounceable issues, share splits, consolidations, and dividend distributions.

9. 0 remuneration means that there are no executives in the firm that earn greater than $100,000.

10. Beta×ned: $p = 0.619$; beta×share percent: $p = 0.302$; beta×tr: $p = 0.853$.

REFERENCES

Aggarwal, R. K., & Samwick, A. A. (1999). The other side of the trade-off: The impact of risk on executive compensation. *Journal of Political Economy, 107*(1), 65–106.

Agrawal, A., & Knoeber, C. R. (1996). Firm performance and mechanisms to control agency problems between managers and shareholders. *Journal of Financial and Quantitative Analysis, 31*(3), 377–397.

Baliga, B. R., Moyer, R. C., & Rao, R. S. (1996). CEO duality and firm performance: What's the fuss? *Strategic Management Journal, 17*(1), 41–53.

Banker, R. D., Lee, S. Y., & Potter, G. (1996). A field study of the impact of a performance-based incentive plan. *Journal of Accounting and Economics, 21*(3), 195–226.

Bathala, C. T., & Rao, R. P. (1995). The determinants of board composition: An agency theory perspective. *Managerial and Decision Economics, 16*, 59–69.

Beatty, R. P., & Zajac, E. J. (1994). Managerial incentives, monitoring and risk bearing: A study of executive compensation, ownership and board structure in initial public offerings. *Administrative Science Quarterly, 3*(2), 313–335.

Bloom, M., & Milkovich, G. T. (1998). Relationships among risk, incentive pay, and organizational performance. *Academy of Management, 41*(3), 283–296.

Brickley, J. A., Smith, C. W., Jr., & Zimmerman, J. L. (1997). *Managerial economics and organizational architecture.* Chicago: Irwin.

Carr, L. L. (1997). Strategic determinants of executive compensation in small publicly traded firms. *Journal of Small Business Management, 35*(3), 1–12.

Coles, J. W., McWilliams, V. B., & Sen, N. (2001). An examination of the relationship of governance mechanisms to performance. *Journal of Management, 27*, 23–50.

Conyon, M. J., & Peck, S. I. (1998). Board control, remuneration committees, and top management compensation. *Academy of Management Journal, 41*(2), 146–157.

Copeland, T. E., & Weston, J. F. (1988). *Financial theory and corporate policy.* Reading, MA: Addison-Wesley Pub. Co.

Core, J. E., Holthausen, R. W., & Larker, D. F. (1999). Corporate governance, chief executive officer compensation, and firm performance. *Journal of Financial Economics, 51*, 371–406.

Crawford, A., Ezzell, J., & Miles, J. (1995). Bank CEO pay-performance relations and the effects of deregulation. *Journal of Business* (April), 231–256.

Dalton, D. R., Dailey, C. M., Ellstrand, A. E., & Johnson, J. L. (1998). Meta-analytic reviews of board composition, leadership structure, and financial performance. *Strategic Management Journal*, *19*(3), 269–290.

Elitzur, R. R., & Yaari, V. (1995). Executive incentive compensation and earnings manipulation in a multi-period setting. *Journal of Economic Behavior and Organization, 26*, 201–219.

Evans, J., & Weir, C. (1995).Decision processes, monitoring, incentives and large firm performance in the U.K. *Management Decision, 33*(6), 32–37.

Fama, E., & Jensen, M. (1983). Agency problems and residual claims. *The Journal of Law and Economics, 26*(2), 327–349.

Gomez-Mejia, L. R., & Balkin, D. B. (1992). *Compensation, organizational strategy and firm performance*. Cincinnati: Southwestern Publishing Co.

Gomez-Mejia, L. R., & Wiseman, R. M. (1997). Reframing executive compensation: An assessment and outlook. *Journal of Management, 23*(3), 291–374.

Hermalin, B. E., & Weisbach, M. S. (1991). The effects of board composition and direct incentives on firm performance. *Financial Management, 20*(4), 101–112.

Jensen, M. C., & Meckling, W. H. (1976). Theory of the firm: Managerial behaviour, agency costs and ownership structure. *Journal of Financial Economics, 3*(4), 305–360.

Jensen, M. C., & Murphy, K. J. (1990). Performance pay and top management incentives. *Journal of Political Economy, 98*, 225–264.

Kosnik, R. D., & Bettenhausen, K. L. (1992). Agency theory and motivational effect of management compensation. *Group and Organisation Management, 17*(3), 309–330.

Kren, L., & Kerr, J. K. (1997). The effect of outside directors and board shareholdings on the relation between chief executive compensation and firm performance. *Accounting and Business Research, 27*(4), 297–309.

Morck, R., Shleifer, A., & Vishney, R. W. (1988). Management ownership and market valuation: An empirical analysis. *Journal of Financial Economics, 20*, 293–315.

Munter, P., & Kren, L. (1995). The impact of uncertainty and monitoring by the board of directors on incentive system design. *Managerial Auditing Journal, 10*(4), 23–34.

Murphy, K. J. (1993). Executive compensation in corporate America 1993. *United Shareholders of America*.

Sanders, W. G., & Carpenter, M. A. (1998). Internationalization and firm governance: The role of CEO compensation, top team composition, and board structure. *Academy of Management Journal, 41*(2), 158–178.

Singh, H., & Harianto, F. (1989). Management-board relationships, takeover risk and adoption of golden parachutes. *Academy of Management Journal, 32*, 7–24.

Skinner, D. (1993). The investment opportunity set and accounting procedure choice. *Journal of Accounting and Economics, 16*, 407–445.

Sloan, R. G. (1993). Accounting earnings and top executive compensation. *Journal of Accounting and Economics, 16*, 55–100.

Stroh, L. K., Brett, J. M., Bauman, J. P., & Rielly, A. H. (1996). Agency theory and variable pay compensation strategies. *Academy of Management Journal, 39*(3), 751–767.

Stulz, R. M. (1988). Managerial control of voting rights. Financing policies and the market for corporate control. *Journal of Financial Economics, 20*, 25–54.

Tosi, H. L., & Gomez-Mejia, M. L. (1989). The decoupling of CEO pay and performance: An agency theory perspective. *Administrative Science Quarterly, 34*, 169–190.

Vafeas, N., & Theodorou, E. (1998).The relationship between board structure and firm performance in the U.K. *British Accounting Review*, *30*, 383–407.

Weir, C. (1997). Corporate governance, performance, and take-overs: An empirical analysis of U.K. mergers. *Applied Economics*, *29*, 1465–1475.

Zhou, X. (2001). Understanding the determinants of managerial share ownership and the link between ownership and performance: Comment. *Journal of Financial Economics*, *62*, 559–571.

CORPORATE REPUTATION AND INVESTMENT PERFORMANCE: THE U.S. AND U.K. EXPERIENCE

Sam Y. Chung, Kristina Eneroth
and Thomas Schneeweis

ABSTRACT

Corporate reputation is often regarded by academics and practitioners as indicative of a firm's current and future financial performance. In this study, the relationship between a firm's equity performance and reputation ratings published in the Economist (U.K.) and Fortune (U.S.) magazine is investigated for the period of 1990–1999. On a total return basis, monthly equity-returns of high-reputation firms are shown to outperform those of low-reputation firms both in the year prior and following the 'reputation' reporting month. As for other studies, the results indicate that the size of a firm's market capitalization positively affect the firm's reputation. This study shows that, unlike previous studies, it is primarily a firm's equity performance in the pre-survey and survey period that affects the published ranking of the firm's reputation and the published ranking has little impact on the firm's future risk-adjusted equity return.

Social Responsibility: Corporate Governance Issues
Research in International Business and Finance, Volume 17, 273–291
Copyright © 2003 by Elsevier Science Ltd.
All rights of reproduction in any form reserved
ISSN: 0275-5319/PII: S0275531903170122

1. INTRODUCTION

Corporate reputation is often regarded by academics and practitioners as indicative of a firm's current and future financial performance. For instance, Shefrin and Statman (1994, 1995) have presented a behavioral capital asset pricing model in which investors' perception of a firm's 'quality' may impact the firm's risk and return. Their theoretical model suggests large (small) firms may be perceived as good (bad) firms and it is consistent with corporate reputation survey evidence that large firms have superior corporate reputation in both U.K. and U.S.[1]

For the United States and Britain, empirical results also exist on the correspondence between a firm's equity performance and external evaluators' perceptions of the firm's qualitative attributes (e.g. quality of management, capacity to innovate). For instance, Antunovich and Laster (1998) have argued that *Fortune* reputation ratings are directly related to a firm's future equity performance in the U.S. They report the most admired firms in the U.S. achieve high equity return performance after corporate reputation publication while the less admired firms generally underperform.[2] For other studies, however, little correlation has been found between perceived management quality and future risk-adjusted equity returns for both U.S. (McGuire et al., 1988, 1990; Shefrin & Statman, 1994, 1995) and British firms (Nanda et al., 1996).

In this paper, the relationship between a firm's published reputation rankings and its equity performance is investigated in: (1) pre-survey period, post-survey period and during the survey period; and (2) pre and post publication month. As in other studies, results show that: (1) the 'high-rated' firms on their reputation outperform, on a total equity return basis, the 'low-rated' firms; and (2) larger firms generally have a higher reputation scores than smaller firms. This study also shows that the impact of firm size is due primarily to the manner of corporate reputation survey collection and the approach taken to risk-return analysis. The results show that: (1) little relationship exists between corporate reputation ratings and a firm's future risk-adjusted equity performance; and (2) changes in corporate reputation ratings are related to changes in a firm's equity return performance in the pre-survey and during the survey period and, thus are not solely due to firm size. Therefore, unlike previous studies, the result in this study shows that a firm's equity return performance in the pre-survey and survey period affects published rankings of a firm's reputation qualities and that the publishing of these rankings has little impact on a firm's future risk-adjusted returns.

In the next section, previous literatures about the relationship between a firm's financial performance and published corporate reputation are reviewed. The data and methodology are presented in Section 3. Results are presented and discussed in Section 4. We conclude in Section 5.

2. LITERATURE REVIEW

Financial theory has supported the use of corporate reputation in assessing a firm's future financial performance. Firms perceived as excellent along an array of dimensions have an easier access to financial capital or have a lower cost of businesses. Managerial capacity has been cited to be of prime interest on evaluating security selection (Bodie et al., 1997). A firm's corporate reputation quality may affect its ability to deal in 'cheaper' implicit contracts (e.g. non-union employees) in contrast to more 'costly' explicit (e.g. union employees) contracts (Cornell & Shapiro, 1987).

As important, previous empirical research has directly addressed the correspondence between a firms' financial performance and external evaluators' perceptions of the qualitative attributes (see Fig. 1; Solt & Shefrin, 1989).

Some researchers have provided evidence that investing in high-reputation firms can be a profitable strategy. For instance, Clayman (1987) finds that the returns of investing in an equally weighted portfolio of 29 firms featured in the book *In Search of Excellence: Lessons from America's Best-Run Corporations* outperform the S&P 500 by 1.1% a year from 1981 to 1985. Antunovich and Laster (1998) have also argued that *Fortune* survey's reputation rankings are directly related to a firm's future equity performance. They report 'the most admired' firms in the *Fortune* survey achieve high ex-post return performance (post ranking publication) while the 'less admired' firms generally underperform. Specifically, their empirical results suggest that a portfolio of the most admired firms earns an abnormal return of 3.2% in the year after the survey is published and 8.3% over the three years. In contrast, the least admired firms earn a negative abnormal return of 8.6% in the nine months through the end of the year.

For other studies (McGuire et al., 1990; Nanda et al., 1996; Shefrin & Statman, 1995, 1997), little correlation, however, is found between perceived management quality and future risk-adjusted security returns for either U.S. or U.K. firm. Shefrin and Statman (1995, 1997) show that the *Fortune* survey gives high ratings to firms with large market capitalizations and high market-to book ratios, hypothesizing that firms rated highly in the *Fortune* survey underperform the market. To test this hypothesis they regress one-year equity returns on the Fortune rating on value as a long-term investment, with mixed results. The reputation measure has a positive coefficient in eight years and a negative coefficient in five years; the pooled regression has a coefficient that is negative and marginally significant.

Thus, theoretical and empirical evidence exists on the external perception of a firm's performance across a wide variety of qualitative attributes as indicative of the ability of firms to lower costs of capital, to lower various contracting costs, to increase investor interest, and to achieve superior future financial performance.

Author	Title	Sample	Major Finding
Antunovich, P. and D. Laster, 1998	Do Investors Mistake a Good Company for a Good Investment ?	Fortune Survey, 1983-1995 published by AMAC DataBook (13 years)	*A portfolio of the most admired firms earns a significant abnormal return in the year after the survey is published (well admired firms are not overpriced). *The least admired firms earn a significantly negative abnormal return after the publication (the timing of returns to least admired firms provides evidence of window dressing).
Shefrin, H. and M. Statman, 1997	Behavioral Porfolio Theory	Fortune Survey, 1997 (1 year)	*Fortune survey gives high rating to firms with large market capitalizations and high market-to-book ratios. *Firms rated highly in the survey underperform the market.
Nanda, S., T. Schneeweis and K. Eneroth, 1996	Corporate Performance and Firm Perception: The British Experience	The Economist 1989, 1991, and 1992 (3 years)	*Differences may exist between US and UK in the use of qualitative survey data on a firm's strategic attributes as a forecast of a firm's future quantitative performance measures. *For small firms, certain qualitative factors may be of importance in forecasting accounting and security market returns.
Shefrin, H. and M. Statman, 1995	Making Sense of Beta, Size and Book-to-Market	Fortune Survey, 1994 (1 year)	*Investors tend to indifferent to the stock's beta when ranking a company. *The qualitative measure (e.g., value as a long-term investment) has a negative relationship with the standard deviation of return on a security.
McGuire, J., T. Schneeweis and B. Branch, 1990	Perception of Firm Quality: A Cause or Result of Firm Performance	Fortune Survey, 1983 (1 year)	*Financial measures of both risk and return influence perceptions of firm quality. *Perceptions of firm quality more closely related to prior financial performance than to subsequent financial performance.
Solt, M. and H. Shefrin, 1989	Good Companies, Bad Stocks	Fortune Survey, 1987 (1 year)	*When analyzing managerial performance, investors review both qualitative factors as well as financial performance such as profit margin.
McGuire, J., A. Sundgren and T. Schneeweis, 1988	Corporate Social Responsibility and Firm Financial Performance	Fortune Survey, 1983 and 1986 (2 years)	*Financial performance influence variables of social responsibility more than the reverse. *Reduction of firm risk is an important benefit of social responsibility.
Clayman, M., 1987	In Search of Excellence: The Investors' Viewpoint	U.S. firms based on market/book and P/E ratio.	*U.S.'s best-run companies beat the S&P 500 by 1.1% a year from 1981 to 1985. * A portfolio of "unexcellent" S&P 500 firms with allow growth, low profitability, and low market-to-book ratios outperforms the index by 12.4 percent a year.

Fig. 1. Selected Research Regarding a Relationship between a Firm's Corporate Reputation and Financial Performance.

However, current reputation ratings may not necessarily be related to future equity performance. Finance theory generally accepts the position that corporate stock prices incorporate all past and current information such that unless published reputation ratings contain new information that affect firms' expected risk and return, published reputation rankings should not affect future risk-adjusted equity returns.

3. DATA AND METHODOLOGY

Rankings of public perceptions of firms' qualitative attributes are obtained from surveys commissioned by The Economist (U.K. firms) and *Fortune* magazine (U.S. firms). For U.S. and U.K. firms, these surveys have been published yearly over the time period of analysis 1990–1999. For U.K., survey participants are asked to rate companies on eight attributes; quality of management, financial soundness, quality of products and services, ability to attract, develop and retain top talent, value as a long-term investment, capacity to innovate, quality of marketing, and corporate social responsibility. For U.S., survey participants are asked to rank companies on similar attributes.[3] For both countries, a total 'firm quality' score is computed by averaging firm ratings over the eight dimensions. Firms are ranked on a scale of 0 (poor) to 10 (excellent).[4]

Monthly return data are determined for the sample firms, the S&P 500, and FTSE all share index. In addition, monthly return data for size-based market indices; Frank Russell 100, 250 and 2000 and the FTSE 100, 250 and small cap indices, are determined. For the U.K., approximately 200 firms are rated each year, while for the U.S., approximately 350 firms are rated. For the U.K., sixty-seven firms' monthly return data are available from Datastream and those are ranked in all across the sample-period (1990–1999). No consistent industry bias is indicated from the sample firms. For the U.S., given the large number of firms, tests are conducted on a data set insured between group variance (high vs. low rankings). In each year the top ten and the bottom ten firms in total ratings are obtained for the high and low group, respectively. While the top ten firms remain relatively stable in their group, the bottom ten firms are changed such that over time a total of approximately 100 firms are listed in those groups.

The portfolio size measured by the market value of equity is also determined for the high- and low-rated portfolio. For instance, in the U.K. sample, the average market value of the firms' equity in high-rated portfolio in the year 1990 is £5,4341 million while the low-rank portfolio is £1,486 million. The relative firm-size remains similar in future years. The firm-size difference between high- and low-portfolio is also evident for the U.S. sample. The average market value of the firms' equity in the high-rated portfolio of the year 1990 (US$20,865 million) is approximately five times larger than that of a low-rated portfolio (US$5,111 million).

Portfolio abnormal returns (AR) are determined by both the 'market-adjusted return' and the 'risk-adjusted return' basis:

$$AR_{it} = R_{it} - R_{mt}$$

where, R_{it} = return on a portfolio i in period t. R_{mt} = return on a market index m in period t.

We also define

$$SAR_{it} = \frac{AR_{it}}{\sigma_i},$$

notice that σ_i is calculated from the prior three years data to the year before the publication

$$CSAR_t = \sum_{k=-12}^{k=t} SAR_{ik},$$

where $k = -12, -11, -10, \ldots 0, \ldots, 9, 10, 11$.

In brief, ARs are determined after subtracting the market return on the appropriate market index from the returns of high-, mid-, and low-rated portfolio in each year. Standard errors from the prior three years data to the year before publication are used to determine the Standardized Abnormal Returns (SARs) for the year before and after publication. Cumulative Standardized Abnormal Returns (CSARs) are reported as means to track the relative performance of the high-, mid-, and low-rated portfolios. ARs are presented for both the pre-publication versus post-publication period and pre-survey versus post-survey period (see Fig. 2).

Time Table: Survey vs. Publication

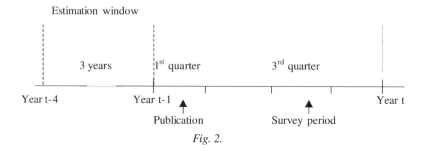

Fig. 2.

Abnormal returns over the window of twenty-four months, one-year prior to and after the publication, measure the impact of the published reputation ranking on the equity performance of the firm. If the relative market performance affects respondents' ratings, then high (low) rated firms should find their CSARs to be rising (falling) in the survey period of the previous year. If the market incorporates the information of the reputation rankings before publication, the pattern of CSARs for the high and low rated portfolio should be similar after the publication month. In addition, if the respondents' ratings affect the firm's equity performance in the months following the survey period, then high (low) rated firms should find their CSARs rising (falling) in the months following the survey period.

As noted earlier, a firm's reputation rating by itself may not indicate equity performance impacts, especially, if the a firm is rated in the same category (high, mid, or low) across publication years. However, for firms with an increase or decrease in rankings, the change in rankings may be due to recent market performance. For firms experiencing a dramatic shift in reputation (e.g. high to low or low to high), one may expect to see rising or falling CSARs during the pre-survey or survey period relative to firms staying in the same portfolio across the sample years.

4. RESULTS AND DISCUSSION

4.1. Corporate Reputation and Market Performance

Previous research (McGuire et al., 1988, 1990; Nanda et al., 1996; Shefrin & Statman, 1994, 1995) indicate that a firm-size (market capitalization) may be a primary determinant of corporate reputation ratings. Similarly, Antunovich and Laster (1998) suggest that firm size may be a primary determinant in firm quality assessments and subsequent return performance based on this quality assessment.

In Fig. 3A (relative performance in the year before the publication) and B (relative performance the year after the publication), the return and correlation results show the close correspondence between market indices based on firm size and portfolios based on corporate reputation. For the U.K., the average correlation between firm-size and the corporate reputation score for the sample period is 0.47.[5] For the high-, mid-, and low-rated portfolios, the average corporate reputation rate and firm-size over the sample period are as follows; high rank (7.45; £5,341 million), mid rank (6.29; £2,302 million), and low rank (4.99; £1,486 million). Given the relationship between corporate reputation rate and firm-size, it is expected that the return of the high-ranked portfolio has its highest correlation with the return of the FTSE 100 index. And the return of the mid-ranked portfolio has a higher correlation with the return of the FTSE 250 (mid-cap) index than that of the FTSE

(A)

Average Monthly Returns*: from 1/89 to 12/ 95

	FTSE100	FTSE250	FTSE Small	High Rank	Mid-Rank	Low Rank	FTSE100-FTSE small	High Rank-Low Rank
Jan.-Mar.	0.90%	1.80%	2.20%	1.40%	1.40%	0.90%	-1.30%	0.50%
Apr.-Sept.	0.90%	0.50%	0.10%	1.20%	0.20%	-1.00%	-0.10%	2.20%
Oct.-Dec	2.10%	1.60%	0.20%	0.90%	0.80%	-0.30%	1.90%	1.20%
All month	1.20%	1.10%	0.70%	1.20%	0.70%	-0.40%	0.50%	1.60%

Average Monthly Standard Deviations*:from 1/89 to 12/95

	FTSE100	FTSE250	FTSE Small	High Rank	Mid-Rank	Low Rank	FTSE100-FTSE small	High Rank-Low Rank
Jan.-Mar.	4.80%	5.20%	5.60%	4.70%	4.70%	6.30%	-0.80%	-1.60%
Apr.-Sept.	4.70%	5.50%	5.00%	4.10%	4.10%	5.70%	-0.30%	-1.60%
Oct.-Dec	3.70%	4.20%	4.30%	2.80%	3.60%	4.80%	-0.60%	-2.00%
All month	4.50%	5.10%	5.00%	3.90%	4.20%	5.60%	-0.50%	-1.70%

Return/Risk Ratio: 1/89-12/95

	FTSE100	FTSE250	FTSE Small	High Rank	Mid-Rank	Low Rank	FTSE100-FTSE small	High Rank-Low Rank
Jan.-Mar.	0.19	0.35	0.39	0.30	0.30	0.14	-0.21	0.16
Apr.-Sept.	0.19	0.09	0.02	0.29	0.05	-0.18	0.17	0.47
Oct.-Dec	0.57	0.38	0.05	0.32	0.22	-0.06	0.52	0.38
All month	0.27	0.22	0.14	0.31	0.17	-0.07	-1.00	-0.94

Correlation Table: 1/89-12/95

	FTSE100	FTSE250	FTSE Sma	High Rank	Mid-Rank	Low Rank
FTSE100	1.00					
FTSE250	0.91	1.00				
FTSE Small	0.77	0.92	1.00			
High Rank	0.81	0.60	0.51	1.00		
Mid-Rank	0.73	0.80	0.69	0.84	1.00	
Low Rank	0.74	0.79	0.75	0.55	0.79	1.00

(B)

Average Monthly Returns*: from 1/90 to 12/ 96

	FTSE100	FTSE250	FTSE Small	High Rank	Mid-Rank	Low Rank	FTSE100-FTSE small	High Rank-Low Rank
Jan.-Mar.	0.20%	1.40%	1.80%	1.00%	1.20%	1.40%	-1.60%	-0.40%
Apr.-Sept.	0.80%	0.40%	0.20%	1.00%	0.60%	0.10%	-0.40%	0.90%
Oct.-Dec	2.10%	1.70%	0.70%	1.30%	1.60%	2.30%	1.40%	-1.00%
All month	1.00%	1.00%	0.70%	1.10%	1.00%	0.90%	0.30%	0.20%

Average Monthly Standard Deviations*:from 1/90 to 12/96

	FTSE100	FTSE250	FTSE Small	High Rank	Mid-Rank	Low Rank	FTSE100-FTSE small	High Rank-Low Rank
Jan.-Mar.	3.70%	4.60%	5.30%	3.30%	3.80%	5.00%	-1.60%	-1.70%
Apr.-Sept.	4.60%	5.50%	5.20%	4.20%	4.90%	6.50%	0.30%	-2.30%
Oct.-Dec	2.90%	3.40%	3.20%	2.50%	3.60%	4.30%	-0.30%	-1.80%
All month	4.00%	4.80%	4.80%	3.60%	4.30%	5.70%	-0.80%	-2.10%

Return/Risk Ratio: 1/90-12/96

	FTSE100	FTSE250	FTSE Small	High Rank	Mid-Rank	Low Rank	FTSE100-FTSE small	High Rank-Low Rank
Jan.-Mar.	0.05	0.30	0.34	0.30	0.32	0.28	-0.29	0.02
Apr.-Sept.	0.17	0.07	0.04	0.24	0.12	0.02	0.14	0.22
Oct.-Dec	0.72	0.50	0.22	0.52	0.44	0.53	0.51	-0.01
All month	0.25	0.21	0.15	0.31	0.23	0.16	-0.38	-0.10

Correlation Table: 1/89-12/95

	FTSE100	FTSE250	FTSE Smal	High Rank	Mid-Rank	Low Rank
FTSE100	1.00					
FTSE250	0.90	1.00				
FTSE Small	0.75	0.92	1.00			
High Rank	0.84	0.74	0.68	1.00		
Mid-Rank	0.81	0.87	0.75	0.85	1.00	
Low Rank	0.71	0.80	0.76	0.57	0.85	1.00

*Average monthly returns and standard deviations are calculated by monthly stock return data
from Datastream over the period.

Fig. 3.   Size Effects and Firm Image – U.K. Results for Pre-Publication Year (A) 1989–1995
and (B) 1990–1996.

Small-Cap index, while the low-ranked portfolio has a higher correlation with the FTSE Small-Cap index than with any other FTSE indices (see the correlation tables). As important, the performance of the different FTSE indices reflects the performance of the U.K. high-, mid-, and low-ranked portfolios. For instance, over the period 1990–1999, as shown in Fig. 3B, the average monthly returns for the large-cap/small-cap FTSE index (1.0%/0.7%) and high/low reputation portfolio (1.1%/0.9%) reflect the relatively higher performance of both the large cap and the associated large firms (high-ranked firms in reputation) in the months following the published rankings. Similarly, for the period 1990–1999, the differential performance between the FTSE small-cap/large-cap index (1.8%/0.2%) as well as the low-rank/high-rank reputation portfolio (1.4%/1%) reflects the traditional small cap effect (higher performance of small firms for the first quarter of the year). When the relative risk (standard deviation) is adjusted, however, the performance of the two portfolios is not significantly different.

Of importance is that in contrast to the first quarter of the year, during the survey months (especially in the pre-publication year) as shown in Fig. 3A, the large-cap index and high-ranked firms (0.9%/1.2%) outperform the small-cap index and low-ranked firms (0.1%/−1.0%). Thus, during the survey period, large firms generally outperform small firms. The results are consistent with respondents' view that the better return performance of the larger firms is indicative of higher quality. Thus, survey ratings are reflected in the higher correlation between large-cap/small-cap market indices and high-rank/low-rank portfolios in the following year.

In Fig. 4A and B, the similar return and correlation result also shows the close correspondence between corporate reputation and firm size for the U.S. firms. For the U.S., the overall correlation between firm-size and the reputation score is 0.52. For the high-, mid-, and low-ranked portfolios, the representative corporate reputation score and firm size are as follows; high rank (8.25/US$20,865 million), mid rank (7.39/US$16,740 million) and low rank (5.62/US$5,111 million). Given the relationship between corporate reputation score and firm-size, it is also expected that the returns of the high-ranked portfolio have the highest correlation (0.88/0.89) with the Russell 200 in the pre- and post-publication years and the returns of the mid-ranked portfolio have the highest correlation (0.92/0.91) with the mid-cap Russell, while the low-ranked portfolio has a higher correlation with Russell small-cap index (0.74/0.82). As important, the performance of the different Russell indices reflects the performance of the U.S. high-, mid-, and low-ranked portfolios. For the period between January, 1990 and March, 1997, as shown in Fig. 4B, the average monthly returns for the large/small cap Russell index (1.3%/1.1%) and high/low ranked portfolio (1.54%/0.4%) reflect the relatively

(A)

Average Monthly Returns*: from 1/89 to 12/95

	FR200	FR MID	FR2000	High Rank	Mid-Rank	Low Rank	FR200-FR2000	High Rank-Low Rank
Jan.-Mar.	1.00%	1.60%	2.00%	0.70%	1.50%	2.60%	-1.00%	-1.90%
Apr.-Sept.	1.10%	0.90%	0.50%	1.80%	0.50%	-0.01%	0.00%	1.81%
Oct.-Dec	1.60%	1.40%	1.10%	2.00%	1.00%	-0.60%	0.50%	2.60%
All month	1.20%	1.10%	1.00%	1.60%	0.90%	-0.10%	0.20%	1.70%

Average Monthly Standard Deviations*:from 1/89 to 12/95

	FR200	FR MID	FR2000	High Rank	Mid-Rank	Low Rank	FR200-FR2000	High Rank-Low Rank
Jan.-Mar.	3.20%	3.60%	4.70%	3.70%	3.20%	6.00%	-1.50%	-2.30%
Apr.-Sept.	3.40%	3.90%	4.20%	4.00%	3.60%	5.20%	-0.80%	-1.20%
Oct.-Dec	3.10%	4.10%	4.40%	3.00%	4.10%	6.10%	-1.30%	-3.10%
All month	3.30%	3.90%	4.40%	3.70%	3.60%	5.80%	-1.10%	-2.10%

Return/Risk Ratio: 1/89-12/95

	FR200	FR MID	FR2000	High Rank	Mid-Rank	Low Rank	FR200-FR2000	High Rank-Low Rank
Jan.-Mar.	0.31	0.44	0.43	0.19	0.47	0.43	-0.11	-0.24
Apr.-Sept.	0.32	0.23	0.12	0.45	0.14	0.00	0.20	0.45
Oct.-Dec	0.52	0.34	0.25	0.67	0.24	-0.10	0.27	0.77
All month	0.36	0.28	0.23	0.43	0.25	-0.02	-0.18	-0.81

Correlation Table: 1/89-12/95

	FR200	FR MID	FR2000	High Rank	Mid-Rank	Low Rank
Frank Russell 200	1.00					
Frank Russell MID	0.90	1.00				
Frank Russell 2000	0.76	0.92	1.00			
High Rank	0.88	0.69	0.59	1.00		
Mid-Rank	0.81	0.92	0.71	0.70	1.00	
Low Rank	0.58	0.73	0.74	0.35	0.74	1.00

(B)

Average Monthly Returns*: from 1/90 to 12/96

	FR200	FR MID	FR2000	High Rank	Mid-Rank	Low Rank	FR200-FR2000	High Rank-Low Rank
Jan.-Mar.	1.50%	2.10%	2.30%	1.30%	2.00%	2.90%	-0.80%	-1.60%
Apr.-Sept.	0.90%	0.60%	0.30%	1.10%	0.20%	-0.40%	0.10%	1.50%
Oct.-Dec	1.90%	1.70%	1.50%	2.40%	1.20%	-0.30%	0.40%	2.70%
All month	1.30%	1.30%	1.10%	1.50%	0.90%	0.40%	0.20%	1.10%

Average Monthly Standard Deviations*:from 1/90 to 12/96

	FR200	FR MID	FR2000	High Rank	Mid-Rank	Low Rank	FR200-FR2000	High Rank-Low Rank
Jan.-Mar.	2.90%	2.80%	4.10%	3.30%	2.70%	5.00%	-1.20%	-1.70%
Apr.-Sept.	3.30%	4.00%	4.60%	3.40%	3.40%	4.70%	-1.30%	-1.30%
Oct.-Dec	3.40%	4.10%	4.20%	3.20%	4.10%	5.50%	-0.80%	-2.30%
All month	3.20%	3.70%	4.40%	3.30%	3.50%	5.10%	-1.20%	-1.80%

Return/Risk Ratio: 1/90-12/96

	FR200	FR MID	FR2000	High Rank	Mid-Rank	Low Rank	FR200-FR2000	High Rank-Low Rank
Jan.-Mar.	0.52	0.75	0.56	0.39	0.74	0.58	-0.04	-0.19
Apr.-Sept.	0.27	0.15	0.07	0.32	0.06	-0.09	0.21	0.41
Oct.-Dec	0.56	0.41	0.36	0.75	0.29	-0.05	0.20	0.80
All month	0.41	0.35	0.25	0.45	0.26	0.08	-0.17	-0.61

Correlation Table: 1/90-12/96

	FR200	FR MID	FR2000	High Rank	Mid-Rank	Low Rank
Frank Russell 200	1.00					
Frank Russell MID	0.88	1.00				
Frank Russell 2000	0.72	0.92	1.00			
High Rank	0.89	0.73	0.60	1.00		
Mid-Rank	0.87	0.91	0.73	0.74	1.00	
Low Rank	0.58	0.73	0.82	0.55	0.79	1.00

*Average monthly returns and standard deviations are calculated by monthly stock return data from Datastream over the period.

Fig. 4. Size Effects and Firm Image – U.S. Results for Pre-Publication Year (A) 1989–1995 and (B) 1990–1996.

higher return of both the large-cap and the associated high-ranked portfolio in the months following the publication. In contrast, the differential performance between the Russell small/large cap index (2.3%/1.5%) and the low/high ranked portfolio (2.9%/1.3%) in the first quarter of the year also reflects the traditional 'small cap effect' (higher performance of small firms for the first quarter of the year).

Again, in contrast to the first quarter of the year, during the survey months of the pre-publication year, as shown in Fig. 4A, the large-cap index and high-ranked firms (1.1%/1.8%) outperform the small-cap index and low-ranked portfolio (0.5%/−0.01%). Thus, during the survey period, larger firms outperform smaller firms, which is the consistent result with the U.K. analysis.

Similarly, the reported superior performance of the high-rank portfolio relative to the low-rank portfolio after the publication month may be due solely to the seasonal pattern of the firm-size return differential. For the six month period (April–September) following the reputation ranking publication, as shown Figs 3B and 4B, the large-cap FTSE/Frank Russell indices (0.8%/0.9%) outperform their low-cap FTSE/Frank Russell indices (0.2%/0.3%). Similarly for the U.K. and U.S. the high-rank portfolio (1.0%/1.1%) outperforms their correspond-ing low-rank portfolio (0.1%/−0.4%) during the six months period. Thus, to the degree that the reputation ratings reflect firm-size, portfolio per-formance after the reputation ranking publication may be less a result of reputation effects than firm size effects. More appropriately, after adjusting relative-risk (standard deviation), the actual performance of the two portfolios, large-cap/small-cap or high-rank/low-rank, is not significantly different in either country.

In brief, the relationship of the portfolio returns for the high, mid, and low rated firms in the U.K. and the U.S. is consistent with previous results; that is a firm-size alone may be seen as a basis for the relative firm ratings and their equity performance in the post reporting period. Moreover, there is evidence that for both the U.S. and the U.K., the high-rank (large-cap) portfolio outperforms the low-rank (small-cap) portfolio. However, the variability in return and the lack of consistent yearly pattern make any long-term investment policy questionable.[6]

Moreover, the seasonal pattern of the return performance of small/large firms may provide further insight as to the impact of a firm's equity performance on the firm's corporate reputation. Since large firms consistently outperform medium and small firms during the second and third quarter or the survey period (July–September), to the degree that a firm's equity performance affects respondents' perception of the firm's quality, larger firms may dominate smaller firms in their reputation ratings of the following year's publication.

4.2. Corporate Reputation and Risk-Adjusted Equity Performance

In the previous section, results indicate the consistency between the corporate reputation and the equity performance especially in regard to a firm's size (market capitalization). In Figs 5 and 6, we describe the risk-adjusted returns (Cumulative Standardized Abnormal Returns) of high, medium and low ranked firms across the U.K. and U.S. for the entire sample period (pooled sample results).[7]

Results are presented relative to both the publication month and the survey period. In Fig. 5A, results show that for the U.K. high-rank portfolio the CSARs increases (3.13) while the low-rank portfolio decreases (−5.94) in the year before the publication month. In the year after publication, the CSAR of the high rank portfolio increases on average (0.30) while that of the low rank portfolio decreases (−0.57). Neither the increase in CSARs of the high rank portfolio or the decrease in CSARs of the low ranked portfolio is significant in the year after publication. The difference between the two CSARs is statistically larger in the pre-publication period than in the year following publication. This is indicative of the inability of reported scores to obtain abnormal returns on risk-adjusted basis for U.S. firms.

Similarly, for U.S. firms in Fig. 6A, results show that for the high rank portfolio the CSARs increases (3.21) in the year before the publication date while the low rank portfolio decreases (−4.59) in the year before publication. In the year after publication the CSAR of the high rank portfolio increases on average (1.62) while that of the low rank portfolio decreases (−3.45). Again, in the year after publication, neither the increase in CSARs of the high rank portfolio or the decrease in CSARs of the low ranked portfolio is significant. The difference between the two CSARs is also statistically greater in the pre-publication period than in the post-publication period. This is again indicative of the inability of reported scores to obtain excess risk-adjusted returns and the fact that the equity return performance during the pre-publication period may be a primary driver for the respondents' perceptions of the firms' reputation.

4.3. Changes in Firms' Rankings and Securities' Performance

In the previous section, the risk-adjusted performance for the each portfolio is compared. The results could be impacted by firms having no change in reputation ratings from one year (year $t - 1$) to the next year (year t). If survey respondents are less willing to change the ratings of a previously high or low ranked firm, the reputation classification may simply be affected by the current reputation ranking of the firm.

This section reports the CSARs for the four U.K. and U.S. portfolios based on changes in reputation rankings from year $t - 1$ to year t; (1) High-rank to

(A)

	High Rank	Mid Rank	Low Rank
1 year Pre-Publication	3.13	-1.86	-5.94
1year Post-Publication	0.30	0.07	-0.57

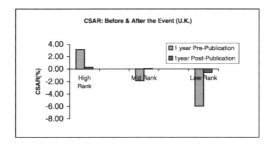

(B)

	High Rank	Mid Rank	Low Rank
Jan-June	2.35	-2.06	-3.06
July-Sept	-0.35	0.13	-1.05
Oct-Dec	0.98	-0.40	-1.65

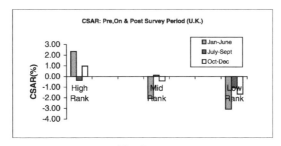

Fig. 5

(A) CSAR of Pre & Post Publication (U.K.)*. (B) Pre-Survey, Survey, Post-Survey Period (U.K.)**. *Note:* Cumulative Standardized Abnormal Return (CSAR) is calculated by:

$$\text{CSAR} = \sum \frac{R_{it} - R_{mt}}{\sigma_i}$$

For more information, refer to page 8.

*UK Most Admired Companies' rankings are published on January of each year on average.
**UK Most Admired Companies are surveyed between July and September on average.

High-rank portfolio (HH), (2) Low rank to High-rank portfolio (LH), and (3) High-rank to Low-rank portfolio (HL) and Low rank to Low rank portfolio (LL).

If a current market performance has more impact to the respondents' perception for a firm's reputation than the general market characteristics does, the CSARs of

(A)

	High Rank	Mid Rank	Low Rank
1 year Pre-Publication	3.21	-3.81	-4.59
1year Post-Publication	1.62	-3.61	-3.45

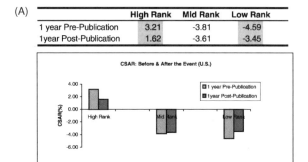

(B)

	High Rank	Mid Rank	Low Rank
July-Sept	0.79	-1.53	-1.84
Oct-Dec	1.18	-1.09	-1.80

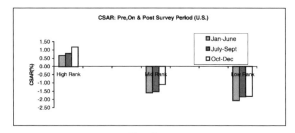

Fig. 6
(A) CSAR of Pre & Post Publication (U.S.)*. (B) Pre-Survey, Survey, Post-Survey Period
(U.S.)**. *Note:* Cumulative Standardized Abnormal Return (CSAR) is calculated by:

$$\text{CSAR} = \sum \frac{R_{it} - R_{mt}}{\sigma_i}$$

For more information, refer to page 8.
*US Most Admired Companies' rankings are published on January of each year on average.
**US Most Admired Companies are surveyed between July and September on average.

the increasing firms in their rankings (LH portfolio) should outperform those of
decreasing firms in their rankings (HL portfolio) both before and during survey
period. Similarly, relative to LL (HH) portfolios, the HL (LH) portfolios should
have a greater decrease (increase) in CSARs. In other words, if a firm's pre-
and current market performance affects the respondents' perception of a firm's
quality, then large shift in their reputation rankings should have unusual market
performance pre- and during the survey period.

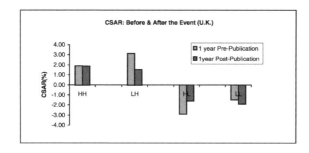

(A)	HH	LH	HL	LL
1 year Pre-Publication	1.88	3.14	-2.88	-1.46
1year Post-Publication	1.85	1.51	-1.56	-1.86

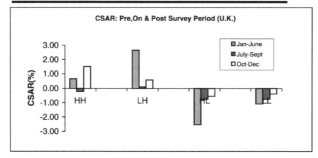

(B)				
Jan-June	0.65	2.66	-2.52	-1.07
July-Sept	-0.21	0.10	-0.76	-0.75
Oct-Dec	1.51	0.59	-0.55	-0.39

Fig. 7

(A) CSAR of Pre & Post Publication (U.K.)*. (B) Pre-Survey, Survey, Post-Survey Period
(U.K.)**. *Note:* Cumulative Standardized Abnormal Return (CSAR) is calculated by:

$$\mathrm{CSAR} = \sum \frac{R_{it} - R_{mt}}{\sigma_i}$$

*US Most Admired Companies' rankings are published on January of each year on average.
**US Most Admired Companies are surveyed between July and September on average.

Results for both the U.K. and U.S. are reported in Figs 7 and 8.[8]

Results are presented relative to both the publication date and the survey period.
In Fig. 7A, results show that for the U.K. the CSAR of decreasing firms in their
rankings (HL portfolio) falls (−2.88%) in the year before publication while that of
increasing firms in their rankings (LH portfolio) increases (3.14%). Similar results

(A)

	HH	LH	HL	LL
1 year Pre-Publication	3.50	3.30	-0.79	-1.92
1year Post-Publication	0.92	-1.62	-0.80	1.91

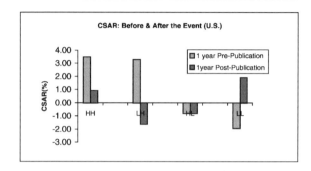

(B)

	HH	LH	HL	LL
Jan-June	2.51	0.31	-0.11	0.19
July-Sept	1.08	-0.84	-1.46	-1.06
Oct-Dec	0.76	-0.09	-0.27	-2.82

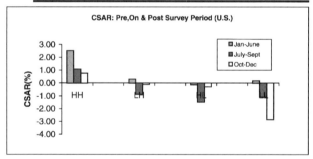

Fig. 8

(A) CSAR of Pre & Post Publication (U.S.)*. (B) Pre-Survey, Survey, Post-Survey Period (U.S.)**. *Note:* Cumulative Standardized Abnormal Return (CSAR) is calculated by:

$$\text{CSAR} = \sum \frac{R_{it} - R_{mt}}{\sigma_i}$$

*US Most Admired Companies' rankings are published on January of each year on average.
**US Most Admired Companies are surveyed between July and September on average.

are presented for the U.S. firms. The U.S. survey respondents are also affected by market performance over the survey period. In Fig. 8A, results show that for the U.S. the CSAR of the HL portfolio decreases (−0.79%) in the year before publication in comparison to the CSAR of the HH portfolio (3.30%).

5. CONCLUSION

In this paper, the impact of corporate reputation is shown to be due primarily to the manner of reputation survey collection and the approach taken to risk-return performance analysis. Therefore, unlike previous studies, the result in this study shows that a firm's equity market performance in the pre-survey and survey period primarily affects published ratings of a firm's reputation and the publishing of these ratings has little impact on a firm's future risk-adjusted returns.

Empirical results indicate that, for the time period of analysis (1990–1999), large firms tend to outperform small firms in the second and third quarters of the year and small firms tend to outperform large firms in the first quarter of the year. As a result, respondents generally witness higher equity returns for large firms relative to small firms during the survey period (July–September). Consequently, if a firm's equity performance affects respondents' perception of the firm's quality, large firms may dominate small firms in reported rankings of the following year. Moreover, given no new information over the following year, respondents may use the last year's ranking as a 'naive' basis for the next year's rating. The result of this study also indicates that a firm's equity performance in the survey period affects its reputation rating; that is, firms which perform poorly (well) in their equity performance in the survey period decline (rise) in their reputation rankings. This result is also indicative of 'non-naive' respondents who use the equity market performance as a basis for reputation ratings. Thus firm size is not a sole determinant of reputation ranking.

Lastly, little relationship between firms' risk-adjusted equity performance and their published rankings is also indicative of the lack of a market reaction to the information of reputation rankings. It is important to realize that information about individuals' view about a firm should be immediately reflected into the today's equity price. Only future unexpected changes in firms' corporate activities would affect future equity prices. Investors or corporate managers who use reputation rankings as a basis for future investment or as indicative of future risk-adjusted performance may only be capturing the expected returns underlying the fundamental risk and return patterns of the firm.

NOTES

1. Empirical result suggests both the *Fortune* and *The Economist* survey tend to give high ratings to firms with large market capitalizations (firm size).
2. For the U.S., our results differ from Antunovich and Laster in that the survey period is assumed to be in the third quarter of the year and the publication month in the first

quarter. For the U.S. over the period of analysis the actual month of publication differs from January to March. However, in all cases, the survey was conducted in the previous year. In addition, we report on the basis of changes in ranking in contrast to ex-post portfolio performance. It should also be noted that this study concentrates on the statistical significance of the risk adjusted performance. Lastly, the issue of window dressing is not directly analyzed in this study. To the degree that window dressing exits, research has concentrated on fund managers' reaction to the published information. Given that the published information is in the first quarter of the year, any window dressing impacts (buy best/sell worst) should be found in the quarter immediately following the publication of the survey.

3. For the U.S. the measured attributes are similar; that is, ability to attract, develop and keep people; innovativeness; financial soundness; community and environmental responsibility, use of corporate assets; value as a long term investment, quality of management, and quality of products.

4. To our knowledge, the *Economist* and *Fortune* magazines are the most comprehensive and widely circulated surveys of firms' qualitative attributes.

5. Correlations between firm-size and corporate reputation for the each individual year are also measured and available from authors.

6. Authors also conduct several statistical tests for the seasonal return-patterns of the large/small firms and high/low reputation firms and the results are available upon request.

7. Results for the individual years for both the U.S. and the U.K. are available from authors.

8. Results for the individual years for both the U.S. and the U.K. are also available from authors.

REFERENCES

America's Most Admired Corporations (1990–1999). *Fortune.*
Antonovich, P., & Laster, D. (1998). Do investors mistake a good company for a good investment? Federal Reserve Board, New York – Working Paper.
Bodie, Z., Kane, A., & Markus, A. (1997). *Investment* (3rd ed.). Irwin.
Clayman, M. (1987). In search of excellence: The investors viewpoint. *Financial Analyst's Journal*, *43*, 54–63.
Cornell, B., & Shapiro, A. (1987). Corporate stakeholders and corporate finance. *Financial Management*, *16*, 5–14.
McGuire, J., Naroff, J., & Schneeweis, T. (1988). Effect of cabinet appointments on shareholder wealth. *Academy of Management Journal*, 201–212.
McGuire, J., Schneeweis, T., & Branch, B. (1990). Perceptions of firm quality. *Journal of Management*, *16*, 167–180.
McGuire, J., Sundgren, A., & Schneeweis, T. (1988). Corporate social responsibility and firm financial performance. *Academy of Management Journal*, *31*, 854–872.
Nanda, S., Schneeweis, T., & Eneroth, K. (1996). Corporate performance and firm perception: The British experience. *European Financial Management*, *2*, 197–221.
Shefrin, H., & Statman, M. (1994). Behavioral capital asset pricing theory. *Journal of Financial and Quantitative Analysis*, *29*, 323–349.

Shefrin, H., & Statman, M. (1995). Making sense of beta, size, and book-to-market. *The Journal of Portfolio Management, 21,* 26–34.

Shefrin, H., & Statman, M. (1997). Behavioral portfolio theory. Santa Clara University, Working Paper.

Solt, M., & Shefrin, H. (1989). Good companies, bad stocks. *The Journal of Portfolio Management, 15,* 39–44.

U.K. Most Admired Firms (1990–1999). *The Economist.*

PARALLEL LINES – HOW SOCIAL ACCOUNTABILITY REPORTING IS DEVELOPING IN NEW ZEALAND

Will Low and Eileen Davenport

ABSTRACT

Two approaches to social accountability reporting are "competing" for acceptance in New Zealand; stand alone social audits based on the Social and Ethical Accounting, Auditing and Reporting standards (ISEA, 2001) and Triple Bottom Line Reporting (Elkington, 1997) based on standards promoted by the Global Reporting Initiative (GRI, 2000) and the World Business Council for Sustainable Development. Using information and case studies from New Zealand, this paper contrasts the limited use of social reporting in the corporate sector with its more extensive use in the not-for-profit sector. The conclusion is that social auditing and TBLR will continue to develop along parallel lines. Social auditing will continue to be favoured by "values-driven" organisations (both private and not-for-profit) and TBLR will continue to be favoured by mainstream companies.

1. INTRODUCTION

Social accountability reporting is crucial for organisations claiming to practice corporate social responsibility and corporate citizenship (Gray et al., 1996; Mathews, 1993). Reporting is essential for engaging with stakeholders, and

Social Responsibility: Corporate Governance Issues
Research in International Business and Finance, Volume 17, 293–308
ISSN: 0275-5319/PII: S0275531903170134

establishing a dialogue that leads to mutual learning and action (Greenwood, 2001; Zadek et al., 1997). It is also a governance issue: by pursuing a reporting agenda, the organisation is formalising the degree of transparency it is "comfortable" with in opening itself up to public scrutiny, and establishing certain rules of engagement.

This paper contends that two approaches to social reporting are "competing" for acceptance in New Zealand: stand alone social audits based on the Social and Ethical Accounting, Auditing and Reporting standards (ISEA, 2001) and Triple Bottom Line Reporting (Elkington, 1997).

Firstly, we outline the development of social accountability reporting, differentiating between social auditing and triple bottom line reporting. Social reporting and triple bottom lining are not mutually exclusive. However, this paper argues that social reporting as it is being practiced by a number of organisations is not simply a complement to triple bottom line reporting, but tends to be qualitatively different, being process driven and requiring active, ongoing engagement with stakeholder groups.

Secondly, we look at the extent of social auditing and TBLR within New Zealand, in the corporate, not-for-profit and public sectors. We contrast the limited use of social reporting in the New Zealand corporate sectors to its use in the not-for-profit sector. Thirdly, we examine social reporting as undertaken by two prominent New Zealand companies and identify the critical role played in both cases by the company founders in driving social reporting. Finally, we outline how social auditing and TBLR are likely to move forward in parallel in New Zealand.

2. FINANCIAL, TRIPLE BOTTOM LINE, AND SOCIAL REPORTING

Under company law, firms must report on their financial performance in order to fulfil their fiduciary responsibility to shareholders. Some form of environmental reporting is legislatively required in France, Denmark, Sweden, the Netherlands, Australia and Canada. There is no such requirement attached to the social "bottom line".

The requirement in law to audit financial accounts has evolved as a way of protecting shareholders and demonstrating the economic sustainability of the enterprise. The accounting standards framework in New Zealand is governed by the Financial Reporting Act 1993. This Act requires all reporting entities (i.e. most companies and all public issuers of securities) to prepare financial statements and group financial statements annually. The Financial Reporting Act and company law require the financial statements of companies and issuers to be externally audited, in terms of audit report requirements set out in the Act.

However, there has also been a long-standing concern that companies should go beyond the bottom line of revenue and sales, and profit and loss. Zadek and Evans (1993, p. 8) point out that as far back as the 1970s in the U.K., the Confederation of British Industry and the British Institute of Management encouraged members "to accept codes of corporate behaviour and to publish statements of their social responsibilities". However, changes in both law and practice were slow and by 1985 the U.K. Companies Act only required company directors to take into account the interests of employees in general (*ibid.* p. 9).

Such tentative steps towards acceptance of the concept of stakeholders, so prominent in the business literature today (e.g. Wheeler & Silanpää, 1997), resulted in largely external accounts of the social impact of business. Early social "audits" and reports were largely driven by local communities, trade unions and the consumer movement (op cit, p. 9). The process of social accounting was therefore often confrontational and reactive to specific events such as plant closures or environmental catastrophes.

Accountability and disclosure go hand-in-hand with stakeholder theory and have direct implications for corporate governance and practice. Wilson (2000, p. 51) cites as one of his new rules of corporate conduct: *"The corporation must be thought of, managed, and governed more as a community of stakeholders, and less as the property of investors"*.

A number of pressures and changes have resulted in a virtual explosion of social and environmental accounting and reporting. Increasing concern about the environment and the rise of environmental pressure groups, the retreat of government from many areas of social provision, and economic restructuring and globalisation resulting in economic decline in geographic locations and industrial sectors, have increased the acceptance and use of a variety of social and environmental reporting mechanisms (Wilson, 2000, p. 52).

Perhaps the most prominent development in the 1990s has been the emergence of the environment as a (silent) stakeholder. John Elkington (1997), who coined the term Triple Bottom Line, suggests; "the notion of reporting against the three components of economic, environmental and social performance is directly tied to the concept and goal of sustainable development . . . if properly implemented (it) will provide information to enable others to assess how sustainable an organisation's or community's operations are".

Yet despite the fact that the environmental bottom line has been developed more recently, in many respects it has overtaken the social bottom line in terms of prominence and technical development. At a recent Prince of Wales Business Leaders Forum event, Elkington (Sustainability, 1999) made the point that if we were to score the current state of development of different types of triple bottom line accounting on a scale of 1–10, we would find the following:

- financial accounting would probably come in at around 8 (while noting that financial accounting does not capture all the economic impacts associated with a business);
- environmental accounting might come in at around 3–4; and
- social and ethical accounting would be hard pressed to score 1–2.

This low score for the social bottom line perhaps reflects a greater interest in the economic and environmental bottom lines, which more easily lend themselves to quantification. At the same time there has been a re-emergence and subsequent development of the stand-alone social reporting processes, especially social audit. Social auditing has been defined as "a process of defining, observing and reporting measures of an organisation's ethical behaviour and social impact against its objectives, with the participation of its stakeholders, and the wider community" (Zadek & Evans, 1993, p. 7).

The head of the social audit team at KPMG in London, David Wheeler, believes that companies are turning to social auditing and reporting as the next avenue to address sustainability (quoted in Watts, 1999). Wheeler notes that:

> Last financial year, over 70% of the top 100 listed companies (in the UK) included environmental auditing and reporting in their annual reports . . . All signs are that the same thing will occur with social auditing and reporting (as) companies are coming under increasing pressure to be accountable for their social impacts.

Social auditing is at one and the same time the terminology adopted early on for describing social reporting, a convenient shorthand for the wider ideas of social and ethical accounting, auditing and reporting (SEAAR), and the most widely implemented approach to SEAAR.

Below we present two tables contrasting the international use of accountability reporting around the world. Table 1 illustrates three things: first, the wide range of SEARR activities, with social audit constituting just one approach; second, the spread of SEAAR from companies like The Body Shop and Ben and Jerry's which purport to start from "alternative" values and worldviews to mainstream organisations such as Shell International; and, third, how relatively few firms use stand-alone social reports, despite (or perhaps because of) the variety of forms these reports can take.

Table 2 contrasts the international experience of firms using different types of accountability reporting. The table is taken from a study by Low and Davenport (2002) which analysed almost three hundred companies whose reports are available from one website www.csrwire.com to understand the popularity of TBLR relative to standalone social reporting.

Reports available through csrwire.com were classified according to the title of the report. How the companies describe their own reports is likely to be indicative

Table 1. Contemporary Approaches to SEAAR.

Approach	Description	Examples
Capital Valuation	Regularly disclosed process to understand, measure, report upon and manage various forms of capital (including intellectual, social, environmental and financial capital).	Skandia
Corporate Community Involvement reporting	Describes, illustrates and measures community involvement policies and activities through occasional reports.	Grand Met British Petroleum
Ethical Accounting	Regularly disclosed process, based upon shared values which stakeholders develop through ongoing dialogue, aimed at designing future plans.	Sbn Bank Scandinavian Public Sector
Ethical Auditing	Regular, externally verified process to understand, measure, report on and improve an organisation's social ethical and environmental performance through stakeholder dialogue.	The Body Shop International
Social Auditing	Regular, externally verified process to understand, measure, report on and improve an organisation's social performance through stakeholder dialogue.	VanCity Credit Union Black Country Housing Association Coop Italia UNIPOL
Social Balance	A regular reconstruction and aggregation of financial data across stakeholder groups which specifies stakeholder costs associated with "social activities".	
Statement of Principles and Values	Develops and describes an organisation's principles in meeting social, financial and environmental responsibilities.	Shell International
"Sustainability" Reporting	An evolving reporting process which identifies and reports on options and actions for progress towards sustainability principles.	Interface

Adapted from Gonella, Pilling and Zadek (1998), Making Values Count: Contemporary Experience in SEAAR, Executive Summary, p. 5.

of the relative importance they place on the different forms of accountability. The evidence from the table indicates that over 40% of these companies place prominence on the environment, issuing a stand-alone Environmental Report. Adding in the sustainability and HSE reports, 78% of the sample predominantly report on environmental impacts. Only 9% produce stand-alone social reports.

Triple Bottom Line Reports fall between the environmental and social reporting camps but these reports form only a small proportion of the total. By definition, Triple Bottom Line Reports will include some social accounting, along with the environmental. The same is true for Health, Safety and Environment reports. And, as suggested already, it is hard to imagine a sustainability report that does not refer

Table 2.   International Experience of Accountability Reporting.

Type of Report (assignment by title of the report)	Number of Companies	Percentage
Environmental	124	43.5
Health, Safety and Environment	52	18.2
Sustainability	46	16.1
Social	26	9.1
Triple Bottom Line	21	7.4
Other: Annual, CSR, etc.	16	5.6
	285	99.9

to the social dimensions of sustainability, of the firm itself (e.g. its employees) or in general (i.e. the environmental impact of operations on people and communities). What is less clear from a report's title itself is how much, if any, attention is paid in a stand-alone Environmental Report to broad social impacts of the company.

Finally, a small number of the listed reports are Annual Reports with environmental and social information or carry other titles such as Corporate Responsibility Report.

3. AN OVERVIEW SOCIAL AND TRIPLE BOTTOM LINE REPORTING IN NEW ZEALAND

Interest in social reporting in New Zealand goes back at least as far as the late 1970s (Robertson, 1977). However, just as elsewhere, interest waned through the 1980s and early/mid – 1990s. Social reporting in New Zealand was only "rediscovered" in the late 1990s – somewhat later than the U.K. and Europe (see Davenport & Low, 2000; Goldberg, 2001).

Triple Bottom Line Reporting was established in 1999 through the creation of the New Zealand Business Council for Sustainable Development (NZBCSD). NZBCSD member companies are committed to a Sustainable Development Reporting initiative implementing triple bottom line accountability principles such as the Global Reporting Initiative. The popularity of stand-alone environmental reports (illustrated internationally in Table 2) does not extend to New Zealand: in a KPMG survey of environmental reporting, New Zealand ranked 13th and last (Milne et al., 2001).

Below (see Table 3) we summarise the New Zealand experience of producing stand-alone social audits and Triple Bottom Line/Sustainability reports. As such, we have not examined company reports which may include social and environmental impact statements, or stand-alone environmental reports.

4. WHO DOES WHAT, AND WHY?

Some commentators have suggested organisations with a high degree of specialisation, little centralisation, and few status differences are the most open to change and new ideas, and consequently most willing to adopt a SEAAR process (Blake et al., 1976; Bouckaert & Vandenhove, 1998; Wokutch & Fahey, 1986). However, Tables 1–3 show the huge diversity of organisations undertaking various forms of social accountability reporting.

Table 3 shows that nine of the ten social audits were produced by not-for-profit organizations. The only private sector company undertaking a social audit process is The Warehouse Limited. Nine organisations have completed either Triple Bottom Line or Sustainability Reports: two public sector organizations and seven companies. Once all the 37 existing NZBCSD members, six more "public" sector entities will have reported on their triple bottom lines. New Zealand local and central government is committed to developing triple bottom line reports sometime in the future. Below we consider in more detail the experiences of the not-for-profit and for-profit sectors in New Zealand.

4.1. The Not-for-Profit Sector

COMMACT Aotearoa[1] helped to introduce social auditing to New Zealand by inviting John Pearce of Community Enterprise Consultancy and Research to speak to a group of community organisations in 1997. Following this meeting, a pilot project was developed involving twelve not-for-profit organisations from across the country.

The fact that the community sector took the lead in social auditing is perhaps not surprising. There is a strong emphasis on openness and accountability to stakeholders in not-for-profit organisations (Pearce et al., 1996). With its emphasis on assessing organisational performance against indicators derived (with involvement of stakeholders) from the values of an organisation, SEAAR is an ideal way of examining performance in values driven organisations.

Not-for-profit organisations have the added pressure of being evaluated on a regular basis as a condition for their legitimacy or accreditation, and as a specific requirement for continued funding from outside sources such as government and foundations (Drucker, 1989). Raynard (1998, p. 1472) refers to Fowler who suggests that not-for-profits have traditionally focussed on project-based

Table 3. Social Accountability Reporting in New Zealand.[a]

Social Audit		TBLR/Sustainability Report	
Raeburn House (North Shore) (1999)	Not-for-profit, dealing with housing issues	Sanford Limited (1999/2000)	Private sector, fishery company
Auckland Unemployed Workers Rights Centre (1999)	Not-for-profit, assisting unemployed people	Hubbard Foods (2001)	Private sector, breakfast cereal producer
Far North Regional Economic AP (1999)	Not-for-profit, working for community development	The Warehouse Limited (2001)	Private sector, general merchandise retailer
Auckland Youth Law Project (1999)	Not-for-profit, working for youth on legal issues	Interface Agencies Ltd. (2001)	Private sector, floor coverings
Auckland Peoples Centre (1999)	Not-for-profit, working for community development	Landcare Research Inc. (1999)	Crown Research Institute
Parent to Parent (national) (1999)	Not-for-profit, working with families	Meridian Energy (2000)	Crown Owned Enterprise, electricity generator
Just Dollars Trust (1999)	Not-for-profit, local economic development	Urgent Couriers (2001)	Private sector, courier company
Trade Aid Importers (2000)	Not-for-profit, fair trade organisation	URS New Zealand (2001)	Private sector, engineering and environmental management
Water for Survival (2000)	Non governmental development organisation	Waimangu Volcanic Valley Limited (2001)	Private sector, eco-tourism provider
The Warehouse Limited (unpublished)	Private sector, general merchandise retailer		

[a] Comalco NZ is a subsidiary of Rio Tinto Zinc, which has released a TBLR for the overall Comalco group, and so Comalco NZ is not listed separately.

evaluations in contrast to organisation-based assessment processes. Project based evaluation is most often externally driven and therefore out of the control of the organisation itself. Raynard (*ibid.*) also suggests that as a result, not-for-profits have been keen to find more holistic approaches they could adopt for themselves to understand the performance of their organisation.

The willingness to adopt SEAAR within the not-for-profit sector may also reflect a greater familiarity with stakeholder engagement and democratic process. Whereas firms are more likely to be outcome oriented and work efficiently towards fulfilling these goals, the not-for-profit sector is more process oriented and so SEAAR fits its values and ethos very well.

In the New Zealand social audit pilot project six of the twelve pilot organisations completed full reports and released them to their stakeholders. Five of the organisations completed various stages of the process. In one interesting case, the Auckland Unemployed Workers Rights Centre decided to go into recess as a result of undertaking a social audit process. The organisation decided that it needed to reassess and redefine its mission in light of the changes in the social and political environment since it was established over ten years ago.

The evaluation report on the pilot recommends the continuation and expansion of the social audit model in the community sector using a refinement of the social auditing process introduced by Pearce and developed through the pilot project (Knowland-Foreman & Jukes, 2001). This develops social auditing as a capacity building process that seeks to build organisations through the positive engagement of their stakeholders. Since the pilot project a number of other not-for-profit organisations have engaged in a social audit process and a training course in social auditing for the not-for-profit sector organised through UNITEC polytechnic in Auckland is growing.

4.2. The Corporate Sector

No systematic trial of social auditing has been done in the New Zealand for-profit sector to match that described above in the not-for-profit sector. According to New Zealand Businesses for Social Responsibility (1998, p. 3), as late as 1998, "no publicly listed companies presently publish complete social accounts. If any privately held companies are producing Social Accounts, none has yet made that fact public".

Since 1998 a number of companies have produced triple bottom line reports including Sanfords Ltd. in 1999 and Meridian Energy in 2000. The establishment of the New Zealand Business Council for Sustainable Development has been instrumental in pushing forward a sustainability reporting agenda.

Two companies central to New Zealand's CSR activities are highlighted as case studies below. Hubbard Foods, a privately owned company not part of the NZBCSD initiative, issued its TBLR in mid-2001. The Warehouse Group Limited (TWL), a key member of NZBCSD released its triple bottom line report in early 2002. TWL is also the only New Zealand company known to be developing an as yet unpublished stand-alone social audit, which it calls a Values Report.

4.3. Hubbard Foods Ltd.

Hubbard Foods (established under the name Winner Foods in 1988) is an interesting case study, being a private company without publicly traded shares. As a private company Hubbard Foods is not even required to release financial data under the Financial Reporting Act. The decision to issue a triple bottom line report is a reflection of the company's stated commitment to a stakeholder approach to its business activities.

Economic performance occupies only two of the Report's twenty four pages. The company reveals sales of over NZ$24 million in the financial year 2000–2001 and a market share for breakfast cereals of 18.5%. In that year, the company also established a staff profit share scheme paying out NZ$94,000 to its one hundred and sixteen staff allocated according to length of service.

Social performance is allotted nine pages in the Report. Some of the information was collected through a separate exercise, a Stakeholder Perceptions survey. Some employees were also interviewed about what they valued most in their jobs. Other stakeholders discussed in the report include: the Service and Food Workers Union; an "extended family" of four companies for whom Hubbard Foods represent at least 40% of their annual turnover; consumers of the product; trade customers; and, the local community.

Environmental performance is reported in two pages. Some of the information comes from an external consultant's environmental report on the company. Issues of waste and energy use are addressed, with measures provided but no trends available. Finally, the report identifies a range of "dilemmas" faced by Hubbard Foods, such as whether or not to use genetically modified organisms in production. A critique of the Hubbard's Triple Bottom Line Report appears in Higgins (2001).

4.4. The Warehouse Group Limited

The Warehouse Group Limited (TWL) is New Zealand's biggest general (non-food) merchandise retailer, with interests in Australia through one hundred and seventeen Clint's Crazy Bargains and Silly Solly's stores. The retailer was established twenty years ago in 1982. In 2001, sales from TWL's trans-tasman operations were NZ$1,665m from two hundred and twenty five stores. Employees numbered 11,503.

Its Triple Bottom Line Report 2001 runs twenty-five pages in total, including a feedback form for stakeholders to comment on the report. Rather than divide the report along the triple bottom lines, TWL report has opted to make the stakeholder central to the reporting process. This approach does make it difficult to classify how much of the report is dedicated to each of the bottom lines, but instead is intended to give "... a clearer account of the impact on these groups to the reader".

Coverage of team members (staff) is allotted two pages in the report. Included in these pages are the findings from a six-monthly "People First" survey to questions such as "I am proud to work for The Warehouse". The result shows a fairly stable proportion (between 88 and 90%) of respondents are proud to work for TWL over the last five surveys. No commentary is reported about why team members do or do not respond positively to this question. Staff attrition is specifically identified under the heading of challenges. However, TWL does not compared itself to similar retail companies to clarify how significant its attrition really is, nor is any change suggested to deal with this.

Financial performance is allotted three specific pages in the report, giving both standard information on earnings and profits. Profiles of TWL and of customers also contain financial performance information but appear elsewhere in the report.

Reporting on customers makes up two pages, including: a count of customers; the average basket size per customer; product recalls; and, customer complaints. The customer section also included results of a survey asking "the community" about views of sustainability, and implementation of zero waste policies by providing recycling facilities to customers.

Community issues are reported in two pages. TWL has acquired a high profile as a "good" corporate citizen, for example providing space and resources for community group to run BBQ's outside its stores which raised NZ$900,000 in 2001. Evidence from a parallel social auditing process of TWL's impacts on small communities is also reported in some detail.[2]

Discussion of supplier issues is used to highlight efforts to promote ethical and sustainable sourcing, such as sourcing timber products approved by the Forest Stewardship Council. Another issue raised is sourcing from New Zealand producers. TWL has been heavily criticised in some circles for predominantly importing "cheap" goods from China (Rogers, 2001).

Waste and energy use issues are discussed over two pages. TWL has been prominent in developing "zero waste to landfill" practice by reducing packaging and wrapping when goods are delivered to its shops. In 2001, forty-eight of its seventy-five stores were identified as "in the programme" (The Warehouse, 2001, p. 19), without being clear about how many actually achieved the zero waste objective.

Finally, the report makes explicit reference to the Global Reporting Initiative Standard indicators (GRI, 2000). The report does not however identify which of the many possible indicators were selected or why. In the absence of this analysis, it is difficult for stakeholders to assess how well TWL's Triple Bottom Line Report conforms to the standards on which it is based. As a first report, there is limited opportunity for TWL to compare its own performance over time. Nonetheless, relatively few specific targets are set to monitor improvement in its "challenges".

5. WHERE TO NOW FOR NEW ZEALAND ACCOUNTABILITY REPORTING?

The leading role in SEAAR taken by the not-for-profit sector is not unique to New Zealand. A huge range of SEAAR processes are now found, for example, throughout the community sector in the U.K. and Europe. However, despite the inherent affinity that values driven organisations have with SEAAR processes, the sector in New Zealand and overseas faces severe resource constraints in conducting social reporting. The pilot project in New Zealand was partially funded by the Department of Internal Affairs and the Lottery Grants Board. Similarly Trade Aid, a "fair trade" company like Traidcraft who pioneered social auditing in the U.K., made use of a special funding facility for monitoring and evaluation from the Ministry for Foreign Affairs and Trade to conduct its social audit.

In New Zealand, even the private companies conducting TBLR have been assisted by government through the Ministry for the Environment (MfE). The Ministry supports the NZBCSD and pays for thirty hours of consultant time to assist each participating company in the TBLR pilot. This support is crucial when one considers that estimates of the cost of a social reporting cycle range from Can$100,000 for VanCity Savings Credit Union to $US750,000 for the Body Shop International (GRI, 2000).

At its launch, the Hubbard Foods Triple Bottom Line Report was estimated to have cost up to NZ$10,000, though it was unclear if this included the cost of the consultant's time paid by MfE, the Stakeholder Perception study conducted in the previous year, and the environmental report. Nor was management time included, as Dick Hubbard considered this "an investment and not a cost".[3]

While the remaining members of the NZBCSD are committed to TBLR in the future, the extent of social reporting in New Zealand is likely to be limited unless it continues to be supported by the government.

The public sector may increase its own use of social reporting and TBLR. The current government has reiterated its commitment to sustainability and specifically to triple bottom line reporting.[4] To date only Landcare Research Inc. and Meridian Energy have completed sustainability reports; the former plans a triple bottom line report in 2002. Landcare's sustainability report is notable for its overall focus on the economic and environmental bottom lines. Landcare's involvement in providing consultancy services for TBLR and the prominence of the Ministry for the Environment as a driver of sustainability reporting means New Zealand is likely to score higher for reporting on the environmental than the social bottom line, as suggested earlier by Elkington. Progress on social reporting may require a balancing role being played by a social agency, just as the government is developing the policy role of the new Ministry of Social Development as a counterweight to the policy advice offered by the Treasury.

The emphasis placed by Hubbard Foods Ltd. and The Warehouse Group Ltd. on social reporting is also likely to remain relatively unique, even when the remaining members of the NZBCSD complete their reports. The role played by both Dick Hubbard and Stephen Tindall can not be underestimated. Dick Hubbard was a founder of the New Zealand Businesses for Social Responsibility. Stephen Tindall is the current Chairman of the NZBCSD and heads his own philanthropic trust, the Tindall Foundation, while occupying the Office of the Founder in TWL. Both have been prominent is promoting CSR in the face of continuing opposition by the New Zealand Business Roundtable which subscribes to the view that CSR and sustainability reporting are recipes for inefficiency and reduced shareholder value (NZ Herald, 2001).

Finally, social accountability has not realised its potential amongst indigenous organisations and businesses in New Zealand. None has completed social reports to date and none are members of NZBCSD. The stakeholder approach to engagement and disclosure would appear to fit well with Maori protocols such as *hui*: communal meetings where important issues facing the extended family, clan and "tribe" are discussed. The Maori perspective on values and ethics in business and the relationship of people to the environment would have much to offer the development of CSR ideas. A model of social reporting developed from this perspective would be particularly interesting.

6. CONCLUSIONS

This paper has examined how and why SEAAR and triple bottom line reporting have followed largely parallel lines of development in New Zealand. The New Zealand experience in social accountability reporting is not dissimilar to experience elsewhere in the world. SEAAR has been adopted and developed primarily in the community/not-for-profit sector which has a "natural" affinity to process driven stakeholder approaches to impact assessment. TBLR has become the "standard" for the private sector which favours more quantifiable and close-ended reporting procedures (TWL being the notable exception in New Zealand).

This split is not surprising for another reason. Social auditing is being promoted through one organization, Social Audit New Zealand, which originates from within the community sector. TBLR is being promoted by NZBCSD, an organisation rooted in the business community. As a result, these two approaches to stakeholder engagement and accountability are unlikely to become more closely aligned, as commentators like John Elkington would endorse. Vested interests and the dearth of opportunity for cross-fertilisation between the two sectors work against closer ties.

The mediating factor may be the role New Zealand government has played indirectly, encouraging social reporting by organisations of all types, and directly, financially supporting the development of both social auditing and TBLR. At the same time, the public sector is explicitly embracing the triple bottom line approach in its own reporting.

The conclusion of this study is therefore that social auditing will continue to be favoured by "values-driven" organisations (predominantly not-for-profit but with a few private companies) and TBLR will continue to be favoured by mainstream companies.

NOTES

1. COMMACT Aotearoa is the New Zealand chapter of the Commonwealth Association for Local Action and Economic Development. COMMACT is recognised by the Commonwealth Foundation as the professional body of practitioners of community-based local economic development.

2. Social Audit New Zealand, a "company" established by COMMACT Aotearoa to develop social auditing in New Zealand, was engaged to undertake independent research and analysis of this issue.

3. Comment made at the launch of the Hubbard Foods Ltd. Triple Bottom Line Report, August 28, 2001.

4. Speech by Prime Minister Helen Clark to the Redesigning Resources Conference, 25–27 June 2000, accessed through http://www.redesigningresources.org/2000_conference/clark.cfm

REFERENCES

Blake, D., Frederick, W., & Myers, M. (1976). *Social auditing, evaluating the impact of corporate programmes*. New York: Praeger Publishers.

Bouckaert, L., & Vandenhove, J. (1998). Business ethics and the management of non-profit institutions. *Journal of Business Ethics, 17*(9/10), 1073–1081.

Davenport, E., & Low, W. (2000). *Filling in the gaps: Options for developing social and ethical reporting in a triple bottom line framework*. Wellington: Ministry for the Environment.

Drucker, P. (1989). What business can learn from nonprofits. *Harvard Business Review, 67*(4), 88–93.

Elkington, J. (1997). *Cannibals with forks: The Triple Bottom Line of 21st century business*. London: Capstone Publishing.

Goldberg, E. (2001). *Profit, people, planet: Policy issues and options around Triple Bottom Line Reporting*. Wellington: Ministry for the Environment.

Gonella, C., Pilling, A., & Zadek, S. (1998). *Making values count: Contemporary experience in SEAAR* (*executive summary*). London: ACCA.

Gray, R. H., Owen, D. L., & Adams, C. (1996). *Accounting and accountability: Social and environmental accounting in a changing world*. Hemel Hempstead: Prentice Hall.

Greenwood, M. R. (2001). Community as a stakeholder: Focusing on corporate social and environmental reporting. *Journal of Corporate Citizenship, 4*, 31–45.

GRI (2000). www.globalreporting.org/GRIGuidelines/June2000GuidleinesA4.pdf

Higgins, C. (2001). Triple Bottom Line Reporting: The importance of consistency. In: D. Birch & J. Batten (Eds), *Governance and Corporate Social Responsibility in the New Millennium*. Melbourne: Deakin University.

Hubbard Foods Ltd. (2001). *Triple Bottom Line Report*. http://www.hubbards.co.nz/triple_bottom_line/triple_bottom_line.htm

Institute for Social and Ethical Accountability (2001). *Accountability Quarterly*, 1st quarter, London: ISEA.

Knowland-Foreman, G., & Jukes, Q. (2001). COMMACT Aotearoa Social Audit Pilot Project 1998–1999, final report, April, Wellington: COMMACT.

Low, W., & Davenport, E. (2002). Social report's next challenge – overcoming the middle child syndrome, mimeo.

Mathews, M. R. (1993). *Socially responsible accounting*. London: Chapman Hall.

Milne, M., Owen, D., & Tilt, C. (2001). Corporate environmental reporting: Are New Zealand companies being left behind? *University of Auckland Business Review, 3*(2), 24–36.

New Zealand Business for Social Responsibility (1998). *Tomorrow. A quarterly newsletter from New Zealand Business for Social Responsibility* (Issue 1).

New Zealand Herald (2001). Corporate social responsibility a case of misguided virtue, June 28, A18.

Pearce, J., Raynard, P., & Zadek, S. (1996). *Social auditing for small organizations: A workbook for trainers and practitioners*. London: New Economics Foundation.

Raynard, P. (1998). Coming together: A review of contemporary approaches to social accounting, auditing and reporting in non-profit organisations. *Journal of Business Ethics, 17*(13), 1471–1479.

Robertson, J. (1977). Corporate social reporting by New Zealand companies, occasional paper No. 17, Department of Business Studies, Massey University, Palmerston North.

Rogers, W. (2001). The rise and rise and stall of big red. *North & South*, November, 36–47.

Sustainability (1999). The Triple Bottom Line in action: Executive summary. http://134.146.2.37/shellreport98/report_Shell_TBL_Working_Paper_execsumm.htm

The Warehouse (2001). *Triple Bottom Line Report 2001*. http://www.eaglenet.co.nz/superstore/twh/report%20pdfs/triplebottom.pdf

Watts, T. (1999). Social auditing – the KPMG U.K. experience, *Australian CPA*, September.

Wheeler, D., & Silanpää, M. (1997). *The stakeholder corporation*. London: Pitman.

Wilson, I. (2000). *The new rules of corporate conduct: Rewriting the social charter*. Westport: Quorum Books.

Wokutch, R., & Fahey, L. (1986). A value explicit approach for evaluating corporate social performance. *Journal of Accounting and Public Policy*, *5*(3), 191–214.

Zadek, S., & Evans, R. (1993). *Auditing the market*. London: Traidcraft and New Economics Foundation.

Zadek, S., Pruzan, P., & Evans, R. (1997). *Building corporate accountability: Emerging practices in social and ethical accounting, auditing and reporting*. London: Earthscan.

PART III:
GOVERNANCE ACTION PROPOSALS

FOSTERING INFORMED AND RESPONSIBLE MANAGEMENT: THE FAILURE OF THE CORRUPTION TREATIES' PROVISIONS ON ACCOUNTING AND CONTROL

Peter W. Schroth

ABSTRACT

A key aspect of corporate governance in the United States, informed management through management accounting and internal controls, is described explicitly in the Inter-American Convention Against Corruption, but not required to be implemented, and left implicit in the OECD's Convention on Combating Bribery of Foreign Public Officials in International Business Transactions, despite the latter's enumeration of mandatory accounting provisions. Most of the 53 countries that are parties to one or both of these treaties have claimed compliance with these provisions while doing nothing, but the on-going dialogue initiated by the OAS and the OECD can be used to make the treaties more effective in this respect. This is an opportunity that should not be ignored, especially because five countries have signed but not yet ratified one of these treaties, while some 30 more have expressed interest in acceding to the OECD Convention.

Social Responsibility: Corporate Governance Issues
Research in International Business and Finance, Volume 17, 311–335
Copyright © 2003 by Elsevier Science Ltd.
All rights of reproduction in any form reserved
ISSN: 0275-5319/PII: S0275531903170146

As context for its thesis, the paper describes the context of international anti-bribery and anti-deductibility efforts and the "business judgment rule" that protects directors from liability for mere negligence in most countries and the "new corporate law" or federalization of this area of the law in the United States, in part through the Foreign Corrupt Practices Act of 1977. It proceeds to the accounting and internal controls provisions of the two treaties and analysis of the national reports on this aspect of their implementation. The last section discusses the lessons to be drawn from this experience, noting in particular that it should provide valuable guidance to the drafters of corporate governance provisions in the planned United Nations convention against corruption.

1. INTRODUCTION

This paper makes a claim about too narrow interpretation – or, arguably, too narrow drafting – of two treaty provisions and advocates increased attention to the aspect of corporate governance of which those treaty provisions ought to be read as a key example. The treaty provisions are:

(1) Article 8 of the OECD *Convention on Combating Bribery of Foreign Public Officials in International Business Transactions* (the "OECD Convention", reprinted in Exhibit 1), which has been drained of its substance by a reading that ignores the rest of the treaty, a reading by which almost all the State Parties claim that they have always been in compliance and need do nothing more at all, and
(2) Article III (10) of the Inter-American Convention Against Corruption (the "OAS Convention", also reprinted in Exhibit 1), which states its corporate governance objective in clear terms, but requires only that States consider possible steps and not that they take them.

The aspect of corporate governance is the responsibility of the board and the management to manage, which depends on their knowledge of the most important information – not all information, of course, but the most important information – about the conduct of the business.

Read fairly in the context of the whole treaty and the historical developments that led to it, Article 8 of the OECD Convention requires that management have that information about payments to foreign government officials, but almost all of the national reports to the OECD read it merely as forbidding false financial statements. The corresponding provision in the United States (subsection 13 (b)(2) of the Securities Exchange Act, also reprinted below in Exhibit 1, p. 329), which is twenty years older and on which Article 8 was based, was the first major step by the United States toward requiring managers to know the most important information about the conduct of their businesses and has often been described as heralding a "new era" or a "sea change" in corporate governance (Schroth, 2002b and sources cited therein; also p. 320). Steps in the same direction would be beneficial in many countries. There are other ways the same results could be achieved, but the opportunity presented by the OECD Convention, already ratified by 34 States and signed by one more (see Exhibit 5), and the OAS Convention, already ratified by 24 States and signed by five more (see Exhibit 6) should not be wasted. It is relevant also that some 30 additional States have expressed interest in acceding to the OECD Convention.

This paper begins with a very brief review of the history of transnational law against bribery (covered in much more detail in Schroth, 2002b) and of the movement against tax deduction of foreign bribes (covered in more detail in Schroth, 2002a). The discussion of accounting and controls begins with the easy standard called the "business judgment rule" in common law jurisdictions, which protects directors from liability for mere negligence in most countries. It continues with a review of the history of subsection 13 (b)(2) in the United States and consideration of the two major Conventions that speak to the same issue. The paper concludes with a discussion of the lessons for comparative study and drafting of international treaties in the area of corporate governance, such as the planned United Nations convention against corruption.

2. THE BACKGROUND IN THE UNITED STATES

There are three threads to the web of transnational laws against corruption: anti-bribery laws, elimination of the tax deductibility of foreign bribes and improvement of corporate governance through accounting and controls requirements. All three originated in the United States. The first and third of these have their roots in the same ground, the first – and for many years the only – transnational law against corruption, namely the unilateral act of the United States called the Foreign Corrupt Practices Act of 1977. The scandals that led to enactment of the FCPA were brought to light by the special prosecutors and the Senate committee charged with investigation of the Watergate affair, in which burglars hired by President Nixon's re-election campaign were convicted of entering and planting listening devices in the headquarters of the opposition party. By 1974, these investigations had turned up evidence not only of another burglary and assorted "dirty tricks" by the Nixon campaign, but also of numerous instances of illegal campaign contributions, of laundering of such money through foreign countries and of the use of campaign funds to bribe foreign officials. As a result of these disclosures, the Securities and Exchange Commission began its own investigation of illegal foreign payments by U.S. corporations. The reports of all these investigators and Congress's General Accounting Office led to President Nixon's resignation, on 8th August 1974, but the corruption hearings continued.

Over the next three years, these hearings and investigations led to *admissions* to the SEC of foreign bribery totalling over $300 million by over 400 American corporations, of which 177 ranked in the Fortune 500. The SEC brought criminal charges in some cases, including a few against corporations that had not responded to its request for voluntary disclosures. It is important to notice here that the FCPA didn't yet exist. The SEC had already been requiring increasingly accurate account-ing and public disclosure by the companies it regulated, relying on the Securities Exchange Act of 1934, and these mid-1970s anti-bribery enforcement actions were based on the 1934 Act. Some of the better known defendants were Ashland Oil Company, Gulf Oil Corporation, Northrup Corporation, Philips Petroleum and United Brands.

3. THE FOREIGN CORRUPT PRACTICES ACT OF 1977

Despite the efforts of United States diplomats in the 1970s to persuade other countries to join in multilateral measures against international corruption, the various international organizations produced, at best, strongly worded policy statements, with no provisions for enforcement or even monitoring. The opposition of America's Western European allies in the Tokyo Round of GATT negotiations and in the Economic and Social Council were expressed by what one commentator called "deafening silence" (Rubin, 1982, p. 320).

Rather than waiting decades for a multinational response, Congress enacted the FCPA, which was signed into law by President Carter in December 1977. The FCPA attacks foreign bribery by persons subject to United States jurisdiction in two ways: first by requiring recording-keeping, internal accounting controls and disclosure, and second by outlawing certain categories of payments. It has been amended twice, in 1988 & 1998, the latter to conform to the OECD Convention following U.S. ratification.

Beginning in 1993, the Clinton administration made international action against corruption a priority of the executive branch, seeking to persuade the governments of European countries and Japan to support the proposals of U.S.

diplomats in several international organizations and institutions. These initiatives were supported by the newly organized Transparency International – a worldwide NGO devoted to fighting corruption – and, in the wake of new corruption scandals in Europe, by the press and public opinion.

In 1994, anti-bribery recommendations began to appear from the OECD. In 1995, the European Union adopted a rather limited Convention on the Protection of the European Communities' Financial Interests, which, however, has not yet been ratified by enough countries to come into force. In 1996, the Organization of American States adopted the broad Inter-American Convention Against Corruption, covering both accounting and disclosure and anti-bribery measures, which entered into force in 1997. At the end of that year, the OECD members and five other countries signed the similarly broad Convention on Combating Bribery of Foreign Public Officials in International Business Transactions, which entered into force in 1999. The Council of Europe adopted its Criminal Law Convention on Corruption, not yet in force, in 1999.

4. TAX DEDUCTIBILITY OF FOREIGN BRIBES

The other thread of transnational laws against corruption is the movement against tax deductibility of foreign bribes. It was never clear that foreign bribes could be deducted as ordinary and necessary business expenses in the United States, but Congress eliminated the possibility by adding a provision to the Internal Revenue Code explicitly denying such deductions in Public Law 85–866, passed on 2nd September 1958.

In many other countries, however, at least in principle, foreign bribes were as deductible as any other business expense, although deduction of domestic bribes was always forbidden. (Sources for this and the subsequent paragraphs of this section are mainly ITA, 2001; Milliet-Einbinder, 2000; OECD, 2001 and my own research and experience.) Some of the countries in this category are Austria, Australia, Belgium, Denmark, France, Germany, Iceland, Luxembourg, New Zealand, Norway, Portugal and Switzerland. As I have explained elsewhere (Schroth, 2002a), the deduction was everyday practice for companies in some of these countries but rare in others. Several countries' tax laws – including those of Denmark, Iceland, Norway and Sweden – said that foreign bribes could not be deducted *unless* payment of such bribes was customary in the recipient's country, but it is clear that it was generally accepted that there were many countries in which bribery was customary and necessary in order to do business.

Here are the years in which some of the countries that had allowed tax deduction
of foreign bribes, at least if they were customary where paid, changed their laws
to forbid it:

Australia 2000	Denmark 1998	Norway 1996
Austria 1998	France 2000	Portugal 1998
Belgium 1999	Iceland 1998	Sweden 1999
Canada 1999	Luxembourg 2000	Switzerland 2001
Czech Republic 2000		

In some countries, especially outside the EU, only the tax deductions expressly
enumerated in the tax code are permitted, and foreign bribes are not on the lists
of permissible deductions.[1] Closely related to this, or perhaps the same thing
in some cases, is categorizing all foreign bribes as "entertainment expenses" or
a comparable category other than business expenses, then disallowing deduction of that category regardless of the purpose.[2] My interpretation is that this
is a result of the different structures of tax codes, not of different attitudes toward bribery. Some tax codes, such as that of the United States, tax net income of business, so that all ordinary and necessary business expenses – even
of criminal business – are deductible unless there's a rule limiting or prohibiting the deduction.[3] Others allow only the deductions that are enumerated in the
tax code. Apparently putting a deduction for "foreign bribes" in the tax code
in so many words is too much for legislators to stomach, because I haven't
found even one example of a tax law structured the second way that allows the
deduction.

In the United Kingdom, a payment cannot be deducted if it was a violation of
British law, which ought to mean the deduction of foreign bribes ends when Britain
outlaws foreign bribery. The United Kingdom ratified the OECD Convention in
1998 without adopting, or even proposing, any implementing legislation, asserting,
in the words of Brian Wilson, Minister for Trade, that "... the U.K.'s existing
anti-corruption legislation is sufficient to meet the obligations arising from the
Convention . . .." This was nonsense, as I and others pointed out (Lowry & Schroth,
1999). The correction came at the end of 2001, in §§ 108–110 of the Anti-terrorism,
Crime and Security Act, 2001, Chap. 24, when Parliament at long last amended
the old British statutes[4] to bring them into compliance with the OECD Convention
(for details, see Schroth, 2002b). The result is that foreign bribery by a British
company or subject apparently remained tax deductible in principle until then if
committed entirely outside U.K. territory, because the U.K. criminal law, so far, did
not reach bribery committed entirely outside U.K. territory. Just lately, however,

Britain too may be counted among the countries that have eliminated the deduction by legislation.

5. THE BUSINESS JUDGMENT RULE: FRAUD, GROSS NEGLIGENCE, ETC.

One more matter must be explained to set the stage for the main argument: in most countries, the standard of care applicable to directors and corporate officers (which in many systems are not separate categories) is much lower than ordinary negligence.[5] In 1872, the House of Lords held that directors could be liable only if "they were cognisant of circumstances of such a character, so plain, so manifest, and so simple of appreciation, that no men with any degree of prudence, acting on their own behalf, would have entered into such a transaction as they entered into" (*Overend & Gurney Co. v. Gibb* (1872) LR 5 HL 480, 487–488). In another leading English case, it was said that "Their negligence must not be the omission to take all possible care; it must be much more blameable than that; it must be in a business sense culpable or gross". (*Lagunas Nitrate Co. v. Lagunas Syndicate* (1899) 2 Chap. 392, 435.)

> In view of the low standard of care which the court has traditionally exacted from directors, namely, the care which they would be expected to show if acting on their own behalf, it is not surprising that in most of the decided cases the defendant directors have been acquitted of negligence (Pennington, 1995, p. 802).

In Delaware, America's most important state for corporations law, a modern decision of the highest court held that "the concept of gross negligence is . . . the proper standard for determining whether a business judgment reached by a board of directors was an informed one" (*Smith v. Van Gorkom*, 488 A.2d 858, 873 (Del, 1985)). In Germany, the statutory duty of directors and managers is "the care of a proper businessman" ("die Sorgfalt eines ordentlichen Geschäftsmannes", Art. 93 I 1 AktG, Art. 43 I GmbHG), but the Bundesgerichtshof refused to read this as anything stricter than the business judgment rule: management must be granted "broad range for action" ("ein weiter Handlungsspielraum") "without which businesslike action is simply impossible" ("ohne den unternehmerisches Handeln schlechterdings nicht möglich ist") (*ARAG/Garmenbeck*, BGHZ 135, 244, 1997).

Gross negligence remains the standard in the law of Delaware and many other states, but for decades this has not really mattered, because the state law of corporations has been overtaken, in this respect, by federal securities law. One aspect of this federalization – of the "new corporate law" (Seligman, 1993) – is described in the next section.

6. ACCOUNTING AND INTERNAL CONTROLS AGAINST INTERNATIONAL CORRUPTION: THE USA

The FCPA added a new subsection 13(b)(2) to the Securities Exchange Act of 1934, applicable to every corporation or company that is an "issuer" as defined in the 1934 Act, that is, any (natural or juridical) person who issues a security in the United States or is required to file periodic reports with the SEC. An issuer could be domestic or foreign; for example, the SEC brought an enforcement action against Montedison, S.p.A., an Italian company whose American depositary receipts were traded on the New York Stock Exchange, for disguising in its accounting an alleged $400 million in bribes. Everything was alleged to have taken place outside the U.S., except that some of the allegedly false accounting statements were filed with the SEC. (*Securities & Exchange Commission v. Montedison, S.p.A.*, SEC Litigation Release No. 15164, 3 FCPA Reporter 699.450 (D.D.C., 1996).)

Issuers have other, quite extensive public disclosure obligations under the 1934 Act, such as annual form 10K reports and quarterly form 8K reports. Subsection 13(b)(2) adds the requirement that any unlawful payments and transactions be disclosed "in reasonable detail" and identified in a way that calls attention to their impropriety. Each issuer must devise and maintain a system of internal accounting controls sufficient to provide "reasonable assurances" that all transactions are authorized by management and recorded in conformity to generally accepted accounting principles (GAAP). See generally Lacey and Crutchfield (1998), Spindler (1998).

Subsection 13(b)(2) often receives less attention than the anti-bribery provisions, but it seems safe to say that it has been a far more effective deterrent to corrupt payments. It was the first provision in federal law requiring corporations to adhere to corporate governance standards and "changed the mandate of the [SEC] by giving that agency the means for regulating the internal management of domestic corporations. Thus, the FCPA heralds a new era" (Crutchfield & Dundas, 1980, pp. 866–867.)

Issuers are responsible for requiring their majority-owned subsidiaries, wherever they may be located in the world, to have adequate internal accounting controls; since the 1988 FCPA amendments, however, issuers need make only a "good faith attempt" to establish such controls in foreign companies in which they hold minority interests. If an issuer has complied to this extent, it has been generally accepted that it is not responsible for the inaccuracies of which it is unaware in the books of a majority owned subsidiary. Settlements are inherently uncertain as precedents, but the recent consent order in *Securities and Exchange Commission v. International Business Machines Corporation* may indicate a change (SEC Release No. 43761, 21 Dec, 2000). In that case, IBM's wholly owned Argentine subsidiary paid bribes and failed to reflect them in its accounting, all without the knowledge of the parent, which took "immediate corrective action" when it learned the facts. IBM agreed to a cease-and-desist order and a U.S. $300,000 civil penalty for the books and records violations; the SEC did not charge IBM with bribery.

Unlike these accounting and control provisions, the anti-bribery provisions of the FCPA make acting "corruptly" an essential element of each crime defined. "Corruptly" was meant by Congress to have about the same meaning as in earlier federal statutes outlawing domestic bribery, namely that the defendant have an "evil intent" to influence an official act. It might seem from this that not too much should be made of the original "knowing or having reason to know", but, on the contrary, the issue of greatest concern to business was potential criminal liability of the corporation or its officers for the acts of subordinate employees, foreign subsidiaries and agents. The Senate Report offered some comfort, suggesting that careful supervision by the board of directors and senior management, plus compliance with the FCPA's accounting provisions, would be indications that the corporation and its management did not have "reason to know" of the misbehavior of rogue employees (S. Rep. No. 95–114, 95th Cong., 1st Sess. at 11, 1977). The same Report pointed out that failure to account properly – i.e. "in reasonable detail"– for the actions of the rogue briber would constitute a violation of subsection 13(b)(2) by a U.S. company, and the SEC promptly took the same position in enforcement actions. However, with "reason to know" defined neither in the statute nor in the legislative history, advising business on practices likely to reduce the risk, such as corporate codes of conduct and scrutiny of the background and activities of local agents, became a substantial industry.

7. ACCOUNTING AND INTERNAL CONTROLS IN THE OAS AND OECD CONVENTIONS

Members of the Organization of American States signed the OAS Convention in 1996 and it accumulated enough ratifications to enter into force the following year. Compared to Article 8 of the OECD Convention, Article III (10) of the OAS Convention is an almost exactly opposite form of ineffective provision. Here the purposes are clearly stated, including "sufficient internal accounting controls to enable their officers to detect corrupt acts". However, the OAS Convention requires only that "the States Parties . . . consider the applicability of measures within their own institutional systems to create, maintain and strengthen" institutions for those purposes.

The OECD Convention – drafted after and with full knowledge of the OAS Convention – was signed by all members of the Organization for Economic

Cooperation and Development in 1997 and entered into force in 1999. Each provision of its Article 8 is introduced by "each State shall", but the only purpose stated in the Article itself is rather vague: "In order to combat bribery of foreign public officials effectively...." Several accounting evils are specified clearly – much more clearly than in the OAS Convention – but the corporate governance words, "sufficient internal accounting controls to enable their officers to detect corrupt acts", are never uttered.

Thus, one Convention proclaims the corporate governance purpose, but requires no action at all, while the other requires the parties to deal with enumerated topics, but leaves it unclear whether the purpose is corporate governance or, say, criminal prosecution. The point is nicely illustrated by Argentina, a party to both Conventions. In its report to the OECD (an excerpt from which is reprinted in Exhibit 3), Argentina says that its laws have always forbidden false accounting. There is no mention of corporate governance or internal controls. In its report to the OAS (an excerpt from which is reprinted in Exhibit 4), on the other hand, Argentina says (in my translation):

> As to mechanisms designed to require commercial companies to maintain internal controls permitting their personnel to detect acts of corruption, although no such specific provisions exist, Company Law no. 19,550 establishes, for commercial stock corporations and limited companies larger than U.S. $2,100,000, obligatory internal controls ...

One version of the OAS questionnaire asked, "Do these measures include the obligation for publicly held companies and other types of associations to maintain sufficient internal accounting controls to enable their personnel to detect corrupt acts"? Three of the four countries that answered this question, namely Bolivia, Chile and Panamá, simply replied "No", without elaboration, while Venezuela made it a full sentence: "Venezuelan law does not provide for the types of accounting controls mentioned in the question" (http://www.oas.org/juridico/english/Bolivia.English.add5.doc, http://www.oas.org/juridico/english/Chile.Inglish.add.7.doc, http://www.oas.org/juridico/english/corrupcion.Panama.Ingles.doc, http://www.oas.org/juridico/english/venezuela.Inglish.add13.doc). Is this not better than most of the responses regarding Article 8 of the OECD Convention, which amount to "Yes, because you didn't ask me the right question"?

The paragraphs on Article 8 of the reports to the OECD from France (Exhibit 2) are typical. Like almost all other countries reporting, France states that its general standards for financial accounting and auditing prohibit everything Article 8 requires to be prohibited, that they apply to all relevant business entities and that the potential penalties for violations are severe. It mentions no new laws or regulations to comply with Article 8. It never mentions informed management or internal controls. Twenty-six of the 28 reports on the OECD web site are similar in this respect, including, most disappointingly, even that of the United States.

In March 2002, a team from the OECD Working Group on Bribery was in the United States to examine its compliance with the OAS Convention as part of Phase II of the Convention's monitoring process. The exercise was much more likely to educate the examiners in the kinds of institutions – large staffs of government employees, specialized private lawyers, corporate compliance departments – that make the FCPA effective, and that were not contemplated by most of the State Parties. In several of their reports on the Conventions, and in meetings with their counterparts from other parties, the Commerce and State Departments have provided education of this sort. Sadly, however, the United States responses to the OAS questionnaire did not take advantage of the opportunity to educate other parties by explaining how management accounting and internal controls contribute to corporate governance. The U.S. response to the same question answered by Argentina reads in full:

> The following sections of U.S. law are designed to prevent and deter the bribery of domestic and foreign government officials: Title 18, United States Code Sections 201 and 666 (domestic officials) and Title 15, United States Code, Section 78dd-1 et. [*sic*] seq. (the Foreign Corrupt Practices Act)

(http://www.oas.org/juridico/english/cp07334.pdf)

However, one of the very few exceptions to the pattern of ignoring the purpose of Article 8 is Australia, a country similar in many ways to the United States. Australia's national report to the OECD says (http://www1.oecd.org/daf/no-corruption/pdf/report/Australia.pdf):

> The Australian authorities state that the Federal Parliamentary Joint Standing Committee on Treaties recommended that an examination be undertaken of the benefits and practicalities of introducing a requirement that payments of bribes be disclosed in business accounts.[6] This recommendation is addressed by subsection 70.4(3) of the Criminal Code amendments, by requiring that a record of facilitation payments be kept.

In Greece, Act 2656/1998, by which the OECD Convention was ratified, added new accounting provisions. These are described thus in its report to the OECD:

> when the establishment of off-book accounts, the making of off-book or inadequately identified transactions, the recording of non-existent expenditures, the entry of liabilities with incorrect identification of their object and the use of false documents are intended to assist or conceal the bribery of a foreign public official, the offence is punishable by imprisonment for up to three years, or more where other statutory provisions provide. (http://www1.oecd.org/daf/nocorruption/pdf/report/Greece.pdf, page 13.)

That Article 8 was read in a bribery context by Greece, a civil law country whose commercial law has much in common with that of Germany, and by Australia, a common law country whose company law is based on that of England, underlines that at least the bribery point is available to be taken by those who will. That it is just as easily ignored, however, is underlined by the 26 reports to the OECD (including that of the United States, which missed a similar opportunity in its OAS report, as noted on p. 323) in which Article 8's requirements are reported on as if they had no context. Not one of the 28 reports on Article 8 mentions its management accounting and corporate governance objectives, so perhaps they aren't really there at all.

8. LESSONS

The focus of this paper is not exactly transparency, but is related to transparency: in principle, management can be well informed without sharing its knowledge with others, but even to enforce this much, others must be able to determine whether or not management is well informed. One way – perhaps not the only way, but surely the simplest way – is to require that management be informed in a manner transparent to some suitable third party, such as shareholders and perhaps other stakeholders, independent auditors or a securities and exchange commission. On the other hand, transparency, in the limited sense of accurate accounts, is not enough, because accurate accounts may be silent on important matters. The real point must be to bring the information to the attention of management, so that management can behave responsibly, or, at least, be held accountable for its knowing failure to do so.

Any claim that an institution is transferable from one system of corporate governance to another deserves to encounter some skepticism (Jacoby, 2000; Licht, 2001). In each system, various complementary and mutually dependent institutions have co-evolved, assigning roles that differ in many details, and often in fundamental respects, to law, non-legal norms, financial markets, labor markets and so forth. It is important to note, however, that advancement of informed management appears unlikely to be a value advanced by one side of the usual divide[7] and rejected by the other. It should not be affected, for example, by the choice of stakeholders, because it requires effective management in the interests of whatever stakeholders there may be: the requirement is only that management be adequately informed and take responsibility for what is done.

The requirement of informed management ought not, however, to be imposed precisely through a particular set of (management) accounting requirements, despite the resemblance of that approach to the U.S. model. The right way to proceed is usually at a higher level of abstraction, but even this is not easily stated as a rule. My best effort, so far, is that a functional result should be specified, defined on the basis of comparative study so as to approximate the level or range of levels of abstraction at which the desired outcomes first converge within the various systems considered. In this paper, but without being certain there would be agreement on the point, I have proceeded on the basis that assuring management knowledge of the key information is the correct level of abstraction. If so, then Article 8 of the OECD Convention ought to have required each State Party to demonstrate that it had taken effective steps, within the context of its own system of corporate governance, to make possible and then to require sufficient management knowledge of all payments to government officials, to enable management to determine whether corruption was involved and to take steps against corrupt payments in time to prevent them. As it stands, the point of Article 8 may not even be clear to many outside the U.S., because it depends on institutions that exist within the U.S. By aiming too low – by specifying a means that is effective in the United States, rather than the result to be achieved – and indeed by leaving the result implicit rather than stating it plainly, the drafters of the OECD Convention made it easy for the State Parties to avoid taking any action at all and, at the same time, to claim full compliance.

The most important feature of the United States Foreign Corrupt Practices Act of 1977 is not its anti-bribery provisions, but its addition of subsection 13(b)(2) to the 1934 Act, requiring effective corporate governance with regard to management's control over transactions; the reader is invited to search for any reference to corruption or bribery in that subsection and to consider the consequences of the result. Whether by choice or through failure to understand the differences between corporations in the United States and elsewhere, however, the counterpart of this provision in the OECD Convention was not drafted in such a way as to convey the concept of internal controls and management accounting. Because management accounting – in contrast to financial accounting – is not a familiar concept in many countries, the point would have benefited from special emphasis; instead, the drafters chose the opposite extreme of bland generality in articulating Article 8's purpose.

This is an argument for "the use of cultural differences in the design and analysis of corporate governance systems" (Licht, 2001, p. 149), but, unlike the drafters of Article 8, I do not offer a specific solution to the problem under discussion. On the contrary, I assert it is unlikely the same solution will fit all countries and therefore those knowledgeable about each country's path dependencies and institutional interrelationships should be put to work on that country's individualized approach, with judgments to be reserved for effects, rather than methods. In the particular case of Article 8, it may be observed that even those countries whose corporate governance systems most resemble that of the United States – such as Canada and the United Kingdom – have been able to read Article 8 so narrowly as to render it meaningless.

In December 2001, a United Nations working group began meeting, with the goal of completing a U.N. convention against corruption by the end of 2003. (See U.N.G.A. Res, 55/61, 4 Dec, 2000; U.N.G.A. Res, 55/188, 20 Dec, 2000; relevant materials are collected at http://www.undcp.org/crime_cicp_expertgroup_ corruption.html.) At this time of writing, it is a matter of some concern that the U.N. convention might set a lower standard than do the OAS Convention and the OECD Convention, in which event some countries that might otherwise have been persuaded to adhere to the higher standard will be able to resist on the ground that they comply with the most universal standards, namely those established by the United Nations. An American Bar Association working group, of which the author of this paper is a member, has urged that instead the U.N. convention be designed to complement, not undermine, existing instruments, such as the OAS and OECD Conventions. One way in which it might do so is by requiring commitments to implement preventive measures – such as codes of conduct and disclosure rules for public officials; transparent systems for government procurement, accounting and auditing, together with independent oversight bodies; statutory protection for whistleblowers; denial of tax deductibility for bribes – as distinguished from the "soft law" exemplified by Article III of the OAS Convention, under which parties agree to consider adopting such measures. Another is by including in a treaty with a much broader range of parties measures for international cooperation comparable to those applicable to the parties to the existing conventions.

In the drafting of the U.N. convention against corruption, it seems clear from our experience with the OAS and OECD Conventions that the corporate governance provisions should make management accounting and controls objectives explicit but somewhat abstract, as in the OAS Convention but not the OECD Convention, and mandatory, as in the OECD Convention but not the OAS Convention.

The OECD's Working Group on Bribery ought to press for a contextual interpretation of Article 8. Failing that, countries such as Australia and the United States could press for it. Whether they do or not, however, any country can strengthen its own law. In the application of Article 8, the corporate governance objective spelled out in Article III(10) of the OAS Convention should be applied without asking whether minimal compliance with the treaty requires it, for the objective of each country should be the best practices appropriate to its circumstances, not the minimum tolerable to its sovereign peers.

As this is written, Kenneth Lay and Jeffrey Shilling have just been telling Congress and the world that they didn't know about the multi-billion dollar schemes – such as LJM2 Co-Investment LP – by which Enron's huge losses were disguised as huge profits. Can we hope for a system in which these assertions would constitute the basis for criminal prosecutions and civil lawsuits against them, for their failure to implement sufficient management accounting procedures to keep management informed and sufficient internal controls to prevent such schemes from being implemented without management authority? Can we hope for a system in which we will be able to say to management, "It is your duty to know. If in fact you did not know, then that is itself what must be punished or otherwise remedied"?

NOTES

1. Some of the countries that appear to fall into this category are Argentina, Bulgaria, Finland, Greece, Hungary, Ireland, Italy, Korea, Mexico, Spain and Turkey.

2. Some of the countries that appear to fall into this category are Japan, Korea, the Czech Republic and the Slovak Republic.

3. That is, with some statutory exceptions, in the U.S. the net income of a criminal business is taxed just as is the net income of a lawful business. This does not affect criminal penalties, but sometimes the only punishment that government has successfully imposed on a "crime boss" has been income tax evasion.

4. Namely the Public Bodies Corrupt Practices Act (1889), the Prevention of Corruption Act (1906) and the Prevention of Corruption Act (1916).

5. The details vary considerably, but, at this level of generality, the principle holds true in every one of the dozens of countries in whose law I have looked for it. An interesting, but temporary, exception was Article 99 of the French loi no. 67-563 of 13 July 1967, which provided for the liability to creditors, when the assets of a company are insufficient, of "all directors of the company, whether *de jure* or *de facto*, acknowledged or secret, paid or not" ("tous les dirigeants sociaux, de droit ou de fait, apparents ou occultes, rémunérés ou non"). That much is not very different from other countries' law, but the 1967 law continued: In order to avoid liability, the implicated directors must prove that they have provided to the management of the company's business all necessary action and diligence. ("Pour dégager leur responsabilité, les dirigeants impliqués doivent faire la preuve qu'ils ont apporté à la gestion des affaires sociales toute l'activité et la diligence nécessaires.")

This clause reversing and greatly increasing the burden of proof was repealed by loi no. 85-98 of 25 January 1985. The current version, which appears in article L. 624-3 of the Nouveau Code de commerce, ordonnance no. 2000-912 of 18 September 2000, is interpreted as requiring fraud or "fault in management distinctly characterized and sufficiently serious to contrast strongly with the typical behavior of an unfortunate manager acting in good faith" ("faute de gestion nettement caractérisée et suffisamment grave pour trancher avec le comportement habituel du commerçant malheureux de bonne foi"). (Bourges, 3 June 1998, *Juris-classeur périodique, édition Entreprise*, 1999, no. 37, p. 1417.)

6. At the time that the review was prepared, the details of the examination had not yet been released, but it appeared likely that the Government would give serious consideration to the recommendations of the Joint Standing Committee.

7. Oversimplified in the usual ways, these are: (1) common law/many shareholders/ dominance of equity markets/investor protection through law and (2) civil law/concentrated ownership/dominance of banks/investor protection through ownership.

REFERENCES

Convention on combating bribery of foreign public officials in international business transactions, OECD/DAFFE/IME/BR(97) 16/FINAL (18 December 1997). *International Legal Materials, 37* (1) (1998).

Crutchfield, G. B., & Dundas, M. J. (1980). Responsibilities of domestic corporate management under the foreign corrupt practices act. *Syracuse Law Review, 31,* 865.

Inter-American Convention Against Corruption, OEA/Ser. K/XXXIV.1, CICOR/doc. 14/96 rev. 2 (29 March 1996). *International Legal Materials, 35,* 724.

International Trade Administration (ITA, 2001). United States Department of Commerce, *Addressing the Challenges of International Bribery and Fair Competition 2001,* http://www.mac.doc.gov/ tcc/anti_b/oecd2001/BriberyReport2001.pdf

Jacoby, S. M. (2000). Employees and corporate governance: Corporate governance in comparative perspective: Prospects for convergence. *Comparative Labor Law & Policy Journal, 22,* 5.

Lacey, K. A., & Crutchfield, B. G. (1998). Expansion of SEC authority into internal corporate governance: The Accounting Provisions of the Foreign Corrupt Practices Act (a twentieth anniversary review). *Journal of Transnational Law & Policy, 7,* 119.

Licht, A. N. (2001). The mother of all path dependencies: Toward a cross-cultural theory of corporate governance systems. *Delaware Journal of Corporate Law, 26,* 147.

Lowry, H. P., & Schroth, P. W. (1999). Survey of 1998 Developments in international law in Connecticut. *Connecticut Bar Journal, 73,* 349.

Milliet-Einbinder, M. (2000). Writing off tax deductibility. *OECD Observer* (26 May).

Organization for Economic Cooperation and Development (OECD, 2001). Update on the Implementation of the OECD Recommendation on the Tax Deductibility of Bribes to Foreign Public Officials in Countries Parties to the Bribery Convention (update 1 June, 2001), http://www.oecd.org/pdf/M00018000/M00018527.pdf

Pennington, R. R. (1995). *Company law* (7th ed.). London etc.: Butterworths.

Rubin, S. (1982). International aspects of the control of illicit payments. *Syracuse Journal of International Law & Commerce, 9,* 315.

Schroth, P. W. (2002a). Forty-three years of transnational law against corruption (of which 40 in the United States alone). In: D. Birch & J. Batten (Eds), *Governance and Corporate Social Responsibility in the New Millennium: Proceedings of the 2001 Conference.* Burwood, VIC, Australia: Deakin University.

Schroth, P. W. (2002b). The United States and the International Bribery Conventions. *American Journal of Comparative Law, 50* (supplement forthcoming).

Seligman, J. (1993). Accounting and the new corporate law. *Washington & Lee Law Review, 50,* 943.

Spindler, M. S. (1998). What you always wanted to know about the accounting provisions of the Foreign Corrupt Practices Act (but were afraid to ask). *Alberta Law Review, 36,* 473.

APPENDIX

Exhibit 1: Legal Texts

OECD Convention, Article 8:

In order to combat bribery of foreign public officials effectively, each Party shall take such measures as may be necessary, within the framework of its laws and regulations regarding the maintenance of books and records, financial statement disclosures, and accounting and auditing standards, to prohibit the establishment of off-the-books accounts, the making of off-the-books or inadequately identified transactions, the recording of non-existent expenditures, the entry of liabilities with incorrect identification of their object, as well as the use of false documents, by companies subject to those laws and regulations, for the purpose of bribing public officials or of hiding such bribery.

Each Party shall provide effective, proportionate and dissuasive civil, administrative or criminal penalties for such omissions and falsifications in respect of the books and records, accounts and financial statements of such companies.

OAS Convention, Article III(10):

Preventive Measures

For the purposes set forth in Article II of this Convention, the States Parties agree to consider the applicability of measures within their own institutional systems to create, maintain and strengthen:

***

10. Deterrents to the bribery of domestic and foreign government officials, such as mechanisms to ensure that publicly held companies and other types of associations maintain books and records which, in reasonable detail, accurately reflect the acquisition and disposition of assets, and have sufficient internal accounting controls to enable their officers to detect corrupt acts.

Securities Exchange Act, Subsection 13(B)(2), 15 U.S.C. § 78m(B)(2)

(2) Every issuer which has a class of securities registered pursuant to section 78*l* of this title and every issuer which is required to file reports pursuant to section 78o(d) of this title shall –

(a) make and keep books, records, and accounts, which, in reasonable detail, accurately and fairly reflect the transactions and dispositions of the assets of the issuer; and

(b) devise and maintain a system of internal accounting controls sufficient to provide reasonable assurances that –
   (i) transactions are executed in accordance with management's general or specific authorization;
   (ii) transactions are recorded as necessary (I) to permit preparation of financial statements in conformity with generally accepted accounting principles or any other criteria applicable to such statements, and (II) to maintain accountability for assets;
   (iii) access to assets is permitted only in accordance with management's general or specific authorization; and
   (iv) the recorded accountability for assets is compared with the existing assets at reasonable intervals and appropriate action is taken with respect to any differences.

Exhibit 2: France's OECD Report – Article 8

8. ARTICLE 8 – ACCOUNTING

8.1 Book-Keeping and Accounting Statements

According to the French authorities, all the acts proscribed by Article 8 of the Convention (establishment of off-the-books accounts, the making of off-the-books or inadequately identified transactions, the recording of non-existent expenditures, the entry of liabilities with incorrect identification of their objects, the use of false documents) are prohibited generally by French accounting law, irrespective of the aim involved. There are no special provisions applicable to cases where such practices are used to bribe a foreign or French public official. The legislative and regulatory sources of French accounting law are, on the one hand, Articles 8 to 17 of the Commercial Code and the related implementing provisions (Articles 1 to 27 of the amended decree of 29 November, 1983) and, on the other, the chart of accounts as resulting from the amended ministerial decree of 27 April 1982, all of which form a consistent whole in the view of the French authorities. In the case of commercial companies, the Act of 24 July 1966 and the related implementing decree of 23 March 1967 lay down rules for drawing up consolidated accounts, disclosure and auditing of annual accounts, the documents that must accompany them, and other accounting information that must be provided.

8.2 Enterprises Subject to These Laws and Regulations

Under Article 8 of the Commercial Code, all traders, natural or legal persons, are subject to the rules regarding accounting, pursuant to the Commercial Code. The law of 24 July 1966 applies to commercial companies. Lastly, the chart of accounts, the rules of which are identical to those in the Commercial Code and the Law of 24 July 1966, apply to all industrial and commercial companies.

8.3 Penalties for Omissions or Falsifications

The Criminal Code, the 1966 Company law and Law No 85–98 of 25 January 1985 on compulsory reorganisation and company liquidation by a decision of the courts, impose stiff criminal penalties for infringements of French accounting law.

Offences and sanctions provided by the criminal code

- The making and use of forged documents by natural persons is punishable by a prison term of three years, a fine of FF 300 000 (Article 441, paragraph 2) and further penalties provided by Article 441–410 of the Criminal Code (i.e. loss of civic rights, ban on doing business, disqualification from public contracts and confiscation).
- The making and use of forged documents by legal persons is punishable by a fine of FF 1,500,000 and further penalties provided in Article 131–139 of the Criminal Code (i.e. winding-up of the company, ban on engaging in business, judicial supervision, definitive or temporary closing-down, disqualification from public procurements, definitive or temporary ban on soliciting funds from the public, ban on writing certain types of cheques, confiscation of the assets which were used or intended for committing the offence, posting or publication of the decision).

Offences and sanctions provided by the Law of 1966:

- Omitting to compile accounting documents – punishable by a fine of FF 60 000.
- Presentation of accounts that do not give a true and fair view – punishable by a prison term of five years and fine of FF 2 500 000 (or one or the other in the case of managers of a SARL – private limited liability company).
- Distribution of fictitious dividends – punishable by a prison term of five years and a fine of FF 2 500 000 (or one or the other in the case of managers of a SARL).

Offences and sanctions provided by Law No 85–98 of 25 January 1985 in respect of compulsory reorganisation and the winding up of a company by decision of the courts

- Patrimonial penalties of personal assets placed in compulsory reorganisation
- Criminal penalties for criminal bankruptcy
- Personal sanction: personal bankruptcy

Furthermore, under Article 233, paragraph 2 of the 1966 Company Law, public auditors are bound to "inform the public prosecutor of offences that have come to their knowledge", at the risk of a term of imprisonment of five years and a fine of FF 120 00.

Source: http://www1.oecd.org/daf/nocorruption/pdf/report/France.pdf,   pp. 23–25. The original of the quoted portion includes 9 footnotes not reprinted here. The last quoted "fine of FF 120 00" is an error and should read "fine of FF 120,000". Art. 457, L. 24 juill. 1966, as amended by L. no. 67–16, 4 janv. 1967.

Exhibit 3: Argentina's OECD Report – Article 8

8. ARTICLE 8. ACCOUNTING

Article 8 of the Convention requires that within the framework of its laws and regulations regarding the maintenance of books and records, financial statement disclosures and accounting and auditing standards, a Party prohibits the making of falsified or fraudulent accounts, statements and records for the purpose of bribing foreign public officials or of hiding such bribery. The Convention also requires that each Party provide for persuasive, proportionate and dissuasive penalties in relation to such omissions and falsifications.

8.1/8.2 Accounting and Auditing Requirements/Companies Subject to Requirements

Accounting Standards

The Argentine authorities state that the Law on Business Associations (Law No. 19.550) provides the general framework, including accounting standards, which companies have to comply with. Pursuant thereto, entities subject to obligations under this law include: general partnerships, statutory limited partnerships, limited liability companies, corporations, and companies registered abroad that establish branch offices, etc. in Argentina. Moreover, the Code of Commerce provides for accounting requirements applicable to "traders", which is defined in Article 1 as "all natural persons, who, having legal capacity to enter into contracts, exercise on their own acts of commerce, in a manner that becomes a usual profession" and to co-operative associations. Foundations, civil associations, mutual associations and public entities (including state-owned or state-controlled companies) are not subject to the requirements under these laws; however, they are subject to accounting standards or governmental supervision under specific law.

Pursuant to Article 120 of the Law on Business Associations, entities subject to this law are obliged to keep separate accounts, and to submit them to the relevant bodies provided for in the law. Pursuant to Article 3 of the Law No. 22.315, corporations (except the ones controlled by the National Securities

Commission), savings and loan companies, limited liability companies, etc. submit financial statements to the General Inspectorate of Companies. Moreover, under the Law on Business Associations, joint stock companies and limited liability companies whose stock capital exceeds 2,100,000 Argentine Pesos must submit annual financial statements, which include a balance sheet, profit and loss account and additional notes (Articles 62–65). The directors of companies must provide information in the annual report on the company situation (Article 66). In addition, registered offices of companies must keep copies of the balance sheet, profit and loss account and the statement of the net equity evolution, as well as the additional notes and information and make these documents available to partners and shareholders. Furthermore, "copies of the management", annual reports and the auditor's report shall also be available "when appropriate" (Article 67).

Under the Code of Commerce, all "traders" must report their transactions and keep commercial accounts in which a true description and clear justification for each transaction are recorded (Article 43). Traders must keep a "book of original entries" and "inventory and balance sheet" (Article 44). All transactions shall be entered in the book of original entries on a daily basis in chronological order and balance sheets must reflect a true and accurate financial situation of the company (Articles 45, 51). In keeping books, the insertion, deletion and modification of entries, etc. are forbidden (Article 54). Books "considered as indispensable" under the Code of Commerce shall be submitted to the Companies Registry of the domicile (Article 53).

In addition, Argentine law provides for accounting requirements which are applicable to specific categories of entities. For instance, with respect to insurance companies, there are requirements under the Insurance Companies and their Control (Law No. 20.091) to record and keep books, submit an annual report, a general balance sheet, profit and loss account, etc. to the supervisory authorities and publish an annual balance sheet. With respect to financial entities, under the Statute on Financial Entities (Law No. 21.526) and the regulations, accounting records, books, correspondences, documents and papers of the financial entities shall be available for auditing, etc. by officers appointed by the Central Bank of the Argentine Republic, which is the supervisory body of financial entities.

The Argentine authorities confirm that pursuant to these requirements, the establishment of off-the-books accounts, the making of off-the books or inadequately identified transactions, the recording of non-existent expenditures, the entry of liabilities with incorrect identification of their object, as well as the use of false documents, are prohibited.

Argentina states that financial statements and the auditor's report, which are submitted to the public supervisory bodies (e.g. the General Inspectorate of Companies), are publicly available.

Audits

The Argentine authorities state that in general, entities are subject to auditing requirements under different legal norms. Some of them are subject to internal audits or independent (external) audits, and in some cases governmental supervision is also required. For instance, corporations are subject to internal audits and those who fulfil one of the conditions under Article 299 of the Law on Business Associations (e.g. operate licenses or public services or have a capital stock exceeding 2,100,000 Argentine Pesos) are also subject to governmental supervision. Mutual associations are subject to internal audits and governmental supervision. Cooperative associations and financial entities are subject to external audits and governmental supervision. In addition, financial statements submitted to the General Inspectorate of Companies (see the discussion above under "Accounting Requirements") must be accompanied by an opinion of a public accountant duly registered.

According to Argentina, with respect to governmental supervisions, the independence of auditors is guaranteed since the auditors are public officials that have no relationship with the audited entity. With respect to "syndics" (i.e. internal auditors), it is guaranteed indirectly, to the extent that he/she will be liable under the APC (Article 300.3, see below 8.3 "Penalties") if he/she authorises, etc. falsification of the records, etc. In addition, the Law on Business Associations contains some provisions on disqualification in the case of a conflict of interest. Moreover, the Code of Ethics, which is the regulation for accountants, states that professionals shall always act with integrity, veracity, independence and objectivity. It also provides for several norms to avoid conflicts of interest. Additionally, the Technical Resolution No. 7 of the Argentine Federation of the Professional Council of Economic Sciences states that external auditors must be independent from the entities being audited. It also provides for some examples of conflicts of interest where independence would not be guaranteed.

Under the Statute on Money Laundering (Law No. 25.246), professionals whose activities are regulated by the Professional Councils of Economic Sciences are obliged to report to the Financial Information Unit (FIU) any suspicious transactions, irrespective of the amount involved. In addition, auditors are required to report suspected criminal activities to the management of the entity. However, management is not obliged to report them to the competent authorities. Additionally, under the Law No. 22.315 the General Inspectorate of Companies can report suspected criminal activities and submit complaints to the police authorities, etc.

8.3 PENALTIES

Article 12 of the Charter of the General Inspectorate of Companies (CGIC) states that "the General Inspectorate of Companies shall impose penalties on the corporations, associations and foundations, on their directors, syndics or administrators and on every individual or entity that does not fulfil its obligation of furnishing information, provides false data or that in any way, infringes the obligations established by law, by-laws or regulations, or hinders the performance of their duties". The Argentine authorities confirm that such penalties are applicable to omissions and falsifications in respect of the books, records, accounts and financial statements in accordance with Article 8.2 of the Convention.

Pursuant to Article 13 of the CGIC and Article 302 of the Law on Business Associations, penalties for corporations and companies organised abroad which ordinarily conduct business in Argentina would be an administrative fine up to 6,801.47 Argentine Pesos or a warning, etc. A fine may also be imposed on their directors and syndics. Pursuant to Article 14 of the CGIC, penalties for companies engaged in capitalisation and savings transactions, associations and foundations, would be an administrative fine up to 115,438,623 Australes or a warning, etc.

In addition, Article 300.3 of the APC states that "imprisonment from six months to two years shall be imposed on the incorporator, director, administrator, liquidator or syndic of a corporation or operating company or another legal person who, knowingly publishes, certifies or authorises an either false or incomplete inventory, balance sheet, profit and loss accounts, or the related reports, minutes, annual reports, or informs at the shareholders' meeting, falsely or reluctantly, on material events to assess the company's financial position, whatever the purpose sought when verifying them may be".

Source: http://www1.oecd.org/daf/nocorruption/pdf/report/Argentina.pdf. The original of the quoted portion includes 13 footnotes not reprinted here.

Exhibit 4: Argentina's OAS Report – Article III(10)

SECCIÓN OCTAVA. ARTÍCULO 10 – SOBORNO DE FUNCIONARIOS PÚBLICOS Y CONTROLES CONTABLESPREGUNTA 11.

Con respecto a la existencia de legislación en materia contable para prevenir, impedir y sancionar el soborno de funcionarios nacionales y extranjeros, se debe responder en forma negativa, toda vez que no existe una normativa específica sobre esta cuestión.

No obstante ello, la ley de sociedades N° 19.550 que regula la actividad de las sociedades comerciales, establece la obligación general para todos los tipo de sociedades de presentar en sus balances un detalle exhaustivo y detallado de sus activos y pasivos (Art. 63).

En lo que respecta a ciertas cuestiones específicas que se deben contestar, esta normativa no autoriza a que los controles contables internos incluyan cuentas sin ser incluidas en los registros contables, o que se realicen asignaciones o pagos sin ser incluidos en dichos registros, o que exista un registro de transacciones inexistentes, o que se registren las transacciones financieras alterando su objetivo, o que se incluya documentación falsa.

Sanciones: Por otro lado, se debe mencionar que el organismo de la administración pública creado para fiscalizar a las sociedades por acciones, la Inspección General de Justicia, en caso de violación a la ley de sociedades, puede aplicar sanciones de apercibimiento, apercibimiento con publicación, o multas a la sociedad, sus directores y síndicos (Art. 13 de la ley n° 22.315 -creadora de la Inspección General de Justicia-, que remite al Art. 302 de la ley n° 19.550).

Con respecto a mecanismos concebidos para obligar a las sociedades mercantiles a mantener controles contables internos que permitan a su personal detectar actos de corrupción, si bien no existen específicamente tales mecanismos, la ley de sociedades 19.550 establece para las sociedades comerciales por acciones, o para las sociedades de responsabilidad limitada que superen los U.S. $2.100.000, una fiscalización interna obligatoria (Arts. 157, 284 y 299 de la ley citada).

Los tipos societarios por acciones son: las sociedades anónimas, la sociedad anónima con participación estatal mayoritaria y la sociedad en comandita por acciones.

Source: http://www.oas.org/juridico/spanish/cp07419.pdf, page 33. This report is not available in English.

Exhibit 5: List of Countries Reporting to the OECD

The reports filed with the OECD by State Parties to the OECD Convention are posted on its web site. Links to these reports are found at http://www1.oecd.org/daf/nocorruption/report.htm. At this writing, the following country reports are available:

Argentina	Germany	Netherlands
Australia	Greece	Norway
Austria	Hungary	Poland
Belgium	Iceland	Slovak Republic
Bulgaria	Italy	Spain
Canada	Japan	Sweden
Czech Republic	Korea	Switzerland
Denmark	Luxembourg	United Kingdom
Finland	Mexico	United States
France		

The OECD Convention has been ratified by the above 28 countries plus Brazil, Chile, Mexico, New Zealand, Slovenia, Turkey. It has been signed, but not yet ratified, by Ireland.

Source for signatures and ratifications: http://www.oecd.org/pdf/M00017000/M00017037.pdf.

Exhibit 6: List of Countries Reporting to the OAS

Argentina
Bolivia
Canada
Chile
*Colombia
Dominican Republic
Ecuador
*Honduras
*Mexico
Panamá
Perú
United States
Venezuela

Just printing the above list exaggerates the information provided by these reports. Some of them (indicated by ∗) are merely comments on the questionnaire and the appropriateness of certain questions, rather than answers to the questions. Those countries providing answers responded to different drafts of the questionnaire, so the responses often are not directly comparable from country to country.

Source: http://www.oas.org/juridico/english/replies_to_the_questionnaire_on_.htm

The Inter-American Convention has been ratified by the above 13 countries plus The Bahamas, Costa Rica, El Salvador, Guatemala, Guyana, Jamaica, Nicaragua, Paraguay, Saint Vincent and the Grenadines, Trinidad and Tobago, Uruguay. It has been signed, but not yet ratified, by Barbados, Belize, Brazil, Haïti, Suriname.

Source for signatures and ratifications: http://www.oas.org/juridico/english/sigs/b-58.html.

EMBEDDING CORPORATE SOCIAL RESPONSIBILITY INTO CORE BUSINESS: CREATING AN ENABLING ENVIRONMENT[☆]

David Birch[†]

ABSTRACT

Over the last few years there has been a considerable amount of aspirational rhetoric promulgating new directions for business to take with respect to corporate social responsibility and corporate citizenship. Senior CEOs of global companies have taken to this with considerable energy. But, at the end of the day, we are left facing the question whether the aspirations and visions are actually seriously embedded into the core business of the companies espousing the principles.

This chapter explores the rhetoric with specific reference to one major mining company, Rio Tinto, and examines, through the Rio Tinto "Business with Communities" programme, the sort of enabling environment

---

☆Parts of this paper were originally delivered as "The Triple Bottom Line as a Business Basic? The Rio Tinto "Business with Communities" Program", Keynote Opening Address, Environmental Justice and Global Citizenship Conference Copenhagen 14–16 February 2002 and in a staff-student seminar in the newly formed International Centre for Corporate Social Responsibility, University of Nottingham, U.K., February 21 2002.

† David Birch is currently funded to work on research into corporate citizenship by a number of large corporations and organizations in Australia, including Rio Tinto.

Social Responsibility: Corporate Governance Issues
Research in International Business and Finance, Volume 17, 337–367
© 2003 Published by Elsevier Science Ltd.
ISSN: 0275-5319/PII: S0275531903170158

required to translate aspiration into everyday reality within a large global company.

1. INTRODUCTION

Corporate Responsibility is not philanthropy – it is good business.

James D. Wolfensohn

In a survey of 20,000 companies worldwide conducted in August 2001, management consultants A. T. Kearney, tracked the performance over 5 years of the companies that make up 98% of worldwide stock market capitalisation. The survey concluded "that revenue growth rather than profitability is the key to the creation of shareholder value, and companies that out-perform the industry average are willing to accept short-term profit volatility to keep the growth story going" (Dabkowski, 2001, p. 1). The key issue here is that in a new economy, growth cannot be simply interpreted against a single financial bottom line. The survey made it clear that good internal vision about a strategic vision was an important aspect of successfully run companies (p. 1), and increasingly everything is now pointing to the importance of triple bottom line thinking as a business basic to the continuation and development of that success. This lies at the heart of new economics thinking, which positions people, not just economic growth, at the centre of a sustainable economics for society overall (see Birch, 2002; Zadek et al., 2000). This is not a difficult lesson for many in business to accept – in principle or in the rhetoric of their publicity material, charters of value, mission statements and the like – but it is a seriously difficult issue for those wanting to embed it into core business on an everyday basis.

This paper is about this "seriously difficult issue", looking in particular at the commitments made by the most senior executives of the world's second largest mining company, Rio Tinto, to corporate social responsibility principles, and how these can be translated into everyday core business policy and practice, as real-life, genuine, expressions of strategic corporate citizenship. As the 1998 stakeholder report on Rio Tinto by the International Federation of Chemical, Energy, Mine and General Workers' Unions made clear, "Rio Tinto must fulfil not only its fiduciary duty, but also its wider social duty to all those stakeholders who have contributed, and continue to contribute, to the survival and success of the company" (ICEM, 1998, Foreword). My basic premise in this paper is that fulfilling these duties effectively and translating leadership vision into core business reality is impossible without an enabling environment being put in place, irrespective of the number of drivers and key performance indicators, measures and resources that might be put in place within the company. Because it is that enabling environment which is needed in order for new cultural vocabularies to be learnt. Without these new cultural vocabularies, drawn from all sectors of society, business, government and civil society, change will be impossible, and the translation of rhetoric into reality never achieved beyond a simple old economics concentration on program outputs and outcomes. Within the context of Rio Tinto, I suggest that such an effective enabling environment is its "Business with Communities" Program.

2. WORLD ECONOMIC FORUM 2002

At the World Economic Forum held this month in New York, 35 leading CEOs and Chairs of Boards of global companies, released a joint action statement headed *Global Corporate Citizenship: The Leadership Challenge for CEOs and Boards* recommending a framework for action that companies can use to develop a strategy for managing their company's impact on society and its relationships with stakeholders (WEF, 2002, p. 1). Using the language of corporate citizenship, the framework is designed to produced a "template for a leadership process" so that corporate citizenship issues in the company are not an add-on but fundamental to core business operations (p. 1).

Companies like Anglo American, Coca-Cola, Diageo, Boots, McDonalds, Statoil, WMC and Rio Tinto all signed, stating very clearly that business has an important role to play in partnership with others in the public and private sectors and civil society, to help spread the benefits of development more widely by the manner in which we pursue our primary business activities. "We believe", they wrote, "that a commitment on our part to listen to and work with these other groups makes sound business sense and will enable us to better serve the interests of our shareholders and other key stakeholders, especially over the long term" (p. 2). They then ask "what does this mean in practice" for both business leaders and business in general? (p. 2). Their answers are:

(1) Our companies' commitment to being global corporate citizens is about the way we run our own business and a "key element of this is recognising that the frameworks we adopt for being a responsible business must move beyond philanthropy and be integrated into core business strategy and practice" (p. 2).
(2) Our relationships with key stakeholders are fundamental to our success inside and outside our companies (p. 2) and this includes stakeholders in the main spheres of the company's influence – in the workplace, marketplace, along supply chains, at the community level and in public policy dialogue.
(3) Ultimate leadership for corporate citizenship rests with Chief Executives, Chairmen (*sic*) and Board Directors. So that:

(a) they provide leadership in corporate citizenship;
(b) they define what corporate citizenship means for the company;
(c) they make it happen;
(d) they are transparent about it.

This, then, is their *Framework for Action*:

• provide leadership;
• define what corporate citizenship means;
• make it happen;
• be transparent about it.

And they make it very clear that there is a compelling case for taking action on issues relating to global corporate citizenship:

• First, an individual business case, that in today's world good corporate citizenship makes sound business sense. It is increasingly in the shareholders' interests for a company to have a clear purpose and set of values, not just a matter of public relations and avoiding negative publicity.
• Second, a broader case that business prospers in societies that are prosperous (p. 10).

So does society agree?

A *Business Week*/Harris Poll reported in *Business Week* in September 2000 certainly found that only 4% of Americans agreed that U.S. corporations should have only one purpose – to make the most profit for their shareholders – 95% agreed that U.S. Companies should have more than one purpose and that they also owe something to their workers and communities in which they operate (Little, 2001 cited in WEF, 2002, p. 10). Many polls worldwide support these findings including the very extensive Millenium Poll on Corporate Social Responsibility conducted in 1999, which surveyed thousands of citizens in 33 countries worldwide.

Last year, the U.S.-based Conference Board, and the Asian Institute of Management, Instituto Ethos in Brazil and the International Business Leaders Forum, surveyed leading CEOs the world over. Seven hundred responded, ranking the two factors as most important to their future success in addressing broader social issues were: more effective management within the company of the company's external involvements and clear leadership from Government (cited in WEF, 2002, p. 11).

As such, business cannot afford to ignore the wider social economic and environmental impacts of its activities, both positive and negative. By supporting governments, inter-governmental organizations and civil society in creating such an enabling environment and building such societies, business will prosper, "over the long term" (WEF, 2002, p. 11).

A very significant issue to be addressed, of course, is how the aspirational CSR views of CEOs and Chairs of Boards, like the ones at the World Economic Form, and the increasing number of people whose views are now being reflected by these senior leaders, can be translated into real, everyday, core business policy and practice for ordinary managers and workers – via *strategic corporate citizenship*. It's not easy – there are conflicts and contradictions in the dominant economic paradigms that rule both business and government worldwide, which would seem to mitigate very strongly against effective development here.

Nevertheless, it is a real issue which we need to engage with very seriously to determine if those who say they are committing their companies to these principles actually go beyond rhetoric and are doing what many of them say they should be doing – making sure that Corporate Social Responsibility/Corporate Citizenship is really being integrated into core business.

In relation to that, the Copenhagen Centre, a leader in the field of CSR, asks the following, very pertinent, questions:

> Will the business community engage in broader societal processes with combined social and financial purposes? Can business develop its values and culture through strong and visionary leadership to support a new understanding of how social and environmental responsibility and accountability can form the foundations for both long-term market competitiveness and contributing to meeting social aims? (Copenhagen Centre, 2000).

What follows in this paper is an exploration of how I interpret some of the ways in which one company, Rio Tinto, might offer answers to these questions in order to meet the challenges of becoming, in the words of Simon Zadek, "a civil corporation" (Zadek, 2001b; see also Zadek, 2001a). This does not mean that my analysis is Rio Tinto's analysis, nor does it mean that some of the possibilities of interpretation that I raise in this paper have actually been thought through by Rio Tinto. Some may have been, some may not.

3. CORPORATE SOCIAL RESPONSIBILITY PRINCIPLES IN RIO TINTO

Rio Tinto, through its Executive Chairman, Sir Robert Wilson, its Deputy Chairman, Leon Davis, Senior Advisers like Lord Richard Holme, and senior CEOs and Executives like Leigh Clifford and Barry Cusack, are very vocal in this area, and have been for some years now. Rio Tinto is represented on most, if not all, of the leading bodies in this field, like the World Business Council for Sustainable Development, and is a signatory to many of the leading initiatives in this area like the UN Global Compact; the OEC Guidelines on multinationals, and the Global

Sullivan Principles, and a closer examination of how the world's second largest mining company comes to grips with some of these issues will form the basis of this paper. Sir Robert Wilson, for example, is one of the 35 who signed the joint statement released at the World Economic Forum, and he is on the Executive Committee of the World Business Council for Sustainable Development which has just released an important paper "The Business Case for Sustainable Development. Making a Difference toward the Johannesburg Summit 2002 and Beyond" (WBCSD, 2002) as a preliminary position paper prior to Rio+10 at Johannesburg.

The WBCSD defines sustainable development as "forms of progress that meet the needs of the present without compromising the ability of future generations to meet their needs" (WBCSD, 2002, p. 2).

The Council's position on Corporate Social Responsibility (CSR) is that 'companies should first determine what they really stand for – their vision and values, their "corporate magnetic north"'. They should then integrate corporate social concerns into the business strategy (WBCSD, 2002, p. 6). In particular, companies should:

- focus on individuals since CSR reaches out to all stakeholders but will be judged by its implications for individual employees, managers and citizens.
- determine a corporate legacy by installing an ethic of education and learning and by instituting processes to foster this ethic.
- put employees first as business's best assets and ambassadors, and also know their neighbours, both their communities and cultures.
- establish a system for keeping CSR debates and dialogues transparent and continuous.
- form smart partnerships, not for publicity or cover, but to realise CSR goals.
- measure and account for what they do.
- report externally but report in ways that reach all stakeholders, not just those on their mailing list or on the internet.

Overall, the WBCSD argue that "A coherent CSR strategy, based on integrity, sound values, and a long term approach, offers clear business benefits to companies and a positive contribution to the well-being of society" (WBCSD, 2002, p. 6).

To do this, they recognise that to move toward 'corporate concern for the "triple bottom line" – financial, social and environmental performance – "requires radical change, throughout the corporation" (p. 7). "It's not", they say, "either or". The new paradigm is "and also"' (p. 7).

Stakeholder dialogue is absolutely key to developing this new paradigm. "Progress toward sustainable development", the WBCSD argues, requires many more – and more complex – partnerships. "Smart companies", they say "are recognising that the most effective way to leverage change in our interdependent world is through common endeavour with others, and learning from experience" (WBCSD, 2002, p. 8).

Smart partnerships like this, they argue, not only "combine skills and provide access to constituencies that one partner may not have, but they also enhance the credibility of the results – results that might be less effective and believable if they came from any business, or any civil society, or any government" (WBCSD, 2002, p. 8).

To that end, Sir Robert Wilson has publicly welcomed what he calls "the flowing of interest in the concepts of corporate social responsibility", believing that "responsible behaviour is essential for the creation of long-term shareholder value" (Wilson, 2000, p. 17). But he also recognises that while there are positive advantages to business – there are also risks, so that, in his words, "As businesses, we should be careful not to overstate our contribution and role: we can and should act responsibly but by ourselves we cannot hope to achieve the careful balancing of economic, environmental and social outcomes which sustains the development demands" (Wilson, 2000, p. 17).

So, while he recognises that "responsible behaviour makes good business sense" (p. 17) he is careful to emphasise that the debate is currently focusing very heavily upon the private sector and "As business", he says "we need to be careful not to create unrealistic expectations about what we can deliver by ourselves" (p. 19). There is a crucial role for government, civil society and "other actors". Rio Tinto's Deputy Chairman, Leon Davis, talks about this in terms of a company's "social conscience", "insofar as it is a call for business", he says "to obey the moral imperative to behave decently and harmoniously" (Davis, 2001, p. 4). But he also makes it clear that it is not in the interests of the community for business to simply act as a substitute for government, and he clearly recognises that it is much easier to talk about than to actually do it (p. 6). Nevertheless, in 1995, Leon Davis led the way for Rio Tinto in actually doing it by recognising that "it is imperative to incorporate new competencies into the core of the company's professionalism" (p. 6). These were new competencies that "went beyond the traditional economic and technical professions to include social and cultural expertise" (p. 6). Today, all Rio Tinto operations have to produce detailed five-year community plans "which contain assessments of the social, economic and cultural characteristics of their host communities" (p. 6). Along with this Rio Tinto, and its component businesses, produce annual non-mandatory social and environment reports outlining performance in these areas against targets and goals set in the previous year. Unlike many companies, which are only just beginning to do this, Rio Tinto produced its first separate report in 1996.

The year before, Rio Tinto published its Aboriginal and Torres Strait Islander policy, and since then over 30 separate agreements have been developed with Aboriginal communities across Australia.

There is a very clear business case behind these Agreements, of course. Rio Tinto would not be able to access new land for new operations without good community support – and in 1995 made a very radical departure for any mining company by recognising that the Aboriginal communities on the lands where Rio Tinto operates should not simply be consulted but they should be seen as key stakeholders in Rio Tinto. In 1995, this was revolutionary for a mining company, because it begins to redefine the business case, beyond a company simply trying to find smarter ways of being able to earn its licence to operate in a community. The move is not, in the words of Bruce Harvey, Chief Adviser Aboriginal and Community Relations in Rio Tinto, "about philanthropy; rather it is all about developing robust regional economies". "Through capacity building", he says "in the hinterland of our operations, we create a virtuous circle of business and community interaction. In this way, our communities help make our mines more competitive and the legacy we leave will survive the eventual closure, or continuation of the mining operations. We want Rio Tinto operations'", he says "to act as a catalyst that unites company, government and community in ways that strengthen and diversify local economies" (Rio Tinto, 2000, p. 3).

Sir Robert Wilson defines the Rio Tinto catalyst Bruce Harvey talks about as "going beyond the outmoded model of paternalistic philanthropy, towards partnership models within local communities" (Wilson, 2002, p. 4). Interviewed in the January 2002 issue of *Ethical Corporation*, Wilson recognises that this requires a different approach and level of awareness from our local management who know they have to take this on board as being an integral part of their operating responsibilities (p. 4). Not only should this not be delegated, he says, "to someone providing local charities with donations", but the way we talk about it, and understand it, needs to also go beyond the outmoded language of corporate social responsibility which has concentrated so much on social *impact* – "as if", he says, "it's a one-off effect that our activities have on local communities. It's more about social interaction, a continuing dynamic process, rather than just a one-off event" (p. 5).

Several years ago Wilson was arguing that "Today's and tomorrow's mineral producers require not only a wider range of management and technical skills to realise the wealth contained in the earth's crust but also a keen sense of their contribution to improving the human condition. Those who do not have that perspective", he said, will struggle to interpret change, as social and environmental forces better them. "Those that do", he said, "those who remember their history and have learned from it, will be far better placed to satisfy both their customers and neighbours as well as those who have invested their careers and their savings in this most fascinating of businesses" (Wilson, 1999, p. 5).

We know this is good business. The companies listed in the Dow Jones Sustainability Index consistently outperform those that are not. Leon Davis, Deputy Chair of Rio Tinto, knows this too, arguing that "Businesses that enter into partnership with the community, and do so with conviction and professionalism, are going to be seen as modern, responsive and to have a competitive advantage". And, "he says", "investors already know this" (Davis, 2001, p. 8).

Richard Holme, co-chair of the WBCSD working group on corporate social responsibility, and a senior adviser now to Rio Tinto, makes it very clear, "if companies behave irresponsibly, in social or environmental terms, then no amount of good-cause giving will tilt their overall contribution to society back from the negative to the positive" (see Holme & Watts, 2000). This is reflected in the *Rio Tinto Communities Policy*, which states "Wherever the Group operates, good relations with its neighbours are different, the policy of Rio Tinto is that every group operation shall strive to understand and interact constructively with its local communities and to assist their development in ways, which apply the following principles:

• mutual respect;
• active partnership;
• long term commitment.

Mutual respect is essential to lasting beneficial interactive relationships between the Group's operations and local communities. This requires continuing and effective two-way communications and realistic expectations on both sides.

Active Partnership determines the way the Group works with local communities as well as with regional and national governments and other affected parties by seeking mutual commitment and reciprocity based on trust and openness so as to reach agreed objectives and shared involvement.

Long term commitment to local communities is sought so that social and economic wellbeing is safe guarded and, where possible, enhanced throughout the mine's life and beyond (*Rio Tinto Communities Policy*).

This goes well beyond the sort of corporate philanthropy and sponsorship of communities and community organizations and activities that often come under the banner, and for many companies still actually define that banner, of corporate social responsibility. Writing a cheque is easy. What Rio Tinto has been thinking through for several years now is very difficult – it is not an add-on to core business, like most CSR activities are in most companies – it is positioned by Rio Tinto's most senior executives as a business basic. It is about the company and the communities in which it operates seeing each other – interacting with each other – as mutual stakeholders. The challenge is how to translate this thinking from the corporate entity of Rio Tinto into its multiple businesses, and within those businesses to embed it all into everyday core business by all employees.

That challenge began in earnest some years ago when Rio Tinto recognised that "The public expectations of corporate responsibility have intensified", and that "the issue of community relations has become more challenging" (Rio Tinto, 2001a, p. 2) so much so that "A company that becomes seriously out of touch with the views of its host communities and other stakeholders puts itself at risk just as surely as a company that loses touch with changes in its marketplace" (Rio Tinto, 2001a, p. 3). The Rio Tinto approach to this has been to concentrate on professionialising its corporate social responsibility programs and activities into three main (and related) areas:

- Bilateral partnerships;[1]
- Multilateral trusts and foundations;[2]
- Agreements with government departments and organisations.[3]

This reflects a view in the Company "that good business is about developing positive relationships" (Rio Tinto, 2001a, p. 6) and that "Rather than dissipate funds over a wide variety of activities, a limited number of strategically appropriate partnerships are supported" (Rio Tinto, 2001a, p. 7). What governs the choice of these partnerships is very strategic:

- they must fit in with Rio Tinto's business focus;
- there must be potential for the partner to benefit from the partnership;
- the partner needs to be able to make effective and efficient use of the funds and skills provided by Rio Tinto;
- there must be an opportunity for Rio Tinto people to be directly involved;
- there must be potential for a long term relationship.

The Rio Tinto policy position, and this is very clear in its 2001b publication *Community Relations Global Business, Local Neighbour*, is that "Contemporary relationships need to be rooted in mutual respect and mutual interest. Implementing a communities policy is not easy. Partnership building is a highly complex process that relies on trust, consultation, common objectives, positive relationships and the active involvement of local people" (p. 2).

Not easy at all, and throughout the rest of this paper I will explore some of this in more detail, concentrating in particular on how the publicly expressed views of Rio Tinto's most senior executives over a period of several years now, are translated (or can be translated) into everyday core business reality, beginning with the most significant move towards translating these ideas into business reality. I argue in this paper that to do so requires the development of an enabling environment, and from this environment the development of a strategic corporate citizenship agenda in order to put new cultural vocabularies into all participating organizations. From these new vocabularies new understandings about mutual stakeholders in sustainability can better enable the rhetoric of CSR to be translated into everyday core business through the initial development of more effective stakeholder engagement.

4. STRATEGIC CORPORATE CITIZENSHIP IN RIO TINTO – STAKEHOLDER ENGAGEMENT

Stakeholder input has been crucial to Rio Tinto's implementation of difficult policies like these – not just traditional stakeholders – but understanding the challenges of the many "new" key stakeholders – local communities. In 2000, for example, Rio Tinto invited 400 community leaders throughout Australia to participate in a survey designed to identify priority initiatives relating to Aboriginal and Torres Strait Islander people and Rio Tinto's involvement in these initiatives. The main findings (Rio Tinto, 2001a) indicated that the most important activities for a mining company to be involved in relating to Aboriginal and Torres Strait Islander people are those that:

- recognise Aboriginal culture;
- improve employment options through training and skill development programs;
- provide opportunities for Aboriginal and Torres Strait Islander people to be employed;
- encourage economic independence and sustainable development for regional communities by promoting their active participation in regional economies.

Serious challenges for any business. The mining industry has been very proactive in this area; the real issue, however, is whether the rhetoric of the policy is translating into real engagement. And the difficulty here is that we currently lack effective measures of this. Companies can, and do, count a range of outcomes and report on them every year with ever increasing sophistication and coverage, but no company is yet reporting effectively upon outcomes of interactions – we lack the vocabulary to do this. We need radically new measures which go well beyond anything currently provided for in frameworks like the Global Reporting Initiative and the London Benchmarking Group. Nevertheless, what we can do is to first of all see what a company says "it stands for"; what it believes in and its position on policy, and then see what processes and practices have been put in place within the company to implement these policies.

The International Council on Metals and the Environment in a 1998 report, for example, aimed at the mining and metals industries recognised that "Developing

environmental and social codes of practice to gain greater public acceptance of
corporate activities has required a more open and proactive dialogue with a wider
variety of interest groups in the local community and in society at large" (ICME,
1998, p. 1). One of the major means of doing this has "included developing
improved consultation processes and partnership arrangements with all parties affected by their operations as well as building up the capabilities of their workforces
and other local community members to adjust to new circumstances" (ICME,
1998, p. 4).

"Corporations", the ICME recognised, "do not operate in a social vacuum",
and "The need to reach out to local mining communities and to the broader
society at large, in both the industrialised and developing worlds, has given
rise to new sensitivities towards the social dimension of industry activities"
(ICME, 1998, p. 6). As a result some companies, like Rio Tinto, have adopted
a multi-stakeholder approach to social issues, following the success of similar
approaches in environmental issues (ICME, 1998, p. 10). But "community
development", the ICME makes clear, "requires much more than communication
and consultation – to be successful it requires the full participation of all parties in
development as well as the integration of complementary activities" (ICME, 1998,
p. 10). The Global Mining Initiative, of which Rio Tinto is a founding member,
has picked up on many of these issues, designed as it is "to provide leadership
as the industry faces the complex challenges of sustainable development" (Hall,
2002, p. 13).

Complex challenges indeed, and relatively easy to talk about – though of course
many companies are still not even talking about it – but very difficult to implement
into core business. James Rose, CEO of Integrative Strategies in Australia, puts
it this way: "Business futures must be mapped on a social landscape as well as
on a balance sheet. The Board Room", he says, "is now very much part of the
domain of public policy", and he goes even further by suggesting that, "It may
soon be at its centre" (Rose, 2001, p. 10). For many, both within business and
outside it, the idea of business being at the centre of public policy would be their
worst nightmare, but if business is genuinely serious about change – about taking
on board sustainability as core business and not simply as a rhetorical stance –
then a more prominent public policy voice is quite clearly needed from business
(see Birch, 2001a, 2002; Birch & Glazebrook, 2000).

5. NEW CULTURAL VOCABULARIES

One way of moving a company closer to that public policy platform – something
that clearly cannot be done overnight – is to break down the silo mentality that

is often at the heart of corporate culture, negatively positioning the company as somehow separate from society. Engaging with stakeholders, and recognising new ones, is a good beginning in that process of breaking down corporate isolationism, and Rio Tinto, for example, has made significant moves in this direction in recent years. The company makes it very clear that, "Good business is about developing positive relationships", and in order for them to "continue mining successfully or to gain access to new sites for exploration or possible development, it is important for us to operate in a positive environment and be accepted as a company with expertise and integrity".

In that respect, then, Rio Tinto is well ahead of the field of many other businesses in recognising that effective stakeholder dialogue will create mutual benefit for both business and communities, and, as such, has been active in stakeholder surveys for several years. In 1999 the company published *Rio Tinto in Australia – Community Survey*, which made it clear, in the words of its recently retired Australian Managing Director Barry Cusack, that "Rio Tinto recognises that its long-term success depends not only on the quality of its operations, but on developing productive relationships with host communities" (Rio Tinto, 1999, p. 1).

Companies cannot, however, simply march into those communities and declare them mutual stakeholders. It takes time, trust and more importantly, the willingness of both sides to learn new cultural vocabularies, which will enable them to be able to talk more effectively with each other by better understanding their cultural differences. Not easy for a mining company more used to hard headed engineering cultures, and not easy for communities and community organizations nervous about powerful mining companies. Learning a new language requires patience – but it also requires practice. A significant way of getting that practice is by bridging the gap between business and the local community through the development of business partnerships with community organizations who can help introduce the new community language needed for business and the new business language needed for communities.

Rio Tinto, has established all sorts of relationships and partnerships with community groups in all of its operations, but probably one of the most significant, and I would suggest is somewhat unrecognised within the Rio Tinto group overall for its importance, is the setting up of the "Business with Communities" Program, several years ago. This program was designed to engage in serious partnerships with particular community organizations, which would involve exchange and interaction between the two parties. The partnership was designed to be much more than simply a financial transaction, going well beyond some of the more traditional corporate philanthropy models like "Doing good things in the community", either socially or environmentally; building up a brand; advertising Rio Tinto or opening up new markets. The program was designed to take serious consideration of very detailed stakeholder surveys conducted by Rio Tinto in Australia, which called for mutual benefit relationships to be established with community groups and organizations which went well beyond the company feeling good about getting involved in local communities or simply supporting sports or the arts.

This program, which has proved to be very challenging; extremely resource intensive for both Rio Tinto and the community organizations it has partnered with, and, at times potentially very risky for all parties (see Birch, 2001c) was thought through to create what the Copenhagen Centre, a leading business community partnership agency and think tank in Europe, now talk about as an "enabling environment", where engagement and interaction between the parties becomes considerably more important than the money, projects or activities that are involved in the partnership. The intangibles of the partnership itself – like access, interaction, engagement, dialogue – not the more tangible programs within the partnership – are the major benefits.

This takes a lot of learning, on both sides, where business, for example, is so used to a very hands-off corporate philanthropy model of community engagement, and where community groups are used to companies walking away once the cheque has been passed over. In the Rio Tinto "Business with Communities" program both organizations, and all the various players involved in the business community partnership, need to have a very clear picture of what constitutes the specific means needed to enable value to be added to the core business of both organizations and to the specific social, environmental, community and cultural goals and targets of the partnership and its programs. Not easy. All players in the partnership need to be aware of the big picture issues of the partnership, and not simply a narrowly focused awareness of specific program goals and targets. Again, not easy. Understanding what constitutes community, social, environmental and cultural profitability, as well as financial return, is key for both organizations, and that means recognising the partnership as a capital investment (financial, cultural, intellectual, reputational and so on), and it also means looking after that investment in the same rigorous way as any other capital investments made by the organization by ensuring that processes are put in place to add value to the investment. Seriously not easy.

But, I would argue, establishing close, long-term, partnerships with leading community organizations is a significant means of beginning the process – establishing that "enabling environment", where the aspirational rhetoric of CSR can be translated into strategic corporate citizenship. Business community partnerships the world over are developed and talked about mostly in terms of their immediate short term benefits – financial or otherwise. Corporate Annual Reports tend to concentrate on measuring short-term outcomes and outputs as indicators of corporate community involvement and investment. The thinking in most business and community organizations is still very firmly based on these outcomes and outputs because we are generally comfortable with the language that is used to measure such things. But, in the long run, these are not very good measures at all. They say little or nothing about a company's ability to translate visionary/aspirational CSR rhetoric into every-day core business policy and practice. They remain, as measures, firmly within an old economics paradigm, which understands how to measure impact through enumerating concrete, tangible, outputs. What we need to be able to do is to determine measures of the more intangible, like social well being and social inclusion.

Again, not easy, but one major way of beginning this process is to open up some key avenues of access for different parties to be able to interact with each other, and then, from that interaction, develop the new cultural vocabularies that are needed in order to break down the social exclusivity barriers that currently exist in order to create better synergies between all groups in society – surely the agenda at the very heart of the push for more sustainable societies – and by so doing create the enabling environment that, long-term, will see the rhetoric of CSR become core business reality.

Whether they couch it in these terms or not, Rio Tinto, began this process several years ago, recognising that the company needed to integrate some of these "newer" values into its everyday business activities "so that our employees understand the issues and incorporate the option of being a good corporate citizen into their normal way of thinking" (Duncan & Fenney, 2000). The "Business with Communities" program was launched in Australia with the stated aim of being able to create value for both the business and the communities in which it operated by operating to three main community principles: mutual respect, active partnerships and long-term commitment. It now has the most extensive business with community partnership program in Australia, and was recognised last year with a special award from the Prime Minister's Community Business Partnership.

But does such a program enable corporate social responsibility principles to become core business? I don't believe it does, nor do I believe, it should be expected to. What such a program can do, and is doing in part very well within Rio Tinto, though I believe there is still a long way to go, is to create an enabling environment where new cultural vocabularies are introduced in order to better enable people, who a few years ago would probably not have spoken with each other, to come together in non-antagonistic ways, to share challenges and opportunities. Corporate citizenship cannot be measured by the outcomes of programs or activities, but those programs and activities need to be put into place in order to be the vehicles of access and interaction – to bring people together in the first place (see, for example, the Proceedings of a joint conference in 2000 between Rio Tinto and Deakin University which brought the "Business with Communities" partners together for the first time, Birch, 2001b).

Learning new cultural vocabularies is the means of beginning the process of translating the aspirations of CSR into the core everyday activities of business and community. The specific deliverables of corporate community programs and activities will not do this, but they will bring people together in order to share and learn those new vocabularies. Whether everyone in Rio Tinto management across the world has realised or expressed it in these terms or not, and many have not yet, the Rio Tinto "Business with Communities" Program is a significant means to achieve this through its concentration on the importance of partnership development and not simply program outcomes As such it is at the leading edge of enabling the processes of translating CSR rhetoric into everyday business reality. It has a long way to go – learning new vocabularies takes time, but it is an important first step along the difficult road to sustainability, and one which most companies in the world have not yet taken, preoccupied as they are with short-term community transactions, and not long-term community interactions.

Partnerships in Rio Tinto are not a new thing. For example, the RBM (Richards Bay Minerals) Business Advice Centre was set up by Rio Tinto in Mbonambi, South Africa, in 1986 to promote local business. Over 2,500 jobs have been created and close to 900 businesses established, with the RBM winning the Worldwide Development Award for the Business Advice Centre's project on micro-credit in 1996 (Warhurst, 2001, p. 9). Partners in the scheme include Richards Bay Minerals, the African Council for Hawkers and Informal Business (ACHIB), the National Economic Initiative of local traders (Warhurst, 2001, p. 9). As Alyson Warhurst points out "The concerns of NGOs and other groups advancing such issues as bio-diversity conservation or human rights, or targeting specific problems at particular project sites, are also driving companies to work in collaboration on social and environmental concerns" (p. 11). Rio Tinto, for example, through the Rio Tinto Rossing Foundation has partnered with the Environment Education Network at Weseldsend in Namibia, together with the Endangered Wildlife Trust, the Save the Rhino Trust and the Department of Wildlife, Conservation and Tourism, to promote environmental training and scholarships with a particular emphasis on drought relief.

I'd like to develop this concept of partnership much further though, by examining in detail Rio Tinto's current partnership with the Earthwatch Institute, particularly in the light of Leon Davis' comments when CEO of Rio Tinto, that "it is essential that we use opportunities like the Earthwatch partnership to improve our understanding of the complexities of both environmental and social issues in the countries where we work".

6. EARTHWATCH INSTITUTE AND RIO TINTO

One of the most effective partnerships established by Rio Tinto is with the Earthwatch Institute. This began as a local Earthwatch Australia partnership and is now developing into a global partnership involving Earthwatch Institute (Europe). A primary aim of the partnership "is to demonstrate a shared commitment to environmental responsibility by using the resources of both organizations to contribute to environmental improvement through support for field research and conservation projects, skills development and public awareness and education" (Duncan & Fenney, 2000). Overall, "Rio Tinto's objectives are to raise the level of environmental awareness within the company, to support areas of Earthwatch's work that are relevant to its business strategies and objectives, develop within the company skills and knowledge relevant to the environment, and also to provide opportunities for employees to contribute their expertise to the work of Earthwatch as part of its overall employee development programme. To support capacity building and community outreach opportunities. To enhance the company's reputation as an organization that is environmentally responsible" (Duncan & Fenney, 2000).

But the real value of such a partnership lies well beyond the social or environmental outcomes of particular projects. The serious value lies in the interaction between NGO and corporate, and the long term, sometimes very slow, cultural changes that such an interaction can develop in both parties. As Jane Gilmour, Director of the Earthwatch Institute (Australia) says, "What we seek to do through these interactions is to influence the value systems within companies so that they are more sensitive to natural and cultural heritage issues and more likely to take a proactive role in environmental responsibility", and continues, "We firmly believe that the ability to integrate different perspectives and develop new competencies will be critical to the sustainability of companies in coming years. Companies will need to look outside their own operations to draw on expertise that is present in other parts of society" (Gilmour, 2002, p. 12). It is these new competencies that Rio Tinto talked about long before any others in the mining industry, and it is these that will bring about the sort of cultural change which will enable Rio Tinto's policies to have real and embedded ownership at all levels of the company. Without this embedding, these policies will remain simply aspirational rhetoric. Cultural change is slow, often imperceptive, but Rio Tinto's "Business with Communities" Programme is an innovative (and seriously challenging) means to bridge the rhetoric with action. The Earthwatch partnership is an excellent example of how this can work.

Earthwatch Institute promotes the sustainable conservation of the world's natural resources and cultural heritage by supporting scientific field research and conservation. They do this by both financial support and also by engaging members of the public as volunteers to work as field assistants with the scientists. Each year over 4000 people worldwide become involved. In line with this policy of making a difference to the world by this sort of active involvement, Earthwatch Institute does not seek to be a confrontational environmental NGO, and seeks, to work closely, and harmoniously with both individuals and corporates, to achieve its mission. In the last 27 years, Earthwatch worldwide have supported over 1,000 research projects in 120 countries in marine, life, earth and social sciences, from its four institutes in Europe, USA, Japan and Australia, involving grants of approx. $U.S.4 million per annum.

"Earthwatch", in the words of Earthwatch Institute (Europe) Chairman Herschel Post, "has always set out to fill the gaps in conservation and environmental understanding which are not being dealt with by other organizations".

On July 1st 1999 Rio Tinto London Ltd, Rio Tinto Services Ltd (Australia) Earthwatch Institute (Europe) and Earthwatch Institute (Australia) signed a Memorandum of Understanding bringing together all four parties on a global basis "with the common objective of promoting environmental improvement" in what is formally known as the "Rio Tinto Earthwatch Partnership".

This partnership, built on a previous formal partnership agreement signed in 1996 between the then CRA (now Rio Tinto Services (Australia)) and Earthwatch Institute (Australia), and several years of prior support by Rio Tinto London to Earthwatch Institute (Europe), is "a jointly-designed programme of activities based on the themes of capacity building and education, to promote the protection of biodiversity through understanding the planet's ecology and history". The partnership is "based on the philosophy that relationships between business and non-government organizations with compatible activities and interests can provide significant benefits for both organizations, as well as the wider community".

6.1. Desired Outcomes

There are four main desired outcomes of the Partnership Agreement:

- To increase scientific data and improved conservation outcomes on a range of issues relevant to both Earthwatch and Rio Tinto globally.
- To enhance scientific capacity in developing countries.
- To increase awareness among Rio Tinto employees and stakeholders of the role played by Earthwatch and Rio Tinto in promoting environmental outcomes.
- To increase public understanding of biodiversity and the issues surrounding conservation.

6.2. Programmes

The following programmes are in place in order to achieve these desired outcomes:

- Field research involving Rio Tinto employees being awarded an Employee Fellowship to take part in selected Earthwatch Institute projects around the world.
- Capacity building fellowships for country nationals in developing countries – currently Africa and Indonesia.
- Public education and stakeholder communication events.
- Support for scientific programme development.

6.3. Employee Fellowship Programme

The aim of Earthwatch Institute (Europe) is to offer an Employee Fellowship to 12 Rio Tinto employees from operations in Europe, Africa, and North America each year. Earthwatch Institute (Australia) recruits Fellows from Rio Tinto operations in Australia, Asia and South America, and similarly, offers 12 Fellowships each year. Two thousand information packs are sent out each year covering both areas, together with publicity material, posters, etc., and candidates complete a formal application.

In 1999 from the 1000 packs sent out by Earthwatch Institute (Europe), 64 Rio Tinto employees applied and the following year saw a significant increase in interest with 99 applying and in 2001, 102 applied. Similarly, in 1999, 71 employees applied through Earthwatch Institute (Australia) with an increase to 133 in 2000 and 167 in 2001. Any employee can apply, and so far, successful Fellows have come from a wide range of roles within Rio Tinto companies.

Both Earthwatch Institute (Europe) and Earthwatch Institute (Australia) report that the main reasons candidates apply is to gain:

- Increased environmental awareness;
- Increased cultural awareness;
- An increased reputation for the company;
- An opportunity to contribute to international projects.

This was tested in December 2000 when Earthwatch Institute (Europe) surveyed the 24 Fellows of 1999–2000. From 13 returned surveys it was confirmed that:

- 77% applied because of interest in the environment;
- 77% because of an opportunity to contribute to environmental research;
- 69% because of the challenges posed;

- 62% thought that the programme developed environmental ambassadors for the company;
- with 69% saying that the programme shows an enhanced company commitment to the environment;
- and 77% that it increased employee awareness of environmental issues.

Earthwatch Institute (Australia) gained similar results where, out of a maximum score of 5, the average score from fellows surveyed was:

- Experience of international team work – 4.9;
- Benefits to personal knowledge – 4.6;
- Benefits to professional knowledge – 3.9;
- Overall experience – 4.6.

These results from both Europe and Australia correlate (qualitatively) well with the three main desired outputs of the Fellowship Programme for Rio Tinto, namely:

- Personal development of Rio Tinto employees, including cross-cultural awareness;
- Improved environmental literacy and understanding of employees;
- Raised awareness among all employees of the company's support for the environment and the Rio Tinto Earthwatch Partnership.

Each successful Fellow

- joins a specific Earthwatch Field Research Project, (six projects are supported each year);
- acts as a field assistant to the scientists involved;
- completes a detailed report on return;
- completes a short evaluation survey;
- presents a talk (or talks) to colleagues.

Of the Fellows so far (1999–2001), all had given a talk to their colleagues, 92% had written something for an internal publication, and 69% were involved in voluntary activities in their local communities.

From 1999–2001, 36 Rio Tinto employees have been awarded fellowships to take part in Earthwatch Institute Field research projects. The projects covered in 1999–2001, selected, with input from Rio Tinto London and Rio Tinto Melbourne, from a total of 140 Earthwatch Institute projects in 50 countries were:

- Kenya's Wild Heritage;
- Great Russian Lakes;
- Conserving the Rainforests of Kalimantan;
- Conserving Platypus in Agricultural Landscapes;

- Brazil's Rainforest Wildlife;
- Zambia's Park Survey;
- Bees and Orchids of Brazil;
- Green Turtles of Malaysia;
- Australia's Forest Wildlife and Ecology;
- Australia's Vanishing Frogs;
- Cameroon's Rainforests;
- Icelandic Glaciers.

Fellowships were awarded/offered in 1999–2001 to employees in the following companies of the group:

- Anglesey Aluminium Metal;
- Argyle Diamonds;
- Borax Europe;
- Boyne Smelters;
- Coal and Allied;
- Comalco (Qld);
- Comalco (Tas);
- Cordero Rojo Complex/Kennecott Energy;
- Dampier Salt;
- Hamersley Iron;
- Iron Ore Company of Canada;
- Jacobs Ranch Mine/Kennecott Energy;
- KEM Indonesia;
- Kennecott Energy – Colowyo Coal;
- Kennecott Utah Copper;
- KPC Indonesia;
- New Zealand Aluminium Smelters;
- Pacific Coal;
- Palabora Mining Company;
- QIT Fer et Titane Inc.;
- QIT Madagascar Minerals;
- Richards Bay Minerals;
- Rio Paracatu Mineracao;
- Rio Tinto Coal;
- Rio Tinto Foundation;
- Rio Tinto Indonesia;
- Rio Tinto Iron and Titanium;
- Rio Tinto Melbourne;
- Rio Tinto London;

- Rio Tinto Technical Services;
- Rio Tinto Zimbabwe;
- Rossing Uranium;
- Spring Creek/Kennecott Energy;
- TBN Paraguay.

6.4. Fellowship Benefits

By 2001, 48 Rio Tinto employees had been placed for two weeks in Earthwatch projects around the world, coming from a wide range of companies in the group, from all over the world. I asked each of these 48 Fellows, through a simple survey, "What do you believe you have contributed to Rio into and the wider community from your involvement on the Fellowship Program?" and received the following responses:

- Realistic appreciations of challenges;
- A positive perspective on Earthwatch and its goals;
- Recognition of Rio Tinto's values and commitment to environmental issues;
- Ability to communicate the values of Earthwatch to Rio Tinto colleagues;
- Recommending to others this sort of involvement;
- Recognising different perspectives and perceptions;
- Reinforcing Rio Tinto's commitment to the environment;
- Better recognising that the environment is a global issue;
- Increased customer and community awareness of Rio Tinto's environmental efforts;
- Increasing internal environmental awareness in Rio Tinto;
- Encouraging colleagues to become involved;
- Getting people at work thinking and talking about the issues more;
- Spreading knowledge;
- Helping to promote Rio Tinto as a company who cares about the environment and which actually contributes something back to the environment;
- Eroding preconceptions of others;
- Promoting Rio Tinto in the local community;
- Enthusiastically sharing the experience amongst family, friends and colleagues;
- Better understanding underprivileged communities;
- Recognising the dedication and commitment of scientists and others to this work;
- Raising environmental awareness;
- Sharing Information;
- Meeting people from different cultures;

- Boosting Rio Tinto's image;
- Resolution of problems requires cooperation and unified approach;
- Better understanding biodiversity;
- Better awareness of the fragility of the environment;

6.5. *Capacity Building Programme*

The object of the Capacity Building Programmes is to provide training in field research skills specifically in the identification and conservation of biodiversity for developing country nationals involved in their normal work as research staff, NGO workers, protected area managers and other relevant positions, using Earthwatch projects as training sites. Earthwatch Institute (Europe) operates a programme in Africa and Earthwatch Institute (Australia) operates one in Indonesia. Earthwatch Institute (Australia) clearly states the objective on its application form:

"An opportunity for Indonesians working in science, conservation or natural resource management to gain hands-on experience working for two weeks as part of an international team of participants on a professional field research project".

The aim is to:

- Increase the Fellows' field experience and data collection abilities;
- Increase the Fellows' understanding of local and global environmental issues;
- Increase the Fellows' contacts with international scientists and other disciplines of fieldwork.

On returning from the project placement each fellow is asked to complete a project evaluation form.

Twenty-five country nationals from Africa have already participated through Earthwatch Institute (Europe) (1999–2000) in the context of the Rio Tinto partnership, though many more have been involved in the programme that pre-existed the Rio Tinto partnership, and a further 11 participated in 2001. This is, in fact, an example of where Rio Tinto London accepted a programme that was already in place and which may not necessarily have suited its best interests (Brazil would probably have been more relevant to Rio Tinto London than Africa). It is likely that the Partnership itself, and its other benefits, became more important than Rio Tinto insisting on establishing a specific program more relevant to its direct interests. The fact that Earthwatch Institute (Europe) could resist Rio Tinto's request for a capacity building programme in Brazil, for example, would suggest either a very strong indication of the strength of the relationship between the two organizations, or that those requests were not pressed very strongly, or, more likely, a combination of both, indicating overall that a healthy and dynamic dialogue partnership exists between the two parties. The challenge to Rio Tinto is how to add value to this particular capacity building program so that it makes sense to Rio Tinto's stakeholders as part of the company's overall approach to sustainability and good corporate citizenship.

Fellows were selected by Earthwatch Institute partner organizations in Madagascar, Namibia, South Africa, Uganda and Zimbabwe, involving projects in Tanzania, Kenya, Cameroon, Zambia and South Africa, and in 2001, Ghana covering

- Tanzanian Forest Birds;
- Rare Plants of Kenya;
- Cameroon's Rain Forests;
- Zambia's Park Survey;
- South African Wildlife;
- Ghana's Hippo Sanctuary.

Visits have also been made to QMM Madagascar, Rossing Foundation, Windhoek, Namibia and Palabora Foundation, South Africa.

A total of 11 fellows from Indonesia have been placed by Earthwatch Institute (Australia) (three in 1999 and four in 2000) and four placed in 2001. Forty-two applied in 1999 with six Fellowships offered. Of these, three withdrew with the others drawn from conservation NGOs, Government and a National Park. After some revisions to the programme, enabling it to concentrate much more on NGO capacity building, 10 applications were received in 2000, with four Fellows accepted, all from NGOs. Two have since gone onto pursue Ph.D.s. There were 44 applicants in 2001. The Indonesian Fellows were involved in the following projects.

- Saving Borneo's Rainforest;
- Green Turtles of Malaysia;
- Australia's Vanishing Frogs;
- Kakadu's Waterbirds.

And in 2001

- Saving Philippine's Coral Reefs.

Earthwatch Institute (Europe) considers, through evaluations with the Fellows so far, that the benefits to individual Fellows (out of a maximum score of 5 and rated as follows) are:

- Experience of international teamwork (4.2);
- Benefits to institution/community (4.3);
- Enhancement of personal knowledge (4.45);

- Enhancement of professional knowledge (4.25);
- The overall experience (4.25).

Unlike Earthwatch Institute (Europe), Earthwatch Institute (Australia) has only been involved with the capacity building fellowship programme in Indonesia since 1999, whereas the Rio Tinto/Earthwatch Institute (Europe) Africa programme, is part of a much larger African Fellowship programme in place before the signing of the July 1999 Global Partnership Agreement, and unlike their European counterpart Earthwatch Australia, have much fewer resources to apply to what is still a developing programme.

While Rio Tinto's environmental policies would still be developed, whether or not the partnership exists, it is generally acknowledged that a leading benefit of the partnership is the confidence gained in knowing that the development of those policies is firmly grounded on leading edge environmental relationships with leading edge stakeholders. The balance that needs to be established, however, is one where Earthwatch Institute is not seen simply as a de facto consultant to Rio Tinto but a serious mutual stakeholder.

Rio Tinto see the benefits of the partnership within the context of enabling policy formulation, for example, the developing biodiversity strategy, to be carried out from a platform of confidence gained from knowing that (though not always necessarily formally using) the expertise of a leading global NGO is available. Membership of the Corporate Environmental Responsibility Group, established by Earthwatch Institute (Europe), gives Rio Tinto access to seminars, other corporates and leading edge developments and information, and positions the company, along with its many other commitments in this area, at the leading edge of environmental issues. In turn, it is acknowledged by Earthwatch that a significant partnership with a major company like Rio Tinto helps considerably in its developing professionalisation as a global NGO – not least of which comes from Rio Tinto's expectations of Earthwatch's performance.

Rio Tinto, therefore, sees the Earthwatch partnership much more within the context of a world's best practice "Business with Communities" program, where much wider and more potentially "risky" stakeholder driven concerns are an every-day reality for mining operations. Partnering with a leading environmental NGO like Earthwatch enables these stakeholder concerns to be fully on the agenda – and similarly, the partnership gives Earthwatch access to Rio Tinto business units and communities it might otherwise have more difficulty accessing. Increasingly, though, as a result of the partnership, all parties are recognising that each is a stakeholder of the other, which, in turn, acts as a powerful model for the development of other relationships on both sides.

7. MUTUAL STAKEHOLDER RELATIONS AS AN ENABLING ENVIRONMENT FOR NEW WAYS OF DOING BUSINESS

There are significant opportunities, then, for Rio Tinto to contribute in a major way to the development of new thinking about business community partnerships by further developing a role for expert NGOs and other organizations who, in long-term relationship building with Rio Tinto, can contribute effectively in a partnership where each recognises the other as committed mutual stakeholders of their respective organizations. Currently this is taking place with very significant partnerships in the Rio Tinto "Business with Communities" program involving WWF; Conservation Volunteers; The Australian Science Olympiads; The Centre for Appropriate Technologies, Alice Springs; The Royal Botanic Gardens, Kew; Birdlife International and The World Conservation Monitoring Centre. As John Hall, Manager of Corporate Relations Rio Tinto Australia, says, "While it remains fashionable in some quarters to be cynical and dismissive of corporate initiative in the social sphere, often from an ideological perspective, that view is increasingly outmoded and wrong. The days when companies could rest on their technical and commercial competence, and leave other issues to governments and bureaucracies, are over – particularly for businesses operating internationally" (Hall, 2002, p. 12).

Organisations involved in a long-term business community partnership need, therefore, to recognise, as Rio Tinto has done, that these are not the same relationships as short term financial transactions. They go beyond fund-raising and good corporate PR. Both organizations need to be able to fully engage with the consequences of how such partnerships can constitute core business to both organizations, especially with respect to the disciplined management and development of both the partnership itself and the various programs and activities that may exist within the partnership. To do that, both organizations need to understand each other's business, mission and strategic directions on how each intends to "grow their business" in the future. They need to understand the partnership as a strategic capital investment – financial, cultural, intellectual, reputational capital, for example – and understand, therefore, each other's strategic purpose in developing a long-term business community partnership.

Jane Nelson, one of the world's leading experts on business community partnerships, argues that such partnerships are "very much about a new way of doing business" (Nelson, 1996, p. 19). She argues that we have only just seen the beginning of this crucial trend. "Business leaders of the future", she says, "will need to be skilled partnership builders" (Nelson, 1996, p. 19), making the important point that "the creation of shareholder value and societal value are not mutually exclusive and are in fact mutually reinforcing in many cases" (Nelson, 1996, p. 23). Without necessarily referring to Jane Nelson's specific work, Rio Tinto in the past ten years or so, have sought to build a "Business with Communities" program that has at its very heart the understanding that "the creation of shareholder value and societal value are not mutually exclusive". Not because it sees itself as a do-gooding company, but because it sees very good business sense for all sectors of society to be able to work together strategically to grow business together in sustainable ways.

Nelson concludes in her report with Simon Zadek, *Partnership Alchemy*, (Nelson & Zadek, 2000) that "New social partnerships are not a panacea. Nor are they easy. Even when they have the potential to solve a particular societal problem or set of problems, they often fail".

As the Copenhagen Centre makes clear: "The future of the social partnership depends critically on whether it can prove capable of delivering societal benefits that cannot be achieved more effectively through other means. To be effective it will need to demonstrate clear added value at the local level in building sustainable livelihoods and improving quality of life in a way that actively and practically engages local communities and beneficiary groups and also, at the strategic level, in helping national and international government bodies to create an enabling environment for addressing socio economic problems". It's too early to say whether Rio Tinto have achieved this, but they have started by putting programs in place which take a major step in developing appropriate enabling environments to develop.

There are seriously significant opportunities for organizations to create such an enabling environment, not only for their own interests, but also for significant social and environmental – multiple bottom lines – benefits. What this effectively means, therefore, is for both organizations to leverage added value from a partnership – in better, and more clearly articulated and strategic ways than perhaps has been done so far – to ensure that the rhetoric of corporate social responsibility espoused by senior executives of companies will, one day, via the vehicle of strategic corporate citizenship, and the enabling environment it creates for the learning of new cultural vocabularies, be effectively translated into the everyday reality of core business.

8. CONCLUSION

There is no doubt that developments in corporate citizenship and sustainability are taking place, in some companies at least, at a fairly rapid rate now. The number of external agencies, guidelines, standards, principles and codes is multiplying quickly, and many companies are signing up to them. Rio Tinto has clearly demonstrated at its most senior executive level a significant commitment to these developments. It has translated these commitments into policies, and publicly declared its commitment through its mandatory and non-mandatory reports each year. Furthermore, it has sought ways to engage with the communities in which it operates, and those which consider themselves to have either a direct or indirect interest in Rio Tinto's affairs, and has actively developed a comprehensive approach to stakeholder engagement, out of which has emerged the "Business with Communities" program which seeks to establish long-term partnerships with some of those key stakeholders. This partnership program has the potential to act as a significant enabling environment for the sharing and learning of new cultural vocabularies, through which the vision of the senior executives of the company can be translated into everyday core business. The following Circle of Corporate Citizenship demonstrates the strengths so far of developments in this area in the Company, but marks out one connection (to the Businesses themselves) which needs to be strengthened in the future if the vision of the leadership of Rio Tinto is to find a way of being embedded more fully into core business activity (Fig. 1).

It is by better connecting the enabling environment of the "Business with Communities" program to the individual businesses of the Company that Rio Tinto now has a major opportunity for ensuring that the vision of its leaders like Sir Robert Wilson, Leigh Clifford, Leon Davies and others, becomes an everyday reality for all of its employees in all of its businesses. For example, more value

Fig. 1.   Circle of Corporate Citizenship.

could be added to the Fellows of the Rio Tinto/Earthwatch partnership as they return to the many businesses of the Group that they represent. It is these people, and others like them involved in other partnerships, that can actually help ensure that the new vocabularies that are being learned can move from the corporate entity into the day to day activities of the businesses. Building upon their experiences on the Earthwatch Fellowship program, these Fellows can help drive and establish new agendas of community/stakeholder partnerships and relationships within the businesses themselves, making the link between partnerships as an enabling environment at the corporate level to the everyday core activities of the businesses.

Without this absolutely crucial link, the equation that will enable the vision of corporate social responsibility to become the everyday reality of Rio Tinto's core business will never be completed. People are the link that will enable the vision to become core business. There is clearly no shortage of people in Rio Tinto wanting to learn new cultural vocabularies; the key strategic challenge for the company to maintain its leading edge developments in corporate social responsibility and sustainability, is, therefore to add value to these people through the growth of business-oriented strategic corporate citizenship. This is the missing link, so far, in Rio Tinto's corporate citizenship profile, and one which it is very well placed to complete, difficult though the development of such partnerships and relationships may be.

NOTES

1. Current partnerships in Australia for example include the Australian Science Olympiads, Conservation Volunteers Australia, Centre for Appropriate Technology, Alice Springs, Earthwatch Institute (Australia) and World Wide Fund for Nature, Australia. Others worldwide include Birdlife International, BTCV, Kew Gardens and Earthwatch Institute (Europe).

2. Current Rio Tinto Community Trusts and Foundations in Australia directly involving Rio Tinto businesses include Central Highlands Community Employment Trust (Pacific Coal); Coal and Allied Community Trust; Tarong Coal Community Development Fund and the Rio Tinto Aboriginal Foundation.

3. Some of the most significant Rio Tinto agreements with government organisations in Australia include a 1998 MOU with the Aboriginal and Torres Strait Islander Commision (ATSIC) and 1998 MOUs with the then named Department of Education, Training and Youth Affairs (DETYA), and the Department of Employment Workplace Relations and Small Business (DEWRSB).

REFERENCES

Birch, D. (2001a). Corporate citizenship. Rethinking business beyond corporate social responsibility. In: J. Andriof & M. McIntosh (Eds), *Perspectives on Corporate Citizenship* (pp. 53–65). London: Greenleaf Publishing.

Birch, D. (Ed.) (2001b). Strategic corporate citizenship. Proceedings of the Second National Conference on Corporate Citizenship (16–17th November 2000). Corporate Citizenship Research Unit, Deakin University, Melbourne.

Birch, D. (Ed.) (2001c). Australasian perspectives on corporate citizenship. *Journal of Corporate Citizenship, 4* (Winter, special issue).

Birch, D. (2002). Social, economic and environmental capital: Corporate citizenship in a new economy. *Alternative Law Journal, 27*(1), 3–6.

Birch, D., & Glazebrook, M. (2000). Doing business – Doing culture: Corporate citizenship and community. In: S. Rees & S. Wright (Eds), *Human Rights, Corporate Responsibility. A Dialogue* (pp. 41–52). Annandale: Pluto Press.

Copenhagen Centre (2000). Publicity flyer for Nelson & Zadek.

Dabkowski, S. (2001). Profit is not king, survey shows. *The Age* (Business Monday, August 20), 1.

Davis, L. A. (2001). The social responsibility of corporations. *The Corporate Citizen, 1*(4), 2–8.

Duncan, T., & Fenney, H. (2000). Business with communities – A strategic approach to corporate philanthropy. Unpublished paper, Rio Tinto, Melbourne.

Gilmour, J. (2002). Can partnerships be an agent for change in corporations? *Alternative Law Journal, 27*(1), 11–12.

Hall, J. (2002). The social responsibility of corporations. *Alternative Law Journal, 27*(1), 12–15.

Holme, R., & Watts, P. (2000). *Corporate social responsibility: Making good business sense.* WBCSD http://www.wbcsd.org

ICEM (1998). *Rio Tinto. Behind the façade. 1998 stakeholders report.* International Federation of Chemical, Energy, Mine and General Workers' Unions. Brussels.

International Council on Metals and the Environment (1998). *Changing values, changing corporate cultures: The way forward, an illustrative framework for the mining and metals industry.* ICME, Ottawa, http://www.icme.com

Little, A. D. (2001). *The business case for corporate citizenship.* http://www.weforum.org/corporatecitizenship

Nelson, J. (1996). *Business as partners in development creating wealth for countries, companies and communities.* The Prince of Wales Business Leaders Forum with the World Bank and the United Nations Development Program, London.

Nelson, J., & Zadek, S. (2000). *Partnership alchemy. New society partnerships in Europe.* Copenhagen Centre, Copenhagen.

Rio Tinto (1999). *Rio Tinto in Australia – Community survey.* Melbourne.

Rio Tinto (2000). *Social and environment review.* London: Rio Tinto Plc.; Melbourne: Rio Tinto Ltd.

Rio Tinto (2001a). *Corporate citizenship in Australia. The Rio Tinto Business with communities program.* Melbourne: Rio Tinto Ltd.

Rio Tinto (2001b). *Community relations. Global business, local neighbour.* London: Rio Tinto Plc.; Melbourne: Rio Tinto Ltd.

Rio Tinto (undated). *Communities policy guidelines.* London: Rio Tinto Plc.; Melbourne: Rio Tinto Ltd.

Rose, J. (2001). Blame it on the Rio Tinto movement. *The Australian Financial Review* (12–16 April), 10.

Warhurst, A. (2001). Corporate citizenship and corporate social investment: Drivers of tri-sector partnerships. MERN Mining and Energy Research Network. Warwick, U.K.: Warwick Business School.

Wilson, R. (1999). The mining industry: In recuperation or revision. unpublished paper delivered at the Securities Institute of Australia, Melbourne (7 December).

Wilson, S. R. (2000). Big business: Neither sinner nor saviour. *Visions of Ethical Business 3, Financial Times*, Warwick Business School in Association with Price WaterHouseCoopers and the Council on Economic Priorities, London, 17–19.

Wilson, S. R. (2002). Interview. *Ethical Corporation* (Issue 2, January), 4–5.

World Business Council for Sustainable Development (2002). *The Business case for sustainable development. Making a difference toward Johannesburg 2002* http://www.wbcsd.org

World Economic Forum (2002). *Global corporate citizenship: The leadership challenge for CEOs and boards.* WEF, Geneva, January http://www.weforum.org

Zadek, S. (2001a). *Third generation corporate citizenship. Public policy and business in society.* The Foreign Policy Centre in association with AccountAbility, London.

Zadek, S. (2001b). *The civil corporation. The new economy of corporate citizenship.* Earthscan in association with the New Economics Foundation, London.

Zadek, S., Hojensgard, N., & Raynard, P. (2000). *The new economy of corporate citizenship.* The Copenhagen Centre, Copenhagen.

ROLE OF CIVIL SOCIETY IN TRADE NEGOTIATIONS: A CASE STUDY OF FOOD SAFETY REGULATIONS

Tracy Murray and Maryvonne Lassalle-de Salins

1. INTRODUCTION

Mike Moore (1999), Director-General of the World Trade Organization (WTO), warned that if governments and international organizations are not inclusive to civil society and their concerns, they cannot expect public support for trade policies. This warning occurred one month prior to the Ministerial Meeting of the WTO in Seattle. We all know of the outcome of that meeting, and subsequent meetings of international economic organizations in Washington, DC, Prague, and Quebec City, to name only a few.

The Uruguay Round opened to the silence of public apathy. The early negotiations only drew the attention of those significantly and directly affected by the outcomes. But times have changed. Hundreds of non-governmental organizations (NGOs) are now concerned about the issues of globalization and international trading relationships. Some groups criticize what they think is wrong with globalization while others are providing suggestions for improved outcomes. Both groups, however, perceive that the interests of the many are being excluded, i.e. that there is a democracy deficit.

The result has been protest. The protestors come from many walks of life including trade unions fearing for jobs, farmers seeking a continuation of their subsidies, environmentalists concerned about ecological degradation and biodiversity, humanitarians calling for improved living conditions for the poor,

Social Responsibility: Corporate Governance Issues
Research in International Business and Finance, Volume 17, 369–382
ISSN: 0275-5319/PII: S027553190317016X

supporters of animal rights and endangered species, and the list goes on. The views of the various NGOs are often contradictory, and some even internally inconsistent. The protestors mainly come from rich countries, but their interests are often global. Not all of civil society is civil, but neither is all of civil society wrong. Some NGOs are well intended, professionally managed, better funded than many of the governmental agencies dealing with particular international economic policy negotiations. Many NGOs have something of value to contribute.

By civil society we normally refer to national, regional or international organizations that are not related to a government or group of governments. They typically are self organized, self financed and not-for-profit; some are more democratic than others. We will generally use an inclusive definition. Civil society will include industry associations, labor unions, consumer associations, parties directly or indirectly affected by a particular trade issue, and parties that are vocal in order to draw attention to unrelated issues. For example, proponents of animal rights may be vocal in negotiations relating to food safety even though animal abuse is unrelated to the safety of food derived from animals.

In Mike Moore's address he quoted President Clinton: "Globalization is a reality not a policy option". It cannot be stopped by international agreement or by national policies. But more important, globalization is not all bad. The challenge is not to design policies to slow the rate of globalization, rather it is to design policies to harness the benefits of globalization and to achieve the socio-economic objectives of both the rich and poor countries. In so doing we must recognize that cultural values often come into conflict with trade considerations (Echols, 2001).

2. GLOBALIZATION, GOVERNANCE AND CIVIL SOCIETY

The international rules governing trade are mainly negotiated in the World Trade Organization. The resulting rules sometimes conflict with national rules governing commerce and, therefore, impinge on national sovereignty and impose costs on importing countries such as lost jobs, lower safety or quality of products, and lower environmental qualities. On the other hand, international trade is mutually beneficial. Moreover, international cooperation that promotes increases in the volumes of trade, increases the gains from trade. While these outcomes are undeniable, it is also true that increased trade alters the distribution of income within nations. This leads to special interest preferences for greater or lesser trade targeted to specific sectors. But it also leads to concerns of others about the impact of trade on the poor, the environment, the quality and safety of goods available in the market, endangered species, animal welfare, sustainable development, quality of life, human rights, child labor, fair working conditions, fair pricing of commodities, and so on.

Intergovernmental organizations (IGOs) are institutions whose membership consists of governments. It is governments who send representatives to meetings, these representatives present positions of their governments, and it is governments who decided the outcomes. In most IGOs some governments have greater influence than others. It is also true that some governments are more democratic than others. Civil society claims that international negotiations fail to incorporate the views of the many and pay too much attention to the views of the few powerful self-interest groups. The leaders of various civil society organizations argue that the omission of the views of the many is unacceptable. And as long as the views of the many are omitted, the general public will not consider the outcomes of international trade negotiations to be in their interest. Protests will become more frequent and more deafening.

Some member governments would argue that they have procedures to provide opportunities for civil society to participate in the process of establishing national positions on issues under negotiation in international fora. If all member governments were to do the same, the views of civil society would be included in IGO decision-making. However, problems would still exist. The heavy weight of special interest groups in establishing national positions is still prevalent. And what about voting. Assuming one country one vote, the vote of one Icelander (population 300,000) would count more than the votes of 4,000 Chinese (population 1.27 billion). Of course, alternative voting schemes could and have been designed to reduce this problem.

But clearly global governance is complex. Many global problems are difficult to solve on the basis of bilateral agreements among sovereign governments. And no one today is seriously proposing the creation of a global government. IGOs are one approach to addressing these problems.

The remainder of this paper reports a case study of a particular IGO in which various groups from civil society have participated for many years. The IGO of concern is the *Codex Alimentarius*. Briefly, this is an effort to establish international food standards to upgrade the quality and safety of food in poor countries, to protect the health of humans and to contribute to fair practices in food trade.

3. CODEX ALIMENTARIUS: A CASE STUDY

3.1. Brief History of Codex

Since the early ages governing authorities have been codifying rules to protect consumers from dishonest practices in the sale and trade of food products. These early concerns included correct weights and measures for food grains, purity of beer and wines, and systems to protect consumers from fraud or bad produce. During the Middle Ages, European countries set standards for the quality and safety of eggs, sausages, cheese, beer, wine and bread (Codex, 1999). Early modern laws (e.g. Great Britain in 1860 and France in 1905) also dealt with the prevention of fraud. The first U.S. law dealing with food safety per se was enacted in 1906 in response to reports of horrible and unsanitary working conditions in the U.S. meat packing industry.[1]

Over time national laws become more comprehensive. By the early 1900s long-distance transportation of food (chilled and frozen) became feasible. However, the differences in national standards became trade barriers that were of increasing concern to the early food traders. Food trade associations (e.g. The International Dairy Federation founded in 1903) developed international standards (including efforts toward the harmonization of national standards) to facilitate international trade in food.

Consumers' concerns were also to play a role. In the 1940s significant advances were made in food science and technology. Knowledge about the quality and health hazards of food became widely disseminated. Most of this information was designed to assist consumers to obtain safer, more nutritious and cost effective foods. However, some of the reporting was sensationalistic and incorrect. Regardless of the purpose of the information, it did raise public awareness and concerns about food safety. This awareness went beyond the traditional concerns such as underweight content, size variations, misleading labelling and poor quality. The new awareness often emphasized the invisible attributes, e.g. health hazards which could not be seen, smelled or tasted, such as micro-organisms, pesticide residues, environmental contaminants and food additives.

In the mid-1950s, Austria actively pursued the creation of a regional food code for Europe called Codex Alimentarius Europaeus.[2] In 1960 a regional conference for Europe was sponsored by the FAO; this conference endorsed the concept of international minimal food standards. Pursuant to resolutions adopted by the Food and Agricultural Organization of the United Nations (FAO) in 1961 and the World Health Organization (WHO) in 1963, the Joint FAO/WHO Programme on Food Standards was created resulting in the *Codex Alimentarius* system of food standards. The primary purposes of the *Codex Alimentarius* are to protect the health of consumers and ensure fair practices in food trade (Codex, 1999, Article 1).

The term "Codex" has dual meanings. It refers to the Codex Alimentarius Commission which oversees the work programme; it also refers to the Codex Alimentarius which is a ledger where food standards, guidelines and recommendations are registered. The desired outcome is a set of harmonized international food standards that all countries might adopt. This effort involves an international sharing of information on available technologies to improve the safety and quality of food which, in turn, contributes to an improvement in the safety and quality of food supplies in developing countries. The harmonization of food standards also reduces barriers to trade resulting from food safety regulations.

3.2. Codex and the WTO

In the beginning, Codex was a relatively unknown programme of meetings of government officials and industry advisors. However, the completion of the Uruguay Round and creation of the World Trade Organization (WTO) beginning January 1, 1995, has forever altered national food safety regulation. From the beginning of the Uruguay Round negotiations it was recognized that a trade liberalizing Agriculture Agreement that increased disciplines on non-tariff measures applied to trade in agricultural products might be countered by governments resorting to other regulations to protect domestic markets (Josling & Warley, 1996). It was further determined that the Technical Barriers to Trade Agreement of the Tokyo Round was inadequate. Food safety risks often vary by source country and by destination country. Thus, measures to deal with such risks might violate the "most-favored nation" and "national treatment" provisions. Thus, a separate agreement was needed to deal with sanitary and phytosanitary measures (Roberts, 2001).

Under the WTO Agreement on the Application of Sanitary and Phytosanitary Measures (SPS Agreement), member countries do retain the right to regulate food production and marketing for the protection of human health. On the other hand, the SPS Agreement requires that such measures be transparent, consistent and based on science; moreover, if alternative measures are available to achieve the same level of protection, the country is to choose those measures having the least restrictive effects on trade. Members are encouraged to based their SPS measures on international standards.[3] Members may have SPS measures that provide a higher level of SPS protection than would exist under international standards provided there is scientific justification or the SPS measures are based on a risk analysis that is appropriate for the circumstances of the country.

The SPS Agreement has created a conflict between national sovereignty and international obligations, partly owing to imprecise language in the agreement and partly to the differences across countries in the trade-offs between food safety and other aspects of food production and marketing. This has resulted in a number of allegations filed before the WTO Dispute Settlements Body. In resolving such disputes, the SPS Agreement states:

> Sanitary or phytosanitary measures which conform to international standards, guidelines or recommendations shall be deemed to be necessary to protect human, animal or plant life or

health, and presumed to be consistent with the relevant provisions of this Agreement of the
GATT 1994 (WTO, 1995, Article 3.2).

Consequently, Codex standards have become a reference point for resolving
WTO disputes. In those cases involving higher national SPS measures the WTO
Dispute Settlements Panels and Appellate Bodies have carefully addressed the
justifications for the higher level of protection, i.e. science and risk analysis
(Goh & Ziegler, 2001; Stanton, 2001; Victor, 2000).

The resolution of these disputes has required governments in some cases to
modify or reform certain national food safety regulations. The central role played
by Codex international standards has raised the stakes for Codex deliberations.
And as a consequence, the Codex programme itself has taken on a much higher
profile.

It is important to note that this paper is about trade negotiations, yet the case
study involves an IGO that is more concerned with safety of humans than the
trade implications per se. While the deliberations leading to the elaboration of
international food standards emphasize science rather than costs and prices, there is
an undeniable link between the resulting national food safety regulations and trade.
It is this link and the new emphasis placed on Codex standards by the WTO Dispute
Settlements process that makes Codex deliberations pseudo trade negotiations.
Clearly, the trade implications of potential Codex standards are uppermost in the
minds of national representatives involved in Codex decision-making.

3.3. How the Codex Works

The scope of the work programme is quite complex. It covers a wide range of
issues such as food standards for commodities, guidelines for contaminants,
codes for hygienic or technological practices, the evaluation of pesticides, food
additives and veterinary drugs, etc. It is also an ongoing process because new
food products are being developed continuously and new scientific discoveries
provide new technologies related to food safety.

The organizational structure of Codex is complex as well. The top authority
is the Codex Alimentarius Commission (CAC) which meets every other year.
An Executive Committee has been established to manage the work programme
between CAC sessions. The main work is accomplished by subsidiary committees
which meet regularly. The committees include general subject committees,
commodity committees, ad hoc intergovernmental task forces, and regional
coordinating committees. The general committees deal with issues that apply
across commodities such as general principles, methods of analysis and sampling,
pesticide residues, food additives, and food import and export inspection and

certification. Commodity committees deal with standards applicable to specific commodities, e.g. fats and oils, milk and milk products, etc. Ad hoc task forces function like committees but with narrow terms of reference and precise objectives; they are established for limited time periods. Regional coordinating committees deal with issues of importance to a specific group of countries. Since many questions are relevant to different committees there is a complex linkage across committees. Issues are often sent from one committee to another and back in an interactive fashion. For example, the committee on food additives may suggest labelling, which requires that the draft standard also be reviewed by the committee on food labelling.

The decision-making process is straightforward. It is initiated by CAC or the Executive Committee with a decision to establish a Codex standard. A proposed draft standard is prepared and sent to the Members and observers for comment. The relevant Committee reviews the comments and prepares a revised proposed draft standard for submission to CAC or the Executive Committee. If the proposed draft standard is adopted by the CAC or the Executive Committee it becomes a draft standard. The above process is repeated with the revised draft standard being submitted to CAC. If the draft standard is adopted by CAC it becomes a Codex standard. If there is no consensus on the draft standard it may remain at a given stage in the process or it may be returned to a prior stage to prepare a revised draft standard to be sent to the Members and observers for comment.[4]

Once a Codex standard has been established by CAC, it is entered into the *Codex Alimentarius* ledger. Members are to submit notifications regarding their adoption of the standard. Members have four options:

(1) Full Acceptance: The Codex standard is incorporated into the Member's national food safety regulations; food products which meet the standard (both imported and domestically produced) can be sold in the country and food products that do not meet the standard cannot be sold.

(2) Acceptance With Specific Deviations: The Member notifies which aspects of the Codex standard it does not accept, typically because there are differences between the Codex standard and existing national food safety regulations.

(3) Free Distribution: The Member does not accept the Codex standards but will allow food products that meet the Codex standard to be sold. For example, if the national standards are lower than the Codex standard, imported products meeting Codex standards can be sold without changing conditions for domestic producers who meet the existing lower national standards.

(4) Do Not Accept: The Member will not incorporate the Codex standard into the Member's food safety regulations. Members who have higher existing national food safety regulations are reluctant to adopt the lower Codex standards.

In many cases the industrialized countries have existing food safety regulations that provide a higher level of protection than Codex standards. In such cases the Member might not accept the Codex standards. On the other hand, many developing countries do not have comparable food safety regulations. Thus, many developing countries use Codex standards as a basis for national food regulations.

The membership of the CAC is open to all Members of FAO and WHO which have notified their desire to be a Member of CAC. However, not all eligible countries chose to actively participate in Codex. In 1963, there were roughly 30 Members who were active in Codex – 20 industrialized countries and 10 developing countries. By 1989 country participation increased but still less than 40 developing countries participated. Since almost all of the industrialized countries have participated from the beginning, their numbers have not changed. During the past decade Member participation in Codex has increased dramatically. Today, 167 countries are Members of CAC (23 industrialized countries and 144 developing countries). At the last meeting of the CAC held in Geneva in 2001, 21 industrialized countries and 65 developing countries were present.[5]

Countries which are not members of FAO or WHO but are Members of the United Nations can request observer status. IGOs and International Non-Governmental Organizations (INGOs) can also request observer status.[6] Observers can submit documents and participate in sessions but cannot actively take part in decision-making or vote. Member delegations are led by an official of the government but can include alternates and advisors including advisors from industry, technical experts, academicians and consumer representatives. There are currently 147 INGOs registered with Codex and, thereby, eligible to participate; representatives from 45 INGOs were present at the most recent CAC meeting in Geneva 2001 (Codex, 2001b).

As mentioned above, the importance of Codex standards has been greatly enhanced by the WTO SPS Agreement. This increased importance makes the process of setting standards much more political; it also slows the rate at which new Codex standards are elaborated. Another factor which is likely to slow the rate of progress is the increased attention Codex debates are receiving from countries and organizations that previously took little note. As reported above, the number of Member countries participating in Codex meetings has increased three-fold, i.e. from 30 in 1963 to almost 90 today. The presence of advisors from industry and consumer groups in national delegations is a long standing practice. However, these delegations had much stronger representation from industry than consumer groups. This would appear to be continuing if one merely counts the number of industry representatives versus consumer advocates in national delegations. A similar impression would be gleaned by counting the number of INGOs which represent industry interests versus those which represent consumer interests.

Table 1. The Codex Alimentarius Ledger.

Activities	Number
Food standards for commodities	237
Codes of hygienic or technological practice	41
Pesticides evaluated	185
Limits for pesticides residues	3,274
Guidelines for contaminants	25
Food additives evaluated	1,005
Veterinary drugs evaluated	54

Source: Codex (1999).

A counterweight to these simple counts is the very active, and well prepared, participation of a few consumer interest INGOs (e.g. Consumers International).

A final point. This trend of greater participation is also accompanied by a greater awareness of the interdependence between Codex standards, national food safety regulations and international trade flows in food and food products. Member representatives today carefully scrutinize each and every Codex document, word by word, to be certain that they understand the economic and trade implications of each Codex standard being considered. In this environment, consensus is much more difficult to achieve. When consensus does not exist, the draft standard is either returned to an earlier step or is put on hold to be revisited at a later meeting.

Indicators of progress to date can be gleaned from Table 1.

3.4. The Role of Civil Society in Codex

It must be recognized that the opportunities for interested parties to influence the work of Codex is quite difficult to assess. First, there are many interested parties. Each of the NGOs has an opportunity to join with other organizations to participate in INGOs which have or can obtain standing before Codex. Each also has an opportunity to participate in the process of building national positions on issues of interest to Codex. Channels exist in each of the Codex Members for civil society to participate, though the channels differ across Members. Governments often hold public hearings, publish draft positions for public comment, and formalize national positions in public view. However, it is not always clear what the impact of the inputs from civil society have on the final positions. Recognizing that the final national position is a political decision, many fear that the politically powerful dominate the process. On the other hand, the checks and balances of democratic societies should assure that over time all interests are included in formulating national positions.

Our focus here is on the "visible" role of civil society groups in Codex, as revealed by Codex documents. The participants are INGOs which have observer status. We will examine a particular issue which has proven to be quite controversial in Codex.

Codex has become a science-based activity soliciting inputs from experts and specialists to ensure that Codex standards comply with the highest level of scientific information. At the same time, when elaborating a standard, Codex "will have regard, where appropriate, to other legitimate factors relevant for the health protection of consumers and for the promotion of fair practices in food trade" (Codex, 2001a, Appendix). Thus, Codex standards shall be based on science but factors other than science might be included in the information on which a standard is based. With different countries having different views, conflicts might arise. Consider the following story which gave rise to this exception for "factors other than science".

In 1991 the CAC considered a draft standard for growth-promoting cattle hormones. Following normal procedures the Joint Expert Committee on Food Additives (JECFA) reviewed the relevant science and reported to the Codex Committee on Residual Veterinary Drugs in Food (CCRVDF). Based on the scientific advice provided by JECFA, CCRVDF concluded that animals treated with the natural bovine growth hormones β-estradiol, testosterone and progesterone would not bear residues of bovine hormones higher than naturally occurring background levels and therefore that neither a finite maximum residue limit (MRL) nor any other regulatory restriction of food from bovine growth hormone-treated animals was needed to protect human health. A finite MRL was proposed for a synthetic growth-promoting agent, zeranol. Thus, the scientific evidence supported a conclusion that beef raised using these growth hormones was safe for human consumption. The CCRVDF recommended to CAC final adoption of the proposed standards setting no minimum levels for the naturally occurring substances and a finite MRL for zeranol.

In the CAC, delegates from several countries opposed adoption on the grounds that consumers in their countries objected to the use of hormones in food production. These delegates agreed that the use of natural bovine growth hormones would not pose any risk to public health, but opposed nonetheless because of consumer concerns. Delegates supporting adoption of the standard argued that the presence of consumer concerns was an insufficient reason for not adopting a measure which, all generally agree, was scientifically supported as not posing a risk to public health. A consensus could not be reached and a vote was taken. CAC voted not to adopt the standards concerning growth-promoting cattle hormones by a vote of 12 for, 27 against and 12 abstentions (Codex, 1991).[7]

It is easy to conclude that the power of public opinion in several Members of Codex was the driving force behind this decision. And this may well be the case.

However, the outcome is also consistent with the thesis that the opposing Members were searching for an argument to justify protecting their domestic producers from imports which happened to originate in countries that use growth-promoting hormones.

There is circumstantial evidence to support both of these views. Civil society is certainly vocal on the issue of growth-hormones. If, in fact, consumer concerns are genuine and widespread, governments which incorporate these views are acting in a democratic manner. On the other hand, if the views of civil society come from a few very vocal NGOs representing a small minority of society, one becomes more suspicious of the underlying reasons for the opposing governments position on this issue in Codex.

It is not our purpose to criticize governments on either side of this issue nor to attribute underlying reasons for the votes. Rather it is our purpose to point out that this practice in Codex of taking into consideration "factors other than science" in reaching Codex decisions is evidence that the views of civil society are entering into the calculations that result in Codex food standards.

In Codex debates most of the INGOs are passive; only a few trade associations and consumer groups participate. This is true of the debates on issues relating to "factors other than science" as well. As a general statement, the positions of the active INGOs can be put into two categories.

INGOs whose membership consists of industry and trade associations favor standards based on sound scientific evidence. Other factors such as animal welfare, consumer preferences, environmental protections, socio-economic factors, religious preferences, and sustainable agricultural concerns are considered not relevant for consumer health or fair trade. These INGOs highlight concerns that the inclusion of such "other factors" presents significant risks of protectionism. To illustrate: in the eyes of the International Council of Grocery Manufacturers Association (Washington, DC), Codex has "witnessed a steady and unmistakably erosion of the integrity of science-based standard-setting processes" because of consumer activities.[8] "Food safety will not be advanced by the exercise of cultural, societal or other non-scientific justifications".[9]

In contrast, INGOs whose membership consists of consumer unions favor the inclusion of other factors in addition to science. Issues of concern include consumer concerns, societal factors, ethical questions, and environmental considerations. At the same time, consumer groups support the inclusion of science in decision making, but only as one of several considerations. Importantly, consumers wish the right to know in order to choose. Clearly, many of the issues for which consumers wish the right to choose have nothing to do with food safety. Concern for the environment may lead some to prefer shade-grown coffee over plantation coffee or traditional foods rather than foods derived from biotechnology, dolphin safe tuna (animal safety), shrimp harvested with devices to safeguard sea turtles (endangered species), free range poultry (animal rights), and so on. And these preferences prevail even at higher prices, as is the case of organic foods which are produced under conditions considered to be environmentally friendly although not safer than foods produced using modern agricultural methods.[10] Consumers International (an international consumer union) favors decisions that avoid negative impacts on internationally agreed environmental standards.[11]

But in the final analysis, Codex decisions are taken by consensus or votes of the Member government representatives. INGOs can participate in the meetings but cannot vote or delay decisions through disagreement. In most cases, Members' positions are determined prior to a Codex meeting and are not altered by INGO interventions. If INGOs are to have an influence in the final decisions, it must be through the strength of their arguments in submitted documents and in discussions during the earlier stages of the decision-making process. It should also be noted that Codex consensus is built by Members who often disagree among themselves. Thus, the process of consensus building is one of compromise. The fact that one or more INGOs might disagree with particular Members differs little from the fact that Members often disagree among themselves.

INGOs often interact with officials and advisors in Member delegations with a view to influencing the Member positions on Codex issues. INGOs might also interact with governmental officials and associations at the national level either directly or through their national membership. Recall that INGOs are organizations whose membership are national NGOs. Thus, the INGOs might influence a particular Member government's position through NGOs in that country. It is also possible that officials of a particular NGO are included in that nation's Codex delegation. But again, it is difficult to document the extent to which such interactions and interventions actually influence decision making.

4. DISCUSSION

As mentioned at the beginning of this article, the Director-General of the WTO warned the Member countries a full year in advance of the ministerial meeting in Seattle that if the views of civil society were not considered, the outcomes of trade negotiations would not be well received by the public at large. Since then, the WTO has taken steps to improve its relationships with civil society; however, the steps taken have been insufficient to conciliate its critics. International cooperation, by its very nature, requires that each Member country sacrifice a degree of national sovereignty. Such sacrifices must be offset by benefits coming from the resulting global governance. These trade-offs are seldom easy and are impossible to structure without imposing hardships on at least some groups in each society.

We have attempted to explore the methods used by Codex to include civil society in its deliberations leading to the elaboration of international food standards. Codex has formalized the participation of INGOs in its deliberations without the INGOs actively participating in decision-making or voting. Even with such arms – length participation, the INGOs have brought the concerns of civil society into the work of Codex. In particular, the issue of the consideration of factors other than science in Codex deliberations is now accepted – though not without controversy. While it is difficult to attribute influence to consumer concerns versus protectionism, there is little doubt about the support of consumer groups (and opposition by producer groups) for the inclusion of factors other than science in Codex deliberations. One can only anticipate that consumer concerns will become more influential in international trade negotiations in the future.

NOTES

1. An influential novel by Upton Sinclair (1906) provides graphic descriptions of conditions in the Chicago slaughterhouses and conditions of workers and quality of the meat and meat products being produced.

2. This term is derived from *Codex Alimentarius Austriacus*, a collection of standards and product descriptions developed during the Austro-Hungarian Empire (Codex, 1999).

3. Article 3.4 of the SPS Agreement specifically mentions Codex standards as the relevant international standards; see also Annex A, 3(a) for the definition of international standards for food safety.

4. Decisions of CAC are taken by a majority of the votes cast, each Member having one vote. However, in practice significant efforts are taken to reach consensus. Voting occurs only if efforts to reach consensus fail. This procedure of decision-making by consensus has been formalized by an amendment to the *Procedural Manual* in 1999 (Codex, 2001a).

5. The developing country list includes Brazil, Korea (South), Malta, Mexico, Singapore, Turkey, high income countries of the Middle East and the countries of Eastern Europe. Of the medium to less advanced developing countries, only about one-third participate in Codex mostly from Africa (including North Africa) and Latin America (Codex, 2001b).

6. Purely national non-governmental organizations cannot have standing in Codex. They are to work through their own nation's procedures for developing national positions on Codex issues.

7. However, this vote was reversed in 1995 with 31 for, 29 against and seven abstentions (Codex, 1995).

8. Codex document for the 24th session of the Codex Alimentarius Commission, CAC/LIM 9, July 2001.

9. "ICGMA carries banner for global processed food industry". World Food Chemical News, 25 October 2000,Vol. 7 No.12.

10. There is a Codex standard for organic foods (Codex Standard Reference CAC/GL 32-1999).

11. Codex document for the 24th session of the Codex Alimentarius Commission, CAC/LIM 1, July 2001.

REFERENCES

Codex (1991). Report of the Codex Alimentarius Commission (19th Session). Document Alinorm 91/40.

Codex (1995). Report of the Codex Alimentarius Commission (21st Session). Document Alinorm 95/37.

Codex (1999). *Understanding the Codex Alimentarius*. Rome: FAO/WHO.

Codex (2001a). *Procedural Manual* (12th ed.). Rome: FAO/WHO.

Codex (2001b). Report of the Codex Alimentarius Commission (24th Session). Document Alinorm 01/41.

Echols, M. A. (2001). *Food safety and the WTO: The interplay of culture, science and technology*. London: Kluwer Law International.

Goh, G., & Ziegler, A. (2001). Implications of recent SPS dispute settlement cases. In: K. Anderson, C. McRae & D. Wilson (Eds), *The Economics of Quarantine and the SPS Agreement* (pp. 75–101). Adelaide: Centre for International Economics Studies and AFFA Biosecurity Australia.

Josling, T., & Warley, T. K. (1996). *Agriculture in the GATT*. London: Macmillan.

Moore, M. (1999). Challenges for the global trading system in the new millennium. WTO Press Release 139. Washington, DC.

Roberts, D. (2001). The integration of economics into SPS risk management policies: Issues and challenges. In: K. Anderson, C. McRae & D. Wilson (Eds), *The Economics of Quarantine and the SPS Agreement* (pp. 9–28). Adelaide: Centre for International Economics Studies and AFFA Biosecurity.

Sinclair, U. (1906). *The jungle*. New York: Doubleday, Page & Co.

Stanton, G. H. (2001). The WTP dispute settlement framework and operation. In: K. Anderson, C. McRae & D. Wilson (Eds), *The Economics of Quarantine and the SPS Agreement* (pp. 53–74). Adelaide: Centre for International Economics Studies and AFFA Biosecurity.

Victor, D. (2000). The sanitary and phytosanitary agreement of the world trade organization: An assessment after five years. *Journal of International Law and Politics*, *32*, 865–937.

WTO. (1995). *Agreement on the application of sanitary and phytosanitary measures (SPS Agreement)*. Geneva: World Trade Organization.

METHOD TO THEIR MADNESS: DISPELLING THE MYTH OF ECONOMIC RATIONALITY AS A BEHAVIORAL IDEAL

John Dobson

ABSTRACT

Although not immediately apparent, the discipline of behavioral finance is rapidly adopting an implicit prescriptive agenda. Behavioral finance does not merely describe financial market reality, it shapes it. Economic rationality is taken as the ideal toward to which individuals 'should' strive.

In this paper I show that, as a behavioral ideal, economic rationality is unjustified both from a strictly economic perspective, and from a moral perspective. In short, there is nothing inherently "wrong" with economically irrational participants in the business environment. Indeed such participants will actually enhance the efficiency, and the ethicality, of business.

1. INTRODUCTION

rationality itself, whether theoretical or practical, is a concept with a history: indeed, since there are a diversity of traditions of enquiry, with histories, there are ... rationalities rather than rationality (Alasdair MacIntyre, *Whose Justice, Which rationality*, 1988, p. 9).

Social Responsibility: Corporate Governance Issues
Research in International Business and Finance, Volume 17, 383–394
Copyright © 2003 by Elsevier Science Ltd.
All rights of reproduction in any form reserved
ISSN: 0275-5319/PII: S0275531903170171

The rapidly growing discipline of behavioral finance is generally viewed as a value-free descriptive subject that makes no pronouncements on how agents "should" behave. Behavioral finance, most academics and practitioners would argue, attempts merely to describe and account for how individuals and groups actually behave in financial environments. In other words, the general consensus is that "behavioral finance" implies no particular moral or ethical agenda.

On closer inspection, however, behavioral finance does espouse a ˌˈescriptive ideal of how economic agents "should" behave. Consider the following statement in a recent behavioral finance article that appeared in the *Financial Analysts Journal*: "The way the world *should be* (the rational economic paradigm) and the way the world is (behavioral tendencies) will always be in tension, but the introduction of psychological antecedents into the analysis of financial anomalies is not a negation of the rational economic paradigm". Note the view that the way individuals "should" behave in financial markets is in a manner consistent with the rational economic paradigm. The authors compound this implication by referring to behavior that is inconsistent with economic rationality as "errant" (p. 56) behavior.

Many other financial economists who write about behavioral finance seem to think it natural to set up a dichotomy between actual observed behavior on the one hand, versus some behavioral ideal on the other; where the behavioral ideal comes from financial-economic theory's concept of rationality. Financial economists often refer to irrational behavior as behavior "off the equilibrium path", as if those individuals who behave irrationally are in some way straying or deviating from an ideal route.

Even in the formative stages of the discipline, therefore, behavioral finance has adopted a normative (i.e. prescriptive) agenda. Behavioral finance is not merely about the application of the theories and methodology of psychology in an attempt to explain behavior. Albeit implicitly, behavioral finance is also about prescribing how agents should behave: agents should behave rationally, where rationality is defined strictly in terms of financial economic theory.

In this paper I analyze behavioral finance's implicit normative agenda. Specifically, I argue that it is unjustified and injustifiable from both an economic and a moral perspective to espouse financial-economic rationality as a behavioral ideal. In short, there is no meaningful way in which we can say that investors, managers, brokers, or anyone else for that matter "should" behave in a way consistent with economic rationality.

The remainder of the paper is split into three parts. First, I describe exactly what is meant by financial-economic rationality. Second, I show why such a rationality concept is unjustified as a normative ideal from a strictly economic perspective.

Third, I show why such a rationality concept is injustifiable as a normative ideal from a strictly moral perspective.

2. WHO IS THE RATIONAL AGENT IN FINANCIAL ECONOMICS?

Rationality in financial economics is founded on the five axioms of cardinal utility, as first enumerated by von Neumann and Morgenstern (1947), plus one additional axiom. These original five axioms are *comparability, consistency, independence, measurability, and ranking*:

- comparability; the individual can make comparisons between preferences.
- consistency; these comparisons are consistent over an array of alternatives.
- independence; original preference orderings are independent of new preference alternatives.
- measurability; preferences are measurable.
- ranking; preferences can be consistently and ordinally ranked.

In essence, the five axioms define rationality in terms of an individual's ability to make consistent preference orderings over a broad spectrum of choices: "We wish to find the mathematically complete principles which define "rational behavior" for the participants in a social economy, and derive from them the general characteristics of that behavior" (p. 31). Furthermore, "people are assumed to be able to make these rational choices among thousands of alternatives" (Copeland & Weston, 1988, p. 80).

The axioms are thus based on a very mathematical and instrumental notion of what it means to be rational: they are all concerned with defining instrumental rationality in terms of the consistent ranking of preferences. For example, if you are an investor choosing stocks in which to invest, and you prefer IBM to Microsoft, and you prefer Microsoft to Netscape, then to be rational you must prefer IBM to Netscape; furthermore your degree of preference for IBM over Netscape, along with your preferences for thousands of other securities, must stay constant no matter how many more stocks are added to your opportunity set.

Note that these five axioms make no normative statement concerning whether the agent has any specific goal, or what the goal of the agent should be; the axioms simply require that the agent act in a consistent manner in ordering preferences.

Financial-economic theory's *sixth* axiom, however, has just such prescriptive implications. As Thomas Copeland and Fred Weston's leading finance text puts it: "Having established the five axioms we add to them the assumption that individuals *always* prefer more wealth to less" (1988, p. 80, my emphasis). Personal wealth maximization is thus a rational agent's *sine qua non*: no matter what the context, no other ultimate objective is allowed or considered.

In relating the five axioms to this sixth axiom, a useful distinction can be made between *instrumental* rationality and *substantive* rationality. In *The Protestant Ethic and The Spirit of Capitalism*, Max Weber made this distinction in labelling two types of rationality as "zweckrationalitat" (formal or instrumental rationality) and "wertrarationalitat" (values-based or substantive rationality). In essence, instrumental rationality concerns how the agent goes about achieving the desired objective, whereas substantive rationality concerns identifying the desired objective itself. Jennifer Moore distinguishes between the two concepts as follows:

> The primary feature of instrumental rationality is that it does not choose ends, but accepts them as given and looks for the best means to achieve them. In instrumental rationality, reason is subordinated to and placed at the service of ends outside itself. In . . . [*substantive rationality*], in contrast, reason is free ranging. It is not the servant of any end. Rather, it subjects every end to its *own* standards of evaluation and criticism (1991, p. 63).

von Neumann and Morgenstern's five axioms clearly pertain to instrumental rationality. They do not stipulate an ultimate objective but merely require that agents pursue some given objective in a consistent and logical manner. The substantive rationality premise of financial economics is provided by the sixth axiom: the opportunistic and atomistic pursuit of material gain ad infinitum. No justification is supplied in the finance literature in the form of empirical evidence to support this substantive rationality premise (indeed there is ample evidence that in many environments individuals are not motivated primarily by personal wealth maximization); nor is any normative argument supplied to defend the notion that this is how agents *should* behave.

The six axioms are merely a framing effect: a way of placing behavior in a relatively simple mathematical context. They make no claim to factual accuracy in all situations, or even in most situations, in which finance professionals find themselves. Nor are the axioms meant to make any moral claim to the effect that this is how individuals should behave in any given situation. As John Boatright observes: "Economics does not make any value judgement about the goods that people prefer or about the selfishness that is assumed" (1999, p. 48). Financial-economic rationality is a simplifying assumption, and nothing more.

3. WHY THE "RATIONAL" AGENT CANNOT BE VIEWED AS AN *ECONOMIC* IDEAL

> I carved a massive cake of beeswax into bits and rolled them in my hands until they softened . . .
> Going forward I carried wax along the line, and laid it thick on their ears. They tied me up, then,

plumb amidships, back to the mast, lashed to the mast, and took themselves again to rowing. Soon, as we came smartly within hailing distance, the two Sirens, noting our fast ship off their point, made ready, and they sang ... The lovely voices in ardor appealing over the water made me crave to listen, and I tried to say 'Untie me!' to the crew, jerking my brows; but they bent steady to the oars (Homer, c. –900, pp. 227–228).

A significant contributor to the canon of financial-economic theory is Stewart Myers. In "The Determinants of Corporate Borrowing" (1977), Myers employs the above excerpt from Homer's Odyssey to illustrate the paradoxical nature of rationality in financial economics. The Sirens' song in financial economics is the opportunistic pursuit of personal material gain. The term "opportunistic" implies that the agent will do whatever is necessary in the interests of this pursuit. The agent will lie, cheat, steal, etc., so long as this behavior is construed as wealth maximizing. Agents are "lashed to the mast" in the sense that they are assumed always to act opprtunistically. In Myers' model of equilibrium in debt markets, for example, borrowers pay a higher interest rate in order to compensate lenders for the assumed opportunism of borrowers: borrowers will renege on loan agreements as soon as it is in their material self-interest to do so. There is no "benefit-of-the-doubt" given here, opportunistic wealth maximization (i.e. the six axioms) is the only rationality premise considered.

What is important to note here is that no one actually gains from this opportunistic wealth maximization; it is self-defeating. Returning to Myers' model, the borrowers have to pay higher interest costs and so borrow less, which in turn hurts the lenders. So economic rationality ensures that its own self-declared objective is never attained: wealth is not maximized for borrowers, for lenders, or indeed for the economy in aggregate. But why *must* this be so?

To answer this question we must look more closely at the behavior, and specifically the interaction, of these "rational" agents. To model behavior, Myers employs game theory, and it is through applying game theory to financial markets – what is generally called agency theory – that we can see the self-defeating nature of economic rationality. Indeed, as a theoretical discipline, behavioral finance can be seen as an application of agency theory. From its humble beginnings in the corporate finance theory of Myers and others, the 1970s agency theory has now become the predominant methodoloy of theoretical finance.

Agency theory analyses the situation, ubiquitous in financial markets, in which "one or more persons (the principal(s)) engage another person (the agent) to perform some service on their behalf which involves delegating some decision-making authority to the agent" (Jensen & Meckling, 1976, p. 308). These agency-theory models can be loosely categorized into two types, namely *adverse-selection* and *moral-hazard*. The difference between these two categories is essentially a function of the nature and degree of uncertainty inherent in the contractual situation.

Consider first moral-hazard-type agency problems, here the contractual situation is ostensibly a simpler one in which there is only one *type* of agent. There may be no informational asymmetry and the agency problem may simply stem from the principal's inability to *control* the actions of the agent. Or there may be informational asymmetry in which case the agency problem stems from the principal's inability to observe directly some information that affects the actions or the performance of the agent (e.g. it might be hard for the principal to discern whether a stockbroker was genuinely committed to executing a client's security transaction at the best available price).

The classic agency problem of this type is managerial perquisite consumption. As a firm moves from private to public ownership, there is a separation of ownership and control. The owners bear the cost of managers' perquisite consumption (e.g. business lunches, corporate jets, generous stock-option packages, etc.), but the managers make the decisions on how many "perqs" to consume. Barring effective accountability – in other words barring a resolution to the agency problem – a "rational" wealth-maximizing management, who no longer bears the full cost of its perqs, may be predisposed to consume perqs to an excessive degree: specifically, to a degree that compromises the value of the firm as a whole. Potential shareholders and bondholders, cognizant of management's "rational" predisposition, will lower the price at which they are willing to buy the firm's equity or debt.

Once again, therefore, the *cost* of agency is invariably borne by the agent. Hence the "finance paradox" that assumes agents are unable to resist the Sirens' Song of opportunism, even though they must rationally realize that such a predisposition is self-defeating. In short, a predisposition to opportunistic wealth maximization does not maximize wealth for either the individual opportunist, or for the economy in aggregate: it is second best.

This point is illustrated clearly by the following simple game.

Figure 1 illustrates a simple game between two players: "A" and "B". Each player represents a stakeholder or group of stakeholders. So, for example, player "A" might represent a group of shareholders considering an investment in a company whose management is represented by player "B". David Kreps summarizes the game's play as follows:

> First A must choose whether or not to trust his opponent. If he (A) elects not to trust B, then both A and B get nothing. If he elects trust, B is made aware of this fact and is given the option either to honor that trust or to abuse it. If A trusts B and she (B) chooses to honor that trust, both get $10. But if A trusts B and she chooses to abuse it, B gets $15 and A loses $5 (1984, p. 12).

Assume that each player's payoff from the game is common knowledge. In other words there is no informational asymmetry and, to the extent that there is an agency problem, it would be characterized as one of simple moral hazard. As Kreps

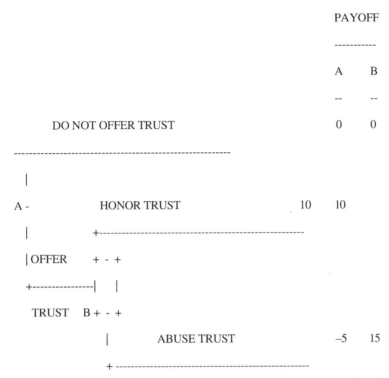

Fig. 1. A Game Tree Illustrating a Contractual Relation between Two Parties in which an Inherent Conflict of Interest Exists.

explains, the game begins with player "A" deciding whether or not to trust player "B". If he ("A") does decide to trust "B", then she ("B") must decide whether to honor or abuse that trust. Readers familiar with Game Theory will recognize Fig. 1 as a one-sided version of the infamous *Prisoners' Dilemma* game. If we assume that both players are rational and thus are primarily motivated to maximize their payoff, then presumably, if called upon to move, "B" will abuse the trust vested in her by "A". Realizing this, "A" will never offer trust and a contract between these two players will not be entered into. The most "reasonable" outcome for this game, therefore, is for each player to receive a payoff of $0. Formally, this is the unique *Nash* equilibrium, in which each player's move is "rational" given the move of the other player.

Such an outcome is clearly not the most desirable, however, either from the point of view of the two players as individuals or from the point of view of the economy as a whole, in that the maximum total payoff of $20 is not attained (this would be the *first-best* outcome). The unwillingness of player "A" to trust player "B" has cost both players $10. But then why should "B" honor trust when her immediate payoff is maximized by abusing it? And whatever "B" might actually plan on doing, why should "A" assume "B" is going to honor trust when he can see that abusing it yields her the higher payoff? In short, economically "rational" agents are unable to reach the desirable outcome; once again simple self-interest has proved self-defeating.

But, returning to Fig. 1, what if the game were repeated. In reality individuals generally deal with one another more than once, and in such a repeated-game environment would not a rational agent now honor trust? Thus, could not enlightened self-interest thus overcome the contractual impasse?

This is the much vaunted "reputation solution" in game theory: the agent honors trust and cooperates in order to build a reputation for cooperation. Game theory, however, indicates that equilibria based on reputation are quite fragile. In the context of Fig. 1, for example, Dave Kreps shows that reputation will enforce a contract between the two players only when there is some uncertainty about the length of the game (i.e. the number of iterations), or when there is uncertainty about the rationality of one of the players (i.e. whether they are both self-interested wealth maximizers). Indeed, even when one of these conditions is met, the agent's desire to maintain her reputation may induce her to honor the contract only some of the time. Similarly, in one of the most extensive game-theory models yet developed – namely Diamond's (1989) model of reputation acquisition in debt markets – agents never actively strive to build reputations. Some merely acquire reputations for timely debt repayment through luck. Once acquired these reputations *may* be actively maintained until the endgame is reached: at which point agents revert to opportunistic behavior.

The economic undesirability of "rational" self-interest becomes even more apparent when we consider adverse-selection, where the uncertainty stems from an *asymmetry of information* that precludes the principal from costlessly identifying the *type* of agent. For example, imagine two stockbrokers: "Churn-and-burn" and "Buy-and-hold". Buy-and-hold tends to offer relatively superior long-run returns to clients than does Churn-and-burn, however prospective clients are not able readily to observe this difference. In other words, the different earnings prospects of the two brokers is not readily apparent from their financial statements or other generally available information. Thus, the contractual environment is one characterized by informational asymmetry.

The ability of the principals, in this context the clients, to make optimal (i.e. wealth maximizing) investment decisions is a function of their ability to distinguish between the two agents, in this context the two brokers. "Buy-and-hold" must in some way signal unambiguously to investors that he/she is superior to "Churn-and Burn".

With this signalling solution to adverse-selection-type agency problems, the challenge is for the "good" agent to devise a signal that cannot be mimicked by the "bad" agent. In addition, this signal must not be so costly that it is uneconomic for even the good agent to emit. If the good agent is able to devise and emit such a signal then it engenders what agency theorists term a *separating equilibrium* in which the two agents become distinguishable to principals and thus the informational asymmetry is overcome. If such a signal does not exist, then the informational asymmetry endures and a *pooling equilibrium* ensues (Spence, 1976).

Even if a separating equilibrium is achieved, however, there are generally costs involved. Whatever form the signal takes, the "good" agent bears the cost of emitting the signal. In other words, if there had been no initial informational asymmetry or if the "bad" agent chose openly to reveal its type, then the bad agent would be no worse off and the good agent would be better off through not having to fund the signal. Formally, the equilibrium is said to be *second-best* because there is a deadweight or "dissipative" cost levied on the economy in aggregate (a cost to the good agent not recouped by the bad agent). Jensen and Meckling (1976) label this deadweight cost the "residual loss"; it results directly from the contractual enforcement problem between principal and agent. Thus, agency problems, even if they are overcome, are not zero-sum games. We are not dealing merely with a redistribution of wealth from principal to agent, but rather with an absolute wealth loss to the economy in aggregate. This absolute wealth loss is a direct result of the bad firm's pursuit of self-interest "with if necessary guile and deceit" (Noreen, 1988, p. 359). Note that in equilibrium the bad firm does not benefit from this opportunistic behavior. Indeed, as part of the economy, it too suffers the consequences of the dead-weight loss.

Reputation or signalling, therefore, may work as contractual enforcement mechanisms in some stages of some contractual situations. But the above studies indicate that there are many environments in which they will not work, or at least not work costlessly. Furthermore, in equilibrium, the cost is invariably borne by the agent. Thus, once again, agents do not benefit from opportunistic behavior; wealth maximization is not achieved, either for the individual or the aggregate. In a broader context, Bowie makes a similar observation; "It only pays to lie or cheat when you can free ride off the honesty of others . . . The conscious pursuit of self-interest by all members of society has the collective result of undermining the interests of all" (1991, pp. 11–12).

Economic game theory, therefore, provides no normative justification for viewing financial-economic rationality as a behavioral ideal. An economy populated with agents adhering strictly to the above six axioms of rationality would, at best, be an inefficient economy; and would, at worst, degenerate into what the Eighteenth Century moral philosopher Thomas Hobbes called a "war of all against all" in which life is "nasty, brutish, and short"!

4. WHY THE "RATIONAL" AGENT CANNOT BE VIEWED AS A *MORAL* IDEAL

In the case of economic efficiency, this paper has made clear that opportunistic agents inevitably engender equilibria that are inefficient in that wealth is not maximized either for the agents involved or for the economy in aggregate. The equilibria are "second-best". But, regardless of their economic efficiency, are economically "rational" agents morally desirable?

Even the most cursory review of ethical theory reveals that this notion of rationality as essentially economic opportunism is not a favorable behavioral attribute. About the best moral defense that one could make is that it is harmless: it is merely a behavioral assumption that expedites finance theory and has no impact on actual behavior. But, as we've already seen, even within their theoretical constructs these agents are not harmless in that they levy a cost on the financial system. More importantly from a moral perspective, several recent empirical studies find evidence that these behavioral assumptions have influence beyond the boundaries of financial modelling. These studies find that the assumptions of financial theory influence financial practice: "is" does indeed imply "ought". For example, from his experience as a business professor, Norman Bowie supplies anecdotal evidence that exposure to this narrow rationality paradigm and related rubrics modifies behavior: "They [MBA students] believe that they will have to be unethical to keep their jobs. They believe that everyone else will put their [own] interests first" (p. 9). But he goes on to note that "the evidence here is not merely anecdotal . . . economics graduate students are more inclined to behave in a self-interested fashion" (p. 9).

For example, in one recent study involving 267 prisoners'-dilemma-type scenarios, economics students defected (i.e. failed to cooperate) 60% of the time, while non-economists defected only 30% of the time. Also, when compared to students in different disciplines, economics students were found to be less honest in hypothetical situations, and both economics students *and professors* were found to be less likely to donate to charity (Frank, Gilovich & Regan, 1993). Bowie observes that "people change their behavior when confronted with assumptions about how other people behave" (1991, p. 9). In *Challenging The Egoistic Paradigm*, he concludes that "[l]ooking out for oneself is a natural, powerful motive that needs little, if any, social reinforcement . . . Altruistic motives, even if they too are natural, are not as powerful: they need to be socially reinforced and nurtured" (p. 19). Such nurturing is not to be found in the behavioral assumptions of finance.

In a broader context, the susceptibility and suggestibility of human behavior was made very clear in the famous laboratory experiments conducted by Stanley Milgram. In these experiments volunteers were asked to administer progressively stronger electric shocks to some individual. Even though these volunteers could see the "victim" in considerable distress from the shocks, the volunteers were generally willing to administer ever higher voltages given the encouragement of an "authority figure". Milgram concluded that:

> Ordinary people, simply doing their jobs, and without any particular hostility on their part, can become agents in a terrible destructive process . . . even when the destructive effects of their work become patently clear, and they are asked to carry out actions incompatible with fundamental standards of morality, relatively few people have the resources needed to resist authority (1974, p. 6).

Similarly, Gregory Dees argues that the value systems of business theory influence those of business practice. He observes that "how concepts are introduced in an academic setting can have a significant influence on their use later on" (1992, p. 38). While commenting on the value system underlying business theory, Ronald Duska notes that "as it gets accepted as a legitimating reason for certain behavior in our form of life, it becomes subtly self-fulfilling" (1992, p. 149). Thus, the behavioral finance paradigm presents itself as morally neutral, but fails to recognize that its narrow and rigid invocation of self-interest has *moral* implications. Alasdair MacIntyre makes a similar point:

> Managers themselves and most writers about management conceive of themselves as morally neutral characters whose skills enable them to devise the most efficient means of achieving whatever end is proposed. Whether a given manager is effective or not is in the dominant view a quite different question from that of the morality of the ends which his effectiveness serves or fails to serve. Nonetheless there are strong grounds for rejecting the claim that effectiveness is a morally neutral value (1984, p. 74).

Models developed within the behavioral finance paradigm, therefore, do not merely endeavor to explain observed phenomena. They do not present merely a morally neutral perspective. To a significant degree they promote a rationality concept that lacks a defensible moral foundation.

5. CONCLUSION

Behavioral finance does not merely describe financial market reality, it shapes it. Economic rationality is taken as the ideal toward to which individuals "should" strive. In this paper I show that, as a behavioral ideal, economic rationality is unjustified both from a strictly economic perspective, and from a moral perspective.

By assuming away other motivations and thus elevating wealth-maximization to the status of a necessary law of nature, behavioral finance may be sanctioning behavior that society at large regards as, at best, morally questionable, and, at worst, strictly immoral. In the corporate milieu, by assuming unbridled self-interest, behavioral finance promotes unbridled self-interest. Furthermore, even if empirical evidence were to overwhelmingly support wealth maximization as the dominant motivation among contemporary economic agents (which, as we've just seen, it does not), behavioral finance's normative dimension would still obligate it to consider alternatives.

REFERENCES

Copeland, T., & Weston, F. (1988). *Financial theory and corporate policy* (3rd ed.). Addison-Wesley.
Dees, G. J. (1982). Principals, agents, and ethics. In: N. E. Bowie & R. E. Freeman (Eds), *Ethics and Agency Theory*. New York: Oxford University Press.
Diamond, D. W. (1989). Reputation acquisition in debt markets. *Journal of Political Economy, 97*, 828–861.
Duska, R. F. (1992). Why be a loyal agent? A systematic ethical analysis. In: N. E. Bowie & R. E. Freeman (Eds), *Ethics and Agency Theory*. New York: Oxford University Press.
Frank, R., Gilovich, T., & Regan, D. (1993). Does studying economics inhibit co-operation? *Journal of Economic Perspectives* (Spring).
Jensen, M. C., & Meckling, W. H. (1976). Theory of the firm: Managerial behavior, agency costs and ownership structure. *Journal of Financial Economics, 3*(4), 305–360.
Kreps, D. (1984). Corporate culture and economic theory. Stanford University, Working Paper.
MacIntyre, A. (1984). *After virtue* (2nd ed.). Notre Dame: University of Notre Dame Press.
MacIntyre, A. (1988). *Whose justice? Which rationality?* Notre Dame: University of Notre Dame Press.
Milgram, S. (1974). *Obedience to authority*.
Moore, J. (1991). Autonomy and the legitimacy of the liberal arts. In: R. E. Freeman (Ed.), *Business Ethics: The State of The Art* (p. 63). New York: Oxford University Press.
Myers, S. C. (1977). Determinants of corporate borrowing. *Journal of Financial Economics, 5*, 147–175.
Noreen, E. (1988). The economics of ethics: A new perspective on agency theory. *Accounting Organizations and Society, 13*, 359–369.
Spence, A. M. (1976). Job market signalling. *Quarterly Journal of Economics, 87*(3), 355–374.
Weber, M. V. (1948). *The protestant work ethic and the spirit of capitalism*. New York: Scribner's, (quote in text p. 182).

REFORMING INDONESIAN CORPORATE GOVERNANCE – A LEGAL-SOCIOLOGICAL PERSPECTIVE

Benny Simon Tabalujan

ABSTRACT

This paper focuses on reforming Indonesian corporate governance from a legal-sociological perspective. It builds on two of my earlier papers which have been published elsewhere. In these two earlier papers, I had postulated that, at least in Indonesia, culture matters to corporate governance.

In this paper, I begin by summarising the findings of my earlier work, providing a condensed version of the case studies of corporate governance among three Indonesian banks during the 1990s. Then I touch on the contemporary debate on convergence of corporate governance systems, using Indonesia as an example. In this context, I discuss the recent work of Amir Licht who utilises insights from the field of cross-cultural psychology to create a framework of testable hypotheses which can be used to examine the correlations between cultural value dimensions and corporate governance. I describe Licht's approach and evaluate its strengths and limitations.

Then, I consider whether the evidence from Indonesia supports the view that corporate governance systems are converging to a final destination, a favourite hypothesis among some of the leading comparative corporate governance experts today. Finally, based on my analysis, I draw out some practical implications for the reform of the Indonesian corporate governance system.

Social Responsibility: Corporate Governance Issues
Research in International Business and Finance, Volume 17, 395–421
Copyright © 2003 by Elsevier Science Ltd.
All rights of reproduction in any form reserved
ISSN: 0275-5319/PII: S0275531903170183

1. INTRODUCTION

This paper focuses on reforming Indonesian corporate governance from a legal-sociological perspective. It builds on two of my earlier papers which have been published elsewhere. In the first paper (Tabalujan, 2001), I sketched the legal and business context of the Indonesian corporate governance framework during the 1990s, with specific reference to the banking sector. That paper showed that, during the 1990s, despite some negative issues like cronyism and corruption, overall, significant improvements had been made in the "hardware" – the rules, institutions and technical framework – of Indonesian corporate governance.

In the second paper (Tabalujan, 2002), I undertook three case studies relating to Indonesian banks which showed that actual corporate governance behaviour during the 1990s was far from the standard to be expected. I chose three banks (Bank Duta, Bank Summa and Bank Pikko) simply because banks were (and still are) among the most highly regulated companies in Indonesia and may thus be considered the bellwether of Indonesian corporate governance. In order to explain the significant divergence in the case studies between formal corporate governance principles on the one hand and actual corporate governance phenomena on the other, I turned to the concept of "legal culture" – a concept championed by Lawrence M. Friedman, a legal sociologist from Stanford University Law School. I postulated that the gap between stated principles and actual practice was due to the fact that Indonesian legal culture was not yet ready to embrace the changes brought about by reformist rules and institutions which sought to improve the Indonesian corporate governance system.

This paper elaborates some aspects of my hypothesis that, at least in Indonesia, culture matters to corporate governance. In particular, I focus on the recent work of Amir Licht who utilises insights from the field of cross-cultural psychology in order to create a framework of testable hypotheses which can be used to examine the correlations between cultural value dimensions and corporate governance. I begin the paper by summarising my findings to date, including a condensed version of the three case studies. I then enter the contemporary debate on convergence of corporate governance systems, using Indonesia as an example. I discuss Licht's approach and evaluate its strengths and limitations. Then, I consider whether the evidence from Indonesia supports the view that corporate governance systems are converging to a final destination, a favourite hypothesis among some of the leading comparative corporate governance experts today. Finally, based on my analysis, I draw out some practical implications for the reform of the Indonesian corporate governance system.

2. INDONESIAN CORPORATE GOVERNANCE BEHAVIOUR IN THE 1990s

In this section, I summarise my three case studies on Indonesian banks: Bank Duta, Bank Summa and Bank Pikko.[1] I undertook the case studies because, until recently, there has not been much published work on Indonesian corporate governance.[2] The absence of a satisfactory theoretical framework for analysing Indonesian corporate governance led me to forsake theory temporarily and instead focus on actual behaviour. This was done with the hope that real events could provide pointers as to what affected the Indonesian corporate governance phenomenon and how it might evolve in future.

2.1. Bank Duta

The first case involved Bank Duta. When the Bank Duta debacle unfolded in 1990, the bank was one of 12 private banks listed on the Jakarta Stock Exchange (JSX) and was the fourth largest private bank in Indonesia (Jakarta Post, 5 September 1990). At listing in June 1990, Bank Duta was majority owned and controlled by three wealthy and influential foundations (*yayasan*) whose chairman was then President Soeharto. In aggregate, the three foundations held about 73% of the bank's issued shares.[3]

In September 1990, it was revealed that Bank Duta had experienced a staggering Rp 782 billion (U.S.$419 million) foreign exchange loss (Jakarta Post, 5 September 1990). No intimation of this loss could be found in the prospectus issued by Bank Duta several months earlier or in the public accountant's report contained in that prospectus. Shortly after the loss was revealed, the bank announced that the three foundations as major shareholders would inject U.S.$419 million cash into the bank as "pure grants" (*hibah murni*) in order to cover the loss (Kompas, 5 October 1990).

Two aspects of the Bank Duta case require comment. The first aspect relates to the accountability of the bank's corporate officers and professional advisors for the loss. The final outcome was that only the vice-president director was prosecuted and convicted. Remarkably, it seems that no other civil or criminal proceedings were issued against any other bank officer or professional advisor, including the public accountant whose report appeared in the prospectus. The second aspect related to the grants of U.S.$419 million injected into the bank by the three substantial shareholders. The grants were not given in exchange for existing or new shares or any other valuable consideration. The grants were not loans and did not have to be repaid. They were a gift in the purest sense of the word.

These two aspects of the Bank Duta scandal leave a set of unanswered questions. Why were there no civil actions against the company officers and public accountant of Bank Duta? Why did the majority shareholders make the grants for no consideration whatsoever? Where did they obtain such large amounts of money? Little was available to answer these questions. Indeed, writing almost a decade later, Ross McLeod from the Australian National University commented:

> The [Bank Duta] rescue operation was non-transparent, however, and whether there was any *quid pro quo* for the individuals concerned remains a matter for speculation (McLeod, 1999, p. 278).

In these circumstances, what actually happened seemed illogical and inconsistent, or at the very least highly unusual, from the perspective of the prevailing rules and underlying concepts of corporate governance.

2.2. Bank Summa

The second case study involved Bank Summa in 1992. At that time, Bank Summa was controlled by the Soeryadjaya family – one of the prominent business families of South East Asia. The family patriarch was (and still is) William Soeryadjaya, an Indonesian national of Chinese ethnic descent, who was one of the wealthiest individuals in Indonesia.[4] At that time, the Soeryadjaya flagship was PT Astra International which held the lucrative licences for manufacturing and distributing Toyota vehicles and Honda motorcycles in Indonesia.[5] In late 1992, Astra International was the largest company on the stock exchange, accounting for 11% of total JSX market capitalisation (Indonesian Capital Market Journal, 1993).

The Summa Group, was headed by Edward Soeryadjaya, the eldest child in the Soeryadjaya family. At the time of its collapse, the Summa Group had more than 70 subsidiaries involved in activities ranging from banking (the flagship Bank Summa), hotels, construction, real estate, insurance, textiles and transportation (Daulay, 1993, pp. 162–164). Through rapid growth, by December 1990 Bank Summa had become one of the ten largest private banks in Indonesia (Daulay, 1993, p. 14). Then things began to sour. In particular, the bank's ratio of non-performing loans began to rise. The decline was partly caused by external factors and also what some alleged to be poor management decisions and lax administrative controls (Info Finansial, 25 November 1992). By July 1991, Bank Summa was categorised as "unsound" (*tidak sehat*) by the central bank.[6]

Subsequently, the Soeryadjaja family took steps to revive the ailing bank. In May 1992, William Soeryadjaya publicly affirmed his commitment to handle the emerging financial crisis developing within the bank (Suara Karya, 29 May 1992).

He was quoted as stating that the Soeryadjaya family "will be responsible for and is capable of facing this responsibility" (Angkatan Bersenjata, 29 May 1992). Among other steps, the family injected fresh capital amounting to Rp 700 billion (U.S.$350 million) into Bank Summa (Kompas, 20 November 1992). It was reported that William also issued a written undertaking in favour of the central bank in which he personally undertook to repay certain loans extended by the central bank to Bank Summa and, if necessary, to sell his family's Astra International shares in order to fulfill this undertaking (Daulay, 1993, pp. 211–215).

Despite these efforts, on 12 November 1992 Bank Summa was unable to fulfill its local inter-bank clearing obligations due to insufficient liquidity (Kompas, 14 November 1992). The central bank immediately suspended Bank Summa's clearing rights effective from Friday, 13 November 1992 (Kompas, 14 November 1992). Shortly thereafter, it was reported that it had non-performing loans totalling Rp 1.7 trillion (U.S.$850 million), of which Rp 1.4 trillion (U.S.$700 million) was owed by related entities in the Summa Group (Tempo, 28 November 1992, p. 36; Daulay, 1993, p. 172).[7] If this figure is correct, then this meant that Bank Summa had grossly contravened the central bank's legal lending limit ("the 3L-rule") prohibiting banks from lending more than 30% of their paid-up capital to parties related to shareholders.[8]

Even after the loss of clearing rights, William Soeryadjaya sought out parties to bail out Bank Summa. These additional rescue attempts did not work. On 14 December 1992, the Minister of Finance revoked Bank Summa's banking licence and ordered the directors of Bank Summa to liquidate the company under the supervision of the central bank. This was the first time since the banking sector was deregulated in 1988 that the government had revoked the licence of a private bank resulting in the bank being liquidated (FEER, 24–31 December 1992).

There are two corporate governance aspects regarding the Bank Summa saga which are of particular interest. First, it raised questions regarding the account-ability of the bank's company officers. The question on many people's minds was: who would be blamed for the collapse? There was talk of possible corporate crimes (Pelita, 19 December 1992) and a potential criminal prosecution (Forum Keadilan, 10 December 1992; Forum Keadilan, 7 January 1993). However, my research found no media report of any criminal prosecution initiated or any criminal sanctions imposed by the authorities against Bank Summa, its corporate officers or its shareholders as a result of the breach of the 3L-rule or the collapse generally. Similarly, although there was talk concerning the potential civil liability of the bank's officers and shareholders (Suara Karya, 4 January 1993), my research again found no report of any civil action initiated by depositors or the regulatory authorities against Bank Summa corporate officers or shareholders. Thus, several years later, Richard Borsuk, the seasoned Asian correspondent of the *Asian Wall Street Journal*, wrote:

> Indonesia does not lack laws, but it certainly has lacked credible administration of business law. There has been plenty of crime without punishment. In 1992, [the] . . . monetary authorities revoked the licence of Bank Summa, which had grossly violated limits on how much it could lend to its owners. But the correct action of shutting the bank, which rattled the whole banking system, was not followed up with prosecutions of any of the shareholders or directors. The main owner, Edward Soeryadjaya, simply stayed out of Indonesia for years while people forgot about Summa (Borsuk, 1999, pp. 140–141).

The second aspect surrounding the Bank Summa collapse which requires consideration is the role of family relationships. The remarkable fact was the extraordinary lengths to which the Soeryadjaja family, especially William Soeryadjaja, sought to save Bank Summa. Granted, the directors, commissioners and shareholders of Bank Summa might have owed certain duties to the bank. However, these duties did not extend to bailing out the bank with fresh capital in cases of loss. Indeed, one of the main reasons why individuals all over the world use corporate entities in business undertakings is to minimise personal liability. In other words, had the Soeryadjaya family simply allowed Bank Summa to collapse, it was doubtful whether any creditor or affected party could successfully claim against the Soeryadjaya family or the family's assets (Angkatan Bersenjata, 1 December 1992). This was because Bank Summa was incorporated as a separate legal entity.

Instead, through their efforts in bailing out Bank Summa, and the express comments of William especially, it became clear that the family viewed the crisis as the responsibility of the entire Soeryadjaya family. They assumed responsibility when there was no legal – as opposed to moral or ethical – obligation to do so. If so, this raises an interesting paradox on the issue of accountability and corporate governance. Why was no one – the bank's officers, shareholders or professional advisors – implicated in Bank Summa's collapse? On the other hand, why did William Soeryadjaya and his family strive so hard to bail out Bank Summa when they had no legal obligation to do so? Thus, the Bank Summa case again exemplifies the key dilemma of Indonesian corporate governance: why corporate governance practice diverges so much from principle.

2.3. Bank Pikko

The third case study focuses on PT Bank Pikko Tbk, a private bank listed on the JSX. It revolves around the alleged manipulation of Bank Pikko shares by certain parties in April 1997. The purpose of the case study is to evaluate how the regulatory authorities such as the JSX and Bapepam (*Badan Pengawas Pasar Modal*), the powerful Indonesian securities watchdog, responded in this instance.[9] Whereas the Bank Duta and the Bank Summa case studies focused on the actions of shareholders and company officers, the Bank Pikko case study shifts the spotlight to Indonesia's corporate regulators. This will help ascertain the contribution of the regulatory authorities and judicial system towards Indonesian corporate governance generally.

Bank Pikko was first listed on the JSX in January 1997. Among the 25 banks listed on the JSX at that time, Bank Pikko was one of the smallest in terms of capitalisation and business operations. After its debut, its share price during January – March 1997 was unremarkable, fluctuating within a comfortable band of between Rp 800 – 1,050 (U.S. 35–45 cents).[10]

Despite its unremarkable size and beginnings as a listed public company, Bank Pikko has become a landmark in Indonesian capital market history. Its claim to fame lay in the alleged manipulation of its shares on 8 April 1997 when its share price increased sharply from Rp 1,300 to Rp 4,050 (U.S. 54 cents – U.S.$1.70) within about 204 minutes of trading. That day has been dubbed "Bloody Tuesday" (*Selasa Berdarah*) and is considered to be one of the most controversial days in the recent history of the JSX (Kompas, 19 May 1997). It also resulted in Bapepam imposing its most severe administrative sanction at that time upon an individual investor – in the form of a fine of Rp 1 billion (U.S.$415,000) – for an alleged case of market manipulation (Kompas, 16 May 1997).

On 15 May 1997, barely five weeks after Bloody Tuesday, Bapepam announced that its investigations revealed that two individuals had allegedly created a false market (*gambaran semu*) in an attempt to manipulate Bank Pikko shares in contravention of prevailing capital market regulations (Suara Pembaruan, 15 May 1997). Bapepam simultaneously announced a string of sanctions imposed upon various parties linked with the Bank Pikko transactions. In particular, two men, Benny Tjokrosaputro and Pendi Tjandra, were fined Rp 1 billion (U.S.$416,000) and Rp 500 million (U.S.$208,000) respectively, for allegedly being the masterminds of the attempted manipulation in Bank Pikko shares. Tjokrosaputro, a youthful 28-year old businessman, responded by acknowledging his readiness, "as a good Indonesian citizen [to] wholeheartedly surrender the profit of Rp 1 billion [U.S.$416,000]" in compliance with the sanction imposed upon him (Suara Pembaruan, 16 May 1997).[11]

However, the issue was whether Bapepam had the legal authority to impose the sanctions it did and, if it did not, why did no one challenge it? Pursuant to Arts 100–101 Capital Market Law 1995 (Tabalujan, 1997), Bapepam clearly had the power to initiate inspections and investigations. But it could only impose administrative sanctions, not criminal sanctions. The prosecution of criminal offences was to be undertaken by the Attorney-General's Office, consistent with the general procedures under Indonesian criminal law, and the imposition of criminal sanctions was the prerogative of the courts.

The point was that, in the Bank Pikko case, the alleged manipulation appears to constitute a criminal offence (Kompas, 16 May 1997). This point was noted by no less a person than Hasan Zein Mahmud, a former president director of the JSX. Moreover, even if it was argued that the alleged manipulation constituted a non-criminal offence, there was still doubt as to whether Bapepam had authority to impose administrative sanctions upon an individual investor. Article 102(1) of the Capital Market Law states:

> Bapepam may impose an administrative sanction for a contravention of this Law and/or its implementing regulations committed by any Party who has a licence or approval from or registration with Bapepam.[12]

The official explanatory memorandum (Elucidation) to Art 102(1) extends the scope of the provision to apply to any person who owns at least 5% of the shares of a listed public company. The available facts indicate, however, that Tjokrosaputro at the relevant time held less than 5% of the issued shares of Bank Pikko. If so, Bapepam had no jurisdiction to impose the sanctions it did. Or, to put it differently, those who had the administrative sanctions imposed upon them theoretically could have challenged Bapepam's decision in the courts.

Yet none did so. Tjokrosaputro and Tjandra made no indication of challenging Bapepam's jurisdiction to impose the sanctions. Neither did any of the securities firms which had sanctions imposed upon them. Indeed, the acquiescence of Tjokrosaputro in paying the fine is reminiscent of a schoolboy caught playing truant rather than the actions of a sophisticated stock market manipulator. Once again this case highlights the key dilemma of Indonesian corporate governance: why corporate governance practice diverges so much from principle.

3. CULTURE AND INDONESIAN CORPORATE GOVERNANCE[13]

How can the discrepancy between the formal corporate governance system and the actual corporate governance behaviour be explained? Why did the foundations inject U.S.$419 million into Bank Duta for what appears to be no consideration whatsoever? Why did the Soeryadjaya family sacrifice so much of their personal assets for Bank Summa when they had no legal obligation to do so? Why did the alleged perpetrators of the Bank Pikko stock price manipulation not challenge Bapepam's jurisdiction when there seemed to be good grounds for doing so?

I suggest that the answer lies with the concept of "legal culture" – a somewhat neglected notion articulated by Lawrence M. Friedman in the 1960s. Friedman, a legal sociologist at Stanford University Law School, postulates that a legal system comprises of three sets of basic components: legal structure, substantive law, and legal culture.[14] Structure refers to the institutions and processes within a legal system; it is "the body, the framework, the long-lasting shape of the system" (Friedman, 1977, p. 6). It includes elements such as the court system, the legislature and the banking and corporate system. Substantive law refers to the laws – both the substantive and procedural rules – and norms used by institutions and which bind the structure together (Friedman, 1975, p. 14).

However, according to Friedman, the third element – the one which gives life to a legal system – is "legal culture". Legal culture refers to the "attitudes, values, and opinions held in society, with regard to law, the legal system, and its various parts" (Friedman, 1977, p. 76). It is "those parts of general culture – customs, opinions, ways of doing and thinking – that bend social forces toward or away from the law and in particular ways" (Friedman, 1977, p. 15). Among the three components, legal culture is the most elusive to describe and yet the most important because it "is the legal culture which determines when, why and where people use law, legal institutions or legal processes; and when they use other institutions or do nothing . . . It sets everything in motion" (Friedman, 1977, p. 76). Writing almost two decades later, Friedman further defined legal culture to mean "the ideas, values, attitudes and opinions people in some society hold, with regard to the law and the legal system . . . Legal culture is the source of law – its norms create the legal norms" (Friedman, 1994, p. 118). According to him, from legal culture "flow lines of force, pressures, and demands that envelop legal institutions and ultimately define their shape" (Friedman, 1990, p. 4).

Friedman's concept of legal culture is not without its critics. Roger Cotterrell in Britain has argued that Friedman's concept "lacks rigour" and is "ultimately theoretically incoherent" (Cotterrell, 1997, p. 14). Friedman responded by pointing out that the lack of precision in the term "legal culture", which he freely admitted, did not necessarily make it incoherent; indeed, the term shares a similar lack of precision with other equally important concepts such as "structure", "legal system" and "public opinion" (Friedman, 1997, p. 33). In my view, Cotterrell is right to highlight the difficulties in handling the concept of legal culture. But he is wrong to conclude that the concept is incoherent because of its lack of specificity. A concept as complex as legal culture, by its very nature, tends to be somewhat elusive. This is evidence of its social pervasiveness rather than a sign of its conceptual weakness.

In my view, for developing and transitional countries, the concept of legal culture becomes especially important. This is because these countries often import from Western nations legislation, codes or even entire legal systems in their attempt to modernise their domestic legal frameworks. Problems, however, arise when such legal transplants are implemented without due consideration of the domestic legal culture (Watson, 1993). If the domestic legal culture is not receptive to the imported foreign legal structure or substantive law, it is likely that these imports will not be implemented properly.

In respect of Indonesia, this point had been recognised as early as 1972 by foreign commentators (Lev, 1972). Lev in fact acknowledged the work of Lawrence M. Friedman on legal culture (Lev, 1972, p. 247). Moreover, legal culture was specifically mentioned in 1982 by the highly-respected former Indonesian Minister of Justice, Mochtar Kusumaatmadja, when he wrote:

> The law development process here embraces the development and strengthening of institutions, processes as well as attitudes, besides revision of existing laws. Law development here in effect means the development of a new legal culture (Kusumaatmadja, 1982, p. 6).

However, legal culture appeared to have been forgotten among policy makers in the past two decades. My research reveals that, apart from Lev's 1972 article, little (if any) additional work was published in English during the next 25 years concerning Indonesian legal culture. During the late 1990s, legal culture, rather be-latedly, began to be recalled by those involved in Indonesian law reform (Lindsey, 1997; Neilson, 1999). In particular, Tim Lindsey from the University of Melbourne Law School, when describing problems associated with reforming the Indonesian legal system, uses the terms "hard law" to refer to black letter law and "soft law" to legal norms and everyday practices (Lindsey, 2000, p. 284). Clearly, Lindsey's "hard law" can be roughly equated with Friedman's legal structure and substantive law while his "soft law" seems equivalent to Friedman's legal culture. Unfortunately, such express acknowledgement of legal culture does not appear to be widespread. A recent paper by two leading Indonesian commentators on the 1997 financial crisis and prospects of Indonesian corporate governance reform, simply ignored the role of legal culture (Simanjuntak & Salim, 2001).

4. CONVERGENCE OF CORPORATE GOVERNANCE SYSTEMS – THE CULTURAL FACTOR

How can the preceding case studies and my conjectures on legal culture contribute to the contemporary corporate governance convergence debate? In this part of the paper, I discuss the current state of this debate and focus, in particular, on the recent work of Amir Licht which attempts to draw insights from the field of cross-cultural psychology to further inform the convergence debate.

A useful starting point for obtaining a snapshot of the current debate is the recently published paper by Douglas M Branson from the University of Pittsburg Law School (Branson, 2001). According to Branson, the debate essentially revolves around whether "the governance structure and practices of larger corporations all over the world will soon take on a resemblance to one another" (Branson, 2001, p. 323). On the one side, proponents of the convergence hypothesis claim that a host of factors – such as the telecommunications revolution, globalisation of financial markets, pressure from international fund managers, and the fact that stock exchanges and regulators are racing to adopt best-practice benchmarks – are currently working together, forcing corporate governance systems to move inexorably towards one another (e.g. Cheffins, 1999; Cunningham, 1999; Gordon, 1999). Moreover, given the dominance of the United States financial markets, compounded by weaknesses in other governance systems as revealed by the 1997–1999 Asian financial crisis and Japan's continuing poor economic performance throughout the 1990s, some proponents argue that the American model of corporate governance should or will be the final destination in the evolution of national corporate governance systems (Hansmann & Kraakman, 2001). This preference for the U.S. model was also implicit in the actual responses of the World Bank – IMF to the Asian financial crisis when these multilateral organisations recommended substantive corporate governance reforms to various Asian countries, including Indonesia, along the lines of the U.S. model (Lane, 1999). If so, then the "end of history" for corporate governance may already be in sight (Coffee, 1999).[15]

As the title of his paper suggests, Branson is skeptical of the claim that there is global convergence. Among other things, he criticises some of the leading convergence proponents on several grounds. Firstly, he claims there is "inbred scholarship", pointing in particular to two well-known authors whom he accuses of showing a preference towards citing works of their own or those from an "inner circle of elites" (Branson, 2001, p. 333). Secondly, he claims that their views are based on a "narrow and unrepresentative" sample of jurisdictions (Branson, 2001, p. 334). As for actual examples of unsuccessful attempts of exporting legal institutions and legal harmonisation, Branson pointed to the failure of the Russian corporate law reform and the stalled European Union Draft Fifth Company Law Directive, first mooted in the early 1980s, which seeks to impose co-determination in company boards along the German model (Branson, 2001, pp. 336–337).[16] He goes further to debunk globalisation as a "myth" (Branson, 2001, p. 340) and to highlight the role of culture as a critical factor in hindering the global convergence phenomenon (Branson, 2001, pp. 341–346).

Branson is not alone in his criticism of the convergence hypothesis. Other scholars have also argued that path dependency – formed by factors including "sunk adaptive costs, complementarities, network externalities, endowment effects" and the self-interest of rent-seeking groups – will constrain the future of corporate governance systems and hinder convergence (e.g. Bebchuk & Roe, 1999; Bratton & McCahery, 1999; Courchene, 1996; Legrand, 1996; Licht, 1998; Roe, 1996). From this perspective, the notion that the U.S. model represents "the evolutionary pinnacle of corporate governance" is clearly not self-evident but instead becomes a point of contention (Gilson, 1994, p. 132).

Between these two polarities of convergence and non-convergence, Ronald Gilson from Stanford University Law School appears to offer a middle ground (Gilson, 2000). In simple terms, Gilson holds the view that national corporate governance systems may be converging in function, but not necessarily in form. He cites evidence which suggests convergence in specific corporate governance functions, for example, in the way management performance is monitored in the U.S., Germany and Japan. He notes, however, that evidence of institutional or formal convergence is relatively scarce, concluding that this is because formal convergence is "costly" (Gilson, 2000, p. 13). On Branson's part, his paper does not appear to deal at length with the possibility of functional convergence. His conclusion, however, suggests that while he acknowledges the possibility of functional convergence in "discrete areas such as financial accounting or disclosure standards", he opposes the view that global convergence of entire systems will occur (Branson, 2001, p. 362).

Overall, although I generally concur with Branson's views, it appears that, at least in some parts of his paper, he has overstated his case. For example, he may be going too far in his claim that convergence proponents are characterised by "inbred scholarship". Granted, in the article by Hansmann and Kraakman referred to by him (Branson, 2001, pp. 333–334), the authors had limited citations for published works on labour participation in governance. Taking the Hansmann and Kraakman paper, as a whole, however, it appears that this may be an isolated case; elsewhere in the paper a diversity of references by other authors are cited. Similarly, it is puzzling that Branson places the 1999 paper by Bebchuk and Roe on the same side with the Hansmann and Kraakman paper (Branson, 2001, p. 334). For one thing, the main thrust of Bebchuk and Roe's paper is to explain differences in corporate ownership and governance systems in advanced economies by attributing these to path dependence factors. That paper was not a defence of the convergence hypothesis as such. In fact, it sought to highlight the differences among corporate governance systems rather than their similarities.

Nevertheless, although Branson's claim of "inbred scholarship" among proponents of the convergence hypothesis may be overstated, I believe that he is correct in his basic contention that the global convergence of corporate governance systems is highly uncertain. In particular, his reference to cultural factors and

Granovetter's "embeddedness of economic actions" add an important aspect to the debate (Branson, 2001, pp. 341, 347).[17] The reference to cultural factors is all the more important because the mainstream corporate governance literature has largely ignored the role of culture in corporate governance. For example, an authoritative 1,238-page tome on comparative corporate governance published in 1998 omitted mentioning culture explicitly as a key factor in corporate governance systems.

On the other hand, it is clear that cultural factors has not been totally absent in the literature. In fact, there appears to have been a discernible shift since the 1990s, especially from the mid-1990s onwards, towards greater recognition of the effect of culture on corporate governance phenomena. One early piece in 1990 by Robert Tricker attempted to explore the links between corporate governance and culture (Tricker, 1990). Prominent corporate governance scholars in the United States such as Bernard Black (Black, 1992, p. 831) and Melvin Eisenberg also mentioned, albeit in passing, the importance of cultural and social norms (Eisenberg, 1989, p. 1473). Other scholars examined corporate governance systems of specific countries like Japan and Germany and discussed the possibility of culture as a significant influence (Henderson, 1991; Mahoney, 1990; Milhaupt, 1996; Pfeil, 1996). In 1996, James Fanto published an important paper examining specifically the cross-cultural aspects of corporate governance and securities regulation (Fanto, 1996).

More recently, one Japanese scholar expresses the view that a community's "cultural tradition" as one of the factors which determines how the community views the nature of its corporations (Iwai, 1999, p. 586). From the private sector, it is noteworthy that CalPERS (California Public Employees Retirement System) – the largest pension fund in the United States with well over U.S.$100 billion in assets – now explicitly recognises the impact of culture on corporate governance (Licht, 2001, p. 153). Moreover, multilateral institutions such as the OECD are also acknowledging the influence of social and cultural factors on corporate governance systems (OECD, 1999).[18] From the academic perspective, with the current burgeoning literature on norms or non-legal rules, the issue of culture and corporate governance appears to have started to become entwined with the literature on norms (Milhaupt, 2001).

However, where culture is acknowledged as having an effect on corporate governance phenomena, the tendency is to regard cultural factors as a "black box" of imponderables touched upon in passing, without rigorous analysis (Mann & Milhaupt, 1996, p. 323). This tendency is probably due to the difficulties associated with undertaking inter-cultural and intra-cultural research. Undertaking research using testable hypothesis and a viable theoretical framework in order to determine what cultural elements are critical and how they shape corporate governance phenomena is not easy. In the Indonesian context, this means developing a research methodology to answer questions such as: what exactly is Indonesian legal culture? How does it affect the corporate governance system? What cultural factors played a role in driving the key players in the Bank Duta, Bank Summa and Bank Pikko case studies to do what they did?

Answering these questions is fraught with difficulty. Lawrence Friedman himself noted that "statements about legal culture rest on shaky evidence at best" (Friedman, 1975, p. 204). Fortunately, there is some hope that this legal-sociological gap in corporate governance research may be tackled soon. There is a novel approach proposed by Amir Licht, a Harvard-trained law academic based in Israel, which attempts to use insights from cross-cultural psychology (Berry, 1997), in particular the concept of cultural value dimensions, in order to analyse the impact of culture on corporate governance systems (Licht, 2001). Licht relies on work undertaken by leading cross-cultural researchers in order to map the values which characterise various cultures. For each community, these values form "the bases for specific norms that communicate to people what is appropriate [behaviour] in various situations" (Licht, 2001, p. 168). At the societal level, these values reflect the society's culture.

The next step is to create a framework through which these values can be measured across cultures. Here, Licht refers to the empirical work of two prominent researchers, Geert Hofstede and Shalom Schwartz (e.g. Hofstede, 1984, 1991; Schwartz, 1999). Essentially, these researchers postulate "value dimensions" (Hofstede) or "value types" (Schwartz) and attempt to characterise a community's culture along these dimensions. Hofstede, for example, focuses on four value dimensions: power distance (legitimacy of unequal distribution of power); individualism/collectivism (caring for self or for the group); masculinity/femininity (valuing achievement, heroism, material success or valuing relationships, modesty and interpersonal harmony); and uncertainty avoidance (preference for ambiguity or certainty). Schwartz focuses on three dimensions: embeddedness/autonomy (maintenance of status quo or personal autonomy); hierarchy/egalitarianism (obeying role obligations or transcendence of selfish interests); and mastery/harmony (active self-assertion or fitting in with the environment).

Based on massive questionnaire data collected over many years – Hofstede surveyed over 117,000 respondents in 50 countries while Schwartz had a sample of over 35,000 in 49 countries (Licht, 2001, p. 174) – these researchers have created maps as to how various cultures differ in terms of their value dimensions. For example, Licht notes that both Hofstede and Schwartz found that East Asian countries tend to accept unequal hierarchical relations more than continental European countries, while on individual-group relations, Western countries emphasise personal autonomy more than East Asian countries (Licht, 2001, p. 178).

The findings from such cross-cultural research have been used in various scholarly disciplines including economics, management studies, and international accounting. However, Licht pointed out that such findings have hardly been used in the legal field, let alone corporate governance (Licht, 2001, p. 180). He then explains the ways in which these findings can provide additional insights to various aspects of the corporate governance phenomena, including shareholding structures, insider trading regulation, and levels of disclosure (Licht, 2001, pp. 187–199). The strength of Licht's approach is that, based on the empirical work of cross-cultural researchers such as Hofstede and Schwartz, statistical values for value dimensions of specific countries can be used as independent variables in order to create testable hypothesis concerning the corporate governance characteristics in various countries. To that extent, therefore, specific hypotheses concerning cultural aspects of corporate governance are now capable of being empirically tested.

In a subsequent unpublished paper by Licht and two other colleagues (including Schwartz), Licht put his theoretical approach to work (Licht et al., 2001). Using the work of Hofstede and Schwartz, Licht and his colleagues analysed the relationship between national cultural profiles and one aspect of corporate governance, investor's legal rights, as contained in the landmark 1996 work by La Porta and others (La Porta et al., 1996). La Porta pioneered the use of statistical analyses of investor's legal rights, structure of capital markets, and corporate governance systems among countries from different legal families. By marrying La Porta's work with those of Hofstede and Schwartz, Licht is attempting to create a set of testable hypotheses based on cultural values which can yield insights which, in turn, will add breadth to the law and economics approach of studying corporate governance phenomena. The analysis yielded by Licht's unpublished paper, although preliminary, suggests that such an approach at the very least offers a way to "identify systematic relations between culture and corporate governance laws" (Licht et al., 2001, p. 33).

Although Licht's novel approach appears promising, several cautionary remarks are in order. Firstly, although the approach brings to the table valuable insights from the field of cross-cultural psychology, by the same token, it also brings with it the academic debate in that field including issues concerning methodology. For example, Licht acknowledges that the testing of cross-cultural hypotheses about corporate governance using data from the Hofstede and Schwartz studies raises the joint hypothesis problem (Licht, 2001, p. 202). More pertinently, there has been some criticism against using Hofstede's cross-cultural methodology in the accounting and legal fields (Gernon & Wallace, 1995; Jackson, 1997). It is important, therefore, that anyone intending to apply Licht's approach be adequately informed regarding the criticisms against and limitations surrounding cross-cultural research.

Secondly, in creating his framework, Licht acknowledges that he is side-stepping various issues raised by cognitive psychology – such as bounded rationality, bounded will-power and bounded self-interests – in order to focus on issues raised by cross-cultural psychology (Licht, 2001, p. 183). Such a step is reasonable if it is proven that the issues of cognitive psychology, which are focused at the personal or individual level, are shaped by culture. The problem is that this relationship may not be only one-way. It is possible that the relationship between individuals and culture is two-way: individuals can initiate cultural change while culture, at least initially, shapes and forms individual thinking and behaviour. If so, then the input from both cognitive psychology and cross-cultural psychology may be useful and one should not be used to the exclusion of the other when examining corporate governance issues.

Thirdly, Licht's approach is primarily statistical in nature and deals with culture at the societal level. He acknowledges that his approach should not be used to the exclusion of other approaches towards studying law and culture, such as the anthropological approach of using "thick" descriptions in the study of social phenomena (Licht et al., 2001, p. 6). The idea of "thick" descriptions of culture was made popular by the noted Dutch anthropologist, Clifford Geertz, and refers to the approach of reporting and recording social phenomena within a community in a heavily descriptive manner providing richness and depth (Geertz, 1973). In fact, the case study approach has been used quite extensively to document corporate governance practices in specific countries (e.g. Fanto, 1996, p. 120). The three case studies of Indonesian corporate governance in my earlier paper follows this tradition. The value of such case studies is that they provide a greater depth of understanding of a particular phenomenon within the overall context of a society. In contrast, the value of Licht's approach is that it provides a statistically-testable method to compare such phenomena across societies. Hence, these two approaches should be used in conjunction with and not to the exclusion of each other in order to improve our understanding of comparative corporate governance.

Fourthly, Licht's novel approach, although useful in highlighting the correlations between cultural factors and corporate governance phenomena, does not appear to provide a framework for analysing changes in corporate governance systems over time. His discussion of the dynamic aspects of causality and change is brief and, unlike the rest of his work, rather unspecific and his conclusion perhaps a little premature. He states that the internationalisation of capital markets "will strain culturally induced features of corporate governance" and that this, and other changes, "[t]o a certain extent . . . will undoubtedly lead to the emergence of an international culture of corporate governance" (Licht, 2001, pp. 199–202). The problem, however, is that such a statement appears unwarranted given the past and continuing debate as to convergence and divergence in cross-cultural management studies (Bartholomew & Adler, 1996). This debate parallels the current debate as to whether corporate governance systems are converging. On this point, it seems that Licht's approach, which tends to be static and based on historical data, has limited contributions to make. Much more work must be done to theorise and operationalise a framework capable of analysing dynamic shifts in corporate governance systems before a definitive answer can be reached.

5. IMPLICATIONS FOR REFORMING INDONESIAN CORPORATE GOVERNANCE

What then are the implications of Licht's pioneering work as far as the study and reform of Indonesian corporate governance are concerned? In my view, Licht's preliminary findings concerning the relationship between culture and corporate governance are significant for Indonesia in at least four aspects. These are elaborated upon below.

Firstly, Licht's comment – that "[o]ne important inference from our findings is that cultural values could impede legal reforms that conflict with them" (Licht et al., 2001, p. 34) – provides a possible explanation for the gap between the formal framework and actual practice of Indonesian corporate governance during the 1990s, as shown by the three case studies summarised earlier in this paper. The formal framework was the result of various economic and law reform initiatives undertaken throughout the 1980s and the 1990s. Licht's comment suggests that the gap between the formal system and actual behaviour may be attributed to specific Indonesian cultural values which impede the implementation of these earlier reforms.

However, the task of identifying which cultural values impede reforms is very problematic when the subject is a nation as large and complex as Indonesia – a mélange of 230 million people from over 250 ethnic groups with equally numerous languages and dialects – as well as a chequered history which included almost 350 years of Dutch colonial rule.[19]

At this juncture, a thorough exposition of Indonesian cultural values is beyond the scope of this paper. However, it is possible to mention one potentially key element of Indonesian culture which appears capable of directly affecting corporate governance behaviour. I venture to suggest that this element is patrimonialism. Patrimonialism, as a sociological concept, owes much to the ideas of Max Weber and refers to a patriarchal system of relationships where a father-figure, similar to that found in a family, exerts authority in social, business or political contexts.[20] Commentators have noted the influence of patrimonialism upon many aspects of Indonesian affairs, including Indonesian legal development (Crouch, 1979;

MacIntyre, 1994; Quinn, 1999). Is it possible that patrimonial tendencies also affect Indonesian corporate governance, such that corporate institutions and relationships are viewed through a familial, as opposed to legal, perspective?

If patrimonialism does in fact influence Indonesian corporate governance such that a corporation is viewed as existing within a network of familial relationships rather than legal relationships, then the giving of the U.S.$416 million grant to Bank Duta by its three shareholder foundations potentially becomes less enigmatic. Similarly with the case of the Soeryadjaya family's ill-fated attempt to bail out Bank Summa. The reasoning is that, in a family context, when one family member suffers, others come to his aid. Thus, a father who sees his child weighed down by excessive debt may choose to repay the debt using the father's funds without requiring any compensation from the child. Such an act is motivated by a sense of family obligation, responsibility and honor which can be quite different from the notion of legal obligation or legal duty.

In the case of Bank Pikko, the alleged mastermind of the market manipulation on the JSX in April 1997, Benny Tjokrosaputro, appeared deeply repentant over the affair. Such an attitude is remarkable. It is not at all consistent with the image of the typical rogue investor who seeks to manipulate the market for personal gain. Again, Tjokrosaputro's response becomes more understandable if there is an assumption that patrimonial attitudes to law and punishment pervade Indonesian society generally.

Of course, much more detailed research is required before any suggested linkage between patrimonialism and Indonesian corporate governance as described above can be substantiated. Here, Licht's approach, especially using the previous work of Hofstede and Schwarz, may be especially useful as a means to determine the extent to which patrimonialism, or its key manifestations, is a significant cultural value in Indonesia and, if so, its possible influence on corporate governance behaviour.

Secondly, Licht's findings appear to be generally consistent with Bebchuk and Roe's view that "[c]ulture and ideology, not only value maximization and self-interest, might influence a country's choice of corporate law" (Bebchuk & Roe, 1999, p. 168). Such findings appear to lend support to the view that culture does matter to corporate governance. If this is correct, then global convergence of corporate governance systems is not likely to happen soon. This flows from the basic premise that corporate governance is embedded in a society's culture. Of course, one may be tempted to think that the post-Cold War economic, political and military dominance of the Unites States will force corporate governance systems worldwide to gravitate towards the United States model. But it is doubtful whether this will happen in a wholesale way. Granted, there may be some convergence in certain areas – what Ronald Gilson dubs functional convergence. But if culture changes, it changes slowly. As Gary Goodpaster, the former resident head of the large USAID-funded ELIPS Indonesia Law Reform Project concluded near the end of his term in 1998:

> Frankly, even with the best of legal-economic analyses supporting legal system and law reform, Indonesia does not appear ready for a global change to a rule of law system. There are now, of course, great pressures on Indonesia to move in that direction. I think, however, this shift – a cultural transformation actually – if it is ever to be made, will be made incrementally over a long period of time (Goodpaster, 1999, p. 30).

This suggests that convergence, if it happens at all, will be slow and be limited, at least initially, to certain functional areas. The *New York Times* columnist, Thomas L. Friedman, made a similar point when he coined the term "glocalisation" (Friedman, 1999, p. 236). What he meant was that globalisation is forcing a certain degree of uniformity in economic and financial systems worldwide; at the same time, the fiercely tribal and communal part of societies resists this process and creates a backlash. Glocalisation is the conciliating process through which these two conflicting trends can be accomodated. Through glocalisation, useful aspects of globalisation can be assimilated into a local culture without overwhelming it.

To speculate a little, the outcome of corporate governance reforms worldwide may be the creation of distinct corporate governance clusters with common characteristics shared among them due to functional convergence. For example, one shared characteristic which might be common to all clusters could be greater corporate disclosure and transparency as financial markets worldwide become even more integrated with each other. On the other hand a cluster might be distinguishable from other clusters by virtue of certain cultural traits shared by the systems within that cluster but which are absent from the systems within other clusters.

Thus, there could be an Anglo-American cluster of corporate governance systems characterised by companies with a high level of shareholder activism; a European-Japanese cluster characterised by companies with interlocking shareholdings dominated by large banks; and an East Asian-Latin American cluster characterised by family-owned or family-controlled companies whose management boards operate with patrimonialistic tendencies. If so, we would end up with customised and culturally sensitive corporate governance systems which nevertheless share some common characteristics, thus reconciling the perennial tension between universalism and particularism. In this way, Indonesian corporate governance can work towards attaining world-class standards while still respecting some of the uniqueness of Indonesian culture.

Thirdly, Licht further suggests that his framework may provide "yardsticks for measuring the suitability of transplanting legal mechanisms from one nation to another" as well as provide data which can be used "to prevent transplant rejection"

(Licht et al., 2001, p. 34). This may be especially relevant in the Indonesian context where corporate governance reform is a key element of the broader push towards reforming the broader economic, banking and legal systems. The point is that Licht's approach might be capable of being used to distill a set of cultural values which reflect Indonesian society and also to examine specific corporate governance reform proposals in order to determine their suitability with such values.

For example, if German or French corporate governance reform initiatives appear to have a better fit with Indonesian cultural values, then serious consideration should be given towards adopting these rather than initiatives which are based on the Anglo-American model. The goal is to use Licht's approach to take into account cultural considerations when evaluating the suitability and likely success of corporate governance reform proposals. By so doing, policy makers will be able to minimise the likelihood of such proposals failing in their implementation as a result of cultural resistance. In other words, just as a proposal for a major industrial project is typically required to be accompanied by an environmental impact study, perhaps it is a good idea for future corporate governance law reform proposals to be accompanied by a cultural impact study.

The fourth implication which emerges from Licht's work is the critical need to adopt a multi-disciplinary approach towards studying the corporate governance phenomenon. The current reality, however, is not the case. Much of the current corporate governance literature is authored by lawyers and economists and, to a degree, finance experts and accountants. Some have scant or no familiarity (or worse, respect) for disciplines such as sociology or cognitive psychology which can provide rich insights into the behaviour of key individuals and groups in any corporate environment. Yet such insights may be especially important in the field of comparative corporate governance (Farrar, 2001).

As a typical example, consider two recent attempts by a respected multilateral agency, the Asian Development Bank, when it commissioned studies into legal development and corporate governance in selected Asian jurisdictions. The relevant reports were published in 1999 and 2000, respectively (Pistor & Wellons, 1999; Zhuang, 2000). Both reports provide various useful insights but pay relatively scant attention to the social and cultural issues involved in legal development and corporate governance. This is not surprising given that the 1999 study was undertaken by a team of lawyers and economists while the four co-authors of the 2000 study comprised of three economists and a professor of finance. The concern here is that, by not considering the impact of social and cultural factors, the studies may be inadvertently overstating the rate of progress in the growth of legal and corporate governance systems in these countries, while understating the actual problems faced by development initiatives and the time required to implement them – especially through ignorance of the cultural resistance which may stifle such initiatives.

In conclusion, I can do no better than quote my former law teacher and the founding chairperson of the Asian Law Centre at the University of Melbourne, Mary Hiscock. As someone with substantial law reform experience in Asia, she put it this way:

> Law is a plant that grows out of the roots of the people, and it is an important way of educating people to change. If what is sought is a ready-made law, it can be bought "of the peg" from any consultant. But all there is then is a law. People still do the same things they always did. Nothing changes. That is the lesson of Asian history (Hiscock, 1997, p. 46).

Or, as Harvard historian David Landes puts it:

> If we learn anything from the history of economic development, it is that culture makes all the difference (Landes, 1999, p. 516).

NOTES

1. This part of the paper is drawn and condensed from Tabalujan (2001). Currency exchange rates used were those prevailing at the relevant times.
2. Among the works available are: Tabalujan (2001, 2002); Simanjuntak and Salim (2001); Fitzpatrick (2000); and Fitzpatrick (1998). For an early article on Indonesian corporate law see: Tabalujan (1996).
3. The names of the three foundations and details of their representatives and share-holdings are found in: Business News, 21 September 1990. Prior to listing, the three foundations in total owned 90% of Bank Duta's issued shares, with the remaining 10% being held by the bank's employees cooperative: Bank Duta (1990, p. 62).
4. According to reports, William Soeryadjaya, a peranakan Chinese, was born on 20 December 1922 in Majalengka, West Java (Kompas, 16 November 1992). He is often referred to as "Om Willem" – "Om" (or Oom) being a respectful but friendly Dutch honorific which means "uncle" and "Willem" being the Dutch equivalent of the English "William". His Chinese name is reputedly "Tjia Kian Liong" (Suryadinata, 1988, p. 272). The publication which appears to come closest to a biography of William Soeryadjaya is: Daulay (1993).
5. In addition, Astra International also distributed Daihatsu, BMW, Renault and Isuzu vehicles (PT Astra International, 1993, p. 3).
6. A bank is classified under one of four categories: sound (*sehat*), sufficiently sound (*cukup sehat*), poor (*kurang sehat*) and not sound (*tidak sehat*): see Hendrobudiyanto, (1994, p. 166).
7. In another report, Minister of Finance Sumarlin was quoted as stating that approximately Rp 1.1 trillion (U.S.$550 million) or 70% of Bank Summa loans was extended to shareholders and directors of the bank and related parties (Forum Keadilan, 24 December 1992).
8. On the 3L rule, see: Binhadi (1995, p. 92).
9. There are many other rumours of alleged stock market manipulation. However, the Bank Pikko case is possibly the most spectacular case and is useful for this case study because, unlike several other cases of alleged share manipulation, this one was widely publicised and subsequently came to a firm conclusion.

10. Share prices as quoted in the daily section "Bursa Efek Jakarta", (Kompas, 9 January 1997; Kompas, 31 March 1997).

11. It is unclear whether the Rp 1 billion (U.S.$416,000) he paid represented part or all of his profit from the alleged stock manipulation exercise.

12. For an alternative translation of Art 102, see: Pakpahan (1996).

13. An earlier version of this section appeared in Tabalujan (2002).

14. Friedman's earliest exposition of these concepts appears to be in 1969: Friedman (1969a); and Friedman (1969b). It is also found in his subsequent books: Friedman (1975, pp. 11–16); Friedman (1977, pp. 6–9).

15. Hegel's term "end of history" was made famous by Francis Fukuyama's widely read work, The End of History and the Last Man (New York: Free Press, 1992).

16. For the case of Russian corporate law reform, Branson cited Black (2000). For the stalled EU Draft Fifth Company Law Directive, he cited Blackburn (1993).

17. The notion of "embeddedness" was made popular by the sociologist, Mark Granovetter (1985).

18. The OECD Ad Hoc Task Force on Corporate Governance in OECD Principles of Corporate Governance (Paris: OECD, 1999) 3, states:

> The [corporate governance] principles are non-binding and do not aim at detailed prescriptions for national legislation ... They can be used by policy makers, as they examine and develop their legal and regulatory frameworks for corporate governance that reflect their own economic, social, legal and cultural circumstances ... [Italics added].

For similar views echoed by IMF staff, see Licht (2001, p. 155).

19. For an introduction to Indonesian culture, see Koentjaraningrat (1971). For insights into Indonesian legal history, see: Ball (1982); Resink (1968); and, for a brief but more recent survey, Linnan (1999).

20. The literature by and on Weber is enormous. For a start, see: Weber (1978) and Rheinstein (1967).

REFERENCES

Angkatan Bersenjata (1992). Belum diketahui, berapa saham All Milik William Akan Dijual (29 May), 3.

Angkatan Bersenjata (1992)Angkatan, B. (1992). Krisis Bank Summa dan Tanggung Jawab Terbatas. Reprinted in: CSIS, 1993, Document Clippings Service No 336/E/III/1993 Bank Summa Jilid III. Centre for Strategic and International Studies, Jakarta (1 December), 87.

Ball, J. (1982). Indonesian legal history 1602–1848. Sydney: Oughtershaw Press.

Bank Duta (1990). Bank Duta prospektus. PT Bank Duta, Jakarta, 62.

Bartholomew, S., & Adler, N. J. (1996). Building networks and crossing borders: The dynamics of knowledge generation in a transnational world. In: P. Joynt & M. Warner (Eds), Managing Across Cultures: Issues and Perspectives (pp. 20–32). London: Thomson Business Press.

Bebchuk, L. A., & Roe, M. J. (1999). A theory of path dependence in corporate ownership and governance. Stanford Law Review, 52, 127.

Berry, J. W., et al. (Eds) (1997). Handbook of cross-cultural psychology (3 vols, 2nd ed.). Boston: Allyn & Bacon.

Binhadi (1995). *Financial sector deregulation, banking development and monetary policy: The Indonesian experience 1983–1993*. Institut Bankir Indonesia, Jakarta.

Black, B. S. (1992). Agents watching agents: The promise of institutional investor voice. *UCLA Law Review, 39*, 811.

Black, B. S., et al. (2000). Russian privatization and corporate governance: What went wrong? *Stanford Law Review, 52*, 1731.

Blackburn, T. L. (1993). The Societas Europea: The evolving European corporation statute. *Fordham Law Review, 61*, 695.

Borsuk, R. (1999). Reforming business in Indonesia. In: G. Forrester (Ed.), *Post-Soeharto Indonesia: Renewal or Chaos* (p. 135). Singapore: Institute of Southeast Asian Studies.

Branson, D. M. (2001). The very uncertain prospect of 'global' convergence in corporate governance. *Cornell International Law Journal, 34*(2), 321.

Bratton, W. R., & McCahery, J. A. (1999). Comparative corporate governance and the theory of the firm: The case against global cross reference. *Columbia Journal of Transnational Law, 38*(2), 213.

Business News (1990). Tiga Kemungkinan Untuk Mengatasi Kasus Bank Duta, reprinted in CSIS, 1990, Document Clippings Service No 223/E/X/1990 Kasus Bank Duta. Centre for Strategic and Information Studies, Jakarta (21 September), 65.

Cheffins, B. R. (1999). Current trends in corporate governance: Going from London to Milan via Toronto. *Duke Journal of Comparative & International Law, 10*, 5.

Coffee, J. C. (1999). The future as history: The prospects for global convergence in corporate governance and its implications. *Northwestern University Law Review, 93*, 641.

Cotterrell, R. (1997). The concept of legal culture. In: D. Nelken (Ed.), *Comparing Legal Cultures* (p. 13). Aldershot: Dartmouth Publishing.

Courchene, T. J. (1996). Corporate governance as ideology. *Canadian Business Law Journal, 26*, 202.

Crouch, H. (1979). Patrimonialism and military rule in Indonesia. *World Politics, 31*(4), 571.

Cunningham, L. A. (1999). Commonalities and prescriptions in the vertical dimension of global corporate governance. *Cornell Law Review, 84*, 1133.

Daulay, A. H., et al. (1993). *William Soerydjaya: Kejayaan dan Kejatuhannya*. Jakarta: PT Bina Rena Pariwara.

Eisenberg, M. A. (1989). The structure of corporation law. *Columbia Law Review, 89*, 1461.

Fanto, J. A. (1996). The absence of cross-cultural communication: SEC mandatory disclosure and foreign corporate governance. *Northwestern Journal of International Law & Business, 17*, 119.

Farrar, J. H. (2001). In pursuit of an appropriate theoretical perspective and methodology for comparative corporate governance. *Australian Journal of Corporate Law, 13*(1), 1.

FEER (Far Eastern Economic Review) (1992). Cost of indecision: Indonesia closes crisis-ridden Bank Summa (24–31 December), 75.

Fitzpatrick, D. (1998). Corporate governance, economic crisis, and the Indonesian banking sector. *Australian Journal of Corporate Law, 9*, 178.

Fitzpatrick, D. (2000). Indonesian corporate governance: Would outside directors or commissioners help? In: C. Manning & P. van Diermen (Eds), *Indonesia in Transition: Social Aspects of Reformasi and Crisis* (p. 293). Singapore: Institute of Southeast Asian Studies.

Forum Keadilan (1992). Mungkinkah Edward Dituntut Pidana? (10 December), 93–94.

Forum Keadilan (1992). Bank Swasta Tak Dipercaya Lagi? (24 December), 80–81.

Forum Keadilan (1993). Celah Jalan ke Penjara (7 January), 88.

Friedman, L. M. (1969a). Legal culture and social development. *Law & Society Review, 4*, 29.

Friedman, L. M. (1969b). On legal development. *Rutgers Law Review, 24*, 11.

Friedman, L. M. (1975). *The legal system: A social science perspective*. New York: Russell Sage Foundation.

Friedman, L. M. (1977). *Law and society: An introduction*. Englewood Cliffs: Prentice-Hall.

Friedman, L. M. (1990). *The Republic of choice: Law, authority and culture*. Cambridge, MA: Harvard University Press.

Friedman, L. M. (1994). Is there a modern legal culture? *Ratio Juris, 7*, 117.

Friedman, L. M. (1997). The concept of legal culture: A reply. In: D. Nelken (Ed.), *Comparing Legal Cultures* (p. 33). Aldershot: Dartmouth Publishing.

Friedman, T. L. (1999). *The Lexus and the olive tree: Understanding globalization*. New York: Farrar, Straus & Giroux.

Geertz, C. (1973). Thick description: Toward an interpretive theory of culture. In: C. Geertz (Ed.), *The Interpretation of Cultures* (p. 3). New York: HarperCollins.

Gernon, H., & Wallace, R. S. O. (1995). International accounting research: A review of its ecology, contending theories and methodologies. *Journal of Accounting Literature, 14*, 54.

Gilson, R. J. (1994). Corporate governance and economic efficiency. In: M. Isaksson & R. Skog (Eds), *Aspects of Corporate Governance* (p. 131). Stockholm: Juristforlaget.

Gilson, R. J. (2000). Globalizing corporate governance: Convergence of form or function. Working Paper No 192, Stanford University Law School, John M. Olin Program in Law and Economics.

Goodpaster, G. (1999). The rule of law, economic development & Indonesia. In: T. Lindsey (Ed.), *Indonesia: Law & Society* (p. 21). Sydney: Federation Press.

Gordon, J. N. (1999). Pathways to corporate governance? Two steps on the road to shareholder capitalism in Germany. *Columbia Journal of European Law, 5*, 219.

Granovetter, M. (1985). Economic action and social structure: The problem of embeddedness. *American Journal of Sociology, 91*, 481.

Hansmann, H., & Kraakman, R. (2001). The end of history for corporate law. *Georgia Law Journal, 89*, 439.

Henderson, D. F. (1991). Securities markets in the United States and Japan: Distinctive aspects molded by cultural, social, economic and political differences. *Hastings International & Comparative Law Review, 14*, 263.

Hendrobudiyanto (1994). Bank soundness requirements: A central bank perspective. In: R. H. McLeod (Ed.), *Indonesia Assessment 1994: Finance as a Key Sector in Indonesia's Development* (p. 158). Singapore: Institute of Southeast Asian Studies.

Hiscock, M. (1997). Contemporary law modernisation in Southeast Asia: A personal perspective. In: V. Taylor (Ed.), *Asian Laws Through Australian Eyes* (p. 31). Sydney: LBC Information Services.

Hofstede, G. H. (1984). *Culture's consequences: International differences in work-related values*. Beverly Hills: Sage Publications.

Hofstede, G. H. (1991). *Cultures and organisations: Software of the mind: Inter-cultural cooperation and its importance for survival*. London: McGraw-Hill.

Indonesian Capital Market Journal (1993). Effect of Bank Summa's problems and the economy on the JSE index and transactions. *Indonesian Capital Market Journal, VI*(1), 6.

Info Finansial (1992). Lilu-Liku Krisis Bank Summa, reprinted in CSIS, 1993, Document Clippings Service No 334/E/III/1993 Bank Summa Jilid I. Jakarta: Centre for Strategic and Information Studies (25 November), 43.

Iwai, K. (1999). Persons, things and corporations: The corporate personality controversy and comparative corporate governance. *American Journal of Comparative Law, 47*, 583.

Jackson, J. D. (1997). Playing the culture card in resisting cross-jurisdictional transplants: A comment on 'legal processes and national culture'. *Cardozo Journal of International & Comparative Law*, *5*, 51.
Jakarta Post (1990). Government steps in as crisis hits Bank Duta (5 September), 1.
Koentjaraningrat (Ed.) (1971). *Manusia dan Kebudayaan Indonesia*. Jakarta: Penerbit Djambatan.
Kompas (1990). Hibah Murni Tutup Kerugian Bank Duta (5 October), 1.
Kompas (1992). BI Blokir Bank Summa Ikut Kliring (14 November), 1.
Kompas (1992). William: Keluarga Soeryadjaya Tidak Akan Lepas Tangan (16 November), 1.
Kompas (1992). Haruskah Oom Willem Dibiarkan (20 November), 1.
Kompas (1997). Bursa Efek Jakarta (9 January), 2.
Kompas (1997). Bursa Efek Jakarta (31 March), 2.
Kompas (1997). Benny: Saya Rela Bayar Rp 1 Miliar Karena Salah (16 May), 2.
Kompas (1997). Transaksi Semu Tindakan Kriminal (16 May), 2.
Kompas (1997). 'Selasa Berdarah' dari Saham Bank Pikko (19 May), 2.
Kusumaatmadja, M. (1982). Law and development in the ASEAN region: The Indonesian experience. *ASEAN Law Journal*, *1*, 1.
Landes, D. S. (1999). *The wealth and poverty of nations: Why some are so rich and some so poor.* New York: W. W. Norton & Co.
Lane, T., et al. (1999). IMF-supported programs in Indonesia, Korea and Thailand. Occasional Paper No 178, International Monetary Fund, Washington, DC.
La Porta, R., et al. (1996). Law and finance. National Bureau of Economic Research Working Paper No. 5661. Washington, DC: National Bureau of Economic Research. Later published as: R. La Porta et al. (1998). Law and finance. *Journal of Political Economy*, 1113.
Legrand, P. (1996). European legal systems are not converging. *International and Comparative Law Quarterly*, *45*, 53.
Lev, D. S. (1972). Judicial institutions and legal culture in Indonesia. In: C. Holt (Ed.), *Culture and Politics in Indonesia* (p. 246). Ithaca: Cornell University Press.
Licht, A. N. (1998). International diversity in securities regulation: Roadblocks on the way to convergence. *Cardozo Law Review*, 20, 227.
Licht, A. N. (2001). The mother of all path dependencies: Towards a cross-cultural theory of corporate governance systems. *Delaware Journal of Corporate Law*, *26*, 147.
Licht, A. N., et al. (2001). Culture, law and finance: Cultural dimensions of corporate governance laws. Social Science Research Network Working Paper (June). Available from: http://papers.ssrn.com/sol3/papers.cfm?abstract_id=277613
Lindsey, T. C. (1997). Paradigms, paradoxes and possibilities: Towards understandings of Indonesia's legal system. In: V. Taylor (Ed.), *Asian Laws Through Australian Eyes* (p. 90). Sydney: LBC Information Services.
Lindsey, T. (2000). Black letter, black market and bad faith: Corruption and the failure of law reform. In: C. Manning & P. van Diermen (Eds), *Indonesia in Transition* (p. 278). Singapore: Institute of Southeast Asian Studies.
Linnan, D. K. (1999). Indonesian law reform, or once more unto the breach: A brief institutional history. *Australian Journal of Asian Law*, *1*(1), 1–33.
MacIntyre, A. (1994). Power, prosperity and patrimonialism: Business and government Indonesia. In: A. MacIntyre (Ed.), *Business and Government in Industrialising Asia* (p. 244). Ithaca: Cornell University Press.
Mahoney, P. G. (1990). Securities regulation by enforcement: An international perspective. *Yale Journal on Regulation*, *7*, 305.

Mann, R. J., & Milhaupt, C. J. (1996). Foreword. *Washington University Law Quarterly, 74*, 317.

McLeod, R. (1999). Control and competition: Banking deregulation and re-regulation in Indonesia. *Journal of the Asia Pacific Economy, 4*, 258.

Milhaupt, C. J. (1996). A relational theory of Japanese corporate governance: Contract, culture, and the rule of law. *Harvard International Law Journal, 37*, 3.

Milhaupt, C. J. (2001). Creative norm destruction: The evolution of non-legal rules in Japanese corporate governance. *University of Pennsylvania Law Review, 149*(6).

Neilson, W. (1999). The rush to law: The IMF legal conditionalities meet Indonesia's legal culture realities. In: D. Duncan & T. Lindsey (Eds), *Prospects for Reform in Post-Soeharto Indonesia* (p. 4). Victoria, BC: Centre for Asia-Pacific Initiatives.

Pakpahan, N. S. (1996). *Introduction to the new capital markets law of Indonesia.* Jakarta: Lembaga Pelayanan Hukum Ekonomi Indonesia.

Pelita (Jakarta) (1992). Kejaksaan Harus Selidiki Kemungkinan Ada Kejahatan Korporasi dalam Kasus Bank Summa (19 December), 1.

Pfeil, U. C. (1996). Finanzplatz Deutchland: Germany enacts insider trading legislation. *American University Journal of International Law & Policy, 11*, 137.

Pistor, K., & Wellons, P. (1999). *The role of law and legal institutions in Asian economic development 1960–1995.* Oxford University Press & Hong Kong: Asian Development Bank.

PT Astra International (1993). *Annual report 1992.* Jakarta: PT Astra International.

Quinn, B. (1999). Indonesia: Patrimonial or legal state? The law on administrative justice of 1986 in socio-political context. In: T. Lindsey (Ed.), *Indonesia: Law and Society* (p. 258). Sydney: Federation Press.

Resink, G. J. (1968). *Indonesia's history between the myths: Essays in legal history and historical theory.* The Hague: W. van Hoeve.

Rheinstein, M. (Ed.) (1967). *Max Weber on law in economy and society.* Cambridge, MA: Harvard University Press.

Roe, M. J. (1996). Chaos and evolution in law and economics. *Harvard Law Review, 109*, 641.

Schwartz, S. H. (1999). A theory of cultural values and some implications for work. *Applied Psychology International Review, 48*, 23.

Simanjuntak, D., & Salim, F. (2001). Transition to good corporate governance in post-crisis Indonesia: High barriers and windows of opportunities. paper presented at the Corporate Governance Forum, Conference on Indonesian Economic Institution Building in a Global Economy, Jakarta, Indonesia (6 September).

Suara Karya (1992). William: Saya Tanggung Jawab Cegah Keruntuhan Summa-Edward (29 May), 1–2.

Suara Karya (1993). Bank Summa Dan Tanggung Jawab Pengurusnya, reprinted in CSIS, 1993, Document Clippings Service No 336/E/III/1993 Bank Summa Jilid III. Jakarta: Centre for Strategic and Information Studies (4 January), 104.

Suara Pembaruan (1997). Bapepam Ambil Tindakan Terhadap Kasus Bank Pikko (15 May), 5.

Suara Pembaruan (1997). Buntut Lonjakan Saham Bank Pikko Benny Tjokro Ikhlas Serahkan Rp 1 Milyar Kepada Negara (16 May), 1.

Suryadinata, L. (1988). Chinese economic elites in Indonesia: A preliminary study. In: J. W. Cushman & G. Wang (Eds), *Changing Identities of the Southeast Asian Chinese Since World War II* (p. 261). Hong Kong: Hong Kong University Press.

Tabalujan, B. S. (1996). The new Indonesian company law. *University of Pennsylvania Journal of International Economic Law, 17*, 883.

Tabalujan, B. S. (1997). Indonesia's new capital market law. *Asia Business Law Review, 15*, 14.

Tabalujan, B. S. (2001). Corporate governance of Indonesian banks: The legal & business contexts. *Australian Journal of Corporate Law, 13*, 67.

Tabalujan, B. S. (2002). Why Indonesian corporate governance failed – Conjectures concerning legal culture. *Columbia Journal of Asian Law, 15*, 141.

Tempo (1992). Utang Dibayar Utang (28 November), 36.

Tricker, R. I. (1990). Corporate governance: A ripple on the cultural reflection. In: S. R. Clegg & G. S. Redding (Eds), *Capitalism in Contrasting Cultures* (p. 187). Berlin: Walter de Gruter.

Watson, A. (1993). *Legal transplants: An approach to comparative law* (2nd ed.). Athens, GA: University of Georgia Press.

Weber, M. (1s978). *Economy and society*. G. Roth & C. Wittich (Trans., and Eds) (2 vols). Berkeley: University of California Press.

Zhuang, J., et al. (2000). Corporate governance and finance in East Asia: A study of Indonesia, Republic of Korea, Malaysia, Philippines, and Thailand. Manila: Asian Development Bank.

IN SEARCH OF SOCIETY: REDEFINING CORPORATE SOCIAL RESPONSIBILITY, ORGANISATIONAL THEORY AND BUSINESS STRATEGIES

Jan Jonker

ABSTRACT

The present CSR movement is a "first generation" attempt to discuss and redefine the role and position of business organisations in contemporary society. Although the debate has been promising so far, it has reached a point where numerous parties appear to agree that some fundamental action is required. What seems to be needed is the operational translation in order to develop the business case for CSR. To understand the meaning of the business case, understanding of the business of business is a prerequisite. This contribution will mainly focus on the nature of the business enterprise thus giving way to an interrogation of underpinning organisational theory. Finally it will focus on emerging contemporary corporate strategies, enabling the "translation" of CSR into the going concern of the organisation.

INTRODUCTION[1]

The way the business enterprise operates in a global marketplace has become the subject of a lively debate within (Western) society at large. Trying to redefine

Social Responsibility: Corporate Governance Issues
Research in International Business and Finance, Volume 17, 423–439
ISSN: 0275-5319/PII: S0275531903170195

and recapture the role of organisations – in particular the business enterprise – is unmistakably a crucial element in this debate. In general this is referred to as the need for "corporate social responsibility" (CSR). At the surface this debate is reinforced by a growing general consciousness of the need to protect the environment, concerns about the depletion of natural resources and awareness of social and societal inequality around the world. At a more fundamental level, CSR refers to a growing appeal asking organisations to take more "social responsibility", behaving accordingly, as "good corporate citizens". The central underlying notion is that organisations should act beyond their classic "business" boundaries, not only generating profit but also (and at the same time) contributing to the "glue" and "cohesion" of society, taking into account the social and ecological environment. Although CSR is undoubtedly gaining increased attention, it still remains a fuzzy concept. The last decade has witnessed much effort being expended to develop programs and approaches to implement ideas derived from this notion within and outside organisations. Unfortunately these efforts can be characterised in general as piece-meal, mainly aiming at one function (e.g. environment, marketing or reporting) at best leading to "local" improvement.

It is argued here that at present, the CSR movement is a "first generation" attempt to discuss and redefine the role and position of business organisations in contemporary society. Real encompassing CSR seems to require a different (world) view, one that takes into account the fundamental shift in societal power balances that has taken place in the past decades. It also seems to imply a more "responsible" behaviour of the business enterprise embedding a variety of nondescript social obligations. This perspective is based upon the generally accepted recognition that an enterprise operates within a societal network of stakeholders, who are influencing directly or indirectly the results of the enterprise. The contemporary debate regarding CSR can be looked upon as a – sometimes contradictory – complex of symptoms referring to a society indeed in the midst of a fundamental transition. Despite all this, talk is far more prevalent than walk. Although the debate has been promising so far, it has reached a point where numerous parties appear to agree that some fundamental action is required. As one of the leading CSR-advocates is arguing: "There is little doubt that many businesses need to open their eyes to opportunities linked to societies" changing values and expectations . . . and make them operational across many international markets" (Zadek, 2002, p. 9). This plea for the operational translation is often referred to as "developing the business case for CSR". In order to really develop the business case, organisations will need to develop new corporate strategies, with many of those currently in use becoming obsolete. Or, to quote Zadek (2002, p. 33) once more; "The real win-win challenge is how to create companies that have the vision, the will (. . . and guts; JJ) and the competencies to turn . . . aspirations . . . into business models that can outperform their dirtiest and meanest competitors. Yet, to really understand the true nature of the business case, it seems useful to refresh our common understanding of the business of business. After a concise overview of the present debate regarding CSR, this contribution will therefore mainly focus on the nature of the business enterprise, thus giving way to an interrogation of its underpinning organisational theory. This will also allow some light to be shed on the meaning of "responsibility" in relation to the business enterprise. As a whole this contribution is above all an attempt to create theoretical building blocks to support the business case for CSR. Finally it will focus on emerging contemporary corporate strategies, enabling the "translation" of CSR into the going concern of the organisation.

THE DEBATE[2]

Unmistakably, there is a growing yet "fuzzy" societal, organisational and political movement often referred to in one undefined go as "Corporate Social Responsibility" (CSR). Tentatively and temporarily labelled under various and sometimes confusing and overlapping headings such as "Corporate Citizenship", "New Social Partnerships" or "Sustainability", it is difficult to assess the size, growth, true nature and impact of this movement. There is, however, no denying the existence of such a movement, given the increasing public, political and business attention it receives on a daily basis in both Europe and other places in the world (in particular Canada, The Americas and Australia). Although it can be argued that there has been steadily increasing interest in the topic in the past thirty years, it is only during the last decade that the issue of CSR has really become a major item on the agendas of governments and businesses. It is for example certainly promising that the notion of "greening" and "operational ecology" have become well-established items on the organisational agenda. Still, given the environmental problems mankind will face in the next decades (see, for example, the websites of the United Nations Environment Programme, The World Resources Institute or The WorldWatch Institute) much work is required. As a result, there is widespread yet still developing awareness about CSR. Hardly any country or government can now avoid entering into the debate (see e.g. "CSR; A Dutch Approach" by the Ministry of Economic Affairs of the Netherlands). Although promising ideas and concepts abound, they take all kinds of shapes and sizes ranging from traditional community sponsoring activities, zero-based material budgeting (K4 and K10), socially responsible investment (SRI), international engagement in the protection of Human Rights or against child labour and so on. There is little wonder that it is hard to define what "CSR" really means – as if in the end one ultimate definition would be the panacea to all (scientific) doubts. At present a working definition is probably the most attainable. For that purpose, CSR can be defined as: the extent to – and the way in which – an organisation consciously is responsible for – and justifies – its action and non-action and the impact of it on its legitimate stakeholders.

The central argument in the CSR-debate at large is that businesses ought to play a more prominent societal role, given their dominant (economic) position. There is a certain substance to that argument. Orts (1998, 1952) provides the following commentary on the business enterprise. "This century (the twentieth; JJ) the for-profit business corporation became the primary engine of economic enterprise in the world. By 1990, business corporations accounted for more than 90% of total sales and receipts in the United States, and the 7000 largest corporations, with assets of $250 million or more, accounted for more than half of all sales and receipts. The largest business firms in most countries are corporations. In the late twentieth century, the exponential growth of multinational or trans-national corporate enterprise qualifies as one of the most important historical developments. From 1969 to 1990, the number of multinationals tripled from around 7000 to almost 24,000. These multinational companies are often structured as parent-subsidiary groups. By 1994, there were approximately 37,000 multinational parents, which accounted for more than 200,000 foreign affiliates or subsidiaries. The largest 300 multinational corporations account for about one quarter of the world's total productive assets. Half of all parents of multinational groups are incorporated in one of four countries: the United States, Great Britain, Germany, or Japan". Although similar overviews can be found, it becomes clear that a limited number of corporations are responsible for the (economic) prosperity in the world. This prosperity only applies to one-fifth of the world population receiving 82.7% of the world income (ENDAP, Human Development Report, 1992), while the poorest one-fifth only receives 1.4%. This leads to a debate around the use of natural resources, inequality (new) power-balances, the role of nations and governments and so forth.

Through e.g. the analysis of annual reports it can be observed that in the past few years many (international) companies have "discovered" the debate covered under headings such as "embedding stakeholders", "transparency" and "accountability". These corporate discoveries have been catalysed through various international events and crises, which have made apparent the "instant" nature of modern risk, which can threaten the continuity of companies – sometimes almost overnight. This has led to, among other things, the recent popularity for risk-assessments of all kinds. Despite these trends, it can also be observed that while many businesses have been quick to adopt the semantics of the debate, they have changed little or nothing at all in their daily practices. This phenomenon – widely researched in the last couple of years – is generally referred to as green-wash, ecological hijacking or simply ethical window-dressing. In itself it is a fine example of talk being far more prevalent than walk. Sometimes it is also referred to as the "knowledge-doing gap"; the lack of organisational competencies to turn policies into business activities. Turning ideas and words into real actions seems to be the real pitfall in an appealing avalanche of semantics. As Zadek states quite precisely: "The business case for "doing good" is the holy grail of the corporate responsibility movement. In fact, the view that win-wins exist that allow profit to be made from doing good is the movement's single most important proposition about the way business and markets do, or can work" (Zadek, 2002, p. 9).

Despite this, in the meantime a growing number of companies are seriously and deliberately trying to translate stepwise this lively debate into their ongoing business activities (e.g. Shell, BP, Rio Tinto, Volkswagen, Unilever and many others). Quite often, the decision to really start this internal process is fed (in a negative sense) by the lack of (national) governmental support. Many global businesses now consider CSR as a strategic issue – yet still to be discovered – necessary to assure business continuity in the long-term. The operationalisation of such ideas is often done through the development of a vision and mission underpinned by business principles. This should lead to the adaptation of existing – or the development of new – business strategies. It is these strategies that provide the framework for the actual "behaviour" of a company. Developing and adopting such a strategy – moving from words into normal day-to-day business actions – would in most of the case require a transformation. As such CSR can be considered the first step towards a strategic corporate transformation.

Despite everything that is going on, one observation remains quite clear. Although numerous models, concepts, codes of conduct, business principles, standards and other "instruments" are rapidly emerging, the debate is still hardly scratching the surface of mainstream business practices. If observed more closely, it appears that two elements are missing. First, it is difficult to discern a real theoretical basis underpinning the CSR movement. Many sources can be found within established academic disciplines such as business ethics, sociology, social-psychology and economics that all deliver a contribution to the debate. Yet, fundamental inquiry leading towards a contemporary theory of the firm seems to be absent. This might explain why the current debate is rather "evangelical" and lacks business realism. This realism doesn't simplistically imply that "the aim of business is just doing business" (to paraphrase a common viewpoint), but rather that, at present, there is little ability to translate growing ideas (and practices) around CSR into actionable perspectives within the business community. To quote Zadek once more: "The business case is about business, not some absolute and abstract cost-benefit calculus" (Zadek, 2002, p. 33).

The translation of ideas, concepts and principles into an actionable business perspective seems to be lacking a common denominator to provide the appropriate values and the supportive arguments. Without such a perspective the implementation of already known codes, instruments and the imitation of (local) best-practices will at best remain just piece-meal improvement. What also seems to be missing is a conversion of these ideas into adequate business strategies that "fit" a specific organisation operating in a particular (local, national or international) context. So at present the CSR debate leads to a rich and intriguing variety of fundamental questions in which (redefining) the nature business enterprise is fundamental. What is the nature of business? Profit driven or based upon principles? Who can or needs to provide a fundamental driver to the ongoing debate and the CSR movement? Business itself? Government? Civil Society? Are businesses to become campaigners, taking a leading role in the exploration and implementation of the current CSR debate? No wonder many significant parties are influencing the present debate. To start answering some these questions a clear conception of what a business is all about seems to be a first requisite.

THE BUSINESS OF BUSINESS

Consideration of the nature of the business enterprise, has received renewed attention in recent years from both scholars and management practitioners. Over the past decades – if not from early in the 20th century – businesses have become the dominant economic entities in our world. This has led to a fundamental shift in power between organisations, governments and civil society. At present an almost religious devotion to the "power" of the corporation can be observed. It is viewed as the master creation of modern society, a vehicle by which human society has become capable of creative power never before imagined, the natural outgrowth of the marvellous market mechanism whose "invisible hand" allows coordination of human economic activity, and it guarantees both the highest possible level of production and the most optimal patterns of distribution and allocation. Its universal nature allows for application in virtually any domain, thus guaranteeing the satisfaction of needs for the majority of people.

One outcome of that heightened interest (of an inter – and multi-disciplinary character) is a widespread agreement, that the business enterprise is not only a profit maximising machine – though profit is central to enterprise success (Schrader, 1993). The business enterprise is a complex, knowledge based, profit seeking, searching, living and learning "social organism" that draws both sustenance and purpose from the various and varying needs and expectations of stakeholders. Stakeholders are those individuals or groups (including shareholders, customers, management and staff), who in the judgement of management are believed capable of actions that can threaten enterprise viability, or inflict unacceptable damages (Birkin & Woodward, 1997; Demsetz, 1997; Metzger & Dalton, 1996; Putterman & Kroszner, 1996). Unfortunately, all the impassioned pleas that can be heard in the public forum about "protecting people and the environment from the giant corporations" or about "getting the government of business back" fail to reflect an understanding of the modern business corporation matching their passion. Those pleas serve relatively little purpose. Understanding the corporation, however, is crucial to the wellbeing of contemporary society.

Against a background of declining public esteem and increasing social significance it is not surprising that when the question of the purpose of business is raised, it often evokes unease (Raiborn & Payne, 1996). Responding to the criticism of being driven by greed, business has sometimes become confused about its own motives, priorities and aims. Statements such as Milton Friedman's (1970) that "the social responsibility of business is to increase its profits", do not find ready support with a business community wanting public approval and a public increasingly concerned with the environment and consumer and employee rights. Of course it is understandable that business does not want to be viewed as rapacious and unconcerned about, and unresponsive to, society's concerns with its impact on social values. A now widely expressed desire of business is to be seen as a "good corporate citizen". Still, as Charles Handy (1985) has said: "It is the organisation's job to deliver; it is not its job to be everyone's alternative community, providing meaning and work for all for life".

Little value can be achieved by discussing the role of business and the strategies it adopts any further without a clear understanding of the nature of the business enterprise. The issue of what is the aim of business is not a semantic exercise. On the contrary, identification of the business aim is crucial to the development of management theory (Metzger & Dalton, 1996). To ask why the business enterprise exists and what are its aims is not to suggest that business has a special or pre-eminent position, and other organisations are in some way inferior (Vallance, 1995). Clearly, other organisations are not inferior; they simply do not share the business aim. The business enterprise is a limited and specific form of activity and asking what is its purpose forces explicit identification of those characteristics that differentiate it from other forms of activity. Those characteristics provide the criteria necessary to conduct a rigorous and objective assessment of the business relevance for CSR. The purpose of business is to make profits by selling its goods and services. In that process business will need to consider its relationships with a variety of groups, a number of whom have a stake in the business, and in whose interests the business correspondingly has a stake. The need to earn a profit is the defining characteristic of the business enterprise. As Vallance (1995, p. 32) has emphasised: "Where an enterprise aims at this return, it is properly called a business; where it does not, it may be a perfectly legitimate enterprise of another kind, but a business it is not". Realistically, the interests of many people other than shareholders e.g. employees, customers, suppliers, government, the local, national and international community are important to business (Schrader, 1993). However, if that is so, does it follow that business has a duty to society to do more than make profits? Does the need to be sensitive to the needs of staff and the environment, and to be a good corporate citizen, mean that it is now a part of the aim of business, to take care of its employees, customers, the environment, and the local community? The short answer is no. The business enterprise exists to provide goods and services in order to make profits; if it is not making profits, its raison d'étre is violated.

Yet, seeking to provide the conditions for profit making, the business enterprise will ignore staff, suppliers, customers, the environment and community/public interests (represented for the most part by government) at its peril, for these are stakeholders. Business enterprise does not exist primarily to ensure that its employees can be fulfilled human beings or suppliers can feel important or loved. However, many businesses have now come to realise that decently treated employees and appropriately appreciated suppliers are essential to achievement of the business aim (Matthews, 1989, p. 135; Vallance, 1995). As the European Commission (1996, p. 76) has explained: "people orientation is not primarily chosen because of its rightness but because of its effectiveness". Business enterprise is concerned with the development of its staff and the interests of its other stakeholders only to the extent that those actions contribute to the aim of business, which is to create sufficient profit to satisfy the needs and expectations of shareholders (which are one of the stakeholders). As Vallance (1995, pp. 29–30) explains: Other social institutions exist to look after our souls, our physical well-being and the improvement of our minds. Institutions such as churches, schools and universities may well seek to create appropriate financial returns but not as their main aim. To fail to make the distinction of priority of aim, or to collapse the one into the other, is to be confused and confusing. As Rust et al. (1995) comments: "To be successful, a firm must deliver consistently high customer satisfaction while simultaneously satisfying its owners and employees . . . Satisfied owners are more likely to invest in the human resources of the firm, not necessarily by paying employees more, but providing the training, the equipment, and the conditions to make the work more productive and enjoyable. That leads to a dedicated work force, which, in turn, leads to superior products and services, and that leads back to higher customer satisfaction. In short, satisfying customers, employees, and owners is a never ending chain that reinforces itself". While satisfying key stakeholders sounds fairly straightforward, the fact is that most companies do not attempt to do it in a sustained manner.

The Social Responsibility of Business?

So if the primary responsibility of the business enterprise is to make a profit, where does the social responsibility come from? The CSR literature is unclear about the basis or rationale for claiming that business has a "social" responsibility. More specifically, that literature argues that business must respond to wider community because it has a responsibility to respond to wider community and needs, and not because of a responsibility to shareholders. Still, it does appear to rely on the view that business is a social entity. If that is the rationale for ascribing a community responsibility to business, it raises the question of which of the myriad of community needs and expectations should business respond to, and which should it ignore. Clearly business cannot respond to any and every concern that its activities generate. If there is a seemingly infinite number of community values that are impacted by business, how does business discriminate between the important and the unimportant? Expressing and acting upon some (but far from all) of the concerns of the wider community, raises the issue of how to treat the wider community. Management will respond to non-legislative demands only if to do otherwise would threaten accomplishment of the business aim. The responsibility of management in relation to the non-legislative demands is defining its responsibility in relation to the business aim.

Viewed in this way, the social "responsibility" of business is not the business aim but a business strategy, a way of determining direction and creating and maintaining relationships and structures that enhance performance. It is not the responsibility of business to fulfil its employees existentially, rather it is to help them to best achieve what the business asks of them. This means providing not simply appropriate training, but also a culture of trust and decency, freedom and support. Business is not the whole of life and substitute for family, school, club or church. Unless that distinction is explicitly and clearly drawn, there is a danger, as Mahoney (1989) has observed, of "overloading business with social expectations to such an extent that it may be hampered in its actual business activities, which must surely be its primary raison d'étre. Thus, the notion of responsibility relates to the relationship between the business aim and the stakeholder and not to some innate feature or quality of the stakeholder. Stakeholders are distinguished from the universe of interested/affected parties by having both the means of bringing their needs to the attention of management and the means of taking action if their demands are not satisfied.

Stakeholders

The notion that to survive, the business enterprise must consistently satisfy the needs and expectations of more than one stakeholder, and for one stakeholder in particular (shareholder/owner) it is necessary to generate profit, is now widely accepted. Stakeholders are defined as those entities that management believes to be capable of causing the enterprise to fail or cause unacceptable levels of damage if its needs are not met. Who then are the likely stakeholders of the modern enterprise? Though the answer to that question may be different between countries and businesses there is now considerable agreement that few Western organisations could anticipate long-term success if explicit attention were not given to shareholders (investors), management, government, staff, customers and suppliers. Management must meet the needs and expectations of those stakeholders because to do otherwise would breach of their responsibility to achieve the business aim. For stakeholders to be satisfied each must have sufficient knowledge of the state of the enterprise and plans for future actions (in terms relevant to each and providing confidence in the integrity of that information to ensure they will not take action detrimental to the enterprise). Thus, the notion of responsibility relates to the relationship between the business aim and the stake-holder and not to some innate (social) feature of the stakeholder(s). Stakeholders are distinguished from the universe of interested/affected parties by having both the means of bringing their needs to the attention of management and the means of taking action if their demands are not satisfied. It is, of course, possible to ignore stakeholders, to sell the tawdry and shoddy to the ill-informed and gullible, but only if there is no dependence on repeat business. Most businesses, certainly those being discussed here, seek a long-term future. As a consequence, management must devote as much attention to the creation of loyalty and goodwill with customers, staff, shareholders, government and suppliers, as they do to the more obviously profit-related activities of controlling costs or increasing margins.

The stakeholder concept also provides a new way of thinking about (strategic) management, that is, how a corporation can and should set and implement direction (Freeman, 1984). Stakeholders are the broad constituency served by business. As such they have a deemed interest in what a firm does in order to earn profits. While stakeholders have a prima-facie right to consideration in decision-making, it is not sufficient to negate the rights of society to a say in business dealings. In engaging in some practice, the interest of the stakeholders should be taken into account. The necessity for an enterprise to satisfy the needs and expectations of more than one stakeholder has changed both the character and behaviour of management (Crowther, 2002; Schrader, 1993). So the real shift is from considering the aim and behaviour of a profit maximising single stakeholder enterprise to one that is multi stakeholder and profit seeking (Crowther, 2002, p. 31). Enterprise success now depends on management being able to satisfy the perceived present and future needs and expectations of a number of stakeholders whose interests, and the means of satisfying those interests, are often very different, and in constant flux.

DEVELOPING ORGANISATIONAL THEORY

To ground new theoretical concepts and corporate strategies of a business-enterprise that is operating on a multi stakeholder perspective and profit seeking, it is essential to focus on underlying theoretical foundations. Such a concept should be based upon the basic assumption that the relation between organisations and society has fundamentally changed over the past century and a half. One of the more obvious features of this "new" perspective on the business enterprise is its demand for a theory that is holistic and capable of dealing with the often rapidly changing and conflicting needs of a disparate group of stakeholders. At the same time a complicating factor facing today's management is that presented by the enormous number and variety of management theories, methodologies, principles and techniques that compete for attention. Selection of a "theory" and appropriate methodology – or mix of methodologies – from that vast array is made the more difficult by some essentially identical approaches having different descriptions. Many lack empirical and theoretical support (though that is seldom obvious) and others whilst purporting to address the entire management system, deal with only one or a few of its many parts. In the face of those difficulties, management is very often confronted with the prospect of either adopting the newest most popular approach or conducting a lengthy (and inevitably fruitless) search of existing theory and practice. There is now a pressing need to overcome that unsatisfactory situation by developing a "General Theory of Business", which recognises that the long-term viability of an enterprise is determined by the ability of management to simultaneously satisfy the needs and expectations of stakeholders. What is needed is the further development of a contemporary theory of the firm that is consistent with the view of the stakeholder perspective as espoused above.

Theory of Theory

Given the subject of this paper it is appropriate to define what constitutes "theory".[3] Key (1999) defines theory as "a systematic attempt to understand what is observable in the world. It creates order and logic from observable facts that appear tumultuous and disconnected". A good theory would "identify relevant variables and the connections between them in a way that testable hypotheses can be generated and empirically established" (Key, 1999, pp. 317, 770). Key to a theory is the demonstration of associations between variables within a conceptual framework. In a similar vein (Bacharach, 1989, p. 836) has defined theory as "a statement of relations among concepts within a set of boundary assumptions and constraints" (1989, p. 496). He suggests that "good" theory in the social sciences should meet the following criteria: It must be falsifiable, logically coherent, operationalisable, useful and possess sufficient explanatory power in terms of scope and comprehensiveness. Ideally, good theory should have both explanatory value as well as predictive value (Key, 1999, pp. 317, 770). A theory should also include the underlying logic and values that explain the observable phenomenon. It must also be supported by a plausible or logical explanation to suggest how it happens (Labovitz & Hagedorn, 1971, p. 925).

At a more specific level, Brenner (1993, p. 797) has looked at what constitutes a theory of the firm. He suggests that such a theory "posits either a single decision principle or set of principles which explain a significant aspect of the organisation's behaviours" (Brenner, 1993, pp. 206, 797). Brenner and Cochran proposed that a theory of the firm should have three components: a world view, basic propositions and choice process(es) (Brenner & Cochran, 1991, p. 793). Taking this as a concise whole: A theory should offer a conceptual framework grounded upon a world-view (paradigm) containing basic propositions and choices. These should be guided by a set of (boundary) assumptions and principles offering explanatory power in terms of scope and comprehensiveness. As such good theory should create order and logic from observable facts that can be researched.

Building Blocks of a Contemporary Organisational Theory

Attempting to elaborate an organisational theory of the contemporary business enterprise the following building block can thus be defined. It is based upon a view of the firm as a "nexus of contracts". It seeks to explore strategic organ-isational behaviour vis-à-vis stakeholders in terms of the nexus of multilateral (changing) contracts where balancing and satisfying the needs and expectations of stakeholders is key in order to make a profit.

(1) To perceive an organisation – and more in particular the business enterprise – as an "open", "living" deliberately constructed social entity, aiming for profit;
(2) To identify its stakeholders (on regular intervals) – which could be more complicated than might first appear – and their needs and expectations;
(3) To adopt an appropriate management theory and underlying concepts best able to meet those various and changing needs;
(4) To organise through strategic processes (either inside or outside the organisation) the satisfaction of those needs and expectations;

(5) To establish the most effective method(s) of presenting information relating to actions taken or planned by management to meet stakeholder needs and expectations, given the changing and conflicting needs and expectations.

Those with responsibility for managing this "nexus of contracts" (executives and senior managers) operate within the context of multiple interests and expectations. Managers can be seen as "interest balancers" and are judged by their ability to satisfy the needs and expectations of participants. Managers, as one of the coalition of participants, negotiate with other participants to establish both objectives for the organisation and the strategies to achieve those objectives. However, this "negotiation" is not simply at their discretion. When decisions are made that are either not supported by other participants, or the needs and expectations of those participants are either not considered or ignored, then some form of conflict will arise. Given the complexity, the (potentially) conflicting interest and the changing nature of needs and expectations it is no wonder that a cry for " transparency" can be heard. It is literally impossible for any organisation to satisfy all needs and expectations of all participants or stakeholders.[4]

Investing in Dialogue and Social Capital

The assumptions underpinning the perspective include that organisational reality is by definition socially constructed. The organisation is a social artefact defined and successfully operating through a multi-level set of strategic processes of social and material interchange between participants. A contemporary concept of the business enterprise should therefore be focused on the challenge of creating inter-institutional and organisational arrangements, allowing members to participate in constitutional changes on all levels. By entering into dialogues with relevant actors from the political and academic systems or stakeholders from civil society, organisations should develop the necessary ability to take those social demands into account that have an impact on the continuity of the firm. Yet, this process of information exchange also allows the generation of knowledge about the conditions for action from other actors and the stabilisation of reciprocal behavioural expectations, thus allowing transparency in the almost impossible "job" of satisfying contradictory needs and expectations. These rules and regulations, developed within constitutional dialogues, are based on a broad sociological foundation labelled as "the social capital of society". This has important implications for further developing a theoretical perspective on the contemporary business enterprise. Deliberately investing in the development of social capital will involve initiating a transformation process in collaboration with partners, the outcomes of which cannot be fully determined in advance. Investing in social capital is therefore an interactive process where outcomes are not only determined by one's own moves, but also by the moves of one's partner(s). It also has important – but more practical – implications for people in business, politics or NGOs on how to guide and plan projects, based upon a common understanding of responsibility(ies) of different partners involved. Bottom-line, it means that organisations have to engage in a dialogue-process beyond the boundaries of the organisation in order to engage significant stakeholders. A process that will not only lead to more communication and interactions, but finally to a "nexus of trans-actions". The sphere of influence of the firm thus becomes a dynamic space as new transactions develop and change with new partners. In the end, key to this emerging organisational concept is managing the "transactivity" of the organisation.

Neither corporate responsibility nor the investment in social capital should be understood as expecting corporations to take over the paternal role and position held by national governments. It should be clear that the economic and social challenges (either on a local or global level) facing modern organisations are based upon the same societal roots and – structure. Therefore, corporations should not to be seen as a replacement for the family or be requested to solve all social problems. However, for organisations a "community strategy" is becoming a crucial issue in order to attain and maintain success in their social environment while pursuing the satisfaction of needs and expectations of their stakeholders. Organisations have to develop business strategies to invest in their social environment as well as in their natural environment ("natural capital"), just as previously, investment was made in roads, machines and buildings ("physical capital") or the professional training of employees (human capital). Corporate Social Responsibility (CSR) as defined above, can then be relabelled as "Organisational Citizenship" leading to a main-stream strategy to be conceived of as a responsible investment in social capital that generates a win-win for both the organisation and for society.

BUSINESS STRATEGIES

Returning to developing the business case for CSR a (corporate) strategy should interconnect the business aim and what needs to be done to ensure that the aim is achieved. Or, quoting Zadek one last time: " 'Good' companies that survive are going to have to be smarter than the rest. Their competitive edge will not come through the world's understanding of their extraordinary virtue. Being a 'good' company will generate financial benefits ... in taking advantage of emerging opportunities" (Zadek, 2002, p. 33). When contemporary business strategies are considered to deliver a contribution accountable to the organisational responsibility (which is primarily making profit), their potential to contribute to more general solutions of (policy) problems at a societal level becomes evident. The failure to make that distinction is responsible for most of what are confused discussions on the aim of business enterprise. Considerable emphasis has been placed on drawing a distinction between the aim of business enterprise and the strategies necessary to achieve that aim. The reasons for that emphasis are a prerequisite to understanding and effectively managing the modern enterprise. Far too much management literature, and the actual practice, is made unnecessarily complex and confusing because that distinction is not made (Clarke & Clegg, 1998, p. 366). Since (past and present) business strategies are embedded into a theory of the firm, changing those strategies also implies a change of theory. Business strategies are usually analysed through their "internal" operational and tactical logic and through the business values that drive them. Given the dominant position of organisations in society and the comprehensive nature, complexity and interconnectedness of the global problems at hand, that would be a limited if not dangerous approach.

Strategies are considered to be situation-bound normative sets of codes that guide the actual choices of organisational members restricted by a general business proposition within a specific context. The reason for emphasising the nature and role of plans, planning, strategy and strategic thinking and drawing the distinction between each extends beyond the need to describe the strategy. Moreover if enterprise viability depends on the satisfaction of those stakeholder needs and expectations, such planning is unquestionably strategic. An understanding of those issues, and particularly the distinction between them, is regarded as fundamental to an appreciation of the way in which modern management deals with the extraordinarily complex task of identifying and estimating the changing needs and expectations of stakeholders. Being able to plan, to have plans and strategies and to think strategically and not confuse those distinguishable activities is a necessary (but not sufficient) condition for enterprise success. This is not to suggest that it is always possible for management to establish goals and develop strategies that will be accepted and followed and that those goals and strategies will be optimal.

The implication of this for management is that the development of strategy is no longer a matter of adapting the organisation to the changing external reality. Instead, it involves engagement with stakeholders to become involved in the construction of their business reality in order to stay in business. This involves active engagement through valuable (inter)actions on the one hand, and mutual projects and leading to profits on the other, all leading to the satisfaction of various, changeable and sometimes conflicting needs and expectations. Viewed in this way, the social "responsibility" of business is not the business aim but a *business strategy*; a way of determining direction and creating and maintaining relationships and structures that enhance performance.

IN SEARCH OF SOCIETY

There is little doubt that many businesses need to open their eyes to opportunities linked to societies (either local or global). Managing the sphere of influence of the firm has become a dynamic process as new transactions develop and change. In the end, the key issue is managing the "transactivity" of the organisation in order to create profit. Organisational Citizenship should lead to a main-stream business strategy to be conceived of as a responsible investment in social capital that generates a win-win for both the organisation and for society. Really embedding the developed perspective of the contemporary business enterprise implies a transformation that can only be achieved in close collaboration and partnership with significant stakeholders, both inside and outside the organisation. The meaning of the social responsibility of business is a *business strategy*; a way of determining direction and creating and maintaining relationships and structures that enhance performance. The bottom-line is that it will force businesses to rethink and redefine their societal and environmental responsibilities (whatever the specific meaning and consequences) without losing sight of their primary economic responsibilities. For many organisations, this will mean an alteration – if not fundamental shift – in their all too familiar business paradigm. The business case for CSR should interconnect the business aim and what needs to be done to ensure that the aim is achieved, through an adequate (corporate) strategy.

NOTES

1. This contribution can hardly be called "my own work". It is mainly based upon – and inspired by – work in progress of Professor Kevin Foley, working at the University of Technology in Mebourne (Australia). More in particular his forthcoming book entitled "WHAT IS QUALITY MANAGEMENT". I am deeply indebted to him for allowing so much material to be used. Still, although I have used ideas, phrases, quotes and references taken from his work, the result presented here is entirely my own responsibility.

2. This paragraph is primarily based upon a research proposal written by the author in collaboration with Professor Andre Habisch, working at the University of Eichsteatt (Germany).

3. This section was drawn from a paper written by the author and David Foster, working at RMIT (Melbourne – Australia) entitled "QUALITY MANAGEMENT BEYOND THE ENTERPRISE – MOVING TOWARDS THE SOCIETAL EMBEDDENESS OF THE FIRM". The paper is a contribution to the 7th TQM World Conference to be held in Verona (Italy) during (June 2002). It hasn't been published yet.

4. This section was taken from "work in progress" by the author and David Foster (RMIT – Melbourne – Australia). See note 3 for further references.

REFERENCES

Bacharach, S. (1989). Organizational theories: Some criteria for evaluation. *Academy of Management Review, 14*, 496–515.

Birkin, F., & Woodward, D. (1997). Management accounting for sustainable development, Part 3: Stakeholder analysis. *Management Accounting, 75*, 858–860.

Brenner, S. N. (1993). The stakeholder theory of the firm and organisational decision-making: Some propositions and a model. *Proceedings of fourth Annual Meeting of the International Association for Business and Society*. San Diego.

Brenner, S. N., & Cochran, P. L. (1991). The stakeholder theory of the firm: Implications for business and society theory and research. *Proceedings of Second Annual Meeting of International Association for Business and Society*. Sundance, Utah.

Clarke, T., & Clegg, S. (1998). *Changing paradigms: The transformation of management knowledge for the 21st Century*. London: Harper Collins.

Crowther, D. (2002). *A social critique of corporate reporting: A semiotic analysis of corporate financial and environmental reporting*. Aldershot, UK: Ashgate.

Demsetz, H. (1997). The primacy of economics: An explanation of the comparative success of economics in the social sciences. *Economic Enquiry, 35*(1), 1–11.

European Commission (1996). *The European way to excellence*. Brussels.

Freeman, E. R. (1984). *Strategic management: A stakeholder approach*. Boston: Pitman/Ballinger.

Friedman, M. (1970). The social responsibility of business is to increase its profits. *New York Times Magazine* (September 13th), 33, 122 and 126.

Handy, C. (1985). *Understanding organisations*. London: Penguin.

Key, S. (1999). Toward a new theory of the firm: A critique of 'stakeholder' theory. *Management Decision, 37*(4), 317–328.

Labovitz, S., & Hagedorn, R. (1971). *Introduction to social research*. New York: McGraw Hill.

Mahoney, J. (1989). *The role of business in society, lecture – series on business and social responsibility*. London: Grisham College.

Matthews, J. A. (1989). New production concepts. *Prometheus, 7*, 129–148.

Metzger, M. B., & Dalton, D. R. (1996). Seeing the elephant: An organizational perspective on corporate moral agency. *American Business Law Journal, 33*(4), 489–532.

Orts, E. W. (1998). The future of enterprise organisation. *Michigan Law Review Association, 96*(6), 1947–1963.

Putterman, L., & Kroszner, R. S. (Eds) (1996). *The economic nature of the firm: A reader*. Cambridge: Cambridge University Press.

Raiborn, C., & Payne, D. (1996). TQM: Just what the ethicisit ordered. *Journal of Business Ethics, 15*(9), 963–1002.

Rust, R. T., Zahorick, A. J., & Keiningham, T. L. (1995). Return on quality (ROQ): Making service quality financially accountable. *Journal of Marketing, 59*, 58–70.

Schrader, D. E. (1993). *The corporation as anomaly*. Cambridge: Cambridge University Press.

Vallance, E. (1995). *Business ethics at work*. Cambridge: Cambridge University Press.

Zadek, S. (2002). Companies should look for the business case for integrating responsible social and environmental policies. In: *Ethical Corporation Magazine* (5 May, pp. 9–33).

BANKING AND SOCIAL RESPONSIBILITY

Jonathan A. Batten and Warren P. Hogan

ABSTRACT

A debate on governance and social responsibility in banking is crucial given that banking remains at the core of financial systems in both the developed and undeveloped world. A unique feature of their operations is the settlement afforded by the payments system whereby banks may write cheques against themselves. In light of the essential culture of credit at the heart of banking operations then the structures of corporate governance should reflect the supervision and management of risks and credit especially so. Corporations must be alert to those arrangements whereby the perceived voting rights of stakeholders impose conditions where a weighted average of interests represents the final outcome.

1. SYNOPSIS

Banks are at the core of the financial system in any market economy. The unique feature of their operations is the settlement afforded by the payments system whereby banks may write cheques, or electronic equivalent claims, upon themselves. Even though official management and supervision of the payments system has been greatly enhanced in the past decade, the integrity of the payments system rests upon the quality of the participants. That integrity is essential to ensuring the completion of transactions in the real sectors of the economy as well as those involving the transfer of ownership of financial assets and liabilities.

Social Responsibility: Corporate Governance Issues
Research in International Business and Finance, Volume 17, 441–455
© 2003 Published by Elsevier Science Ltd.
ISSN: 0275-5319/PII: S0275531903170201

In light of the banking culture being a culture of credit, the heart of all banking operations lies in the management of risks. Thus, structures of corporate governance in banking are about the means by which board and management secure the optimisation of risk-reward structures. The analysis of risk is supported by other banking functions such as the generation of information about clients and potential ones.

New developments reflecting legislative changes and proliferation of stakeholder interests, emphasise the need for institutions to account for their social responsibilities beyond the maximisation of shareholders' returns. New tasks for board and management are imposed by these requirements whether formal or otherwise. Yet there are complicated issues as to what these requirements mean and how they should be analysed. While the analysis of obligations arising in the banking sphere reach well beyond the financial services sector, the concerns for establishing the basis for testing whether or not the new requirements or goals have been achieved are important. The paper sets out to establish what formal meanings may be attached to goals of social responsibility and their interpretations for testing outcomes.

The paper aims at providing a framework for discussion of what social responsibilty means for banks and other deposit-taking institutions.

2. THE SETTING

This paper has as its purpose an examination of the roles of corporate governance and social responsibility in the conduct of banking.[1] Notwithstanding the process of disintermediation and a shift towards market mechanisms, banks remain at the core of financial systems, particularly in the developing world and are crucial for the efficient allocation of capital.[2] Nevertheless the treatment of the two themes of corporate governance and social responsibility does call for some general appraisal before turning to matters specific to banking. Moreover, it is not the intention to look into all features of the financial services sector even though some banks, and most of the larger ones, pursue activities other than banking such as funds management, general and life insurances and discount broking. Some reference to the differences will be made where necessary to aid understanding of issues.

Corporate governance is about the ways in which business organisations conduct themselves and to what purposes. In the Australian context, the Australian National Audit Office (1999, p. 1) has defined corporate governance as the "process by which organisations are directed, controlled and held to account". There are many interpretations of the issues involved in the analysis of corporate governance, for example a perspective on the differing corporate governance regimes by Stilpon and Thompson (1999) highlights the effect of the legal bases, whether civil or common law. Overall, three central features may be identified. First, there are owners of business organisations however legally constituted as corporate entities, various forms of partnerships or cooperative societies. Secondly, the organisation has a board of directors supervising the workings of management responsible for day-to-day operations. Thirdly, the organisation must have a set of objectives towards which the entity is directed and against which results are measured. The organization is then a nexus of contractual arrangements[3] between claimants to the products and earnings, a view that dates back to Coase (1937).

At issue in corporate governance is the extent to which the business organisation must take into account the ways in which its activities affect others being individuals, households and legal entities. This feature has come to be called stakeholder interests. These may be viewed as the users of the outputs of the business organisation or the providers of inputs to reflect upon two such stakeholder interests. These may be seen as distinct and separate from those of the owners, the shareholders, being the providers of the equity capital.

Mention is made of this distinction of interests at the outset because it blends into the other theme of corporate social responsibility. This amorphous term appears to embrace not just the claims of stakeholders, as distinct from shareholders, but the wider communities in which the business organisations operate. For example, the claim may be advanced about any one business benefiting from the community in which it operates while not many members of the community benefit from its presence. This aspect points to a claim being made for compensatory payments to the socially disadvantaged, in effect a wealth transfer or redistribution. However, it is important to understand the looseness of the concept of social responsibility so that what the term embraces is all too often in the eye of the beholder. It is a reflection of those abstractions and generalisations devoid of scope for testing.

Before turning to matters of corporate governance and social responsibility, it is essential to develop an understanding of the ways in which the banking system, and each bank within it, works so that essentials are identified. In this way it should be possible to clarify the roles of banks and what this means for the claims of others than the owners and management. The following section offers an analysis of the workings of banks and what this means for the economy.

3. THE FUNCTIONS AND MECHANISMS OF BANKING

In this segment the focus is on three features; the functions of banking, the mechanisms for asset management being about credit first and foremost, and the constraints on the conduct of banking business. The three are connected and relate to ways of thinking about the connections between banking and provision of goods and services across the economy.

3.1. Functions

For an understanding of the functions performed by any one bank, an appraisal should start with the proposition that the bank under scrutiny is in equilibrium. This means the bank is "fully lent". This means the bank is not in a position to lend more money because it has utilised its cash reserves and liquidity support to meet the scale of assets deployed given the risk-return relationships desired by the bank's board and management. Technically, in terms of the analysis of a bank's revenue statement and balance sheet, the equilibrium would be described as the condition where the marginal net revenue from making loans is equal to the total marginal cost of maintaining and servicing deposits which includes interest payments, marginal operating costs and marginal liquidity cost. In short it is a matter of marginal funding costs in relation to lending opportunities. Given these conditions there is no confusion with banking mechanisms, which are the subject of the following sub-section.

The purpose of this appraisal of functional relationships in banking is to clarify the ways in which some activities pursued by banks are not dissimilar from other entities in the financial services sector while others are distinctly different. There are six basic functions that may be distinguished.

3.1.1. Clearing and Settlement
The payments system ensures the completion of the exchanges of goods and services as well as financial assets and liabilities between individuals and entities in the economy. The clearing and settlement arrangements bring certainty to transactions in goods and services. The main characteristic is the electronic and paper transfers between banks holding accounts, known as exchange settlement accounts, at the central bank, for example in the case of Australia is the Reserve Bank of Australia (RBA). These obligations are "written" by any one bank's customers against that bank's reserve being largely the sums held at the RBA. Other bank customers have claims against cheques that will be lodged in payment thus counterbalancing more or less the depletion in reserves brought about by the payment of obligations. Thus, clearing and settlement afforded by the payments system whereby banks may write cheques against themselves is a feature unique to banking.

3.1.2. Pooling and Divisibility
This function is about the means used to take a flow of funds reflecting small and large collections from households and amongst legal entities and then convert them

into sums for lending to bring about production and asset creation such as with residential mortgages to fund housing and apartment construction. Pooling and divisibility are more familiar in terms of intermediation being the primary activity of banks as distinct from direct financing being the raising of funds through equity and debt issuance on securities markets.

3.1.3. Resource Transfers

Resource transfers concern the real effects in the economy of the activities associated with the monetary values embodied in the pooling and divisibility function. This aims for the optimal allocation of resources, subject to uncertainty, most of all with respect to capital spending and the efficient location of plant and equipment. These resource transfers are also about lifetime and intergenerational allocations so timing as well as location are important to assessments of optimality.

3.1.4. Risk Management

This is about managing the uncertainties associated with borrowing and lending. Until some three decades ago, measures to manage risk were embedded in the contracts associated in one or other activity. Historically insurance companies were the progenitors of risk management through the offering of contracts as "policies" freeing the buyer of the contract from exposure to risk of some activity not being successful. From the early 1970s the separation of risk bearing from real investment outlays became possible on a comprehensive basis with the growth of markets for trading financial futures and then options. Later there were further developments with derivative contracts to allow switching of interest rates between fixed and variable rates over the life of a contract as well as to permit substitution of currencies. The latest development is with credit derivatives; their purpose is to transfer the credit exposure explicit to a loan agreement from the originating lender to another financial entity, which takes the full credit exposure for a fee.

The effect of all these new developments starting in the early 1970s is to make possible the pure lending function from the risks associated with a loan. In turn this means that risk management may be seen as a separate function from borrowing and lending. One cannot underestimate the importance of these tasks. Incorrect risk assessment and measurement has been largely responsible for the underlying weakness of the domestic banking systems in Asia and Japan (Khan, 2001) and directly contributed to the Asian financial crisis. It is also interesting to note that contrary to popular belief, recent financial collapses (the most spectacular being the Barings Group) usually have little to do with the specific risks associated with derivative contracts, but rather the failure of management to monitor and analyse trading activities and the risks associated with them (Hogan & Batten, 2001).

3.1.5. Information

Financial transactions in whatever market they are developed depend for their implementation on information about the entities incurring obligations. Bear in mind that this type of commitment applies to the traditional instruments used by borrowers from banks and the counterparties to transactions in various derivative and securities markets. That information may come from public sources or be privately held. The larger companies listed for trading in stockmarkets are reliant on the publicly available information demanded of them as part of listing requirements. Separately but with the same outcome, rating agencies secure information to ensure an informed market, so far as is possible, in which the equity and debt issues of the companies are traded. Larger companies have choices whether or not to fund their positions by borrowings from banks or to raise funds through new issues to the stockmarket.

This is not so with the smaller to medium size company or partnership. Few could afford the costs of listing and where they chose to do so would find trading in their shares infrequent to the point where trades would be infrequent and thus illiquid. Similarly the costs of securing assessment by a rating agency would be prohibitive. Thus, for the great bulk of smaller and medium size business the information about the company is privately held by the lender. In this context the bank making the loan is acting in place of the market to verify the quality of the loan in terms of its characteristics but most of all its credit quality.

The existence of rating agencies shows how the information function is not the preserve of the banks. Rather it is the cost of gleaning information which confines their activities to the larger companies wanting recognition for their qualities to justify their securities being funded by institutions.

3.1.6. Completion

This function is about the measures taken to ensure that all parties to a contract are equally informed about the conditions of contracts, transparency in arrangements during the course of a contract and the means to secure completion in terms of the original contract. The critical theme is to minimize the costs of enforcing contract terms, which means setting incentives to bring mutual benefits to the parties. The risk of exposure to moral hazard is the major issue because of the unobservability of some contingent possibilities.

Part of the issue in this context is the aim of banks to ensure the loans made are used for the purposes specified in the lending contract. This is not necessarily secure should the range of items in the balance sheet of the borrowing entity not be fully disclosed or understood. This lack of understanding can permit an osmotic process to adapt priorities for resource allocation not readily apparent to the lender.

This summary appraisal of the six functions identified with banking business is revealing of much which banks have in common with other financial institutions. Historically many of the activities of insurance companies, whether life or general, are similar to those of banks when perceived in terms of information and risk management quite apart from the aggregation of funds especially in the life sphere. Funds management in general, not just in life insurance, is about pooling and divisibility as well as resource transfers.

Indeed the only function amongst the six listed is the one associated with the payments system, namely clearing and settlement. This has been historically the responsibility of banks because each had to honour the claims on them presented by other banks as a result of liabilities created by their customers. Now any legal entity may be a member of the payments system provided they can meet the prudential standards laid down for banks. The implications for issues in corporate governance and social responsibility are onerous.

With corporate governance the inability of board and management of a bank to manage the risk-return requirements bringing potential instability and systemic risk might deprive that bank's customers of access to clearing and settlement as well as bringing hardship and increased costs to the real sectors of the economy. The social responsibility issues must be treated in terms of efforts of interested groups to thwart an activity deemed to be unfriendly in some way or other which were it to be realised would bring lack of access to the payments system which would mean prohibition on business activities owing to failure to gain completion to its contracts with no means of clearing and settlement.

In an open democratic society, prohibitions on business activities should be exercised only by government rather than be inflicted on business organizations. This does not mean that institutions not commanding access to essential functions for business should be placed in the same position. Then choices can be made whether or not to accept claims of the need to act in socially responsible ways.

3.2. Mechanisms

The preceding discussion of functions was based upon a premise which recognised the equilibrium condition of banks or a single bank. Its sole purpose was to concentrate on functions. But equilibrium is a rare condition for any bank to find itself in, as there is need to adapt to shifting circumstances as the reserves and liquidity conditions change; for example when a central bank adapts liquidity in its economy to bring about policy targets.

Disequilibrium is the order of the day for banks and, most often, the banking system as a whole. The mechanism for adjusting the balance sheet structure is the growth of assets under conditions where the bank is holding excess reserves and liquidity. Where a bank is faced with a loss of reserves and potential illiquidity, the task for management is the running off of loans and the disposal of securities held in trading portfolios to restore stability in the balance sheet. The speed and extent of the adjustment is influenced by the rate at which loans mature and overdrafts may be called in. This means the expansion of credit by means of additional loans and similar financial instruments as well as the acquisition of securities traded in markets.

This mechanism serves to emphasise the essential feature of banking activity. Above all else banking is about the management of credit. The information and risk management functions are about the provision of material to inform the decisions on the granting of credit or its rejection. There are other features to risk in the banking milieu such as market risk being exposures to variability in values and volume of financial instruments in markets where they are traded, operational risk related to the failure of management systems to measure and record accurately the contracts associated with assets and liabilities, and variants reflecting market volatility such as interest rate and currency risks. Clearing and settlement involves exposure to risk that parties will not complete, most obviously where counterparties collapse or cannot secure foreign currency to meet obligations internationally. Yet this settlement risk is, simply put, a particular example of credit risk in the setting of completion.

The implications are straightforward. The basic element of banking is credit. The banking milieu is a culture of credit. It cannot be anything else because a failure to grasp the overwhelming task of credit management across the entire asset portfolio puts at risk the stability of any one bank. No less significant is the way the performance in asset management determines the capacity to fund liabilities to support liquidity as well as fund assets themselves.

3.3. Constraints

Given the importance of the payments system to the workings of the real economy, and the implications of any breakdown in arrangements for employment, investment and output, there can be no surprise about the ways the activities pursued by banks are circumscribed by authorities and market participants. In short banks are beholden to others in the economy thus constraining the types and range of activities undertaken. Thus, efforts of board and management to provide shareholders with maximum value or returns on an on-going basis are constrained by the actions of regulatory authorities to monitor and supervise prudent behaviour, or respond to the potential for systemic risk.

Other constraints are found in the efforts of the tax authorities in delineating the bases by which incomes are earned and measured though this relationship can be a testing one. Then there are market constraints. For example, the rating agencies make judgements about the quality of any one bank's performance just as they do for any other listed public company. This rating process impinges on the cost of raising funds and may help or hinder earnings. Another role is played by the debtholders of bank securities issued in debt markets. The covenants associated with the borrowing contracts by which the debt securities are issued bind the behaviour of banks in the same way as for any other company. In an important sense these participants are no less "stakeholders" than any other set of people or entities having relationships with banks.

4. CORPORATE GOVERNANCE

In the context of the modern financial system with its suppliers and users of funds, the practice of corporate governance has developed to ensure that those that supply finance to modern corporations are assured of its return along with a reward commensurate with the underlying risk of the contract. This practice is now more critical given the move towards disintermediated forms of corporate financing evident in many developed and developing countries. Under these circumstances providers of funds – both debt and equity – must attend to both the task of monitoring and to ensure the quality of mechanisms that facilitate these activities. As Hart (1995) argues, the inability to create perfect contracts then necessitates a need for corporate governance. Thus, corporate governance issues arise wherever contracts are incomplete and agency problems exist.

The empirical investigation of corporate failures during the 1980s highlights these concerns, with corporate governance proposed as a general prescription. Various investigative reports[4] suggest the development of codes though these recommendations have been questioned because the costs appear to place onerous restrictions on smaller firms compared with the benefits they would receive. While initially the primacy of the board of directors remained firmly entrenched in the governance literature, more recently there has been an increasing awareness that an intricate set of relationships, both internal and external, affect the way corporations are governed.

One must differentiate between three broad categories of agency problems arising in modern corporations. The first concerns conflicts of interest between managers and shareholders, the second between shareholders and bondholders, and the third between old and new shareholders due to information asymmetry problems. The modern finance and microeconomics literature has largely focused on problems arising from the separation of ownership between managers and shareholders with solutions found in corporate law, capital markets, signalling and financial intermediation, and corporate governance. The latter aims to overcome, or at least mitigate, incentive concerns.

There is no one perspective on corporate governance owing to cultural, social and political differences across economies.[5] However, as many authors have observed (for example Zhuang, 1999), the nature of corporate governance reflects a country's financial and legal system and on this basis there are clearly two main models: the Anglo-American market-based system and the European-Japanese relationship-based system. The first has its foundations in common law, with the latter in civil law. In a recent series of papers, La Porta, Lopez-De-Silanes, Shleifer and Vishny (1998, 2000a, b) (LLSV) investigate the relationship between legal origin, investor protection and finance. Their findings suggest that investor protection, consisting of legal protection and ownership concentration, varies depending on a country's legal regime. Specifically, common law countries were found to have greater legal protection, whereas in civil law countries there is evidence of higher ownership concentration. Thus, Shleifer and Vishny (1997, p. 769) suggest "that both the legal protection of investors and some form of concentrated ownership are essential elements of a good corporate governance system . . . legal protection and large investors are complementary in an effective corporate governance system".

Pertinent to this paper is the recent study commissioned by the ADB (2000) to investigate the corporate governance structures of the Asian Crisis Economies. In the comprehensive analysis, drawn from five individual case studies of Indonesia, Korea, Malaysia, Thailand and the Philippines, the ADB provided a comparison of governance structures, focusing on ownership, finance and control. They found, on the whole, that the governance structures of the Crisis Economies closely resembled each other. Generally, the elements were high ownership concentration (allowing insiders to dominate control), bank-centric financial systems, ineffective shareholders rights and low transparency.

The Anglo-American emphasis lies in the maximization of shareholder value subject to some variations associated with the nature of bankruptcy law treating the extent of protection afforded debtors from their creditors. The arguments in favour of the maximization of shareholder value are succinctly expressed by Tirole (2001, p. 32): (a) it makes up for the dearth of pledgeable income; (b) it provides more focus and sharper incentives for managers; and (c) undivided control prevents foot-dragging and deadlock in decision-making. There is considerable empirical evidence to support these claims. For example, Johnson and Greening (1999), investigating the effects of corporate governance and institutional ownership types in U.S. firms conclude that the presence of managerial equity holdings does increase managerial attention to stakeholder interests.

In essence this approach to corporate governance relies upon market discipline to ensure commitments to the pursuit of shareholder value and the maximization of returns. The equities market becomes in these circumstances a market about corporate control. There is always the possibility for a company to be subject to challenge by merger or takeover from a rival company while the board and management of any one company may be open to ejection through the acquisition of a sufficient shareholding by those who see the means to do better than the incumbent with the assets of the company.

But this is not the only approach to corporate governance. Other countries do not have the same approaches to equities trading. Germany has a system historically which revolved around the role of the universal banks. Their functions were to manage the arrangements of companies and sponsor their development to the point when they could be floated on the stockmarket. Even then the universal banks remained the custodian of the companies they had sponsored and held shares for themselves as well as acting as agent for other shareholdres including voting their shares. Thus, the bank and the company had a symbiotic relationship involving a great measure of interaction about strategy and management. The stockmarket was not a market for corporate control. Similar manifestations are present in the Japanese and French experiences with the former emphasising the role of the banks with the latter much more that of the state.

5. SOCIAL RESPONSIBILITY

The applicability of social responsibility concepts to banking may be better understood by first providing an overview of key arguments central to this debate. The position from the viewpoint of ethics is clear; social responsibility is both morally correct and should be considered even if this involves an unproductive resource allocation. Such an allocation may over the long-term be rational since firms may be able to extract concessions from society and government and enable product differentiation between less socially responsible competitors (Jones, 1996, 1999).

It is interesting to record the evidence on this point provided by Johnson and Greening (1999, p. 574). Their study of U.S. firms suggests that outside directors are more predisposed to non-profit goals since they believe this will be in the best long-term interests of shareholders. This view focuses on the development of quality products and a positive environmental reputation and suggests that board diversity and a corporations' positive attitude to social responsibility are likely to be correlated. On the other hand the alternate perspective based on institutional function, or property rights, and its paradigm centred on the primacy of shareholder wealth maximization above other stakeholder interests. This perspective concerns the extension of stakeholder arguments into all those relationships involving users of bank services as well as providers of inputs. But why and under what circumstances would a bank not look to the interests of customers, who are not necessarily shareholders, because without them there would be no business?

The best answer lies with the failure of markets due to the presence of a monopoly (or oligopoly) and an inability to freely enter and exit a market. However in the banking sector there is clear evidence of market segmentation despite deregulatory efforts to open up these markets. It must be remembered that banking is ultimately a transaction-based business and the non-regulatory barriers to entry, such as those applying to scale and scope economies, are breaking down due to electronic access and internet-based activities. The emergence of community-based banks as competitors at the retail end of the market also bodes well for the efficiency of the market mechanism.

Then there are the wider issues of looking after those dispossessed by change. How far does the responsibility of corporate entities extend as compared with government? And in the event that a subsidy be agreed (as perhaps applies to the provision of services in remote areas) should it not be explicit? These are important questions which have preoccupied intellectual debate. Tirole (2000, p. 1) amongst others would argue that the implementation of a broader stakeholder society strikes three rocks, "dearth of pledgeable income, deadlocks in decision making, and lack of a clear mission for management".

The concept of pledgeable income requires the return from a project to be greater than the outlay to investors in order to ensure that the project is financed. Thus, investors require sufficient pledgeable income, a position that may force an entrepreneur to relinquish rights to prospective cash flows (for example firms with weak balance-sheets during a start-up phase have little equity, collateral and guaranteed income and so usually relinquish rights to venture capitalists). Clear mission and management decisions assists the process of holding managers accountable for their actions. Should the fiduciary duty of managers be expanded to a broader concept of stakeholders then how should this duty be measured?

This brief illustration of the complexities associated with the notion of social responsibility requires some further explanation. In the corporate setting there appear to be three layers to ways in which corporate responsibility should be exercised positively. There are the connections to suppliers and users of services as well as to those who may be acting as agents on behalf of the corporate entity. In all these instances, as has been noted earlier, it is hard to think why any company would act to thwart these groups when success as measured by earnings depends heavily upon good relationships. The second category or layer is about general business practices and policies which amount to matters associated with reporting and accountability. There exist strong legal requirements for many of these activities in most market economies though examples of transgressions are most prominent at this time. Even so the spirit of transparency in accounting for actions is not honoured in the detail and extent a positive approach to corporate social responsibility might warrant. The third layer or category is about wider community participation. In some respects contributions are of long-standing when recognition is given to the support of charities by companies. Nonetheless the "new" social responsibility goes much wider to questions about community investment and initiatives.

These last matters merit close scrutiny. They are often couched in language, which implies their purpose is to build "social capital" though the precise implications of that term are hazy. There is a meaning which seems to be about some strategic involvement with community groups to address a limited range of social issues. These are beyond matters of environmental protection though various interpretations are on offer, some of which would place this topic as one of the social issues. In effect there is a looseness to the claims for social responsibility which places the current appraisals as something akin to hostages to fortune and the machinations of interest groups.

In light of this brief discussion the focus might turn back to banking. Consider concerns readily expressed about the environment and the opposition of some proportion of the population in many countries to the mining of uranium. What is one to make of any claim on grounds of social responsibility for a bank not to be associated with the financial activities of a uranium mining company? Given the singular position of banks in the payments system, to which reference was made in an earlier section, a prohibition would effectively mean the cessation of this mining. Yet so long as the national government does not preclude uranium mining this exercise of social responsibility would be tantamount to abrogating the role of government.

The example serves to illustrate the potential quandary arising with the advancement of claims for the exercise of social responsibility by companies. Actions by special interest groups with any community could see opportunities to secure outcomes which might not be accessible to them through ordinary democratic processes. In effect this means some risk of adding to a range of entities and the like who seek decisions by extra-parliamentary means and with the specific authority in legislation.

6. CONCLUSIONS

A debate on governance and social responsibility in banking is crucial given that they remain at the core of financial systems in both the developed and undeveloped world. Initially this discussion considered the functions of banking, the mechanisms for asset management and the constraints on the conduct of banking business. A unique feature of their operations is the settlement afforded by the payments system whereby banks may write cheques against themselves. The strictures here apply to banks as in banking and not in their other functions such as funds management. In light of the essential culture of credit at the heart of banking operations then, the structures of corporate governance should reflect the supervision and management of risks and credit especially so. The debate on the role of corporate governance in the modern corporation highlights the relevance of the legal environment and the institutional arrangements in which the corporation operates. The applicability of social responsibility concepts to banking was then considered. While there may be a moral basis underpinning stakeholder theory, this basis must be translated into law. Thus, corporations must be alert to those arrangements whereby what is tantamount to the "voting rights" of stakeholders impose conditions where a weighted average of interests represents the final outcome. Such an outcome may not necessarily be one which maximizes firm value in either the short, or the long term.

NOTES

1. The views expressed are those of the authors and do not reflect judgements and opinions of organisations with which they are associated or have been associated.
2. See Beck and Ross (2001) concerning industry growth and the role of banks versus market-based financial systems. Wurgler (2000) demonstrates the positive correlation between the level of financial market development and the efficient allocation of capital.
3. See Easterbrook and Fiscel (1989) and Kornhauser (1989).
4. For example, the (1999) Commonwealth Association for Corporate Governance, Guidelines. The (1998) OECD Principles of Corporate Governance – primarily based on Western legal and ethical concepts "focus on governance issues that result from the separation of ownership and control" (OECD, 1999, p. 2).
5. See Macey and O'Hara (2001) for a discussion of these perspectives.

REFERENCES

Asian Development Bank (2000). *Corporate governance and finance in East Asia: A Study of Indonesia, Republic of Korea, Malaysia, Philippines, and Thailand, 1* (A consolidated report) Asian Developent Bank.
Beck, T., & Ross L. (2001). Industry growth and capital allocation: Does having a market or bank-based system matter. World bank working paper (March).
Commonwealth Association for Corporate Governance (1999). *CACG Guidelines, Principles for Corporate Governance in the Commonwealth: Towards global competitiveness and economic accountability.*

Coase, R. H. (1937). The nature of the firm. *Economica, 4.*

Easterbrook, F., & Fischel, D. (1989). The corporate contract. *Columbia Law Review, 89.*

Hart, O. (1995). Corporate governance: Some theory and implications. *The Economic Journal, 105*(May), 678–689.

Hogan, W., & Batten, J. (2001). Corporate governance issues in Barings' failure. Issues in international corporate control and governance. *Research in International Business and Finance, 15,* 331–351.

Johnson, R., & Greening, D. (1999). The effects of vorporate governance and institutional ownership types on corporate social responsibility. *Academy of Management Journal, 42*(5), 564–576.

Jones, M. (1996). Missing the forest for the trees: A critique of the social responsibility concept and discourse. *Business and Society, 35*(1), 7–41.

Jones, M. (1999). The institutional determinates of social responsibility. *Journal of Business Ethics, 20,* 163–179.

Khan, H. (2001). Corporate governance of family business in Asia. Asian development bank conference on corporate governance working paper.

Kornhauser, L. (1989). The nexus of contracts approach to corporations: A comment on Easterbrook and Fiscel. *Columbia Law Review, 89.*

La Porta, R., with Lopez-De-Silanes, F., Shleifer, A., & Vishy, R. (1998). Law and finance. *Journal of Political Economy, 106*(6) (December), 1113–1155.

La Porta, R., with Lopez-De-Silanes, F., Shleifer, A., & Vishy, R. (2000a). Agency problems and dividend policies around the world. *The Journal of Finance, 55*(1) (February), 1–34.

La Porta, R., with Lopez-De-Silanes, F., Shleifer, A., & Vishy, R. (2000b). Investor protection and corporate governance. *Journal of Financial Economics, 58* (October), 1–2, 3–27.

Macey, J., & O'Hara, M. (2001). The corporate governance of banks. FRBNY *Economic Policy Review,* 1–17.

Organisation for Economic Co-operation and Development (1999). Principles of corporate governance (p. 2) (see www.oecd.org/daf/governance.htm).

Shleifer, A., & Vishy, R. W. (1997). A Survey of Corporate Governance. *Journal of Finance, 52*(2) (April), 737–783.

Stilpon, N., & Thompson, J. (1999). Corporate governance patterns in OECD countries: Is convergence under way? *OECD Conference on corporate governance in Asia: A comparative perspective,* Seoul (3–5 March).

Tirole, J. (2000). Corporate governance. *Econometrica, 69*(1), 1–35.

Wurgler, J. (2000). Financial markets and the allocation of capital. *Journal of Financial Economics, 58,* 187–214.

Zhuang, J. (1999). Some conceptual issues of corporate governance. EDRC Briefing notes, number 13. *Economics and development resource center, Asian development bank,* Manila, Phillipines.

THE INFORMATIONAL COMPLEXITY APPROACH AS A CRITERION FOR MODEL SELECTION IN FINANCE

Amitabh S. Dutta, Hamparsum Bozdogan,
M. Cary Collins and James W. Wansley

1. INTRODUCTION

This paper proposes the use of Bozdogan's Informational Complexity (ICOMP) criterion to help determine empirically for a sample of firms whether institutional ownership is endogenous or exogenous to the system of equations determining the relation between equity ownership and corporate policy.

Empirical financial analysis has often debated about selecting the most appropriate methodology for determining relations amongst variables of concern to researchers. Some questions have been addressed by partial correlation analysis. Other approaches have focused on methods such as factor analysis, maximum likelihood estimation, or auto regressive conditional heteroscedasticity. By far, most empirical research though utilizes multivariate regression analysis. Multivariate regression analysis itself has multiple options, from simple OLS to nonlinear simultaneous equations regression.

Regardless of the chosen form or system of multivariate regression analysis, one question facing researchers is the choice of the model that best fits the available data. However, besides goodness of fit, researchers are aware that the model must also be parsimonious. It is generally accepted that some criterion other than purely R^2 (or even, adjusted R^2) needs to be used to choose the best model. The two

Social Responsibility: Corporate Governance Issues
Research in International Business and Finance, Volume 17, 457–462
ISSN: 0275-5319/PII: S0275531903170213

criteria that should be used jointly to judge the best model are goodness of fit and model parsimony.

Bozdogan (1988, 1990a, b) has developed a new Informational Complexity (ICOMP) criterion for model selection in general multivariate linear and nonlinear structural models. Bearse, Bozdogan and Schlottmann (1997) apply ICOMP to their econometric modeling of food consumption.

The format of the paper is as follows. Section 2 gives a brief introduction to the informational approach to model evaluation and a more detailed explanation of Bozdogan's ICOMP criterion. Section 3 proposes one potential use for ICOMP and discusses the methodology of doing so. Section 4 summarizes and concludes the paper.

2. INFORMATION-THEORETIC APPROACH TO MODEL EVALUATION

Bozdogan (1990a) defines a statistical model as a mathematical formulation that expresses the main features of the data in terms of probabilities. Any model used to fit available data is an attempt to clarify the underlying relations amongst the variables of concern. Since the exact nature of the variable interdependencies is not known – all models will be inexact representations of the true model. Thus, model selection criteria have been developed as objective measures of model performance. The best model is the one with the lowest criterion value.

2.1. Akaike's Metric, AIC

Akaike's (1973) Information Criterion is a sample estimate of the expected log likelihood, or equivalently, the expected Kullback and Leibler (1951) (K–L) information in a set of data. Bozdogan (1987) proves how AIC may be applied to compare models in a set of competing models. In words, AIC can be interpreted as:

$$\text{AIC} = -2\log(\text{maximized likelihood}) + 2\,(\text{no. of free parameters in the model}) \quad (1)$$

The first term is a measure of the lack of fit (model inaccuracy or bias). The second term is a penalty for increased unreliability of the bias in the first term due to additional free parameters in the model. This application of AIC emphasizes comparing goodness of fit across models – while adjusting for the principle of parsimony.

2.2. Bozdogan's ICOMP

As an alternative to AIC, Bozdogan's ICOMP criterion is designed to test the lack of fit of a particular model to a given data set. Given several different multivariate linear (and non-linear) structural models, this measure estimates the lack of fit for each model. The model with the lower ICOMP is chosen to be the best model, that is, the model most likely to reflect the true relation between the endogenous and exogenous variables.

Though the analytic formulation of ICOMP has the spirit of AIC, it utilizes a generalization of the entropic covariance complexity index of Van Emden (1971). The design of ICOMP is to estimate a loss function for each model tested where:

$$\text{Statistical Model} = \text{Signal} + \text{Noise} \qquad (2)$$

and

$$\text{Loss} = \text{Lack of fit} + \text{Lack of Parsimony} + \text{Profusion of Complexity} \qquad (3)$$

The above is achieved by using the additive property of information theory and the developments of Rissanen (1976) in his *Final Estimation Criterion (FEC)* for estimation and model identification problems, as well as Akaike's (1973) AIC, and its analytical extensions in Bozdogan (1987).

ICOMP incorporates a measure of the complexity of the model into the penalty term. Empirically, complexity is defined to be a measure of the cohesion or interdependence among the components of a random vector. Larger values of complexity indicate higher interaction among the variables. Therefore, in model evaluation, the concept of complexity plays an important role. As Rissanen (1976) notes, without a measure of model complexity, any model evaluation criterion overlooks estimating the internal cohesion of the model. The interactions among the residuals and the covariance matrix of the parameter estimates are considered by the evaluation criterion through the complexity measure.

ICOMP, as an information-theoretic model evaluation criterion for linear and non-linear statistical models, uses an information-based characterization of the covariance matrix properties of the parameter estimates and the error terms starting from their finite sampling distributions.

The first approach to ICOMP results in:

Proposition 2.1. For a multivariate linear or non-linear structural model, the maximal information-theoretic measure of complexity called ICOMP is defined by

$$\text{ICOMP (Overall Model)} = -2 \log L(\varepsilon|\theta) + 2[C_1(\text{Cov}(\theta)) + C(\text{Cov}(\varepsilon))] \qquad (4)$$

In Eq. (4), while the first term measures the lack of fit, the second term incorporates the complexity of the model due to the covariance matrix of the parameter estimates and due to the covariance of the error terms. If the error terms are uncorrelated, the second part of the second term, $C(\text{Cov}(\varepsilon))$, tends to zero. Among a portfolio of competing models, the model with the minimum value of ICOMP is chosen to be the "best" model. Thus, the "best" model will be the one that achieves the optimum trade-off between lack of fit, accuracy of the parameter estimates and interactions among the residuals.

3. AN APPLICATION FOR FINANCE

Rather than study the impact of managerial decision-making on debt and dividend policy separately, Ravid and Sarig (1991) theorize on the simultaneity of the decisions management makes regarding debt and dividend policy. Jensen, Solberg and Zorn (1992) (JSZ) test the jointness of the relation between insider holdings, debt and dividend policy.

Arguably, since the Jensen et al. study, the U.S. equity market has become institutionalized. Some evidence has been presented by case studies which show institutional investors actively involved in determining the debt and dividend policies of corporations.

While the above studies document the role of individual institutional investors as monitors of corporate management, they do not address the question whether such ownership, in general, is exogenously or endogenously determined. Researchers in the field of finance have put forward theoretical hypotheses whereby institutional owners (earlier referred to as "large shareholders", which could be either individuals or institutions) could function either endogenously or exogenously in determining the debt and dividend policies of firms.

Thus, there is no clear cut prior expectations on the role of institutional holdings in the joint determination of corporate ownership and corporate policy. In such a situation, ICOMP would be an ideal tool to help determine whether institutional ownership is endogenous (that is, a dependent variable) or exogenous (an explanatory variable only) to the system of equity ownership and corporate policy.

3.1. Methodology

Prior research has demonstrated that ownership and corporate policy choices are determined contemporaneously. This has been modeled by performing simultaneous systems regression analysis, with debt, dividends, and insider ownership as the three endogenous variables. To study the impact of institutional equity ownership on the dynamics of these variables, a suitable sample of firms needs to be collected. Building on prior research, first one would incorporate institutional ownership as an explanatory variable in the three structural equations of debt, dividends, and insider holdings. Next, the model would be modified and the model would take the variable, institutional ownership, and treat it as endogenous. Thus, the system would be modified into a four-equation system, with dividends, debt, insider ownership, and institutional ownership as the four endogenous variables.

3.1.1. The ICOMP (IFIM) Criteria

For an empirical study, ICOMP can be operationalized by using the system-weighted R^2 of the regression analysis and (Cov(θ)), the covariance matrix of the parameter estimates, as under:

$$\text{ICOMP(IFIM)} = -N\log(1 - R^2) + 2C_1(\text{Cov}(\theta))$$

where: $N =$ Total sample size; $C_1(\text{Cov}(\theta)) = 0.5s\log[(\text{tr Cov}(\theta))/s] - 0.5$ $\log(\det\text{Cov}(\theta))$; $s = \dim(\text{Cov}(\theta)) = \text{rank}(\text{Cov}(\theta))$; $\det(\text{Cov}(\theta)) = $ determinant $(\text{Cov}(\theta))$.

In the above equation, the first term, $-N\log(1 - R^2)$, measures the lack of fit of the model. The second term, $C_1(\text{Cov}(\theta))$ represents an information-theoretic maximal complexity measure of Cov(θ), the covariance matrix of the parameter estimates of the simultaneous regression system of equations.

Model Selection. After the simultaneous regressions have been performed, the study would determine whether, for the compiled data set, the institutional ownership variable is endogenous or exogenous to the system. It is possible that where the relation between ownership structure and the choice of corporate policies is concerned, institutional ownership may be an endogenous or dependent variable, that is, such ownership has an effect on the system being studied and is affected by the system. On the other hand, institutional ownership may function as an exogenous variable or independent variable, simply having an effect on the system but not affected by the system.

The method of determining the above would be resolved by statistical model selection, using the informational approach proposed by Bozdogan (1988). This is the most appropriate test given the nature of the model, a multivariate simultaneous system of equations. Bozdogan's (1988, 1990a, b) Informational Complexity Criterion, ICOMP, are designed for "model selection in general multivariate linear and nonlinear structural models" (Bearse, Bozdogan & Schlottmann, 1997).

4. SUMMARY AND CONCLUSIONS

In this paper, Bozdogan's ICOMP criterion is introduced. Then, a simple application is proposed in Section 3 – to assess whether institutional ownership is endogenous or exogenous to the system of relations among corporate policy choices and equity ownership. One way to operationalize ICOMP is by using the ICOMP(IFIM) method, described in Section 3.1. In the field of economics, ICOMP has been used to measure food consumption in the Netherlands. Section 3 puts forward but one potential application for financial research. The potential usage for this criterion is manifold. Any research situation in which two (or more) competing models need to be evaluated to determine which is better, can use ICOMP to resolve the issue.

REFERENCES

Akaike, H. (1973). Information theory and an extension of the maximum likelihood principle. In: B. N. Petrov & F. Caski (Eds), *Second International Symposium on Information Theory* (pp. 267–281). Budapest: Academiai Kiado.

Bearse, P., Bozdogan, H., & Schlottmann, A. (1997). Empirical econometric modeling of food consumption using a new informational complexity approach. *Journal of Applied Econometrics, 12,* 563–592.

Bozdogan, H. (1987). Model selection and Akaike's Information Criterion (AIC): The general theory and its analytical extensions. *Psychometrika, 52,* 345–370.

Bozdogan, H. (1988). ICOMP: A new model selection criterion. In: H. H. Bock (Ed.), *Classification and Related Methods of Data Analysis* (pp. 599–608). Amsterdam: North-Holland.

Bozdogan, H. (1990a). On the information-based measure of covariance complexity and its application to the evaluation of multivariate linear models. *Communications in Statistics, Theory and Methods, 19,* 221–278.

Bozdogan, H. (1990b). Multisample cluster analysis of the common principal component model in K groups using an entropic statistical complexity criterion, invited paper presented at the International Symposium on Theory and Practice of Classification, Puschino, Soviet Union.

Jensen, G. R., Solberg, D. P., & Zorn, T. S. (1992). Simultaneous determination of insider ownership, debt, and dividend policies. *Journal of Financial and Quantitative Analysis, 27,* 247–263.

Kullback, S., & Leibler, R. (1951). On information and sufficiency. *Annals of Mathematical Statistics, 22,* 79–86.

Ravid, A., & Sarig, O. (1991). Financial signalling by precommitting to cash flows. *Journal of Financial and Quantitative Analysis, 26,* 165–180.

Rissanen, J. (1976). Minmax entropy estimation of models for vector processes. In: R. K. Mehra & D. G. Lainiotis (Eds), *System Identification* (pp. 97–119). New York: Academic Press.

Van Emden, M. H. (1971). An analysis of complexity. *Mathematical Center Tracts,* 35. Amsterdam.